India's Risks

India's Risks

*Democratizing the Management of Threats
to Environment, Health, and Values*

Edited by

RAPHAELLE MOOR
AND
M.V. RAJEEV GOWDA

OXFORD
UNIVERSITY PRESS

OXFORD
UNIVERSITY PRESS

Oxford University Press is a department of the University of Oxford.
It furthers the University's objective of excellence in research, scholarship,
and education by publishing worldwide. Oxford is a registered trademark of
Oxford University Press in the UK and in certain other countries

Published in India by
Oxford University Press
YMCA Library Building, 1 Jai Singh Road, New Delhi 110001, India

ISBN-13: 978-0-19-945045-9
ISBN-10: 0-19-945045-5

Typeset in Dante MT Std 10.5/13
by Alphæta Solutions, Puducherry, India 605 009
Printed in India by Sapra Brothers, New Delhi 110 092

Contents

Section Three   Science and Technology

Acknowledgements

This book is the culmination of a study (http://steps-centre.org/ project/risk/) run jointly by the Centre for Public Policy at the Indian Institute of Management Bangalore and the STEPS Centre at the University of Sussex. This project was only made possible thanks to generous funding by the UK India Education Research Initiative: http://www.ukieri.org/index.html.

We would like to thank all the people who attended the conference we held in India in February 2011, from where the idea of this book arose, including all the contributors in this volume as well as Professor Ian Scoones, the convenor of this study and our partner at the University of Sussex, Dr Les Levidow (Open University), Professor Shreekant Gupta (Delhi University), Muhammad Ali Khan (special advisor to Sri Jairam Ramesh), Dr V. Thiruppugazh, Dr Aditi Iyer (IIMB), Dr Saraswathy Ganapathy (Belaku Trust), R.D. Jakati, Professor V. Ranganathan (IIMB), N. Ravi (IIMB), Sreedhar Ramamurthi (Mines, Minerals and People), Dr K.K. Narayanan (Metahelix Life Sciences), Sanjay Sridhar (EMBARQ India), and Ripin Kalra.

All royalties from the sale of this book will go directly to the Environment Support Group, an NGO based in Bangalore coordinated by Leo Saldanha (a contributor to this volume). The Environment Support Group (http://esgindia.org/) works with a variety of environmental and social justice initiatives across India and the world. They pro-actively address issues and concerns, collaborating across sectors and disciplines, and keeping the interests of local project-affected communities and voiceless ecosystems in primary focus. The spirit of their involvement is to be sensitive to contextual complexities so the solutions are environmentally and socially, just, and deeply democratic. Started informally in 1996 and formally registered as a Public Charitable Trust in 1998, ESG's not-for-profit initiatives respond through a variety of actions involving research, education, campaign support, and advocacy. They are amongst the foremost proponents in India for the reform of environmental decision-making processes, working to make them people friendly and just.

Raphaelle Moor—I must also acknowledge my family's tremendous patience, encouragement, and support over the last few years, which never faltered, even from 5,000 miles away. And neither would this book have been possible without my friends: Nicky, Carsten, Shreekanth, Arundhuti, and Vidhula—who all made India feel like home.

Abbreviations

AAI	Airports Authority of India
AEC	Atomic Energy Commission
AERB	Atomic Energy Regulatory Board
ALARP	As low as reasonably practicable
AMTSL	Active management of the third stage of labour
ANM	Auxiliary Nurse Midwife
APAC	AIDS Prevention and Control Programme
ART	Anti-retroviral Therapy
ASE	Additional safety assessments
AYUSH	Ayurveda, Yoga & Naturopathy, Unani, Siddha, and Homoeopathy
BARC	Bhabha Atomic Research Centre
BARCCIS	Bhabha Atomic Research Centre Channel Inspection System
BATNEEC	Best available technology not entailing excessive cost
BEE	Bureau of Energy Efficiency
BHEL	Bharat Heavy Electricals Limited
BJP	Bharatiya Janata Party
BPA	Bisphenol A
BPEO	Best practical environmental option
BPL	Below Poverty Line
BRAI	Biotechnology Regulatory Authority of India
CAC	Codex Alimentarius Commission
CAG	Comptroller and Auditory General

CAM	Community Asset Management
CBDRR	Community-based Disaster Risk Reduction
CBO	Community-based organization
CDC	Centre for Disease Control
CDF	Centre for Development Finance
CDP	City Development Plan
CDRMF	Comprehensive Disaster Risk Management Framework
CIP	COWAM in Practice
COWAM	Community Waste Management in Practice
CPCB	Central Pollution Control Board
CSE	Centre for Science and Environment
CSR	Corporate Social Responsibility
CSW	Commercial Sex Worker
DADA	Decide, Announce, Defend, and Abandon
DAE	Department of Atomic Energy
DDMA	District Disaster Management Authorities
DLB	District Local Bodies
DRM	Disaster Risk Management
DTE	Down to Earth
ECS	Évaluations complémentaires de sûreté
EDF	Environmental Defense Fund
EIA	Environmental Impact Assessment
EPA	Environmental Protection Agency
EPCRA	Emergency Planning and Community Right to Know Act, 1986
EPR	European Pressurised Reactor
ESCo	Energy Saving Companies
FAO	Food and Agriculture Organisation
FDI	Foreign Direct Investment
FSC	Forum on Stakeholder Confidence
FSW	Female Sex Workers
GE	General Electric
GEAC	Genetic Engineering Approval Committee
GM	Genetically Modified
GMO	Genetically Modified Organism

GoM	Government of Maharashtra
GRP	Green Rating Project
GSACS	Goa State AIDS Control Society
HBM	Health Belief Model
HDI	Human Development Index
HIV/AIDS	Human Immunodeficiency Virus/Acquired Immune Deficiency Syndrome
HLFPPT	Hindustan Latex Family Planning Promotion Trust
HRG	High-risk Group
HRO	High Reliability Organization
HSE	Health and Safety Executive
HUDCO	Housing and Urban Development Corporation
IAEA	International Atomic Energy Agency
ICAO	International Civil Aviation Organisation
IDSP	Integrated Disease Surveillance Project
IDU	Injecting Drug Users
IFA	Iron and Folic Acid
IFRC	International Federation of Red Cross and Red Crescent Societies
IHR	International Health Regulations
IIMB	Indian Institute of Management Bangalore
IIPH	Indian Institute of Public Health
IIPS	International Institute for Population Sciences
ILW	Intermediate-level waste
IMR	Infant mortality rate
INES	International Nuclear Event Scale
INSAG	International Safety Advisory Group
IRGC	International Risk Governance Council
ITER	International Thermonuclear Experimental Reactor
JE	Japanese Encephalitis
JIRM	Joint Implementation Review Mission
JNPP	Jaitapur Nuclear Power Plant
JnNURM	Jawaharlal Nehru National Urban Renewal Mission

JSY	Janani Suraksha Yojana
KARP	Kalpakkam Atomic Reprocessing Plant
LAEC	Local Area Environment Committees
LBW	Low birth weight
LDF	Left Democratic Front
LEPC	Local Emergency Planning Committee
LLW	Low-level waste
MDC	Municipal Planning Committee
MDGs	Millennium Development Goals
MECL	Minerals Exploration Corporation Ltd.
MEERP	Maharashtra Earthquake Emergency Rehabilitation Programme
MGI	McKinsey Global Institute
MIIB	Major Incident Investigation Board
MIC	Methylisocyanate
MMR	Maternal mortality ratio
MoHFW	Ministry of Health and Family Welfare
MOSPI	Ministry of Statistics and Programme Implementation
MoU	Memorandum of Understanding
MSL	Mean sea level
MSM	Men who have sex with men
MSSR	Mangalore Area Control Radar
MTPA	Million Tonnes per Annum
MWe	Megawatt electric
NACO	National AIDS Control Organisation
NACP	National AIDS Control Programme
NAS-NRC	National Academy of Sciences-National Research Council
NCAER	National Council for Applied Economic Research
NCDC	National Centre for Disease Control
NDA	National Democratic Alliance
NDMA	National Disaster Management Authority
NEA	Nuclear Energy Agency
NGO	Non-governmental Organization

NGT	National Green tribunal
NIMBY	Not in my back yard
NIMHANS	National Institute of Mental Health and Neuro Sciences
NIV	National Institute of Virology
NPC	Nuclear Power Corporation
NPCIL	Nuclear Power Corporation of India Ltd
NPPs	Nuclear Power Plants
NRC	National Research Council
NREGS	National Rural Employment Guarantee Scheme
NRHM	National Rural Health Mission
NSRA	Nuclear Safety Regulatory Authority
OECD-NEA	Organisation for Economic Cooperation and Development-Nuclear Energy Agency
OFC	Orbitofrontal Cortex
OPEC	Organization of Petroleum Exporting Countries
OSHA	Occupational Safety and Health Administration
PCB	Pollution Control Boards
PCBs	Polychlorinated Biphenyls
PCI	Press Council of India
PEs	Peer educators
PFI	Population Foundation of India
PIB	Public Information Bureau
PHC	Primary Health Centre
PIL	Public Interest Litigation
PMANE	People's Movement Against Nuclear Energy
POSCO	Pohang Iron and Steel Company
PPRP	Pandemic Preparedness and Response Plan
PPSS	Pratirodh Sangram Samithi
PRA	Probabilistic risk assessment
PRB	Population Reference Bureau
PTI	Press Trust of India
PWD	Public Works Department
QRA	Quantitative Risk Assessment
QUALY	Quality-adjusted Life Years
RCC	Reinforced Cement Concrete

RCT	Randomized Control Trials
RESA	Runway End Safety Area
RFF	Rescue and Fire Fighting
RGICD	Rajiv Gandhi Institute of Chest Diseases
RTI	Right to Information
RWM	Radioactive waste management
SACO	State AIDS Control Organisation
SAR	School of American Research
SARF	Social Amplification of Risk Framework
SDMA	State Disaster Management Authority
SERC	State Emergency Response Commission
SLS	Same language subtitling
SPCB	State Pollution Control Board
STD	Sexually Transmitted Disease
STS	Science and Technology Studies
SUPSI	Scuola Universitaria Professionale Della Svizzera Italiana
TLD	Thermoluminescent Dosimeter
TMI	Three Mile Island
TRAI	Telecom Regulatory Authority of India
TRI	Toxics Release Inventory
TSU	Technical Support Units
UDF	United Democratic Front
ULB	Urban Local Bodies
UNEP	United Nations Environment Programme
UNFPA	United Nations Population Fund
UPA	United Progressive Alliance
USAID	United States Agency for International Development
US NRC	US National Research Council
WHO	World Health Organization
WOCL	Window of Circadian Low
WTF	Waste tank farm

RAPHAELLE MOOR

M.V. RAJEEV GOWDA

Introduction

India has been widely touted as a superpower in the making. It is a nuclear nation dabbling in biotechnology, with a wealth of natural resources, one of the world's largest young demographics, a burgeoning middle class, and also globally competitive businesses. India, however, is also grappling with a bewildering array of risks—risks that it has long had to confront and new types of risks associated with its particular model of economic growth. Even as women still die in childbirth at a shamefully high rate, at the same time India celebrates the launch of ballistic missiles. Floods, earthquakes, and cyclones wreak colossal devastation every year, blighting the lives of communities for decades to come. A creaky healthcare system, already struggling to deal with the rapid spread of Human Immunodeficiency Virus (HIV), flounders in the wake of the 2009 H1N1 outbreak. Fatalities are a frequent feature in rail and road accidents. Urban infrastructure is crumbling, and pedestrians run the risk of being electrocuted by overhanging wires or falling through poorly constructed pavements. The government faces a stumbling block as citizens angrily contest the official assessment of the risks of Bt brinjal. Activists perpetually decry India's unsustainable and inequitable path of development as both the environment and vulnerable communities are subject to collateral damage in the ongoing thrust towards growth. The spectre of Bhopal's unresolved tragedy hovers over India's aggressive investments in nuclear technology, pursued in the name of energy security and prosperity. Meanwhile, the Japanese nuclear disaster at Fukushima has heightened the fears of local communities neighbouring India's nuclear power plants.

Needless to say, India abounds with risk. It has been struggling to stay on top in the presence of an onslaught of destructive natural hazard and health risks which batter often those already vulnerable communities. Most of these risks, such as dying in childbirth, are easily preventable and have long been conquered in other countries. Due to either natural or human activity, too many risks are routinely faced yet elicit nothing more than shrugs of resignation. They persist year after year unabated. Yet, even as some risks are accepted as part of the humdrum of daily life, others have become the subject of vicious and passionate disputes. The government has been attracting much of the public's rancour as it forges ahead with large projects using advanced technologies bearing potentially devastating and unknown risks. Many citizens are worried that those who are charged with safeguarding their interests and creating a safe environment may also be endangering their well-being or threatening the life they want to lead. To these citizens the State itself appears to be a source of many risks.

India's policy of science-, technology-, and innovation-led economic growth has created phenomenally high rates of GDP growth within a short space of time, and yet, there is a dark side to this success. The rapid expansion of India's cities, in particular the spectacular transformation of Bangalore from a hill station into an intensely concentrated urban sprawl, has created noxious and intolerable pollution levels that have created new health risks. Growing pressures on land and urban infrastructure have severely impacted public transport, waste services, water, and power supplies. Flooding in Bangalore is now a perennial problem. In Punjab, fly ash from coal burnt at thermal power plants, and the rampant use of pesticides, fertilizers, and other chemicals during the Green Revolution are alleged to be the source of the high uranium levels in the groundwater. Greater Bangalore's groundwater has similarly been polluted by toxic leachates released by overflowing illegal landfills. These risks are now a part of life in India, but for some people this burden is heavier than for others.

It is, inevitably, the poorest, uneducated, most vulnerable and marginalized sections of the society which bear the brunt of these risks.

Development projects have displaced between 60–65 million people in India since Independence, of whom 40 per cent are estimated to be tribals and another 40 per cent are dalits and other rural poor. How do smallholder farmers earn their livelihood when they are thrown off their land by the IT sector? They lack the skills, education, and access to finance to participate and benefit from this technology-led model of economic growth. Neither can they afford to escape the worst of these risks; unlike the urban elite living in secure enclaves kitted out with power backup systems, air-conditioning units, and private water supplies. Moreover, they have an ambivalent relationship with risky activities or products, which, while risky to their health and safety, are often central to their livelihoods. Unorganized and poorly protected workers, mostly women and children, have, for example, been unknowingly risking their health on e-waste scrap heaps, using strong acids to extract precious materials such as gold.

The emergence of new risks, and the degree to which a population is vulnerable to risk, is largely a product of governmental policies and institutional processes. This is true of health, environmental, and science and technology risks; as this volume will show. There are numerous examples showing how the current path of development has created an unfettered and lopsided model of economic growth which has increased poor people's vulnerability to risks. Even natural hazards, which are external events that are mostly beyond our immediate control, need not become disasters if the government is well prepared. If we look at major floods in India, these have been caused by unregulated and haphazard housing developments that encroach on flood plains, or due to poorly built and maintained structures such as the dams in Bihar. The field of disaster management has a well-defined formula for risk:

$$\text{risk} = \text{natural hazard} \times \text{vulnerability} \times \text{exposure}$$

Vulnerability refers to the physical, social, economic, and environmental factors or processes that increase a community's susceptibility to hazards. Whilst the occurrence of natural hazards is largely beyond the government's control, the degree to which a population is vulnerable to natural hazards falls well within the political domain.

Clearly, decisions concerning the distribution, prioritization, and minimization of risks are entirely political. To reduce risks, the government not only needs to design appropriate policies and institutional arrangements, but also decide which ones should be reduced first and to what level. There are innumerable risks around every corner, but the government has a limited amount of resources, and therefore it needs to prioritize. How does it decide which risks deserve more attention than others? Furthermore, how much of the public resources should be invested in social safety nets to redistribute risks and cushion people from adverse effects? Jairam Ramesh, the Minister of Rural Development, jokingly remarked that for the cost of just one Rafale aircraft, 126 of which are being bought by the defence ministry at a total cost of USD 20 billion, 1,000 village panchayats could afford to get bio-digester toilets. What is more important to the government, a fighter plane or toilets; defence or sanitation?

Regardless of whether the source of risk is 'natural' or 'manufactured', both the existence of risks and people's exposure and vulnerability to them are the product of political judgements. The concept of 'risk', however, tends to hold very strong technical connotations. Governments, the world over, often give the impression that their decisions for taking or avoiding risks are dictated by supposedly 'objective' expert-given technical assessments. The public is, in turn, portrayed by these policymakers as being ruled by irrational fears and follies, 'misperceiving' and 'misinterpreting' risks. Yet, the process of identifying, characterizing, and assessing risks is, from start to finish, loaded with normative considerations. Policymakers and scientists are not uniquely blessed with the ability to engage in a neutral, value-free process of risk assessment. This is why, across the world, we see such vastly different understandings and assessments of risk, as well as diverse regulatory styles and cultures.

What will count as 'risk' is fundamentally very different for different people. People's political and cultural values, education, background, interests, and vision of the 'best' direction for society's development will give rise to very different understandings, and thus assessments, of risk. Take, for example, the oft-heard comment during the Bt brinjal debate that biotechnology is a purely scientific issue, not to be hijacked by peripheral socioeconomic concerns. These advocates strongly believed that biotechnology would uniformly be in society's best interests and attempted to frame the problem as though it were purely scientific, which they equated with 'neutral'. However, deciding what evidence should count in the assessment of biotechnology's risks is a value judgement. As is the implicit assumption that biotechnology will be in everyone's best interests. Others participating in the debate had a very different idea of what their best interests were, highlighting, for example, its uncertain impact on the livelihood of petty farmers and the consumer's right to choose what they eat.

With such a multitude of competing constructions of risk, whose understanding, and thus assessment, of risk counts? Who decides which risks should be taken and which should be avoided? Are these people even politically accountable? Crucially, what questions are being asked and whose knowledge is considered relevant for assessing risks? Deciding what knowledge is relevant and legitimate to 'know' risks is clearly a value judgement that will elicit a wide variety of opinions. For example, those who construct risks in purely technical and scientific terms will invariably only seek the expertise of scientists in deciding on an 'acceptable' level of risk, rather than that of communities or social scientists.

The notion of 'acceptability' is itself, of course, a subjective judgement. The outcomes of projects and technologies do not speak for themselves—governments must decide how to characterize and interpret different possible effects. Evidence cannot compel a particular decision—this is often known as *Hume's Law* (Hume 1739). Hume stated that you cannot get an 'ought', in other words a normative statement about what *should* be done, from an 'is', which is a descriptive factual statement. What level of 'proof', for example, is needed to establish 'safety'? Where does the line of 'safety' lie—does something have to be 'safe', 'safe enough', 'tolerable', or 'best practice'? (See Chapter 13.) How should different forms of harm be compared (for example, young v. old, present v. future generations)? Decisions to reduce certain risks also sometimes paradoxically increase other risks. Technologies such as nuclear power or biotechnology are a means of overcoming the risk of climate change, energy and food shortages, yet governments must weigh these risks against new, uncertain, and potentially apocalyptic risks. What criteria should be used in these risk–risk trade-offs? When governments choose risks because the associated benefits are seen to be greater, exactly the same questions as above apply: what counts as 'benefits', according to whom, how should these be calculated, and what criteria should be used to decide when the benefits outweigh the harms?

When is it acceptable to take or avoid risks and whose principles or values are being invoked in the process? Cries of 'development' and 'progress' are often bandied around; but development and progress for whom?

Since Chauncey Starr's paper on technological risk (Starr 1969), and Mary Douglas' paper on environmental risk (Douglas 1972), psychologists, sociologists, anthropologists, political theorists, philosophers, and scientists in the West have vigorously debated these various issues around risk. This multidisciplinary field of academic research on risk, however, has been curiously absent in India. Shiv Visvanathan in his article remarked on this when he pointed out that 'STS [Science and Technology Studies] in an academic sense has been the case of a missing discipline that democracy in India urgently needs but cannot access' (Visvanathan 2001). The academic field of STS looks at how scientific and technological knowledge has been produced by people and institutions and how this knowledge has, in turn, shaped the social context. Broadly, it examines science in society and society in science and it has been hugely influential in shaping science policy in the West. In India, however, the critical questions that form the core of STS have only been found in social movements. There has been very little in the way of academic and policy research on issues such as the role of scientific expertise in the characterization and assessment of risks, or how the public should engage with science. This framework is equally applicable in examining health and natural hazard risks—it can probe the dominant perspectives of risk and knowledge that exist and how these have shaped and moulded risk management policies, legislations, and institutions.

In light of this, an international conference was organized at the Indian Institute of Management Bangalore (IIMB) in February 2011, from which the idea of creating this volume originated.[1] Reflecting the truly multidisciplinary nature of the field of risk analysis, we brought together scholars and practitioners in disciplines ranging from anthropology, economics, social psychology, public health, political science, philosophy, physics, architecture, urban planning, law, and

---

[1] This conference was part of a project funded by the UK India Education Research Initiative, given jointly to IIMB's Centre for Public Policy and the STEPS Centre at the University of Sussex. The presented papers were revised and updated for their inclusion in this volume as the respective chapters.

disaster management. Academics from the UK and Europe furnished insights from the field of risk, and provided a window into how risks have been governed in the West. Indian academics and practitioners, not all of whom were necessarily as familiar with the risk literature, shared examples of risk-related controversies in India. Both the conference and subsequent discussions during the editing process sought to bring together the theory of risk with lessons from the West and the realities of risk in India.

This edited volume thus offers a unifying conceptual lens that draws attention to the inherently political, social, and ethical nature of risk. It uses the tools, vocabulary, and critical insights from the multidisciplinary risk literature to systematically deconstruct the various meanings, attitudes, assessments, and approaches to risk that exist in India. Delving into the meaning of risk in India, we ask what it signifies for policymakers and different factions of society. What are the political, social, and economic dynamics that have shaped the very different constructions of risk that exist in India? How have India's aspirations to become the next leading superpower framed policymakers' assessments of scientific and technological risks? How have their understandings of 'development' and 'progress' shaped subsequent risk assessments? We examine what knowledge and expertise officials tend to consider relevant to include in their risk assessments, and what knowledge has been overlooked as a result. Are those risks that policymakers have identified and chosen to address consonant with those constructed by the community? Are their assumptions about people's behavioural patterns even correct? Why have we yet to see policy and behavioural changes which would minimize death and destruction from health and natural hazards, given that people and governments have had eons of experience?

Many of the chapters in this volume offer suggestions for how governments can reconcile radically different assessments of the same risk. Public's and experts' understandings of risks frequently diverge, and for some people a given risk is wildly unacceptable and unethical, whilst there might be others who see the same risk as safe and tolerable. Government's assurances, risk assessments, and expert committees frequently fail to allay the public's concerns, but why? Is it really fair to claim that the public is unreasonable in their fear or opposition to industrial projects and new technologies? Who has set down the parameters for rational and irrational behaviour?

Whilst various disciplines in India have had their own approaches to addressing health, natural hazard, technological, and industrial risks, each shedding light on a particular dimension, rarely have they been brought together under one overarching framework. Yet analysing different risks and disciplinary domains through the same analytical framework can generate a cross-fertilization that adds new perspectives to each of these areas of study. We have divided this volume into three sections—disasters and the environment, public health, and science and technology, and we hope that the readers will delve into each of these and recognize some of the recurring themes and issues about how risk has been governed in India. We have highlighted some of these themes below and Chapter 1 particularly attempts to connect the dots and present a more multi-dimensional lens to risk. Each of these chapters point out that natural risks are equally as political as risks that are the product of human activity, that risk assessment cannot be separated from how risks are understood, perceived, and defined, and that all these risks are profoundly intertwined and cannot be effectively governed in isolation from each other. A few of the central themes are explored as follows.

THEMES

Technical, Instrumental, and Managerial Risk Discourse

During the conference discussions, Les Levidow remarked that 'risk is stereotypically seen as an inherent property of a thing or a situation which then becomes an object of management and therefore conceals and structures the relations of power that determine and seek to legitimize the degree of risk we face'. Across every domain, in the governance of health, natural hazard, technological, and environmental risks, the Indian government has shown a tendency to approach risks through an avowedly scientific and techno-optimistic framework. Crucial policy decisions are left in the hands of technical 'experts' and their scientific and technical solutions are privileged over those put forward by communities or social scientists. Science has been seen as vital 'in ridding this country of the ancient scourges of poverty, ignorance and disease' (Jawaharlal Nehru), a sentiment that was recently echoed by Manmohan Singh when he said that 'our problems as a nation are in many ways overwhelming and they need scientific and technological solutions' (Newstrack 2012). Experts have been typically charged with calculating and mapping the probabilities and magnitudes of various outcomes to produce a supposedly 'objective' and quantitative picture of risk. According to this approach, experts can capture a neutral and objective picture which is free from politics, culture, and any pre-existing interests, unlike the public's supposedly 'biased' and cloudy perceptions.

The risk literature has forcefully challenged this technical and managerial approach to risk regulation, which attempts to masquerade political judgements as neutral, value-free science. Knowledge is not formed in a vacuum, but is shaped by wider social, economic, and political values and interests. A number of the chapters in this volume point to the interests, principles, and values which have underpinned how the Indian government and scientists have framed and assessed risks in India (see, in particular, Chapters 9 and 13). These, however, have either remained buried or been dismissed as uncontroversial. For example, meeting 'developmental challenges', achieving 'self reliance', and 'nation building' are all objectives which are lauded by the Indian government as being fairly benign and in 'the public's interest'. The motivations and purposes for taking these risks have largely been left unchallenged and unexamined, and alternative paths of development are overlooked.

Myth of Control and Blame Games

India's predominantly technical and managerial risk discourse understates uncertainty, projects an image of absolute control, and favours technical fixes. In Chapter 10, M.V. Ramana investigates the nuclear establishment's 'no-risk ideology', which ranges from a refusal to acknowledge the risk that nuclear facilities *may* pose to the health of neighbouring populations to the current Atomic Energy Commission (AEC) Chairman's bold assertion that nuclear reactors in India are 100 per cent safe. Risk management, however, is often 'an effort to know the unknowable' (Power 2004: 59). Reducing uncertainties into calculable risks promotes not only a dangerous illusion of control but it is also 'irrational, unscientific and potentially misleading' (Stirling 2007). When these uncertainties come to light and the Indian government's image of control is shattered, it switches between denial, spin, or blaming others. Either way, trust is rapidly eroded.

Conflicts in India have given rise to an insidious atmosphere of blame and moral outrage as India's society is mentally divvied up into the victims and the beneficiaries, the winners and the losers, those at fault and those who have been wronged. In the case of H1N1 in India, a game of pass the hot potato emerged as political parties either tried to pin the blame for the mismanagement of H1N1 on their rivals, to shift the responsibility for risks to other state structures and hospitals, or to blame the public themselves for their own misfortune (see Chapter 7). This is equally true within organizations, where management has 'externalized the risk problem' by blaming any mishaps and accidents on its employees (see Chapter 10). This blame game works against creating institutions which are accountable for their actions and can learn from their failures, as well as fuelling feelings of injustice. Government policies which have identified and blamed vulnerable risk groups are also counterproductive to creating an accurate understanding of the risks and how they arise, as we will see in Chapter 6 on HIV/AIDS.

Political, Economic, and Social Roots of People's Risk Behaviour

Risk communication and management policies often fail because the Indian government does not understand or recognize the political, economic, and social roots of people's risk behaviour (see Chapters 5, 6, and 8). There exists a mismatch between the government's and communities' constructions of risk. Whilst the government and its institutions tend to construct risk in technical or scientific terms, people hold a more multifaceted understanding. In narrowly limiting the discussion to one of 'safety', government (and the scientific community) ignores the fact that not everyone equates 'risk' with physical risk (see Chapter 6). Risks to one's livelihood, finances, status in the community and reputation sometimes outweigh or are ranked alongside risks to life and limb. As Kilaru et al. point out in Chapter 5 on the risk behaviour of pregnant women: 'death and morbidity are part of a constellation of risk in which death prevention may not always be the priority'.

Whilst the Indian public is often seen to be acting irrationally or unreasonably, and is told as much, this is based on a limited understanding of rationality that ignores people's experience, background, cultural values, and political judgements (see Chapter 1). People see risks as not just potentially threatening their lives, but the kind of person they wish to be, or the lives they want to lead. Douglas and Wildavsky (1982: 2) argued that 'fear of risk, coupled with the confidence to face it, has something to do with knowledge and something to do with the kind of people we are'.

Public Deliberation and Community Engagement

In India, public participation has mostly involved 'educating' citizens about risks in order to remove opposition. Experts and policymakers frequently express frustration when debates escape the boundaries of science, as happened during the Bt brinjal debate. It is thus seen as a means to an end; a way of bringing the public's perception of risks in line with the experts 'true' and 'objective' assessments. Public deliberation has become a mere *product* to tick off the 'to do' checklist, rather than one of the *processes* for assessing risk. The direction of India's development and what should count as 'progress' is more often than not decided with little input from the public. For example, the Prime Minister, Manmohan Singh, was recently quoted saying that 'in due course of time we must make use of genetic engineering technologies' to increase agricultural productivity (Hindustan Times 2012)—appearing to dismiss the predominantly negative public opinion that emerged during the Bt brinjal debates. There is also a strong sense that risk communication strategies are principally concerned about managing reputational risk rather than the risks themselves; as is apparent in Ranjani Ramaswamy's chapter on the communication of H1N1 in India (Chapter 7).

Attempts at public participation in India have typically degenerated into ugly debates as fingers are pointed, derisory remarks casually tossed around and viewpoints are ridiculed and disparaged. Why 'can we not disagree, if we have to, without being disagreeable?' cried Minister Jairam Ramesh in his 2011 convocation address delivered at IIT Guwahati (2011: 10). One answer, as this volume argues, is that participation should not be a means of forcing publics to accept one, often technical and scientific, meaning of risk. Rather, it should uncover and debate these different constructions of risk so that an understanding of risk is negotiated which reflects shared public values. Publics are not 'consumers' or 'passive beneficiaries' of science and technology (Leach et al. 2005). They have knowledge, experience, and understandings of risk that should be fed into the initial 'upstream' stages where the risk agenda is framed. This is the route to creating more socially acceptable, robust and trusted policies (see Chapters 1, 10, and 12). Whilst governments may be sceptical of the value that non-specialist publics can bring to the decision-making process, many of the chapters in this volume provide examples that prove otherwise. In Chapter 12, Mays presents evidence from the West's experience with radioactive waste management (RWM), arguing that local communities should not just be 'affected' by RWM plans, but become active partners in creating safe and sustainable waste management solutions that will fit in, adapt to, and contribute to their way of life.

In the event of health and natural hazard risks, failing to grasp communities' cultural constructions of risk and how people behave ultimately results in a failure to effectively mitigate and reduce communities' vulnerability to risk. Overlooking or dismissing various local knowledge and experiences denigrates the identity and way of life of communities and only exacerbates existing economic, social, and physical vulnerabilities—this is particularly clear in Chapter 4 on the policy of post-disaster reconstruction after the Marathwada earthquake. Many of the chapters argue that it is necessary to redefine what counts as 'expert' knowledge. This should be extended to incorporate the range of local and contextual knowledge of communities, which is typically more suited to the given conditions and constraints.

Appreciating the Wider Context and the Interplay of Risks and Vulnerabilities Across Society

Risks cannot be effectively regulated and mitigated in one domain as long as there are wider socioeconomic vulnerabilities and little inter-departmental coordination. The situation is akin to Nandan Nilekani's observation that 'successive governments have often tended to view the problems across our education, health, industry, and infrastructure policies in isolation to each other, where each problem is separately an 'aching tooth that can be taken out' (Nilekani 2009: 2). India has large inequality, 'invisible' social groups, a large informal labour market, weak social safety nets, fragile institutions, patchy enforcement and regulation of policies, and inadequate resources, expertise, and capacity. This context abets the perpetual reproduction of risks. It not only significantly increases the likelihood and severity of risks, but also limits the population's capacity to resist, recover, and adapt to risk events (Porto and Fernandes 2006). Indian policymakers thus need to pay greater attention to any underlying physical, social, and economic vulnerabilities, and how risks and vulnerabilities across society interact and reinforce each other.

These limitations, however, are often disregarded and decisions are made by the government as though it were faced with a perfectly controlled environment. India is supremely confident in its nuclear energy program, yet Chapter 10 sketches a history of small accidents and notes a deficiency in technical staff and testing facilities in the Atomic Energy Regulatory Board (AERB). Chapter 5 details the erratic medical and drug supplies in hospitals, the poor equipment facilities, and inadequate medical training. The government, however, has pursued a policy to reduce maternal mortality by increasing the number of hospital births rather than the all-important need for better quality of care. Similarly, urban local bodies have inadequate financial and technical resources, yet these are the bodies ultimately charged with implementing the national disaster risk management framework. Rather than see only what they want to see—a blinkered trait we are all guilty of from time to time—policymakers should instead work backwards from an understanding of the local context to devise creative solutions which will function well, given the existing limitations (see Chapter 8).

There has occasionally been some appreciation of these limitations by Indian policymakers. Notably Jairam Ramesh, whilst Minister of Environment and Forests, admitted that India's regional offices do not have the capacity to monitor industry's compliance with the conditions attached to environmental approvals. Regardless, approvals continue to be granted at an alarming rate with sometimes up to 120 conditions per project. The Indian government's appraisal of risks largely appears to be divorced from the wider context and the reality of the situation at hand. Perhaps, as Saldanha and Rao argue in their chapter (Chapter 2), this situation has occurred because the Indian government's strong economic and political imperatives to grow have frequently obscured the risks on the grounds that such growth entails.

The Devil Is in the Detail

Many of the chapters have pointed to numerous instances where the government has failed to define key concepts, guiding principles, frameworks, and processes of risk assessment. For example, the parameters of risk assessment are missing from the Biotechnology Regulatory Authority of India (BRAI) Bill (Chapter 9). Furthermore, the 2006 Environmental Impact Assessment (EIA) legislation only stipulates that stakeholder consultations be held 'close by'; essentially leaving the decision to consultants who often hold these consultations miles away from the concerned village (Chapter 2). Similarly, governmental frameworks provide no clear definition of disaster management, nor do they even make a reference to the comprehensive risk management framework. It is left at the discretion of consultants completing City Development Plans (CDPs) whether they choose to commission hazard maps or integrate risk mitigation measures into their investment plans. A critical opportunity is often missed to plan and design disaster-resilient infrastructure.[2]

The devil is always in the detail. In failing to notice these details, critical opportunities to reduce risk are missed, or controversial and unexamined value judgements are hidden. The latter is particularly apparent when examining India's scientific and technological controversies, which, at first glance, appear to play out in the same language— the language of science. At the same time as new data is volleyed back and forth, terms such as 'risk', 'safety', 'uncertainty', 'development', and 'progress' are batted back and forth. Whilst the same words are employed in each party's invective, on closer examination it is clear that their understanding of these concepts is fundamentally different.

The protests at the nuclear power plant in Kudankulam are one of the most high-profile examples of this mismatch in the different understandings of 'risk' and 'development'. Officially the protests were declared to be 'overdone' and the product of a lack of 'good sense'. Prime Minister Singh hoped that they would end soon as the government had gone 'out of the way to assure the villagers about the safeguards of the facility' (Bipindra 2011). Hammering home the need for greater energy security, the government has insisted that there is no alternative and nuclear power is the only viable option. On the other hand,

[2] Ripin Kalra's conference paper.

People's Movement Against Nuclear Energy (PMANE) co-ordinator S.P. Udayakumar said, 'This is a classic David-Goliath fight between the ordinary citizens of India and the powerful Indian government supported by rich Indian capitalists, MNCs, imperial powers and the global nuclear mafia'. This statement provides a telling glimpse into how the protestors construct and understand the risks of nuclear power. Although the government frames the discussion of nuclear power in terms of opportunity, necessity, and safety, for the protestors it is mostly a question of fairness and past experience. They are concerned about transparency, indignant at being lectured to by scientists, wary as corruption leaves no institution intact and outraged to be presented with a lifestyle that they do not want. Assurances of safety and adequate expertise have unfortunately been belied too many times in the past, and when the rules have been broken there has been little effective redress and justice, as in the case of Bhopal. Unpacking and openly addressing the different concepts of 'risk', 'fairness', 'development', and 'progress' that have been at play in India can be the first step towards developing institutional arrangements that can negotiate constructively between these different positions.

A Call for the Social Sciences

This volume points to the very real and urgent need for the multi-disciplinary social sciences to be encouraged in India so that they may find their place alongside technical risk analyses. Scientific and technical knowledge has been revered by India's policymakers, whilst the expertise of those from fields such as STS has been eclipsed. India has created structures of decision-making and regulatory frameworks which have privileged scientific expertise and sought to exclude 'irrational' and 'secondary' public concerns that they believe will hamper 'progress', that is, their vision of development. This has fuelled a number of risk conflicts. As we have seen, social scientists can probe the non-scientific judgements and assumptions underpinning scientific risk assessments (see Chapter 9), and have a role in promoting an understanding of the different cultural constructions of risk to encourage the development of socially acceptable policies. Social scientists can help create regulatory frameworks and safety cultures that are appropriate to the national context and cultural attributes (see Chapters 11 and 13). In the domains of health and natural hazards they can provide an understanding of people's behavioural patterns and the social, political, and economic roots of their risk behaviours.

Drawing on the expertise of sociologists, psychologists, and anthropologists, amongst others, will capture other aspects of reality, such as people's behavioural patterns and ways of knowing the world. Perhaps, even by putting oneself in other people's shoes, a degree of humility and self-awareness may emerge that can help move past the socially destructive conflicts that are plaguing India. Developing such a multidisciplinary research platform will enable academics, policymakers, and activists to critically reflect upon and constructively contribute to the management of risks in India.

BRIEF OVERVIEW OF THE CHAPTERS

Delving into the sociological risk literature in Chapter 1, Moor expands on each of the themes raised in the previous section, exploring the limitations of the technocratic risk framework. She begins by challenging the particularly narrow understanding of rationality embodied in the technocratic risk framework, which fails to understand how people practically reason and the 'sociological, cultural and ethical basis of human judgement'. Proponents of the technocratic risk framework assume that the 'facts will show the way' and an assessment of risks can be stripped from the polluting effects of politics, emotions, ideologies, etc. However, publics, scientists, regulators, and governments alike select and 'frame' risks according to their cultural values, politics, and past experiences. This technocratic risk framework, as Moor illustrates, has been present in the Indian context. After analysing the multiple discourses surrounding risk in India and the bias in its knowledge economy towards the hard sciences, this chapter concludes that a broader array of perspectives, framework, and disciplines should be employed to capture the many dimensions of risk that elude scientists and technical experts. After all, risks originate, are defined, and experienced in a social context.

Disasters and the Environment

Saldanha and Rao, in Chapter 2, critically explore some of these buried policy judgements and assumptions, arguing that the government's ruling mantra has long been that the risks are worth taking in the interests of India's 'progress'. But what does the Indian government understand by 'progress' and 'development', and how has this shaped the appraisal of risks in environmental decision-making? Saldanha and Rao begin by locating their analysis within India's wider political and economic context, particularly pointing to the tensions between Article 39 in the Constitution of India, which states that development must serve the wider public good, and the government's policies, which have failed to trickle down to the poor. In some depth they proceed to analyse two case studies involving projects of economic, technological, and strategic significance—Mangalore Airport and Pohang Iron and Steel Company (POSCO). These case studies reveal the extent to which there was an utter lack of discipline and rigour in the processes of risk appraisal, with tragic consequences in the case of Mangalore Airport. Where there was some uncertainty or ambiguity faith was placed in the project developer and the evidence and assurances that they submitted. India's economic policies, its structure of environmental decision-making and the two case studies evaluated in this chapter lead Saldanha and Rao to conclude that 'progress' and 'development' only favour the elite and those with agency.

In Chapter 3, Gowda and Idiculla examine how information provision can be harnessed in the Indian context to strengthen environmental compliance and to induce sustainable practices on the part of corporations. Recent years have witnessed the emergence of innovative policy instruments—such as emission trading and other market-based instruments—to induce corporations to manage environmental risks more carefully. One such policy tool involves having corporations disclose publicly their emissions into air, water, and land. The aftermath of the Bhopal tragedy resulted in the United States employing this policy measure in the form of the Superfund Amendments and Reauthorization Act, or SARA Title III, or the Community Right-to-Know Act. Once such information is publicly available, it can be used by non-governmental organizations (NGOs) to highlight the risks posed by corporations to the communities within which they operate. Such information can result in adverse public perceptions and put pressure on corporations to change their practices.

Jigyasu, in Chapter 4, examines why in India, despite enormous investments, post-disaster reconstruction outcomes have continued to differ distressingly from their objectives. In order to understand this, he argues that we must probe policymakers' fundamental risk assumptions and the 'development' ideologies that they have subscribed to. Evaluating the reconstruction policy following the Marathwada earthquake in 1993, Jigyasu argues that decision makers had a one-dimensional hazard-centric focus which overlooked underlying pre-disaster vulnerabilities. This only reinforced and even created new physical, sociocultural, and economic vulnerabilities. The development ideology of the time also deemed local knowledge, skills, and materials to be outdated and reconstruction was seen as an opportunity to 'develop' these 'backward' communities. Communities were treated as disaster *victims* rather than people who could legitimately strengthen the reconstruction process. This chapter concludes that post-disaster reconstruction is not simply the remit of engineers, nor is it just about providing earthquake resistant houses. It needs to be designed with an appreciation of the wider social context and developmental processes—a central theme in this volume.

Public Health

Kilaru et al., in Chapter 5, narrate the sadly familiar story of an India plagued by the high risks of maternal mortality. The government has successfully increased facility-based childbirth over the last decade, but, they ask, are these hard-pressed services successfully recognizing women's health risks in pregnancy, birth, and, post partum stage? Is there an understanding of women's health behaviour and the risks they perceive and prioritize? This chapter explores the quality of health services in two studies conducted nearly 10 years apart in rural Karnataka, during which time there was a 47 per cent increase in institution-based births. They show that both women's as well as their family's perception of maternal mortality risks is mediated by cultural and socioeconomic factors. Conversely, the healthcare system has tended to construct risks in a biomedical framework. The healthcare system fails to understand why women switch their planned place of delivery after labour begins or do not access appropriate care during labour and in the post-partum period seeing this as irrational and illogical behaviour. Consequently, the causes of India's persistently high maternal mortality rate remain unaddressed. Furthermore, the process of identifying, assessing, and managing these health risks has not been located in an institutional framework of accountability that prioritizes its patients. This chapter proposes that the government should adopt a more culturally attuned approach that would strengthen the quality and, not simply, the coverage of healthcare services.

Bailey, in Chapter 6, employs an organizing framework drawn from anthropology to examine the 'culture of' and the 'culture in' HIV/AIDS. Building on a case study in Goa, this chapter first looks at the 'culture of' HIV/AIDS; this refers to the organizational culture that has developed to handle this epidemic and the norms, assumptions and priorities encoded in national policies and intervention strategies. Bailey shows how the politics of risk and blame has marginalized and alienated certain groups, and, in targeting them, has critically overlooked the changing nature of risk groups in India. He further examines the impact of national policies and international aid on the people delivering these interventions at the grassroots level. In examining 'culture in' HIV/AIDS risk management, this chapter shows how the cultural construction of risk (including whether words for risk exist in the local language) affects people's behaviour and understanding of HIV/AIDS. This chapter makes a strong case for the inclusion of more culturally grounded knowledge and practices in risk management, which will help in both reducing the risk of HIV and better management of the risk for those living with the virus.

Ramaswamy, in Chapter 7, traces the Indian government's risk communication strategy during the H1N1 pandemic; from the first suspected case in April 2009 to the period of full-fledged panic when the first confirmed H1N1 death was reported on 3 August. She sketches the multiple and diverse narratives that were constructed of this pandemic by the media, the government, healthcare providers, and the private sector. While media was bloodthirsty for real-time drama and sensationalism, the government was preoccupied with the immediate political ramifications of the pandemic and alternated between issuing empty statements that the pandemic was under control to shifting the onus of the blame to private hospitals and state governments. A haphazard and uncoordinated risk communication approach resulted in a deficiency of credible information, contradictory, and damaging advisories from health authorities, media sensationalism, and public hysteria. Effective risk communication strategies rely on trust, confidence, and credibility. In the Indian context where, Ramaswamy argues, neither the government nor the media are seen to be particularly trustworthy, and the health system clearly does not have the capacity to withstand a pandemic, what risk communication strategies should be developed? This chapter articulates a set of vital recommendations for the design of risk communication strategies, particularly stressing the need for locally grounded research and data to fill the void in communication research in India.

In Chapter 8, Sgaier presents the Bill and Melinda Gates Foundation's 'game changing' approach to tackling India's rapidly escalating HIV/AIDS epidemic. Given the urgency and scale of the epidemic, the Avahan Programme's objectives were to provide HIV/AIDS services to 300,000 high-risk groups (HRGs) and over five million men at risk simultaneously across 600 towns in 83 districts within the first 2–3 years. To effectively roll out this ambitious initiative, the programme drew on many of the lessons and principles underlying the strategy of a large-scale service or retail company. First and foremost, a successful business needs to understand its market in order to design an appropriate business strategy. It identifies and gathers information on the behavioural patterns of its potential consumers, the best locations to set up retail outlets, investigates the demand for its good and how it can quickly reach its targeted consumers. It develops strong management structures and processes throughout its delivery chain, securing the relevant expertise for its business, and ensures that secure foundations are created to sustain the business in the years to come. These structures are designed to be flexible, adaptable, and responsive to continually monitored data regarding its performance and the demand for its goods and services, without which the company would not survive. Sgaier presents Avahan's equivalent 'business management framework' and takes us through each of these steps in the delivery of its innovative programme.

Science and Technology

In Chapter 9, Millstone asks what should be the appropriate division of labour between 'experts' and policymakers. How should scientific and policy considerations be separated or integrated? The Indian Ministry of Environment's public consultation process in the Bt brinjal case very openly brought these issues to a head in India. Millstone begins by outlining the technocratic and Red Book models of science in regulatory policymaking which have evolved in the US and Europe. Discarding these models because of their unrealistic assumptions about the completeness and certainty of scientific knowledge, and the artificial dividing line they maintain between science and politics, he sets out a new analytical 'co-dynamic' framework. Using this framework to explore the assessment of the possible risks from GM brinjal, or Bt brinjal, Millstone exposes the non-scientific and unacknowledged policy assumptions and judgements underlying Mahyco's assessment of risks, an assessment the Genetic Engineering Approval Committee (GEAC) endorsed. These assumptions determined the framing of the questions, what and how much evidence was sufficient, and the criteria for interpreting the evidence about Bt brinjal. Commenting on the Indian government's bizarre decision to re-impose a technocratic framework with the tabling of the BRAI Bill, Millstone concludes that it is time for the policy stakeholders to recognize that their scientific assessments are framed by 'up-stream' policy judgements and assumptions.

Chapter 10 by Ramana investigates the Department of Atomic Energy's (DAE) claim that 'Safety is accorded overriding priority in all activities. All nuclear facilities are sited, designed, constructed, commissioned and operated in accordance with strict quality and safety standards... As a result, India's safety record has been excellent in over 260 reactor years of operation of power reactors and various other applications.' (GOI 2007: 3) Is this diagnosis correct? Ramana explores whether India's track record measures up against international safety criteria relating to hazardous technologies. Evaluating numerous small accidents in India's various reactors and processing plants, he concludes that this confidence is misplaced and absurd; a theme that echoes throughout the volume. Exploring some of the reasons for this poor safety record, Ramana points to a host of issues we raised at the beginning of this introduction. There is the nuclear establishment's 'techno-optimistic' risk assessment approach, which underplays uncertainties and denies the possibility of many risks associated with nuclear energy. Also to blame is the DAE's unaccountable and technocratic risk framework. Finally, Ramana addresses a crucial weak point—India's AERB, highlighting its lack of financial, technical, and organizational independence from the nuclear establishment it is tasked with surveying.

Poumadère, in Chapter 11, points to the complex spectrum of technical, social, political, economic, organizational, and psychological issues that India must examine in shaping its path on nuclear energy. There has not yet been any serious research on the reasons underlying the Indian public's appreciation of nuclear energy, how they respond to the government's framing of the issue of nuclear energy, and their attitude towards scientists/experts. The range of risk perception studies Poumadère presents on Western publics' diverse reactions to nuclear energy, both before and after Fukushima, may be useful for India to take on board. He particularly stresses that for India to design appropriate deliberation mechanisms, effective risk communication strategies, and a contextually appropriate safety culture, these must be rooted in understanding of India's cultural dimensions—at the national as well as local level, amongst communities neighbouring nuclear power plants (NPPs), as well as NPP workers.

In Chapter 12, Mays looks at the hard lessons that have been learnt over the past three decades in Europe, North America, and Asia on the need for early and meaningful public engagement in RWM. Top-down efforts to site RWM facilities mostly met with failure in the face of strong public resistance. India's AERB, though, has stated that technical regulation and control should provide 'adequate assurance' to the public and secure their trust and confidence. Will this be sufficient to secure a 'social license to operate'? She investigates the factors that may positively or negatively influence the Indian public's confidence in the Indian nuclear establishment—factors that the government should be aware of if it is to shape a trusted RWM strategy. Experience in the West has shown that to dispel negative perceptions of radioactive waste and break down the 'us versus them', 'David versus Goliath' attitude afflicting the relationship between communities and institutions, the nuclear establishment should take publics into confidence and work with them to develop trusted RWM strategies. She also traces the various successful partnership arrangements and governance processes operating in Europe, where some communities now volunteer and compete to host these facilities. Working in partnership with governments and other stakeholders, they investigate technical issues, socioeconomic concerns, and design community benefit packages. Mays concludes that technical soundness is not sufficient to gain the trust of citizens or develop sustainable and socially acceptable RWM solutions—procedural fairness is of equal importance.

Chapter 13 presents the key challenges to Health and Safety regulations in the 21st Century. Bouder first explores the pros and cons of hazard-based v. risk-based regulation; echoing a central debate in India about whether risks should be avoided or managed. He then proceeds to explore different Health and Safety regulation models in the US and Europe and how they have dealt with 'risk' and 'uncertainty'. These different models and styles have evolved out of each country's political and administrative culture, and in response to their own history of accidents. Whilst these models are unique to each country, undertaking such a comparative analysis may be useful for India to reflect upon its own regulatory model. Finally the chapter examines how health and safety regulators need to keep pace with, and adapt risk management procedures to, changing societal expectations—lessons that could prove useful in the Indian context.

BIBLIOGRAPHY

Adam, B., U. Beck, and J. van Loon (eds) (2000). *The Risk Society and Beyond, Critical Issues for Social Theory*. London: Sage Publications.

Beck, U. (1999). *World Risk Society*. Cambridge: Polity Press.

Bipindra, N.C. (2011). 'Kudankulum Protests Overdone Says PM', *Hindustan Times*, 17 December, available at http://www.hindustantimes.com/world-news/kudankilam-protests-overdone-says-pm/article1-783721.aspx, last accessed on 7 April 2014.

Borthakur, A., and S. Singh (2012). 'Electronic Waste in India: Problems and Policies', *International Journal of Environmental Sciences*, 3(1), available at http://www.ipublishing.co.in/ijesarticles/twelve/articles/volthree/EIJES31033.pdf, last accessed on 7 April 2014.

Caplan, P. (ed.) (2000). *Risk Revisited*. London: Pluto Press.

Chamberlain, G. (2009). 'India's Generation of Children Crippled by Uranium Waste', *The Observer*, 30 August, available at http://www.guardian.co.uk/world/2009/aug/30/india-punjab-children-uranium-pollution, last accessed on 13 October 2013.

Douglas, M. (1986). *Risk Acceptability According to the Social Sciences*. London: Routledge and Kegan Paul.

———— (1992). *Risk and Blame: Essays in Cultural Theory*. London: Routledge.

Douglas, M., and A.B. Wildavsky (1982). *Risk and Culture: An Essay on the Selection of Technical and Environmental Dangers*. Berkeley: University of California Press.

Financial Express (2005). 'A Wiser Approach to E-Waste', 14 November, available at http://www.financialexpress.com/news/a-wiser-approach-to-ewaste/159134/, last accessed on 13 October 2013.

Gandhi, D. (2012). 'Garden City Lost Two-thirds of its Vegatation in Four Decades', *The Hindu*, 18 April, available at http://www.thehindu.com/news/cities/bangalore/article3325346.ece, last accessed on 13 October 2013.

Giddens, A. (1999). 'Risk and Responsibility', *The Modern Law Review*, 62: 1–10.

Government of India (2007). *National Report to the Convention on Nuclear Safety*, available at http://www.infraline.com/power/nuclear/NationRepp ConventNuclearSafety-Sep07.pdf, last accessed on 13 October 2013.

Hindu (2012). 'Ground Water Contaminated, Punjab Battles Uranium Curse', *The Hindu*, 13 July, accessible at http://www.thehindu.com/health/medi cine-and-research/article3635131.ece, last accessed on 13 October 2013.

Hindustan Times (2012). 'Jairam differs with PM, says no NGO forced Bt Brinjal ban', *Hindustan Times*, 25 February, available at http://www.hindustantimes. com/india-news/jairam-differs-with-pm-says-no-ngo-forced-bt-brinjal-ban/article1-816910.aspx, last accessed on 7 April 2014.

Hume, David (1739). *A Treatise of Human Nature*.

Jasanoff, S. (1999). 'The Songlines of Risk', *Environmental Values*, 8: 135–52.

——— (2002). 'Risk, Precaution and Environmental Values', *Carnegie Council*, available at http://www.carnegiecouncil.org/media/683_jasanoff.pdf, last accessed on 1 December 2012.

——— (2004). *States of Knowledge: The Co-production of Science and the Social Order*. London: Taylor and Francis.

——— (2009). 'Governing Innovation', *India Seminar*, 597, available at http://www.india-seminar.com/2009/597/597_sheila_jasanoff.htm, last accessed on 13 October 2013.

Kalam, A., and S. Singh (2011). 'Nuclear Power is Our Gateway to a Prosperous Future', 6 November, *The Hindu*, available at http://www.thehindu.com/opinion/op-ed/article2601471.ece, last accessed on 13 October 2013.

Krimsky, S., and D. Golding (eds) (1992). *Social Theories of Risk*. Westport: Praegar.

Lash, S., B. Szerszynski, and B. Wynne (eds) (1996). *Risk, Environment and Modernity: Towards a New Ecology*. London: Sage Publications.

Leach, M., I. Scoones, and B. Wynne (eds) (2005). *Science and Citizens: Globalization and the Challenge of Engagement*. London: Zed Books.

Löfstedt, R., and L. Frewer (eds) (1998). *Risk & Modern Society*. London: Earthscan.

Lupton, D. (2006). 'Sociology and Risk' in G. Mythen, and S. Walklate (eds), *Beyond the Risk Society: Critical Reflections on Risk and Human Security*. Buckingham: Open University Press.

Mukherji, A. (2012). 'India Uproots Most People for "Progress"', *The Times of India*, 4 June, available at http://articles.timesofindia.indiatimes.com/2012-06-04/india/32030869_1_internal-displacement-shivani-chaudhry-land-rights-network, last accessed on 13 October 2013.

Newstrack (2012). 'Manmohan Singh promises new national policy on science and technology by year-end', *Newstrack India*, 2 June, available at http://www.newstrackindia.com/newsdetails/2012/06/02/308-Manmohan-Singh-promises-new-national-policy-on-science-and-technology-by-year-end.html, last accessed on 13 October 2013.

Nilekani, N. (2009). *Imagining India: The Idea of a Renewed Nation*. New York: The Penguin Press HC.

Porto, M., and C. Freitas (1996). 'Major Chemical Accidents in Industrialising Countries: The Socio-Political Amplification of Risk', *Risk Analysis*, 16(1): 19–29.

Porto, M.F.D.S., and L.D.O Fernandes (2006). 'Understanding Risks in Socially Vulnerable Contexts: The Case of Waste Burning in Cement Kilns in Brazil', *Safety Science*, 44: 241–57.

Power, M. (2004). 'The Risk Management of Everything: Rethinking the Politics of Uncertainty', *Demos*, available at http://www.demos.co.uk/files/riskmanagementofeverything.pdf, last accessed on 13 October 2013.

Ramesh, J. (2011). 'Nehru's Scientific Temper Recalled', Text of 13th Convocation Address delivered at IIT, 27 May, Guwahati.

Starr, C. (1969). 'Social Benefit versus Technological Risk'. *Readings in Risk*, 183–94.

Stirling, A. (2007). 'Risk, Precaution and Science: Towards a More Constructive Policy Debate', *EMBO Reports*, 8: 309–15, available at http://www.nature.com/embor/journal/v8/n4/full/7400953.html, last accessed on 13 October 2013.

———— (2009). 'Risk, Uncertainty and Power', *India Seminar*, 597, available at http://www.india-seminar.com/2009/597/597_andy_stirling.htm, last accessed on 13 October 2013.

———— (2012). 'Opening Up the Politics of Knowledge and Power in Bioscience', *PLoS Biology*, 10(1), available at http://sro.sussex.ac.uk/40172/1/journal.pbio.1001233.pdf, last accessed on 7 April 2014.

Stirling, A., and A. Scott (2011). 'Risky Advice and Immeasurable Uncertainties', *Aljazeera*, 6 June, available at http://www.aljazeera.com/indepth/opinion/2011/06/201163124740332864.html, last accessed on 13 October 2013.

Suraiya, J. (2012). 'Fighters Vs Toilets: Walking the Tightrope Between Defence and Development', *The Economic Times*, 15 August, available at http://articles.economictimes.indiatimes.com/2012-08-15/news/33216755_1_defence-minister-defence-budgets-india-and-pakistan, last accessed on 13 October 2013.

Visvanathan, S. (2001). 'Democracy, Governance and Science: Strange Case of the Missing Discipline', *Economic and Political Weekly*, (29 September to 5 October), 36(39): 3684–8.

Wynne, B. (1992). 'Misunderstood Misunderstandings: Social Identities and Public Uptake of Science', *Public Understanding of Science*, 1(3): 281–304.

——— (1996). 'May the Sheep Safely Graze?', in S. Lash, B. Szerszynski, and B. Wynne (eds), *Risk, Environment and Modernity, Towards a New Ecology*. London: Sage Publications.

1

RAPHAELLE MOOR

Adopting a Multi-dimensional Lens to Approaching Risk in India

This chapter ties together a number of the themes that are dealt with in detail in the following chapters, and draws on insights and personal research conducted in India between 2010 and 2012. This period was a particularly an opportune time for studying debates concerning risk in India, with the spotlight on Jairam Ramesh's public crusade at the Ministry of Environment and Forests, the seminal Bt brinjal debates, the protracted nuclear power protests at Jaitapur and Kudankulam, and the drafting of the Nuclear Liability Bill and Biotechnology Regulatory Authority of India (BRAI) Bill. A key observation that emerges from examining all these developments is that the responsibility for managing risk in India has remained within the tight grip of the technically minded, that is, the scientists and engineers. Public consultations are mostly still confined to discussing alleged scientific facts rather than broader societal or ethical concerns, and deviating from the limits that have been set down prompts refusals to engage with what is considered irrational and hysterical behaviour.

Each of the chapters in this volume, however, invariably shows that risks originate, are defined and experienced within particular social contexts. Firstly, the identification and assessment of risks does not take place in an apolitical bubble; as will be elaborated upon in this chapter. Secondly, scientific risk assessments cannot settle many of the political conflicts surrounding risk and should not be used to 'dictate' policies. This is David Hume's 'is-ought' problem which states that a normative statement cannot be inferred from a descriptive one (Pielke 2007). Lastly, a solely technical assessment of risk ignores the social, economic, and political conditions that are often the reason that risks become reality. This chapter thus makes the case for opening up India's institutions and policies to other disciplines, perspectives, and frameworks which will capture the dimensions of risk that elude scientists and technicians.

TECHNOCRATIC RISK FRAMEWORK

Conventionally, risk assessment is understood to involve predicting certain outcomes and the probability that these will arise in order to arrive at a single sound quantitative picture of risk (Stirling 2012). This purely scientific and technical approach to risk analysis argues that experts, armed with knowledge about the 'true' risk involved and wielding their toolbox of various technical fixes, will be able to rationally decide what should be done to ensure our safety. This is a typical technocratic risk framework—where attempts are made to turn policymaking into a purely technical exercise. The role of the government and their chosen experts within this framework is to educate us about the true risks at large so that we may accordingly adjust our 'misperceptions' and our behaviour to match their constructions of risk. Those who endorse this approach believe that if we are given the real facts about man-made risks, shown that we have accepted similar, if not worst, risks in the past, and told what benefits these risks will bring, then our subjective perception of risk will automatically fall into step with the expert's ostensibly 'objective' calculation of risk. This is the renowned 'information deficit model', and it often goes hand in hand with the technocratic risk framework.

The information deficit model suggests that the public resists new technologies or projects because they lack the right information, and are incapable of processing it; because they are ruled by irrational fears, are uneducated or 'backward'; because they foolishly expect zero risk;

or simply because they distrust those in authority. Such technocratic approaches assume that the public suffers from 'cognitive failure', irrationality, and ignorance. Essentially they see the public as 'fools' (Douglas 1992: 13). In reaction to the mass protests at Kundakulum's nuclear power plant in Tamil Nadu, for example, mental health specialists were sent to 'counsel' protestors. Others were charged with 'sedition' and 'waging war against the state' (The Hindu 2012). In another attempt to mollify the opposition, the Nuclear Power Corporation of India Ltd (NPCIL) released a comic book saying, '[I]f you have to, then protest against misconceptions and wrongs and not against progress' (Basu 2012)—as though 'progress' was uni-directional. Under the technocratic risk framework public deliberation is therefore typically seen as a brake on progress and an 'inefficient bottleneck' (Scoones 2012) which only risks 'demoralising scientists' (Agriculture Minister Sharad Pawar on Bt brinjal moratorium in Chaudhury 2010).

SOCIOLOGICAL, CULTURAL, AND ETHICAL THEORY OF HUMAN JUDGEMENT: PROCESSING RISK

The technocratic approach suggests that risks can and, most peculiarly, *ought* to be analysed within a social vacuum. But do risks, that is, the possibility of undesirable outcomes, make sense detached from their contexts? What people consider to be acceptable or undesirable will always depend on their values and preferences. Most people are not just concerned about minimizing risk and physical harm, or even maximizing their payoffs; they often see greater value in the equitable distribution of risk, fairness, and individual rights. Many demand the right to not be unnecessarily and dangerously exposed to risks they never agreed to, or which solely benefit others. Some may believe that risks to children outweigh those to older people, or consider the risk of poverty to take priority over risks to animals and the environment. Others may heavily discount the future and prioritize risks to the present generation.

There are also those who consider the morality of an action, not just the different outcomes and probabilities. Who exposes whom to risk and why, is one such pivotal question. For example, what are the intentions of the person who has decided to take an action that may pose a risk to others and what assessment have they taken prior to this decision? Who may be impacted by their action and what is their relationship to those who may be affected—is there an imbalance of power? (Hayenhjelm and Wolff 2001; Hansson 2003).

> Compare, for instance, the act of throwing down a brick on a person from a high building to the act of throwing down a brick from a high building without first making sure that there is nobody beneath who can be hit by the brick. The moral difference between these two acts are not obviously expressible in a probability calculus. (Hansson 2003: 302)

The public may equally be concerned about the procedure of decision-making. What are the processes for obtaining consent from communities being exposed to risk, for example? Compensation is sometimes a means of securing consent, yet to offer compensation to those who can least afford to turn it down may seem exploitative. Less compensation will need to be offered to tribal communities than to the inhabitants of a gated community in Delhi, in the unlikely event of it being torn down. Many will also have strong views about whether it is acceptable for the government to engage in risky projects when there is neither an adequate safety net nor the requisite resources and expertise to deal with a potential fallout.

The process of reasoning and forming judgements about risk includes many other considerations and concerns (as seen above) than just information on the magnitude and probability. When people think about and judge risk it is rarely in quantitative terms; people 'reason dramatically, not quantitatively' (Dowie 1980: 108, cited in Caplan 2000: 157). In making decisions about risks—what counts as risk, which to take or avoid, which to prioritize—emotions, values, principles, and experience, all feed into the decision-making process. It is natural to call on previous experience; ask about the values, integrity, trustworthiness and track record of those providing facts and assurances of 'safety'; consider the processes through which this evidence is gathered, which may be illegitimate and lack transparency; ask who is responsible if things go wrong and reflect on what hidden agendas and interests may be at stake. None of these can be expressed in technical quantitative terms (Fischer 2005: 56).

Mary Douglas and Aaron Wildavsky, pioneers of the cultural theory of risk, argued that the risks people select and the blame they apportion for being subject to those risks is a 'normal strategy for protecting a particular set of values belonging to a particular way of life' (Douglas and Wildavsky 1982: 8.) They famously said: '[T]he choice of risk and the choice of how to live are taken together' (1982: 8). It would be entirely foolish and irrational for citizens not to consider their values, past experience, and the social context to which technologies or projects may be introduced.[1] Interesting studies by Sandman (cited in Fischer 2005: 59) even showed that when experts were asked to think of themselves as only fathers, rather than engineers, they discarded their technical model of decision-making and instead considered issues of trust and past experience, that is, they reasoned practically.

What does this mean for the technocratic risk framework that we outlined here earlier? Firstly, it becomes clear that technical risk discourses, which demand that publics should reason quantitatively, are irrational as they ignore how people practically reason and the 'sociological, cultural, and ethical basis of human judgement' (Douglas 1992: 3). Secondly, by not recognizing the cultural dimensions and context within which attitudes towards risk form, this approach fails to grasp why certain risks become politicized. Thirdly, technical risk discourses 'banalise moral dilemmas' (Visvanathan, cited in Leach, Scoones, and Wynne 2002: 4) and bury the political and value judgements involved in assessing and regulating risk. As Erik Millstone aptly put it, technical risk discourses are 'often a polite way of talking about politics without making it sound too political' (Millstone, conference discussions).

CAN FACTS SHOW THE WAY?

Scientists and technical experts may recognize that politics will creep into the regulation of risks, yet in an attempt to be free of all bias they regularly insist that they can still bracket-off the polluting effects of politics, emotions, and ideologies to get at the 'real essence' of risk (Douglas 1992). Proponents of the technocratic risk framework essentially believe that facts will show the way. Facts are seen to come first and politics after; muddying the waters and pushing people further

[1] See Chapter 12 for an interesting discussion of the range of factors that citizens are likely to weigh up in assessing India's radioactive waste management strategy.

away from 'rational' behaviour. Buried under all these normative considerations on justice, fairness, and the 'good life' is there not, they argue, a measure of risk that can first be objectively determined by experts and the politics dealt with later?

To answer this, consider how people, scientists included, process and construct the world around them. When people inwardly or outwardly express what they are seeing, their minds do not first passively notice the facts 'out there' and *then* verbalize this information. Perception and expression are in fact one process. Language and thought processes cannot momentarily be escaped in order to impartially judge how well these capture reality. Information is selected, ordered and generally made sense of according to intellectual frameworks, values, emotions, culture, past experience, and social context. This is not to say that there is no real world 'out there' to perceive. Rather, as the poet Wordsworth suggests, you half-create the world you see; your mind is both a 'creator and receiver' (Bronck 2009: 258).

Recent neuro-scientific studies have in fact shown: '[I]f it weren't for our emotions, reason wouldn't exist at all' (Lehrer 2009: 20). Studying the behaviour of patients who had damaged their orbitofrontal cortex (OFC), it was found that whilst they initially seemed fine and were found to score the same on IQ tests, they were completely unable to make decisions and were strangely devoid of any emotion. It was discovered that the OFC connects feelings generated by the amygdala, the 'primitive' brain, to conscious thought and decision making. When this connection was severed patients were unable to take a decision. Essentially, '[A] brain that can't feel can't make up its mind' (ibid.: 22). The perceived dichotomy between reason and emotion, where emotions are typically seen to lead us astray from rational decisions—is no longer tenable.

It is therefore understandable that each of us filters, processes, and interprets the chaos of world around us in different ways. A group of individuals observing the same situation will hone in and select very different features and harmful agents, find and establish very different patterns, and, through this, impose a semblance of order and control that will reflect their understanding of the world. This is nowhere more obvious than in the case of risks. Risk is a word that refers to the future, a future which can only exist in our imaginations (Adams 2009). Images of risk are constructed by people not through pristine lenses but through those shaped by cultural values, politics, and history. These cognitive devices are otherwise known as 'frames'. Therefore if people have very different ideas of 'how the world is, then it is only to be expected that they will have very different ideas of what risks are out there' (Douglas and Wildvasky 1982: 147).

The use of frames is not just limited to the lay public, but to experts, regulators, and policymakers alike. Regulators and policymakers routinely decide what count as the costs and benefits of a project, and how to compare and calculate the two. They choose between utilitarian or rights-based approaches to justice and define what is meant by 'progress'. They decide what role public engagement should play in risk analysis, how the consultation agenda should be framed, how the issues should be discussed and who should participate. Expert risk assessments are equally shaped by pre-existing assumptions and value judgements as Stirling (2005) explains:

> The choice of policy questions, the bounding of institutional remits, the prioritizing of research, the inclusion of disciplines, the accrediting of expertise, the recruitment of committees, the setting of agendas, the structuring of enquiries, the forming of hypotheses, the choice between methodologies, the interpretation of uncertainties, the setting of base lines, the exploring of sensitivities, the definition of metrics, the characterization of decision options, the prioritizing of criteria and the constitution of 'proof' all provide ample latitude for contingency or agency. (ibid.: 224)

Since the criteria for risk assessment are matters of social judgement, is there no way of judging whether one process of risk assessment is more accurate or robust than others? (Zwanenberg and Millstone 2000) Can we ever decide what counts as legitimate knowledge? Revealing the social and cultural roots of competing knowledge claims does not necessarily throw us into a dizzying spiral of relativism where anything goes. Firstly, in arguing for the inclusion of non-official, non-technical, lay perspectives into risk assessment this is in effect a statement on how to *improve* risk assessments. Secondly, as we will see in Erik Millstone's chapter on the assessment of Bt brinjal in India, '[O]nce we have learnt how some sets of scientific claims have been constructed, we can sometimes determine which ones have merely been shoddily or opportunistically constructed and contrast them with others that are demonstrably more robust' (Zwanenberg and Millstone 2000: 277). New empirical observations regularly force us to adjust our theories and methodologies. Accepting that there is not a neutral method for defining and assessing risk is certainly not a rejection of science. It is rather a very strong argument for including other perspectives which can capture different aspects of risk. This is more likely to improve risk assessments, as well as arrive at solutions which are socially acceptable.

'OBJECTIVE' SCIENCE MEDIATES RISK CONFLICTS IN INDIA

The lack of scientifically rigorous, credible, and independent studies of Bt brinjal was raised by activists, consumers, independent scientists, and state governments during the Bt brinjal consultations initiated by Jairam Ramesh, the Minister of Environment and Forests in 2010. There were real concerns that the data had been manipulated by commercial interests to show negligible impacts on the environment, human and animal health. Alongside doubts about the 'safety' of Bt brinjal, there were issues with labelling and the consumer's right to choose what they consume, the absence of a liability regime to compensate farmers in the event of damage, foreign control of the Indian seed market, and the need for Bt brinjal given the presence of alternative solutions to the problem of pests. The Bt brinjal debates, though criticised for being predominantly middle-class and consumer-led, were heralded by many as a significant moment in finally assessing Bt brinjal in terms of India's societal needs and concerns. Finally Jairam Ramesh announced:

> It is my duty to adopt a cautious, precautionary principle-based approach and impose a moratorium on the release of Bt brinjal, till such time *independent scientific studies* establish, to the satisfaction of both the public and professionals, the *safety of the product* from the point of view of its long-term impact on human health and the environment, including the rich genetic wealth existing in brinjal in our country. (PIB 2010: 17, emphasis added)

The final decision officially hinged on 'independent scientific studies' to establish the 'safety' of Bt brinjal (Gupta 2011). Very serious political, social, and ethical concerns were laudably raised by numerous stakeholders. Regardless, science was given the 'arbiter's role' to mediate and settle this conflict (Nandi 2010). The call on science to 'prevail' over 'public sentiment' and 'lead the way' in decisions concerning technological risks is a regular feature in Indian debates over nuclear power, biotechnology and industrial projects. For example, discussing the Bt brinjal moratorium, Science and Technology Minister Prithviraj Chavan said, 'slogan shouting and protests should not cloud scientific vision in the country'.

Jawaharlal Nehru's principle of scientific rationality can be seen to epitomize this privileging of science in India:

> It is the scientific approach, the adventurous and yet critical temper of science, the search for truth and new knowledge, the refusal to accept anything without testing and trial, the capacity to change previous conclusions in the face of new evidence, the reliance on observed fact and not on pre-conceived theory, the hard discipline of the mind—all this is necessary, not merely for the application of science but for life itself and the solution of its many problems. (Jawaharlal Nehru cited in Ramesh 2011)

Manmohan Singh drew on Nehru's principle recently in calling for younger generations to adopt a science-based value system as 'complex issues, be they genetically modified food or nuclear energy or exploration of outer space, cannot be settled by faith, emotion and fear, but by structured debate, analysis and enlightenment' (Sunderarajan 2013). A questioning mind, humility, and self-awareness are all valuable qualities that we should certainly encourage, and which Nehru hoped would break India from its stultifying habits and dogmatic beliefs, push boundaries, and broaden outlooks in India. Yet, as we have seen, we cannot disconnect from our emotions. Secondly, in most policymaking contexts, 'observed facts' cannot point us in the right direction. A good example of this is the case of the abortion, taken from Roger A. Pielke Jr's book *The Honest Broker* (2007). Scientific information will never be the most relevant information in a debate on abortion; where there are widely different commitments based on differing values, that is, pro-life v. pro-choice. No amount of scientific information will reconcile these different values and allow policymakers to arrive at a decision. Pielke (2007) explains that science cannot 'compel action' in circumstances where there are different values about both the desired outcomes and the means to achieve those outcomes, nor in instances where knowledge is contested and there is significant uncertainty. The debate on Bt brinjal in all respects appears to be one such case where scientists cannot 'compel action' for policymakers.

What is needed is rather to uncover and debate these 'pre-conceived theories', otherwise, 'instead of objectivity, we find ideological entrenchment' (Douglas 1992: 13). If what people mean by risk is intimately bound up with their ways of seeing the world, then experts are not the sole possessors of the 'truth' about risks, and 'laypeople' do not have a distorted picture of its 'true' image. This demands a complete re-evaluation of the interaction between experts, government, and society in order to determine a socially acceptable approach to risk. As a number of the chapters highlight 'science can only be on tap, not on top'.

POLITICAL, SOCIAL, AND ECONOMIC DYNAMICS OF PUBLIC DELIBERATION IN INDIA

It is when people attempt to impose their understanding of risk on others, their views on how the world should be, that society becomes riven with conflict and distrust. Those who try to frame and define risk solely from one angle and exclude the perspectives of others are in effect discarding their values, experiences, and primary concerns. This criticism holds true for all parties in a debate; the government, activists, scientists, and communities.

Kudankulam is a useful case study to explore. Many of the local protestors and the People's Movement Against Nuclear Energy (PMANE) have interpreted the government's attitude towards the risks of nuclear power as symptomatic of a society shot through with corruption, guided by political opportunism and skewed towards promoting elite and corporate interests. Shiv Visvanathan (2011) had shrewdly observed when discussing Bhopal: '[C]orruption normalizes a disaster in India'. In other words, corruption provides a familiar framework with which people can understand risk, disasters and conflicts. With the current political dynamics in India this is perhaps unsurprising. The political class has been losing its legitimacy and the Maoist conflict continues in force. As political parties feel their foothold loosening, rather than push through much needed political reforms, they have focused on short-term populist measures to try and secure a loyal vote-bank. Social fragmentation has also deepened as economic benefits fail to 'trickle down', identity politics has weakened the civic bond, the moral fibre of India's society has been waning as corruption and cronyism reign, and, to many, democracy seems to be only in name. As the litany of scandals has taken down one institution after another the public mood has continued to sour (Gopal 2011; Guha 2012; Kapur 2005).

Conversely, the conflict has been glibly described by the government as being instigated by foreigners, Naxalites, and characterized by an irrational hysteria which should not be reasoned with. Given the anti-establishment agenda traditionally associated with activists, a fear of the growing reach of Naxalites, and the political class' predominantly 'techno-optimistic' outlook, it is not altogether surprising to hear this line of attack either. India's immediate development challenges, its push to achieve 'self reliance' and become a global superpower appear to have particularly shaped the government's approach to risk. The risks on the ground from nuclear power, biotechnology, and industrial projects are frequently dismissed as insignificant. They are seen to be substantially overshadowed by the risks of not achieving energy and food security, failing to appear investor friendly or being left behind in an increasingly high-tech, globalized world.

The Indian government's attitude towards risk also appears to be shaped by the image and identity that India wants to project to the rest of the world. In Chapter 7, Ranjani Ramaswamy writes that: 'India faced strong compulsions to display preparedness and publicly echo the dominant beliefs of other powerful global actors about H1N1', even though, as she proceeds to illustrate, India was anything but adequately prepared. A particularly powerful example is India's position on nuclear power, captured by former President Abdul Kalam, who wrote in response to the recent nuclear power protests that: '[W]e cannot afford to lose the opportunity to emerge as the energy capital of the world, which coupled with the largest youth power, will be our answer to emerge as the leading economy of the world' (Kalam and Singh 2011).

These multiple discourses surrounding risk, in other words, the frameworks of meaning within which risks are understood, are grounded in India's political, social, and economic dynamics. Past and present relationships between the government and its citizens, centre and state, scientists, and Non-governmental Organizations (NGOs), have constructed these various attitudes towards risk. These fears and frustrations, historical grievances and ambitions, have dominated and shaped how both the government and public have framed certain risks

and approached each other in risk debates. Through these social interactions group identities are not only challenged and threatened, but also
constructed in opposition to others.

Entrenched in their positions, many people are wary and suspicious
of the intentions of others, seeing only 'evil' plots and political agendas.
Yet, adopting such overtly critical and dissidence-oriented approaches,
and always seeking 'others' to blame (Douglas 1992), simply results in a
failure to connect constructively. Neither does it help to see these scientific and technological controversies as being primarily problems of risk
communication. This is typical of technocratic risk frameworks which
see the public as in need of 'educating' about the 'true' risks involved.
When the problem has been framed as 'one of communication, there is
no need to question the appropriateness of existing procedures, established patterns of access to decision-making, institutional prerogatives,
and power distributions' (Rayner 2004: 358). From observing nuclear
power and biotechnology debates it is clear that it is the latter which
has been fuelling the wrath of protestors and is in dire need of being
addressed. What the public appears to be demanding is for risk management by transparent and accountable institutions which reflect a diversity of views, are reflexive, have integrity and technical competence
(Rayner 2007). In many respects, these dimensions are currently lacking
from India's institutions.

INDIA'S SKEWED KNOWLEDGE SOCIETY

This chapter has shown that it is problematic when some people define
risk for others, and by extension also decide who is deemed to be behav-
ing rationally or irrationally. Risks are often defined and legitimized
on the basis of assumptions, ethical principles, and value judgements
about 'development' and the 'good life' which are not always shared,
and most importantly have not always been negotiated or debated in
advance. These beliefs and knowledge systems do not just interpret
the world; they simultaneously construct it (Jasanoff 2004). The government will privilege certain forms of knowledge and expertise over
others, shaping the society we live in. On the basis of this officially
certified knowledge, institutions and regulatory frameworks are created, assessment methods designed, and expert committees chosen to
organize, control, and assess the technological risks that we face.

Susan Cain recently wrote a powerful book *Quiet* (2012), which looked into the implications of America's prevailing ethos on the pool of knowledge and expertise in the work place. She argues that America has become an extrovert culture, where it is the loud, impulsive risk-takers with exuberant characters that are seen as successful and talented, and thus are more valued in the workplace. Extroverts rush, and speak and do, leading, Cain argues, to crises like the bank meltdown of 2008, whilst introverts sit back and think before acting. She quotes Richard Hofstadter (Cain 2012: 155) on the consequences of this extroverted culture on policymaking: 'Tocqueville saw that the life of constant action and decision which was entailed by the democratic and business like character of American life put a premium upon rough and ready habits of mind, quick decision, and the prompt seizure of opportunities—and that all this activity was not propitious for deliberation, elaboration, or precision in thought'.

In the case of India, the government has overwhelmingly privileged scientific and technical expertise. This has moulded the views of professionals and state officials, and taught them that science alone can solve India's developmental challenges and lead to nation-building. The National Knowledge Commission report pays little attention to the social sciences, and the humanities such as philosophy and art barely find a mention, whereas management, engineering, and legal education are discussed in depth (Gowda 2009). The following quotes perfectly capture the bias in official representations of India's knowledge society: 'Indian governments have long recognized the need for any country that aspires to call itself a modern nation to invest heavily in science and technology' (Hon'ble Minister of State for Science and Technology and Earth Sciences, Shri Kapil Sibal 2003). Inaugurating the Science Congress, Manmohan Singh said: '[I]f India has to emerge as a knowledge power in the 21st century, then it can only be through a strong capability in science and technology' (India Government Report).[2] And famously, of course, Nehru said: '[I]t is science alone that can solve the problems of hunger and poverty, of insanity and illiteracy, of superstition and deadening custom and tradition, of vast resources running to waste, of a rich country inhabited by starving people... The future

---

[2] See http://pib.nic.in/newsite/erelease.aspx?relid=56577, last accessed on 17 March 2014.

belongs to science and those who make friends with science' (cited in Irwin and Wynne 2004: 6).

India's knowledge society has been heavily skewed towards the hard sciences, whilst the social sciences and humanities are sadly overlooked by the government. Each of the chapters in this volume very clearly illustrates this bias. Maternal mortality is officially tackled through a medical framework which does not investigate the reality of people's lives or consider the social, economic, and cultural roots of their health behaviour (Kilaru et al., Chapter 5 of this volume). Earthquake reconstruction efforts are dominated by engineers and technical experts, and the economic, political, and social roots of physical vulnerability are overlooked (Jigyasu, Chapter 4 of this volume). Similarly, nuclear power has remained firmly within the hands of scientists and engineers, and while the benefits of nuclear power are vehemently asserted, the risks and uncertainties are downplayed or denied (Ramana, Chapter 10 of this volume). Developing a sound safety culture, however, requires multidisciplinary expertise to investigate Indian cultural attributes and patterns of behaviour in relation to decision-making and authority (Poumadère, Chapter 11 of this volume). An investigation of this type was carried out in Japan on the causes of the Fukushima disaster, blaming the 'ingrained conventions of Japanese culture: our reflexive obedience; our reluctance to question authority; our devotion to "sticking with the program"; our groupism; and our insularity' (BBC News 2012). A similar investigation was regretfully never officially carried out in India after the Bhopal disaster.

By approaching and framing risks solely in technical terms, other societal concerns and meanings are ignored. While the Bt brinjal debates raised many of these concerns, the BRAI Bill proposed the establishment of a body that will leave the assessment, regulation, and authorization of biotechnological crops in the hands of scientists (See Chapter 9). A recent study by Jayanthi et al. (2012) on nanotechnology developments also criticizes the lack of attention paid to societal concerns, which are seen by the government as inimical to progress. There has yet to be any research on the environmental, health, and safety aspects of nanotechnology, which has remained within the domain of scientists and engineers. They do note that this is not entirely surprising given that in the past three science and technology statements only that in 1983 makes a passing reference to the need to analyse the environmental impact of technologies. Not only are publics' perspectives and definitions of 'progress' not factored into the process of risk analysis, but the various local knowledge and experiences of communities are regretfully overlooked. Rohit Jigyasu (Chapter 4 of this volume) suggests creating partnerships with local communities who can provide a cost-free source of knowledge on the risks and vulnerabilities of their environment, as well as create and maintain a more disaster-resilient infrastructure appropriate to the local conditions.

In the country, of Bhopal it is amply clear by now that the context within which technologies come to rest will constitute the riskiness of technologies. Victims of Bhopal were let down by India's woefully deficient emergency response structure, and then again by its judicial system, which, twenty years on, has yet to assign legal culpability for the accident or distribute all of the financial compensation (Jasanoff 2007). In Ravi Rajan's (2002a) analysis of the Bhopal disaster he concluded that India's vulnerability to disasters partly lay in the state's 'missing expertise'. This 'refers to the phenomenon wherein the production of the potential for risk is not matched by a concomitant creation of expertise and institutions with the wherewithal to help mitigate a crisis, should one ensue' (ibid.: 237). Persistently, however, India's institutional capacity and wider vulnerabilities are ignored in the official assessment and regulation of risks. The nuclear liability bill, for example, was drafted without the involvement of the health ministry, even though they would be responsible in the event of a nuclear accident and disturbingly claimed that there was not the medical capacity to deal with radioactive fallout (See Chapter 10 by M.V. Ramana). It appears that risks in India are largely still assessed and managed as though they exist in ideal, fully controllable, laboratory like conditions, a criticism earlier raised by Brian Wynne in relation to the European context (Wynne 1992, 1996). Risks are officially assessed and managed in isolation from their wider context, including existing resource and staffing constraints, India's history of regulatory failures, and how they interact with other risks and vulnerabilities in society.

The frame needs to be widened to include the social context and recognize the pre-existing social, economic, and physical vulnerabilities that can give rise to such disasters. This can partly be achieved by accepting the need for the expertise of social scientists to be ranked alongside that of engineers and scientists, and by their inclusion to trigger a cultural shift in the knowledge privileged in Indian society. Social scientists can debate and help frame the questions given to scientists. They can also probe and question society's prevailing ethos—what knowledge, expertise, and people are most valued in society—and thus encourage a broader range of perspectives to be included in the assessment of risks.

CONCLUDING NOTES: MULTIDISCIPLINARY APPROACHES TO RISK ANALYSIS

Wordsworth warned:

> In weakness we create distinctions, then
> Believe that all our puny boundaries are things
> Which we perceive and not which we have made
> (quoted in Bronck 2009: 285)

Pre-conceived theories are inevitable. They efficiently direct people's attention and resources to the problem at hand, thus focusing their vision. Yet they can also blind people to other aspects of reality. Thomas Kuhn argued that paradigms are intellectually self-reinforcing. Using one theoretical framework people risk only seeing what their model reveals and either overlooking anomalies or twisting and fitting reality to the theoretical model. As Paul Krugman wrote: '[T]he act of modelling has the effect of destroying information as well as creating it' (quoted in Bronck 2009: 278). It is therefore important to use a plurality of perspectives and frameworks that will provide a richer understanding of risk.

India has been officially dominated by the hard sciences, which has inevitably produced a particularly technical understanding of risk. But, as we have seen, much eludes this narrow perspective. In this chapter I have particularly concentrated on the limitations of such a purely scientific approach with respect to technologies such as nuclear power and biotechnology, yet this is also true of the fields of health and natural hazards. Epidemiology has been a particularly dominant approach in public health research and practice, relying on statistical methods and large scale surveys. It has however, been criticized for its 'narrowly quantitative methods, framed in positive assumptions' which 'treat data as an aggregation of individual cases' and tend to 'rely on technical fixes' (Bujra 2000: 64). Sociological accounts instead gather qualitative data and examine the meaning of risk behaviours, why diverse peoples behave the way they do, the relationship between communities and health professionals, the influence of cultural and religious practices on health behaviour, gender inequality, and of course the impact of economic, social, and political vulnerabilities.

Similarly, disaster management has historically belonged to the fields of the natural and applied sciences—the geologists, seismologists, meteorologists, geographers, and engineers. Information is gathered on the physical aspect of natural disasters, modelling systems are employed to calculate the physical vulnerability to hazards, and new building materials and safer construction standards are developed. Yet, this method gives little attention to the social, economic, and political factors underlying this physical vulnerability. Rapid and uncontrollable urbanization processes, demographic pressures, environmental degradation, poverty, and structural economic vulnerability not only increase a community's physical vulnerability to disasters, but also limit their ability to adapt and recover from natural hazards. A purely technical approach to disaster management overlooks the fact that disasters are in fact a product of their natural and social environments.

Social scientists, using a range of different perspectives and frameworks, can explore people's risk behaviours and study the socially embedded character of policymakers', scientists', and communities' knowledge and constructions of risk (Wynne 1992). They can map out the social context within which risks originate and are experienced—the social, political, and economic factors that may increase the severity and probability of risks occurring and people's vulnerability to these risks. Looking at the cause of the 2007 economic and banking crisis, Richard Bronck (2009), explains:

> You cannot fully explain or predict economic and market behaviour unless you have learned to empathise with (the better to interpret) the various mind-sets and conceptual structures that influence beliefs and reasons for action. Without analytical imagination—the conscious effort and unconscious ability to place yourselves in the conceptual shoes of other market participants—you are always liable to miss key aspects of what is going on. (Bronck 2010)

Similarly, you cannot fully explain or predict risk behaviours unless you understand the 'various mindsets' and 'conceptual structures' shaping people's attitudes towards risk. Risk crises will continue as long as policymakers fail to design policies which are not attuned to people's behaviour. Furthermore, it is necessary for policymakers and scientists alike to prise open and explore the values and principles underlying their own assessments and understandings of risk. There is a need on their part for 'self-reflexive humility, awareness, and debate' (Leach et al. 2005: 6). In her book *Quiet* (2012), Susan Cain states that

> it often pays to be quiet and gracious, to listen more than talk, and to have an instinct for harmony rather than conflict. With this style, you can take aggressive positions without inflaming your counterpart's ego. And by listening, you can learn what's truly motivating the person you're negotiating with and come up with creative positions that satisfy both parties. (p. 216)

From each of these books, be it poetry, behavioural economics, risk literature, or popular psychology, the message remains the same—to engage in more critical introspection and reflection, to put oneself in other people's shoes and be open to new perspectives, theories, systems of knowledge, and disciplines. Risk management needs to take place in transparent and accountable institutions which reflect a diversity of views (Rayner 2007). If India were to move beyond the technocratic risk framework and open up its institutions to the expertise of social scientists and the value of people's different worldviews and knowledge this will help create safer, more effective, and socially acceptable risk policies.

BIBLIOGRAPHY

Adams, J. (2009). 'Risk Management: The Economics and Morality of Safety Revisited', in C. Dale, and T. Anderson, (eds), *Safety Critical Systems: Problems, Process and Practice*. London: Springer.

Basu, M. (2012). 'Waging a "Nuclear" War, With Comics & Cartoons', *Indian Express*, 16 July, available at http://www.indianexpress.com/news/waging-a-nuclear-war-with-comics-&-cartoons/975010/2, last accessed on 21 October 2013.

BBC News (2012). 'Fukushima Report: Key Points in Nuclear Disaster Report', *BBC News*, 5 July, available at http://www.bbc.co.uk/news/world-asia-18718486, last accessed on 21 October 2013.

Bidwai, P. (2011). 'No Margin for Error', *Hindustan Times*, 4 June, available at http://www.hindustantimes.com/News-Feed/ColumnsOthers/No-margin-for-error/Article1-865997.aspx, last accessed on 21 October 2013.

Bipindra, N.C. (2011). 'Kudankulam Protests Overdone, says PM', *Hindustan Times*, 17 December, available at http://www.hindustantimes.com/News-Feed/World/Kudankulam-protests-overdone-says-PM/Article1-783721.aspx, last accessed on 21 October 2013.

Bowonder, B. (1987). 'The Bhopal Accident', *Technological Forecasting and Social Change*, 32: 169–82.

Bradbury, J. (1989). 'The Policy Implications of Differing Concepts of Risk', *Science Technology Human Values*, 14: 380.

Bronck, R. (2009). *The Romantic Economist: Imagination in Economics*. Cambridge: Cambridge University Press.

——— (2010). *The Romantic Economist Addresses the Limits of Knowledge in Markets*, 28 April, available at http://www.gresham.ac.uk/lectures-and-events/the-romantic-economist-addresses-the-limits-of-knowledge-in-markets, last accessed on 21 October 2013.

Bujra, J. (2000). 'Risk and Trust: Unsafe Sex, Gender and AIDS in Tanzania', in P. Caplan (ed.), *Risk Revisited*. London: Pluto Press.

Cain, S. (2012). *Quiet: The Power of Introverts in a World That Can't Stop Talking*, New York: Crown.

Caplan, P. (ed.) (2000). *Risk Revisited*. London: Pluto Press.

Chaudhury, S. (2010). 'The Gene Gun at Your Head', *Tehelka Magazine*, 7(9), available at http://archive.tehelka.com/story_main44.asp?filename=Ne060310coverstory.asp, last accessed on 21 October 2013.

Douglas, M. (1986). *Risk Acceptability According to the Social Sciences*. London: Routledge and Kegan Paul.

——— (1992). *Risk and Blame: Essays in Cultural Theory*. London: Routledge.

Douglas, M., and A.B. Wildavsky (1982). *Risk and Culture: An Essay on the Selection of Technical and Environmental Dangers*. Berkeley: University of California Press.

Fischer, F. (2005). 'Are Scientists Irrational? Risk Assessment and Practical Reason', in M. Leach, I. Scoones, and B. Wynne (eds), *Science and Citizens: Globalization and the Challenge of Engagement*. London: Zed Books.

Fischoff, A. (1995). 'Risk Perception and Communication Unplugged: Twenty Years of Process', *Risk Analysis*, 15(2): 137–45.

Giddens, A. (1999). 'Risk and Responsibility', *The Modern Law Review*, 62: 1–10.

Giridharadas, A. (2011). *India Calling: An Intimate Portrait of a Nation's Remaking*. India: HarperCollins Publishers.

Gopal, N. (2011). 'The Search for a Moral Compass: India after Globalization', presented at the Foresight Brazil Conference at Sao Paulo, available at http://www.yorku.ca/drache/Canada%20Watch/canada-watch/pdf/fall2011/GopalJayal.pdf, last accessed on 21 October 2013.

Gowda, C. (2009). 'Thin Encounters with Knowledge', *India Seminar*, 597, available at http://www.india-seminar.com/2009/597/597_chandan_gowda.htm, last accessed on 21 October 2013.

Guha, R. (2012). *Will India Become a Superpower*, available at http://www2.lse.ac.uk/IDEAS/publications/reports/pdf/SR010/guha.pdf, last accessed on 21 October 2013.

Gupta, A. (2011). 'An Evolving Science-Society Contract in India: The Search for Legitimacy in Anticipatory Risk Governance', *Food Policy*, 36: 736–41.

Hansson, S.O. (2003). 'Ethical Criteria of Risk Acceptance', *Erkenntnis*, 59: 291–309.

——— (2004). 'Fallacies of Risk', *Journal of Risk Research*, 7(3): 353–60.

Hayenhjelm, M. and J. Wolff (2011). 'The Moral Problem of Risk Impositions: A Survey of the Literature', *European Journal of Philosophy*, 20(S1): E26–E51, June 2012.

Hindustan Times (2012). 'Jairam Differs with PM, Says No NGO Forced Bt brinjal Ban', 25 February, available at http://www.hindustantimes.com/News-Feed/India/Jairam-differs-with-PM-says-no-NGO-forced-Bt-Brinjal-ban/Article1-816910.aspx

Irwin, A., and B. Wynne (eds) (2004). *Misunderstanding Science?: The Public Reconstruction of Science and Technology*. Cambridge: Cambridge University Press.

Irwin, A. (2001). 'Construction of the Scientific Citizen: Science and Democracy in the Biosciences', *Public Understanding of Science*, 19(2): 147–54.

Jasanoff, S. (1999). 'The Songlines of Risk', *Environmental Values*, 8: 135–52.

——— (2002). 'Risk, Precaution and Environmental Values', *Carnegie Council*, available at http://www.carnegiecouncil.org/media/683_jasanoff.pdf, last accessed on 1 December 2012.

——— (2004). *States of Knowledge: The Co-Production of Science and the Social Order*. London: Taylor and Francis.

——— (2007). 'Bhopal's Trials of Knowledge and Ignorance', *Isis*, 98: 344–50.

——— (2009). 'Governing Innovation', *India Seminar*, 597, available at http://www.india-seminar.com/2009/597/597_sheila_jasanoff.htm, last accessed on 21 October 2013.

Jayanthi, A., K. Beumer, and S. Bhattacharya (2012). 'Nanotechnology: "Risk Governance" in India', *Economic and Political Weekly*, 47(4): 34–40.

Kapur, D. (2005). 'India's Promise? Conflicting Prospects for the World's Most Populous Democracy', *Harvard Magazine*, available at http://harvardmagazine.com/2005/07/indias-promise.html, last accessed on 21 October 2013.

Kalam, A., and S. Singh (2011). 'Nuclear Power is Our Gateway to a Prosperous Future', 6 November, *The Hindu*, available at http://www.thehindu.com/opinion/op-ed/article2601471.ece, last accessed on 21 October 2013.

Krimsky, S., and D. Golding (eds) (1992). *Social Theories of Risk*. Westport: Praegar.

Lash, S., B. Szerszynski, and B. Wynne (eds). (1996). *Risk, Environment and Modernity: Towards a New Ecology*. London: Sage Publications.

Leach, M., I. Scoones, and B. Wynne (2002). 'Citizenship, Science and Risk', *IDS Bulletin*, 33(2): 1–12.

———— (2005). *Science and Citizens: Globalization and the Challenge of Engagement*. London: Zed Books.

Lehrer, J. (2009). *The Decisive Moment: How the Brain Makes up its Mind*. Edinburgh: Canongate.

Lofstedt, R., and L. Frewer (eds) (1998). *Risk & Modern Society*. London: Earthscan.

Lupton, D. (2006). 'Sociology and Risk', in G. Mythen, and S. Walklate (eds), *Beyond the Risk Society: Critical Reflections on Risk and Human Security*. Maidenhead: Open University Press.

Ministry of Environment and Forests (2010), 'Decision on Commercialisation of Bt-Brinjal', 9 February, available at http://moef.nic.in/downloads/public-information/minister_REPORT.pdf, last accessed on 21 October 2013.

Nandi, J. (2010). 'Brinjal Reheated', *Times of India*, 1 October, available at http://articles.timesofindia.indiatimes.com/2010-10-01/developmental-issues/28232793_1_bt-brinjal-gm-crops-premier-science-academies, last accessed on 21 October 2013.

Pielke Jr., R.A. (2007). *The Honest Broker: Making Sense of Science in Policy and Politics*. New York: Cambridge University Press.

Porto, M., and C. Freitas (1996). 'Major Chemical Accidents in Industrialising Countries: The Socio-Political Amplification of Risk', *Risk Analysis*, 16(1): 19–29.

Porto, M., and L. Fernandes (2006). 'Understanding Risks in Socially Vulnerable Contexts: The Case of Waste Burning in Cement Kilns in Brazil', *Safety Science*, 44: 241–57.

Power, M. (2004). 'The Risk Management of Everything: Rethinking the Politics of Uncertainty', *Demos*, available at http://www.demos.co.uk/files/riskmanagementofeverything.pdf, last accessed on 21 October 2013.

Press Information Bureau (PIB) (2010). 'Decision on Commercialisation of Bt Brinjal', Government of India, 9 February, available at http://pib.nic.in/newsite/erelease.aspx?relid=57727, last accessed on 7 April 2014.

Rajan, R. (2002a). 'Disaster, Development and Governance: Reflections on the "lessons" from Bhopal', *Environmental Values*, 11: 369–94.

———— (2002b). 'Missing Expertise, Categorical Politics and Chronic Disasters: The Case of Bhopal', in S. Hoffman, and A. Oliver-Smith (eds), *Catastrophe and Culture: The Anthropology of Disaster*. Oxford: School of American Research (SAR) Press, Santa Fe and James Currey.

Rajan, R. (2005). 'Science, State and Violence: An Indian Critique Reconsidered', *Science as Culture*, 14(3): 1–17.

——— (2011). 'Nuclear Energy and Responsible Governance: Toward a Regime of Disaster Preparedness', *The Hindu Survey of the Environment*.

Ramesh, J. (2011). 'Nehru's Scientific Temper Recalled', Text of 13th Convocation Address, 27 May. Guwahati: IIT.

Rayner, S. (2004). 'The Novelty Trap: Why Does Institutional Learning About New Technologies Seem So Difficult?', *Industry and Higher Education*, 18(5): 349–55.

——— (2007). 'The Rise of Risk and the Decline of Politics', *Environmental Hazards*, 7: 165–72.

Rediff (2010). 'The Nuclear Liability Bill Needs a Rethink', *Rediff News*, 25 August, available at http://news.rediff.com/column/2010/aug/25/the-nuclear-liability-bill-needs-a-rethink.htm, last accessed on 21 October 2013.

Renn, O., and D. Levine (1991). 'Credibility and Trust in Risk Communication', in R.E. Kasperson, and P.J.M. Stallen (eds), *Communicating Risks to the Public*. Dordrecht, The Netherlands: Kluwer Academic Publishers.

Renn, O. (2005). 'Risk Governance: Towards an integrative approach', White Paper No. 1, available at http://irgc.org/wp-content/uploads/2012/04/IRGC_WP_No_1_Risk_Governance__reprinted_version_3.pdf, last accessed on 21 October 2013.

Ruparelia, S., S. Reddy, J. Harriss, and S. Corbridge (eds) (2011). *Understanding India's New Political Economy: A Great Transformation?* London: Routledge.

Scoones, I. (2012). 'Getting Hotter: Regulating Biotechnology in India', 24 February, available at http://stepscentre-thecrossing.blogspot.co.uk/2012/02/getting-hotter-regulating-biotechnology.html, last accessed on 21 October 2013.

Shah, E. (2011). '"Science" in the Risk Politics of Bt brinjal', *Economic and Political Weekly*, 46(31): 31–8.

Sibal, K. (2003). Science and Technology Policy 2003, available at http://www.dst.gov.in/stsysindia/stp2003.htm, last accessed on 21 October 2013.

Singh, M. (2010). 97th Indian Science Congress Inauguration Speech, available at http://www.isro.org/newsletters/scripts/newslettersin.aspx?page8jan2010mar2010, last accessed on 21 October 2013.

Skinner, J. (2000). 'The Eruption of Chances Peak, Montserrat, and the Narrative Containment of Risk' in P. Caplan (ed.), *Risk Revisited*. London: Pluto Press.

Slovic, P. (1999). 'Trust, Emotion, Sex, Politics, and Science: Surveying the Risk-Assessment Battlefield', *Risk Analysis*, 19(4): 689–701.

——— (2003). 'Going Beyond the Red Book: The Sociopolitics of Risk', *Human and Ecological Risk Assessment*, 9: 1–10.

Stirling, A. (2005). 'Opening Up or Closing Down? Analysis, Participation and Power in the Social Appraisal of Technology', in M. Leach, I. Scoones, and B. Wynne (eds), *Science and Citizens*. London: Zed Books.

——— (2007). 'Risk, Precaution and Science: Towards a More Constructive Policy Debate', *EMBO Reports*, 8: 309–315, available at http://www.nature.com/embor/journal/v8/n4/full/7400953.html, last accessed on 21 October 2013.

——— (2009). 'Risk, Uncertainty and Power', *India Seminar*, 597, available at http://www.india-seminar.com/2009/597/597_andy_stirling.htm, last accessed on 21 October 2013.

Stirling, A., and A. Scott (2011). 'Risky Advice and Immeasurable Uncertainties', *Aljazeera*, 6 June, available at http://www.aljazeera.com/indepth/opinion/2011/06/201163124740332864.html, last accessed on 21 October 2013.

Stirling, A. (2012). 'Opening Up the Politics of Knowledge and Power in Bioscience'. *PLoS Biology*, 10(1).

Sunderarajan, P. (2013). 'Manmohan for Approaching Complex Issues Through Debate Analysis', *The Hindu*, 3 January, available at http://www.thehindu.com/news/national/manmohan-for-approaching-complex-issues-through-debate-analysis/article4268986.ece, last accessed on 21 October 2013.

Suraiya, J. (2012). 'Fighters vs. Toilets: Walking the Tightrope between Defence and Development', *Economic Times*, 15 August, available at http://articles.economictimes.indiatimes.com/2012-08-15/news/33216755_1_defence-minister-defence-budgets-india-and-pakistan, last accessed on 21 October 2013.

Szerszynski, B., S. Lash, and B. Wynne (1996). 'Introduction: Ecology, Realism and the Social Sciences', in S. Lash, B. Szerszynski, and B. Wynne (eds), *Risk, Environment and Modernity, Towards a New Ecology*. London: Sage Publications.

The Hindu (2012). 'Suppressing Dissent with "Sedition" Taint', *The Hindu*, 17 September, available at http://www.thehindu.com/todays-paper/tp-national/suppressing-dissent-with-sedition-taint/article3905533.ece, last accessed on 7 April 2014.

Varma, S. (2012). 'Will India Learn from Fukushima and Make its Indian Plants Safe?', *Times of India*, 6 July, available at http://articles.timesofindia.indiatimes.com/2012-07-06/india/32565640_1_fukushima-industrial-safety-agency-nuclear-plants, last accessed on 21 October 2013.

Visvanathan, S. (2011). 'Tsunamis of the Mind', *Tehelka*, 8(14), 9 April, available at http://www.tehelka.com/story_main49.asp?filename=Ne090411ESSAY.asp, last accessed on 21 October 2013.

Waldman, L. (2011). *The Politics of Asbestos, Understandings of Risk, Disease and Protest*. London: Earthscan.

Wolff, J. (2006). 'Risk, Fear, Blame, Shame and the Regulation of Public Safety', *Economics and Philosophy*, 22: 409–27.

Wynne, B. (1992). 'Misunderstood Misunderstandings: Social Identities and Public Uptake of Science', *Public Understanding of Science*, 1(3): 281–304.

———— (1996). 'May the Sheep Safely Graze', in S. Lash, B. Szerszynski, and B. Wynne, (eds), *Risk, Environment and Modernity: Towards a New Ecology*. London: Sage Publications.

Wynne, B. (2009). 'Daring to Imagine', *India Seminar*, 597, available at http://www.india-seminar.com/2009/597/597_brian_wynne.htm, last accessed on 21 October 2013.

Zwanenberg and Millstone (2000). 'Beyond Skeptical Relativism: Evaluating the Social Constructions of Expert Risk Assessments', *Science Technology & Human Values*, 25: 259.

DISASTERS AND
THE ENVIRONMENT

2

LEO F. SALDANHA
BHARGAVI S. RAO

Article 39 and Environmental Decision-making in India

The policy of being too cautious is the greatest risk of all.

This statement ascribed to Jawaharlal Nehru, former Prime Minister of India, is a widely echoed sentiment amongst public administrators in India. Former President Dr A.P.J. Abdul Kalam leaned on this rationale to justify the need for a highly controversial mega nuclear power plant in the coastal village of Kudankulam situated at the Southern tip of India, and in the process dismissed massive local concerns that the plant is not tsunami safe. He confidently stated: 'Anybody having any issues on safety can meet me. Nuclear energy like hydroelectricity and solar energy is safe and clean' (Times of India 2011). Thousands of local villagers, whose concerns over the safety of the plant have only deepened in the post-Fukushima scenario, are not convinced, and continue to rally against the plant, braving very harsh police action and the risk of arrest under charges of sedition.

What is of concern here is that Nehru's tongue-in-cheek remark seems to have become, rather disconcertingly, a foundational mantra guiding the decisions relating to major policies and mega projects, the basis being that India's 'progress' demands such action. Such utilitarian pledging is evident in decisions relating to the building of large dams, mining in forests, industrialization in ecologically sensitive areas, and also in major policy decisions such as allowing foreign direct investment (FDI) in the retail sector. Prime Minister Manmohan Singh parroted this approach when he defended his decision to allow FDI in the retail sector, saying, 'it will take courage and some risks but it should be our endeavour to ensure that it materializes. The country deserves no less' (IBN Live 2012). It is commonly believed by the Government that the consequences of not taking such risks will result in policy paralysis and a lack of development.

But what counts as 'progress', and according to whom, has been an extremely controversial issue in recent times. A widely held view in India is that the phenomenal economic growth of the past two decades has largely benefited only those with access to privilege and power, while leaving behind the majority, who are poor. Hope remains that someday the benefits will 'trickle down'. Pandurang Hegde, leader of the *Appiko* movement in Karnataka, poignantly highlighted in a workshop organized by the Environment Support Group the contradictions inherent to the mega developmental project which was promoted in the environmentally sensitive Uttara Kannada district of Karnataka. He cited what a villager had said to him, 'In the olden days people were asked to sacrifice for the freedom of the mother land and nation but now when the country is free, for whose sake should I sacrifice? Why should I sacrifice for the people of Bangalore and Davanagere?' (ESG Report 2007).

This calls to attention the crucial question: Who defines risks and how are they deemed acceptable in the 'public's interest'? Whilst technical tools may guide and inform an assessment of the risks, first and foremost, the risk agenda must be 'framed'. What should count as harm, how should benefits be compared with harm, and how should different types of harm (injury to the poor or the rich, present versus future generations) be compared? Why are the risks being taken, and whom do they benefit? Further, what alternatives have been foregone, and what are their impact on values such as justice, equality, and human rights?

Based on these introductory remarks, in this chapter, we examine India's current economic developmental choices and the inequalities it has generated. By analysing the government's fundamental priorities and concerns we show, with the use of two case studies, how this has structured the prevailing approach to environmental decision-making, that is, the process of risk assessment, its approach to uncertainty, the way it frames 'risk', and whose knowledge and values are considered when determining the ultimate outcome. In such a context we question the extent to which the prevailing process of decision-making safeguards or furthers the 'publics' interest' as required per Article 39 of the Constitution of India.

RISK AND PRECAUTION

The Tamil Nadu and Indian governments have been keen not to waste any time commissioning the Kudankulam nuclear power plant, which has seen an investment of Rs 15,000 crore, and have decided to initiate the loading of the fuel. However, this position disregards local opposition from a community that remains unconvinced by both local and central governments' claims that the plant will be tsunami safe. Hope invested by local communities in the Madras High Court's capacity to address these concerns was dashed when the Public Interest Litigation (PIL) demanding a stay on operating the plant was dismissed. This decision was immediately appealed in the Supreme Court. The question put to the court was whether it was safe to commission the plant when only six of the seventeen critical safety conditions recommended by an Expert Committee, appointed by the Indian government following the Fukushima disaster, had been complied with. The government informed the court that it would take up to two years to meet all the conditions, which would make the enterprise uneconomical if it was now stayed. The issue has, once again, brought to the fore sharp divisions between public safety concerns and the government's notion of 'progress'. The Supreme Court refused to stay the commissioning of the plant but admitted the appeal observing '[P]ublic safety is of prime importance. There are poor people living in the vicinity of the plant and they should know that their life would be protected' (PTI 2012).

An important light-post in guiding such complex decisions is the Supreme Court of India's judgement in 1999, relating to the risk of industrial pollution seeping into Hyderabad's drinking water supply (A.P. Pollution Control Board v. M.V. Nayudu). Invoking the

Precautionary Principle into Indian jurisprudence the Supreme Court
held that

> if the environmental risks being run by regulatory inaction are in some
> way 'uncertain but non-negligible', then regulatory action is justified.
> This will lead to the question as to what is the 'non-negligible risk'. In such
> a situation, the burden of proof is to be placed on those attempting to
> alter the *status quo*. They are to discharge this burden by showing the ab-
> sence of a 'reasonable ecological or medical concern'. That is the required
> standard of proof. *The result would be that if insufficient evidence is presented
> by them to alleviate concern about the level of uncertainty, then the presumption
> should operate in favour of environmental protection*. (emphasis added)

Since then the Precautionary Principle has become a major imperative in shaping the outcomes of environmental decision-making in India.
In actual practice though, the tendency has still been to rely on technical
and quantitative risk assessments, even in conditions of uncertainty. This
tension between two very different conceptual frameworks of enquiry—
the reductive framework of quantitative risks assessment and the
Precautionary Principle—seems to pervade public policy in India today.
When the Indian Environment Minister Jairam Ramesh imposed a moratorium on the controversial decision to approve the commercial release
of Bt brinjal (India's first food Genetically Modified Organism [GMO])
on 9 February 2010, based on a series of unprecedented nation-wide
public consultations, he did so by invoking the Precautionary Principle:

> [W]hen there is no clear consensus within the scientific community *itself*,
> when there is so much opposition from the state governments, when
> responsible civil society organisations and eminent scientists have raised
> many serious questions that have not been answered satisfactorily, when
> the public sentiment is negative and when Bt-brinjal will be the very first
> genetically-modified vegetable to be introduced anywhere in the world
> and when there is no over-riding urgency to introduce it here (in India),
> it is my duty to adopt a cautious, precautionary principle based approach
> and impose a moratorium on the release of Bt-Brinjal…. (Ramesh 2010:
> 17, emphasis added)

Jairam Ramesh highlights two key points in his statement. Firstly,
he points out the significant scientific uncertainty concerning the
possible immediate and long-term effects of Bt brinjal on human and
animal health, as well as its impact on indigenous brinjal varieties in
the environment. Second, the social, political, and ethical concerns

raised by numerous stakeholders challenging how the issue of Bt brinjal has been 'framed'. In other words, if a different set of questions were posed and other expertise, knowledge, and values sought during the analysis of Bt brinjal then a radically different set of answers would have been produced concerning its 'acceptability'. Stakeholders raised concerns about what should be counted as the benefits and harms of Bt brinjal, how it should be compared to the alternatives, if it was even necessary, and issues of labelling, consumer rights and the foreign dominance of the domestic seed market. Attempting to reduce these uncertainties and ambiguous issues into quantifiable risks, rather than adopting the Precautionary Principle, would have proven to be a profoundly unsound, irrational, and unscientific approach (Stirling 2007).

Compared to the Precautionary Principle, however, 'reductive–aggregative risk assessment' (Stirling 2008: 102) is typically considered to be a 'sophisticated, comprehensive, rational and robust' process of appraisal (ibid.: 101). Critics portray the Precautionary Principle as anti-scientific, value based, and an ad hoc decision rule; a sign that the government has buckled to public pressure and the influence of environmentalists. This is certainly a criticism that was thrown at Jairam Ramesh by some pro Bt brinjal scientists and government ministers following the moratorium. What Stirling (2008) has shown is that the Precautionary Principle is in fact a 'sophisticated, comprehensive, rational and robust' process of appraisal itself under conditions of uncertainty, ambiguity, and ignorance. The Precautionary Principle is a broader process of appraisal which evaluates the 'issues that are addressed, the questions posed, the options considered, the possibilities examined, and the perspectives included in appraisal' (Stirling 2008: 104). As with any process of appraisal, including the process of scientific risk assessment, the Precautionary Principle involves value judgements, as does the process of scientific risk assessment. In fact it is more explicit about the value judgements involved in appraising technology, thus opening these to scrutiny and debate.

Whilst Jairam Ramesh invoked the Precautionary Principle during the Bt brinjal appraisal process, the same Minister frenetically cleared almost all the projects that came to it for statutory forest and environmental clearances. As reports reveal:

> Out of the 1,689 projects that the environment ministry decided upon from 2008 up to August 2011, only 19 were rejected. The ministry cleared

186 thermal power plants in the same period. Another 641 building and construction projects got the nod from the government and not a single project was rejected. Forty-five hydroelectric projects were given green sanction without any rejection. (Sethi 2011)

One particular instance when the Minister chose to step away from a Precautionary-principle-based decision-making framework was when he infamously shuffled clearances for the mega steel-power-port-mining township project benefiting the Korean giant company POSCO (Pohang Iron and Steel Company). In doing so he overlooked serious objections to the project from three committees that had thoroughly reviewed the evidence on his invitation. This case, which is discussed in some depth later on, was justified on the basis of the 'categorical assurance' extended by the Orissa government: '[L]aws on environment and forests (would) be implemented seriously' and that such compromises were essential to 'projects such as that of POSCO (which) have considerable economic, technological and strategic significance for the country' (Ramesh 2011: 3–4).[1]

In such deeply political and strategic situations, environmental decision-making in India is like performing a tight-rope walk. Having clearly pledged support for the Precautionary Principle in the Bt brinjal case, it is to be expected that the same yardstick could be applied to concerns raised for Kudankulam or POSCO. However, in mega project decisions, and also in the procedural clearances for hundreds of industrial, mining, and infrastructure development projects, ritual, or scant attention is being paid to environmental and social impacts. This demands a deeper consideration of the wider and overarching political and economic factors that influence environmental decision-making in India.

ADDRESSING THE WIDER CONCERNS IN POLICY FORMULATION

Article 39, which is a part of the Directive Principles for the state, is amongst the most progressive features of the Indian Constitution. It

---

[1] A detailed critique of the environmental decision-making processes relating to the POSCO project is available in Saldanha and Rao (2011).

requires that any development must serve the wider public good, first and foremost, and therefore, by implication, development that only benefits a few is not really development at all. Measured by this yardstick, India's progress in the post-colonial phase is found to be woefully inadequate and has perhaps even failed this particular Constitutional mandate. Such a test is extremely relevant in assessing the past two decades of neoliberal economic reforms in India. This is important because the reforms were introduced with the promise that it would liberate the country from its sluggish growth rates and from poverty itself, thus guaranteeing a reasonably improved quality of life for all.

Unprecedented investment and prosperity has indeed followed economic reforms. India leapfrogged the traditionally sluggish 'Hindu' annual rate of growth of about 3 per cent GDP, as its growth rate spiralled to 6–8 per cent, and thereafter succeeded in securing a prime position in the world economy (Swamy 2002). With competitiveness being promoted as a core value to achieve success, not only has the nature of business transformed over the past two decades, but that of politics as well. Economic policies have created a fierce climate of competition amongst states. Regional governments, in their enthusiasm to secure investment and sustain high rates of growth, have aggressively adopted policies even when it involved the whittling down of regulatory standards supporting environmental and social concerns. To many, this appears as a race to the bottom. The implications are deep and wide-ranging and have also affected the nature of federalism in India. We now observe a clear departure from the cooperative framework that the Constitution demands—which should exist between states, as well as the states and the centre—transformed into one of intense competition.

An early assessment of current economic policies was made in the Republic Day address in 2000, to the nation by the then President of India, late Dr K.R. Narayanan. This speech is widely perceived as a formal criticism of the economic reforms process and the following is an excerpt:

> Fifty years into our life in the Republic we find that Justice—social, economic, and political—remains an unrealized dream for millions of our fellow citizens. The benefits of our economic growth are yet to reach them. We have one of the world's largest reservoirs of technical

personnel, but also the world's largest number of illiterates; the world's largest middle class, but also the largest number of people below the poverty line, and the largest number of children suffering from malnutrition. Our giant factories rise from out of squalor; our satellites shoot up from the midst of the hovels of the poor. Not surprisingly, there is sullen resentment among the masses against their condition erupting often in violent forms in several parts of the country. Tragically, the growth in our economy has not been uniform. It has been accompanied by great regional and social inequalities. Many a social upheaval can be traced to the neglect of the lowest tier of society, whose discontent moves towards the path of violence. Dalits and tribals are the worst affected by all this.

Dr Narayanan (2000) also brought out starkly the impacts of such developmental policies by remarking that

the unabashed, vulgar indulgence in conspicuous consumption by the *noveau-riche* has left the underclass seething in frustration. One half of our society guzzles aerated beverages while the other has to make do with palmfuls of muddied water. Our three-way fast-lane of liberalization, privatisation and globalisation must provide safe pedestrian crossings for the unempowered India also so that it too can move towards 'Equality of Status and Opportunity'

Can 'safe pedestrian crossings for the unempowered' sufficiently address the demands of equity and justice for all? This especially when little or no attention is paid to such warnings and the benefits accrued by those with access to privilege and agency are so substantial? As a Forbes survey (Forbes 2011) revealed, there are 57 billionaires in India today, an astronomical figure, considering that in the pre-reform era, there were hardly any. A study by Mckinsey and Co. suggests that India will also become the world's fifth-largest consumer market by 2025 due to the ever-increasing purchasing power of its middle and upper-middle classes (McKinsey and Company 2007). Yet, India is still amongst the poorest countries in the world and is 134th in the Human Development Index, alongside Solomon Islands, Republic of Congo, Laos, and Myanmar (UNDP 2011).

EXCLUSION FOR MANY, PROFIT TO FEW

So who are the ones benefiting from these reforms? The most comprehensive survey in recent years on this question was undertaken by the

Indian National Commission for Enterprises in the Unorganized Sector, and its findings were published in the 'Report on Conditions of Work and Promotion of Livelihoods in the Unorganized Sector', commonly known as the Arjuna Sengupta Report (Sengupta 2007). This report exposed the inequity that has become a norm, and has even accentuated over the past two decades, in the time when neoliberal economic reforms were aggressively promoted. Highlighting the feeble support the poor have received from the state, the report indicates, '[I]t is only reasonable that when faced with choices, governments should place the highest priority on the poor and the weak, and ensure that these groups are adequately compensated whenever their livelihoods are threatened by specific policies, laws and regulations' (Sengupta 2007: 174). Coming as it did a decade and a half into the reforms process, proponents of current economic policies within and outside the government found it extremely difficult to justify the purportedly utilitarian approach ingrained in the economic reforms, which now had been empirically proven to not benefit the poor at all.

To ward-off the scathing criticisms regarding the reforms, that it were failing the larger masses, the Congress-I led United Progressive Alliance (UPA) government at the Centre promoted an ambitious and unprecedented job creation project, National Rural Employment Guarantee Scheme (NREGS), recently named after Mahatma Gandhi (MGNREGA).[2] A few years later, though, the most vocal critic of this programme Jean Dreze, a welfare economist who is considered one of the architects of the original scheme, asks, 'Where is work for all, minimum wages, timely payment...?' (Jeelani 2010).

Such criticisms, however, have not deterred Deputy Chairman of the Planning Commission, Dr Montek Singh Ahluwalia, one of the key proponents of economic reforms, to claim that the lot of the poor has actually improved. To justify his claim, he scandalously, and comically, asserted that anyone who spends over Rs 32 per capita in urban areas is not poor, the equivalent for rural areas is Rs 26. A petition was

---

[2] Recent studies reveal that while this scheme has helped secure employment for up to 100 days in rural areas, it has not helped in substantially diminishing the biting poverty suffered by majority of Indians. A critique of how this scheme has been implemented across India and an analysis of its outcomes is offered in: Banerjee and Saha (2010).

submitted to the Supreme Court slamming Dr Ahluwalia for fudging numbers to escape responsibility for the policies that exacerbated poverty in India. In an affidavit submitted to the Court he claimed '...that Rs 4,824 per month for a family (of five persons) to define poverty is not comfortable but it is not all that ridiculous from Indian conditions' (PTI 2011).

Such polemical debates on the efficacy of the ongoing reforms process notwithstanding, it is important to note that the unprecedented economic growth in India over the past two decades has also witnessed a concomitant increase of conflicts over resource management, resource extraction, over access to the commons, and on the sharing of the products of the prevailing paradigm of development. This has resulted in widespread dislocation, disharmony, and environmental degradation, particularly amongst communities dependent on natural resources, who constitute a majority of India's population. This tension is most poignantly captured in *Gaon chodab nahi* (We will not leave our village), a short clip based on a folk song by noted filmmaker K.P. Sasi[3] and this is an excerpt:

> They built dams, drowned villages and built factories.
> They cut down forests, dug out mines and formed sanctuaries.
> Without water, land and forest, where do we go?
> Oh God of Development, pray tell us, how to save our lives?

The video uses visuals of Indian cricketer M.S. Dhoni guzzling a Cola in a TV promo, quickly followed by those of women filtering filthy water for drinking, as the song asks:

> You may drink your colas and bottled water, but how shall we quench our thirst with polluted waters?

It is a hugely popular video, particularly in rural and forested areas of India, and its success, in many ways, indicates the increasing feeling of disenfranchisement of the millions. One major representation of this discontent is the increase in the influence of Naxalism across India, said to now affect about 220 districts, which corresponds roughly

---

[3] This clip is accessible at: http://www.youtube.com/watch?v=8M5ae MpzOLU.

to half the geographical area of India. This has caused great unease among the ruling classes. Their method of overcoming such a ground-swell of opposition to the ongoing reforms process has been to demand a strong state action against the protestors and quell the resistance. The determination involved in this reaction is best epitomized by what India's Finance Minister P. Chidambaram said in his previous role as Home Minister, that the government was 'willing to tolerate debate, and perhaps even dissent, as long as it does not come in the way of 8 per cent growth' of the Indian economy (Hindu Business Line 2006).

HOW REFORMS HAVE IMPACTED ENVIRONMENTAL DECISION-MAKING IN INDIA

In such a context, it is not at all surprising that there is a weak appre-ciation, and even neglect, of the critical need to put major policy and project decisions to deep democratic debates. Consequently, there is only a marginal and ritual consideration of environmental and social issues in economic policy decision-making, a process that seems to have become systemic to governance. A clear indicator of this shift is the complete acceptance of the recommendations of the Govindarajan Committee on Investment Reforms, which was first promoted by the right wing Bharatiya Janata Party (BJP)-led National Democratic Alliance (NDA) that ruled the country between 1999 and 2004. This Committee almost entirely consisted of hand-picked bureaucrats favour-ing the current economic policies. Two years after carefully perusing various laws and policies, the Committee identified the strong demo-cratic regulatory mechanisms that existed to protect the environment, forests, and human rights, as significant bottlenecks for foreign and Indian investment. It recommended that such statutory procedures, which had evolved over several decades in response to numerous studies, movements, and peoples struggles, must be whittled down to allow investments to flow in. Meanwhile the World Bank financed the Environmental Management Capacity-building Programme in India, which broadly supported the nature of reforms promoted by the Govindarajan Committee. Ever since, these 'reform' processes are fundamentally reshaping environmental laws, procedures, and norms of India.

The most representative example of this transition is in the way the Environmental Impact Assessment (EIA) notification was comprehensively amended in 2006. This subordinate legislation is extremely critical to advancing ecological security as it oversees the administration of environmental decision-making at all levels of governance. When promoting amendments to this notification in 2005, as a critical review has since revealed (Saldanha et al. 2007: 1), the Indian Ministry of Environment and Forests had claimed that it would:

- Incorporate necessary environmental safeguards at planning stage;
- Involve stakeholders in the public consultation process; and
- Identify developmental projects based on impact potential instead of the investment criteria.

Instead, the new EIA notification promotes opaqueness, concentrates power (either with the Centre or States) in violation of constitutional requirements that require decentralization and devolution of power, and unnecessarily creates new layers of bureaucracy that have a disempowering effect on local communities, while adversely affecting the environment and public health. The review has found that the legislation has resulted in:

- Further weakening the review of environmental and social impacts of projects;
- Substantially reduced involvement of local governance bodies and the wider public in environmental decision-making;
- And essentially forestages investment over environmental and social concerns. (Saldanha et al. 2007: 1)

Large protests against these reforms from various impacted communities and people's movements were overlooked in the process.[4] Several years later, this new EIA law has proven to have caused widespread environmental destruction in the country, and has resulted in a

[4] The most comprehensive representation of such protests is *MoEF Suno!* and *MoEF Chalo!*, initiated collectively by Campaign for Environmental Justice—India, a network of environmental justice groups, movements and impacted communities, in 2005. A public hearing was held as a part of this initiative in Delhi on 13 November 2005, that witnessed the deposition by communities impacted by bad environmental decisions from across India. Since the officials

situation, according to Jairam Ramesh, where 'approvals and the rate of sanctions is over 92 per cent, which is unhealthily high' (Pathak 2009). He admitted that in the decade of the 2000s, at least 7,000 projects were approved on the basis of environmental conditions and safeguards, when there is no 'system of monitoring compliance with...standards' (ibid.). Consequently, '[M]any approved projects have not fulfilled the conditions associated with the clearance' (ibid.). Ramesh, in another interview, stated: 'The acceptance rate for environment projects has been very high—almost 98 per cent. We are putting a system in place whereby projects go through the whole drill. We have to bring down this unhealthy rate of acceptance' (Buchar 2009). But as has been discussed before, neither during his term as Environment Minister, or under the term of Jayanthi Natarajan who succeeded him, has any significant departure been made from this admitted *status quo*. In some ways, this admission summarily exposes the lack of serious intent to incorporate environmental and social considerations in decision-making. In what follows, we look at two case studies, one involving the expansion of the Mangalore airport in Karnataka and the other, the POSCO project in Orissa, to understand the consequences of this environmental decision-making framework.

QUALITY OF PROJECT RISK ASSESSMENT AND TRAGIC CONSEQUENCES OF NEGLIGENCE

In the late 1990s, the ecologically sensitive coastal region of *Dakshina* (South) Kannada in Karnataka was aggressively promoted as a major destination for a variety of mega industrial and infrastructure investments, overlooking widespread opposition from local communities

---

from the Ministry of Environment and Forests did not turn up for the hearing despite several appeals, the following day a protest march was led into the highly fortified Paryavaran Bhavan in Delhi (the Headquarters of the Ministry); the functioning of the Ministry was blocked for the day and a symbolic *Death Certificate* of the Ministry was served to the Prime Minister of India. Details of this campaign are available at the website of the Environment Support Group, http://static.esgindia.org/campaigns/moefsuno2005/index.html, last accessed on 7 April 2014.

on environmental and social impact grounds. Local business associa-
tions, keen to position the coastal city of Mangalore as a major commercial and trading hub, lobbied to expand the airport at Bajpe so it
could handle international flight movements. Reliable air-connectivity
was considered an essential prerequisite to secure investment in the
region as the alternative was to travel eight hours over the mountains
to Bangalore.

The Karnataka government supported this demand from investors.
It had two choices in deciding how to expand the existing airport.
The first was to add a second runway extending towards Bajpe town
from the existing one, involving acquisition of agricultural land of
large landholders. The second option was to take the runway in the
opposite direction onto a mountain strip surrounded by deep valleys,
a location that supported a fairly dense colony of Dalit communities
who had been rehabilitated post independence after being rescued from
bonded labour. The government chose the second option, yielding to
pressures from the highly influential and politically well-connected
large landowners, one of whom was then district-in-charge Minister.
In the process, a third option that existed for building a new airport
30 kilometres to the north, in a location that complied with all norms
for aerodrome construction, was not given the slightest consideration.
The State quickly moved to acquire Dalit lands claiming that the site
was fully compliant with all norms and that it also involved a lower
displacement factor.

The impacted Dalit communities under the banner of *Vimana
Nildhana Vistharana Virodhi Samithi* (Kannada for Airport Expansion
Resistance Committee), that involved various local activists and voluntary organizations,[5] staunchly resisted their dislocation on the basis of
highly technical arguments. It was submitted that building the runway
onto the mountain strip was unsafe and in comprehensive violation of
applicable Indian and International Civil Aviation Organization (ICAO)
aerodrome design standards. However, the government brushed aside
all these considerations arguing that the presumption of risk raised by
the Dalit communities was exaggerated and that the new runway would

---

[5] The Environment Support Group systematically supported this struggle for
over a decade, which included a variety of efforts including advocacy, press
mobilization, lobbying, and also litigation.

be absolutely safe and meet all norms, a contention that they continue to maintain to this day (Kamila 2006).

Unwilling to accept the government's argument, the Samithi initiated a PIL in the High Court of Karnataka challenging the airport expansion on various legal and technical grounds:

* The strip was surrounded by a deep valley on three sides providing insufficient emergency landing space;
* In the case of an accident, access to emergency and rescue teams would be substantially hampered;
* The physical limitations of the site precluded further airport expansion;
* The presence of the city's landfill, mega refineries, and industrial activities in the vicinity of the airport posed a significant risk to the safety of flight movements particularly given that it was table-top and located in a high rainfall zone;
* The decision was in comprehensive violation to various legal procedures that demanded due consultation of the affected public; and,
* An EIA study was not undertaken to establish the environmental and social impacts of the project.

The High Court of Karnataka admitted the petition (*Arthur Pereira and Ors. v. Union of India and Ors.* [1997]) but dismissed it with the following ruling:

It is stated (by the Airports Authority of India on behalf of the government) that the fear of the petitioners that the runway is insufficient for any emergency landing of a plane is without any basis since before the project is to proceed, the authorities will be meeting the recommendations of the ICAO. It is also stated that there is no basis for the allegations made by the petitioners to the effect that the various safety measures have not been followed. That on the other hand they will be getting all the relevant materials described by the petitioners which will be followed in letter and spirit without which the airport would not have been conceived in the first place. Thus it can be seen that the expansion of Bajpe airport *project is at the initial stage* and the second respondent has in their objections mentioned above unequivocally stated that all the safety measures etc., stated by the petitioners in their writ petition will be followed during the progress of the project and *nothing can be said before the lands are handed over to the second respondent.* Considering these facts, we are of the view that *the petitioners have rushed to this court before commencement of the project itself and the writ petition is premature.* It is not, therefore, necessary to consider the various grounds taken by the petitioners in the writ petition to allege that the respondents have been proceeding with the project in a casual manner. *There is nothing to doubt about the statement made by the second respondent in their objection statement and we are sure that the respondents will be taking all necessary measures under the different enactments etc…, before proceeding with the project in question.* The writ petition stands dismissed'. (Order of the High Court of Karnataka, 1997, emphasis added)

The petitioners were disappointed with the court's ruling and felt that the implications of the lack of compliance with applicable standards had not been fully appreciated. The court, it seemed, had merely placed reliance on an unsubstantiated written assurance from the Airports Authority of India (AAI), in response to the petition. The following is an extract of this assurance:

It is submitted that as regards the apprehensions of the petitioner that the Length and width of the runway is insufficient for a plane making an emergency landing, the same is without any basis. It is respectfully submitted that all the requirements as per the ICAO recommendation will be met and that there has been no infringement of any of the recommendation and limitation therein. (Airports Authority of India Response to the PIL 1997)

Resistance continued on the ground for several years, and the project was delayed as land acquisition could not be initiated. The Samithi returned to the Karnataka High Court a few years later with a fresh and more thoroughly prepared petition (*Arthur Pereira and Ors. v. Union of India and Ors.* [2002]) contesting that the assurance extended by AAI was false and that the project did not meet the applicable standards. This petition was dismissed at the admission stage on the following grounds:

No doubt, in an appropriate case, this Court can issue directions, if there is gross violation of fundamental rights *or if the issue touches the conscience of this Court*, but not for personal gain or political gain. The construction of 2nd Runway and Terminal Tower in Mangalore Airport will otherwise be in the interest of public. Learned Counsel has not been able to show how the construction of 2nd Runway and Terminal Tower in Mangalore

Airport will be against the public interest. On consideration and in the facts of the given case no direction as prayed for can be issued in this PIL. The authorities concerned have to complete all formalities as per law before commencement of the project. Accordingly, this Writ petition is dismissed. However, it is made clear that dismissal of this petition will not preclude the concerned Authorities to take all necessary precaution and to complete the formalities as per law before proceeding with the project in question.' (Karnataka High Court order in *Arthur Pereira and Ors. v. Union of India and Ors.* [2002], emphasis added)

Once again the court had not thoroughly verified the issue of compliance with applicable standards, so the disappointed petitioners preferred an appeal in the Supreme Court against the High Court ruling. This too was dismissed at the admission stage with the following direction:

We see no reason to interfere with the impugned order. Accordingly, the special leave petition[6] is dismissed. We, however, clarify that in constructing the Airport, the Government shall comply with all applicable laws and also with environmental norms. (*Environment Support Group and Ors. v. Union of India and Ors.* [2003] SLP(C) 1172 of 2003)

Bolstered by this decision, the AAI quickly proceeded to displace communities and acquire the land required for the expansion of the second runway in Mangalore. Subsequent enquiries revealed that none of the safeguards prescribed were complied with, even following the Supreme Court's directive, and with devastating consequences.

On 22 May 2010, an early morning Air India express flight arriving into Mangalore from Dubai attempted to land, the pilots, realizing it was an 'un-stabilized landing', attempted to abort the landing by attempting a take-off, but by then it was too late. The plane reached the end of the runway, found the critical Runway End Safety Area (RESA) occupied by a concrete instrument landing system, crashed into it, caught fire and plunged 100 metres into the valley killing 158 people, including the crew. Only eight survived the inferno. Most of the people killed were migrant workers and many were sole breadwinners for their families in India. When it was exposed that the accident could have been averted had the standards of airport design been strictly complied with, there

---

[6] An appeal against a lower court's ruling to the Supreme Court.

was national outrage.[7] The authorities, though, defended their decision claiming that it was the fault of the pilots.

As per procedure, a court of enquiry was set up under the chairmanship of Air Marshal B.N. Gokhale, PVSM, AVSM, VM (retd.), and former Vice Chief of Air Staff, Indian Air Force. The enquiry committee, following an exhaustive review of the material, which included visiting the crash site, examination of the vicinity of the airport, the backgrounds of the pilots, and on the basis of public hearings conducted in Mangalore and Delhi, released its report in October 2010 and held as follows:

Direct cause of the Accident:

The Court of Inquiry determines that cause of this accident was the Captain's failure to discontinue the 'un-stabilised approach' and his persistence in continuing with the landing, despite three calls from the First Officer to 'go around' and a number of warnings from EGPWS.

The contributory factors were:

(a) In spite of availability of adequate rest period prior to the flight, the Captain was in prolonged sleep during flight, which could have led to sleep inertia. As a result of relatively short period of time between his awakening and the approach, it possibly led to impaired judgment. This aspect might have got accentuated while flying in the Window of Circadian Low (WOCL).

(b) In the absence of Mangalore Area Control Radar (MSSR), due to un-serviceability, the aircraft was given descent at a shorter distance on DME as compared to the normal. However, the flight crew did not plan the descent profile properly, resulting in remaining high on approach.

(c) Probably in view of ambiguity in various instructions empowering the 'co-pilot' to initiate a 'go around', the First Officer gave repeated calls to this effect, but did not take over the controls to actually discontinue the ill-fated approach. (B.N. Gokhale 2010: ix)

Clearly the report confirms that pilot error was a substantive causative factor of the accident. But the report also highlighted that:

Mangalore being a table top runway with deep valleys and gorges on either ends of airport, there should be no downward slope in the

---

[7] One major debate on this accident was on *Times Now* TV channel, which can be accessed at http://www.timesnow.tv/Debate-Air-tragedy-in-Mangalore/videoshow/4345737.cms, last accessed on 17 March 2014.

overshoot area. This is particularly in view of a large number of accidents recently,[8] which have occurred during takeoff and landing phases, resulting in runway excursion (ibid.: 96).

Inspection of RESA at Mangalore had revealed that at the time of accident, localiser antenna and *some temporary concrete platforms for ILS calibration were located within RESA*.[9] It also lacked regular maintenance. *The RESA did not have adequate sand refilled as the concrete mounting structure of approach lights were protruding above the surface.* … Regular ploughing of this area would have prevented such growth (ibid.: 96, emphasis added).

Due to the constraints of terrain, the strip width is only 150 metres as against the mandated 300 metres. This limitation is one of the major permanent concessions sought by AAI for licensing of Mangalore airport. Two points emerge from this concession. Firstly, there should be no further erosion of strip width and necessary engineering precautions need to be taken to ensure this. Secondly, all operators would need to impose crosswind limitations during take-off and landings, so as to avoid aircraft excursion laterally (ibid.: 97).

On impact with the ILS structure, major portion of the right wing and engine had separated from the aircraft. As a result of this impact, the parts had caught fire, which were extinguished by the first RFF (Rescue and Firefighting) (which was Airport Rescue and Firefighting) vehicle. When the aircraft finally came to rest in the gorge, the aircraft had caught fire. This resulted in suffocation and burn injuries, leading to death of crew and passengers, other than 8 survivors. A number of parts of the aircraft had also been consumed in the fire. *The RFF crew of Mangalore had responded well but owing to the distance and difficult terrain could not reach the site quicker than about 4-5 minutes by which time the aircraft had been engulfed in fire.* With sustained and involved efforts by the airport staff and civil fire department the fire was brought under control so that the charred bodies could be removed from the aircraft wreckage. The RFF crew would have contributed to better rescue operations, if the Hazard identification and risk management exercises would have taken into account possibility of crash outside the airport. Mock drills conducted catering to such circumstances would have highlighted the need for better access roads (ibid.: 98–9, emphasis added).

[8] This refers to the high frequency of accidents in India, and also the near misses, in contrast to the world average.

[9] As per ICAO standards in Annexure-14, which are mandatory, the RESA area has to be free from any interference; permanent or temporary.

While it was established that pilot error was a causative factor, it was also established that the runway did not comply with several of the necessary safeguards to prevent an accident or limit damage when one took place. The hazardous nature of the runway is in fact highlighted as a serious cause of worry, especially the fact that emergency rescue teams cannot rapidly reach an aircraft in distress if it slips into the surrounding valley. All this suggests that the airport is extremely high-risk as it provides very little margin for error and a minor technical glitch could potentially result in a major disaster. These are risk considerations that the petitioners had unsuccessfully attempted to secure the attention of the court in its effort to protect the wider public interest.

RISKING THE CYCLONE FOR THE POSCO PROJECT

With an initial capital outlay of Rs 51,000 crore (USD 12 billion at 2005 exchange rates), the Korean POSCO's iron ore mining, steel-power-port-township project in Orissa, is India's single largest industrial foreign direct industrial investment ever. Such has been the eagerness to secure the project that the Orissa government concluded a Memorandum of Understanding (MoU) with POSCO immediately after the company made an initial offer. The MoU signed on 22 June 2005 made the project a sweetheart deal for the Koreans as the state guaranteed that 'the Government of Orissa will assist the Company in obtaining all clearances' and 'will make best efforts and provide all possible assistance to POSCO for expeditious clearance of applications' (POSCO MoU: Section vi).

With such aggressive support for the project, POSCO India Pvt. Limited, the Korean giant company's Indian subsidiary, quickly demanded 4,004 acres of land (about 3,000 acres of which is forest land) in the ecologically sensitive Jagatsinghpur district in coastal Orissa. Here the company proposed to establish a massive steel plant with a production capacity of 12 million tonnes per annum (MTPA), backed by a 400 MW coal-fired thermal power plant and a massive captive port capable of berthing cape size ships (the largest commercial ships ever built). About 1,000 acres would accommodate a large fly ash dump. In addition, the project required 2,000 acres of land for a township to accommodate its large workforce, and more land to support the project's water, fuel, and transport (road and rail) linkages. On top of this the mining component of the project ostensibly required 6,000 acres of forestland, about 300 kilometres from the plant site.

The diversion of forest land for industrial use is subject to various provisions of the Forest Conservation Act and Forest Rights Act, requiring detailed assessments of the environmental impact, coastal regulation norms, town and country planning standards, etc. The steel plant component of the project alone could displace a large number of rural, coastal, and forest dependent communities, with the number of directly affected ones estimated to be well over 20,000. Only if the actual social displacement and environmental impacts of the project's mining, pipeline, road/rail networks and township development are comprehensively and accurately assessed, can the true extent of the impact of this project and its consequences to Orissa be seen.

Instead, in a deliberate act of downplaying the actual environmental and social impacts of the project, POSCO and the Orissa government sought statutory clearances in a piecemeal manner. An environmental clearance application was submitted for only 4 MTPA capacity of the steel plant, when in fact project documents reveal that a 12-MTPA plant was proposed along with a captive port to export the iron ore mined and steel produced. The environmental and social impacts of the ancillary facilities, such as the rail/road network, the township and the massive mining component, were also not reviewed. The cumulative impact of the project has been comprehensively ignored.

The region where the steel plant is to be sited is ecologically sensitive and has also been in the eye of fierce cyclones that hit the region frequently. The 1999 super-cyclone severely affected the Jagatsinghpur district with an estimated death toll of 30,000 (Actionaid India 2007). Local people report that a major cyclone hits the region every decade on an average. The Orissa State Disaster Management Authority has a record of all the cyclones that have hit the state since 1737. The 1885 cyclone is recorded as a super-cyclone, as is the one in 1999. Over the past sixty years, the authority has recorded over seven cyclones, three being designated super-cyclones and four as 'very severe cyclonic storm[s]'.

POSCO has considered the risk from cyclones and taken steps to safeguard its plant. It has proposed raising the base height of the plant site from 0 MSL (mean sea level) to 5 MSL, which was the height of the crest of the wave that slammed the coast in 1999—the highest ever recorded tidal surge to hit a coast. The measures POSCO has proposed could possibly safeguard its plant from the worst of a cyclone, but the consequences of such massive landform transitions on the surrounding fertile deltaic region has not at all been considered, and could possibly be devastating. Also ignored in their assessment is the high likelihood that climate change could intensify extreme weather events, thus exposing the plant and surrounding areas to high risk.

In securing this investment various regulatory agencies have overlooked the large social and environmental impacts of the projects on local agricultural, riverine, coastal, and forest ecosystems. Records reveal that the region is a critical habitat for the highly endangered Olive Ridley Turtles and the ancient horse-shoe crabs. However, such concerns have hardly played any role in affecting the decision of the Ministry of Environment and Forests when it accorded the project environmental and coastal regulation clearances in 2007, responding largely to pressures from the Prime Minister's Office. Fundamental procedures, such as prior and informed consultation with local communities, were complied with rather ritually and in a climate of fear, where those critical of the project have been systematically arrested on foisted charges. The statutory Environmental Public Hearing was not held in the project affected villages, but happened instead in Kujang town which was 20 kilometres away, to prevent the affected population from participating. Interestingly, such mischievous and highly questionable practices are supported by the EIA Notification of 2006 which permits local authorities to hold statutory hearings 'in close proximity' to the project site, leaving it open to officials to decide what 'close' implies. Quite obviously, this provision has been practiced to the disadvantage of affected communities nation-wide.

Various analysts and research groups have revealed that the project, besides its devastating ecological and social impacts, is also economically disastrous for Orissa and the country as the deal is comprehensively pro-POSCO. One such study by Mining Zone Peoples' Solidarity Group (2010) has attacked a claim in a 2007 POSCO sponsored study by the centrally funded National Council for Applied Economic Research (NCAER) that the project would provide Orissa with 8.7 lakh jobs over 30 years. Instead, they revealed that only 7,000 direct jobs would be created by the investment. Meanwhile, project-affected communities have consistently articulated that the project is of no benefit to them at all. Guided by the POSCO *Pratirodh Sangram Samithi* (PPSS) (Oriya for POSCO Resistance Coordination Committee) they have successfully blocked the investment for several years now by sealing their villages to the entry of project and government officials. In response, the Orissa government has frustrated villagers by denying them their land titles and their traditional and customary rights over the forests. The intent has been to prevent communities from securing their rights under the procedures of the Forest Rights Act, and thus limit their chances of legally blocking the acquisition of land for the project. The authorities have also extensively abused their police powers by foisting a variety of false charges against key leaders, exemplified by the repeated arrests and long periods of incarceration of PPSS leader Abhay Sahoo and others.

In the face of such staunch resistance from local communities, and the harsh response by the Orissa state, the project has assumed an extremely controversial status. This was difficult to ignore for the Government of India, and in an effort to clear the air, the environmental clearance decisions were subjected to thorough reviews by two committees in 2010 and 2011, when Jairam Ramesh was Minister of Environment and Forests. Both Committees returned to report (N.C. Saxena Committee, 2010 and Meena Gupta Committee, 2011) that there had been flagrant violations of the various environmental and forest protection laws. In addition, it was reported that community efforts to secure rights per the Forest Rights Act were being deliberately and illegally discouraged by the Orissa government. It was also highlighted that there had only been a cursory review of the environmental and social impacts of the project, that very little by way of compliance had been done in the three years since POSCO secured clearances for the first phase of the project (the controversial 4 MTPA steel plant) and that it was far from complying with the conditions imposed to accord the port coastal clearance. However, overlooking all these reports and recommendations of the statutory Forest Advisory Committee against diverting forest land and demanding compliance with the findings of the Saxena and Gupta Committees reports, Jairam Ramesh approved the environmental clearances accorded to the project. This decision was based entirely on 'strong assurances' extended by the Orissa government that all legal norms and safeguards would be duly considered and complied with. Notably he said: '[F]aith and trust in what the state government says is an essential pillar of cooperative federalism which is why I rejected the second option (that of rejecting the project for non-compliance with clearance conditions). Beyond a point, the bona fides of a democratically elected state government cannot always be questioned by the Centre' (Ramesh 2011: 3). He did, however, concede that he was under pressure from the highest levels of governance, including the Prime Minister's Office, and thus was compelled to clear the project as it was of 'strategic' national importance. Manmohan Singh was deeply worried that if POSCO was struck down it would hit India's pro-investment image, especially given that he had already assured the South Korean President a number of times that the POSCO project would soon see the light of day.

The POSCO deal is of concern to the public's welfare and interest. On the one hand there are serious ecological and social risks involved in locating the steel plant at Jagatsinghpur, none of which have been factored into the appraisal process. On the other, the MoU backing POSCO, though now expired, promoted an unprecedented package to POSCO allowing it to export 60 per cent of the iron ore mined without any value addition in India. The report of the Mining Zone People's Solidarity Group (2010) notes with concern that '[T]he extraction of iron ore alone allows POSCO to profit to the tune of Rs 6,500 crores per year (about 1.5 billion US dollars) for 30 years, ensuring that its entire investment of 12 billion US dollars in this project is recouped within the first 8 years' (ibid.: i). On the other hand, 'the average loss of income for a cultivator is at an average Rs 40,000 per year per decimal of land under betel vine cultivation, but the latest compensation on offer is a one time payment of Rs 11,500 per decimal. The total loss experienced by a betel vine farmer per decimal over a 30 year time period would be in the range of Rs 12 lakh, thus making the current one time compensation package on offer less than 1 per cent of their cumulative earning potential'. (ibid.: i–ii). This revealing a stunning gap between the NCAER claims in its POSCO sponsored study about the project's benefits and that of the Mining Zone People's Solidarity Group (2010).

The POSCO project has also been challenged in the Orissa High Court and the National Green Tribunal (NGT). While the former court has been reticent in addressing the issues raised, the tribunal has held that the project has to undergo a fresh review based on fresh studies of the impacts and risks involved. In passing this order, though, the tribunal, a specialized environmental court, has shied away from verifying in detail the anticipated risks. It has suspended the project's final clearances, yet offered a veneer of protection to the defendant company in saying that the new studies need not be all that comprehensive 'since some study might have already been initiated in view of the final order dated 31.1.2011' (Prafulla Samantara Case 2012: 31). This potentially leaves the door open for the old studies to be represented as those that technically comply with the tribunal's order, without necessarily addressing any of the environmental and social concerns. It appears that when a review of the risks entailed by a project are subjected to independent review and the reports that emerge are adverse to the project's future, the government assumes the role of an interlocutor favouring the investment. Clearly, a comprehensive and rigorous process of risk appraisal appears to have no major value in decisions where 'strategic' interest is claimed, as in the mega POSCO project. Consequently, the deep political character of such decisions overwhelms all other considerations, however critical or important they may be to different constituencies, resulting in a highly problematic situation where the interests of those with agency prevail.

★ ★ ★

Article 39 of the Constitution of India requires that a state must direct its policy towards ensuring that the 'ownership and control of the material resources of the community are so distributed as best to sub-serve the common good' and that 'the operation of the economic system does not result in the concentration of wealth and means of production to the common detriment'. Our review, however, reveals an innate lack of discipline in appraising all factors diligently, an acute disregard for applicable standards and little concern for broader societal values and other visions of development. In addition to lobby-induced pressures that play a major role in the outcomes of decisions, there are also deeper political reasons that often are left unstated, thus advantaging particular policies and projects, and not necessarily the wider public interest. Be it in the wider economic policies that are now in practice, or project-level decisions such as Mangalore airport, POSCO, and Kudankulam, little attention is paid to assessing and promoting the wider public interest as defined in Article 39 of the Constitution. Consequently, people and communities with an agency seem to profit, as in the case of economic policies supporting the interest of the rich and middle classes, and those without an agency suffer, sometimes with tragic consequences, as in the case of the airport expansion (both displaced and victims of the accident).

Public administration in India has a long way to go in truly comprehending the impacts of its decisions. Assessing risk has become largely ritualistic and the Precautionary Principle is rarely employed, relegated largely to high judicial and ministerial interventions. This has only increased the success of investor-induced interests whilst making wider populations more vulnerable to the consequences of such decisions. Sadly, it has become a game of who wins and who loses. For the poor, the class–caste divide weighs heavily against their interests, as the essential quality of public decision-making today has been to shelter the interests of the elite.

CASES CITED

A.P. Pollution Control Board v. Nayudu. Supreme Court of India. SOL Case No. 53, 27 January 1999.

Arthur Pereira and Ors. v. Union of India and Ors., Writ Petition No. 37681 of 1997, before the High Court of Karnataka, accessible at http://static. esgindia.org/campaigns/bajpe/docs/Writ_1997.htm, last accessed on 25 October 2013.

Arthur Pereira and Ors. v. Union of India and Ors., Writ Petition No. 20905/2002 in the High Court of Karnataka, available at http://static.esgindia.org/campaigns/bajpe/docs/Bajpe%20HC%20PIL%2020905%20May%202002.htm, last accessed on 25 October 2013.

Environment Support Group and Ors. v. Union of India and Ors., Special Leave Petition No. 1172 of 2003, decided by the Supreme Court of India on 7 February 2003, accessible at http://static.esgindia.org/campaigns/bajpe/docs/BAJPE%20SC%20ORDER%20070203.htm, last accessed on 25 October 2013.

Order of the High Court of Karnataka (1997). WP No. 37681 of 1997, delivered by the Principal Division Bench constituted by Chief Justice Y. Bhaskar Rao and Justice A. M. Farooq, available at http://static.esgindia.org/campaigns/bajpe/docs/1998%20Karnataka%20High%20Court%20Judgement.htm, last accessed on 25 October 2013.

Prafulla Samantara v. Union of India and Ors., decision of National Green Tribunal dated 30 March 2012, available at http://www.greentribunal.in/

orderinpdf/8-2011(Ap)_30Mar2012_final_order.pdf, last accessed on 25 October 2013.

BIBLIOGRAPHY

Actionaid India (2007). 'Livelihood Security in Emergencies: Learning from Orissa Super Cyclone', *Actionaid India*, available at http://www.slideshare.net/siddharth4mba/livelihood-security-in-emergencies-learning-from-orissa-super-cyclone, last accessed on 7 April 2012.

Banerjee, Kaustav, and Partha Saha (2010). 'The NREGA, the Maoists and the Developmental Woes of the Indian State', *Economic and Political Weekly*, 45(28).

Buchar, P. (2009). 'Environment Ministry Set for Revamp', 11 July 2009, *NDTV News*, available at http://www.ndtv.com/article/india/environment-ministry-set-for-revamp-5675, last accessed on 25 October 2013.

Environment Support Group Report (ESG Report) (2007). Report on the Release of 'Green Tapism: A Review of the Environment Impact Assessment Notification–2006', 4 June. Bengaluru: Institute for Agricultural Technologists.

Forbes (2011). 'India's Richest', Forbes Survey, *Forbes* available at http://www.forbes.com/lists/2011/77/india-billionaires-11_rank.html, last accessed on 25 October 2013.

Gokhale, B.N. (2010). 'Report on Accident to Air India Express Boeing 737-800 Aircraft vt-axv on 22nd May 2010 at Mangalore', Government of India: Ministry of Civil Aviation, available at: http://indianaviationnews.net/allimages/MangloreCrashReport.pdf, last accessed on 25 October 2013.

Hindu Business Line (2006). 'Dissent will be Brushed Aside if it Impedes Growth', 11 September 2006, available at http://www.thehindubusinessline.com/2006/09/11/stories/2006091102260300.htm, last accessed on 25 October 2013.

Jeelani, M. (2010). 'NREGA's Reality Check: 4 Years. 784 Billion Rupees. Can India's Most Ambitious Legislation Tackle Poverty?' *The Caravan*, 1 May, available at http://caravanmagazine.in/reportage/nrega%E2%80%99s-reality-check, last accessed on 25 October 2013.

Kamila, R. (2006). 'New Runway at Bajpe Airport Meets All Norms', *The Hindu*, 26 May 2006, available at http://hindu.com/2006/05/26/stories/2006052623420100.htm, last accessed on 25 October 2013.

Narayanan, K.R. (2000). 'India Republic Day Speech', 25 January, available at http://www.krnarayanan.in/html/speeches/others/jan25_2000.htm, last accessed on 25 October 2013.

McKinsey and Company (2007). 'The "Bird of Gold": The Rise of India's Consumer Market', May, available at http://www.mckinsey.com/locations/india/mckinseyonindia/pdf/India_Consumer_Market.pdf, last accessed on 25 October 2013.

Mining Zone People's Solidarity Group (2010). *Iron and Steal: The POSCO–India Story*, October, available at http://miningzone.org/wp-content/uploads/2010/10/Iron-and-Steal.pdf, last accessed on 25 October 2013.

Orissa Government (2005). 'Memorandum of Understanding between the Government of Orissa and M/s POSCO for Establishment of an Integrated Steel Plant at Paradeep', 22 June, available at http://www.orissa.gov.in/posco/POSCO-MoU.htm, last accessed on 25 October 2013.

Orissa State Disaster Management Authority, History of Cyclones from 1737 to 1999, available at http://www.osdma.org/ViewDetails.aspx?vchglinkid=GL002&vchplinkid=PL005

Pathak, N. (2009). 'Our Biggest Task is to Create a Domestic Consensus Than Worry About International Ramifications', interview with Jairam Ramesh, Gulf News, 10 October, available at http://envfor.nic.in/downloads/public-information/Interview_GULF_NEWS.pdf, last accessed on 25 October 2013.

Press Trust of India (2011). 'Rs 32 Per Day Poverty Line Not All That *Ridiculous*: Montek Singh Ahluwalia', *Economic Times*, 11 October, available at http://articles.economictimes.indiatimes.com/2011-10-11/news/30266895_1_poverty-line-urban-areas-indian-conditions, last accessed on 25 October 2013.

——— (2012). 'No Stay on Fuel Loading, but SC Will Examine Risk Factor', *The Hindu*, 13 September, available at http://www.thehindu.com/news/national/article3892860.ece, last accessed on 25 October 2013.

——— (2012). 'Courage and Risk Needed to Get Higher Growth: PM', *IBN Live*, 16 September, available at http://ibnlive.in.com/news/courage-and-risk-needed-to-get-higher-growth-pm/291894-37-64.html, last accessed on 25 October 2013.

Ramesh, J. (2010). 'Decision on Commercialization of Bt Brinjal', *Ministry of Environment and Forests*, available at http://moef.nic.in/downloads/public-information/minister_REPORT.pdf, last accessed on 25 October 2013.

——— (2011). 'Posco Final Order', *Ministry of Environment and Forests*, available at http://moef.nic.in/downloads/public-information/Posco-final-orders-02052011.pdf, last accessed on 25 October 2013.

Saldanha, F., and Bhargavi S. Rao (2011). 'Tearing Through The Water Landscape: Evaluating the Environmental and Social Consequences of POSCO Project in Odisha, India', Environment Support Group Report, available at http://esgindia.org/resources/reports/resources/tearing-through-water-landscape.html, last accessed on 9 February 2014.

Saldanha, L., A. Naik, A. Joshi, and S. Sastry (2007). 'Green Tapism: A Review of Environmental Impact Assessment Notification–2006', *Environment Support Group*, available at www.esgindia.org, last accessed on 25 October 2013.

Sengupta, A. (2008). *Report on Conditions of Work and Promotion of Livelihoods in the Unorganized Sector*. National Commission for Enterprises in the Unorganized Sector. New Delhi: Academic Foundation.

Sethi, N. (2011). 'Only 19 Projects Were Denied Green Clearance From 2008 to Aug 2011', *Times of India*, 16 August, available at http://articles.timesofindia.indiatimes.com/2011-08-16/environment/29891715_1_clearance-thermal-power-projects-mining-projects, last accessed on 25 October 2013.

Stirling, A. (2007). 'Risk, Precaution and Science: Towards a More Constructive Policy Debate: Talking Point on the Precautionary Principle', *EMBO Report*, 8(4), European Molecular Biology Organization, available at http://embor.embopress.org/content/8/4/309, last accessed on 25 October 2013.

Stirling, A. (2008). 'Science, Precaution, and the Politics of Technological Risk: Converging Implications in Evolutionary and Social Scientific Perspectives', *Annals New York Academy Science*, 1128: 95–110.

Swamy, S. (2002). 'Assessing India's Economic Reforms' *Frontline*, 19(2), 19 January to 1 February 2002, available at http://www.frontlineonnet.com/fl1902/19020610.htm, last accessed on 25 October 2013.

The Times of India (2011). 'Kudankulam Plant Safe: APJ Abdul Kalam', *The Times of India*, 15 November, available at http://timesofindia.indiatimes.com/india/Kudankulam-plant-safe-APJ-Abdul-Kalam/articleshow/10737594.cms, last accessed on 20 September 2012.

United Nations Development Programme (2011). Human Development Index (HDI)—2011 Rankings, available at http://hdr.undp.org/en/statistics, last accessed on 20 September 2012.

3

M.V. RAJEEV GOWDA
MATHEW IDICULLA

Integrating Information Disclosure with Indian Environmental Policy

Bhopal, 1984: The Union Carbide plant in Bhopal experiences a breakdown leading to leakage of Methyl Isocyanate gas. More than 2,000 people living around the plant are killed when they are exposed to the toxic plume. Tens of thousands of others are injured and there is also significant damage to livestock and crops. Bhopal becomes synonymous with the worst industrial accident in modern history.

Tirupur, 2011: Citizen activists (the Noyyal River Ayacutdars Protection Association) in the thriving textile hub of Tirupur in the state of Tamil Nadu file a contempt of court suit against the Tamil Nadu Pollution Control Board, Public Works Department (PWD), Tirupur Dyeing Factory Owners Association, and the Tirupur Bleaching Units/Industries Owners Association. They allege lack of compliance with earlier court orders to check pollution of the Noyyal River and ground water in the area. In response, the Madras High Court orders the closure of more than 700 bleaching and dyeing units and effluent treatment plants, effectively shutting down the textile industry in Tirupur. The shut units will be allowed to reopen only when they achieve zero liquid discharge of effluents (Narayanan 2011).

After the Bhopal gas tragedy, India understandably focused on legal recourse to ensure that Union Carbide paid compensation to those affected by the disaster. India went on to establish an elaborate legal framework to control environmental pollution. But, as the Tirupur case suggests, uncontrolled toxic emissions continue to wreak havoc on India's people and their environment. This implies that India's regulatory regime has neither been able to create the incentives for better environmental management nor has it been able to enforce and implement its laws effectively.

In contrast to India, changes brought about by the US, in its environment pollution control regime in response to the disaster at Bhopal succeeded in regulating toxic emissions more effectively. In this chapter, we focus on one key change that US made to its regulatory regime: its adoption of disclosure as an instrument of environmental policy. The US mandated that companies formally provide information to the government about their emissions into the air, water, and land. We describe the power and potential of such disclosures to induce changes in corporate management of toxic emissions, drawing attention to how disclosure empowers citizens and activist groups, enabling them to play a part in the overall regulatory framework. We also explore the complexities of disclosure as an instrument of environmental policy, paying particular attention to issues of risk perception. We then discuss the potential of environmental reporting to strengthen India's efforts to protect its people and environment.

THE REGULATORY RESPONSE TO BHOPAL IN THE US

In response to the Bhopal disaster, in early 1985, US Senator Frank Lautenberg asked some critical questions: What percentage of the American public lives in close proximity to facilities that produce or use hazardous chemicals? Is it known what these materials are, and what hazards they present, to adjacent communities? How adequate are the emergency procedures established by the federal and state government to respond to environmental disasters? In short, the Senator wanted to know whether a Bhopal could happen in the US (Fortun 2004).

A few months after the Bhopal catastrophe, a Union Carbide plant in Institute, West Virginia (where methyl isocyanate also happened to be produced), experienced a leak of methylene chloride and aldicarboxime.

Exposure to the toxic cloud caused 134 residents to seek emergency treatment (Coppock 1989). The combination of public concern about Bhopal and the shock to the American public about their own vulnerability because of this incident gave boost to the grassroots environmental movements agitating for stricter regulation of toxic emissions.

The congressional deliberation that ensued resulted in the passing of the landmark Emergency Planning and Community Right to Know Act, 1986 (EPCRA). It established a framework to ensure that state agencies and the private sector work together to control releases of hazardous chemicals. It established commissions at the state and district level to deal with such releases and mandated that companies provide annual reports on environmental releases of specified chemicals (Schierow 2012). Most importantly, it mandated public access to such information (Cole 1986).

Under the EPCRA, states were required to create State Emergency Response Commissions (SERCs) and local emergency planning committees (LEPCs) to plan for emergencies (Sand 2003). Facilities must submit information annually about their on-site chemicals to the LEPC, SERC, and local fire department, and about their emissions into air, land, or water to the Environmental Protection Agency (EPA). EPA compiles the data of toxic chemical releases into a computerized database, the Toxics Release Inventory (TRI). All information about chemicals is made available to the general public, unless the identity of a chemical is a trade secret (Schierow 2012). Every year, each LEPC must insert notices in local newspapers announcing that such information is available to the public (Wolf 1996).

Under the EPCRA, the EPA can command a facility to comply with emergency planning notification requirements. States and local governments can bring suits against facilities for failure to provide emergency planning notification, hazardous chemical inventory forms, etc. Citizens can also bring suits against facilities or the EPA for failure to carry out their reporting responsibilities (Wolf 1996).

SCORECARD

Environmental Defense Fund (EDF), a non-governmental organization (NGO), added a new dimension to the disclosure of environmental information with the launch of the website Scorecard (www.scorecard.org)

in April 1998 (van den Burg 2004). Scorecard's stated goal was 'to make the local environment as easy to check on as the local weather' (Fortun 2004). It made TRI information more accessible to the public by linking quantitative information on emissions to specific health consequences (van den Burg 2004). *Chemical Week* termed Scorecard as 'The Internet Bomb' because of its potential effect on the reputation of chemical companies (The Economist 1999). The environmental activist group Greenpeace referred to Scorecard as the 'gold standard' of environmental information systems as it 'bridges the gap between setting up passive information and creating a collaborative environment for action' (Fortun 2004: 292).

Scorecard also ranks polluting facilities to put a spotlight on the biggest polluters. It allows users to produce customized reports and makes it easy for them to send emails or letters to the EPA or a polluting company. Pollution maps form the centrepieces of the Scorecard site. Based on post office zip codes, these maps display the manufacturing facilities in a particular area and state how many pounds of toxins were released in a given year by a given facility and the probable health risk involved. Scorecard provides information in a manner that enables the public to put pressure on polluting facilities to reduce pollution risks (Fortun 2004).

By using industry-reported data, Scorecard sidesteps industry claims that the information is politically motivated (ibid.). However, health effects are uncertain and encompass a range of possibilities rather than a point estimate (for example, a risk can be characterized as having between 1 in 10,000 and 1 in 1,000,000 chance of causing damage to health). It is possible that EDF, in constructing the risk interpretations available on Scorecard, would choose the higher-end of the range while industry would choose the lower end of the range in their assessments of risk. Thus the data and interpretation on Scorecard is not incontrovertible but can nonetheless be defended as valid because they are based upon industry reports to the EPA.

ADVANTAGES OF DISCLOSURE

The effects of making TRI data publicly accessible have been significant. When the first round of TRI data was submitted in July 1988, the president of Monsanto was so taken aback by the figures, that he pledged to reduce emissions by 90 per cent over the next five years (Fortun 2004). The biggest victory credited to the TRI is that the releases of toxic chemicals into the environment declined by a sizable 46 per cent from 1988 to 1999, even as the American economy grew rapidly (Beierlie 2004). Hence public disclosure has led to significant reductions in toxic emissions, and in a cost-effective manner (because companies are only required to track and report their emissions).

Disclosure as a policy instrument can be supported by three types of rationales: normative, instrumental, and substantive (ibid.). The normative rationale for information disclosure is that citizens have an inherent 'right to know'. It is based on the idea that an individual has a right to self-protection. By extension the community has a right to know about the risks its residents face.

Substantive rationales for information disclosure are that it provides new insights and understanding of environmental problems and how to remedy them. Disclosure also enables companies to learn more about themselves, helps regulatory agencies to use the data to tailor their programmes, and NGOs to use the data to lobby for their cause. Regardless of its effect on environmental quality, disclosure creates a more information-rich environment to assist decisions.

Instrumental rationales require tangible benefits from information disclosure, for instance, by inducing emissions reductions, increasing safety, enhancing pollution prevention or better regulatory compliance. The major instrumental benefit of TRI is that it has helped reduce toxic releases by 46 per cent in 11 years (Beierlie 2004).

Information on TRI creates incentives for better behaviour because different observers can use it in ways that can reduce the market value of a firm. Investors may use high TRI emissions as a signal of the firm's productive inefficiency, as an indicator of poor management practices and increased risk of spills or accidents. Communities may use TRI information to demand lower emissions, in the process affecting the targeted firm's relationship with and standing in their local communities. 'Green consumers' may decide to boycott products produced by firms which have high levels of emissions, even when they are legally permissible. Firms high on the TRI list can be expected to spend resources to keep up with their competitors and to also incur more litigation expenses in potential class action suits. Investors who learn that a firm has high TRI emissions may bid down that firm's stock price. The fear that a firm's stock price will be bid down provides managements with a strong incentive to reduce pollution which could then also lead to a strengthening of the firm's value in subsequent years (Konar and Cohen 1997).

Powers et al. (2011) have identified six basic ways by which disclosure can improve environmental performance. They are:

1. Output market pressures;
2. Input market pressures;
3. Judicial pressures;
4. Regulatory pressures;
5. Community pressures; and
6. Managerial information.

Disclosure creates output market pressures by affecting the demand for firms' goods. If the ability of firms to hire and retain employees is affected by disclosure it is an input market pressure. Judicial pressures may be in the form of private citizens initiating tort law actions against polluters, based on information accessed through disclosure. When disclosure results in new pollution control legislation or better enforcement of existing laws it may be termed regulatory pressure. Community pressure arises when community groups and NGOs draw on disclosure data to pressure companies to cut their discharges. Managerial information refers to the new information managers obtain when they track their plants' discharges, thus providing avenues for reducing emissions (Powers et al. 2011).

Fortun (2004) surveys a variety of other perspectives about the effects of disclosure. Psychologists suggest that when information is particularly shocking, groups may be motivated to act in extraordinary ways and to start protesting against corporate polluters. Scholars working on 'environmental justice' suggest that when citizens learn about the existence of pollution, their sense of comparative justice and anger against being discriminated against would compel them to mobilize against polluters. Researchers studying the media's agenda setting effects show that when the press reports prominently on industrial pollution, environmental issues gain prominence in the minds of local citizens.

Ultimately, disclosure is an instrument that enhances democratization because it enables citizens to access information which they would otherwise not be able to collect on their own. Since disclosure also provides environmental NGOs and communities with the means to target companies with high emissions, it can be seen as empowering civil society and enabling it to act as a countervailing influence on potential corporate excess.

CHALLENGES OF RISK PERCEPTION AND COMMUNICATION

A key challenge affecting the usefulness of disclosure as an instrument of environmental policy pertains to how people perceive and interpret risk-related information (Slovic 1987, 1992, and 1993). Scholars have raised concerns that the public responds 'irrationally' to risk-related information and that legislation in the US panders to such irrational public fears. Breyer (1993) (now a US Supreme Court Justice) argues that a 'vicious circle' of counterproductive regulation is set into motion by political responses to public demands. Similarly, Zeckhauser and Viscusi (1996) urge governments 'to avoid institutionalizing common irrational responses to risk'.

How can and does the public interpret and misperceive risks? It turns out the public's reaction to risks differs substantially from that of experts. For example, people rate risks higher when they involve catastrophes, involuntary exposure, dread, novel threats, and the like. People tend to overestimate rare but catastrophic risks and underestimate risks from frequent but less-dramatic events. People tend to attach disproportionate importance to risks of events that easily come to the mind, ignore evidence that contradicts beliefs and shun information overload (Graham 2002). People find it difficult to think clearly on uncertain data and probabilistic outcomes and hence use judgmental heuristics to simplify complex problems. But the use of such heuristics often can lead to serious judgement errors (Nordenstam and DiMento 1990; Gowda 1999, 2000).

Scholars working on risk perception argue that the public's reactions to risk, far from demonstrating ignorance and irrationality, emphasize a richer conceptualization of risk, taking into account legitimate concerns that are typically omitted from expert risk assessments (Hadden 1991; Slovic 1987, 1992). The concerns affecting the public include qualitative factors such as voluntariness, catastrophic potential, and impact on future generations, which experts typically ignored by restricting their focus to only quantitative factors such as expected mortality and morbidity (Slovic 1992). As Leiss (1992) points out, the public's perceptions of risk have also been affected by its awareness of the historical record of risks being underestimated by governments and industries.

Risk-related information also needs to be communicated carefully. Nordenstam and DiMento (1990) point out that risk communication can give rise to a variety of problems—source problems (who says it), message problems (what is said), channel problems (how is it said) and receiver problems (to whom is it said). Source problems arise from the credibility, competence, and objectivity of the company or agency providing information. Message problems deal with issues like the frequency of message, level of arousing information and understand-ability. Channel problems may originate in either the medium used for information like television or internet and presence of other stimuli competing with the receiver's attention. Receiver problems arise due to the dysfunctional response to risk messages which could be based on personality traits and other issues which can create an 'anchoring' effect (ibid.).

Levels of education are among other factors affecting how disclosure affects environmental outcomes. Terry and Yandle (1997) found a stronger relationship between more highly educated individuals and lower state per capita TRI emissions. More highly educated individuals formed groups, wrote letters, and brought public pressure to bear on emitters. Also where the state owned a larger share of the land there was a larger reduction of emissions. Companies with the largest investment in brand-name capital were the most sensitive to the citizen pressures emerging from TRI data.

The media's coverage of a risk-related event can result in a 'ripple effect' (Lofstedt 2003) leading to direct societal impacts such as stricter regulation of the relevant risk and also 'significant indirect impacts such as liability, insurance costs, loss of confidence in institutions, stig-matization, or alienation from community affairs' (Kasperson 1992). Interestingly, the magnitude of the societal impacts may have little to do with the technically assessed magnitude of the actual risks involved. The Social Amplification of Risk Framework (SARF) (Kasperson et al. 1988) attempts to explain this phenomenon by positing that amplification or attenuation depends on a complex set of behavioural, psychological, social, and cultural processes, rather than objective measures of risk. Factors affecting social amplification included public concern and fears about the risks and attention from the media and active opposition from key individuals and groups in society. These individuals and groups acted as 'amplification stations', often through their societal roles, and helped to convert an individual risk-related incident into a range of socially transforming outcomes (Kasperson 1992).

Thus, along with disclosure, it is important to pay attention to how people react to risk-related information. This is vital because trust plays a central role in societal risk management. But trust is fragile, and once lost, it takes a long time for it to be rebuilt. The consequences are large—public perceptions and acceptance of risk from nuclear and chemical technologies have been shown to be less influenced by technical risk assessments and more by trust (Slovic 1993). There is a direct relationship between high public trust in authority and low perceived risk and vice-versa (Lofstedt 2003).

THE INDIAN CONTEXT

India has an elaborate environmental regulatory structure. It established two major environmental regulatory bodies, the Central Pollution Control Board (CPCB) and various State Pollution Control Boards (SPCBs) under the Water (Prevention and Control of Pollution) Act, 1974. These Boards have been entrusted with powers to control pollution including the power to obtain information, power to take samples, and power of entry and inspection. The Air (Prevention and Control of Pollution) Act, 1981 also endows the state and central Boards with similar powers. SPCBs have been made responsible for the collection and dissemination of information relating to pollution and empowered to call for any information from an industry regarding its emissions. No facility is permitted to discharge pollutants above certain prescribed limits and if any such discharge occurs, it has to immediately intimate its state Board.

More importantly, every industry is required to furnish an environment statement every year which has information on the level of pollution and quantity of waste generated. Industries dealing with hazardous substances must obtain an authorization from the SPCB before commencing operations, have to maintain a record of the hazardous substances in the prescribed form, and also file an annual return containing all details of such substances to the Board. The Board has to maintain a register containing details of authorization granted and conditions imposed and the register must be open for inspection to any interested person.

The Environment (Protection) Act, 1986 was enacted as an umbrella legislation on environment protection. Pursuant to the Act, the central government framed the Environment (Protection) Rules, 1986 which provide the standards of quality of air, water or soil, and the maximum allowable limits of concentration of various environmental pollutants for different areas. The standards provided in the schedules to the rules may be in the form of source standards which restrict the manufacturers from discharging pollutants at the source of production, production standards that regulate the standards of products that can cause pollution or ambient standards which fix maximum amounts of pollutants permissible in the air. Every facility is required to file an environmental audit report to the board that discloses information regarding the quantity of pollutants discharged into water and air, the concentrations of pollutants in discharges, and the percentage of variation from prescribed standards with reasons. Hence, under the current legal framework, though statements on level of emissions are required to be furnished every year, such information is to be provided only to the SPCB and is not required to be publicly disclosed.

However, in practice, neither have industries followed these regulations nor have SPCBs implemented them rigorously. In spite of greater importance given to public participation (Menon and Kohli 2007), the public may be consulted only at the time plants are set up, if at all (Saldanha et al. 2007). Reporting requirements are not adhered to but Boards neither seem to have the manpower or enforcement capability to ensure effective reporting of emissions. Rangarajan (2009) points to the lack of technically trained manpower in pollution control boards (PCB) and their limited financial capability to follow through effectively on their environmental regulatory role. Similarly, the Parliament Standing Committee Report (2008) on the functioning of the CPCB observed that 'a Gujarat SPCB technical person spares 1.77 days to monitor an industry in a year, the Karnataka SPCB technical person 1.72 days a year, and a Maharashtra SPCB technical person 1.23 days a year'.

This state of affairs led the Supreme Court of India to observe in its judgment in the case of *Indian Council of Enviro-Legal Action v. Union of India*:

> If the mere enactment of the laws relating to the protection of environment was to ensure a clean and pollution-free environment, then India would, perhaps, be the least polluted country in the world. But, this is not so. There are stated to be over 200 Central and State Statutes which have at least some concern with environment protection, either directly or indirectly. The plethora of such enactments has, unfortunately, not resulted in preventing environmental degradation which, on the contrary, has increased over the years.... Enactment of a law, but tolerating its infringement, is worse than not enacting a law at all.... Continued tolerance of such violations of law not only renders legal provisions nugatory but such tolerance by the enforcement authorities encourages lawlessness and adoption of means which cannot, or ought not to, be tolerated in any civilized society.

In another case between the same parties, the Supreme Court expressed its 'deep sense of hurt' at the way environmental regulations are enforced in India.

THE CHANGING INDIAN CONTEXT

In recent years, a number of developments are setting the stage for a change in the way India's environmental regulatory environment functions. If these disconnected changes could be coordinated in a synergistic manner, India could potentially bring about a transformation in the effectiveness of its efforts to tackle the scourge of unlawful toxic emissions. Disclosure has the potential to be a key factor in such an integrated regulatory regime.

At the macro level, the policy environment is now receptive to the idea that the public has a right to information about the details of how governments make policy decisions and why. In 2005, after sustained pressure from civil society organizations, India enacted legislation giving people the Right to Information (RTI) Act. With the success of the RTI movement, concepts like 'transparency' and 'accountability' are centre stage. The RTI Act enables citizens to obtain data they can use to further environment-related activism as government has to provide information when requested about project clearances and expenditure on programmes (Kohli 2009). Section 4 of the RTI Act focuses on voluntary disclosure of information by public authorities. This could become the catalyst for a change in how Pollution Control Boards (PCB) enforce emissions reporting requirements.

The Supreme Court of India, in response to public interest litigations (PILs), has played a significant role in initiating and enforcing environmental regulation (Sawhney 2003). In 1995, the Research Foundation for Science, Technology and Natural Resource Policy filed a PIL against the Union of India in the Supreme Court. The petition sought to regulate the movement and handling of hazardous wastes both within the state and between countries. The Supreme Court constituted a 'High-Powered' Committee chaired by Prof. M.G.K. Menon to look into the problems presented by the petition. By an order in October 2003, based on the report of the Committee, the Supreme Court directed the central government to constitute a Monitoring Committee to oversee the compliance of 29 comprehensive directions it issued (Research Foundation for Science, Technology and Natural Resource Policy v. Union of India).

One of the directives to SPCBs was to prepare a toxic inventory regarding the generation of hazardous wastes and to use the data to form a national inventory. The court also directed the SPCBs to ensure that information on Hazardous Wastes is displayed on notice boards and newspapers and communicated through radio, television, and the internet. However it was only in February 2009 that the CPCB published a 'National Inventory of Hazardous Wastes Generating Industries and Hazardous Waste Management in India' which contained state and district-wise data on the toxic waste generated. But no such inventory has come out in subsequent years (Central Pollution Control Board 2009)

In the same order, the Supreme Court ordered the creation of Local Area Environment Committees (LAEC), quasi-judicial structures to monitor hazardous waste management (Rangarajan 2010). In 2004, LAECs were constituted in Delhi, Gujarat, Kerala, Maharashtra, and Tamil Nadu by involving technical experts and members of affected local communities. The LAECs were to report to the Supreme Court Monitoring Committee that was established to supervise their functioning. For a few years, they played an active role in engaging with state boards to improve the effectiveness of environmental regulation.

According to Rangarajan (2010) the 'functioning of the LAEC brought a sense of fear of unpredictability and a kind of *rogue* or militant element in execution keeping the SPCB on its toes as the LAEC was creating tremendous countervailing pressure to take hard decisions'. Over time, SPCBs reconstituted the membership of LAECs and this may have affected their effectiveness. No LAEC is in operation today. However, the LAEC experiment demonstrated that involving citizens in the monitoring and enforcement of environmental regulation enhanced environmental protection. Therefore Rangarajan advocates the revival and refinement of the LAEC model and its institutionalization in a manner that enables LAECs to function effectively and sustainably as part of the broader environmental enforcement regime.

Another set of changes come from the arena of corporate reporting. There is no requirement under either the Indian Companies Act or the accounting standards issued by the Institute of Chartered Accountants of India to disclose non-financial information such as environmental performance in corporate financial statements. However, companies are beginning to volunteer and put up such information on their websites and in their annual reports (Chatterjee and Mir 2008; Sen et al. 2011). This is part of an emerging trend to acknowledge the importance of social and environmental aspects of corporate conduct, captured by terms such as the triple bottom-line and Corporate Social Responsibility (CSR).

In 2009, the Ministry of Corporate Affairs issued 'Voluntary Guidelines for Corporate Social Responsibility' and 'Corporate Governance Voluntary Guidelines' and in 2011 'National Voluntary Guidelines on Social, Environmental and Economic Responsibilities of Business'. None of these guidelines are prescriptive and they are voluntary in nature. They aim to create a transparent and accountable system that harmonizes the needs of business with that of society. CSR guidelines provide that companies should engage with all stakeholders including customers, project affected people and society at large to inform them of inherent risks as well as strategies to mitigate them.

Sahay (2004) has raised concerns that environmental reporting in India is a mere public relations exercise. Companies used environmental reports to publicize their good environmental performance without giving factual data and environmental trends. Their reports provided information that was 'unsystematic, piecemeal, and inadequate' and the lack of common standards for reporting thwarted any efforts to compare environmental performance across companies (ibid.). But the changing policy environment can enable India's civil society organizations and citizen groups to turn this situation around. We consider below an initiative of the Centre for Science and Environment (CSE) as an example of how civil society can play a key role in changing environmental behaviour.

CSE'S GREEN RATING PROJECT

Centre for Science and Environment, India's premier environmental research organization, initiated the Green Rating Project (GRP) in 1997 to monitor, rate, and publicly disclose the environmental performance of Indian companies. CSE first systematically collects information about the environmental performance of industries to create its own alternative database. It then constructs a detailed environmental profile of each plant using the 'Life Cycle Analysis' approach that takes into account the impact of industrial activity from the raw material procurement stage to the end product stage. It shares its reports with the assessed plants for review before releasing the ratings to the public. For each industrial sector, GRP also publishes specific recommendations for improving environmental performance (Powers et al. 2011). GRP has gained credibility because its panels have involved eminent and highly respected representatives from industry, civil society, and the government United Nations Environment Programme (UNEP).

GRP has rated the performance of enterprises in the cement, steel, pulp and paper, automobile, and chlor-alkali sectors. CSE was able to obtain the voluntary participation of 90 per cent of industry members in the latter three sectors. CSE's success in obtaining corporate cooperation arises because it compares companies in the same sector, thus allowing participating companies to demonstrate that they perform better than their competitors.

Powers et al. (2011) evaluated the impact of the GRP on the environmental performance of pulp and paper plants. The study found that the programme drove significant reductions in pollution loadings among dirty plants, but not among cleaner ones. It also found that plants in wealthier communities and single-plant firms were more responsive to GRP ratings. The study concluded that public disclosure programmes can be an effective environmental tool even with weak regulatory institutions and limited political will. It suggested that NGOs would be better in administrating disclosure programmes than government as they would face less resistance from industrial lobbies than would the government (ibid.).

HOW INDIA CAN GAIN FROM DISCLOSURE

The salutary performance of CSE's GRP and the limited effectiveness and sustainability of the LAEC model suggest that India must pay careful attention to organizational design if it intends to involve the public in environmental management. Because of the RTI Act, the context is favourable to mandating disclosure. But careful design requires India to address the following questions: What kinds of information should be made publicly available? What are the modes through which such information should be communicated to the public? How can the interpretation of risk data by affected communities be improved? Which agencies should be given the task of monitoring environmental risks? How can these agencies ensure that risks are avoided and action taken to reduce pollution?

As a fundamental step, India needs to adopt an environmental policy which clearly mandates that any data that has the potential to pollute the environment or cause damage to the lives of people has to be made public. It may be insufficient to make only the data presently required to be submitted to the PCBs publicly available. More information regarding use and storage of chemicals in factories can also be required to be made public.

In order that disclosed information is communicated to the public in a way that helps them understand the risks, the government must first create a central database like TRI for the whole country. This data must be made publicly available through the internet. The website hosting the data should provide a variety of details regarding the level of toxic pollutants discharged. The data must contain area-specific and plant-specific information on environmental risks. The existence of this environmental data should be publicized through TV, radio and newspapers.

However as environmental emission data is very technical in nature, it may be difficult for a lay person to understand. Hence along with raw data, there should also be a simplified representation of the data in a comparative manner. Additional information like the associated health risks (such as provided by Scorecard) may also be useful. The Environmentally Sustainable Finance Group of the Centre for Development Finance (CDF) has already launched a portal, India Pollution Map (www.indiapollutionmap.org) which aims to provide easy information on pollution levels in India. For Tamil Nadu and Maharashtra, the two pilot states of the project, the user generated maps display environmental data from government sources along with demographic and socioeconomic information.

However, ensuring that every plant reports its environmental data and then creating a central database with risk information accessible through the internet does not solve all problems. India's level of internet penetration is quite low and a substantial majority of the population is still illiterate. So putting out environment data, however simplified, on the internet may still leave whole, possibly more vulnerable, sections of society unaware of the environmental risks. This is why we need to see the information disclosure policy in a new light. Environment information is not to be made available only for those who bother to look it up. The thrust should be to make every individual aware of the environmental risks he or she faces.

Other developments that support public involvement and disclosure include the concept of 'social audit' of government programmes by communities. This feature has already been institutionalized under the National Rural Employment Guarantee Scheme (NREGS). However, a critical challenge is that of finding legitimate bodies that represent the public and that can also sustainably engage with SPCBs and local communities. To address this challenge, we suggest that the government should integrate Panchayati Raj institutions into the environmental regulatory process and to also make them part of LEPCs.

Panchayati Raj institutions, local-level democratically elected institutions which consist of the Gram Panchayat, Taluka Samitis and Zilla Parishads (that is, village, block, and district-level councils respectively) were established under the 73rd Amendment to the Constitution of India. Similarly, the 74th Amendment established Urban Local Bodies like Town Municipal Councils and City Municipal Corporations in urban areas. These local governments have been charged with a developmental role and financially empowered as well. If these institutions are also engaged to oversee the enforcement of environmental regulations, their accountability to their electorate would ensure that they would bring pressure on government agencies and companies to mitigate harmful environmental impacts. The Gram Panchayat can also play a role in communicating environmental information to the Gram Sabha, the assembly of people, on a regular basis.

When environmental data becomes localized and democratized through Panchayati Raj institutions, the local public would become aware of the environmental risks in their area. However, they would still need the help of technical experts to communicate credible information on the potential impacts of various emissions in a manner comprehensible to lay citizens; but this is an issue that can be substantially addressed with suitable funding. Another advantage of working with Panchayati Raj institutions is that they can address larger challenges, for example, environmental emissions in the unorganized sector or from small and medium enterprises that often escape regulatory scrutiny. They could also address the challenges of environmental problems caused by other sectors; for instance, excessive fertilizer use that can cause environmental damage through groundwater contamination.

Overall, disclosing environmental information to the public clearly has the potential to reduce environmental pollution and environmental risk. When people become aware of pollution in their environment, they exert pressure on firms to reduce pollution. Media and civil society also inform the public about pollution and environmental risks and also exert pressure on the polluting facility. Pressure from the public, media, and other agencies will cause firms with a stake in their communities to reduce emissions and control environmental risks. Carefully managed, disclosure has the potential to truly improve the capabilities of the people of India (Sen 1999) and enhance their capacity to manage their lives and their environment.

CASES CITED

Indian Council of Enviro-Legal Action v. Union of India, 1996 (3) SCALE 579: AIR SC 1446.

Research Foundation for Science, Technology and Natural Resource Policy v. Union of India and Anr. – Writ Petition No. 657/2005, available at http://www.wbpcb.gov.in/html/suporders/HW_supcourt_order.pdf

BIBLIOGRAPHY

Beierle, Thomas C. (2004). 'The Benefits and Costs of Environmental Information Disclosure: What Do We Know About Right-to-Know?', *Risk Analysis*, 24(2): 335–46.

Breyer, Stephen (1993). *Breaking the Vicious Circle: Toward Effective Risk Regulation*. Cambridge: Harvard University Press.

Centre for Science and Environment (undated). 'About Green Rating Programme', available at http://www.cseindia.org/node/277, last accessed on 23 October 2013.

Central Pollution Control Board (2009). 'National Inventory of Hazardous Wastes Generating Industries and Hazardous Waste Management in India', available at http://www.cpcb.nic.in/upload/NewItems/NewItem_145_hw_inventory_final_report_2009.pdf, last accessed on 23 October 2013.

Chatterjee, Bikram, and Monir Zaman Mir (2008). 'The Current Status of Environmental Reporting by Indian Companies', *Managerial Auditing Journal*, 23(6): 609–29.

Chemical Industry Archive (undated). 'Responsible? Care? As Bad News Mounts and Polls Head South, Chemical Companies Spend Millions on 'Public Perception', available at http://www.chemicalindustryarchives.org/dirtysecrets/responsiblecare/1.asp, last accessed on 23 October 2013.

Cole, Henry S. (1986). 'Toxic Chemical Information Systems and Right-to-Know', *Journal of Public Health Policy*, 7(1): 28–36.

Coppock, Rob (1989). 'Communicating Corporate Disaster: The Aldicarb Oxime Release at the Union Carbide Plant at Institute, West Virginia on August 11, 1985', in Improving Risk Communication Working Papers, Washington, D.C.: National Academy Press.

The Economist (1999). 'www.democracy.com', 1 April, available at http://www.economist.com/node/195325, last accessed on 23 October 2013.

Environment Protection Agency (undated). 'The Toxics Release Inventory (TRI) and Factors to Consider When Using TRI Data', available at http://www.epa.gov/tri/triprogram/FactorsToConPDF.pdf, last accessed on 23 October 2013.

Fortun, Kim (2004). 'From Bhopal to the Informating of Environmentalism: Risk Communication in Historical Perspective', *OSIRIS*, 19: 283–96.

Gowda, M.V. Rajeev (1999). 'Heuristics, Biases, and the Regulation of Risk', *Policy Sciences*, 31(1): 1–20.

———— (2001). 'Enhancing the Effectiveness of Innovative Policy Instruments: The Implications of Behavioural Decision Theory for Right-to-Know Policies', in M.V. Rajeev Gowda and Jeffrey C. Fox (eds), *Judgments, Decisions, and Public Policy*. Cambridge: Cambridge University Press.

Gowda, M.V. (2003). 'Integrating Politics with the Social Amplification of Risk Framework', in Pidgeon, Nick, Roger E. Kasperson, and Paul Slovic (eds), *The Social Amplification of Risk*. Cambridge: Cambridge University Press.

Graham, Mary (2002). 'Is Sunshine the Best Disinfectant? The Promise and Problems of Environmental Disclosure', *The Brookings Review*, 20(2): 18–19.

Hadden, Susan G. (1991). 'Public Perception of Hazardous Waste', *Risk Analysis*, 11(1): 47–58.

Kasperson, Roger E. (1992). 'The Social Amplification of Risk: Progress in Developing an Integrative Framework', in Sheldon Krimsky and Dominic Golding (eds), *Social Theories of Risk*. Westport, Connecticut: Praeger.

Kasperson, Roger E., Ortwin Renn, Paul Slovic, Halina S. Brown, Jacque Emel, Robert Goble, Jeanne X. Kasperson, and Samuel Ratick (1988). 'The social amplification of risk: A conceptual framework', *Risk analysis*, 8(2): 177–87.

Kathuria, Vinish (2009). 'Public Disclosures: Using Information To Reduce Pollution in Developing Countries', *Environment, Development and Sustainability*, 11(5): 955–70.

Kohli, Kanchi (2009). 'A Boost to Transparency in Environment Regulation', *India Together*, 5 January, available at http://www.indiatogether.org/2009/jan/env-transpenv.htm, last accessed on 23 October 2013.

Konar, Shameek, and Mark A. Cohen (1997). 'Information As Regulation: The Effect of Community Right to Know Laws on Toxic Emissions', *Journal of Environmental Economics and Management*, 32(1): 109–24.

Leiss, William (1992). 'Assessing and Managing Risks', *Policy Sciences*, 25(3): 341–9.

Lofstedt, Ragnar (2003). 'Risk Communication: Pitfalls and Promises', *European Review*, 11(3): 17–35.

Menon, Manju, and Kanchi Kohli (2007). 'Environmental Decision-making: Whose Agenda?', *Economic and Political Weekly*, 42(26): 2490–4.

Narayanan, Sumana (2011). 'Tirupur Dyeing Units Told to Close', *Down to Earth*, 28 February, available at http://www.downtoearth.org.in/content/tirupur-dyeing-units-told-close, last accessed on 23 October 2013.

Nordenstam, Brenda J., and Joseph F. DiMento (1990). 'Right-to-Know: Implications of Risk Communication Research for Regulatory Policy', *University of California Davis Law Review*, 23(2): 333–74.

Parliament of India (2008). '192nd Report on the Functioning of the Central Pollution Control Board', Department-related Parliamentary Standing Committee on Science and Technology and Environment & Forests, June 2008.

Powers, Nicholas, Allen Blackman, Thomas Lyon, and Urvashi Narain (2011). 'Does Disclosure Reduce Pollution? Evidence from India's Green Rating Project', *Environmental and Resource Economics*, 50(1): 131–55.

Rangarajan, Rajesh (2009). 'A Review of Implementation Gaps in the Enforcement of Environmental Regulation in India', Working Paper, Institute for Financial Management and Research, available at http://cdf.ifmr.ac.in/

wp-content/uploads/2011/03/Working-paper_env-enf-gaps_final.pdf, last accessed on 23 October 2013.

Rangarajan, Rajesh (2010). 'Lessons from a Model of Public Participation in Environmental Enforcement in India: Local Environment Area Committees', Working Paper, Institute for Financial Management and Research, available at http://cdf.ifmr.ac.in/wp-content/uploads/2011/08/Rajesh_LAEC_final1.pdf, last accessed on 23 October 2013.

Sahay, A. (2004). 'Environmental Reporting by Indian Corporations', *Corporate Social Responsibility and Environmental Management*, 11(1): 12–22.

Saldanha, Leo F., Abhayraj Naik, Arpita Joshi, and Subramanya Sastry (2007). *Green Tapism: A Review of the Environmental Impact Assessment Notification–2006*. Bangalore: Environment Support Group.

Sand, Peter H. (2003). 'Information Disclosure as an Instrument of Environmental Governance', *Heidelberg Journal of International Law*, 63: 487–502.

Sawhney, Aparna (2003). 'Managing Pollution: PIL as Indirect Market Based Tool', *Economic and Political Weekly*, 38(1): 32–7.

Schierow, Linda-Jo (2012). 'The Emergency Planning and Community Right-to-Know Act (EPCRA): A Summary', CRS Report for Congress, RL32683, 5 April, Congressional Research Service.

Sen, Amartya (1999). *Development as Freedom*. Oxford: Oxford University Press.

Sen, Mitali, Kuhali Mukherjee, and J.K. Pattanayak (2011). 'Corporate Environmental Disclosure Practices in India', *Journal of Applied Accounting Research*, 12(2): 139–56.

Slovic, Paul (1987). 'Perception of Risk', *Science*, 236(4799): 280–5.

——— (1992). 'Perception of Risk: Reflections on the Psychometric Paradigm', in Sheldon Krimsky and Dominic Golding (eds), *Social Theories of Risk*. pp. 117–52. Westport, Connecticut: Praeger.

——— (1993). 'Perceived Risk, Trust, and Democracy', *Risk Analysis*, 13(6): 675–82.

Terry, Jeffrey C., and Bruce Yandle (1997). 'EPA's Toxic Release Inventory: Stimulus and Response', *Managerial and Decision Economics*, 18(6): 433–42.

United Nations Environment Program (undated). 'Green Rating of the Indian Industry', available at http://ekh.unep.org/files/Green%20Rating%20of%20the%20Indian%20Industry.pdf, last accessed on 23 October 2013.

van den Burg, Sander (2004). 'Informing or Empowering? Disclosure in the United States and the Netherland', *Local Environment*, 9(4): 367–81.

Wolf, Sidney M. (1996). 'Fear and Loathing About the Public Right to Know: The Surprising Success of the Emergency Planning and Community Right-to-Know Act', *Journal of Land Use and Environmental Law*, 11(2): 217–319.

Zeckhauser, Richard J., and W. Kip Viscusi (1996). 'The Risk Management Dilemma' *Annals of the American Academy of Political and Social Science*, 545: 144–55.

4

ROHIT JIGYASU

Linking Post-disaster Reconstruction to Long-term Risk Reduction

Challenges and Opportunities in India

India is vulnerable, in varying degrees, to a large number of natural disasters, and this has been exacerbated by dramatic changes to the landscape. Out of the total landmass, 58.6 per cent is prone to earthquakes of moderate to very high intensity; over 40 million hectares (12 per cent of land) is prone to floods and river erosion; of the 7,516-km-long coastline, close to 5,700 km is prone to cyclones and tsunamis; 68 per cent of the cultivable area is vulnerable to drought, and hilly areas are at risk from landslides and avalanches. An expanding population, intensified urbanization and industrialization, development within high-risk zones, environmental degradation, and climate change, have only heightened India's vulnerability to the risks from natural disasters. In India, disasters affect over 56 million people, kill over 5,000 people and result in an economic loss of approximately USD 1,884 million, annually. Inevitably any social and economic progress achieved over decades of initiatives by the community can be significantly degraded or devastatingly reversed by natural disasters (Unnikrishan and Sekher 2001).

Human beings have always been exposed to risks from natural hazards such as earthquakes, landslides, floods, and tsunamis. Ironically, human settlements have often evolved in areas that are highly exposed to these hazards due to the abundance of natural resources that these areas provide, especially water and fertile soil needed for sustenance and growth. Over time, human beings have developed various coping mechanisms and have learnt to live with the ever-present threat of natural hazards. In traditional societies, for example, the collective perception of natural disaster risks has resulted in the development of indigenous management systems that build on local capacities and opportunities. In many rural Indian communities, agricultural land is put aside to be collectively owned and managed by the community, and its yield stored for times of crisis. Over the recent decades, however, as disaster risk management has emerged as a formal sector in India, public policies and institutional systems have been set up at the national, state, and district levels, with tools and procedures for risk assessment, mitigation, preparedness, response, and recovery. These formal mechanisms for disaster risk management, which are predominantly top-down, have rarely recognized these indigenous systems, though the latter have sometimes continued to work in parallel.

After such catastrophic events, recovery of the affected communities is undertaken through reconstruction programmes initiated by the Government with the support of international organizations, as well as national and local Non-governmental Organizations (NGOs). Millions of dollars are pumped into these programmes to ensure that the lives of the affected people are speedily rebuilt through the provision of alternative settlement sites, new building technologies, and projects aimed at enhancing societal resilience to natural hazards. Increasingly, reconstruction is seen beyond mere recovery to a pre-disaster state, but rather as an opportunity for 'building back better' and reinforcing the link between 'post-disaster reconstruction' and 'risk reduction'. Yet, in order to enhance the visibility of post-disaster reconstruction, the emphasis is too often placed on 'camcorder'-driven policies that seek to build the maximum number of housing units in the shortest time possible. In spite of massive investments, reconstruction outcomes continue to differ distressingly from their objectives.

The policies and programmes for post-disaster reconstruction in India can be better understood if we learn about the fundamental perceptions and assumptions of decision-makers on 'development' and 'risk reduction'. While the fundamental risk assumptions of decision-makers have shaped the interpretation and implementation of policies and procedures, these can be markedly different from those of local communities. When risk assumptions are one dimensional and limited to a short-term perspective, they often end up reinforcing pre-existing vulnerabilities and creating a whole new set to grapple with in the long run. This chapter will investigate these issues, based on empirical research conducted by the author and his collaborators, on the long-term impact of reconstruction, following the 1993 earthquake in Latur;[1] the first comprehensive programme to be implemented in India on such a large scale.

THE CASE OF MARATHWADA

A devastating earthquake hit Marathwada in the early morning hours of 30 September 1993. Its magnitude was 6.3 on the Richter scale and it left nearly 9,000 villagers dead and around 16,000 injured. In the 52 villages that were most severely affected, some 30,000 houses were destroyed or badly damaged (Jigyasu 2001). The loss of life and property was particularly high in rural areas since traditional constructions, which were already weak and vulnerable, could not withstand the shock of the earthquake.

The initial phase of emergency, rescue, and relief lasted until December 1993. In the next phase, the government evolved a rather comprehensive rehabilitation programme called Maharashtra Earthquake Emergency Rehabilitation Programme (MEERP)—a USD 326 million worth aid programme that targeted over 2,64,500 households in 13 agricultural districts. This was the first of its kind in India, both in

[1] Research is currently being undertaken by the author along with Dr Jennifer Duyne Barenstein and Daniel Pittel within the framework of the project: 'Understanding Habitats, Housing and Social Changes in Post-disaster Traditional and Relocated Rural Settlements in India' with the University of Applied Science and Arts of Southern Switzerland (SUPSI). The research builds on earlier research conducted by the author in 2000 as part of his doctoral thesis titled: 'Reducing Disaster Vulnerability through Local Knowledge and Capacity: The Case of Earthquake Prone Rural Communities in India and Nepal'.

terms of the number of shelters reconstructed and the sheer size of the government's investment, which was funded by a soft loan from the World Bank. The programme had five main components, namely— housing, infrastructure development, economic rehabilitation, social rehabilitation, community rehabilitation, and technical assistance, training, and equipment. However, the programme mainly focused on the housing component, under which the construction or reconstruction of permanent housing was financed.

The villages were divided into three categories based on pre-defined criteria,[2] namely (GoM 1993):

- Villages to be relocated—type 'A' villages
- Villages to be reconstructed in situ—type 'B' villages
- Villages where repairs and seismic strengthening and retrofitting programme would be implemented—type 'C' villages

Within each village the houses were then divided into three categories, where the size of the house plot varied on the basis of the family's landholding prior to the earthquake.[3] Most of the plans of the relocated villages were prepared by engineers in the local Town Planning office. The layouts of these villages were mainly 'city-like' with wide streets forming a grid pattern and row or cluster housing. This is contrary to traditional settlements, which are typically characterized by narrow streets, a hierarchy of public and private open spaces used for religious as well as other activities and clusters of housing with distinct

[2] The villages to be relocated were those where more than 70 per cent of the houses were damaged, where a certain number of deaths were reported, and where the ground had black cotton soil up to a depth of 2 metres. Where the damage was more than 70 per cent but strata was good, that is, soil was less than 2 metres deep, it was decided to reconstruct those villages in situ. The 'C' category villages were decided on the basis of a detailed 'technical' survey by a team of government engineers.

[3] Accordingly 'A' category houses had a carpet area of 250 square feet. These were to be provided to farmers who were landless or had land up to 1 hectare. 'B' category housing of 400 square feet carpet area was provided to those having land-holding between 1 hectare and 7 hectares. All bigger landlords, having more than 7 hectares of land-holding, got 'C' category houses of 750 square feet. The built-up area for these houses was about 10 per cent more than the carpet area to allow for future expansion.

typologies influenced by traditional occupation patterns (See Figures 4.1 and 4.2). Most of the relocated villages were adopted by various public and private agencies and the entire reconstruction activity was primarily contractor-driven, where contractors and labour were hired by donor agencies from outside the region.

Among all other components, housing was given the first priority in the rehabilitation process. Accordingly, 52 villages were to be relocated with essential services and infrastructure, and new standards were set for housing construction to include 'earthquake-resistant technology'.

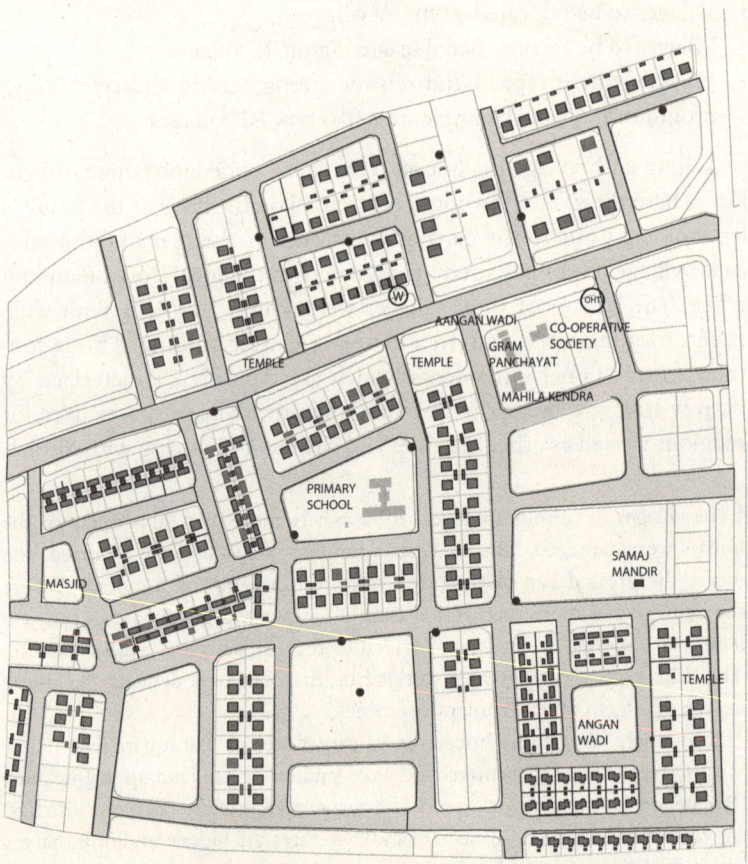

FIGURE 4.1   A Government-proposed Layout for a Reconstructed Village in Marathwada

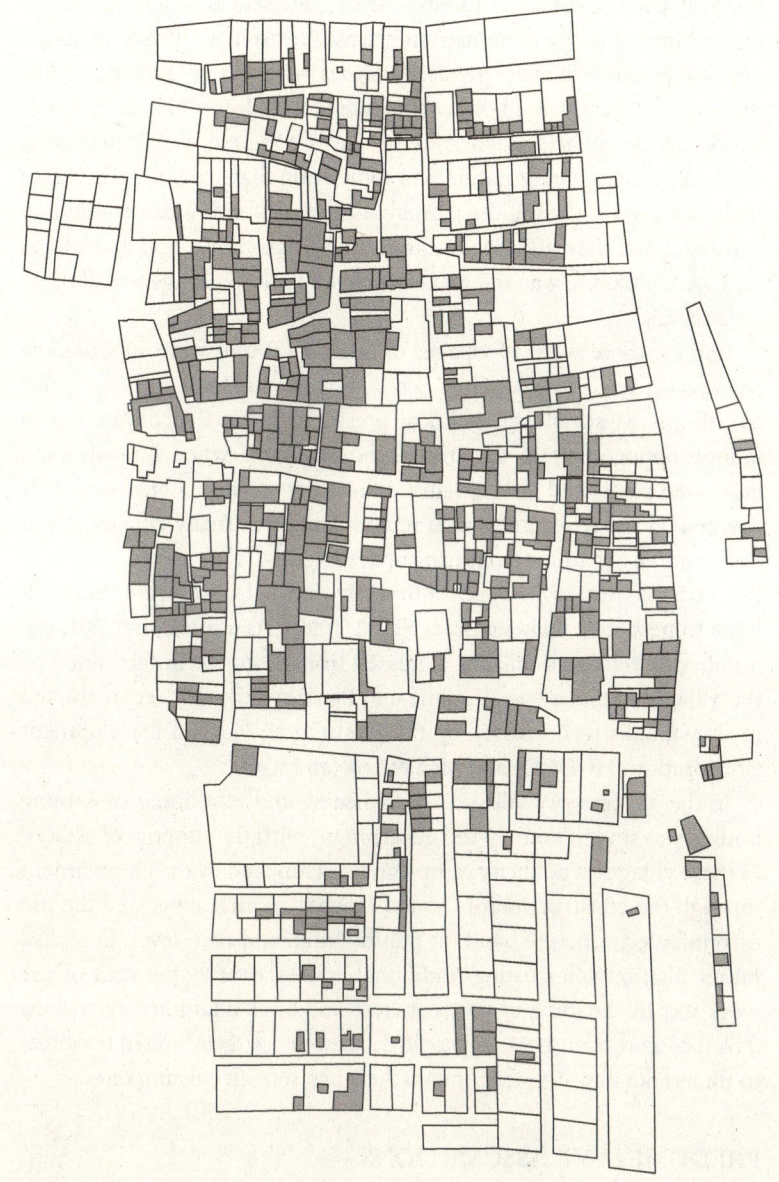

FIGURE 4.2   A Traditional Village Layout in Marathwada

A number of non-governmental agencies (international donor agencies, political parties, and commercial firms) devised a variety of building technologies to demonstrate seismic resistance. These included pre-cast concrete panels, geodesic domes with Ferro cement, in situ reinforced concrete and hollow concrete blocks. It is worth noting that almost all the agencies advocated the use of concrete, a material that is markedly different in its nature and application than traditional building materials used in the region, namely stone and wood. While traditional constructions were affordable, climatically appropriate, and had a local skill base, concrete was an unsuitable building material against all these parameters.

Initially there were 10 villages in category B that were supposed to be reconstructed in situ (GoM 1993), but the number grew to about 22 villages as social and political pressures grew. Panchayats saw a unique opportunity to obtain new houses, even when little damage had taken place, and filed lawsuits demanding in situ reconstruction. It dawned on the government that reconstructing so many villages in situ would entail a mammoth clearing operation of all the rubble. Therefore the Maharashtra government ultimately decided to relocate these villages to new sites (Nikolic-Brezev et al. 1999). As a result, by 2001, the number of relocated villages increased from 52 to 74. In fact, none of the villages except two—Tembhe and Pardhewadi—got reconstructed in situ, thanks to initiatives by the Housing and Urban Development Corporation (HUDCO) and Manav Lok (an NGO).

In the 'C' category villages, strengthening and retrofitting of existing houses was undertaken by the government with the support of NGOs. In these villages, a publicity campaign was launched by the Government through the construction of 'Model Houses', which advocated the use of reinforced concrete bands at plinth, lintel, and roof level. In reality, rather than retrofit existing traditional houses, over 99 per cent of the work was in the form of new concrete and brick additions/extensions (Nikolic-Brzev et al. 1999) as people decided to use their limited resources to undertake new constructions rather than retrofit existing ones.

PREDOMINANT ASSUMPTIONS

The reconstruction policies at Marathwada were based on some predominant risk perceptions that were determined by the special conditions within which the disaster took place. The reconstruction programme in Marathwada primarily focused on reducing risks from a single hazard—earthquakes. However, disaster risk is not just about earthquakes or floods. It is a product of hazards, vulnerability, and exposure in a given place. Earthquake-safe design and construction features were introduced, but measures to mitigate the impact of rainfall and high winds—such as adequate draining and sloping roofs—were overlooked. A fear of short-term risks clearly outweighed long-term considerations and the emphasis was on rapidly delivering ready-made villages and housing for quick, visible results.

The ruling ideologies and notions of development at that time also shaped the policymakers' assessment of the risks and determined their subsequent risk reduction measures. Post-disaster reconstruction was seen as an opportunity for the 'development' of 'backward' rural communities by providing them with 'city-like' formal design and layout of villages and houses. The fundamental assumption was that local knowledge and skills were either non-existent or outdated and the only panacea for reducing risks was the provision of state-of-the-art design and technology. The engineers attributed risks to traditional constructions, which were built of stone and wood, and the local people who had witnessed their loved ones die under collapsed stone houses also subscribed to this view out of fear. As a result the essential focus of the programme was on the immediate provision of permanent shelters built using state-of-the-art earthquake-resistant technologies. This approach, however, was born out of a superficial assessment of the root cause of risks. A more thorough damage assessment would have shown that traditional constructions per se were not the source of the risk; it was rather the economic vulnerability of the region which had led to a deteriorating quality of traditional craftsmanship and thus, an increased physical vulnerability to natural hazards. In order to assess the impact of reconstruction on vulnerability and risk reduction, let us look at those vulnerability factors that created the conditions for the disaster in the first place.

PRE-EARTHQUAKE VULNERABILITIES AND RISKS

The region is essentially agrarian in nature. Prior to the earthquake, the region was already one of the most economically poor regions of

India, primarily because agriculture could no longer meet the basic needs of the people. This was further aggravated by years of neglect of the agricultural sector by the government. Increasing marginalization of the rural community was also linked to the land ownership pattern. Though the Zamindari system[4] was abolished after independence, the big landowners continued to exploit the majority of poor small tenant farmers, who were becoming increasingly weak and powerless socially, economically, and politically. The presence of middle men also posed great hurdles in getting the farmers the right price for their produce. Over and above all these factors were the effects of globalization, market capitalism, and economic liberalization, where many petty farmers were not able to withstand competition from outside.

One of the main consequences of the increased marginalization was that many people were forced to change their traditional occupations. These included local craftsmen who were no longer able to support themselves through the traditional barter system, where food and other materials were exchanged for work. As a result, their knowledge was slowly forgotten, lost, or degenerated. Take the case of *Sutars* (carpenters, who used to make the unique roof pattern called *Malwad*, as well as agricultural tools), *Wadars* (who were involved in extracting and breaking the stones from quarries and used to play a vital role in stone masonry work), and *Patharwat* (who used to decorate house entrances and do stone carving). Sutars continued to make agricultural tools but the practice of Malwad was mostly lost, as wood became scarcer and its market value increased (Jigyasu 2002). Stone masons also gradually lost their knowledge and skills due to a lack of demand, as a result of which stone masonry gradually deteriorated in terms of the quality of stones used and the shape and size needed for proper bonding. Yet, as the quality fell, the thickness of the stone walls continued to increase as this was seen to reflect the household's status.

Poverty increased the vulnerability of existing houses as people were no longer able to maintain them properly. Besides gradual deterioration, certain alterations in the fabric were made out of sheer ignorance, which only added to their physical vulnerability. For example, additional layers of mud were added to the roofs, increasing their thickness.

---

[4] Zamindars were big landowners who employed a lot of petty tenant farmers to work on their lands for meagre sum of money and exploited them.

Behind the seemingly nice facades of vernacular houses, the physical fabric had deteriorated or altered to a significant extent, increasing their vulnerability to earthquakes. When the earthquake struck the region on 30 September 1993 the rural communities were already socially and economically vulnerable. Equally vulnerable was their built fabric with heavy mud roofs, thick stone walls, and weak bonding, especially at the joints.

The subsequent section will elaborate on the long-term impact of reconstruction, in terms of the community's vulnerability and capacity to adapt, through an analysis of rehabilitated villages 18 years after the earthquake (1993–2011).

IMPACT OF RECONSTRUCTION (1993–2011)

Physical Vulnerability

In order to introduce earthquake-safe materials and technology, ten 'Building Centres' were set up in the affected area supported by HUDCO and assisted by the government. These centres were supposed to promote construction activity and generate employment through training programmes for construction artisans, unskilled labour, and unemployed youth. The centres supplied building materials to construction sites and educated people on the use of earthquake-resistant technology. This was a welcome initiative that would have ensured sustainability. Unfortunately, all these building centres were shut down within three to four years as they were completely dependent on external support.

As a result, people in relocated villages undertook extensions to their houses using a variety of materials and technology, which were markedly different than those that were introduced during reconstruction. The walling materials included tin sheets, thatch, and ferrocement, sometimes with bamboo posts, stones and bricks in cement mortar. Interestingly, very few extensions were done using the materials and technology that were originally promoted in reconstructed houses, mostly due to their lack of affordability and availability. The reconstructed houses were also built by contractors with very little involvement from the owners, who did not manage to acquire any knowledge of these earthquake resistant features (Figures 4.3 and 4.4).

FIGURES 4.3 AND 4.4   People have undertaken additions and alterations to their houses in relocated villages using variety of materials

Stone, the predominant building material of traditional houses in the region before the earthquake, was used only to a very limited extent, mostly for boundary walls. All local construction practices were rejected by 'official expert agencies'. Local people, who saw their loved ones die under the heap of stone rubble, also developed an acute fear of stone. Traditional material and techniques were considered 'unsafe', despite the fact that it was the poor quality of construction at the time, and not the material per se, that made these constructions vulnerable to earthquakes.[5] Houses suffered enormous damage, primarily due to the heavy mud roofs and thick stone walls constructed with weak bonding, especially at the joints. This caused a huge loss of life. On the basis of a quick damage assessment immediately after the earthquake, the traditional techniques of vernacular housing were deemed to be the major cause of loss of life. However, a detailed assessment would have shown that it was the loss of knowledge in traditional techniques, the incompatible additions, and a lack of maintenance that in fact caused the extensive damage to traditional houses.

The nature of the materials and the construction system used for the extensions also varied among various economic groups. While the lower economic groups tended to use tin, ferrocement, thatch, and stone, those from the higher strata used bricks and concrete blocks. In many instances, walls were constructed using hybrid materials such as stone and brick. However in most cases tin sheets were used for roofing because they were perceived to be safe in the event of any further earthquakes, due to their light weight. Unfortunately, these tend to get very hot during the day time, causing health problems for the inhabitants.

Ironically, most of these extensions, regardless of the economic group, are still vulnerable to earthquakes due to poor construction

[5] Traditional houses are built using stone and wood; materials that have been available locally. Typically, the walls are made of stone masonry, sometimes more than 600 mm thick and with mud mortar. The most commonly found roof consists of a thick layer of soil serving primarily as roofing. A heavy water-proof and insulating layer is placed on timber under-structure. There is a distinct typology for the housing based on the economic and social status of the household. Houses of people with well-to-do status are characterized by a courtyard surrounded by a colonnaded verandah in front of rooms. A front wall with dressed stone cladding and a massive doorway are other characteristic features of these houses.

practices; such as the hybrid constructions built using incompatible materials and poor masonry, the poor corner joints between walls, the absence of lintel bands, and inadequate foundations. The Reinforced Cement Concrete (RCC) columns, wherever used, were of improper cross-section and did not have adequate reinforcement. In many instances, the tin sheets used for roofing were not fixed with the purlins and just held in place with stones, thereby making them susceptible to high winds or leakage during heavy rains.

The policy of house allocation, which was done on the basis of land-holding, also reinforced the existing socioeconomic disparity among local communities. As a result, landless farmers and craftsmen, who did not own any land, frequently ended up with very small houses or even none at all, often constructing their own using a combination of materials such as thatch, tine, and stone. However, the quality of these self-built houses was very poor, making these highly vulnerable to hazards such as earthquakes and heavy rains.

As mentioned before, retrofitting techniques for existing houses were promoted by the government and NGOs in 'C' category villages which did not sustain much damage. Some pilot projects were initiated in these villages and it was hoped that these examples would be replicated by others. However, 18 years after the earthquake, many inhabitants in the village do not even remember the houses where pilot retrofitting projects were undertaken by either by the government or NGOs. Even the residents of those retrofitted houses only vaguely know the advantages of retrofitting, and can just remember the 'iron angles introduced to strengthen connections between the wall and roof' as one of the distinctive features of these houses, without really understanding how they contribute towards improving earthquake performance. In some of these houses these angles were removed to increase the height of the roof, and were not subsequently reintroduced (Figure 4.5). In other houses, extensions did not incorporate any earthquake-safe features as people did not quite understand the advantages of these measures or simply did not find masons who could undertake such retrofitting measures. While many local masons were trained during the initial retrofitting work undertaken by the government and NGOs, these valuable skills also increased their employability and they left the region to find more profitable work.

FIGURE 4.5   Angles from a retrofitted house meant to strengthen connection between walls and roof, have been removed to increase the height of the roof

One of the long-term impacts of the reconstruction policy has been that traditional building craftsmen have almost disappeared from the region and vernacular constructions in stone and wood have been replaced by highly vulnerable new constructions. The reconstruction process further accelerated the process of marginalization of traditional craftsmen. Construction work is now undertaken by other socioeconomic groups, who have acquired a limited knowledge of brick and RCC constructions. In their drive to maximize profits, local contractors running short apprenticeships are only interested in faster and cheaper constructions, with little emphasis placed on quality.

In some instances, where the traditional houses are still intact, people do not feel safe and prefer to move into tin sheds. Even after so many years of the earthquake, people are still reluctant to employ traditional materials, using wood salvaged from their old houses as firewood and stones for boundary walls. Influenced by the popular architectural vocabulary in the region, locals have also replaced traditional stone temples, which were considerably safe from earthquakes, with those made with brick and RCC. Most of these new constructions also do not follow any earthquake safety standards.

Capacity to Adapt and Recreate

Assessing the long-term impact of reconstruction provides a unique opportunity to understand how people have dealt with these relocated villages and the various layouts and designs that were provided to them after the earthquake. Most relocated villages were designed along the same lines as urban residential neighbourhoods—wide roads, large rectangular plots organized in either rows or clusters, and houses with both front and backyards and frontal access. They were also provided with public buildings such as community halls, schools, and health centres, and large public open spaces to be used as 'parks'. With such planning, the size of a relocated village was sometimes more than three times that of the old village. Yet people have adapted to these alien village layouts and building designs; altering them and recreating the traditional rural morphology and architectural vocabulary of the region.

Within the plots, people changed access points and reconfigured spaces into open or semi-covered courtyards, which are sometimes shared by their neighbours for collective activities. The pattern of these transformations varied according to how plot boundaries were demarcated and entrances defined at the time of reconstruction. Even in the village of Gubbal, the inhabitants adapted to Geodesic domes (earthquake-resistant technology), by creating intimate spaces between the dome and subsequent extensions where they could carry out their daily outdoor activities (Figure 4.6).

Elaborate stone-clad gateways occasionally adorned with paintings, a characteristic of traditional homes, have reappeared in many reconstructed houses, although these are built with new materials such as brick and RCC. In spite of their fear of living in traditional houses, people have used some of the materials that they salvaged from their old houses to reinforce and reconnect with their traditional identity, as well as to save costs. These include beautiful front doorways, dressed stone masonry, and in some places, wooden beams and columns. Other traditional elements such as Tulsi Vrindavan (a platform with a sacred basil plant) have also been reintroduced in the courtyards.

FIGURE 4.6   Reconfiguration of plots and houses in relocated villages according to the socio-economic needs of inhabitants and to reintroduce cultural identity in the built environment

The pattern of these transformations show a marked relationship with the socioeconomic background of the inhabitants. For example, potters have undertaken extensions in such a way that they can have a front yard, where they can carry out pottery-making and sale. Marathas—members of a predominant social group—have introduced courtyards and massive gateways that are reminiscent of the ones in their traditional Wadas.

Most of the relocated villages are also characterized by a growth in vegetation, with big and small trees being planted by house owners in the open areas within plots. These include various medicinal and fruit trees. In fact most of the relocated villages are much greener than traditional villages.

While residents have undertaken creative reconfiguration and densification of their residential plots, open areas designated as parks or clusters have largely remained under-utilized or used for activities associated with agriculture, such as drying and storage of agricultural produce, keeping the cattle or storing cow dung and firewood. It is ironical that while the reconstruction policy in Marathwada on the one hand has reinforced physical vulnerabilities and risks, it has on the other, also brought forward the inherent capacity of communities to adapt and tailor their built environment to suit their sociocultural and economic needs.

Sociocultural Vulnerability

Pre-disaster villages were characterized by a distinct socio-spatial structure for various social, caste, or religious groups. This, of course, meant that certain marginalized groups were forced to stay at the fringes of the settlement. Post-disaster reconstruction was a unique opportunity to initiate social change through mixing various groups. This was also attempted in many relocated villages where an effort was made to bring together people belonging to varied castes or religious groups such as Patels, Marathas, and Muslims. However, at present, one finds that in most relocated villages traditional socio-spatial structures have largely remained unchanged and those marginalized groups or minorities continue to stay at the fringes of the relocated settlements. In many instances main roads along the relocated villages have turned out to be undeclared boundaries between dominant and marginalized social groups. This socio-spatial regrouping took place right from the start as various social groups lobbied to stay together in spite of some attempts to bring about social change.

Furthermore, as the criteria for distributing houses was according to the size of landholdings, house holds were grouped together according to their land assets. This added to the economic segregation of the community, besides reinforcing pre-existing social hierarchy. Due to this continuing socioeconomic segregation, some socially marginalized groups, especially those who did not own any land, were left behind in the old villages to stay in dilapidated houses while most others moved to relocated villages.

Also, many relocated villages were planned with very large public open spaces, which were designated as 'parks'. However there is no tradition of such open green parks in the region, which are particularly unsuitable for the hot weather. In the absence of collective social functions defined for various sections of the community, these have been lying mostly abandoned. This has adversely affected the close-knit social fabric of the community thereby affecting their social vulnerability.

A very significant feature of relocated villages is their continuing spiritual relationship with the old village. Although religious structures have been built in most of the relocated villages, villagers still pay regular visits to old temples and dargahs located in the old village and continue to maintain them. As a result communities have still retained a connection with their old villages although they have largely adapted to their new environs.

Another interesting trend is seen in villages belonging to category 'C'. Many residents have undertaken self relocation to newer parts of the village, or created altogether new settlements near the old village. This is both due to a gradual increase in the population and a persistent fear that traditional houses are unsafe. The result is that the community continues to live in fear and lacks a feeling of stability and unity; exacerbating their social vulnerability.

Economic Vulnerability

Marathwada is predominantly rural and therefore agriculture is the primary occupation of the people, and agricultural lands have traditionally surrounded the villages. However, relocation meant that many villages got shifted further away from agricultural land, sometimes even by more than 5 km. This posed significant problems for the daily commute to work, both in terms of time and money. Whilst relocated villages were located next to the main roads to facilitate travel and connectivity, this distance has created a far-reaching impact on the livelihood pattern of people in these villages. An increasing number of people are leaving agriculture, and working in petty shops that line the roads leading to these villages. However, this has failed to improve people's living conditions as the meagre income cannot compensate for the loss of agricultural land, which is a crucial source of livelihood following a disaster.

FROM RECONSTRUCTION TO VULNERABILITY AND RISK REDUCTION

Assessing the long-term impacts of post-disaster reconstruction in Marathwada has shown how reconstruction policies, for all their good intentions, have reinforced some pre-disaster vulnerabilities and risks while creating new ones. At the same time, it has also brought forward the capacities of local communities to innovate, adapt, and shape their built environment in response to their sociocultural needs—in the process reintroducing traditional elements that have defined their identity. This flies in the face of the dominant reconstruction policy which sees disaster victims as weak, vulnerable, and passive recipients of tailor-made houses.

Clearly, the case reveals how a short-term focus on the risks from earthquakes can overshadow the considerations of risks that may accrue in the long-term. Moreover, it shows that post-disaster reconstruction does not effectively build on local skills and capacities that would have contributed towards a reduction in vulnerabilities. This could have been achieved if local craftsmen were actively engaged in the reconstruction process and their traditional skills updated, rather than stoking fears of traditional materials and promoting solutions alien to the local context. A superficial assessment of the risks and a one-sided risk-communication strategy created long-lasting misconceptions about the safety of traditional dwellings, and ultimately increased the vulnerability of the local community.

Decision-makers tend to consider risks only from the lens of one predominant hazard while overlooking the fact that risks result from multiple hazards and vulnerabilities which interact with each other and are a product of larger developmental processes. In the case of Marathwada, the reconstruction policy focused on promoting earthquake resistant houses. Yet, a long-term assessment reveals that reconstruction is not simply about building safe houses but a holistic planning of villages, that takes into account traditional customs, whilst also recognizing the social, cultural, and economic vulnerabilities that can make buildings vulnerable to hazards in the first place. Failing to recognize this can lead to a superficial assessment of the risks, as in the case of Marathwada, where officials identified traditional construction materials and technology as the source of vulnerability.

While there are now a multitude of policies and institutional systems for disaster risk management in India, these will have little impact as long as the larger development processes which create socioeconomic vulnerability, poor governance systems and ineffective planning processes continue unabated. This perspective is consistent with the vulnerability studies of Kenneth Hewitt (1983 and 1997), Anthony Oliver-Smith (1986), Ann Varley (1994), and others, who demonstrate the historical complexity of disasters and their links to development processes. In their book 'At Risk: Natural Hazards, People's Vulnerability and Disasters' Blaikie et al. (1997) provide one of the most comprehensive and relevant definitions of vulnerability. They state: 'By "vulnerability" we mean the characteristics of a person or group in terms of their capacity to anticipate, cope with, resist and recover from the impact of a natural hazard. It involves a combination of factors that determine the degree to which someone's life and livelihood is put at risk by discrete and identifiable event in nature or society'. This definition is particularly important in that

- it defines natural disasters as the outcome of both physical determinants (such as the type and amount of damage to buildings caused by earthquakes) and sociocultural issues that precede and shape the outcome of disaster events;
- it defines 'vulnerability' not as a social problem (the more popular usage of the term, where people are seen as passive victims due to poverty, age, gender, etc.) but as a process wherein people are actively involved through daily life in both creating and reducing risks; and
- it places peoples' livelihood as the key concept in understanding the impact of disasters and extends this to mean much more than only physical resources.

Post-disaster reconstruction should therefore be seen as a process closely embedded in the context of pre-disaster vulnerability. In order to effectively reduce the gap between the short-term needs of post disaster reconstruction with those of long-term disaster risk reduction, an integrated approach for risk analysis is required that takes into consideration multiple hazards and vulnerabilities, with a greater emphasis on understanding and addressing the conditions that create the latter. The approach would entail considering the physical vulnerabilities of the built environment along with the sociocultural, economic, and institutional vulnerabilities that gave rise to these. Moreover, people's capacity to adapt should be recognized and utilized for reducing vulnerability through post-disaster reconstruction. Policymakers should facilitate owner-driven reconstruction through active engagement of the community in the design and planning of their houses and immediate environment, ensuring that there is scope for future additions and expansions.

Such an integrated approach also calls for institutional mechanisms to link various sectors/line departments for disaster risk reduction. For example, the departments responsible for housing or building construction should be closely coordinated with those in charge of employment and livelihoods, health, environment, and social security. Moreover, risks need to be analysed spatially as well as temporally. Disasters are not just localized events, they have greater economic and ecological knock-on effects, which demands integrated regional planning. With growing rural-urban migration, a disaster that struck Mumbai for example, would also be felt by families across the region relying on money sent from the city. Regional planning would therefore entail dovetailing disaster risk reduction concerns in macro-level policies, strategies, and institutional systems. The temporal consideration would necessitate balancing short-term needs with the long-term considerations of disaster risk reduction and sustainable development. This would necessitate an incremental approach that fulfils short-term temporary shelter needs in the immediate aftermath of the disaster but would facilitate development of safe housing over time through gradual guided additions undertaken by the owners.

Another challenge seen time and again is that of the appropriateness of technology for disaster risk reduction, especially in reconstruction projects. Even regular government housing schemes tend to ignore traditional methods in their design and construction. We are still locked in an unending debate about the suitability of contemporary versus traditional technologies, whilst the larger challenge is integrating the two. Programmes can be driven by local professionals and craftsmen from affected communities, thus building on local skills and experience, while at the same time considering new needs and the opportunities offered by experts and institutions for developing creative solutions. It is crucial to employ the technology and reconstruction methods that are most appropriate to the local economic situation. Physical reconstruction should thus be linked with the rehabilitation of livelihoods after the disaster. Tools and mechanisms that would allow local professionals to proactively assess the vulnerability of traditional dwellings should also be put at the disposal of communities, to reduce their vulnerability to future disasters.

Marathwada reconstruction programme was followed by several large-scale post-disaster reconstruction programmes in India, especially after the Gujarat earthquake in 2001, the Indian Ocean Tsunami in 2004, and the Kashmir earthquake in 2005. Contrary to Marathwada, where most of the reconstruction was contractor-driven, owner-driven reconstruction was promoted on a larger scale in Gujarat and in subsequent programmes. As a result, there certainly has been a greater engagement of local community and NGOs in the design and construction of shelters, and also a greater emphasis on social and economic regeneration. Since 2005, policies and institutional systems for disaster risk reduction have also been set up at national and state levels and the primary approach has undergone a radical shift from post-disaster relief to pre-disaster preparedness mode. However, in spite of these commendable achievements, most post-earthquake reconstruction policies and programmes have had little impact on long-term risk reduction and sustainable development. Post-disaster reconstruction is still seen as a close-ended programme with orientation towards short-term results, largely disconnected from the larger developmental processes that create the vulnerability of communities in the first place. Therefore, in spite of huge investments and robust policies and institutional systems for reconstruction, vulnerabilities continue to be recreated in the long run.

BIBLIOGRAPHY

Blaikie, P., T. Cannon, I. Davis, and B. Wisner (1997). *At Risk: Natural Hazards, People's Vulnerability and Disasters*. New York: Routledge.

Government of Maharashtra (GoM) (1993). 'Proposal for Maharashtra Earthquake Rehabilitation Programme'. Mumbai: Government of Maharashtra.

Hewitt, K. (ed.) (1983). *Interpretations of Calamity: From the Viewpoint of Human Ecology*. Boston: Allen and Unwin.

Hewitt, K. (1997). *Regions of Risk: A Geographical Introduction to Disasters*. Essex: Addison Wesley Longman.

International Federation of Red Cross and Red Crescent Societies (IFRC). (2010). *World Disasters Report 2010–Urban Risk*, available at http://www.ifrc.org/wdr, last accessed on 17 November 2013.

Jigyasu, R. (2001). 'From Natural to Cultural Disaster: Consequences of the Post-Earthquake Rehabilitation Process on the Cultural Heritage in Marathwada Region, India', *Bulletin of the New Zealand Society for Earthquake Engineering*, 34(3): 237–42.

Jigyasu, R. (2002). 'Reducing Disaster Vulnerability through Local Knowledge and Capacity—The Case of Earthquake-prone Rural Communities in India and Nepal', PhD thesis, Norwegian University of Science and Technology, Trondheim.

National Disaster Management Authority and ODR Collaborative (2009). 'Owner-driven Reconstruction: Towards a Policy Framework', Summary report of National Conference held in Delhi, available at http://odrcollaborative.net/odrc_docs/ODRnationalSummary.pdf, last accessed on 17 November 2013.

Nikolic-Brezev, S., M. Green, F. Krimgold, and L. Seeber (1999). *Lessons Learned Over Time*, Vol. 1. Oakland: Earthquake Engineering Research Institute.

Oliver-Smith, A. (1986). *The Martyred City: Death and Rebirth in the Andes*. Albuquerque: University of New Mexico Press.

Salazar, A., and R. Jigyasu (2010). 'Lessons from Marathwada', in S.B. Patel and A. Revi (eds) *Recovering from Earthquakes: Response, Reconstruction and Impact Mitigation in India*, pp. 79–117. New Delhi: Routledge.

Unnikrishnan, P., and K. Sekher (2001). 'Disasters and Disability', Discussion Paper, available at www.aifo.it/english/resources/online/apdrj/frimeet102/disaster.doc, last accessed on 30 April 2012.

Varley, A. (ed.) (1994). *Disasters, Development and Environment*. West Sussex: John Wiley.

PUBLIC HEALTH

5

ASHA KILARU
SHANTI MAHENDRA
BANEEN KARACHIWALA
ZOE MATTHEWS

The Rise of Institutional Births in India

Are Maternal and Newborn Risks Adequately Addressed?

The Government of India's National Rural Health Mission (NRHM) has pursued a policy of promoting institutional deliveries in order to reduce the risk of maternal and newborn deaths. The policy has been viewed as successful because of the increase in institutional deliveries since the launch of the Mission. The Coverage Evaluation Survey 2009–10 showed all-India institutional delivery to be 73 per cent (Karnataka recorded 86 per cent), an increase from 40.8 per cent in 2005–6 (UNICEF 2010; IIPS and Macro International 2006). The question is whether increasingly hard-pressed health services are successfully re-orienting towards recognizing and reducing women's health risks in pregnancy, during birth, and in the postpartum period, as well as reducing unwanted foetal losses and newborn deaths.

Developing systems and staff that effectively address risk is a challenge faced by health systems world-over. It depends on policy, organizational, and clinical dimensions that understand and address health behaviours of the populations they seek to serve. Health behaviour, and its counterpart health education, is inherently complex. What risks do people perceive and what influences these perceptions and their response? What are the dynamics and determinants of risk prioritization at individual and family levels? What risks should institutions address and for which ones should they be held accountable? The risks range from financial risks of treatment expenditure, with potentially devastating social and economic impacts, to social risks arising from exclusion and discrimination, and to immediate health risks or sequelae from poor quality of care.

Trading the narrow view of risk offered by dominant biomedical and economic perspectives (such as the rational actor paradigm that assumes that behaviour adjusts optimally with information) for a multi-dimensional view of risk—including social, historical, cultural, and economic—is necessary if healthcare provision is to be transformed to improve population health with a vision of health-for-all. This becomes critical when we expect that health services must function within a framework of equity and social justice. We consider this wider perspective of risk while examining the results of two prospective studies undertaken by Belaku Trust on healthcare sought during pregnancy, intrapartum stage, and postpartum stage. These studies had similar aims and objectives and were conducted in the same area nearly ten years apart, during a period in which there was a rise in institutional births by 47 per cent. We describe women's perceptions of risks and of the quality of care, and explore indications of change over the last decade. We also identify the reasons why a family's and women's healthcare-seeking may vary from their plans (that is, switching from planned birth locations). Whilst the government has sought to increase the coverage of health services, our research has identified several aspects in the quality of these health services being provided, which need attention if health risks and personal risks that women and their families face during pregnancy, birth, and postpartum stage are to be effectively managed by the health system.

RISKS TO WOMEN DURING CHILDBIRTH

With 63,000 women dying from obstetric-related causes, India had a larger number of maternal deaths[1] than any other country in 2008.

---

[1] Deaths classified as 'maternal' are those that happen to women who are 'pregnant or within 42 days of termination of pregnancy, irrespective of the

This puts the lifetime risk[2] of maternal death in India as high as 1 in 140 women as compared to 1 in 4,300 in developed countries, with it being as low as 1 in 11,400 in Sweden (WHO 2010a). The Indian infant mortality rate (IMR), at 37 per 1,000 live births in the same year, was much higher than the global average of 26 per 1,000 live births (WHO 2010b).

Labour, childbirth, and the first 24 hours after giving birth are the vulnerable periods when most maternal deaths occur. In Asia, the major causes that account for over 2–3 of all maternal deaths (most of which are preventable) are (Khan et al. 2006):

- haemorrhage
- sepsis/infection
- high blood-pressure related problems (eclampsia)
- abortion
- indirect causes of death (examples include malaria, Human Immunodeficiency Virus (HIV), cardiovascular disease)

Other complications such as prolonged or obstructed labour can also prove fatal, if they are not addressed appropriately (Ronsmans and Graham 2006; UN 2010). Women who survive the ordeal often find themselves facing serious life-long ailments which threaten their livelihoods, and also their ability to care for their children. Health risks for women are sometimes linked to their socioeconomic circumstances. For example, women from poor households are more likely to have moderate to severe iron-deficiency anaemia, especially in Asian contexts. Anaemia, in turn, is a risk factor for complications such as heavy bleeding and cardiovascular problems. Anaemic women, who account for over 50 per cent of pregnant women in developing countries, are also at a higher risk of experiencing stillbirths, low birth-weight or prematurely born infants (WHO 2005).

---

duration and site of the pregnancy, from any cause related to or aggravated by the pregnancy or its management but not from accidental or incidental causes' (WHO 2004). International Statistical Classification of Diseases and Related Health Problems, Tenth Revision, 1992 (ICD–10), available at www.who.int/classifications/icd/en/index.html, last accessed on 7 April 2012.

[2] Defined as the probability that a 15-year-old female will die eventually from a maternal cause.

RISKS TO THE NEWBORN

The life of a newborn is inextricably linked to its mother's health. Women's health (including nutritional status) prior to conception, as well as during experience of labour and childbirth exert strong effects on the outcome of pregnancy. Infection, obstructed and prolonged labour, and high blood pressure in a woman can prove fatal for newborns or cause serious long-term damage such as cerebral palsy, learning difficulties, and other disabilities (WHO 2005).

Birth and the immediate hours, days, and weeks after it are when health services can make a dramatic impact on newborn survival and health. A recent UNICEF report states that 40 per cent of the deaths in children under the age of five occurred within the first 28 days of life, an increase of 10 per cent since 1990 levels (UNICEF 2011). The same report states that 30 per cent of all neonatal deaths in the world occur in India. Most of these neonatal deaths occur in the first seven days of life. Complications due to prematurity and low birth-weight, neonatal infections, birth asphyxia, and birth trauma are the main causes of death (The Million Death Study Collaborators 2010). Risk assessment and management at this time saves lives and prevents serious morbidity.

GOVERNMENT'S RISK MANAGEMENT APPROACH: INCENTIVES TO INCREASE INSTITUTIONAL CARE

The roots of maternal and newborn health risks are deeply embedded in the social and economic context of poverty and gender-based discrimination. This context promotes early marriage, low educational status and inadequate employment skills, early child-bearing, and vulnerability to poor health in women. Evidence shows that economic reforms of the 1990s and post-reform policies have done little to decrease health inequities (Sen 2004; Siggel 2010). Instead of addressing these inequities, the government employs a plethora of schemes and programmes, limited in scope, with eligibility criteria that serve as barriers, to enable below-poverty-line individuals to access services needed for health and welfare. From conditional cash transfer programmes to capitation contracts for services, to insurance, there are now several schemes specific to care during pregnancy, birth, and postpartum stage.

However, the extent to which they form a strong continuum of care for poor women is questionable.

How is the country attempting to ensure the survival of women and newborns? As part of the Millennium Development Goals (MDGs) (Ministry of Health and Family Welfare) the Government of India is pursuing a policy of expanding institutional care at childbirth in order to reduce maternal and newborn mortality. This is being pursued through incentives such as the conditional cash transfer programme Janani Suraksha Yojana (JSY). However, other factors such as the corresponding withdrawal of home birth services, and providers' instructions to women during antenatal visits to give birth in institutions are also likely to have influenced this shift. In a country where, until recently, nearly half of all women gave birth at home, this is a major change that must be examined critically.

This chapter presents data that shows the missed opportunities for risk assessment and risk mitigation in the quality of professional care during pregnancy, intrapartum (labour and birth), and postpartum (or newborn) care. It adds to the evidence that the quality of care is poor on multiple counts and questions whether the policy of institutional deliveries will achieve the full range of benefits envisaged. Whilst maternal mortality ratio (MMR) has been declining, there is little evidence to show that institutional deliveries have been hastening this decline, echoing the study conducted by Lim et al. (2010). India will still fail to meet the MDGs by 2015 and may, in fact, be ignoring the negative consequences of poor quality institutional care, such as iatrogenic illness and suboptimal care-seeking, by those discouraged by the cost of care and disrespectful treatment during institutional deliveries.

STUDY DESIGN AND SETTING

The findings presented in this chapter are based on two studies on women's health and healthcare use in pregnancy, labour, delivery, and postpartum stages, conducted in the same region, that is the southern state of Karnataka. The first study was carried out between 1996–8 in 11 villages of a *taluka* (a sub-district administrative unit) in an area that is part of Ramanagaram District and involved a sample of 388 childbearing women. The selected villages covered a population of approximately 25,000. The second study was carried out between 2007–9, in 84 villages of the same taluka and covered 1,50,000 people, based on a sample of 608 pregnant women. Both of the studies were prospective and used face-to-face surveys to arrive at quantitative conclusions. Qualitative data, however, was also collected in both studies. The World Health Organization (WHO) funded both studies. (Details of study design are available in Table A5.1).

The performance of Karnataka is average in terms of women's health and educational status when compared to national data, though it compares unfavourably to its southern neighbours. In terms of health service utilization, a professional healthcare worker attends over 70 per cent of the births in the state and 67 per cent births are facility-based (IIPS and Macro International 2006). Whilst there have been significant improvements for women in the state, urban and rural disparities continue to exist. The taluka in which the study was conducted is predominately rural and one of the largest in the state (Government of Karnataka 2010). A comparison with neighbouring talukas shows that the level of literacy here is lower compared to the surrounding areas.

Pregnancy Care

Early and regular contacts with a skilled care provider during pregnancy is key to reducing maternal risk. These visits provide the opportunity to identify potential or clinical risks and complications, and convey the necessary information to the woman and her family along with appropriate care. Early antenatal contact is part of the recommended package of care in India. About 56 per cent of the women in the first study done over ten years ago, had their first antenatal contact in the first trimester. More than 60 per cent of women reported having at least one contact, and a large majority had at least three check-ups, the minimum number recommended by the Government of India. A closer look at the quality of care during these contacts, however, reveals that they mostly included mandatory routine home visits by the Auxiliary Nurse Midwife (ANM, the first level of nursing in India) who is trained to provide basic maternal and child care. Basic preventive care such as tetanus toxoid injections and iron and folic acid (IFA) tablets were provided at these contacts, but visits were often perfunctory and rarely including crucial advice on how to plan for emergency care. They lacked in-depth clinical examinations, which could detect potential risks.

Ten years later, the timing and number of antenatal visits has increased. Although the content of antenatal care has improved, many gaps remain. Analysing across all ANC visits, nearly 66 per cent of women had their blood pressure checked, and about 64 per cent received IFA tablets, just eight per cent had a urine test, and less than 25 per cent of the women received any advice on how to recognize problems. Only 5 per cent received advice on breastfeeding, and just 2 per cent of women received advice on when to come in for a postpartum visit, information which is especially important to women in their third trimester.

Intrapartum Care

Birth location

A significant change from the first study to the second is the shift from giving birth at home to giving birth at a health facility. Between 2007–9 over 82 per cent of women gave birth in hospitals, ranging from rural primary health centres (PHCs) to large tertiary care hospitals, compared to just 35 per cent ten years ago.

The percentages of women who *planned* to give birth at home instead of health centres between the two studies changed dramatically. In 1996–8, nearly 87 per cent of the women planned a home birth, and a decade later this dropped to 10 per cent (Figures 5.1 and 5.2). Although planned public sector births account for the majority of planned institutional deliveries, a significant proportion expected to deliver in a private institution. This is likely due to the perception that better care is taken at private health centres and there is a lack of faith in government institutions. Although some of the women's narratives indicated positive attitudes towards government facilities, many did not opt for them. A recurring concern with government hospitals was the lack of accountability. As in the words of one woman, 'if we develop problems [during birth] they will say they cannot treat us. What are we to do at that time?'.

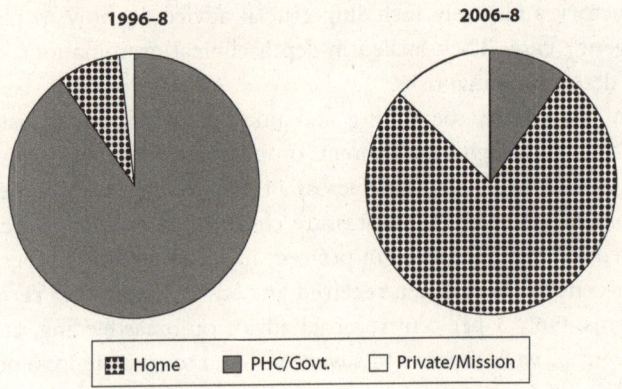

FIGURE 5.1   Planned Place of Delivery

Source: Prepared for this study by Asha Kilaru and Zoe Williams whilst working at Belaku Trust.

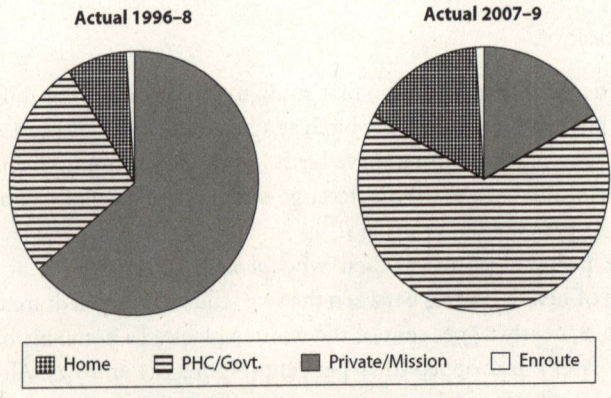

FIGURE 5.2   Actual Place of Delivery

Source: Prepared for this study by Asha Kilaru and Zoe Williams whilst working at Belaku Trust.

Switching

An important aspect of care in the latter part of pregnancy is to advise women and their families to decide on a place of birth, consider arrangements for transport, plan what to do in the event of an emergency, and how to meet the necessary costs. This is referred to as birth preparedness and complication readiness, and it is a programming tool used to reduce risk to the woman and newborn (Maternal and Neonatal Health Programme 2011). However, emergency planning is culturally incongruent among some people in India, as planning for a problem is considered prophetic. Both studies found that a vast majority of women and their families *did* identify a delivery location or provider when asked in the third trimester of pregnancy, but *did not* have a plan of what to do if, either unexpected symptoms or problems developed, or a provider or health centre was unavailable or closed. Comparing planned place of delivery to actual (Figures 5.1 and 5.2), both studies show high levels of 'switching'—changing from anticipated birth location. The first study documented 30 per cent of women switching from planned place of birth. The level is similar a decade later—approximately 33 per cent of the women switched intended location of birth, excluding those who were referred. Including referrals, the percentage of women who changed their intended location of birth increased to 43 per cent in the 2007–9.

Analysing the reasons for switching, in the 2007–9, nearly a quarter of the women said it was because the health centre was closed, and another 24 per cent switched because a family member decided to go elsewhere (usually the woman's mother), anticipating that the provider would not be at the health centre, or because they felt it was better to go to a higher level facility in case a problem arose. These reasons were commonly reported among women who went into labour at night. An additional 9 per cent switched because of a lack of time to reach the planned facility, and another 9 per cent reported a problem finding transport to where they planned to go. Furthermore, of the women who switched, an astounding 90 per cent did so *after the onset of labour*. Switching the planned place of birth when a woman is in labour may add to the psychological stress of coping with labour.

Switching because of medical referrals may affect risk in a number of ways. While referrals should manage risk because the intent is to move a woman as safely as possible to an institution with the capacity to treat her, it often increases risk. This is due to long travel times, delays caused by transportation and its cost (often privately arranged), a lack of stabilizing treatment at the referring centre, the absence of a health provider or a paramedic to accompany the mother, and little or no communication to the referred hospital. The first referral often leads to onward referrals and women move from one facility to another as labour advances. Below is an excerpt from an interview about referral 'switching' and the lack of accountability with which families must contend.

> We wanted to have the delivery done at the local Taluk Hospital. We went there as soon as the delivery pain started. The doctor at the Taluk hospital checked me and said the baby's head has not turned, and that I am very short so the delivery will be difficult, go to [xx] hospital in Bangalore and they will have to do an operation. But there was no time and Bangalore was far so we rushed to a private, local clinic [hiring private transport]. The doctor there did the operation and took the baby out. I stayed for 5 days in the hospital and went home. There were no facilities at the taluk hospital… [for a Caesarean section]. We should not have had to go to a private clinic…we need not have spent so much money. The government hospital should have all the equipment and necessary facilities.

In the absence of inter-institutional arrangements, families handle referrals on their own, usually without an ambulance or paramedic:

> When I started labour, we went by auto to the taluk hospital. The nurse admitted me and gave me two injections and did the delivery but the baby was not breathing and crying. The nurse said it had drunk lot of water and she gave mouth-to-mouth resuscitation and the baby started breathing. The nurse told us to take baby to a local clinic [private]. They said they wouldn't guarantee anything. Then they sent us to a hospital [tertiary care government hospital] in Bangalore. They had no facilities and sent us to Van Vilas hospital—there also there were no facilities so they sent us to Kempe Gowda hospital. They also said they did not have the facilities and sent us to _____ hospital [tertiary care government hospital]. There the baby was kept in ICU for one night and one day and observed the child. For three days he had not taken any breast milk. They did a scan and found the baby's blood had clotted. They kept the child for four days and treated him with lot of injections and medicines, and then the baby recovered. We had to spend a total of Rs 7,000.

Conversations with several doctors showed that none of them were aware that a high percentage of women change their planned place of delivery after labour begins. Providers appeared unaware of the behavioural dynamics of care-seeking. It is revealing that 'switching' remains unrecognized by the health system, and this ignorance is suggestive of a myopic view of risk, uninformed of key aspects of families' behaviour.

Whilst some amount of switching is inevitable, and desirable when it involves moving to facilities with more advanced care when needed, the extent to which it is observed in our studies indicate that there are barriers to accessing chosen providers. Switching reveals the need to improve provider and institution competencies—both clinical and social. In the latter, understanding how families seek care for pregnancy and birth and addressing this during communication with the patients is a key role which the providers must play to reduce risk. Furthermore, medically, unnecessary switching may disrupt continuity of provider. Visiting the same skilled provider through pregnancy and delivery may help catch complications early and should lead to more prompt treatment. However, continuity of care must be maintained with monitored referrals and accountability at all points of the referral chain.

As stated, switching the planned birth attendant persisted over the ten years of the two studies. Even though most women indicated a birth location or attendant late in pregnancy, this did not deter families from late-stage change. From the health system perspective, switching for reasons other than a referral by a provider may be seen as irrational or undesirable. However, families obviously view switching as a rational response to their own perceptions of medical risk and provider's availability and capabilities. This mismatch is the result of the failure of providers to characterize and communicate risks, as well as the general indifference to community health needs (such as what will happen to women whose nearest health centre is unstaffed at night).

We also note a possible increase in medical risk for home births. A decade ago, outreach obstetric services were stronger than they are now. The proportion of home births conducted by a professional birth attendant has declined between the two studies from 38 per cent in 1997–9 to 17 per cent in 2007–9. Untrained lay attendants conducted 49 per cent more home deliveries than a decade past, and during 2007–9 this rose to over 60 per cent (births attended by traditional midwives or Dais have not been included in these percentages). In interviews, government medical officers and midwives said that they are not supposed to attend a home birth when there is time to reach an institution. This unstated policy is also supported by the shortage of staff at institutions and an increased case-load. As much as the government may strive for all women to deliver at institutions, some home births will continue, both out of choice and insufficient time to reach the health centre.

In the more recent study we asked women if they became pregnant again where they would consider giving birth. About 43 per cent (263 respondents) said they would not have another child and were planning to undergo sterilization. Of the remaining, 14 per cent of women said they would prefer a home birth. Failing to attend home births is a clear breach of Indian healthcare system's accountability, and a failing of the objective to provide free or subsidized, and accessible care to the poor. Home births must be viewed as part of a continuum of delivery locations that families will consider. Maternal and newborn services must recognize the different circumstances, conditions, and traditional norms that influence how and where women decide to give birth. These omissions result in an inability of the health system to assess the risks of women labouring and delivering at home and thus provide the necessary services to minimize those risks and increase support.

Financial Costs

Women and their families have their own dynamic process of prioritizing risks, often determined by the financial costs of institution-based care. Several studies have found that out-of-pocket expenses can be crippling, particularly when accessing emergency obstetric care (Borghi et al. 2008). This means that families must negotiate between seeking care at less-advanced facilities (and face an increased risk of morbidity or death), or borrow substantial amounts of money, usually almost immediately and at high interest rates.

Public expenditure on health as a percentage of GDP is notoriously low in India compared to global figures. This percentage slightly increased after 2005, under the NRHM, although India remains in the lowest category for per capita expenditure in the world, much less than USD 15 (White Ribbon Alliance 2009). Low public expenditure on healthcare has resulted in tremendous growth of the private sector, with most health costs paid out-of-pocket by individuals and families.

JSY intends to increase facility-based childbirth by reducing financial barriers to institutional birth (public and private). However, our data show that women and families opted for institutional care expecting the cash entitlement to substantially cover the costs, but were faced with expenditures well beyond this amount. The Rs 700 provided under JSY in the state of Karnataka, where the study took place, was insufficient

FIGURE 5.3   Worldmapper Map of Public Health Spending
Source: http://www.worldmapper.org/display.php?selected=213, last accessed on 9 February 2014.
Note: Territory size shows the proportion of worldwide spending on public health services that is spent there. This spending is measured in purchasing power parity.

FIGURE 5.4   Worldmapper Map of Maternal Mortality
Source: http://www.worldmapper.org/display.php?selected=258, last accessed on 9 February 2014.
Note: Territory size shows the proportion of deaths of women worldwide while pregnant or within 6 weeks of pregnancy and partly due to it, that occur there.

to meet the cost of care even at the PHC, let alone the costs at a higher-level facility and multiple referrals, both of which occur in women experiencing complications. Other studies have found little evidence of a commensurate reduction in maternal or newborn deaths that can be attributed to JSY (Lim et al. 2010; Das et al. 2011). Maternal death reviews conducted in two districts of the state of Rajasthan show that 90 per cent of the deaths occurred in transit to a higher-level facility.

Experts view institutional deliveries as a possible reason for this high incidence of in-transit deaths, as women are taken to grossly inadequate facilities and discharged very soon after birth without the staff following an appropriate observation period (FOGSI 2012, as cited in Dhar 2012). Data from our second study showed that 62 per cent of women left the facility in less than six hours after delivery, even among women who had infants with low birth weight.

Policies and practices around the disbursal of cash incentives can also add to social risk through tensions that arise among family members, and between families and health staff, as they vie for these resources. In one case, the woman who delivered attempted suicide due to the harassment by her father-in-law and husband to surrender the money which she had yet to collect. Finally, her father-in-law approached the ANM and claimed the money on the woman's 'behalf'.

The highest expenditure for a single visit that women in our study incurred during pregnancy ranged from Rs 100–200 for medicines. These costs add up over the course of a few to several antenatal visits. During labour and childbirth, the costs incurred spiralled. For a normal delivery, median costs range from Rs 1,000–1,300 at a PHC or the government taluk hospital and increase to a median of Rs 4,000 at a tertiary-level public healthcare facility in Bangalore or a local private clinic. For a Caesarean section (most of which occurred at institutions outside the taluk) the median costs at a tertiary care public hospital in Bangalore were close to Rs 8,000 and Rs 20,000 at a private hospital. These are financially crippling expenditures to a population of mostly small and landless farmers.

Such costs can deter women from seeking appropriate care, as the following interview extract shows:

> I wanted to have my birth at the [PHC] but even a month after my due date I did not get any labor pain so the PHC doctor said go to [a tertiary care government hospital] in Bangalore. I went to Bangalore and was admitted there for 5 days. They gave me injections to induce pain and I still did not have labour pain. The doctor said he may have to operate. After we paid Rs 2000 he conducted my delivery. I stayed for 3 days in the hospital after the delivery. Bangalore hospital is not for poor people, it's only

for rich people. We spent a total of Rs. 7000. We had problems getting the money. Now when I think of the hospital I get scared about the next time. Next time I shall have the delivery at home even if I have to die.

The narratives reveal that death and morbidity are part of a constellation of risks in which death prevention may not always be priority. This is also an area where we can expect clear gender differences. Women internalize how poorly they are valued in a patriarchal society. They feel shame and stigma about putting the family in debt for their care. A member of the field staff narrated her visit to one of the women in the study whose newborn had died.

> She said that her mother did not have any money on the day she went into labour. She had to use the money reserved to pay the workers. The workers came home and demanded money so her mother had to pawn her anklet to pay to some of them and for others, she had requested time so that she could go for work and earn wages to return their money. She shared with us that there was no cash even to get milk. Her mother had gone for work and she was feeling very bad that her mother had to spend so much on delivery to save her.

Unnecessary Interventions

Oxytocin is a drug that stimulates uterine contractions and is the drug recommended to prevent as well as treat postpartum bleeding. Its more controversial use is to induce labour or hasten prolonged labour. NRHM does not recommend the use of oxytocin to augment labour, and WHO recommends that it is given only when labour fails to progress in a way that the dose can be adjusted while assessing the woman's response. It is recommended for such use only in a facility with an attendant trained in emergency obstetric care, and with a functional operating theatre, since oxytocin can increase the risk of uterine rupture. However, a substantial proportion of the births in both studies used oxytocin during labour, even among women who delivered at home. In the first study, over 90 per cent of the 243 women who delivered at home reported injections to augment labour. In the 2007–9 study, over 50 per cent of the women who had home births were given oxytocin. This decrease is likely due to the decline in skilled birth attendants at home births, discussed earlier. Considering all deliveries in 2007–9, 39 per cent of all women said they received at least one injection for labour augmentation, and nearly 60 per cent of these women said they were given intramuscularly—a method not recommended because the dose cannot be adjusted. Labour augmentation is required in only a fraction of all labours, and thus the data indicate that oxytocin is probably being administered without medical need. Analysing reported complications shows that more than 75 per cent of all women who had complications during labour were given repeated injections of oxytocin to hasten labour (Matthews et al. 2005), although it is not clear whether these were medically indicated.

WHO recommends using oxytocin for the active management of the third stage of labour (AMTSL) and to prevent postpartum haemorrhage. This requires routine administration after the delivery of the baby and before the placenta comes out. Only 16 per cent of the women in the recent study reported having received injections after the baby was born and either before or after the placenta was delivered. Only two respondents said that they were told this was to prevent bleeding after delivery. Since postpartum haemorrhage is the leading cause of maternal death, it is expected that most, if not all, women receive oxytocin during the third stage. It is not clear from the data why this service gap exists—it appears that medical staff is not adequately trained, and that AMTSL procedures are not yet part of routine clinical practice. The absence of AMTSL is another missed opportunity to reduce the risks of bleeding and haemorrhage.

Inappropriate use of oxytocin and the failure to establish a clear evidence base for each intervention have been reported in several places, including India (Buekens 2001). Widespread reports of misuse of oxytocin begs for immediate policy and clinical interventions to stem this practice and train providers in rational drug use. Unnecessary interventions increase medical risk because they increase the likelihood of complications, and increase expenses for families as the cost of care may rise in the long run. In India the costs are usually borne by families with already stretched budgets. An unjust mix of poor care, unnecessary interventions, and high costs coexist. These issues need to be explored in further research, comparing private and government care. Private care operates with little regulation and price control, and very little research has been done on quality of care in this sector. Legislation and enforcement are required to make both the private and government sectors risk-accountable in healthcare.

Social Support: Birth Companions

Social support during birth is crucial for the physical and emotional needs of a woman (Hodnett et al. 2011). The evidence on risk reduction is clear—women with continuous one-to-one support are more likely to have a spontaneous vaginal birth, shorter labour, and less likely to have complications. Yet, in most facility-based births in India women are not allowed a companion in the delivery room (Mathai 2011). The 2009 study showed that only 31 per cent of women who had institutional births had a companion with them in the birthing room, and this was usually the woman's mother. Analyzing the data by facility type, about half of the women in a PHC were allowed a birth companion. However, this was probably because these facilities are small and often have only one nurse during a shift so the companion also assists the nurse or ancillary nurse–midwife. More than 50 per cent of the women in our study who delivered at a PHC, and over 95 per cent of those who delivered at a tertiary public hospital said they were unhappy about not being allowed to have a birth companion. Women's perceptions of their experiences of institutional care are important and are likely to influence further care-seeking in the immediate postpartum period, as well as for the next birth. The Yashodha Mamta programme, which places a non-medical support worker in the hospital to provide labour support and counsel women on newborn care, is an example of a programme that seeks to improve care and comfort to women during birth.

Health Service Providers

Most providers had concordant views of what they think women want during pregnancy and birth. Two government midwives had the following opinions:

> Only pregnant women from rich families think of clean beds and clean surroundings, and if needed they will go to private doctors and spend thousands.
>
> Some people go to private clinics for check-ups but after that they come to government centers. The pregnant women feel that the private doctors, though they give check-ups, do not explain or say anything the way they should be told, so they are not satisfied. In the government hospital they have concern for the baby and the mother and take

responsibility. The families have my telephone number and can contact me at any point.

These opinions were not unusual and reveal commonly held perceptions by providers regarding people's choices of care. Some providers view certain aspects of care as dispensable, such as clean and appealing surroundings—these are the frills of care sought only by those who can afford it. This is the type of care described as offered by the private sector. But many poor women resort to private care, which they know is costly, because they perceive it to be more reliable especially during complications. Much of the government staff say that they have opted to 'serve' people, and suggest that the lack of appealing surroundings in government institutions is made up for by the providers' commitment. Data from women's interviews show varied opinions of government care. Some women share the view expressed by government providers that it is a 'value-for-money' service, in comparison to private care. Other women see government care as highly unreliable—high absenteeism among staff, lack of supplies and medicines, low capacity to handle emergencies, and no accountability; expressed as a refusal to treat if the case is complicated. Most of the women who held this view said that at least treatment is not denied in the private sector if they pay.

There is little mention in the provider interviews about the need for effective communication, empathy, and respectful care. This is of little surprise, given the deeply entrenched attitude of inequality and indifference based on caste and class.

> I started labour at midnight and we went to [the government hospital]. There were two nurses there. My mother went to the nurse and said "look after my daughter", but they behaved irresponsibly. I was unable to bear the pain and the nurse slapped my cheeks. They said I wouldn't deliver now; it would take time. Since we were not familiar with any other hospital and the nurse had made me very tired we stayed there and had the delivery done. Afterwards, they took money and were fighting with each other and told them not to tell the doctor. They took a lot of money from us...we felt frightened. They conduct deliveries but you can't ask them anything.

Overall, a clear policy of respectful care with human resource training and education is desperately needed. This also requires policymakers to address the extremely hierarchical nature of professional relationships in institutions in which fault-finding supervision and concentrated authority thrives. Multi-dimensional risk assessment and management requires good communication, team-based problem solving, and opportunities for feedback and learning within a framework of accountability.

Postpartum Care

Check-ups

Postpartum care has a history of neglect, as typically the child is given more importance in the mother–baby dyad and the focus shifts to the baby after birth. The importance of adequate quality of postpartum care is well known, but continues to be neglected in both public and private sector care for low-income families. Although data from both studies show a large increase over the decade in the percentage of women who had at least one postpartum interaction with a provider, the 'check-up' is still focused on routine immunization and not on carrying out an individual assessment of the woman's and newborn's health (Table A5.2). The content and care of those visits seem to have changed little, with most of the attention (68 per cent of the visits in the second study) on routine immunization for the newborn and sterilization or contraception information for women with two living children. A little over one per cent received advice on postpartum care and 4.3 per cent said they were advised on both.

Since the majority of maternal deaths happen either during birth or in the first 24 hours after birth, it is a critical period to assess the health status and risk of complications in the mother and the newborn (most newborn deaths also occur in the first seven days of life) (Baqui et al. 2006). Advice on postpartum care for the woman and for the newborn is essential to the practice of good quality care, and it was rarely given. Such communication failures can significantly increase risk and these are critical missed opportunities on the part of the care provider.

There is strong evidence for adopting simple measures that result in decreased maternal and newborn morbidity and mortality, such as immediately attending to postpartum bleeding, not bathing newborns and ensuring they are kept warm and within close skin contact, especially for low birth weight infants. In 2007–9, 62 per cent of women in the study with a newborn of normal weight and 56 per cent of those with a low birth-weight baby received advice on newborn care. After a normal delivery the mother and the baby are to be kept under a skilled attendant's observation for 24 to 48 hours. In the first study, the interviews revealed that the women and their babies left the facility within the first few hours, either because they were discharged or because they requested to leave. In the second study, short stay was also observed, with 54 per cent of women who had a normal, institutional delivery reporting they left within six hours after delivery. The percentage of women with low birth-weight babies who left within six hours was even higher at 67 per cent. These findings reveal the need for home-based newborn care, introduced by NRHM but yet to be fully implemented.

CULTURAL MEDIATION AND PERCEPTIONS OF RISK

Perceptions of risk are mediated by culture. The healthcare system and providers construct risk in bio-medical terms, which is not always in coherence with cultural beliefs. The need for care and attention in the postpartum period, or *bananthana*, has strong cultural recognition in this part of southern Karnataka. Older females of the household typically conduct the bananthana. It is a period of confinement for the woman wherein rest, diet, water intake, and bathing, among other aspects, are observed and regulated, and marked by ritual.

In the words of one household member: 'She has a "tender body" (hasi mayi). If we do not do a strict bananthana, she will be weak in later life'.

The newly delivered woman is also considered vulnerable to 'drishti', or evil eye, and also spirit possession. She needs protection from these as well from 'cold', in the form of air passing into body orifices and in the form of a cooling effect created by certain foods. It is also believed that fluids accumulated in the body need to drain and water intake is restricted because the body needs to 'dry out'. Some amount of postpartum bleeding, for example, is considered necessary and beneficial for this reason. In the 42 days after delivery among the women in the 1996–8 study, only half who reported heavy bleeding sought care for their condition. There are similar examples in the case of diarrhoea in young children, which has multiple causes in the cultural context of this study. The first study documented that one 'cause' of diarrhoea in young children occurs from contact with a menstruating woman, and the remedy lies in various rituals either at a temple or with a traditional healer, such as wearing a talisman, prayers, or chants. In contrast, fever is a symptom that prompts care-seeking from professionally trained persons, rather than traditional healers, very likely because its cultural representation demands it.

'*Beethi shanke*' (literally, terror and suspicion) is a locally defined illness, and women in the postpartum period are considered especially vulnerable. It is culturally well-recognized, although local names for it differ by region. Interviews conducted in 1996–8 indicate the stigma associated with this condition for the woman affected. Treatment usually consists of rituals at home or at a temple, in the case of Hindus. These conditions affect the child as well. Usually the baby would be kept away from the mother and breastfeeding may reduce or cease. Physical contact with the mother and breastfeeding are factors that promote well-being. Psychological and physical health risks (such as infection), increase in such infants. In the 1996–8 study, three of the 388 women were reported to have beethi shanke by a family member, and none sought care from the healthcare system. The healthcare system does not recognize beethi shanke in all its cultural modalities. The term is most likely unknown to healthcare providers and since families rarely take women to professional care for this condition, providers are not aware of what to look for. These cases are the tip of the iceberg of mental health problems, and even medically recognized depression goes untreated and not screened by providers during the pregnancy–postpartum continuum. In the earlier study, within a year of completion (which ended at three months postpartum), eight of the 388 women had committed suicide.

Thus, contextual meaning and representation is important to understanding the people's understanding of risk, and the tendency to seek care. Cultural norms during postpartum do not include routine care-seeking from healthcare providers, so women are taken to a healthcare provider only if the condition appears very serious, and by then it is often an emergency as maternal and newborn complications can become life-threatening very quickly. Postpartum haemorrhage can result in death within hours.

This is unrecognized by the healthcare system and therefore also unrecognized by frontline staff (professional midwives, nurses, and doctors).

★ ★ ★

Our results corroborate the large increase in the percentage of institutional births reported across India. More importantly, however, they also reveal the absence of a systematic process of assessing and managing risk by the health system; public as well as private. As a result, the persons delivering care and implementing the policy of institutional births lack adequate guidance and training, and therefore the capacity to identify and handle the multiple risks, medical and other, faced by poor women during pregnancy and all its outcomes.

Having opted to give birth at a facility, women and families face barriers that are firmly entrenched in the healthcare system—barriers of limited human resources, equipment, and medicines; inadequately trained staff, unfriendly and even hostile environments; check-ups that are often perfunctory and of poor clinical content; poor inter-institutional arrangements for referral and care during complications; a lack of outreach and community awareness; insufficient infection control measures, and high costs. Careful assessments are therefore needed to determine whether births at facilities are necessarily less risky than those at home.

Particularly in India, how women and their families perceive and respond to health risks is mediated by their cultural and socioeconomic contexts. Healthcare providers often operate in a bio-medical paradigm that does not always recognize these alternative perceptions. An awareness of the nature of these heterogeneous perceptions and how they influence people's interactions with and response to professionalized institutional care needs to be fostered. In the case of maternal health, at no other time in India have so many women sought institution-based care. In order for this historic change to achieve a greater public health impact, these issues need to be brought into the health and social policy discourse and fed into human resource training, education, and management, thus creating services that are attuned to cultural, social, and economic risk perceptions.

Clinical risk management is a continuous process which requires regular health consultations that assess the status of health through a combination of skilled examinations, and good communication, culminating in advice which will also take into account social or financial constraints. Management information systems in both government and private health centres and hospitals lack this level of monitoring. For example, for a given month, data may be recorded on how many women came in for an antenatal check-up, how many blood tests were done or tetanus toxoid injections given overall, but not the completeness of each individual check-up, or how many women in the catchment area are pregnant, which provides the population denominator. The advent of the NRHM has resulted in an increase in data recording, but it is still focussed on the numbers (and often without denominators, so percentages cannot be calculated) and targets rather than the quality of care.

Simply meeting the target of increased facility-based births does not guarantee that care has improved, nor do checklists sensitize providers who are not trained to understand the social and economic context and risk orientation of the individuals they treat. We need to improve every aspect of the 'risk management chain', from identifying the risks and understanding how the patients characterize and respond to them, to correctly assessing these risks (which needs trained personnel, and strong institutional processes, along with the availability of good equipment and medicines), to effectively managing these risks within a framework of accountability. This chain is founded on good channels of communication—between patients, their families and providers, between providers themselves, and between those on the ground and policymakers. A holistic risk shift would also require inter-departmental, inter-sectoral work—as the risks people face need to be addressed by multiple ministries—food and civil supplies, welfare, labour, agriculture, pension, and the like. While NRHM has improved the supply and management of some aspects of health services, quality care that is evidence-based and respectful is still largely lacking. These are the benchmarks that the healthcare system must privilege in its own standards of care.

APPENDIX A5

TABLE A5.1 Study of Design, Setting, and Sample of Both Studies

	Study 1: 1996-8	Study 2: 2007-9
Research Design	Observational study	Observational study
	Quantitative and qualitative methods used	Quantitative and qualitative methods used
	5 qnrs (1 background, 2 antenatal, 1 immediately post-delivery, 1 about three months postpartum)	1 qnr at third trimester, 1 about one month postpartum
Geographical Coverage	11 villages, total population approximately 25,000	80 villages, total population approximately 150,000
Village Selection	Study villages randomly selected from the villages in the taluk for an earlier study.	39 villages across all PHCs randomly selected, remaining purposively selected to meet enrolment target.
Exclusion Criteria	Women planning to deliver outside the study area	Women planning to study outside the study area
Sample	Population-based sample of all pregnant women from 1996-8 (535 women). 514 women completed the antenatal qnrs, and 388 completed the first postnatal qnr.	Population-based sample of all pregnant women. Enrolment April 2007 to January 2009, data collection ended June 2009 (642 women). Analyses carried out on a subsample of 608 women, excluding 34 women who could not be followed up for the duration of the study.

Note: qnr refers to questionnaire.

TABLE A5.2   Selected Indicators of Quality of Care in Delivery

	Study 1: 1996–8 (number of respondents – 388)	Study 2: 2007–9 (number of respondents – 608)
Birth Weight Recorded	<25%	76%
Length of Stay	Usually few hours	62% < 6hrs (same for women with low birth weight (LBW) infants)
Postpartum/Newborn Advice	Rarely given just after delivery. Of the women who had a postpartum visit, 2% reported some advice received.	56% of women with LBW infants received advice 62% of women with normal birth weight infants received advice

BIBLIOGRAPHY

Borghi, J., S. Tagmatarchi, and V. Filippi (2008). 'Overview of the Costs of Obstetric Care and the Economic and Social Consequences for Households', in F. Richard, S. Witter, and V. Brouwere (eds), *Studies in Health Services Organisation and Policy*, 24, available at http://www.itg.be/itg/Uploads/Volksgezondheid/shsop24/SHSO&P%20n%C2%B024%20-%20ENG_version5_Finale.pdf, last accessed on 23 October 2013.

Baqui, A.H., G.L. Darmstadt, E.K. Williams, V. Kumar, T.U. Kiran, D. Panwar, V.K. Srivastava, R. Ahuja, R.E. Black, and M. Santosham (2006). 'Rates, Timings, and Causes of Neonatal Deaths in Rural India: Implications for Neonatal Health Programmes', *The WHO Bulletin*, 84: 706–13.

Buekens, P. (2001). 'Over-Medicalisation of Maternal Care in Developing Countries', *Studies in Health Services Organisation and Policy*, 17, available at www.itg.be/itg/GeneralSite/InfServices/Downloads/shsop17.pdf#page=199, last accessed on 23 October 2013.

Dhar, A. (2012). 'Most Pregnancy-related Deaths Occur in Transit', *The Hindu*, 20 April, available at http://www.thehindu.com/todays-paper/tp-national/article3334000.ece, last accessed on 23 October 2013.

Das A., D. Rao, and A. Hagopian (2011). 'India's Janani Suraksha Yojana: Further Review Needed'. *The Lancet*, 377(9762): 295–6.

Government of Karnataka. (2010). 'Nanjundappa Report', available at http://planning.kar.nic.in/?q=node/56, last accessed on 23 October 2013.

Hodnett, E.D., S. Gates, G.J. Hofmeyr, C. Sakala, and J. Weston (2011). 'Continuous Support for Women During Childbirth', *Cochrane Database of Systematic Reviews*, 2: CD 003788.

International Institute for Population Sciences (IIPS) and Macro International. (2006). *National Family Health Survey (NFHS-3), India: Karnataka*. Mumbai: IIPS, accessed at www.nfhsindia.org/pdf/Karnataka.pdf, last accessed on 23 October 2013.

Khan, K.S., D. Wojdyla, L. Say, A. Metin Gülmezoglu, and P.F.A. van Look (2006). 'WHO Analysis of Causes of Maternal Death: A Systematic Review', *The Lancet*, 367: 1066–74.

Lim, S., L. Dandona, J.A. Hoisington, S.L. James, M.C. Hogan, and E. Gakidou (2010). 'India's Janani Suraksha Yojana, A Conditional Cash Transfer Programme to Increase Births in Health Facilities: An Impact Evaluation', *The Lancet*, 375: 2009–23.

Maternal and Neonatal Health Programme (2011) National Child Health Resource Centre, National Institute of Health and Family Welfare, available at http://www.nihfw.org/NCHRC/GuidelinesAndManuals.html, last accessed on 25 October 2013.

Mathai, M. (2011). 'To Ensure Maternal Mortality is Reduced, Quality of Care Needs to be Monitored and Improved Alongside Increasing Skilled Delivery Coverage Rates', *British Journal of Obstetrics and Gynaecology*, 118(Suppl. 2): 12–14.

Matthews, Z., J. Ramakrishna, S. Mahendra, A. Kilaru, and A. Ganapathy (2005). 'Birth Rights and Rituals in Rural South India: Care Seeking in the Intrapartum Period', *Journal of Biosocial Science*, 37(4): 385–411.

Ministry of Health and Family Welfare (2005). 'Janani Suraksha Yojana: Guidelines for Implementation' [online], Government of India, available at http://www.ilo.org/dyn/travail/docs/683/Janani%20Suraksha%20Yojana%20%20Guidelines%20for%20implementation%20-%20Ministry%20of%20Health%20and%20Family%20Welfare.pdf, last accessed on 25 October 2013.

Ronsmans, C., and W.J. Graham (2006). 'Maternal Mortality: Who, When, Where, and Why', *The Lancet*, 368: 1189–200.

Sen, Himanshu (2004). 'Poverty and Inequality in India', *Economic and Political Weekly*, 39(38): 4247–63.

Siggel, E. (2010). 'Poverty Alleviation and Economic Reforms in India', *Progress in Development Studies*, 10(3): 247–59.

The Million Death Study Collaborators (2010). 'Causes of Neonatal and Child Mortality in India: A Nationally Representative Mortality Survey', *The Lancet*, 376(9755): 1853–60.

United Nations (UN) (2010). *Millennium Development Goals Report 2010*, available at http://www.un.org/en/mdg/summit2010/pdf/MDG%20Report%20

2010%20En%20r15%20-low%20res%2020100615%20-.pdf, last accessed on 25 October 2013.

UNICEF (2010). 'Coverage Evaluation Survey, 2009, All India Report', New Delhi: UNICEF, available at http://www.unfpa.org/sowmy/resources/docs/library/R309_UNICEF_2010_INDIA_2009CoverageSurvey.pdf, last accessed on 25 October 2013.

―――― (2011). 'Levels and Trends in Child Mortality', estimates developed by the UN Inter-agency Group for Child Mortality Estimation, available at http://www.unicef.org/media/files/Child_Mortality_Report_2011_Final.pdf, last accessed on 25 October 2013.

White Ribbon Alliance (2009). *Atlas of Birth*, available at http://www.atlasofbirth.com/documents/The-Atlas-of-Birth-book.pdf, last accessed on 25 October 2013.

WHO (2004). *International statistical classification of diseases and related health problems*. Vol. 1. World Health Organization.

―――― (2005). *World Health Report 2005: Make Every Mother and Child Count*. Geneva, Switzerland: World Health Organization.

―――― (2010a). 'Trends in Maternal Mortality 1990–2008', available at http://whqlibdoc.who.int/publications/2010/9789241500265_eng.pdf, last accessed on 25 October 2013.

―――― (2010b). 'Global Health Indicators–Part 2', available at www.who.int/entity/whosis/whostat/EN_WHS10_Part2.pdf, last accessed on 25 October 2013.

6

AJAY BAILEY

Culture in and of HIV/AIDS Risk Management in India

C ulture through its various functions provides the meaning system which guides and motivates our behaviour. Understanding culture helps us in situating and contextualizing people's perceptions, knowledge, and behaviour. Though the study of culture and its relation to health and illness has been in the realm of medical anthropology, this relationship has not necessarily permeated into cognate disciplines such as epidemiology and public health. The literature on Human Immunodeficiency Virus/Acquired Immune Deficiency Syndrome (HIV/AIDS) still perceives culture as a dimension that only needs to be examined in non-western societies or marginalized sub-groups, such as homosexuals or sex workers. A number of studies have expressed dissatisfaction with HIV research that fails to include the concept of culture or pay attention to local meanings and cultural variations (Aggleton et al. 1994; Parker 2001; Schoepf 2001). Public health specialists have attempted to develop psychometric tools to examine behaviour change but are limited by their underlying theoretical framework which does not acknowledge culture. On the other hand, anthropologists have provided detailed insights on culture and its interpretations but have typically not been able to translate these into quantifiable concepts. The communication between these two groups has been limited, thus leading to islands of knowledge in terms of the documentation of behavioural practices. However, the sub-discipline of medical anthropology is one space where a dialogue between medical practitioners and anthropologists is proving to be more successful.

In defining medical anthropology, Foster and Anderson (1978) make the distinction between anthropology *of* medicine and anthropology *in* medicine. Anthropology of medicine is the social and cultural study of the medical practice itself. Anthropology in medicine consists of research into the cultural and social factors that influence efforts to improve health levels or change health-related behaviour. In the case of the anthropology of medicine scholars examine how medical practice as an institution has its own rules, norms, knowledge base, and accepted behavioural traditions. These are then reflected in the manner in which medicine and health care is provided to 'lay' people. Anthropology in medicine is the study of the social and cultural milieu, and how this plays a role in the health-seeking behaviour of individuals. Based on Foster and Anderson's distinction, we suggest the existence of culture *of* AIDS and culture *in* AIDS as an explanatory framework. Culture of AIDS reflects the impact that HIV/AIDS has had at different levels in organizing efforts to understand the pandemic, namely, efforts in the fields of research, health care, and health promotion. Culture in AIDS examines how culture permeates the shared domains of human life to contextualize risk and risk behaviour. In this chapter we use this explanatory framework, first, to understand the efforts of Non-governmental Organizations (NGOs) and communities in dealing with the pandemic. Second, the manner in which cultural schemas, norms, and perceptions aid in the cultural construction of risk is discussed. This framework is thus an effort to fill the gap in the literature connecting culture and HIV/AIDS.

Culture of AIDS can be seen as an investigation into the 'organizational culture' of institutions and actors working on halting the pandemic and providing care to those infected and affected by it. AIDS has been around for nearly 25 years now and has had a tremendous impact on science and society. The methods of managing the pandemic and the accompanying discourse has transformed several 'minority' populations (that is, homosexuals, sex workers, drug users, etc.) into 'risk groups', thus emphasizing and projecting a politics of stigma and marginality. On the other hand, Altman (1994) suggests that AIDS has a positive side because it has opened up a space for talking more publicly about what was previously taboo: diverse sexualities, gender identities, and inequalities. Under this part of the framework we will examine the changing nature of risk groups and how changes in national policies affect interventions at the grassroots level.

Culture in AIDS investigates the various social and cultural mechanisms which shape people's construction of risk and the behaviour they engage in. In this chapter we use Geertz's (1973) definition of culture where he says that the analysis of culture is 'not an experimental science in search of law but an interpretative one in search of meaning' (pp. 4–5). Risk assessment and risk behaviour should be examined in terms of the cultural rationality of the group under study. Culture and behaviour are intricately connected to the cognitive mechanisms that motivate people to take action. Cognitive anthropologists such as D'Andrade (1992) explain that shared cognitive schemas guide people's behaviour. Cultural norms could be one such shared cognitive schema that affects risk-related decisions and behaviour. According to Mary Douglas, culture is not a static 'thing' but something which everyone is constantly creating, affirming, and expressing. She writes about 'the admonitions, excuses, and moral judgements by which the people mutually coerce one another into conformity' (Douglas 1986: xxiii). Examining the social construction of risk, Douglas and Wildvasky (1983) looked at it as a way of interpreting how and why individuals form judgements about danger, pollution, and threat. This theory seeks to show that such judgements are formed within a particular social context (Tansey and O'Riordian 1999; Rayner 1992). In the present study, we look at how the socio-cultural context affects the risk perception of HIV, especially in terms of evaluating the social consequences of being infected with HIV. Towards the end, both parts of the explanatory framework are discussed to see what lessons can be learnt from this case study to arrive at a comprehensive HIV and AIDS risk management policy in India.

CASE STUDY AMONG MIGRANT MEN IN GOA

The study presented here is part of a larger project 'Risk Assessment of HIV/AIDS by Migrant and Mobile Men in Goa, India' (Bailey 2008), which was conducted between September 2004 and February 2005. This chapter presents insights using data drawn from 25 in-depth interviews, 16 focus group discussions, and a survey involving 1,259 men.

The selection criteria in both the qualitative and quantitative studies were: married men[1] aged between 20 and 45 years, who were migrants from the neighbouring state of Karnataka and had been living in Goa over the last whole year. Mobile men (truckers and fishermen) were those who had travelled between Karnataka and Goa for work. Migrant men were selected for inclusion in the survey using stratified systematic sampling, which involves compiling a list of eligible households in each area and then visiting every third house. Truckers and fishermen were selected by snowball sampling.[2] As two different sampling techniques were used, the results are presented accordingly. Six male research assistants conducted the survey, in both Kannada and Hindi, and lived close to the migrant settlements to gain a better understanding of the daily life of the migrants. They were given intensive training and field tested for their ability to interact with men on issues of sexuality. In addition to the study described earlier, insights from a study conducted in 2009 are also discussed here, which included observations, in-depth interviews, and focus group discussions on migrants' access to healthcare.

In Goa, HIV prevalence has crossed the five per cent level among high-risk groups (that is, commercial sex workers, or CSWs) and reached one per cent among pregnant women (PRB and PFI 2003). According to the Goa State AIDS Control Society (GSACS), the predominant route of HIV transmission in Goa is through sexual contact, followed by parent to child transmission (GSACS, 2003: 10). Most of the prevention programmes of the GSACS focus on migrants from other states in Goa. More recently, the targeted intervention focus has shifted to CSWs and their clients.

HIV/AIDS IN INDIA: THE OFFICIAL RESPONSE

If one were to compare Goa with the overall context of HIV/AIDS in India, revised estimates show that in 2010, some 2.5–3 million Indians

[1] Married men were selected as they are seen as a bridge population who transfer the HIV virus from the high-risk group (sex workers) to low-risk groups (women attending antenatal clinics).
[2] Snowball sampling is a non-probability sampling technique where existing study subjects suggest future participants so that the sample grows like a snowball.

were living with the virus and HIV prevalence among adults was around 0.3 per cent (UNGASS 2010). The recent trend has shown a decline in the HIV epidemic—the estimated adult HIV prevalence in the country has declined from 0.45 per cent in 2002 to 0.36 per cent in 2006 (NACO 2008). Still 90 per cent of people newly infected with HIV in India are believed to have acquired it during unprotected sex (UNAIDS 2010). HIV and AIDS still differentially affect men and women with women bearing the consequences of her male partner's risk behaviour. According to the Asia Intimate Partner Transmission Study, women are predominantly infected by their husband or intimate partner. For example, recent data on HIV infection patterns in India reveal that 90 per cent of women in India were infected within long-term relationships (UNAIDS 2009).

India's response to the HIV/AIDS crisis is largely driven by the National AIDS Control Organization (NACO). It has so far introduced three phases of programmes to control the spread of HIV, and to provide care for people living with HIV and AIDS. The first phase began in 1991 with interventions geared towards promoting blood safety, prevention among high-risk populations, raising awareness in the general population, and improving surveillance. The second phase began in 1999 when NACO began to decentralize and form State AIDS Control Organisations (SACO). In its third phase, NACO aims to halt and reverse the epidemic over the next five years. Its goals are to expand treatment, care, and support for people living with HIV, continue to target prevention interventions among high-risk groups, and to focus on building infrastructure and human resource capacity.

The official response has been encouraging in the setting up of integrated testing and counselling centres and the rollout of Anti-retroviral Therapy (ART) centres which have resulted in the stabilization of HIV infections at the national level. However, at the micro-level there have been many questionable state interventions which have resulted in serious human right violations. In 2004, while this study was in progress, the Goan government—armed with an order from the High Court in Mumbai and reinforced by the police and civil servants—demolished the cubicles of sex workers and houses of some migrants which bordered the red light area in Baina. The government's claim was that the cubicles and houses were illegally built. The demolition resulted in the marginalization of sex workers and migrants. But it also proved that they could adapt to new circumstances quite swiftly. Following the demolition, sex workers dispersed to smaller towns, highways and to more secluded urban places. The government saw its action as a way to cleanse the space and reduce HIV transmission. This is in line with Douglas (1992), who argues that for every risk that a person has to face or has faced; the community identifies the persons on whom blame can be heaped. In the case of sex workers in Baina, for example, the blame of higher HIV/AIDS rates was put on the women and not on the men who visited them. This counterproductive government intervention underscores the need to educate government officials about adopting a long-term perspective rather than merely pursuing actions which are of short term and driven by economics. Shifting the blame to more vulnerable risk groups actually works against the larger national efforts to empower the same groups to take more informed decisions to protect themselves and their partners.

CULTURE OF AIDS: CHANGING NATURE OF RISK GROUPS

The manner in which risk groups are defined is often a product of the simultaneous interplay between the evidence collected by epidemiologists and the stated priorities of health administrators. These categories then get segregated and become the prime focus for intervention. How their vulnerability is defined is still unclear. What makes them a risk group other than the prevalence rate is very much related to the moral discourse that surrounds HIV prevention policies. By defining certain sub-cultures or occupations as 'high-risk' groups, one excludes other at-risk groups from surveys and thus from interventions and policies. The consequence of such targeted interventions is that certain minority groups are blamed for the spread of the virus. *Othering* the risk of HIV/AIDS to certain individuals because of their minority status or their occupation skews society's perception of this risk. For example, being a truck driver is not a risk factor for acquiring HIV and conversely being a housewife does not put her at any less risk. It is the context that surrounds risk behaviour that needs to be brought under the spotlight.

In India, we can no longer just target these high-risk groups as the virus has spread to almost all sections of society through the bridge populations (UNAIDS 2010: 15–18). Market and business-driven approaches, such as the Avahan initiative, may have professionalized prevention services, but their target-oriented approaches (towards sex workers) fail to reach a broader population. We need to give due attention to the changing nature of risk groups which has shifted from occupation-related groups such as sex workers and truckers, to those in everyday settings such as housewives, office going men, and adolescents. The NACO has partly recognized this in its risk communication posters through the use of models who represent everyday people. Posters depict women with the symbolic markers of marriage, such as vermilion on the forehead and mangalsutra,[3] and men are portrayed as middle class and affluent. The following sections explain the emergence of new risk groups and the manner in which the NGOs in Goa have dealt with covert risk groups.

Risk From Outside to Inside the Neighbourhood

During the interviews and focus groups migrant men referred to 'going out' as a euphemism for going to sex workers. This term was used as CSWs are principally found outside the migrant settlement, and in less crowded places (see Bailey et al. 2011). Migrant men *othered* the risk of HIV/AIDS to sex workers, believing it was a risk that only they harboured. This image was exacerbated by NGOs as their messages stressed that men should not 'go out' as this could put them at risk of Sexually Transmitted Diseases (STDs), particularly HIV/AIDS.

In late 2004, however, I was approached by the NGO Population Services International to examine risk groups comprising non-commercial sexual partners. They could not identify and target this new risk group of women. Such targeting was also risky for the NGO as these relations were carried out secretly. If the NGO failed to manage this issue with tact and sensitivity they risked being expelled from the settlement. In the interviews for this project certain questions were included that would unearth this new risk group. In the interviews, men referred to the women as 'lovers'. The term lover is derived from

[3] It is a chain of black beads and two small gold cups. The constitution of the beads varies with regions. This chain is tied by the groom around the bride's neck on the day of the wedding, and from then on till the death of the husband remains as a symbol for a married woman.

the Bollywood movies where the romantic ideal of love is depicted. The discursive meaning that men attached to this term demonstrated that they preferred to have a lover rather than a sex worker, as they perceived a low risk of HIV infection from the former as compared to the latter. It is quite telling from the quote below that they did not perceive having multiple 'lovers' as engaging in risky behaviour:

> R: I have some lovers and I don't use condoms with them. They are here in this area and in Birla. I feel safe so I don't use condoms. There in Baina (former red light area) it's a different story. There in Baina many people would have come and gone. Here we know that there is no one else. And it's only between me and my lovers.

To know more about these women and why men thought they were of less risk to them we put forth vignettes in the focus group discussions. Both through the interviews and focus group discussions we identified the women to be either neighbours, co-workers or other women. Thus in the survey we included a question about whether men had extramarital relations with a lover in the last six months preceding the survey. Out of 742, 45 migrant men (6 per cent) and 60 out of 507 mobile men (15 per cent) answered in the affirmative.[4] Neighbours constituted the most prominent category among both groups of men. This further emphasizes the point that risky sexual behaviour is not necessarily 'out there' (that is, in the red light areas) but very much in and around the neighbourhood. Risk management and communication efforts should be more focused on the risk of unprotected sex, rather than 'risky' partners per se.

Dealing with Covert Risk Groups

In India same-sex behaviour among many men is based on identities which focus on the individual's role in the sexual act (Asthana and Ootsvogels 2001; Chakrapani 2004). Darak et al. (2003) report that one can identify many terms such as 'panthi' (insertive partner), 'kothi' (receptive partner), 'nirvana kothi' (castrated receptive partner), 'hijras' (trangendered people), and now the urban, western-influenced, self-identified gays. According to NACO (2006), Manipur (15.6 per cent)

---

[4] The number of men reporting having paid for sex was 25 in both groups.

followed by Karnataka (11.6 per cent) have the highest percentages of HIV-positive men who have sex with men (MSM). Only in the third stage of the National AIDS Control Programme (NACP-III) did the NACO acknowledge that MSM required urgent attention. Khan (2001) observes that many men in India may not consider anal sex with other men as 'sex' per se, but just 'masti'.[5] Thus NGOs working with this group use different messages to highlight the risk of HIV transmission but do not necessarily deal with the sexual acts and the bisexual identity. The language used in their messages positions the MSM community as in opposition to the heteronormative society, that is, to the societal norm of opposite-sex relationships.

For example, a message, painted in one of the bus stops in a settlement which is predominantly composed of migrants from Karnataka, deals with the issue of multi-partner sexual relations. Translated, it reads: 'From whom do we have the risk (danger)? Man, Woman, Impotent (men who have sex with men), having unprotected sex with all three can put you at risk (of HIV)'. It was the only one in the settlement which dealt with the sensitive issue of bisexuality and MSM. The wording used in the public message highlights the nature in which the NGO approached the issue of bi-sexual men. The message further adds that the risk of HIV can be from any of the partners irrespective of their sexual orientation. Inadvertently with the use of the term 'Napunsak'[6] the message further stigmatizes and discriminates MSM communities. Though NACO acknowledges that different sexual routes put people at risk, in its broader campaign the different sexual acts are not explicitly highlighted.

CULTURE OF AIDS: NATIONAL POLICIES, AID, AND GRASSROOTS IMPLICATIONS

Policy changes that result in different prevention strategies and targeted interventions do not just impact the groups at risk but also the people

---

[5] The word 'Masti' originates from Hindi and has the colloquial meaning of fun or mischief. Etymologically, masti refers to a state of sexual tension. This state is perceived to reduce the individual's ability to understand the danger of unprotected sex.

[6] Of being neither male or female. This term is also used as an abuse. In this context it is used to refer to MSM.

delivering these interventions at the grassroots level. In this section, I examine first, how constant changes in targeted interventions lead to difficulties at the grassroots level, and second, how international and national aid fails to trickle down to disadvantaged groups. With the arrival of international aid in India, a whole new non-governmental infrastructure was created to deal with the pandemic. NGOs were considered to be in a better position to further prevention efforts, as the governmental machinery had alienated people through its inefficiency, especially in reaching out to marginalized and vulnerable groups. It should be acknowledged that the NGOs in India have been responsible, to a large extent, for reducing the spread of HIV and AIDS. But the very nature of their non-governmental existence makes them more vulnerable to changes in funding policies, which in some cases threaten the survival of smaller organizations. Risk management and communication policies should take into account the sustainability of such organizations, as they are crucial to delivering key services and linking disadvantaged groups to governmental health services. The experience of Thabo, a former out-reach worker in Goa is a case in point of such drastic changes:

> When I first started to work in the Muslim-dominated Charminar (name changed) area in 2003 I met Thabo (name changed) who was then working as out-reach worker with the NGO. She was living in the migrant settlement and knew many people. She was bold enough to enter people's house to talk to them about HIV and AIDS. She could easily converse about different risks to men and women. Her most challenging task was to demonstrate the use of a condom using a wooden penis. In 2004 and 2005 when I came for a longer period of fieldwork she was still very active in the community and aided us in finding people to interview. All this changed in 2006. In one of my visits to the settlements I asked the program manger as to the whereabouts of Thabo as she was not seen in the community. The program manger rued that under the new directions from the Goa AIDS Control Society they could not pay an honorarium for Thabo. Hence she had left the NGO to go find work in a factory. It was now becoming difficult for the NGO to find community volunteers as they feared being let down. The new directives were part of the NACP III guidelines which advocated that community should volunteer for such activities or find peer members such as fellow sex workers. The program manager recently wanted to rehire Thabo for a targeted intervention on sex workers. Thabo tells me, 'How can I join that post (peer educator)? They will think I am also that kind of woman!'

Drastic changes in policies and decisions on the financing of care and prevention have led in some instances, to mistrust in the community and among grassroots NGOs. The sudden redefinition of target groups[7] and interventions, such as the use of peer-educators, alienates the community, as only some groups qualify and many that still need information and care are forgotten.

The structure and flow of international aid has also prompted a shift in national policies and the institutional landscape. The United Nations Population Fund (UNFPA 2009), which examined the flow of resources for STD and HIV/AIDS and family planning activities from 1995 onwards, observed that the expenditures on family planning activities fell from nearly USD 60 million in 1995 to less than USD 10 million in 2008, whereas, the expenditures on STDs, HIV, and AIDS rose from USD 10 million to more than USD 70 million in 2008. This sheer increase in resources contributed to the creation of a large parallel machinery seen through the establishment of NGOs and other community organizations. Though earlier aid relied on governmental institutions, the flow of aid for HIV and AIDS relied on setting up NGOs, both for monitoring and service delivery. Shifting international aid priorities from population control to HIV were also echoed at the national level. According to Sridhar and Gomez (2011), the contribution of the Government of India (GoI) into the NACP phases has drastically increased. In NACP-II the GoI contributed only 10 per cent whereas in NACP-III the contribution was an impressive 41 per cent. Even though there is international aid and the governments are also contributing a significant share in financing health care, India still has the highest proportion of household out-of-pocket health expenditures in the world (Balarajan et al. 2011). During the 2004–5 study in Goa, data showed that when migrant men were asked if they had taken an HIV test or if they knew where to take a test they always pointed towards the NGO. What we gradually realized was that migrant men in Goa had problems

[7] In 2004 the national policy on targeted interventions included fishermen, migrants, and truckers as part of the targeted interventions. By 2008, the fishermen and migrant settlements were excluded from targeted interventions, as the focus narrowed down to sex workers and short-term migrants. The effect was more drastic on the fishermen as no other NGO replaced the government-funded programme at the docks.

accessing public health facilities even for basic care. Thus in 2009, an exploratory study was carried out to understand the accessibility and affordability of care for migrants living in Goa. Migrant labourers were aware of the public health facilities, but wary of losing a whole day's wage,[8] and thus preferred to go to a [quack] doctor in the neighbour-hood, who, in some cases, was also a migrant from Karnataka. In this scenario, where getting basic healthcare is difficult, one can fathom that rollout of the ARTs will be even more difficult for such marginalized groups.

CULTURE IN AIDS: THE CONSTRUCTION OF HIV AND AIDS RISK

The cultural construction of risk is based on the beliefs, norms, and values that people associate with HIV and AIDS. To capture the theoretical understanding of risk, I apply the concepts of perceived susceptibility and perceived severity, as derived from the Health Belief Model (HBM). The HBM was developed by psychologists in the 1950s to explain the widespread failure of people to participate in programmes to prevent or to detect disease (Maiman and Becker 1974). In Kannada, the language of the migrants, there is no term for risk; the interviews revealed that the word risk is synonymous with the term 'possibility' (saadhyathe) and the term 'danger' (apaaya). The conceptualization of risk thus has to be viewed between these two extremes. In the survey (742 migrant men and 507 mobile men), men were asked in three different ways whether they perceived themselves to be at risk of HIV/AIDS. In the first instance, men were asked if there was a possibility that they might have contracted HIV. Of migrant men, 13.3 per cent, and of mobile men, 11.4 per cent, confirmed that there was a possibility. As the risk of HIV is othered to sex workers, in the second question, we asked whether the men might have had a sexual relationship with a person who was at risk of HIV. Only 3.8 per cent of the migrants and 5.1 per cent of the mobile men felt that they might have had. In the third question, we inquired directly if the men felt that they were at risk of HIV.

[8] Due to the location, the waiting time, the costs of travel, food, and medicines for both the patient and the person accompanying, a whole day is often spent seeking treatment. This results in the loss of a day's wages.

Only 3.6 per cent of the migrant men and 3.7 per cent of the mobile men answered in the affirmative, that they were at risk (danger).

When we compare the three questions and the responses from migrant men we see that when risk is phrased as 'possibility' it is perceived to be higher. This perception reflects the external locus of control as they believe that 'anything can happen to them'. Such fatalistic attitudes were seen among both Hindus (concept of Karma) and Muslims (concept of Naseeb) in this study population. Migrant men in this study differentiated between sexual partners; their wives were classified as 'normal' women, from whom the risk was perceived to be the lowest, whilst the risk of HIV infection from sex workers was seen to be the highest. Hence the men believed that to protect themselves from HIV they had to avoid sex with a CSW. Men feared that as CSWs had many sexual partners it was more likely that HIV could spread from them. The risk of HIV infection was largely 'othered' to the CSWs and the men did not perceive themselves as carriers or transmitters of the HIV virus. Hence all other sexual partners (spouses, lovers, and neighbourhood women) were perceived to be safe and there was no need to negotiate for condom use.

As migrant and mobile men are away from their spouses quite often, in response to our statement: 'if a man lives away from his family then he has a higher chance of getting HIV/AIDS', nearly 69 per cent of the migrant men and approximately 63 per cent of the mobile men agreed. For the mobile men who agreed with this statement it showcases their own situation: 75 per cent of them were not living with their spouses in Goa. Truckers were on the road most of the time and fishermen would spend large amounts of time on their boats at sea. Men believe that living away from their spouse and the various opportunities at truck stops or in the neighbourhood make it easier for men to engage in risky behaviour. In the qualitative part of this study truckers and fishermen reported that they perceive sexual feeling to be generating heat in the body and if this heat was not released through sex then they would fall sick. The notions of heat and cold come from the ayurvedic medical paradigm which advocates for a humoral balance in the body.

While collecting data in the migrant settlements, the men often asked us why we came to talk to them about sex and AIDS rather than going to the Goan community. They perceived the Goans as more 'modern' due to their drinking habits and their free socializing with women. To get further insights into this perceived relative risk, we asked if men perceived that Goans (that is, the host population) were more at risk of HIV/AIDS than they were. Nearly 47 per cent of the migrants and 52 per cent of the mobile men agreed. However, a small percentage of the migrant and mobile men felt that fellow migrants and mobile men were equally at risk of HIV/AIDS. Some migrant men felt discriminated against by the Goan government that thought that they were responsible for the spread of HIV.

The cultural perceptions of risk discussed thus far, though specific to the migrant population in Goa, has many pan-Indian cultural norms and values. But such perceptions are not reflected in the risk communication messages of the national programmes as they are mostly focussed on condom use and testing high-risk groups. If the prevention efforts incorporate such varied understandings of susceptibility they will be able to reach a larger group and aid in educating men about unprotected sex rather than focusing on risky partners.

Having examined men's perception of their susceptibility to HIV/AIDS, I move on to describe the perceived severity of HIV/AIDS. This perception was operationalized, as the perceived consequences of getting infected with HIV. In the qualitative data, the economic and social consequences are perceived to be more severe than the health consequences. In NACO's risk communication messages on HIV and AIDS only the long-run health consequences are taken into account whilst the economic and social consequences are ignored. There is also a crucial time dimension which these messages have overlooked, as the poor migrant is more immediately concerned with finding work and feeding his family than what will happen to him in 10 or 20 years' time. This relative perception of severity does not get highlighted in the communication patterns and messages at either the national or NGO level. Different consequences are elaborated upon in the following sections.

CONSEQUENCES

Economic Consequences

A major perceived consequence of contracting HIV was the impoverishment of the family. Men were afraid that if they contracted HIV, there would be no one to earn an income. As men were the sole breadwinners, any wage loss would push the family further into poverty. Men also worried about their parents and siblings back in their village who were economically dependent on them. According to the Hindu religious scriptures, the eldest son is required to provide care and support for his aging parents.

> R: These days the people are also scared of AIDS. They have realised that they should not go to Baina (red light area)…it is not good. They now think that if they get the disease then they will die and then who will look after the family?

In the in-depth interviews men gave instances of families returning to the villages in case of illness because living in Goa is more expensive. Further impoverishment was perceived by more than 60 per cent of the migrant and mobile men. These families had to borrow money, and hence were falling into debt.

> R: See if the person falls ill then he cannot work, so he goes and takes baddi (interest paid on loan). If the family has no money then they sell whatever property they have and go back to the village.

Among the men 67 per cent of the migrants and 75 per cent of the mobile men believed that there would be more debt problems in the household with a person living with HIV/AIDS. Losing a job meant that families had to return to their villages. More than 78 per cent of the mobile men and around 58 per cent of migrant men felt it was better to send a person infected with HIV back to his village.

Social Consequences

The perceived social consequences of contracting HIV/AIDS are isolation from the community, earning a 'bad name', and exclusion from community activities. Having a 'good name' was important to enhance one's social capital. More than 90 per cent of the migrant and mobile men believed that contracting HIV would lead to the loss of family name. As per the survey, social consequences are more important than economic consequences. Loss of family name not only means a lowering of the social status in the migrant community, but also in the place of origin. Loss of social status, as a consequence, was perceived by more than 75 per cent in both groups.

R: If I go to someone else and get the disease then the whole family will get a bad name. If I die then only my wife will be there who will respect her then? For my respect to be there I have to be alive.

Men reported that people living with HIV/AIDS are usually avoided. Nearly 79 per cent of the migrant and mobile men reported that people with HIV/AIDS are generally isolated in the community. Men also feared that if they should die, as well as their wives and children, there would be no one to continue the family name. In the Indian context continuation of one's family name or lineage is through the male progeny. This consequence was perceived by more than 91 per cent of the migrant and mobile men.

R: [I]f I die, then my wife will die, then my children will die and then who will take my family name further? The family is destroyed.

Health Consequences

We sought to understand the perceived severity of the disease with the question: Is AIDS a fatal disease? About 83 per cent among the migrant men and 84 per cent of the mobile men affirmed the fatal nature of AIDS. The qualitative data, however, suggests another perceived health consequence—not death but the process of dying of AIDS. Probing deeper into what 'AIDS as fatal' meant to the men, they refer to visual memories of the slow deterioration of the body. The perceived consequences to health were: loss of weight and weakening of the body.

R: If a person gets AIDS then it's a big thing, he will become weak, his colour of skin changes, you see only his bones. Even if he eats it doesn't bring him strength (maige hathangila). He gets not one but many diseases (bemari) all at once, he might get paralysis.

Men gave instances where persons with AIDS would first go to various doctors to seek treatment, and in the last stages would just remain at home or some, with enough resources, returned to their villages.

Measuring the perceived severity of the disease through these consequences yields a broader picture than narrowly approaching it through a purely medical perspective. To enhance the effectiveness of intervention programmes, I suggest that the programmes use these beliefs and fears to address local risk constructions. The need then is to have a risk communication policy which encourages local programme managers to seek and incorporate local/cultural risk constructions in their awareness programmes.

★ ★ ★

The 'culture of AIDS' and the 'culture in AIDS' explanatory frameworks are useful at contextualizing both organizational and individual efforts in preventing the pandemic (term previously used in Clark-Decès and van Hollen (2011)). Based on the case study of Goa we clearly see that there are multiple actors and multiple agendas which are at work, sometimes even against each other, in their efforts to contain the spread of HIV. Thus to arrive at a comprehensive HIV and AIDS risk-management policy in India we need a more combined approach of bio-medical, behavioural and structural interventions. For such a policy to exist one needs to have a broad-based collaboration between both governmental and the NGOs. The NGOs can provide valuable insights into the cultural and situational context of the sub-populations that they deal with, hence making risk communication more localized and population-specific.

The gaps in connecting the local needs to the global health agendas is a result of a top-down approach to managing HIV/AIDS prevention and care in India. The official response to HIV and AIDS has been encouraging in terms of the organizational structure it has built up, grassroots local organizations, who are dependent on aid only from HIV prevention programmes, have struggled to remain sustainable in the long run. A comprehensive risk-management policy should include and protect the sustainability of local infrastructure so that the link with the community is not lost. In this chapter we saw this alienation at the community level in the discussion on the changing nature of risk groups and the case study of Thabo, where changes in national polices on HIV risk management can sometimes work against the ideal of community development.

The culture in AIDS framework showcased the discrepancies that arise in HIV risk management in Goa. Official messages often construct risk only from the perspective of health whereas for the migrant and mobile men in Goa traditional gender roles, social, and economic consequences were found to influence their risk perceptions.

For risk communication on HIV and AIDS to be successful it needs to be localized to the cultural groups it aims to target. This will reduce cognitive dissonance between the messages projected and the ability of the population to understand the messages. NGOs could use more culture-oriented approaches by highlighting the economic and social consequences in their prevention programmes, rather than solely dealing with health consequences (for example, Wilson and Miller 2003; Arihihenbuwa and Obregon 2000). Inclusion of more culturally grounded knowledge and practices in risk management will help in both reducing the risk of HIV and better management of the risk for those living with the virus.

BIBLIOGRAPHY

Aggleton, P., K. O'Reilly, G. Slutkin, and P. Davies (1994). 'Risking Everything? Risk Behaviour, Behaviour Change and AIDS', *Science*, 265: 341–5.

Altman, D. (1994). *Power and Community: Organizational and Cultural Responses to AIDS*. London: Taylor and Francis.

Arihihenbuwa, C.O., and R. Obregon (2000). 'A Critical Assessment of Theories/ Models Used in Health Communication for HIV/AIDS', *Journal of Health Communication*, 5(suppl.): 5–15.

Asthana, S., and R. Ootsvogels (2001). 'The Social Construct of Male "Homosexuality" in India: Implications for HIV Transmission and Prevention', *Social Science and Medicine*, 52: 707–21.

Bailey, A., I. Hutter, and P.P.P. Huigen (2011). 'The Spatial-Cultural Configuration of Sex Work in Goa, India', *Journal of Economic and Social Geography*, 102(2): 162–75.

Bailey, A. (2008). *Culture, Risk and HIV/AIDS Among Migrant and Mobile Men in Goa, India*. Amsterdam: Rozenberg Publishers.

Bailey, A., and I. Hutter (2006). 'Cultural Heuristics in Risk Assessment of HIV/AIDS', *Culture Health and Sexuality*, 8(5): 465–77.

Balarajan, Y., S. Selvaraj, and S.V. Subramanian (2011). 'Health Care and Equity in India', *The Lancet*, 377(9764): 505–15.

Chakrapani, V. (2004). 'Methodological and Ethical Issues in Conducting Behavioral Research Among Men Who Have Sex With Men (MSM) in India'. Paper presented at 15th International Conference AIDS; Bangkok and Thailand.

Clark-Decès and van Hollen (2011). 'India Responds to the HIV/AIDS Pandemic: Unintended Consequences of Global Health Initiatives', in Clark-Decès (ed.), *A Companion to the Anthropology of India*. Oxford: Blackwell Publishing Ltd.

D'Andrade, R.G. (1992). 'Schemas and Motivation', in R.G. D'Andrade, and C. Strauss (eds), *Human Motives and Cultural Models*. Cambridge: Cambridge University Press, pp. 23–44.

Darak, S., V. Kulkarni, S. Gurjar, A. Bailey, and S. Kulkarni (2003). 'Males But Not Men'. Paper presented at the 4th IASSCS International Conference: Sex and Secrecy, Johannesburg, June 22–5.

Douglas, M. (1986). *Risk Acceptability According to the Social Sciences*. London: Routledge and Kegan Paul.

———— (1992). *Risk and Blame: Essays in Cultural Theory*. London: Routledge.

Douglas, M., and A. Wildavsky (1983). *Risk and Culture: An Essay on the Selection of Technological and Environmental Dangers*. Berkeley: University of California.

Foster, G.M. and B.G. Anderson (1978). *Medical Anthropology*. New York: John Wiley and Sons.

Geertz, C. (1973). *The Interpretation of Cultures*. New York: Basic Books.

Goa State AIDS Control Society (GSACS) (2003). *Containing HIV/AIDS in Goa*. Panaji: Goa Government Publication.

Khan, S. (2001). 'Culture, Sexualities and Identities: Men Who Have Sex With Men in India', *Journal of Homosexuality*, 40: 99–115.

Maiman, L.A. and M.H. Becker (1974). 'The Health Belief Model: Origins and Correlates in Psychological Theory', in M.H. Becker (ed.) *The Health Belief Model and Personal Health Behaviour*. New Jersey: Charles B. SlackInc.

National AIDS Control Organisation (NACO) (2008). 'UNGASS Country Progress Report 2008: India'. New Delhi: Ministry of Health and Family Welfare.

———— (2006). 'HIV Sentinel Surveillance and HIV Estimation', available at http://naco.gov.in/upload/NACO%20PDF/HIV%20Sentinel%20Surveillance%202006_India%20Country%20Report.pdf, last accessed on 10 November 2013.

Parker, R. (2001). 'Sexuality, Culture, and Power in HIV/AIDS Research', *Annual Review of Anthropology*, 30: 163–79.

Population Reference Bureau (PRB) and Population Foundation of India (PFI) (2003). *HIV/AIDS in India*. New Delhi: Population Reference Bureau and Population Foundation of India.

Rayner, S. (1992). 'Cultural Theory and Risk Analysis', in S. Krimsky and D. Golding (eds), *Social Theories of Risk*. Westport, Connecticut: Praeger.

Schoepf, B. (2001). 'International AIDS Research in Anthropology: Taking a Critical Perspective on the Crisis', *Annual Review of Anthropology*, 30: 335–61.

Sontag, S. (1988). *AIDS and Its Metaphors*. New York: Farrar, Strauss and Giroux.

Sridhar, D., and E.J. Gomez (2011). 'Health Financing in Brazil, Russia and India', *Health Policy and Planning*, 26: 12–24.

Tansey, J., and T. O'Riordan (1999). 'Cultural Theory and Risk: A Review', *Health, Risk, Society*, 1(1): 71–90.

UNAIDS (2010). 'Global Report: UNAIDS Report on the Global AIDS Epidemic 2010', available at http://www.unaids.org/documents/20101123_globalreport_em.pdf, last accessed on 10 November 2013.

——— (2009). 'HIV Transmission in Intimate Partner Relationships in Asia', Geneva, available at http://data.unaids.org/pub/report/2009/intimate_partners_report_en.pdf, accessed on 17 October 2010.

UNGASS (2010). *India: Country Progress Report NACO*. Ministry of Health and Family Welfare New Delhi: Government of India.

UNFPA (2009). Financial Resource Flows for Population Activities in 2007 and Resource Flows Project Database, available at http://www.unfpa.org/webdav/site/global/shared/documents/publications/2007/resource_flows_2007.pdf, last accessed on 10 November 2013.

Wilson, B.D.M., and R.L. Miller (2003). 'Examining Strategies for Culturally Grounded HIV Prevention', *AIDS Education and Prevention*, 15: 184–202.

7

RANJANI RAMASWAMY

Exploring H1N1 Risk Communication in India

When the minister of health himself comes to the frontline of the battlefield and shouts 'Don't panic!' Who will not panic? The first directive through media channels was for ill persons to appear at designated centres for collection of specimens for testing. Anyone who saw the crowds either directly or on TV would certainly believe that there was a huge epidemic.

—Virologist Dr T. Jacob John (2009)

On 11 June 2009, World Health Organization (WHO) Director General Dr Margaret Chan declared a global pandemic of H1N1 announcing that there was 'almost universal susceptibility of the world's population to infection' (WHO 2009). A 'bleaker picture' was expected in poorer healthcare settings. As a signatory of the International Health Regulations (IHR), India faced strong compulsions to display preparedness and publicly echo the dominant beliefs of other powerful global actors about H1N1 (IHR 2005).

Before India reported its first case in May 2009, the global newswires were producing two types of narratives. The first was the popular 'worst-case scenario' narrative which revolved around terrifying images of Mexico, large public gatherings in masks, official death toll and infection rate estimates in the millions, as well as vaccine and drug shortages. The second predicted a mild flu season, compared H1N1 to diseases with higher mortality rates like tuberculosis and tried to establish that this was simply a case of media and pharmaceutical industry hype.

Both narratives had its memes in India, but what set the H1N1 India narrative apart is the manner in which official communication (over-confident in its messages about being prepared) clashed with the visibly ineffectual state of public health systems. This clash became more publicly observable when deaths were reported. The first H1N1-related death of a teenage girl in Pune acquired an unusually high level of media prominence and significance (Phadke 2009). The 'global outbreak' story mutated into multiple frenzied narratives across the country. It was then reframed as a local tale of incompetence and negligence by hospitals, testing centres, and the State.

Public officials tried to pre-emptively insulate themselves from blame by invoking colonial epidemic laws and introducing abrupt institutional measures like school and cinema closures. Testing facilities were overloaded, with mild cases delaying care for the critically ill. Millions of doses of expensive vaccines and drugs were hoarded by the centre and deployed later to the states. In a country with over 575 million TV viewers, 302 million newspaper readers, 55 million surfers, and 1.2 million bloggers (Kohli-Khandekar 2010) the story snowballed into a spiral of anger, fear, and panic across states that lasted for several months.

Since the 2005 Asian Avian Flu experience, India has had multiple versions of the Pandemic Preparedness and Response Plan (PPRP) on paper (MoHFW 2009a) which lists out pharmaceutical, non-pharmaceutical, and risk communication interventions. There are ongoing efforts to have a networked decentralized approach to disease surveillance and management such as the World Bank funded Integrated Disease Surveillance Project (IDSP). A draft National Health Bill (2009) is also being circulated to legally recognize health as a basic human right. As commendable as these initiatives sound on paper, they all face overwhelming implementation challenges.

According to economist Lant Pritchett (2009), Indian bureaucrats in official settings give an 'elaborate and intriguing' story about health systems in India which is 'fully backed with data and reports'. However when the realities are witnessed one realizes that 'this description of India's health system (while it may serve as a useful organizing myth) is a complete fiction' (Pritchett 2009: 2).

The fact is that there is no comprehensive capacity to communicate, mobilize, implement, and enforce disease-management strategies across the country, across healthcare delivery systems (private, public, or alternative) or even across medical and scientific professional channels (John and Muliyil 2009). In spite of obvious limitations, India resorted to what has been described elsewhere as a 'hysterical exaggeration of moderate or even small risks' (Sandman and Lanard 2011) and 'the most explicit, excessive, and repeated over-reassurances about (H1N1) containment' (ibid.: 2009).

In terms of the model of Epidemic Psychology (Strong 1990) an outbreak of a disease like H1N1 is usually accompanied by three other psychosocial epidemics—the 'epidemic of fear', 'the epidemic of explanation and moralization', and 'the epidemic of action or proposed action'. Risk communication plays a crucial role in all these psychosocial manifestations and all three occurred in India during H1N1 outbreak in 2009 (referred further as H1N1 2009).

This chapter will explore and analyse key issues and problems in the risk communication during the H1N1 2009 experience in India. The larger purpose of critically examining this event is to appeal for original interdisciplinary evidence-based research on risk communication that is contextually India-specific, which takes into account health dispari-ties, social inequities, history, political frames, and the massive changes in the Indian media landscape that have taken place during the last two decades. There is currently a void in communication research in India. There is very little academic or independent research, other than project reports written by the government and international develop-ment agencies on the successes of their efforts to increase awareness for diseases like Human Immunodeficiency Virus/Acquired Immuno Deficiency Syndrome (HIV/AIDS) (NACO 2008) or Polio (UNICEF 2010). There is little attempt to contextualize what 'lay understanding', 'health literacy', or 'risk acceptability' means in a population with the starkest socioeconomic contrasts and the largest number of adult illiter-ates (over 270 million) in the world (UNESCO 2010). 32.7 per cent of the Indian population fall below the international poverty line of USD 1.25 per day (PPP) (World Bank 2010).

Exploring how H1N1 was communicated in India will hopefully also reveal the difficulties of the unquestioning application of 'global' aca-demic approaches to risk perception, communication, and media studies to developing country settings. The majority of 'global' communication guidelines that currently exist are 'new' (not more than 10 years old) and are predominantly 'Anglo-Saxon in context' (Löfstedt 2010). Current communication and media research mainly emerged from Western Europe and the United States in the late 19th century (McQuail 2005). According to Gunaratne (2010: 474) an 'oligopoly of social science powers' in the UK, US, and other parts of Europe dominated media and communication perspectives, whose scholars were largely ignorant or indifferent about the history and context of the non-West. Western theories and guidelines may be conceptually useful but they were made for the specific contexts that were studied. What is problematic is that these are universalized as perfect substitutes or best practices in other contexts in the absence of rigorous indigenous research. Research agendas in the 21st century need to not only address these concerns but they must also fully accommodate and explore the effects of rapid contemporary changes in media flows which today are so 'multi-vocal, multi-directional, and multi-layered' (Thussu 2007).

For this chapter on H1N1 risk communication in India, the inquiry was conducted using Lasswell's (1948) model, which assumes that in pluralistic societies, messages flow through numerous channels to multiple audiences with different effects; *Who* (Control Analysis), *Says What* (Content Analysis), *In What Channel* (Media Analysis), *To Whom* (Audience Analysis), and *With What Effect* (Effect Analysis)? Lasswell's source-receiver communication model provides a useful typology to describe problems in conveying information about health events (Covello et al. 1986). Problems related to the sources of the risk information, the content of these messages, the channels through which they were disseminated, and the audiences who received the messages were analysed. A set of dominant themes are presented in this chapter.

Personal face-to-face and telephonic interviews were conducted with key officials from the Ministry of Health and Family Welfare (MoHFW), virologists, testing centres personnel, hospital officials, journalists, and doctors based in Bangalore and New Delhi. A literature review of the disease was done by looking at articles and research papers in major scientific and medical publications. MoHFW's dedicated webpage for the H1N1 outbreak; news releases from the Public Information Bureau (PIB), numerous television reports, videos, social media, newspapers, journal articles, and health websites available online were used to frame a coherent narrative.

WHAT IS RISK COMMUNICATION?

Risk communication is defined as: '[T]he flow of information and risk evaluations back and forth between academic experts, regulatory practitioners, interest groups, and the general public' (Leiss 1996: 86). This definition allows us to see that in an environment where risk evaluations and information are constantly flowing *back and forth*, risk communication messages need to be refined and altered in tune with unfolding events and public responses. Messages should be formulated with an awareness of the heuristics and biases (Tversky and Kahneman 1974) governing the different audiences and individuals the government seeks to influence. Risk communication plays an important role in arousing concern or assuaging fears *before a* potential eventuality while crisis communication takes place to help recover when the risk materializes as a full-blown crisis.

Sandman's (1993; also Sandman and Weinstein (2002)) model of risk uses a body of research (Fischhoff et al. 1981) that suggests that people assess risks according to metrics other than their technical seriousness. These researchers believe that risk perception depends qualitatively on factors such as controllability, voluntariness, fear, dread, degree of organized safety, equity, and familiarity (Slovic et al. 1980; Vlek and Stallen 1981) now commonly known as the outrage factors.

According to Sandman, if the tangible death rate (what the experts mean by risk) is the 'hazard' then all the other factors that make people frightened, angry, or otherwise upset about a risk is collectively called 'Outrage'. Outrage is not a distortion of the risk, but rather an intrinsic part of how people perceive risk.

$$\text{Risk} = \text{Hazard} + \text{Outrage}$$

The public typically pays too little attention to hazard; the experts pay absolutely no attention to outrage. In the context of risk-communication research, 'If the message is not appropriately matched to the frame of reference of the audience then the communication may fail (or even prove counter productive)' (Pidgeon 1992: 178 cited in Weyman and Kelly 1999).

H1N1 in India is an example of how some risks acquire higher salience and policy attention (due to a number of factors), even while others, perhaps more significant risks do not receive a similar response. A year after the first positive cases emerged, there were 1,511 H1N1 lab-confirmed deaths (MoHFW 2010a), a fraction of the deaths caused by tuberculosis which kills 1,000 Indians everyday or rabies which kills 20,000 people annually. In Pune, the epicentre of the H1N1 drama, the Serum Institute of India which had frantically set up its own H1N1 vaccine manufacturing unit during the panic phase, had to destroy seven million unused vaccines past their expiration date (Indian Express 2009) because the pandemic was not as serious as expected. The waste of resources and the panic outside testing centres could have been avoided if risk messages had created a level of outrage appropriate to the hazard (Sandman 1993).

The Social Amplification of Risk Framework (SARF) (Kasperson et al. 1988; Kasperson 1992) can help us evaluate the communication chain in India—exploring why H1N1 attracted greater attention than other health risks, and how different social and political processes influenced the filtering of information within this chain. The premise of SARF is that risk events are portrayed through various risk signals (images, signs, or symbols) and interact with complex psychological, social, institutional, and cultural processes in ways that can heighten (amplify) or quell (attenuate) perceptions of risk and result in secondary effects (ripples, such as the loss of public trust). Risk is experienced not only in physical terms but also as a process by which individuals and groups learn to acquire or create interpretations of the risk.

Petts et al. (2001) argue that risk events hold particular 'risk signatures' or 'images' that determine how people interpret a risk and why they accord certain hazards more attention than others. There are four dimensions to these 'risk signatures' which include: 'the specificity of adverse effects; concern for potential effects on others; concern over perceived secrecy or cover-ups by institutions; distrust in institutions due to vested interests; and whether the issue presents moral questions or not' (ibid.: viii). Studying the entire realm of 'risk signatures' associated with H1N1 in India and how these interacted with the multiple psychological, social, institutional, and cultural processes of the time is beyond the scope and scale of this study, which focuses on the government's communication of the event. Hopefully, however, this will encourage more critical in-depth studies into how risk messages that were supposed to influence public debate, policymaking, and personal action towards mitigation ended up exacerbating the impact and significance of H1N1.

THE HOBBESIAN NIGHTMARE

In India the authorities who communicate during health crises are mostly political non-experts with their own agendas and interest groups. 'The public' is a broad generalized mass, encompassing audiences who speak over 29 languages (with over a million speakers each, as per the 2001 census), and a liberalized media setting with over 60,000 newspapers (Kohli-Khandekar 2010), and over 246 TV news channels (Ministry of Information and Broadcasting 2009).

These are ripe conditions for many types of miscommunications during an outbreak. According to Strong (1990: 249) '[U]nder the right conditions, epidemics can potentially create a medical version of a Hobbesian nightmare—the war of all against all.' In the Indian context, the communicator (because of either vested interests or lack of expertise) communicates politically motivated, incorrect, or oversimplified messages through the media. The media (mainly due to its own lack of expertise, apathy, or competitive interests) amplifies or ignores an issue according to its own profit-motives or agendas. These messages are received by the audience who might or might not trust the government or the media. The audience might not even understand some or even all of the messages. We really know very little about what motivates individuals in India to adopt or reject state advisories.

The transition from a singular policy voice claiming to be in 'control' of the H1N1 virus to an all-out blame war happened primarily because the Indian government did not bring about a transition from containment to mitigation measures fast enough, and because they did not address valid public confusions and fears *before* deaths occurred in the community.

CONTAINMENT AND CONTROL

At the end of April 2009, a suspected H1N1-infected passenger travelling back from the US was hospitalized in Hyderabad. At exactly the same time, the WHO raised its pandemic alert level from Phase 4 to Phase 5. Till then H1N1 was perceived largely as a 'foreign' disease affecting the US and Mexico.

Soon after this first case, India went into a full-fledged containment phase with border control and entry screening at 22 airports and seaports (MoHFW 2010b). Tamiflu® (Oseltamivir) stockpiles increased from one million to seven million doses almost overnight, and by 2010 there were over 40 million capsules. Diagnosis, quarantine, and treatment were all under the control of public health authorities and designated public health facilities. Diagnostic and treatment guidelines were given *only* to doctors working in public health facilities when infections were reported. This was surprising in a context where more than three-fourths of health spending in India is in private health facilities and where national household surveys have demonstrated that 'the private sector in the previous two decades has become the main provider of inpatient care' (Balarajan et al. 2011: 508). Why health policy at the time excluded a critical bulk of the health sector from pandemic planning is an important question to consider from a risk management perspective.

Governments traditionally put containment measures in place to buy time. These measures offer no guarantee to stop the disease; they only provide a transitional period which allows the government and the public to get prepared. A new unpredictable virus spreading in a densely overpopulated country of 28 states and seven union territories, with each regional government having starkly different records on public health, could only mean that whatever the government did in terms of containment would have limitations, and people needed to be adequately prepared. The Indian government did not explain its reasons behind implementing containment measures, nor did it publicly acknowledge uncertainties concerning the nature and magnitude of the pandemic or the limited effectiveness of these measures. Instead, it bragged about its preparedness, power to 'control' and 'stop' the spread of the virus: 'Swine flu is totally under control and presence of H1N1 virus is very negligible in the country. Its spread has also been effectively checked as we took extraordinary precautions' (TOI 2009b).

Local WHO officials too seemed remarkably confident about India's ability to handle the potential crisis, as Dr J.P. Narain, Director, Communicable Diseases, WHO said:

> They (India) have tremendous capacity to deal with any kind of situation and it is very much in the forefront of preparedness...capacity is very much there...we have absolutely no doubt about that. (PTI 2009a)

As a public health intervention, containment measures such as airport scanning are expensive, and have no proven track record. Asymptomatic cases can very easily walk through thermal scanners and still spread the disease. In a study of passengers at Singapore's Changi Airport (Mukherjee et al. 2010), scanners picked up only 12 per cent of travel-associated flu cases and many travellers boarded flights despite symptoms.

Officials at the India's Health Ministry said that they were aware of the limited use of containment, thermal scanners, and stockpiling measures to 'stop' the spread of a pandemic (MoHFW, personal communication 2010) but felt it was an essential *trust-building* exercise. They considered it better being seen doing something that reassured the public rather than be blamed for doing nothing.

The Indian media did not question whether containment worked or could even work in India, or why it was implemented months after the disease emerged in Mexico. However, there were a number of media reports asking why the government was not strict enough in enforcing airport screening procedures and attributed such 'lax' containment practices to the disease spreading and the panic over H1N1 (NDTV 2009).

Ghulam Nabi Azad, a former Parliamentary Affairs Minister who was newly sworn in as the Union Health Minister in May 2009, publicly urged the External Affairs Ministry to prevail upon affected countries such as US to have exit screening so that cases were no longer 'exported' out of foreign nations and 'imported' into India (TOI 2009a). Many of the positive cases which were reported in India till June were travellers from the US, Thailand, and Australia and other countries. Exit screening can be useful, but the rhetoric of import and export appeared to be a means of scoring political points, harking back to the aggressive travel restrictions placed on Indian travellers by many countries during the Surat plague scare in 1994. The External Affairs Ministry did not respond, but it was enough to convey the message that the virus was a 'foreign' threat. After deaths were reported in August 2009, the H1N1 narrative of control over the virus changed to a more fatalistic stance about the potential toll of H1N1 in India:

Admitting that no government measure could prevent the spread of the H1N1 influenza in India, Union health minister Ghulam Nabi Azad said on Sunday that around one-third of the Indian population was likely to get infected with the virus over the next two years, in accordance with WHO predictions. But most people would suffer only mild symptoms of the disease, he added. (TOI 2009b)

Contrast this with a 'model example' of pandemic communication by the former Australian Health Minister Tony Abbott during the bird flu:

It's hard to discuss potential disasters outside people's ordinary experience without generating the sort of lurid headlines which make some scoff and others panic. It's important not to over-react to potential threats. On the other hand, people and their governments need to take credible threats seriously and take reasonable and proportionate precautions against them. If a deadly flu pandemic ever seems imminent, no preparations will be enough. But if the current bird flu outbreaks in Asia gradually subside, the Government's investment in a stockpile likely to be time-expired in five years will be the health equivalent of a redundant weapons system. (Sandman and Lanard 2005)

Abbott's risk communication style displays an almost extraordinary level of trust in the public, validating their fears and preparing them for potential uncertainty and distress, all the while setting their expectations at manageable levels. Unfortunately this was not the case in India. And it was not just health officials at the centre with overconfident and misleading messages.

The Principal Secretary of the Government of Karnataka, Department of Health and Family Welfare, I.R. Perumal, became notorious for his unsubstantiated proclamations on H1N1 2009: 'India is the hottest country. The swine flu will not come to India at all. If at all, one or two places it will come. It may be cold there,' he said during one such press conference. This and other ludicrous statements he made about H1N1 were repeated for days on the local tabloid channel *News 9* as a comic gag segment called 'Just for Laughs' (News 9 2009).

Statements like these left the government extremely vulnerable to attacks when mortalities were reported, as these were immediately interpreted as a sign of the state's negligence and incompetence.

EDUCATING THE MASSES

The central government held daily press briefings about the number of infections and deaths for almost a year, established videoconferencing facilities to communicate with designated centres, launched a website for the pandemic, a toll-free helpline, print advertisements and a UNICEF supported TV ad campaign.

Television is extremely powerful in a country where images are the only way to transcend language and literacy barriers (Thussu 1999). In one of the public interest TV advertisements, a man on a crowded red public bus is about to sneeze (Mudra Group 2009). The passengers freeze and recoil in slow motion with overdramatized expressions of fear, suspicion, and revulsion. The bus driver turns around to look fearfully at the passenger and steps on the brakes. The man's mouth is wide open, his body bracing for the impending sneeze. When he ultimately sneezes into a hankie his fellow passengers relax, smile, and give him a standing ovation with the voice-over: 'Simple habits like covering your nose and mouth with a hankie while coughing and sneezing can save many lives and stop deadly diseases like H1N1 from spreading. Stop the infection. Be the Hero!'

Promoting healthy personal protective practices is important in a country where many diseases spread because of overcrowding and unsanitary habits or lack of sanitation facilities. But this hysterical advertisement exaggerated the benefits of personal protection (the protagonist transforms from a social pariah to a hero just by sneezing appropriately) and oversimplified disease information to such a degree that public fear, panic, and stigma associated with H1N1 could only have amplified substantially.

The print advertisements were less visually alarmist but in many ways equally problematic. Advertisements targeting vulnerable groups insisted on the need to get tested at designated public centres: 'Got the flu with any other medical problems? Get tested for H1N1 (Swine flu) immediately' (MoHFW 2009b). The print advertisement goes on to list everything from hypertension and diabetes to pregnancy, heart, and respiratory illnesses as conditions that would make people more vulnerable to H1N1. There are an estimated 62.4 million diabetics (PTI 2011a) in India. This advertisement did not recommend contacting one's local doctor and getting treated early for the flu, or staying at home, but in fact it only pushed for testing. Neither did it say that it would take time to test, since, at the beginning of the H1N1 spread in India, there were only two government testing centres nationwide. Officials at the MoHFW have said (MoHFW personal communication, 2010) that it was the public demand for testing that caused most of the panic outside government centres, but advertisements like these obviously contributed to the public perception that tests were crucial to H1N1 management.

The helpline is said to have received over 35,000 calls related to H1N1 (Kant and Krishnan 2010) but is this really statistically relevant in a country where the overall tele density is around 76.86 per cent with 926.53 million telephone subscribers (TRAI 2012)? There are no publicly available evidence-based impact or reach evaluation studies about these government advertising initiatives. This raises serious questions about how risk communication is strategized and delivered by public health systems in India, the choice of media, and whether resources for these health campaigns were effectively used.

FEAR AT SAMSUNG (BANGALORE) AND GOOGLE (HYDERABAD)

During the second stage of a disease outbreak, when there are positive cases in the community, risk communicators naturally shift to crisis communication mode. This is aimed at helping people accept, manage, and treat the disease. It includes clearing any doubts and misinformation and giving relevant precautionary advice for certain vulnerable groups. Two fairly significant events in June and July 2009 should have motivated officials to shift to crisis communication.

The offices of Samsung in Bangalore were shut down for three whole days when an asymptomatic 27-year-old engineer returned from South Korea in late June 2009, developed flu symptoms, and was tested positive a few days later. Even though only two employees had direct contact with the positive case, over 90 employees swamped the public Rajiv Gandhi Institute of Chest Diseases (RGICD) in Bangalore, clamouring to be tested. RGICD and Victoria Hospital were at the time the only public health facilities allowed to quarantine and treat H1N1 patients in Bangalore.

'I have never seen anything like it', said Dr Shashidar Buggi (2009, through a personal communication), Director of RGICD describing the panic. He also said that the Samsung scare was the tipping 3 point in Bangalore after which for weeks hundreds of people flooded the hospital demanding to be tested:

The communication was top down and not inclusive in its approach. I spent a large part of my time during the panic phase answering all sorts of basic questions over and over again about wearing masks, explaining why some cases clinically did not warrant expensive tests and asking them to stay calm. The government did not talk to businesses, private doctors and stakeholders at the grassroots as a trusted means to convey valuable information about testing and treatment...before the panic button was hit. There was no public-private partnership and no real sense of collaboration between the States and the Centre. (ibid.)

The Samsung scare was not an isolated case. The Google offices in Hyderabad were also shut down for two days and fumigated in July after an employee was tested positive. Central government officials kept insisting that everything was under control and asked people to remain calm, but in press conferences they never detailed the specific pharmaceutical, non-pharmaceutical, and risk-communication guidelines applicable to well-defined stakeholder groups (which are businesses, teachers, general physicians, school children, and private practitioners). Clearly the situation was not under control and there needed to be a greater effort to make information relevant to different stakeholder groups about diagnosis, and the availability, distribution and safety of testing, vaccines, and treatment protocols. From the end of April 2009 to late July 2009, the government had plenty of opportunities to interact with and involve community stakeholders in their H1N1 information campaigns. They could have decentralized state control over Tamiflu® supplies, treatment, and testing facilities so that more people could access these. But they did not do so.

TESTING

The government's limited capacity to test was a recurring theme during the H1N1 narrative. This was also a theme during the SARS of 2003 and the Surat Plague Scare of 1994. In all three crises, government messages stressed on getting tested and treated for the disease only in the public health centres. One lab could test for the plague, two labs (the National Centre for Disease Control (NCDC) and the National Institute of Virology (NIV)) could test for SARS, the same two for H1N1, and in all three this capacity seemed dwarfish compared to the perceived severity of 'killer' diseases spreading across a large population.

During H1N1, the capacity to test increased from initially just two national labs to 18 designated testing centres and finally 42, when people queued outside hospitals to get tested. The message that there were not enough testing facilities was constantly amplified by local cable networks. Health officials never explained that there were limitations in testing capabilities (number of labs and trained personnel issues) and that limited resources had to be used judiciously. Instead, the situation offered them the political opportunity to proclaim that they were increasing the testing capacity of accredited labs and universalizing testing. Karnataka's Principal Secretary (Health), I.R. Perumal, announced that his government was taking steps to increase the capacity of lab testing from 160 swabs a day to 300 and eventually 1,000 (The Hindu 2009), simply reiterating the message that testing was the solution to the H1N1 crisis. Dr V. Ravi, Head of Neurovirology at the National Institute of Mental Health and Neuro Sciences (NIMHANS), one of the first H1N1 testing centres in Bangalore said:

> This was the first time in my career dealing with such a bloated sense of fear, misinformation and media scrutiny during a health crisis. Even the doctors working here at NIMHANS would secretly approach us to get tested for H1N1-09 because that was the message they had gotten, without understanding that test results had nothing to do with treatment, especially under the new guidelines. I went on a few caller shows in Kannada where people asked questions and I answered, but the major news channels were not interested in talking to us unless it was to buffer a sensational premise for a story. Many of these reporters would begin with 'why don't you have enough testing kits?' instead of asking more relevant questions. (2009, personal communication)

The new diagnostic guidelines Dr Ravi mentioned were communicated to the public only two weeks after the first H1N1 death was reported and the panic had reached fever-pitch. They also tried to communicate that getting treated early for flu symptoms was much more important than getting tested and waiting for the results. But the period of passively receiving government messages and explanations was over. A multi-directional 'war of all against all' erupted when news of the first lab-confirmed H1N1 death, a 14-year-old girl Rida Shaikh from Pune was reported on 3 August 2009.

COMMUNICATING DEATH

Personalizing risk narratives is the stuff of headlines and few things are more evocative than the untimely death of a teenager. According to

Covello et al. (1986): '[R]isk calculations are made at a macro-level: what will happen to the community as a whole, while citizens are concerned with the micro-level: what will happen to me and the people I love' (ibid.: 314).

Rida Shaikh from Pune had neither travelled abroad, nor had been in close contact with an H1N1 case. She was in and out of various private hospitals in the end of July 2009, and as her condition worsened she was shifted to the intensive care unit. It was not until a week into her ordeal that her test for H1N1 was sent to a state lab. An earlier private lab test had been negative for Influenza A and B. By the time it was established that she was H1N1 positive, she died. When news of her death was telecast, over 1,000 people a day lined up to get tested for H1N1 outside Naidu Hospital, the main referral testing centre for H1N1 in Pune.

THE SPECTACLE OF BLAME IN REAL TIME

On 3 August, Rida's visibly crushed parents and aunt Ayesha Shaikh gave interviews to the press alleging criminal negligence on the part of two private hospitals and filed criminal and civil charges against the hospitals.

An upset and emotional Sajid Shaikh, Rida's father, said: 'If they (the private hospital) had sent Rida's samples to the NIV earlier, probably my daughter would have been alive today' (Hindustan Times 2009a).

To this there is almost a real-time statement given to the press by the Union Health Secretary Naresh Dayal: 'It appears she was treated late. If she had been treated earlier, she could have been saved' (that is, she should have been given anti-flu medication earlier/visited a public health centre for testing) (Hindustan Times 2009b).

This generalized statement exacerbated panic across the states by implying that Rida's family and the private hospitals were somehow responsible for the death. The next few days saw a panic wave of people thronging the testing facility at the Naidu public hospital, mostly worried parents. Suspected flu or fever cases were indiscriminately sent to the public testing facilities by private doctors without prior screening, fearing that they too will be accused of criminal negligence. Personal precautions extended to hoarding the most expensive N95 masks and buying Tamiflu® off the black market.

Other countries too faced a lot of panic and frenzy when individual deaths were personalized and tabloidized in the media coverage. A comparable case could be that of healthy six-year-old Chloe who died because of H1N1-related complications in West Drayton, England (Clench et al. 2009). She was originally diagnosed with tonsillitis and her H1N1 test result came too late.

There were, however, two fundamental differences between how this was handled in the UK and India. One, while UK health officials commiserated with the grieving family, they urged the public to keep things in perspective, and secondly, Chloe's family gave a statement that even though they felt that she could have been saved had she been diagnosed earlier that they were 'satisfied that the medical care Chloe received at all times was appropriate' (ibid). Perhaps it was a legal requirement but what is evident is that the health officials did not blame the victims and the victims did not blame officials. It was framed as a 'tragedy'.

This was not the case in India. Union Health Minister Azad called for a 'probe' and made statements a few days later saying that Rida *could have* infected at least 80 other people as she was shifted back and forth between various health facilities seeking treatment, further shifting the blame onto not only Rida's family but also the private hospitals and Rida herself. According to Mary Douglas (2002: 56), blaming the victim or their kith and kin is a 'hand-washing ploy' and an effective means to 'silence indictments of the whole system'. Azad's statement created a near-riot situation outside the public hospital in Pune. Rida's family demanded that Azad apologize, which he promptly did by adding that 'I never meant to say that Rida spread H1N1 infection in Pune' (Hindustan Times 2009b).

What ensued was a number of adversarial television interviews where doctors blamed the government, the government blamed private hospitals, private hospitals blamed the state, the state blamed the centre and Rida's aggrieved family blamed them all. Without any clear winner or loser in the blame game, the number of contradictory befuddling messages escalated the level of anger and fear amongst the public.

To resume control, Maharashtra's Health Minister Dr Rajendra Shingne declared that Rida's death was a result of medical negligence and the state invoked the Epidemic Control Act, 1897, which historian David Arnold has termed as 'one of the most draconian pieces of sanitary legislation ever adopted in colonial India' (Arnold 2000: 143). The governments of Delhi, Haryana, and Gujarat also invoked the Act, which allowed the states to ban public gatherings and forcibly hospitalize people who are suspected of being infected. States like Tamil Nadu issued travel advisories directly urging people not to visit Maharashtra (TOI 2009c). All educational institutions in Pune and its surrounding industrial districts were closed for a week. Other public gathering areas like movie theatres and even public courts were also shut for a few days.

STATE VERSUS CENTRE VERSUS STATE

Health is essentially a state subject in India's federal political structure and the centre only has jurisdiction over national infectious disease programmes, medical education, research, and population control. Disease control and prevention in India means working across 28 states with different languages, health indicators, and political parties in power, as well as working across various ministries and departments (the law ministry and the water and sanitation departments for instance). As more deaths were reported and personalized, discourses about the disease became playing fields for party politics and opportunities to manipulate risk perception.

Union Health Minister Azad lambasted states over their inability to curb H1N1. In a meeting, Azad claimed that the centre was 'bloody slogging', while states had 'chickened out' of their responsibility to counter H1N1 (PTI 2009b). A visibly infuriated J.N. Vyas, Gujarat's Health Minister told the media: 'The health minister spoke to us as if he was the headmaster of a school and we were his students' (ibid.).

These public displays of self-righteous indignation may have had little to do with the disease itself. State health officials openly resented criticism from the Union Health Minister. On both ends of these acrimonious exchanges, the reactions were not based on transparent performance appraisals but on which side of the political divide they fell on. Health ministers from states like Gujarat, Bihar, and Madhya Pradesh (all opposition-ruled states) reacted more angrily to Azad's statement (Economic Times Agencies 2009). In Kerala, H1N1 was politically hijacked by the United Democratic Front (UDF) (which had taken over from the communist party-led Left Democratic Front (LDF) in 2011), led by the Indian National Congress (ruling party). The LDF staged a walkout when the new State Health Minister Adoor Prakash from the UDF said that *their* party (UDF) had been more effective in controlling H1N1 since only one person had died out of 78 positive cases till July 2011, while 85 of 1,408 H1N1-affected persons had died during the LDF's tenure the previous year (PTI 2011). There was very little rational, informed discourse about the disease (even months after its emergence) during these bouts of political theatre, except to act out political rivalries and reiterate 'control' over H1N1.

AYURVEDA, YOGA AND NATUROPATHY, UNANI, SIDDHA, AND HOMOEOPATHY (AYUSH)

The MoHFW comprises a number of departments including the department of AYUSH. The purpose of AYUSH is to encourage research and standardize education, quality control, and drug protocols in the largely unorganized sector of alternative indigenous medicine.

What was particularly disconcerting during H1N1 was that without any clinical trials or evidence-based research to back claims, AYUSH was actively promoted as a preventive or curative medicine for H1N1. Every system of medicine in AYUSH claimed to have its own cure for H1N1. Baba Ramdev, a popular yoga master, claimed at a press conference after Rida's death that yoga and ayurvedic medicinal herbs could 'cure' H1N1 and that 'there was no need to panic' (playing on the rhetoric of health officials) (Zee News 2009).

TRUSTING GOVERNMENT SOURCES

A negative performance history creates what is known as the 'velcro effect' (Coombs and Holladay 2001: 338) where the negative history will 'stick to' the organization and eventually lower an organization's reputation (Coombs and Holladay 2001). It is not hard to find negative stories of poor performance that have 'stuck' to the Indian government's reputation.

The 1994 Surat Plague outbreak and 2003 SARS outbreak were similar to H1N1 2009 with similar levels of uncertainty, media scrutiny with equally frightening social and economic costs and public displays of panic and fear. The Surat plague was perhaps the worst manifestation of a fear pandemic (Shah 1997; Garrett 2000), where just 54 people died but the fear of the plague led to two million people fleeing the city. During SARS, individuals were blamed for spreading the virus because they had 'escaped' from quarantine facilities (Nagral 2003). There was so much fear at one point that 45 Air India pilots were suspended because they refused to fly to SARS-affected nations and over a third of doctors and paramedical staff in Kolkata's infectious diseases hospital refused to report to work (Singh 2003).

Why focus on trust in government? In India the government is the primary source of information about potential outbreaks. Unlike other countries, India does not have 'expert' epidemiologists or independent health experts who address and interact with the media and the public, like Richard Besser from the Centres for Disease Control (CDC) in the US. The scientists at India's NCDC and NIV have no such voice or public prominence. There are also less than a handful of reporters nationally who cover health issues and few trained health communication experts, most of whom work as consultants with Non-governmental Organizations (NGOs) and other international institutions on health promotion and behaviour change projects.

In risk communication, trust is said to act as the crucial fulcrum supporting a see-saw between emotions (fear) and facts (Ropeik 2000). Trust, confidence, and credibility are key components of any analytical framework studying risk communication (Renn and Levine 1991; Kasperson et al. 1998; Slovic 1999; Poortinga and Pidgeon 2003). But what if the important fulcrum of trust is broken?

Löfstedt (2009: 4) argues that certain western countries are becoming 'post-trust' societies citing a number of factors for this including 'higher levels of education and greater availability of information resulting in a more sceptical public', 'cronyism in government', 'growth of citizen activism in an era of complex and uncertain risks and multiple messages' and 'regulatory scandals'. Factors, such as 'regulatory scandals', and the 'growth of citizen activism', are relevant to a discussion on trust in India, but Western 'post-trust' discourses cannot be super imposed onto the Indian context. Historical retrospection shows us that India has not neatly transitioned from a trust to post-trust setting. The country for large parts of its post-independent history has been caught in a vicious cycle of similar health scandals marked by corruption, poor performance, apathy and ultimately fatalism.

Viral Japanese Encephalitis (JE), for instance, is a recurring threat, which killed one in four children it affected in 2011, resulting in over 1,133 deaths (Deccan Herald 2011). India has many endemic zones for JE and outbreaks for the most part coincide with wet seasons or wet regions when the possibility of transmission of the disease through vectors like mosquitoes, pigs, and water birds is high. Insecticide spraying, vector control, and vaccination are all virus 'control' measures. But nothing has been done to communicate the risk posed by this 'killer' viral disease by the centre or the states. The public, during high-risk JE periods, still knowingly tolerates this risk year after year because it has no other choice and perceives no means for remedy. Union Health Minister Azad, who gave innumerable press conferences to sound the alarm on H1N1 and participated in all H1N1-related media stories nationwide, was conspicuously silent about the centre's or India's role in 'controlling' JE. The state health officials too were silent, occasionally blaming the virus on people 'not boiling their water' or other unsanitary habits (again shifting the blame onto the public and absolving themselves of the responsibility). The media dubbed it the 'apathy virus' (Frontline 2011). This sensibility differs considerably from the West where for the most part, there is a culturally and morally set baseline for 'acceptable risks' (Hunter and Fewtrell 2001).

In India, the *legally* set baseline for acceptable risks is comparable to the West but the promises inherent in the law to punish individual or institutional transgressors are seldom implemented. Scandals exist from the top to the bottom of the health establishment. In 2008, the World Bank released a 600-page Detailed Implementation Review (DIR) detailing instances of rampant financial fraud and corruption in five multi-million-dollar health projects funded by the Government of India, the World Bank and other donors (World Bank 2008). An estimated 870 million rupees is paid annually in bribes by the poorest Below Poverty Line (BPL) households in India to avail basic hospital services (TII-CMS India Corruption Study 2007). These corruption scandals exist not only within the health sector (at institutional, federal, local, and individual levels) but thrive across sectors in education, telecom, and politics. These are extremely contentious and uncomfortable realities even for the development community who prefer to 'focus excessively on the micro-aspects of corruption improprieties in procurement, shoddy monitoring, and fraudulent project reporting' (Vaishnav 2011) at the cost of delving into the much bigger and more complex picture of how political forces or agendas determine health policies.

There is a great scope for risk studies in socially vulnerable contexts like India in terms of translating these representations of extreme distrust, corruption, apathy and inefficiency and incorporating them into an intelligible pragmatic framework. This will not only be useful for illustrative purposes but also to find more useful ways to address communication challenges in such dire settings.

TRUST AND THE MEDIA

O'Neill (2002), in her Reith Lectures, talks about finding ways to reduce 'deception and lies' in order to restore trust. Can the media, for instance, be a means to call out these deceptions and lies especially during critical periods of a health crisis? It would not seem so at the current moment.

When India became independent it had a free independent press and a state-controlled broadcast media. During the 1990s the Indian media went through a massive transformation where state controls were removed and the monopoly of the state's broadcasting system (Doordarshan) was broken with the introduction of private TV channels. By 2009 there were 512 private TV channels out of which 249 were news channels (Ministry of Information and Broadcasting 2009). Pre-liberalization, in the 1980s, television was used by the state to enforce a uniform national cultural consensus on issues like national integration. Post-liberalization, with no clear monopoly, television news was less about state propaganda and more about TRPs and means to attract consumer segments, especially the booming middle class audience (a population that is estimated to be 580 million people by 2025 according to the McKinsey Global Institute (MGI) 2007).

Historically, the Indian media enjoyed much higher levels of trust and credibility than the government because it was seen as an independent arbiter of the state. Newspapers had intellectual credibility and television was influential since it visually transcended barriers of language and literacy and viewers tended to trust it (Thussu 1999). But some recent results would suggest a different trend. A US PR firm,

Edelman, presented annual findings of their 'trust barometer', which records the trust that respondents in their small selective sample size places on government, business, NGOs, and the media. A few interesting insights from their 2011 study in India (Edelman 2011): The trust in NGOs had gone up dramatically to 61 per cent (+14 points over 2010) and trust in government had flattened at 44 per cent (43 per cent in 2010) while trust in media declined to 50 per cent (−15 points from 2009).

While the media still enjoys better trust levels than the government, it has been caught in a series of scandals involving paid news and more recently the 2G Telecom Scam of 2010, where senior TV broadcasters were accused of wilfully suppressing stories related to government corruption. The most scathing criticism levelled against the media by commentators and many chairs of the Press Council of India (PCI) is what they see as crass commoditization and a lopsided coverage of entertainment over the 'real issues' plaguing the majority of poor and marginalized people:

> Entertainment got 9 times the coverage that health, education, labour, agriculture and environment together got.... The Roman Emperors used to say 'If you cannot give the people bread give them circuses'. This is precisely the approach of the Indian establishment, duly supported by our media. Keep the people involved in cricket so that they forget their social and economic plight. (The Hindu 2011)

The shift from development driven programming in the days of public broadcasting to private profit-driven coverage has had a lasting impact on health coverage in the media where 'the inordinate amount of media attention attracted to a few select medical cases contrasts sharply with the media's relative neglect of other health-related events and issues within the country' (Joseph 2007). Joseph also believes that health coverage is 'susceptible to manipulation that makes a mockery of the ethics of both the media and the medical profession' (ibid.). Private TV channels and newspapers have steered clear of reporting on public health, focussing instead on replicating generic press releases from organizations, pharmaceutical representatives, lobbyists, and health institutions, or reprinting articles from international news agencies and foreign journals (Sosa et al. 2009). Most newspapers and TV channels do not have dedicated health reporters.

For the most part H1N1 stories in newspapers and television did not show proof that government assertions were being independently verified or refuted when there was contrary evidence. There were rare 'investigations' of local scams that sold masks worth Rs 10 for hundreds of rupees. However, the dominant tendency was to reprint the same Press Trust of India (PTI) report or replicate a health official's statement across mainstream channels and newspapers, resulting in the amplification of rather insignificant messages into something far more sensational. Most reporters who covered H1N1 were political reporters or local bureau chiefs who wore grim expressions and face masks and interviewed scared people lining up to get tested. The Bangalore bureau chief of a national TV channel said:

> I usually report on state politics, and I was being honest when I wore a mask when I reported on H1N1 because I was afraid and thought it was a legitimate fear to convey to the public. The government never told us what precautions journalists had to take covering these issues or how we should cover health emergencies'. (personal communication, 2009)

Tabloid and local cable channel coverage were more sensational and created bigger frenzies over testing and medication shortages since the stories they reported on *directly* impacted the lives of their viewership: 'The stories were self-sustaining. Every local doctor, shopkeeper, hospital nurse, and municipal ward officer wanted to participate in the H1N1 story. We kept getting calls from godmen and healers asking to come on the channel because they wanted to create awareness', said a TV9 cable reporter from Bangalore (personal communication, 2009).

When asked about what role journalists need to play during a health crisis, many of those spoken to felt that it was the job of the government to deal with health, education, and other development issues and the journalist's role was to report in an 'unbiased' manner without delving into the complicated task of interpreting the event since they did not believe they had the medical knowledge. Almost all of them acknowledged that training journalists on a regular basis to handle potential health disasters would have helped them ask the right questions.

TOWARDS A NEW PARADIGM

A study of how H1N1 was communicated reveals a complicated and messy web of political opportunism and media apathy which clouds the overall sordid state of healthcare systems in India. There is little doubt that the messages put out by political communicators caused a lot of the frenzy and panic. The government did little to educate the public either about H1N1 or about the choices and decisions they had to make during a health crisis. Their messages were generalized, simplistic, and overconfident. The media reported these simplistic messages without any critical inquiry or investigation of the claims. They contributed even less to the public understanding of the risk.

In the current scenario, where both the government and media are not perceived as particularly trustworthy and there are few health experts in the public domain, it would be worthwhile considering an alternative inclusive approach to risk communication. Articulate individuals from diverse socioeconomic backgrounds (expert and non-expert from different fields), for example, can be socially networked, trained, and given responsibilities across the country to report and communicate risks within their communities during a health crisis.

But what guidelines could we provide these people? Global guidelines do not address challenges faced by communicators in developing country settings. Is it even possible for communicators to articulate both pandemic-related uncertainty as well as the inability of public health systems to withstand a massive epidemic in a country like India without creating fear? How can communicators be transparent and honest if there is every chance of becoming a political scapegoat? How do you create risk messages for differently literate groups speaking multiple languages? To even begin to answer these questions we need to step out of the Western-oriented niche of risk communication scholarship and move towards a more detailed and nuanced understanding of how political economy and health processes converge with the communication and media landscape in India. We need to know how communication and media flows impact various audiences in India in different cultural, economic, linguistic, and social contexts. We need reliable data about the successes and, more importantly, the failures of government health communication programmes. Without locally grounded research and a contextual typology and vocabulary to articulate and address communication issues (especially health related) in India, we will continue to witness similar epidemics of fear repeat themselves with crippling consequences on the management of future eventualities.

BIBLIOGRAPHY

Arnold, D. (2000). *Science, Technology, and Medicine in Colonial India*, Part 3, Vol. 5. Cambridge: Cambridge University Press.

Balarajan, Y., S. Selvaraj, and S.V. Subramanian (2011). 'Health Care and Equity in India' in 'India: Towards Universal Health Coverage', a series of papers, *The Lancet*, pp. 377; 505–15.

Beck, U. (2006). 'Living in the World Risk Society', *Economy and Society*, 35(3): 329–34.

Clench J., A. Lazzeri, and N. Syson (2009). 'Swine Flu Lines are Flooded With Calls', *The Sun*, available at: http://www.thesun.co.uk/sol/homepage/news/2532313/Concern-rises-after-healthy-girl-Chloe-Buckley-6-killed-by-swine-flu.html, last accessed on 1 February 2012.

Coombs, W.T., and S.J. Holladay (2001). 'An Extended Examination of the Crisis Situations: A Fusion of the Relational Management and Symbolic Approaches', *Journal of Public Relations Research*, 13(4): 321–40.

Coppola, D.P. (2011). *Introduction to International Disaster Management*. Amsterdam: Elsevier.

Covello, V.T., D. von Winterfeldt, and P. Slovic (1986), 'Risk Communication: A Review of the Literature', *Risk Communication*, 3: 171–82.

Deccan Herald (2011). '25% Children Affected by Japanese Encephalitis Die: Govt.', *Deccan Herald*, 29 December 2011.

Douglas, M. (2002) [1985]. *Risk Acceptability According to the Social Sciences*. New York: Sage.

Economic Times Agencies (2009). 'H1N1: When Will The States Wake Up?', *Economic Times*, 22 August.

Edelman (2011). 'Insights from India', *Edelman*, available at http://www.youtube.com/watch?v=oHWZSagcQCI, last accessed on 1 February 2012.

Express News Service (2009). 'Maharashtra Invokes Epidemic Diseases Act', *Express News Service*, 5 August.

Fischhoff, B., S. Lichtenstein, P. Slovic, S.L. Derby, and R.L. Keeney (1981). *Acceptable Risk*. New York: Cambridge University Press.

Frewer, L., S. Miles, and R. Marsh (2002). 'The Media and Genetically Modified Foods: Evidence in Support of Social Amplification of Risk', *Risk Analysis*, 22: 701–11.

Frewer L. (2004). 'The Public and Effective Risk Communication', *Toxicology Letters*, 1 April, 149(1–3): 391–7.

Frontline (2011). 'Apathy Virus', *Frontline Magazine*, November, 28(23): 5–18.

Garrett, L. (2000). *Betrayal of Trust: The Collapse of Global Public Health*. New York: Hyperion, p. 754.

Gunaratne, A. (2010). 'De-Westernising Communication/Social Science Research: Opportunities and Limitations', *Media, Culture and Society*, 32: 473.

The Hindu (2009). 'A (H1N1): 60 Private Hospitals Asked To Start Screening People', *The Hindu*, 15 August.

Hindustan Times (2009a). 'We Will Sue The Hospital: Swine Flu Victim's Family', *Hindustan Times*, 4 August.

——— (2009b). 'Azad Sorry for Rida Remark'. *Hindustan Times*, 10 August.

Hunter, P.R., and L. Fewtrell (2001). 'Acceptable Risk', in L. Fewtrell and J. Bartram (eds), *Water Quality: Guidelines, Standards and Health. Assessment of Risk and Risk Management for Water Related Infectious Disease*. London: IWA Publishing, pp. 207–27.

India Today (2009). 'Swine Flu Under Control: Azad', *India Today*, 18 June.

Indian Express (2009). 'Govt Allays Fear of Swine Flu in India', *Indian Express*, 30 April.

Integrated Disease Surveillance Project (IDSP) (2010). *Epidemiological Situation of Communicable Diseases in Kerala (2006–2010)*, Directorate of Health Services, Government of Kerala, available at http://dhs.kerala.gov.in/docs/part1.pdf, last accessed on 5 January 2012.

John, T. Jacob (2009). 'India's Amateur Handling of The H1N1 Pandemic', available at http://infochangeindia.org/public-health/analysis/indias-amateur-handling-of-the-h1n1-pandemic.html, last accessed on 10 November 2013.

John, T.J., and J. Muliyil (2009). 'Editorial: Pandemic Influenza Exposes Gaps In India's Health System', *Indian J Med Res*, 130, August 2009, pp 101–4.

Joseph, A. (2007). 'Media and Health: Who Will Heal Who?', 7 December, India Together, available at http://www.indiatogether.org/2007/dec/ajo-medhealth.htm, accessed on 1 February 2012.

Kant and Krishnan (2010). 'Information and Communication Technology In Disease Surveillance, India: A Case Study', *BMC Public Health* 2010, Vol. 10, Suppl 1, pp.: S11.

Kasperson, R.E., O. Renn, P. Slovic, H. Brown, J. Emel, R. Goble, J.X. Kasperson, and S. Ratick (1988). 'The Social Amplification of Risk: A Conceptual Framework', *Risk Analysis*, June, 8(2): 177–87.

Kasperson, R.E. (1992). 'The Social Amplification of Risk: Progress in Developing an Integrative Framework of Risk', in S. Krimsky and D. Golding (eds), *Social theories of Risk*. New York: Praeger, pp. 153–78.

Katju, M. (2011). 'Justice Markandey Katju on the Role of Media in India'. *The Hindu*, 5 November.

Kohli-Khandekar, Vanita (2010). Appendix II, *The Indian Media Business*, 3rd edition. New Delhi: SAGE Publications.

Kothari, B. (2008). 'Let a Billion Readers Bloom: Same Language Subtitling (SLS) on Television For Mass Literacy', *International Review of Education*, 54: 773–8.

Lasswell, Harold (1948). 'The Structure and Function of Communication in Society', in Lyman Bryson (ed.), *The Communication of Ideas*. New York: Harper and Row.

Leiss, W. (1996). 'Three Phases in the Evolution of Risk Communication Practice', *Annals of the American Academy of Political and Social Science*, 545(1): 85–94.

Löfstedt, R.E. (2009). *Risk Management in Post-trust Societies*. London: Earthscan.

——— (2010). 'Risk Communication Guidelines for Europe: A modest proposition', *Journal of Risk Research*, 13: 1, 87–109.

Mascarenhas, A. (2011). '7 mn Unused Doses of H1N1 Vaccine to be Destroyed', *Indian Express*, available at http://www.indianexpress.com/news/7-mn-unused-doses-of-h1n1-vaccine-to-be-dest/803718/, last accessed on 15 January 2012.

McKinsey Global Institute (MGI) (2007). *The 'Bird of Gold': The Rise of the Indian Consumer Market*. McKinsey and Company, available at http://www.mckinsey.com/insights/asia-pacific/the_bird_of_gold, last accessed on 15 November 2013.

McQuail, D. (2005). 'Communication Theory and the Western Bias'. In Walter de Gruyter (ed.), *Read the Cultural Other: Forms of Otherness In The Discourses of Hong Kong's Decolonization*. Berlin: Walter de Gruyter GmbH and Co. KG.

Ministry of Health and Family Welfare (MoHFW) (2009a). Pandemic Response and Preparedness Plan, available at http://mohfw-h1n1.nic.in/documents/PDF/Preparedness%20and%20Response%20India%20not%20Affected.pdf, last accessed on 20 November 2010.

——— (2009b). *Health Alert: Pandemic Influenza A H1N1*. New Delhi: Government of India, available at http://mohfw-h1n1.nic.in/documents/PDF/do%27s%20n%20-dont%27s.pdf, last accessed on 18 November 2009.

——— (2009c). 'Print Ad for Vulnerable Groups', available at http://mohfw-h1n1.nic.in/link8.html, accessed on 1 February 2012.

——— (2010a). 'Situational Update for May 2010', available at http://mohfwh1n1.nic.in/documents/PDF/SituationalUpdatesArchives/may2010/Situational%20Updates%20on%2011.05.2010.pdf, last accessed on 1 February 2011.

——— (2010b). 'Annual Report to the People on Health (2010)', available at http://mohfw.nic.in/WriteReadData/l892s/9457038092AnnualReporthealth.pdf, last accessed on 10 October 2011.

Ministry of Information and Broadcasting (2009). 'Year-end-Review 2009: Ministry of Information and Broadcasting Highlights'.

Ministry of Statistics and Programmer Implementation (MOSPI) (2005). *Millennium Development Goals India Country Report 2005*, Government of India, available at: http://www.unicef.org/india/ssd04_2005_final.pdf. last accessed on 2 March 2014.

Mudra Group (2009). 'UNICEF Flu Ad (Bus)', available at http://www.youtube.com/watch?v=0xGPHw-_oXA, last accessed on 1 February 2012.

Mukherjee, P., Poh Lian Lim, Angela Chow, Timothy Barkham, Eillyne Seow, Mar Kyaw Win, Arlene Chua, Yee Sin Leo, and Mark I-Cheng Chen (2010). 'Epidemiology of Travel-associated Pandemic (H1N1) 2009 Infection in 116 Patients, Singapore'. *Emerging Infectious Diseases*, January, 16(1).

Nagral, S. (2003). 'Editorial: SARS: Infectious Diseases, Public Health and Medical Ethics', *Issues Med Ethics*, Jul–Sep, 11(3).

National AIDS Control Organisation (NACO) (2008). 'About the 360 degree Surround BULADI Campaign', available at http://www.nacoonline.org/upload/Publication/IEC%20&%20Mainstreaming/About%20the%20The%20360%20degree%20surround%20BULADI%20Campaign.pdf, last accessed on 1 February 2012.

NDTV (2009). 'H1N1 Patient Speaks to NDTV', *NDTV*, available at http://www.youtube.com/watch?v=cONH_rhQt3E&feature=related, last accessed on 15 November 2013.

Neogi, S. (2007.) 'India, World Diabetes Capital', *Hindustan Times*, 3 September.

News 9 (2009). 'Just for Laughs', a video on Aiyoo Perumale, available at http://www.youtube.com/watch?v=Aim6_lZQi4g, last accessed on 1 February 2012.

Office of the Registrar of Newspapers India (2010). *Press in India Highlights for 2010–2011*, available at rni.nic.in, last accessed on 1 February 2012.

O'Neill, O. (2002). 'A Question of Trust', *BBC Reith Lectures*, available at http://www.bbc.co.uk/radio4/reith2002/, last accessed on 15 November 2013.

Pandey, Vineeta (2009). 'No Morning Assembly Teacher to Check Student for Flu, New Guidelines', *DNA*, 17 August.

Petts, J., T. Horlick-Jones, and G. Murdock (2001). *Social Amplification of Risk: The Media and the Public*. Contract Research Report 329/2001. Sudbury: HSE Book.

Phadke, A. (2009). 'Response to an Epidemic of Novel H1N1 Flu in Pune: Need for Introspection', *Indian Journal of Medical Ethics*, October–December, 6(1), available at http://www.ijme.in/174ed176.html, last accessed on 1 February 2012.

Pidgeon, N., R.E. Kasperson, and P. Slovic (eds). (2003). *The Social Amplification of Risk*. Cambridge: Cambridge University Press, p. 448.

Poortinga and Pidgeon (2003). 'Exploring the Dimensionality of Trust in Risk Regulation', *Risk Analysis*, October, 23(5): 961–72.

Press Trust of India (PTI) (2009a) No Suspected Cases of Swine Flu in India, *Outlook* April 30th 2009, accessed http://news.outlookindia.com/items. aspx?artid=659207, last accessed on.

———— (2009b). 'Azad Slams States over H1N1, Gujarat Minister Takes Him On', 21 August.

———— (2011a). '62.4 Million People Afflicted with Diabetes in India', *DNA*, 29 September.

———— (2011b). *LDF Walkout over H1N1 Fever Issue*. 11 July.

Pritchett, L. (2009). 'Is India a Flailing State?: Detours on the Four Lane Highway to Modernization'. HKS Faculty Research Working Paper Series RWP09-013, John F. Kennedy School of Government, Harvard University.

Renn, O. and D. Levine (1991). 'Credibility and Trust in Risk Communication', in R.E. Kasperson and P.J.M. Stallen (eds), *Communicating Risks to the Public*, pp. 175–218. Dordrecht: Kluwer.

Ropeik, D. (2000). 'Let's Get Real About Risk', *The Washington Post*, 6 August.

Sandman, P.M. (1993). *Responding to Community Outrage: Strategies for Effective Risk Communication, American Industrial Hygiene Association*. Fairfax, VA: American Industrial Hygiene Association, available at http://www.psandman. com/book.htm, last accessed on 10 November 2013.

Sandman P., and J. Lanard (2005). 'Superb Flu Pandemic Risk Communication: A Role Model from Australia', available at http://www.psandman.com/ col/abbott.htm, last accessed on 1 February.

———— (2009). 'Containment as Signal: Swine Flu Risk Miscommunication', available at http://www.psandman.com/col/swineflu2.htm, last accessed on 1 February 2012.

———— (2011). 'Over-Reassuring Thai Crisis Communication about the Great Flood: When "Restoring Trust" Is Too Much to Expect', available at http://www.psandman.com/col/Thai-flood.htm, last accessed on 1 February 2012.

Sandman, P. M., and Neil D. Weinstein (2002). "The Precaution Adoption Process Model and Its Application", in Ralph J. DiClemente, Richard A. Crosby, and Michelle C. Kegler (eds), *Emerging Theories in Health Promotion Practice and Research*, pp. 16–39. San Francisco: Jossey-Bass.

Sawant, P. B. (1998). 'Indian Press During the Last 50 Years', paper presented at International Conference of World Association of Press Councils, 4–5 April, New Delhi.

Shah, G. (1997). *Public Health and Urban Development: The Plague in Surat*. New Delhi: Sage Publications, p. 317.

Singh, S. (2003). 'SARS in India', in Chronology, *Outlook*, available at http://www.outlookindia.com/article.aspx?219990, last accessed on 1 February 2012.

Slovic, P. (1999). 'Trust, Emotion, Sex, Politics, and Science: Surveying the Risk-assessment Battlefield. *Risk Analysis*, 19(4): 689–701.

Slovic, P., B. Fishhoff, and S. Lichtenstein (1980). 'Facts and Fears: Understanding Perceived Risk', in W.A. Albers, (ed.), *Societal Risk Assessment: How Safe Is Safe Enough?*. New York: Plenum Press.

Sosa, Anibal de J., Denis K. Byarugaba, Carlos F. Amabile-Cuevas, and Iruka N. Okeke (2009). *Antimicrobial Resistance in Developing Countries*. New York: Springer.

Strong, P. (1990). 'Epidemic Psychology: A Model', *Sociology of Health & Illness*, 12(3), available at http://onlinelibrary.wiley.com/doi/10.1111/1467-9566.ep11347150/pdf, last accessed on 1 February 2012.

Telecom Regulatory Authority of India (TRAI) (2012). 'Highlights of Telecom Subscription Data', available at http://www.trai.gov.in/WriteReadData/trai/upload/PressReleases/869/PR-Dec-11.pdf, last accessed on 10 February 2012.

Thussu, D.K. (1999). *Privatizing the Airwaves: The Impact of Globalization on Broadcasting In India. Media, Culture and Society*, Vol. 21. London and New Delhi: Sage Publications and Thousand Oaks.

——— (2009). *Internationalizing Media Studies*, 1st edition. New York: Routledge.

TII-CMS India Corruption Study (2007). Centre for Media Studies and Transparency International, India, available at: http://www.cmsindia.org/highlights.pdf, accessed on 1 February 2012.

Times of India (TOI) (2009a). 'Health Minister Wants Exit Screening To Tackle H1N1 Flu', *The Times of India*, 10 June.

——— (2009b). '33% Indians Likely to Get H1N1: Azad', 10 August.

——— (2009c). 'TN Lays Down Guidelines to Curb H1N1 Spread', 7 August, available at http://articles.timesofindia.indiatimes.com/2009-08-07/chennai/28200879_1_private-hospitals-h1n1-fresh-guidelines, last accessed on 10 February 2011.

Tversky, A., and D. Kahneman (1974). 'Judgment Under Uncertainty: Heuristics and Biases', *Science*, New Series, 185(4157): 1124–31.

UNESCO (2010). 'Regional Overview: South and West Asia', *Education for All Global Monitoring Report*, available at http://unesdoc.unesco.org/images/0018/001865/186527E.pdf, last accessed on 1 February 2012.

UNICEF (2010). 'India Communication Update', Vol. 1, March, available at http://www.unicef.org/india/ICU_March_2010_1g.pdf, last accessed on 1 February 2012.

Vaishnav, M. (2011). 'Corruption in India's Health Sector: Let's Look at the Bigger Picture', Global Health Policy Blog, Centre for Global Development, available at: http://blogs.cgdev.org/globalhealth/2011/09/corruption-in-india%E2%80%99s-health-sector-let%E2%80%99s-look-at-the-bigger-picture.php, last accessed on 10 January 2012.

Vlek, C., and P. Stallen (1981). 'Risk Perception in the Small and in the Large', *Organizational Behavior and Human Performance*, 28: 235–71.

Weyman, A.K., and C.J. Kelly (1999). *Risk Perception and Risk Communication: A Review of Literature*. Sudbury, UK: HSE books.

World Bank (2008). 'Government of India and World Bank Group Join Forces to Stamp Out Corruption in Health Sector Projects', World Bank Press Release, available at http://go.worldbank.org/YVLEFEQKZ0, last accessed on 1 February 2012.

World Health Organization (WHO) (2009). 'Statement to the Press by WHO Director-General Dr Margaret Chan', 11 June, available at http://www.who.int/mediacentre/news/statements/2009/h1n1_pandemic_phase6_20090611/en/index.html, last accessed on 1 January 2011.

Zee News (2009). 'Yoga Can Cure Swine Flu: Baba Ramdev', *Zee News*, 11 August 2009.

8

SEMA K. SGAIER

A Business Management Framework for Addressing Public Health Risk

The Avahan Experience in Scaling-up HIV Prevention in India

In 2002, studies modelled on the India AIDS epidemic predicted a grim future (Nagelkerke et al. 2002). The studies projected that more than 20 million people would be living with Human Immunodeficiency Virus/Acquired Immune Deficiency Syndrome (HIV/AIDS) by 2010, which would place India as one of the countries most affected by the HIV/AIDS epidemic. An explosive AIDS epidemic on the horizon needed immediate attention, as it could potentially erase India's development gains, just as India was experiencing significant economic growth.

The national response to the HIV/AIDS epidemic until the early 2000s, through the National AIDS Control Programme (NACP) Phase I (NACP-I; 1992–5) and Phase II (NACP-II; 2000–5), focused on four key areas (Claeson and Alexander 2008). These included—raising awareness among the general population through information, education, and communication (such as mass media campaigns); piloting prevention programmes with individuals at the highest risk (such as sex workers);

controlling sexually transmitted infections through treatment in sexually transmitted disease (STD) clinics; and ensuring that all blood transfusions were infection free. Development partners, such as the United States Agency for International Development (USAID) with its AIDS Prevention and Control Programme (APAC) in Tamil Nadu, were also breaking ground in terms of designing interventions for sex workers and collecting data to better understand the nature and magnitude of the problem (APAC 2002).

The Indian epidemic was found to be a 'concentrated' epidemic, similar to others in Asia. Most infections were concentrated in discrete populations who very often engaged in high-risk behaviours such as sharing needles and syringes when injecting drugs, or having multiple sexual partners without the use of protective condoms. The high-risk group (HRG) populations in India included female sex workers (FSWs), men who have sex with men (MSM) and injecting drug users (IDUs). Therefore, an effective response to the epidemic in India needed to ensure that every high-risk individual had access to prevention services (such as condoms, clinical services to treat STD, HIV testing, and treatment) and had the ability to engage in safe behaviours. These populations needed to be at the 'centre' of the policy dialogue in India. Despite the serious threat, there was insufficient political commitment and little acknowledgment of the magnitude of the problem. Crucially, the government failed to adopt an evidence-based approach and respond at an appropriate scale. The government spent most of its resources on large mass media campaigns that targeted the general population rather than supporting prevention programmes with HRGs and taking these to scale across the country.

India needed to bolster its response to the escalating HIV epidemic; in essence, it needed a 'game-changing' approach. The Bill and Melinda Gates Foundation understood that the risk-management approach needed to be re-framed and built on five core principles: focus, innovation, evidence, scale, and sustainability. These are the same principles that underpin any successful business model. In order to win consumers and change their patterns of behaviour, businesses need to first analyse the demand for their product and on that basis design a strategy for supplying goods or services. Similarly the factors that fuelled the HIV epidemic needed to be comprehensively addressed and an appropriate, data-driven and sustainable response developed so that such high-risk behaviour could be changed. The foundation adopted a 'Business Management Framework' and thus *re-defined* the approach to public health risk management. This chapter describes this framework and also discusses the results and challenges of the Avahan programme, drawing lessons from this experience for public health programming.

AVAHAN PROGRAMME AND ITS USP

In 2003, the Bill and Melinda Gates Foundation launched Avahan ('a call to action' in Sanskrit), a large-scale HIV/AIDS prevention programme in India. Unlike previous government initiatives, this programme chose to focus all of its efforts on stopping infections at the source of the transmission chain of HIV. It did this by scaling and saturating prevention programmes that targeted HRGs (FSWs, MSM, and IDUs) and their sexual partners. Avahan is a 10-year programme divided into two phases (Avahan 2008). In Phase I (2003–9), Avahan's goal was to scale up a prevention programme in the most affected geographies to ensure that it had an impact on the epidemic. In Phase II (2009–13), which was ongoing at the time of writing Avahan's goal has been to ensure that its impact is sustained over the long term by transferring the programme to the Government of India and the communities it serves. In this phase the foundation also focuses on disseminating programme lessons within and outside India to inform other HIV prevention projects.

Avahan entered the HIV/AIDS response arena in India with a *complete sense of urgency and the approach of doing business as 'unusual'.* Key questions that Avahan tried to address included:

- Has the response to date been effective, and if not, why;
- Which game-changing choices would turn the tide of the HIV/AIDS epidemic in India;
- What delivery strategies should be undertaken to deliver these choices in the most effective and efficient manner; and
- How the impact of the programme would be sustained?

In light of these questions, the programme made *key strategic choices* that were novel at the time in the field of public health. The programme invested a significant sum in prevention of the Indian epidemic at a time when many agencies were pushing for universal coverage of treatment and when there were little data on the impact of prevention programmes.

It also chose to deliver a comprehensive package of services at scale, in a short time period. The idea of saturating coverage of HRGs within three years of the programme's launch, in a country where most of the target groups were hidden, dispersed, and mobile was seen as nearly impossible. Most importantly, the programme acknowledged that the HRG communities had to be equal partners and be empowered in order to win the war on HIV/AIDS. In an environment where FSWs, MSM, and IDUs were highly stigmatized, Avahan took on the challenge of fostering the formation and building the capacity of hundreds of community-based organizations (CBOs). The guiding rationale for this approach was that empowered and well-organized HRG communities would be able to engage in safe behaviours, become partners in the delivery of the response, and advocate for their needs with various stakeholders (such as local and national government). Given the government's focus on the general population and the sense of urgency at the time the programme started, Avahan chose to directly fund non-governmental organizations (NGOs) rather than working through the government system to scale the prevention programmes.

The Avahan programme has had a *significant impact* on the landscape of HIV/AIDS prevention in India (Ng et al. 2011; Ramesh et al. 2010; Lipovsek et al. 2010; Moses et al. 2008). The programme has shared its results, lessons, tools, and approaches with the government and demonstrated that the rapid scale-up of prevention programmes with HRGs in India is both possible and effective. The National AIDS Control Organization (NACO) also gained momentum from 2007, and, in parallel, scaled up its prevention response through the third phase of the national response (NACP-III; 2007–13). This was largely the result of change in political leadership and a shift towards evidence based programming. Today, India is seen as a global success story of how an evidence-based and scaled-up prevention strategy can work (Sgaier et al. 2012). The collective efforts of both the government and development partners have shown encouraging results. It was predicted that more than 20 million would be living with HIV; instead, it is now estimated that 2.4 million people are affected (UNAIDS 2010; NACO 2010a). Furthermore, there has been a decline in both the prevalence of HIV and incidence of new infections (Arora et al. 2008; NACO 2010b).

The Avahan programme is also *now influencing other prevention approaches globally* and has become a global model for prevention programmes (Rau 2011). For example, Avahan has shared its lessons with Thailand, Ethiopia and Cote d'Ivoire, among others, and is working closely with both the governments of Kenya and South Africa to scale their preventions efforts. Many of the Avahan innovations, such as intensive data-driven techno-managerial support, are also being adapted to prevention programmes with HRGs in Kenya, for example.

The Avahan programme undertook a management-centric approach to scale up delivery of prevention services through the development of a 'business management framework' (Figure 8.1). It drew lessons from how a large-scale service or retail company, for example, would scale-up its services across India. Many of the challenges faced in designing and delivering a scaled public health programme are similar to those dealt with by commercial enterprises on a daily basis. For example, the sheer scale of the initiative involved targeting 300,000 HRGs and close to 5 million men across more than 600 towns in 83 districts, and simultaneously rolling out within two to three years all the necessary infrastructure and services.

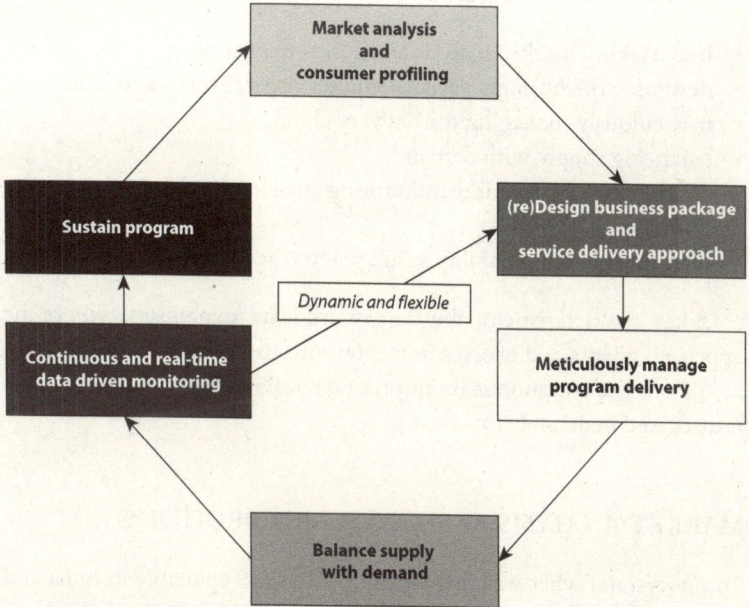

FIGURE 8.1   Avahan's Business Management Framework for Managing Public Health Risk

The first step in designing an effective programme is to clearly identify the desired beneficiaries and obtain data on their current health-seeking behaviours. This is no different from the market segmentation and consumer profiling conducted by businesses to understand their target consumers. Similarly, the questions considered while rolling out health infrastructure are similar to those faced by businesses setting up retail outlets. Which physical location would be most convenient for the beneficiary/consumer to access services? How can we build trust in the service we are providing so the beneficiary/consumer will access the service repeatedly? Finally, the programme worked to establish the right management structures and hire the right talent with expertise in management needed to run a large-scale enterprise. The Avahan team brought business management expertise that was key in running such a large-scale public health programme. This focus on in sourcing management skills was novel at the time in a public health sector dominated by health experts.

In summary, the key components of the Avahan business management framework are (Figure 8.1):

- undertaking market analysis and consumer profiling;
- designing the business package and service delivery approach;
- meticulously managing the delivery chain;
- balancing supply with demand;
- continuous and real-time monitoring at all levels of the management chain; and,
- integrating a sustainability strategy into the design.

A key characteristic of the framework is its 'dynamism,' where the approach adapts and evolves in response to the evidence that is generated from the continuous monitoring data. Each of these components is discussed in detail below.

MARKET ANALYSIS AND CONSUMER PROFILING

To understand what was driving the HIV/AIDS epidemic in India and the effectiveness of the current response, data were required to inform each stage of planning, design, and implementation. Indeed, data-driven decision-making is a core Avahan principle.

Although data was limited at the time, the Avahan design team first conducted a situational assessment of the epidemic. Data from national surveillance and other sources indicated three key aspects of the Indian HIV epidemic (NACO 2003). First, the HIV epidemic was a concentrated one—the groups at greatest risk of HIV were the worst affected. These included FSWs and their clients, MSM, and IDUs. Second, the epidemic was also concentrated geographically, with 70 per cent of infections found across six states (Andhra Pradesh, Tamil Nadu, Karnataka, Maharashtra, Manipur, and Nagaland) (Figure 8.2). Finally, the epidemic was driven by different factors in these six states—in the four southern states of Andhra Pradesh, Maharashtra, Tamil Nadu, and Karnataka, the HIV epidemic was driven by sexual transmission; whereas, in the north-eastern states of Manipur and Nagaland, the use of injecting drug fuelled the epidemic.

Given the important role of HRGs in the India epidemic, the team next sought to understand the extent and coverage of the existing prevention response among these groups in the six high prevalence states. Again, data was very limited. The team therefore conducted extensive visits to each of the states to meet with various experts and

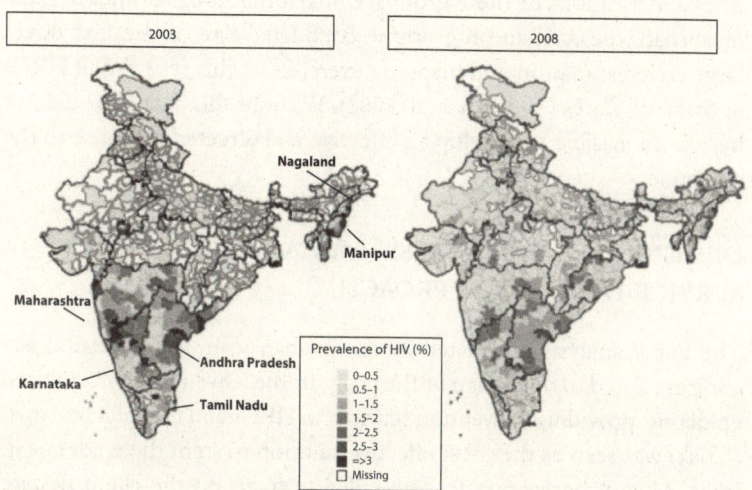

FIGURE 8.2   Prevalence of HIV among Pregnant Women
Source: NACO HIV Sentinel Surveillance.

agencies and gather ground level intelligence. It was immediately clear that there was a huge gap in coverage of HRGs with prevention services (Avahan 2008). While prevention programmes with FSWs were ongoing in the large cities, such as Bangalore, Mumbai, and Chennai, these programmes reached out to only a small fraction of the total FSWs as they were primarily focused in major metropolitans. Most of the so-called 'tier two' cities were characterized by a significant gap in coverage, due to two main reasons. Firstly, no one had conducted comprehensive studies to directly estimate the number of HRGs (such as sex workers) in each of the cities across the six states. The previously used methods provided only rough estimates of the potential size of the population. While some states had better data than others, the data did not provide any accurate details on the relative size of the populations at micro-geographic levels, such as by city. Secondly, little data was available on the nature of the high-risk behaviours, such as, what was the nature of the sex work and the networks within which these individuals operated? Who were their commercial partners? This missing information led to gaps in the reach of prevention programmes, where only some of the visible HRGs, and those in the major cities, were receiving services. Therefore Avahan meticulously mapped the high-risk individuals in these states, describing the numbers, characteristics and locations of these groups. Unlike other programmes in India or abroad, the Avahan programme conducted one of the first direct large-scale estimation and mapping exercises of this type for all HRGs in these six states (Vadivoo et al. 2008). Without this data it would not have been feasible to develop an effective and targeted response to the epidemic.

DESIGNING THE 'BUSINESS' PACKAGE AND SERVICE DELIVERY APPROACH

The initial analysis conducted by the Avahan team led to several key choices related to the design of the programme. Given the concentrated epidemic, providing prevention services to HRGs and their clients (men at risk) was seen as the most effective solution to stem the epidemic in India. Most programmes to date failed to focus on the client despite the fact it was an epidemiologically important population to work with

(Piot 2010). While a few programmes funded by other donors and piloted by government were in operation, these were not implemented at scale, thereby limiting impact (Laga et al. 2010). The programme also decided to focus on the geographies most affected by HIV (the six high prevalence states) rather than cover the whole of India. These six states alone accounted for more than 70 per cent of the infections in the country and hence limiting the coverage to these states would not only be operationally more feasible but also cost-effective. Given that a proven solution from other Asian countries (Commission on AIDS in Asia 2008), such as Thailand (Hanenberg et al. 1994) and India (Jana et al. 1998), for addressing concentrated epidemics was available, the programme decided to scale up a known package of solutions. This package included the distribution of commodities (condoms and sterile injection material), clinical services for the treatment of STD, outreach and behaviour change communication, crisis response systems, linkages to care and treatment, and community mobilization. For high-risk men, two separate programmes were started: a truckers programme along the major trans shipment routes of India and a 'men at risk' programme (NACO 2003).

In addition to key decisions on whom to target and what to implement, the programme also had to determine how to deliver the package of services. Typically, programmes would first implement a small-scale version (pilot) in a defined geography (such as a handful of districts) to determine its effectiveness. Once proven, the programme would then be replicated in other geographies. While this was the recommended approach by many experts in the field, this approach would be very time consuming and would not halt the epidemic quickly. Given the need to move with speed, the programme decided to take an approach of simultaneously scaling up services in all of its target geographies. Over the next three years, Avahan rapidly scaled the provision of services to close to 300,000 HRGs and to over five million men at risk simultaneously in more than 600 towns in 82 districts in six states (Figure 8.3). While the prevention package Avahan was providing was not new, the sheer scale of response and speed of rollout was. The programme concentrated on reaching at least 80 per cent of the defined target population in the intervention area—and it aspired to reach this goal within the first three years of operation (Figure 8.4).

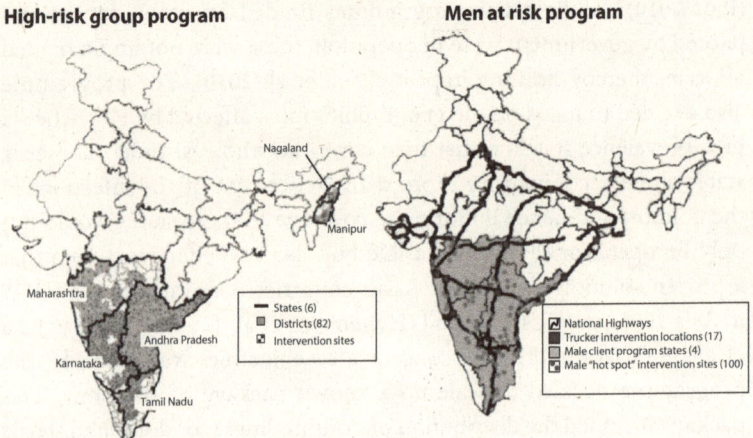

High-risk group program

Nagaland

Manipur

Maharashtra

Andhra Pradesh

Karnataka

Tamil Nadu

- States (6)
- Districts (82)
- Intervention sites

Men at risk program

- National Highways
- Trucker intervention locations (17)
- Male client program states (4)
- Male "hot spot" intervention sites (100)

FIGURE 8.3   The Avahan Implementation Landscape
Source: Avahan (2008).

MANAGING THE DELIVERY CHAIN: PEOPLE, PROCESSES, AND STRUCTURES

To effectively manage such a large-scale programme, Avahan developed a multi-tiered network of partner agencies. The first tier consisted of agencies that directly received grants from the foundation and took on the responsibility of overseeing a state or part of a state (state lead partner). These first-tier agencies were often large, well-established and seasoned NGOs, such as Family Health International or the Hindustan Latex Family Planning Promotion Trust (HLFPPT), or universities that had the capacity and experience of managing programmes. These in turn contracted local NGOs to implement the programmes. The local and smaller NGOs had a good understanding of local challenges, were well integrated into the district machinery, and close to the recipients of the services. The in-country office of the Bill and Melinda Gates Foundation (Avahan programme) closely managed the network. To standardize the delivery of services across the six states, the programme also developed a Common Minimum Programme, a set of guidelines on how to implement each element of the Avahan package (Avahan 2010a). While the guidelines provided a framework for the partners to deliver the services, it also allowed them the flexibility to innovate in

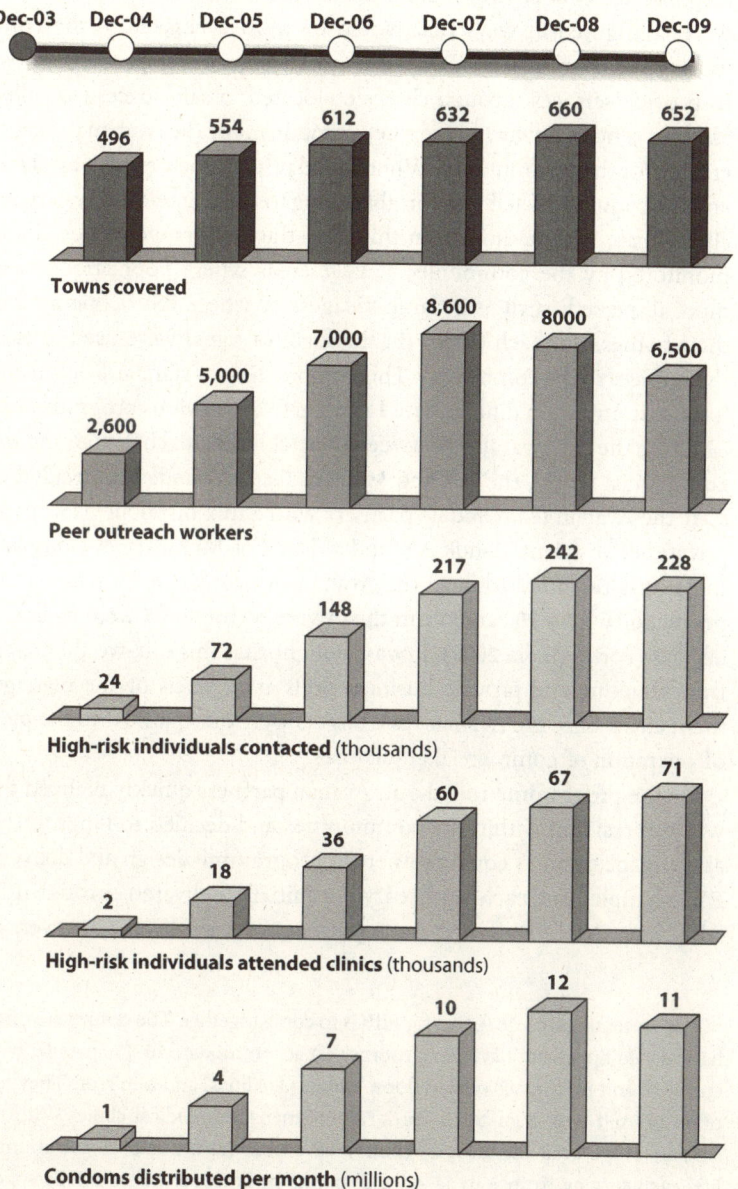

FIGURE 8.4   Avahan Scale Results
Source: Avahan (2008).

response to local environmental needs. For example, clinical services were configured in ways that would be most accessible to the community (Avahan 2010b). For large urban epicentres, partners chose to provide services through clinics co-located in safe spaces (so called 'drop-in centres',[1] which were a key component of the Avahan package) created for the communities. Where good private doctors were available and the community felt comfortable going to them, a referral system for clinical care was developed. In this case, the doctors were chosen and monitored by the community. Finally, areas where populations were more dispersed (such as in large villages) or where FSWs operated in their homes, outreach clinics (in the form of vans) were used to take the services to the community. This combination of standardization and local customization differentiated Avahan from previous programmes.

Given the close parallels between this public health challenge and the commercial world, the Bill and Melinda Gates Foundation decided to staff the Avahan team and its partners with a mix of public health and private sector talent. Ashok Alexander, Head of McKinsey & Company India, was recruited to head the Avahan. Ashok formed a team of 15 people, of whom 10 came from the private sector and 5 were technical experts (Forbes India 2009). It was thought that this mix would enable fresh thinking and provide business skills at all levels of the management chain since the Avahan scale targets were quite similar to the pace of operation of commercial enterprises.

As the programme rolled out, Avahan partners quickly realized the wisdom residing within the communities and decided to tap into this and engage them as equal partners in programme design and delivery. For example, outreach services were initially delivered through PEs who were NGO staff and non-community[2] members. However, in

---

[1] Drop-in centres are safe spaces for HRGs to come together. The centres are often basically equipped but have clean rooms that accommodate 50–150 people, with cushions and mattresses on the floor, bathing facilities, and a mirror. They are often housed next door to the programme-managed medical clinic. With no similar refuge available, drop-in centres have become the hub of community life, each serving from 5 to 11 contact points or hotspots where HRGs solicit and practice

[2] Community in this context refers to members of HRGs such as FSWs, MSM, and IDUs.

those early days the programme was not reaching enough community members. Once the non-community peer educators (PEs) were replaced by community peers, the number of HRGs contacted increased dramatically. Using PEs for service delivery is not a new or novel concept. However, in Avahan, peers were not seen as passive channels of delivery. They were managed and supervised, empowered to use data and tools to better achieve their goals and motivated and rewarded through an honorarium. For example, with the help of the community, Avahan devised a range of pictorial data collection tools that helped peers (who were mostly illiterate) plan, monitor, and execute their work (Figure 8.5). Each peer educator was responsible for providing services to 40–50 other fellow community members (clients). With micro-planning tools, the peer educator recorded the risk profiles and frequency of uptake of service of her/his clients (such as how many condoms she/he needed, whether she/he faced violence, when was the last time she/he visited a clinic). This allowed the peer educator to prioritize, based on need, and track her/his outreach on a weekly basis. Peers were also engaged in other functions, traditionally seen as 'staff functions' such as clinic administration. By engaging community members in the delivery of services and the management of

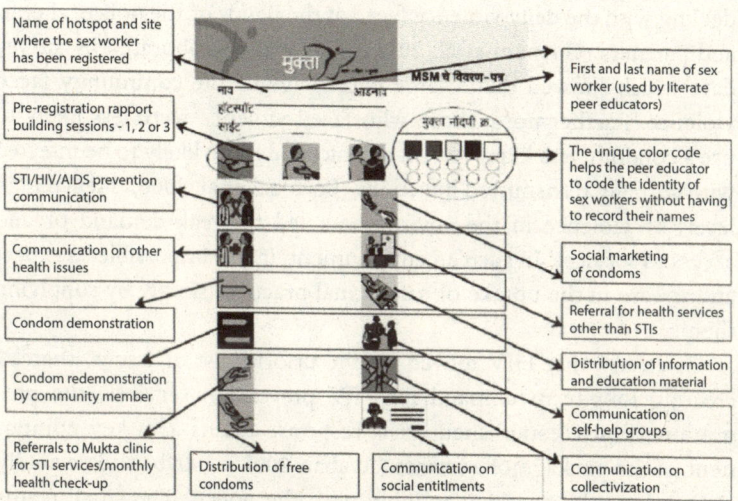

FIGURE 8.5   Pictorial micro-planning tools used by the peer educators
Source: Mukta Project, Pathfinder International.

the programme, a greater ownership was seen and a path created for sustainability of the programme. For example, community members formed clinic committees where they monitored the performance of the doctors and nurses and advocated for changes as needed.

BALANCING SUPPLY WITH DEMAND

The provision and delivery of public health services by themselves are often not enough. Demand for services (in this case prevention services such as condoms and clinical services) also has to be created—both at an individual and collective level. Factors external to the programme can create a sub-optimal environment that can hinder the programme's effectiveness. In the early days, Avahan found that the demand for HIV services among members of the FSW community was low. In fact, HIV prevention was not even a priority in the lives of FSWs despite the fact that they were at great risk. The programme team discovered that beneficiaries in fact rank and rate risks in unexpected ways for the outsider. Understanding this was a key element of the programme design. More pressing issues of concern included stigma, discrimination, earning sufficient daily wages to feed children and family, finding a safe space to sleep at night, and most importantly, dealing with the daily violence faced at the hands of the police, clients, and partners (Gurnani et al. 2011). This was corroborated by survey data which showed that a large percentage of the community faced violence. Furthermore, those who faced violence were less likely to use a condom, less likely to visit a clinic, and more likely to be infected with sexually transmitted infections (Bertozzi et al. 2006). Hence high levels of violence in the environment led to weak demand of and access to services. In such an environment, it was impossible to expect an increase in the uptake of safe sexual practices simply by supplying them.

To ensure that HIV moved up the priority list of issues, thereby creating long-term demand for HIV prevention services, the programme firstly established crisis response teams as a key component of its package of services (Avahan 2009a, 2009b) and secondly engaged in advocacy and training with the police. The small teams consisted of PEs, volunteer community members, a few NGO staff, and a probono lawyer on call. A hotline enabled community members to contact this team whenever they were in need. The team would reach the site within a few hours and help the community member resolve the situation. Community members, NGO staff, and state-led partners of Avahan routinely engaged with the police to make them more empathetic towards the difficulties faced by FSWs. The police received information about the risks faced by sex workers, and about the Avahan programme and what it was designed to achieve. These regular advocacy activities raised awareness among police officers, curtailed unlawful arrests of FSWs, MSM, and IDUs, and cultivated support for the programme within government bodies. In some states, the state-led partners also trained new police recruits on the same issues.

Collectively, these activities addressed individual cases of violence by raising awareness among the community and addressing them when they occurred. Crucially, they also increased the self-confidence and empowerment of the HRGs. As HIV prevention services became an increasing priority for the community, programme coverage and service uptake also improved considerably (Gurnani et al. 2011).

CONTINUOUS AND REAL-TIME MONITORING

A key feature of the Avahan programme was its focus on data. The core belief was that effective management is only possible when people are empowered with data to make choices based on sound evidence. Data was therefore generated and used at all levels. Data was used at the design stage to identify intervention areas and populations to target, and was used to monitor the performance of the programme, to routinely plan activities of all those involved, and to provide information on the effectiveness and impact of the programme. A data-driven programme enabled real-time monitoring of gaps in an ever-changing environment and allowed for quick adjustments to the programme. For example, the redesign of the truckers and male clients programme was guided by feedback from the data. In the trucker programme, the number of halt points with prevention services was substantially scaled down as the strategy of having programmes at all the major stops across the country was deemed inefficient. In fact, by having fewer sites at carefully chosen truck stops, the programme was able to reach most of its target population and at a much lower cost.

INTEGRATING A SUSTAINABILITY STRATEGY

Discussions between the Bill and Melinda Gates Foundation and the Government of India two years into Avahan made it clear that it needed to develop a strategy to ensure that the programme would continue well beyond the life span of foundation funding. Together, the foundation and the Government of India developed a sustainability strategy, which was the main focus of Avahan Phase II (2009–13). The strategy included two elements. First, the programme would be transitioned in a phased manner to its 'natural owners' over a period of five years. The natural owners of HIV prevention programmes in India are both the government—since it is a major funder of prevention programmes across the country (particularly in those states where Avahan did not operate)—and the HRGs. The second component of the strategy was the transfer of Avahan's lessons in implementing a large-scale HIV prevention programme within and outside of India. The first element of the sustainability strategy is discussed in the following section.

In order to build a grassroots sustainability base for the HIV prevention agenda in India, the Avahan programme invested heavily in fostering HRGs and their organizations (CBOs). Across the six states it operates, Avahan has helped develop and foster more than 200 CBOs. While there are many long-term gains of developing and working with CBOs, there are also a number of challenges. Many community members, especially FSWs, are illiterate and therefore CBOs need to in-source certain specialized skills, such as accountants or data managers. Often charismatic community leaders pave the way. However, building a broad leadership base is essential so that the organization does not rely on just a few members. This requires long-term capacity building of human resources. CBOs are also very fragile as they are young institutions. They need nurturing and handholding to build their organizational capacity (including aspects such as governance, leadership, and systems). These community bodies are instrumental in changing sex workers' attitudes towards their rights and entitlements—including the right to be protected from HIV. These platforms have helped transform previously passive recipients of prevention services into active, informed consumers for whom good health is a priority. Sex workers have the opportunity to publicly air their grievances which helps limit the violence and mistreatment they face.

To sustain the prevention programmes and maintain this grassroots base, Avahan entered into an agreement with the Government of India whereby the funding and management of the programmes would be handed over to the NACO over a five-year period. In this model, NACO would contract and manage the same grassroots organizations (NGOs and CBOs) currently contracted by Avahan to deliver the services. In 2009, 10 per cent of HRG interventions were handed over, 20 per cent in 2011, and the remaining 70 per cent will be transferred in 2012. Given that such a large-scale donor-funded programme was being handed over to the government for the first time, a phased handover was designed to ensure that lessons were consolidated along the way from one phase to the next. This phased transition also ensured that the government system was not overloaded at once, given the scale and reach of the Avahan programme.

Avahan has also worked closely with NACO to develop the government's management capacity. It has supported a national team of managers and technical experts to assist NACO in scaling-up its national programme. The government has now implemented a model similar to Avahan by developing Technical Support Units (TSUs); private entities which support NACO's state arms (State AIDS Control Societies) in managing the implementing partners. This novel private–public partnership model is showing immense results. Collectively, these strategies (phased handover and building the management capacity of the government) are helping to ensure that the transition happens smoothly and there is minimal disruption in the programme's delivery on the ground when Avahan exits. This transition strategy has attracted some criticism which is discussed in the 'Challenges Ahead' section.

AVAHAN PROGRAM RESULTS

Emerging evaluation results are encouraging. In a short period of time, the Avahan programme was able to rapidly scale up HIV prevention services in 83 districts in the six high prevalence states of India (Figures 8.3 and 8.4) (NACO 2007). For example, by year three of the programme, 75 per cent of the target HRGs were met monthly, and 85 per cent of FSWs and 64 per cent of MSMs that were contacted received clinical services at least once. External independent assessments also revealed improvements in the quality of programmes delivered over time

(Mogasale et al. 2010). Integrated behavioural and biological surveys conducted with FSWs show declines in both sexually transmitted infections (by 42 per cent for syphilis) and HIV (from 19.6 per cent to 16.4 per cent) and an increase in condom use with clients (from 66.1 per cent to 84.1 per cent with repeat clients in last sexual encounter) in the geographies where Avahan operates (Ramesh et al. 2010). Finally, a statistical analysis of the first five years of Avahan estimated 100,000 HIV infections had been averted by the Avahan programme (Ng et al. 2011; Times of India 2011; BBC News 2011). The key is to consolidate and sustain these gains through the years to come.

CHALLENGES AHEAD

Avahan has faced many varied challenges, which have changed during the course of the programme's lifecycle. Today, most of the challenges facing the programme are related to its on-going handover to the government. These are:

- *Transferring the Business Intelligence*: A key challenge Avahan faces today is the difficulty of transferring the management thinking and techniques—the so-called intangibles of the programme. While processes and tools can be transferred, the dynamic nature of the epidemic means this will not be enough. The programme has always adapted itself to new aspects of the epidemic as revealed by data, and this flexibility is one of the defining features of Avahan, and also one that is challenging to impart to an external entity, such as the government.
- *Transition to Government*: 'Transition' is often seen as a convenient exit strategy for donors rather than a true strategy for sustainability (Rao 2010). However, donors can never substitute for the government, which holds ultimate responsibility for its citizens. Therefore, the messaging around transition remains a challenge. The Avahan programme has also been criticized for its high costs, especially compared to the costs of government-funded prevention programmes (ibid.). However, the Avahan programme only spends 10–25 per cent more than the government on the interventions and these costs are being reduced to government's levels before the handover. Other risks include the derailment or slowing of the transition due to

changes in government leadership, loss of quality of programming, and damaged trust from the community as a result of the handover to the government. Preliminary results suggest that programme indicators have remained high after the handover. Close monitoring of quality is necessary, which Avahan will continue to do for a number of years post transfer and provide technical support to the government as required.

- *Transition to Communities*: Avahan has invested heavily in empowering communities and building CBOs. While the initial projection was that five years of community building would be sufficient to generate a strong platform of communities, Avahan has found that these organizations can be fragile and continued investment, handholding, and capacity building is necessary. Avahan will therefore continue to invest in community capacity building even after handing over the programmes to government for at least 2–3 years.

- *Attribution of HIV Impact to Avahan*: The evaluation design of the Avahan programme has been criticized for not being able to clearly ascertain the attribution of averted HIV infections to the Avahan programme alone (Bertozzi et al. 2010). Experts have suggested alternate models of evaluation. These include randomized control trials (RCT), typically done in public health to prove the effectiveness of interventions, or implementing the programme in a step-wise fashion to prove the effectiveness of the different components of the Avahan package. While these critiques are valid, following the recommended approaches would have been impossible for numerous reasons. An RCT design, for example, mandates that within similar geographies two groups of HRGs would be compared: one receiving the full package of services and the other receiving none. Not only would this have been politically unacceptable in India, but in the early 2000s when the epidemic was seen as an emergency, withholding proven interventions (services) from HRGs would have been unethical. Furthermore, the programme did not operate in a vacuum. The government was scaling up its prevention services and therefore maintaining segregated environments where one group received services and another did not would have been impossible. In light of these challenges, the programme has developed methods to be able to quantify the impact of the programme—such as statistical

(Ng et al. 2011) and mathematical modelling (Pickles et al. 2010)—to prove attribution wherever possible.

LESSONS FROM HIV PREVENTION PROGRAMMING IN INDIA

Important risk-management lessons for public health programmes can be drawn from the Avahan experience in India. There can be immense value in redefining the risk management approach by adopting and adapting frameworks used in the business sector, which the Avahan programme has effectively done for the first time in the area of public health (Figure 8.1). The market and customer-focused approaches developed in business can provide a valuable paradigm for designing and executing public health programmes. Further, lessons from business on the scaling up of programmes can be valuable for the public health sector, where, in a context such as India, only a scaled programme, where more than 85 per cent of the affected geographies and populations are covered with services, will result in positive health gains. Other lessons from business relate to the careful attention that needs to be given to the components of the service package and the mechanism with which to deliver them. Scaled delivery of services further relies on adequate management structures and managers empowered with data to be in place.

The experience in India demonstrates that a focus on service delivery is not enough. Programmes need to pay attention to the environment they operate in and understand how this may affect the delivery and uptake of services. Tackling environmental barriers to service uptake, which are sometimes not obvious, such as violence, is important. Finally, a sustainability strategy should be part of the programme DNA. The sustainability strategy should be conceptualized with all partners (government, implementing partners, and community) early on in the programme. It should also include timelines, deliverables, and guidelines on how to implement and manage each step of the process.

Public health programmes do not operate in a vacuum; rather they are agents within a complex and evolving system consisting of society, other programmes, government policy and response, and the natural dynamics of a disease such as AIDS. Thus programmes have to be flexible and adaptable, as in the case of Avahan, where substantial changes were made to the programme design as a result of continuously monitoring evidence. Concomitantly, the definition of the 'expert', who assesses and addresses the risk, needs to be expanded beyond specialists in public health, to extend to members of the affected communities. Each brings a unique and valuable perspective, and the marrying of views from different angles will result in a more effective response. Hence there is a need to form a 'social contract' and manage risk through a coalition of partners. Together, all these insights drawn from the experience of Avahan demonstrate that risk-management approaches in the world of public health can gain substantially by adopting effective and proven paradigms, such as those from the world of business.

BIBLIOGRAPHY

AIDS Prevention and Control Programme (APAC) (2002). 'HIV Risk Behaviour Surveillance survey in Tamil Nadu Wave VII'. Chennai, India: AIDS Prevention and Control Programme.

Arora, P., R. Kumar, M. Bhattacharya, N.J. Nagelkerke, and P. Jha (2008). 'Trends in HIV Incidence in India from 2000 to 2007', *The Lancet*, 372(9635): 289–90.

Avahan (2008). *Avahan—the India AIDS Initiative: The Business of HIV Prevention at Scale*. New Delhi: The Bill & Melinda Gates Foundation.

——— (2009a). *Community Led Crisis Response Systems: A Guide to Implementation*. New Delhi: The Bill & Melinda Gates Foundation.

——— (2009b). *The Power to Tackle Violence: Avahan's Experience With Community Led Crisis Response in India*. New Delhi: The Bill & Melinda Gates Foundation.

——— (2010a). *Avahan Common Minimum Program for HIV Prevention in India*. New Delhi: The Bill & Melinda Gates Foundation.

——— (2010b). *Treat and Prevent: Avahan's Experience in Scaling Up STI Services to Groups at High Risk for HIV Infection in India'*. New Delhi: The Bill and Melinda Gates Foundation.

BBC News (2011). 'Bill Gates India Scheme "Spared 100,000 from HIV"', *BBC News*, 11 October, available at http://www.bbc.co.uk/news/world-south-asia-15254805, last accessed on 18 November 2013.

Bertozzi, S., N.C. Padian, J. Wegbreit, L.M. De Maria, B. Feldman, H. Gayle, J. Gold, G. Grant, and M.T. Isbell (2006). 'HIV/AIDS Prevention and Treatment'. *Disease Control Priorities in Developing Countries*, Second edition. Washington, DC: The World Bank and Oxford University Press.

Bertozzi, S.M., N. Padian, and T.E. Martz (2010). 'Evaluation of HIV Prevention Programmes: The Case of Avahan', *Sex Transm Infect*, February, 86 (Suppl 1): i4–5.

Claeson, M., and A. Alexander (2008). 'Tackling HIV in India: Evidence-based Priority Setting and Programming', *Health Aff (Millwood)*, 27(4): 1091–102.

Commission on AIDS in Asia (2008). 'Redefining AIDS in Asia: Crafting an Effective Response', Report of the Commission on AIDS in Asia. New Delhi: Oxford University Press.

Forbes India (2009). '$258 Million for Condoms?', *Forbes India*, 6 June, available at http://forbesindia.com/interview/magazine-extra/$258-million-for-condoms/1182/1, last accessed on 18 November 2013.

Gurnani, V., T.S. Beattie, P. Bhattacharjee, H. Mohan, S. Maddur, R. Washington, S. Isac, B.M. Ramesh, S. Moses, and J.F. Blanchard (2011). 'An Integrated Structural Intervention to Reduce Vulnerability to HIV and Sexually Transmitted Infections Among Female Sex Workers in Karnataka State, South India', *BMC Public Health*, 11: 755.

Hanenberg, R.S., W. Rojanapithayakorn, P. Kunasol, and D.C. Sokal (1994). 'Impact of Thailand's HIV-Control Programme as Indicated by the Decline of Sexually Transmitted Diseases', *The Lancet*, 344(8917): 243–5.

Jana, S., N. Bandyopadhyay, S. Mukherjee, N. Dutta, I. Basu, and A. Saha (1998). 'STD/HIV Intervention With Sex Workers in West Bengal, India', *AIDS*, 12(Suppl B): S101–8.

Indian Institute of Public Health (IIPH) (2010). 'HIV/AIDS Situation and Response in Andhra Pradesh: Epidemiological Appraisal Using Data Triangulation', Hyderabad: Indian Institute of Public Health.

Laga, M., C. Galavotti, S. Sundararaman, and R. Moodie (2010). 'The Importance of Sex-worker Interventions: The Case of Avahan in India', *Sex Transm Infect*, 86(Suppl 1): i6–7.

Lipovsek, V., A. Mukherjee, D. Navin, P. Marjara, A. Sharma, and K.P. Roy (2010). 'Increases in Self-reported Consistent Condom Use Among Male Clients of Female Sex Workers Following Exposure to an Integrated Behaviour Change Programme in Four States in Southern India', *Sex Transm Infect*, 86(Suppl 1): i25–32.

Mogasale, V., T.C. Wi, A. Das, S. Kane, A.K. Singh, B. George, and R. Steen (2010). 'Quality Assurance and Quality Improvement using Supportive Supervision in a Large-scale STI Intervention with Sex Workers, Men who have Sex with Men/Transgenders and Injecting-drug Users in India', *Sex Transm Infect*, 86(Suppl 1): i83–8.

Moses, S., B.M. Ramesh, N.J. Nagelkerke, A. Khera, S. Isac, P. Bhattacharjee, V. Gurnani, R. Washington, K.H. Prakash, B.S. Pradeep, and J.F. Blanchard (2008). 'Impact Of An Intensive HIV Prevention Programme for Female Sex Workers on HIV Prevalence among Antenatal Clinic Attenders in Karnataka State, South India: An Ecological Analysis', *AIDS*, 22(Suppl 5): S101–8.

Nagelkerke, N.J., P. Jha, S. J. de Vlas, E.L. Korenromp, S. Moses, J.F. Blanchard, and F.A. Plummer (2002). 'Modelling HIV/AIDS Epidemics in Botswana and India: Impact of Interventions to Prevent Transmission', *Bull World Health Organ*, 80(2): 89–96.

National AIDS Control Organization (NACO) (2003). *Sentinel Surveillance Data*. New Delhi: NACO.

——— (2007). *HIV Fact Sheet Based on Sentinel Surveillance Data in India 2003–2006*. New Delhi: Government of India.

——— (2010a). *Joint Implementation Review Mission (JIRM), December 2010*. New Delhi: Government of India.

——— (2010b). *HIV Declining in India: New Infections Reduced by 50% from 2000–2009; Sustained Focus on Prevention Required*. New Delhi: Government of India.

Ng, M., E. Gakidou, A. Levin-Rector, A. Khera, C.J. Murray, and L. Dandona (2011). 'Assessment of Population-Level Effect of Avahan, An HIV-Prevention Initiative in India', *The Lancet*, 378(9803): 1643–52.

Piot, P. (2010). 'Setting New Standards For Targeted HIV Prevention: The Avahan Initiative In India', *Sex Transm Infect*, 86(Suppl 1): i1–2.

Pickles, M., A.M. Foss, P. Vickerman, K. Deering, S. Verma, E. Demers, R. Washington, B.M. Ramesh, S. Moses, J. Blanchard, C.M. Lowndes, M. Alary, S. Reza-Paul, and M.C. Boily (2010). 'Interim Modelling Analysis to Validate Reported Increases in Condom Use and Assess HIV Infections Averted Among Female Sex Workers and Clients in Southern India Following a Targeted HIV Prevention Programme', *Sex Transm Infect*, 86(Suppl 1): i33–43.

Ramesh, B.M., T.S. Beattie, I. Shajy, R. Washington, L. Jagannathan, S. Reza-Paul, et al. (2010). 'Changes in Risk Behaviours and Prevalence of Sexually Transmitted Infections Following HIV Preventive Interventions Among Female Sex Workers in Five Districts in Karnataka State, South India', *Sex Transm Infect*, 86(Suppl 1): i17–24.

Rao, P.J. (2010). 'Avahan: The Transition to a Publicly Funded Programme as a Next Stage', *Sex Transm Infect*, 86(Suppl 1): i7–8.

Rau, B. (2011). *The Avahan-India AIDS Initiative, AIDSTAR Case Study Series*. Arlington, VA, USA: AIDSTAR.

Sgaier, S.K., C. Claeson, C. Gilks, A. Wadhwani, A. Ramakrishnan, B.M. Ramesh, P.D. Ghys, and K. Chandramouli (2012). 'Knowing Your Epidemic and Tailoring the Response: Lessons from HIV and AIDS in India', *Sex Transm Infect*.

Times of India (2011). 'HIV Project Averted 100,000 Infections in India: The Lancet', *The Times of India*, 11 October, available at http://articles.timesof india.indiatimes.com/2011-10-11/india/30266144_1_hiv-infection-avahan-human-immunodeficiency-virus, last accessed on 18 November 2013.

202 | *India's Risks*

UNAIDS (2010). 'Country Progress Report, India', UNGASS.

Vadivoo, S., M.D. Gupte, and R. Adhikary, A. Kohli, B. Kangusamy, V. Joshua, A.K. Mathai, K. Kumar, M. Mainkar, P. Goswami, and IBBA Study Team (2008). 'Appropriateness and Execution Challenges of Three Formal Size Estimation Methods for High-Risk Populations in India', *AIDS*, 22(Suppl 5): S137–48.

SCIENCE AND TECHNOLOGY

9

ERIK MILLSTONE

Science and Politics in Indian GM Crop Regulation

A U-turn Down a Blind Alley

While scientific evidence and expertise are necessary for regulating technological risks, such as genetically modified (GM) crops, there have been heated debates about whether or not they are sufficient. If other types of considerations are also relevant, then which types of considerations might those be? Also, how can they be differentiated from or coupled with scientific considerations? This chapter will outline several models in terms of which the role of science in technology policymaking has been conceptualized, and then use those resources to characterize the evolving controversy in India over the regulation of Bt brinjal, which was the first GM food crops to be reviewed by Indian regulators. While numerous varieties of Bt cotton have been cultivated in India, they are textiles and not foodstuffs, where issues such as consumer safety and choice are both more relevant and politically explosive.

Prior to October 2009, when the Minister of State for Environment and Forests (Jairam Ramesh) intervened in what had seemed a routine process, GM risk assessment deliberations had been portrayed officially and corporately as if purely scientific. The Indian government's industrial policy was predicated on the assumption that India's economic development should benefit from advances in science and technology—GM crops were approached through this lens. Ramesh initiated a series of open, public consultations across India, before announcing a moratorium on the introduction of Bt brinjal on the grounds of inadequate scientific information on its long-term effects on the safety of humans and the environment. (Hindu 2010). The ministerial intervention in October 2009, along with the release of previously confidential documents following civil litigation under the Right to Information Act, revealed that the deliberations of the scientific advisors had not been purely scientific but were rather replete with unacknowledged non-scientific assumptions and judgements that were distinctly policy-sensitive. Those developments created the conditions in which those judgements and assumptions could be, and deservedly were, exposed and critically appraised. During the ministerial reshuffle in July 2011, Ramesh left the Ministry of Environment and Forests to become the Minister for Rural Development. Shortly after, a revised draft of the Biotechnology Regulatory Authority of India (BRAI) Bill, 2011 (Bill No. 54 of 2011) was published by the Ministry of Science and Technology and Earth Sciences, which end eavoured (once again) to portray GM crop regulatory issues as if they were purely scientific. Optimists had hoped that Ramesh's intervention would set a precedent and bring social engagement and transparency to future GM regulations. Yet, from the government's perspective it appears that too little was learnt from the processes initiated or the information that emerged over the last two years.

MODELS OF SCIENCE IN RISK POLICYMAKING

A diverse range of competing models of the role of science in regulatory policymaking have been developed by scholars and policy analysts (US NRC 1983; US NRC 1994; Oxera 2000; CEC 2002; Millstone 2007). For the purposes of this discussion three contrasting models may suffice. In this context they are referred to as (van Zwanenberg and Millstone 2005):

- the technocratic model;
- the Red Book model; and,
- the co-dynamic model

One very influential portrayal of the role of scientific expertise in policymaking emerged in 19th century France in the work of the positivists Saint-Simon and Comte. They portrayed scientific knowledge as if it was not just necessary but also sufficient for policymaking, and this model is often referred to as a 'technocratic' model. Technocratic models have often appealed to governments and ministers because they provide a narrative that may help them (at least to try) to depoliticize controversial policy issues. Those models also appeal to scientific expert advisors because it attributes a high status to their knowledge, expertise, and influence. The conceptual structure of the technocratic model can be represented schematically in Figure 9.1.

This model implies that scientific facts can on their own be sufficient to determine policy decisions. Advocates of such technocratic approaches adopt remarkably optimistic assumptions about the progress, accuracy, and adequacy of science. They assume that public administration by impartial experts could and should replace governance by those characterized by partiality, biases, ignorance, or vested interests. The technocratic model of policymaking has often been encapsulated in the claim that policy should be based on, and only on 'sound science'. In the USA from the 1950s to the late 1960s, and in much of Europe until the late 1990s, the dominant official narratives were technocratic (Brickman et al. 1985; Ezrahi 1990; Jasanoff 1990, van Zwanenberg and Millstone 2005). Technocratic narratives presuppose that the science and the relevant facts are socially and politically objective and neutral, and that all relevant facts can readily be gathered.

An implication of this model is that responsibility for setting policy should be delegated to expert committees, and the responsibilities of elected ministers can be confined to recruiting the best experts and following their advice. Technocratic models and rhetoric are therefore potentially very vulnerable to criticisms if the evidential base and the understandings of experts are incomplete, unreliable, or equivocal.

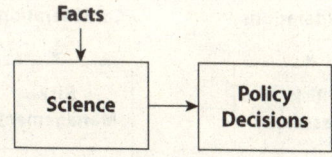

FIGURE 9.1   The Technocratic Model

While technocratic narratives survived in Europe until at least the late 1990s, they became unsustainable in the US during the late 1960s and early 1970s. This occurred in large part because of the passage of the US Freedom of Information Act, which revealed that often the science used to support policy was incomplete and uncertain. Consequently the US authorities needed an alternative model using a new vocabulary. Science-based risk appraisal and decision-making came to be portrayed in the USA as a two-stage process, the first of which is called 'risk assessment' and the second of which is known as 'risk management'. The first of these two stages is typically portrayed as a purely scientific stage and the second as a policy-making stage at which non-scientific and often normative considerations, such as economic, social, and political factors may be taken into account when making policy decisions. On this two-stage model, policymakers (also known as 'risk managers') are informed and influenced by scientific advisors, but the scientific advisory bodies are portrayed as if entirely independent of policy, and of any and all non-scientific considerations. This model was outlined in an influential report from the US National Research Council (NRC) called 'Risk Assessment in the Federal Government: Managing the Process' (US NRC 1983). In what came to be known as the *Red Book* (given the colour of its cover) the NRC has been widely interpreted as asserting that science-based risk policy-making can and should be legitimate, but only if it is conducted in ways that ensures a proper separation of science from policy. The model is linear and unidirectional and its structure can be represented schematically, as shown in Figure 9.2.

This model, often supplemented with a third stage, termed 'risk communication', has been adopted by many powerful policymaking institutions; it became the new orthodoxy in the 1990s, when it spread

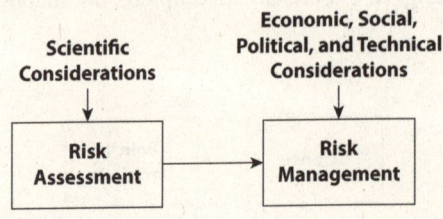

FIGURE 9.2   The Red Book Model

from the USA to multilateral bodies such as the OECD, the European Commission, to many European Union (EU) Member States, and to the World Trade Organization (WTO).

CRITIQUING THE TECHNOCRATIC AND RED BOOK MODELS

Despite their official popularity, science policy analysts and sociologists of scientific knowledge have long been critical of the Technocratic and Red Book models, and for two main reasons. Firstly, both presuppose that the available scientific knowledge is reliable and known (or knowable) with sufficient certainty, and that experts can readily reach a consensus. In practice, the available science is frequently incomplete, uncertain and equivocal, and the scientific community rarely speaks with one voice. Therefore, different groups of scientists frequently provide competing assessments of risks and of benefits, which may be equally scientific or at any rate plausible. In those circumstances, scientific considerations alone cannot determine policy decisions.

Secondly, it presupposes that scientific assessments of risks and/or benefits can be, and routinely are, developed in socially, politically, and ethically neutral settings, and that scientific assessments can be and are constructed solely from scientific considerations. Numerous scholars have documented some of the most important ways in which social, economic, political, and cultural considerations have influenced the agendas, deliberations, and conclusions of official scientific advice on risk issues (Levidow et al. 1997; Jasanoff and Wynne 1998; Millstone et al. 1999; Abraham 1993; Castleman and Ziem 1988; van Zwanenberg and Millstone 2000; Huff 2002). Jasanoff has been right to emphasize that while:

> [P]leas for maintaining a strict separation between science and politics continue to run like a leitmotif through the policy literature, the artificiality of this...can no longer be doubted. Studies of scientific advisors leave in tatters the notion that it is possible, in practice, to restrict the advisory process to technical issues or that the subjective values of scientists are irrelevant to decision making. (Jasanoff 1990: 230)

Accepting this premise entails abandoning both technocratic and Red Book models.

A CO-DYNAMIC LINEAR BI-DIRECTIONAL MODEL

To avoid those difficulties, a new model has been developed. Like the two previous models it is linear, but unlike them its starting point is not a set of scientific facts but a set of normative judgements about what is important, and which policy aims and objectives are to be pursued. Secondly, though linear, it is characterized by reciprocal interactions; it is not unidirectional but bi-directional. This model is termed a 'co-dynamic' model, and its structure can be represented schematically, as shown in Figure 9.3.

This model assumes that science-based technology policymaking depends on both expert scientific assessments and on non-scientific considerations, but instead of portraying expert risk assessments as if they occurred in a policy-free space, the model represents those scientific deliberations as 'sandwiched between' two sets of judgements. On the one hand, there is a set of upstream judgements that provides key assumptions about what is to be assessed and the questions to which scientific answers are expected, and on the other is a set of downstream evaluative judgements about what actions are appropriate in the light of those answers, including comparisons with alternative courses of action and the distribution and acceptability of the associated costs and benefits.

There is evidence indicating that the reasons why different groups of scientific risk assessors reach different conclusions about the risks from

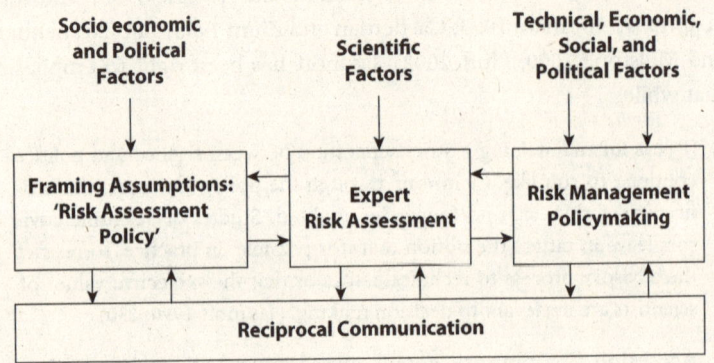

FIGURE 9.3 A Co-dynamic Model

GM crops is not because they are providing competing interpretations of agreed and shared bodies of evidence, but because they have asked and answered different questions, and have therefore reviewed different data sets; in other words they have adopted conflicting risk assessment policies (Millstone et al. 2008).

OPERATIONALIZING A CO-DYNAMIC APPROACH

While co-dynamic analyses have become increasingly accepted amongst science policy scholars and sociologists of scientific knowledge, public policy institutions have been far slower in understanding the implications of co-dynamic analyses, or they have understood them but have been reluctant to accept some or all of their implications.

In the food safety regulatory field, it has been the Codex Alimentarius Commission (CAC) that has been in the vanguard. The CAC was jointly established in 1963 by the Member States of the United Nations Food and Agriculture Organisation (FAO) and the World Health Organization (WHO). It sets food safety standards for internationally traded food products. Until 1994, CAC standards were merely advisory, with no statutory force. Since the establishment of the World Trade Organization in 1995, CAC standards have been adopted as food safety benchmarks below which importing countries can lawfully exclude products. Individual CAC Member States may set higher standards than those adopted by CAC, but if challenged at a WTO Dispute, they would need to justify those standards as 'based on a scientific risk assessment' and as not as discriminatory trade barrier to prevent or inhibit imports (WTO 1998).

Since 1995, with the enhanced role of CAC standards within the WTO regime, regulatory convergence and divergence has become increasingly important and problematic. CAC has struggled to set agreed common standards given the differences amongst the competing standards of Member States. Under those conditions, and given the collisions amongst the risk assessments and regulatory standards of competing CAC and WTO member states, it is unsurprising that explicit attention has been given by CAC to upstream framing assumptions that contribute to the construction of competing risk assessments. CAC is the first major public policy institution explicitly to acknowledge that scientists' assessments of food safety risks are framed by prior upstream framing assumptions, which CAC has termed 'risk assessment policy'.

The CAC has characterized 'Risk Assessment Policy' in the following terms:

- Determination of risk assessment policy should be included as a specific component of risk management.
- Risk assessment policy should be established by risk managers in advance of risk assessment, in consultation with risk assessors and all other interested parties. This procedure aims at ensuring that the risk assessment is systematic, complete, unbiased and transparent.
- The mandate given by risk managers to risk assessors should be as clear as possible.
- Where necessary, risk managers should ask risk assessors to evaluate the potential changes in risk resulting from different risk management options (CAC 2003, Appendix IV paragraphs 13–16).

The introduction of those provisions in the early years of the 21st century represented an important innovation. CAC introduced a novel obligation on its risk management committees to articulate risk assessment policies, though several CAC committees have been struggling with that challenge (Millstone 2009). The implications of these developments may be quite profound although their significance is not yet widely appreciated. Their importance has been hugely reinforced by the fact that at the July 2007 plenary meeting of the CAC, a text on the 'Working Principles for Risk Analysis for Food Safety for Application by Governments' was formally adopted (CAC 2007: 9 paragraphs 56–60). Under the provisions of that agreement, all CAC member states, including India, have accepted the obligation for their domestic risk managers to provide their risk assessors with explicit risk assessment policies prior to the start of the deliberations of those risk assessors.

Whether CAC member states realize it or not, they have, at least implicitly acknowledged that scientific representations of risks and/or benefits cannot be fully separated from policy considerations, though their separate contributions can and should be duly acknowledged and legitimated. On the other hand, few Codex member states are fully implementing the commitments they made (Millstone 2009). In this context, it is important to note that while Ramesh, in his role as India's Environment Minister, deemed the Genetic Engineering Approval

Committee's (GEAC's) risk assessment policy to be inadequate, the Indian government has never yet indicated what alternative policy it would deem appropriate.

The three models of the role of science in policy set out above will be used in the next section to analyse debates about the appraisal of Bt brinjal in India, including the key question of the extent to which the Indian authorities have engaged explicitly with GM food crop risk assessment policies.

THE SCIENTIFIC AND POLICY DEBATES ABOUT BT BRINJAL IN INDIA

Many varieties of brinjal are cultivated and consumed in India; brinjal is a type of vegetable that is known as aubergine in Europe and eggplant in US. In May 2008 an Indian-based corporation called the Maharashtra Hybrid Seed Company (or Mahyco) applied to the Indian government for consent for the commercial release of Bt brinjal seeds, by reference to an 8-volume dossier of information submitted to the Department of Biotechnology. Data in the dossier related to some of the potential risks from, and safety of Mahyco's GM variety of brinjal (Bt brinjal), which the firm had modified so that it expressed a bacterial insecticide known as *Bacillus thuringiensis* (or Bt), making the crop resistant to a pest known as the 'fruit and shoot borer' or *leucibodes or bonalis*. The new variety had been developed by Mahyco in collaboration with the agrochemical company Monsanto. The dossier was submitted to and reviewed by a committee of scientists called the Genetic Engineering Approval Committee (GEAC). In October 2009 the GEAC cleared Bt brinjal for commercial release.

Before that release could take place, the Ministry of Environment and Forests published GEAC's report inviting comments. Those comments were extensive and informed by the disclosure in August 2008 of much of the underlying data, following the intervention of critics of GM crops and adjudications by the Chief Information Commissioner and the Indian Supreme Court (Gupta 2011). Prior to the disclosure of those documents and the data they revealed, the Indian system had been portrayed by Mahyco, by GEAC, and by the Indian government in traditional orthodox technocratic terms, as if only scientific considerations had contributed to regulatory deliberations or decision-making.

The impact of the disclosure of the contents of the Bt brinjal dossier in India had a similar effect to that accomplished by the introduction of Freedom of Information in the USA—it torpedoed the technocratic model below the waterline.

The dossier was scrutinised, analysed, and critiqued by several authoritative and influential scholars, and the following discussion draws both on the text of the dossier and several scholarly critiques (Seralini 2009; Carmen 2010). By revealing that the available science was at best incomplete and at worst equivocal and chronically uncertain, and that numerous non-scientific considerations contributed to GEAC's deliberations and decisions, the evidence deprived technocratic and Red Book narratives of whatever limited plausibility they might previously have enjoyed in relation to India's science-based risk management system.

Even though Mahyco's dossier ran to eight volumes, it does not follow that the underlying data sets were substantial or adequate. The dossier covered a range of topics, though just two main types of possible risks were discussed. Firstly, it commented on possible risks to human health, either directly from consuming Bt brinjal or indirectly from consuming animal products from livestock fed on crop residues from Bt brinjal plants. Secondly, it commented on possible environmental risks to flora and fauna from cultivating this Bt brinjal. A third set of possible risks, namely, those arising as economic or social consequences of commercializing Mahyco's Bt brinjal were not addressed in the dossier, despite their importance to many of Mahyco's potential customers and consumers. Wynne (2012) has recently summarized some of the most controversial aspects of debates about the putative socioeconomic consequences of commercializing GM crop technologies. He explains that a key axis of contestation concerns arguments that GM technologies '[E]xacerbate[s] already-unsustainable high-input industrialised farming and concentrates ownership and control of key resources of the global food-chain in private corporations, while also shaping innovation in their interests...damages the social distribution of production, control, and access to food, especially for the most desperately needy' (Wynne 2012). In this context it is not possible comprehensively to review all of those categories of potential risks; instead the discussion will focus just on the first of those sets, namely food safety risks to consumers, on the understanding that the pattern that emerges is characteristic of debates about all three types of risks.

One set of preparatory remarks may be helpful. Before the use of a new chemical can be authorized as, for example, a pharmaceutical, a pesticide, or a food additive, the set of tests that will be required routinely include a so-called chronic toxicity test. The test is 'chronic' in the sense of requiring repeated daily dosing with the test compound for all or most of the lifetime of a sample of laboratory animals. Mice in labs regularly live for 18 months, while for rats average lifetimes are 30 months. A standardized chronic rodent feeding study is considered sub-standard if fewer than 400 animals are used. The most commonly encountered chronic toxicity protocols use 50 male and 50 female animals, at each of three dosing levels (low, medium, and high), plus one counterpart control set, making a total of 400. Not only should these be repeat-dose studies, protocols require that a broad set of anatomical, physiological, biochemical, and histopathological parameters should be monitored. As the following section explains, Mahyco's tests on Bt brinjal fell a very long way short of those conventional benchmarks.

ASSESSING FOOD SAFETY

A starting point for an attempt to estimate the consumer health and/or environmental impact of Bt brinjal involves a chemical and biological characterization of the product. The Mahyco dossier did include data from some rather limited chemical analyses, along with assertions that they were sufficient to establish 'substantial equivalence' to non-GM brinjal counterparts, concluding that Bt brinjal can safely be consumed. The dossier also provided data from some limited biological and toxicological studies, to supplement the chemical analytical data (Mahyco 2008: Vol. 1, ch. 7). The dossier revealed, however, that those analyses of chemical composition were conducted on just three samples of Bt brinjal and three samples of non-Bt brinjal (ibid.: 104). The parameters included in those chemical analyses did not, however, include data on either amino acids or fatty acids, or levels of enzymes. Data reporting levels of intended protein additions and unintended modifications were also conspicuously absent. Seralini (2009) highlighted the fact that even the slender data set indicated that the dietary calories available from Bt brinjal were some 15 per cent below the average levels for the non-GM brinjal. The text of the dossier discounts those differences as insignificant, and characterized Bt brinjal as unproblematically safe.

The dossier did contain some data on how Bt brinjal might be digested, and the GEAC considered those data. The data were, however, derived only from experimental models contained in laboratory equipment (so called *in vitro* studies), while data from the digestive systems of living organisms (so called *in vivo* studies) were also conspicuous by their absence. GEAC treated the *in vitro* data as sufficient. As Carmen (2010) has argued, however,

> such [*in vitro*] studies are notorious for providing false assurances about the digestibility of GM DNA and proteins. For example, such studies often use unrealistically high levels of stomach acid and digestive enzymes. The level of acid in a human stomach moves towards neutral once food enters it. The only real way to determine how quickly GM DNA and protein are digested is to do experiments in animals or humans.

If such studies had been conducted they were not reported.

Data that had some bearing, albeit indirectly, on the possible allergenicity of Bt brinjal were included in the dossier; not withstanding their limitations GEAC deemed them sufficient. Mahyco conducted a paper-based analysis, which assumed that the GM Bt protein would split into smaller familiar segments and they compared those segments with selected databases of known allergens. Mahyco did not however consider possible allergenic effects of unintended proteins. The paper exercise was supplemented with data from a skin irritation test and a mucous membrane test using vaginal tissue in rabbits. For both of those studies, only three rabbits were included in each treatment group, and they only received single doses, after which they were monitored for just 72 hours, and the results compared to nine control animals. The almost vanishingly small number of animals tested could barely provide an adequate model of effects on a larger population of rabbits, let alone a vastly greater and more diverse group of human consumers. Nonetheless GEAC accepted the data as reassuring and sufficient.

Data from acute toxicity studies in mice were reported by Mahyco and reviewed and accepted by GEAC even though those data were obtained from a test that was not conducted with the specific protein that is expressed in Mahyco's Bt brinjal, which supposedly was being assessed. Their Bt brinjal contains a chimeric Cry1 A protein (C cry1 A) but a different protein (i.e., Cry1 Ac) was used in Mahyco's study. Furthermore only 10 mice per dose group were used, and the only data submitted reported body weight and food intake; apparently tissue samples were taken but not analysed, or at any rate no analyses were included in Mahyco's dossier. Nonetheless, GEAC deemed those few data sufficient and reassuring.

Data from an acute toxicity study on rats were included, but for that study only five rats per gender per dose group were used, and the animals were exposed only to single doses, and they were monitored for just 14 days. Nonetheless, those data suggested that male rats fed with Bt brinjal had a concentration of AST (a liver function enzyme) that was 48 per cent and 63 per cent higher than the rats fed with non-GM brinjal. The GEAC discounted the apparent evidence of toxicity, and deemed the data sufficient and reassuring.

A study was conducted with lactating cows fed on plant material from Bt brinjal. The data from that study suggested that the cows fed Bt brinjal produced significantly more milk after six weeks, approximately 14 per cent more, suggesting that the GM feed had acted like a lactation-enhancing hormone. The GEAC discounted that possibility, but otherwise deemed the data sufficient.

A sub-chronic (that is, 90-day) feeding study was conducted with goats, but only six goats per sex per dose, eating a diet containing Bt brinjal. The results indicated that those fed Bt brinjal-derived material consumed significantly less hay in week 11 when compared to those fed a non-Bt diet. The authors did not interpret that difference as problematic. Moreover the dossier suggested that the feeding trial consisted of six males and three females, but provided no explanation for the disappearance or exclusion of data from the three missing females. Those results were nonetheless deemed sufficient and acceptably reassuring by the GEAC.

Data from a three-month-long (or sub-chronic) feeding study on rats were included in Mahyco's dossier, but only 10 rats per gender per dose were used, and only very few data were reported, especially histological data, that is, data reporting the detailed conditions of particular types of cells. The initial sample of rats was unusually varied; the body weights of some groups varied by as much as 31 per cent. Since there were only 10 rats per group, the intra-group variation could have easily masked any evidence of effects as between different groups. Those data were nonetheless deemed acceptable and sufficient by the GEAC.

Several other possible categories of putative toxicological risks were not covered by the reported studies. In particular, there is no evidence of studies conducted to explore whether the use of antibiotic marker genes, which were deliberately introduced into the Bt brinjal, might provoke resistance to therapeutically important antibiotics, in particular to kanamycin. The GEAC failed to comment critically on that omission. There were, moreover, no data from studies designed to investigate reproductive toxicity, genotoxicity, or carcinogenicity, although they are routinely required for studies of chemicals deliberately added to human diets, even if they are to be used at low levels. Once more, the absence of such data was not discussed in the GEAC report.

In these circumstances it is readily understandable why Seralini (2009) highlighted the tactics repeatedly adopted by Mahyco and the GEAC when discounting evidence that appeared to indicate positive signs of adverse effects. Seralini argued that the potentially significant differences were repeatedly deemed to be 'not biologically meaningful' by both Mahyco and the GEAC (p. 14). The judgments to discount such findings were superficially legitimated by the deployment of several unscientific devices, which included:

- Comparison was carried out with several unnecessary 'reference' groups of animals, including in some cases animals that had eaten a different type of brinjal to that which had been GM (that is, not a sister line but different lines of brinjal).
- The control or reference group was in some cases six times larger than the GMO treated group (in some instances the historical data of the laboratory conducting the experiment served also as references in some files).
- For some effects, the differences in the effects on males and females were interpreted as indicating that the differences were not linked to the GM treatment.
- For some apparently significant effects, the fact that they were only evident during some weeks of the experiment were cited as ground to discount any possible biological significance. Mahyco suggested that unless those differences were evident during the entire duration of the experiment they could be discounted.
- Some apparently adverse effects were discounted because there was no simple linear correlation with the dose level, as if all toxic effects exhibit linear monotonic dose–effect relationships.

While such tactics have been encountered in other contexts that is not sufficient to confer on them scientific legitimacy.

SUMMARY AND ANALYSIS

The foregoing discussion of the assessment of the risks posed by GM Bt brinjal has focussed relatively narrowly on issues of food safety, understood as a concern with consumer health. It has not provided a review of corresponding evidence, questions or debates in relation to possible impacts of cultivating Bt brinjal on the environment, let alone the social and economic consequences of cultivating Mahyco's Bt brinjal in India. While the discussion of food safety has been quite broad, it has not been comprehensive, let alone exhaustive. Nonetheless a clear set of patterns has emerged. Very similar patterns can be discerned in relation to environmental and socio-economic risks, but the scope of this chapter cannot extend to a detailed discussion of those topics.

The patterns that emerged in the Indian Bt brinjal saga show that the deliberations and conclusions of Mahyco's portrayal of the putative risks to consumer health from its Bt brinjal were profoundly influenced by a broad range of non-scientific (risk assessment policy) assumptions concerning how the scientific questions should be framed, about how much (or rather how little) evidence might be deemed sufficient, and about how those evidential fragments could be interpreted. Furthermore it is clear that those assumptions were shared by, and implicitly endorsed by, the GEAC.

In other words, what was represented by Mahyco and the GEAC as if it was a purely science-based technocratic policy-making system was in reality an exemplification of a co-dynamic system, because the presence, characteristics and influence of a set of prior non-scientific framing assumptions determined Mahyco's 'risk assessment' of its own product and GEAC's endorsement of Mahyco's judgements and conclusions. The evidence indicates that Mahyco and the GEAC both repeatedly made non-scientific judgements that consistently favoured Mahyco and that they were relentlessly optimistic about the safety of Bt brinjal and relentless sceptical about any possible risks. So despite their adoption of technocratic narrative, Mahyco and GEAC's portrayal of the putative risks of Bt brinjal can be most comfortably accommodated in a co-dynamic model, which reveals much that Mahyco and the GEAC chose to conceal.

The co-dynamic model cannot yet be comprehensively applied to this saga, but only because (at the time of writing—May 2013) no decision has yet been taken by the Indian authorities to either definitively license or ban Mahyco's Bt brinjal. In the absence of a risk management policy decision, other than an interim decision to delay, it would be premature to conclude that the 'downstream' right-hand-end part of Figure 9.3 fully applies. Nonetheless, the evidence adduced above has shown that Mahyco's risks assessment and GEAC's acceptance of Mahyco's conclusion cannot be comprehended within the resources provided by either a technocratic (see Figure 9.1) or a Red Book (see Figure 9.2) model—they can only be understood as exemplifying at least the centre and left-hand-end of Figure 9.3.

POLITICAL DEVELOPMENTS SINCE OCTOBER 2009

As Gupta (2011) has argued, changes in the regulatory framework in India for GM crops 'have been stimulated by socioeconomic concerns relating to foreign dependence, social need and economic gain (or lack thereof) from transgenic crops...' (Gupta 2011: 737). In particular, when the Minister of State at the Ministry of Environment and Forests (Ramesh), announced in October 2009 that the GEAC's judgements and advice on Bt brinjal were not being accepted, and that further studies and more data would be required before any regulatory decision could be made, his decision could be understood as a repudiation of the technocratic model. His policy judgement clearly indicated that he took the view that too few endpoints and putative risks had been studied or assessed, and that, for those that had been investigated, too few data had been gathered from samples that were too small. Instead, Ramesh initiated a process of public consultation that, amongst other things, addressed issues such as: how wide or narrow the scope of any adequate 'risk assessment' should be, and, how extensive and comprehensive should the requisite studies be. What never emerged from the Indian government was a definitive statement of its risk assessment policy for GM foods and crops. Mahyco was, in effect, told that its risk assessment policies and data sets had been insufficient, but the Indian government did not provide any indication of what might eventually be deemed necessary and sufficient. While this chapter has highlighted how limited the testing had been and how few data were available, neither this chapter nor this author is recommending what should be deemed necessary or sufficient in India. It is intrinsic to the analysis provided here that responsibility for judging how much data of which sorts will be necessary for Indian policymaking purposes is a matter for which Indian ministers should take responsibility, and for which they should be democratically accountable. It is not for a British academic to tell the Indian government or Parliament what it should require and accept. On the other hand, it would be reasonable to assume that if the Indian government set its requirements significantly below those set for the EU, Indian exporters of GM crops might have considerable difficulties gaining access to the EU's single market.

The tactics adopted by the Indian government since the summer of 2011, have, however, been bizarre and perverse. Instead of abandoning the pretence of trying to operate a purely technocratic regime and embracing a more sophisticated and realistic understanding of science-based risk policymaking, the Indian government attempted to turn back the clock and to re-impose a technocratic structure, procedure, and narrative. Once however 'Pandora's box' has been opened, it is not clear that an attempt to re-impose a technocratic orthodoxy can be sustained.

At the end of July 2011, a draft BRAI Bill (Bill No. 54 of 2011) was published by the Ministry of Science and Technology and Earth Sciences. The Bill is a remarkable document; because it is drafted in a way that suggests either that no lessons whatsoever had been learnt from the Bt brinjal or that too many (cynical) lessons had been internalised by the authorities. Some explanatory light on those developments may be cast by Gupta's comment (2011) that: '[T]he regulatory system has sought a balance of authority between concerned governmental actors, with the central axis of conflict being between a proactive Department of Biotechnology under the Ministry of Science and Technology, which aggressively promotes development and adoption of transgenic crops, and a more precautionary Ministry of Environment and Forests' (Gupta 2011: 737).

At the time of writing the position is that, while the Bill was tabled in the summer of 2011, the procedure to debate, amend and decide the Bill has been stalled. The Bill has not been withdrawn, but neither has it progressed, although there was a plan to re-table the Bill in April 2013. What matters however in this context is its text rather than its legislative progress. According to Saldanha and Rao (2011): 'The proposed Bill makes no effort at all to holistically address a variety of concerns associated with the high risks involved in biotechnology. In fact as a legislative effort it brazenly, controversially and questionably proclaims it as a *Bill to promote the safe use of modern biotechnology'* (ibid.: 1). The centre piece of the legislation is the creation of a body to be called the Biotechnology Regulatory Authority of India (or BRAI). This institution is portrayed in the Bill in narrowly technocratic terms; it is to be staffed only by scientists, who are to be chosen and managed by a committee of bureaucrats working under the Cabinet Secretary, with no parliamentary or democratic oversight or accountability (BRAI Bill 2011, Ch. II). Moreover, most of the operational details concerning how risk assessments will be scoped, framed and conducted have been left open-ended and unresolved, as have details of how policy decisions are to be reached; the processes by which they might be decided remain obscure and consequently unaccountable.

The Bill proposes that the BRAI body will have responsibility for all regulatory decisions, rather than merely for providing scientific advice to policymakers. The Bill also proposes that scientists, and scientists alone, should decide to authorise biotechnological crops, with ministerial responsibilities confined to appointing scientists to the BRAI and ensuring that BRAI's decisions are implemented. Members of the BRAI, and especially those named as Chief Regulatory Officers, must undertake to keep the data, by reference to which they reach their decisions, confidential and secret.[1] The BRAI may release some of the data, but only if it is satisfied that: '[T]he public interest outweighs the disclosure of commercially confidential information'.[2] This suggests that the BRAI will decide its own risk assessment policy, to which the BRAI Bill makes no direct reference. It could mean that policy decisions will masquerade as if they were scientific and un-contestable, when in practice they will be non-scientific and potentially very controversial.

The draft Bill endeavours however to restrict controversy, by the inclusion of Clause 62, to the effect that: 'If a person, in connection with the requirement or direction under this Act, provides any information or produces any document that the person knows is false or misleading, he shall be punishable with imprisonment for a term which may extend to three months and also with fine which may extend to

---

[1] BRAI 2011, Ch. V, para 21.5, and para 28(1).
[2] BRAI 2011, Ch. V, para 28(2).

five lakh rupees' (which is about USD 10,000). The implications of this clause are, predictably, controversial but critics of the Bill and of the government's enthusiasm for GM crops interpret that clause as designed to muzzle or silence the critics. The fact that the Bill stipulates that neither the civil courts nor the individual Indian states will have any say in any of these matters is also highly controversial. The draft Bill also assigns no roles or responsibilities to independent scientific laboratories, as if science and scientists can be relied upon to 'speak with one voice' and as if commercial and corporate science could be relied upon to be sufficient and reliable.

The disclosures about Mahyco's dossier on Bt brinjal and GEAC's interpretation of that dossier revealed that the available scientific evidence is far from complete, comprehensive, unequivocal, certain or decisive. They also showed that the choices that Mahyco and GEAC had made, concerning the scope and adequacy of microscopic quantities of data, had been relentlessly optimistic and forgiving. Since the widespread outrage these revelations sparked in India, it is hard to imagine a re-constructed technocratic system of the sort envisaged by the draft BRAI Bill, 2011, being seen to have any scientific or democratic legitimacy; that is why the sub-title of this chapter is 'A U-turn down a blind alley' (Gupta 2011).

The foregoing discussion suggests that if a new regulatory regime for GM crops is to be constructed in India that might deliver both scientific and democratic legitimacy, it will need to be structured in a way that explicitly corresponds to a co-dynamic model, or something rather similar to it, rather than doing so covertly. Heinemann (2012) has, for example, recently published a set of proposals that would contribute significantly to complying with that requirement. His recommendations include:

> The regulatory review process should begin with the participation of all stakeholders, from industry (not just the applicant's industry), civil society and government and seek a consensus endorsement in the scope and nature of the risk assessment. The stakeholder engagement should not begin with an evaluation of the outcome of a risk assessment. A scientific risk assessment should be based on scientific information that is available for review and verifiable (through independent testing) by qualified scientists who have reliable career independence from the commercial incentives pervading both public and privateer search.

In other words, Ministers should consult relevant stakeholder groups, and then take responsibility for setting risk assessment policies for GM crops in India, and expert advisors should be accountable for acting in accordance with that policy guidance. Given, moreover, that in August 2012, a technical expert panel appointed by the Indian Supreme Court recommended a 10-year moratorium on all field trials of GM food crops; the prospects for the rapid adoption of the BRAI Bill seem remote.

Since October 2009 events and disclosures in India have not only undermined the plausibility of technocratic regimes, they have also cut the ground from underneath a regime resembling a Red Book model. If a sufficient proportion of policy stakeholders recognise that scientific assessments of technological risks are invariably framed by prior upstream assumptions, for example about what is to be counted as a risk and how much of which kinds of evidence can be deemed as variously necessary and/or sufficient for policy decisions then both technocratic and Red Book regimes become unsustainable—they lose a minimum requirement for their superficial appearance of legitimacy. As can be seen in many of the other chapters in this book on public health, pollution, natural hazards, and civil nuclear power plants there is a growing need for a general re-appraisal of science-based technological risk management regimes; to turn these inside out and bring to the surface buried policy judgements and assumptions for debate.

BIBLIOGRAPHY

Abraham, J. (1993). 'Scientific Standards and Institutional Interests: Carcinogenic Risk Assessment of Benoxaprofen in the UK and US', *Social Studies of Science*, 23: 387–444.

Biotechnology Regulatory Authority of India (BRAI) Bill (2011). *Biotechnology Regulatory Authority of India Bill*, Bill No. 54 of 2011, available at http://indiagminfo.org/wp-content/uploads/2011/09/BRAI_Bill_2011.pdf, last accessed on 28 March 2012.

Brickman, R., S. Jasanoff, and T. Ilgen (1985). *Controlling Chemicals: The Politics of Regulation in Europe and the USA*. Ithaca: Cornell University Press.

Codex Alimentarius Commission (CAC) (2003). *Procedural Manual*, 13th edition, available at http://www.fao.org/docrep/006/y4971e/y4971e00.htm, last accessed on 17 November 2013.

——— (2007). 'Report of Thirtieth Session of the Joint FAO/WHO Food Standards Programme', available at http://www.codexalimentarius.net/

web/index_en.jspasftp://ftp.fao.org/codex/Alinorm07/al30REPe.pdf, last accessed in January 2008.

Carmen, J. (2010). *The Inadequacy of GM Brinjal Food Safety Studies: A Reply to the ECII Report*, Institute of Health and Environmental Research Inc. South Australia, February 2010, available at http://www.gmwatch.org/latest-listing/1-news-items/11932-the-inadequacy-of-gm-brinjal-food-safety-studies-dr-judy-carman?format=pdf, last accessed on 31 January 2011.

Castleman, B., and G. Ziem (1988). 'Corporate Influences on Threshold Limit Values', *American Journal of Industrial Medicine*, 13: 531–59.

Commission of the European Communities (CEC) (2002). *Communication From The Commission on the Collection and Use of Expertise by the Commission: Principles and Guidelines 'Improving the Knowledge Base for Better Policies'*, Commission of the European Communities, COM, 713 final, Brussels, 11 December 2002.

Ezrahi, Y. (1990). *The Descent of Icarus: Science and the Transformation of Contemporary Democracy*. Cambridge, Massachusetts: Harvard University Press.

Gupta, A. (2011). 'An Evolving Science-Society Contract in India: The Search for Legitimacy in Anticipatory Risk Governance', *Food Policy*, 36: 736–41.

Heinemann, J.A. (2012). 'Suggestions On How to Apply International Safety Testing Guidelines for Genetically Modified Organisms', 27 February 2012, available at http://agrariancrisis.in/wp-content/uploads/2012/03/Jack-Bt-b-further-assessment-forimmediate-release-feb-27-2012.pdf, last accessed in March 2012.

Huff, J. (2002). 'IARC Monographs, Industry Influence, and Upgrading, Downgrading, and Under-grading Chemicals', *International Journal of Occupational and Environmental Health*, 8: 249–70.

Jasanoff, S. (1990). *The Fifth Branch: Science Advisors as Policy-Makers*, Cambridge, Massachusetts: Harvard University Press.

Jasanoff, S., and B. Wynne (1998). 'Science and Decision-making', in S. Rayner and E.L. Malone (eds), *Human Choices and Climate Change: Volume 1–The Societal Framework*. Ohio: Battelle Press.

Levidow, L., S. Carr, D. Wield, and R. von Schomberg (1997). 'European Biotechnology Regulation: Framing the Risk Assessment of a Herbicide-Tolerant Crop', *Science, Technology and Human Values*, 22: 472–505.

Mahyco (2008). 'Toxicology & Allergenicity Studies', 'Environmental Safety Studies', and 'Other Studies', Vol. 1–8 of the dossier on Bt Brinjal. Mumbai, The Maharashtra Hybrid Seeds Company Ltd., Mumbai.

Millstone, E., E. Brunner, and S. Mayer (1999). 'Beyond Substantial Equivalence', *Nature*, 401: 525–6.

Millstone, E. (2007). 'Can Food Safety Policy-making Be Both Scientifically and Democratically Legitimated? If So, How?', *Journal of Agricultural and Environmental Ethics*, 20: 483–508; DOI:10.1007/s10806-007-9045-x.

Millstone, E. (2009). 'Science, Risk and Governance: Radical Rhetorics and the Realities of Reform', *Research Policy*, 38(4): 624–36, doi:10.1016/j.respol.2009.01.012.

Millstone, E., P. van Zwanenberg, Les Levidow, Spök Armin, Hirakawa Hideyuki, and Matsuo Makiko (2008). *Risk-assessment Policies: Differences Across Jurisdictions*, Institute for Prospective Technological Studies, Seville, Spain, EUR Number: 23259 EN, available at http://ipts.jrc.ec.europa.eu/publications/pub.cfm?id=1562, last accessed on 17 November 2013.

Oxera (2000). *Policy, Risk and Science: Securing and Using Scientific Advice*, Oxford Economic and Research Associates, a report to the UK Health and Safety Executive, available at http://www.hse.gov.uk/research/crr_pdf/2000/crr00295.pdf, last accessed on 27 March 2012.

Saldanha, L.F., and B.S. Rao (2011). 'Creating an Undemocratic and Unaccountable Biotechnology Regulator: A critique of the Biotechnology Regulatory Authority of India Bill, 2011, with Particular Emphasis on Environmental laws', Environment Support Group, November, available at http://www.esgindia.org/campaigns/brinjal/press/brai-bill-2011-esg-critique.html, last accessed on 17 November 2013.

Seralini, G. (2009). *Effects on Health and Environment of Transgenic (or GM) Bt Brinjal*, CriiGen, January, available at http://www.somloquesembrem.org/img_editor/file/SeraliniberenjenaIndia.pdf, last accessed on 31 January 2011.

The Hindu (2010). 'It's Moratorium on Bt Brinjal: Ramesh', *The Hindu*, 10 February, available at http://www.hindu.com/2010/02/10/stories/2010021058000100.htm, last accessed in April 2012.

US National Research Council (US NRC) (1983). *Risk Assessment in the Federal Government: Managing the Process*. Washington, D.C.: National Academies Press.

———— (1994). *Science and Judgment in Risk Assessment*, Commission of the Life Sciences, US National Research Council. Washington, D.C.: National Academies Press.

van Zwanenberg, P., and E. Millstone (2000). 'Beyond Sceptical Relativism: Evaluating the Social Constructions of Expert Risk Assessments', *Science, Technology & Human Values*, 25(3): 259–82.

———— (2005). *BSE: Risk, Science and Government*. Oxford: Oxford University Press.

World Trade Organization (WTO) (1998). 'Understanding the WTO Agreement on Sanitary and Phytosanitary Measures', available at http://www.wto.org/english/tratop_e/sps_e/spsund_e.htm, last accessed in January 2008.

Wynne, B. (2012), 'Do We Need GM Food?', *The Times: Eureka Supplement*, 5 April.

10

M.V. RAMANA

Absurd Confidence

Risk and Nuclear Power in India

Such in reality is the absurd confidence which almost all men have in their own good fortune, that wherever there is the least probability of success, too great a share of it is apt to go to them of its own accord.

—Adam Smith (2001: 742)

In the aftermath of Fukushima, several countries, including Germany, Italy, and Japan, rethought their reliance on nuclear power because safety concerns now dominated their assessments of energy choices. In India, however, the Secretary of the Department of Atomic Energy (DAE) assured the viewers of the popular television channel, *NDTV*, that Indian reactors are 'one hundred per cent' safe (Bagla 2011). Other policymakers and senior functionaries were also equally reassuring. The unshakable confidence that the Indian authorities have in the safety and reliability of their nuclear facilities is not new. In the aftermath of the Tokaimura criticality accident of 1999 in Japan, the DAE Secretary then had also asserted that there 'is no possibility of any nuclear accident in the near or distant future in India' (ToI 1999). In another instance, the Reactor Safety Analysis Group of the DAE had confidently declared in 1986: 'For coastal sites, flooding may be due to tropical cyclones, tsunamis, seiches and wind waves. In India, tsunamis and seiches do not occur. Hence cyclones alone have been singled out for detailed study'

(RSAG 1986, cited in Anand (2005)). This assertion was belied by the December 2004 tsunami. There is a profound parallel between the way the DAE has concluded that just because no tsunamis and seiches had hit India till 1986 that they 'do not occur' and the way it concludes from the record, so far, of no catastrophic accidents that its nuclear facilities are safe. In other words, the absence of catastrophic accidents cannot be cited as evidence of absence of *risk* of catastrophic accidents.

Over the decades, there has been a multitude of small accidents, including one that was rated Level 3 on the International Nuclear Event Scale (INES) (Chernobyl and Fukushima were Level 7). The leadership of the DAE has largely ignored these accidents and various other risk signals.[1] India's atomic energy proponents have usually maintained that all nuclear facilities are safe and there is no possibility of a nuclear accident. The rest of this chapter traces the track record of the DAE and its constituent organizations and explores the reasons why this confidence is not justified.

RISK MANAGEMENT

That the production of nuclear power entails significant risks has always been evident, and this concern has been accentuated since accidents in nuclear power plants at Chernobyl and Fukushima. Most countries have also paid attention to those somewhat less catastrophic risks, such as those associated with occupational exposure and radioactive waste disposal. Overall, there has been a strong focus on managing the risks from nuclear power in a socially acceptable manner.

Broadly speaking, there are two dimensions to risk management in the arena of nuclear power: the hardware (technology and safety devices) and software (human factors and safety culture). It is impossible to neatly compartmentalize these two dimensions, however, as human factors also permeate the realm of technology through design choices.

In terms of hardware, the two primary methods of making a system safe, both of which are usually implemented, are in the realm of

---

[1] I use the term DAE as an omnibus descriptor for the many official organizations involved in the production of nuclear energy (and weapons) in India, including five research centres, five government-owned companies ('public sector enterprises'), three industrial organizations, and three service organizations.

design and the use of safety mechanisms. The first method requires that for 'a number of possible accidents the design is such that the reactor recovers and behaves safely and damage does not spread even if no protective action, automatic or deliberate is taken' (Judd 1981: 134). The second approach is to incorporate multiple protective systems so that they would all have to fail before a radioactive release occurs. For example, the cladding surrounding the fuel would have to give way and the integrity of the pressure vessel and containment would have to be lost before a radioactive release occurs. This concept is called defence in depth (Glasstone and Sesonske 1981; Knief 1992). The likelihood of meeting these requirements is enhanced if there is redundancy, with more than one system serving the same function. These technical devices ensuring safety should themselves be reliable, that is, operating as designed when needed, and built with high quality control standards. Furthermore, in another instance of the interplay between the hardware and software aspects to safety, nuclear facilities should be built, maintained, and operated according to design, failing which protective systems may not behave as desired.

As an example of the software side of risk management, we turn to the recommendations advanced by the High Reliability Organization (HRO) School, led by a group of scholars from the University of California, Berkeley. The HRO theorists started with the observation that some organizations operate hazardous technological facilities with what seemed 'an extraordinary level of safety and productive capacity' (La Porte 1996). This prompted a search for explanatory factors that focused on intelligent organizational design and good management practices. The HRO group maintains that they have only uncovered 'conditions that were *necessary* for relatively safe and productive management of technologies' but do not wish to imply that 'these conditions were *sufficient*' (La Porte and Rochlin 1994).

The common ingredients that contribute towards the safe operation of hazardous technologies include: political elites and organization leaders placing a high priority on safety in design and operations; setting and maintaining safety standards and practices; ensuring a healthy relationship between management and workers; redundancy in technical operations and personnel management; allowing compensation for failures; and continuous organizational learning via systematic gleaning of feedback (Sagan 1993; La Porte 1996; Bigley and Roberts 2001).

But does the DAE meet these requirements? To better answer this question, we turn to a couple of accidents that have occurred at the DAE's nuclear facilities.

THE NARORA ACCIDENT

India's most serious accident at a nuclear reactor occurred on 31 March 1993. Early that morning, two blades of the turbine of the first unit at Narora power station broke off due to fatigue. Through a chain of rapid events, this led to a major fire that engulfed the turbine building. Among the systems burnt by the fire were four cables that carried wires and electricity, which caused a general blackout in the plant and rendered the secondary cooling systems inoperable. The fire and smoke forced operators to leave the control room, which could not be re-entered for close to 13 hours. This, coupled with the lack of power, meant that operators had no indications about the condition of the reactor and were, in effect, 'flying blind' (Nowlen et al. 2001). Fortunately, the reactor shutdown systems worked and the chain reaction was stopped.

More worrisome than the accident itself is the evidence that it provides about how the DAE had not met various requirements for safety, both with respect to the hardware and software. Prior to the accident, there were repeated warnings and recommendations that the organization had ignored. There had been a number of fire accidents at the DAE's reactors and elsewhere, but the organization had not taken any serious steps towards fire mitigation (Kumar and Ramana (unpublished); Ramana and Kumar 2010).

In 1989, four years before the accident, General Electric (GE) Company had communicated information to the turbine manufacturer, Bharat Heavy Electricals Limited (BHEL), about a design flaw that had led to cracks in similar turbines around the world. They recommended design modifications, and the manufacturer responded by preparing detailed drawings for the Nuclear Power Corporation (NPC), which operated the Narora reactor. However, NPC did not take any action until months after the accident (Gopalakrishnan 1999a). In addition to GE, the manufacturer of the turbine, BHEL, also recommended that NPC replace the blade design before any accident occurred. But NPC did not act on this advice until after the accident (ibid.). This represents a failure of the necessary maintenance.

Second, even if the turbine blade did fail, the accident might have been averted if safety systems had been operating, which they presumably would have if their power supply had been encased in separate and fire-resistant ducts. By the time the Narora reactor was commissioned, this was established wisdom in the nuclear design community and has been ever since a fire at Brown's Ferry plant in the United States in 1975. The Brown's Ferry accident had resulted in significant changes being mandated at all US nuclear plants (Ramsey and Modarres 1998: 106). Nuclear reactor operators had to make sure that there were physically diverse ways of providing electricity and ensure that these were protected from fires by barriers. Other countries also adopted similar measures.

All of this was well before the Narora plant attained criticality, but the DAE did not take note of this international experience. The plant was constructed with the four backup power supply systems in the same duct, with no fire-resistant material enclosing or separating the cable systems. This setup was perfect for a single cause, a fire, to render these many safety systems inoperable, and constitutes an excellent example of what safety analysts call 'common cause failure'. Narora violated the most basic of technical requirements for a nuclear power plant—that of a design which incorporates adequate levels of safety, specifically the ability to recover from failures.

It appears that the DAE was aware of the necessary measures to reduce the risk from fires. The probabilistic safety assessment for Narora performed by DAE analysts, which included Anil Kakodkar, the future Chairman of the Atomic Energy Commission (AEC), points out that the effects of common cause failures (due to fires or changes in the ambient temperature) would be reduced if 'physical diversity and fire barriers are provided' (Babar et al. 1989: 109). Another paper by safety analysts in the DAE, albeit well after the Narora accident, acknowledges that after 'the Browns Ferry experience in the United States, fire risk evaluation and hazard analysis has been considered as an essential component of safety evaluation and assurance' (Vinod et al. 2008). Thus, it would seem that even though some sections of the DAE were aware of the risks of a common cause failure in the event of a fire, organizational leaders chose not to implement the necessary design modifications.

Another DAE characteristic that may have contributed to the Narora accident is its disregard for precursor events. Risk analysts and safety theorists have repeatedly emphasized the importance of small precursors and the possibility that such precursors could combine with other failures to escalate into a major accident (Perrow 1984). In the case of Narora, not only did the fire have precursors, but so did the events that led to the fire. Specifically, there were many instances of excessive vibrations in the turbine bearings and oil leaks (Ramana and Kumar 2010).

The DAE did not take serious note of these earlier failures. When asked by an interviewer about recurring turbine blade failures at nuclear reactors, the DAE Secretary side-stepped the issue by suggesting 'this kind of failure at Narora has happened for the first time...two blades failing', offering the non sequitur, 'you must remember that as far as nuclear reactor is concerned, there was no problem at Narora. The reactor worked perfectly according to design' (Chidambaram 1993). While the DAE Secretary may have been trying to mystify the interviewer by harping on the difference between the turbine and the reactor, there is little doubt that the DAE had ignored early warnings and set the stage for the Narora failure that led to 'widespread damage to the [turbine generator] set, condenser and caused [a] fire which engulfed the cables, the turbine building and control equipment room' (Ghosh 1996: 30). Events such as fires, turbine vibrations, and leaks have persisted even after the Narora accident, raising questions about what has been learnt from that event.

KALPAKKAM REPROCESSING PLANT

On 21 January 2003, some employees were tasked with collecting a sample of low-level waste (LLW) from a part of the Kalpakkam Atomic Reprocessing Plant (KARP) facility called the Waste Tank Farm (WTF). Unknown to them, a valve had failed, resulting in the release of high-level waste (HLW), with much greater levels of radioactivity, into the part of the WTF where they were working. Although the plant was five years old, no radiation monitors or mechanisms to detect valve failure had yet been installed in that area. Therefore the workers had no way of knowing that the sample they went in to collect was actually emitting high levels of radiation. The accident was recognized only after a collected sample was taken to a different room and processed. In the meantime, six workers had been exposed to high radiation doses (Anand 2003).

Apart from the lack of monitoring mechanisms, a significant cause for concern was the response of the management, in this case the Bhabha Atomic Research Centre (BARC). Despite a safety committee's recommendation that the plant be shut down, the upper management of BARC decided to continue operating the plant. Despite many attempts by employees, the management refused to implement any safety demands. Finally, the employees union leaked information about the radiation exposure to the press.

Once the news had become public, the management grudgingly admitted that this was the 'worst accident in radiation exposure in the history of nuclear India' (Anand 2003). But it claimed that the 'incident' resulted from 'over enthusiasm and error of judgment' on the part of the workers (Venkatesh 2003). The management also tried to 'externalize the risk problem' by blaming the workers for not wearing their thermoluminescent dosimeter (TLD) badges (Subramanian 2003). But this had nothing to do with the accident as TLD badges would not have warned the workers about radiation levels in real time; these badges are periodically processed in laboratories and the workers get to know that they have been exposed to a high level of radiation only well after the actual exposure.[2] For its part, the employees union claimed that the accident was only to be expected as the unrelenting pace of work at KARP and the 'unsafe practices being forced on the workers' have made accidents a regular feature (Anonymous 2003).

OTHER EVIDENCE

There are further indications of poor risk-management strategies, specifically, the inadequacy of organizational learning. One important indicator is the DAE's history of repeated occurrences of similar accidents (Kumar and Ramana (unpublished)). There have been, for example, multiple leaks of heavy water. Despite much effort—partly because heavy water is expensive (Ramana 2007) and has been in short

---

[2] The practice of inadequate methods of detecting high levels of radiation seems to continue. In 2011, workers at the Kakrapar reactor found that the radiation detectors they were given did not record beyond a certain value, whereas they had been asked to work in a zone that had nearly 20 times that level of radiation (Banerji 2011).

234 | *India's Risks*

supply for decades—the DAE has not managed to contain them.[3] Other examples are repeated bursts of the pipes that carry radioactive waste from the Uranium Corporation plant in the Jaduguda area. The first widely reported such burst occurred in 2006 (Krishnan 2007), and was to occur on at least three more occasions over the next couple of years (Tiwari 2008). These repeated occurrences suggest either weaknesses in the regulatory board or an inability to control the technology and operate it adequately. In either case such failures are not conducive to safety.

A related, and disturbing, indication of the lacunae in India's risk-management process is the frequent failure of safety devices. These are the mechanisms that seek to control the reactor under unanticipated circumstances. Therefore, if these do not work as expected then it is more likely that a small event could cascade into a major accident. In the case of the 1993 Narora accident discussed earlier, for example, the smoke sensors in the power control room at Narora did not detect the fire immediately, and the fire was detected only when the flames were noticed by plant personnel (Srinivas 1993).

Once in a while, the callousness of the authorities comes back to bite them, as it were. On one occasion in the mid-1960s, an underground tank at the Trombay reprocessing plant, which was used to store irradiated fuel rods, became severely contaminated. The water was pumped out into the sea and a very high level of radiation built up close to the shore. What happened after that is best described by someone who was part of the DAE at that point:

> The next day the canteen waiters of the plutonium plant, who usually used the shore for ablutions, were severely contaminated. Unaware of this, they served in the canteen and passed on the contamination to the technicians who carried it into the labs. Radiation monitors in the labs went haywire due to the very high levels of nuclear radiation they were exposed to. It was only after a great deal of effort that the problem was

---

[3] Some of these leaks have occurred while a device called BARCCIS (Bhabha Atomic Research Centre Channel Inspection System), which is used to inspect coolant tubes in reactors, was in operation. In March 1999, at the Madras Atomic Power Station, the Atomic Energy Regulatory Board (AERB) had undertaken a review of the BARCCIS system and suggested a number of changes in design, operating procedures, and training (AERB 2004: 18). But in the next few years, there were heavy water leaks at the Narora and the Rajasthan reactors (PTI 1999; AERB 2001, 2004).

traced back to the plutonium plant. Thereafter, Health Physics safeguard inside, outside, and around the plutonium plant were stepped up sharply. But [Homi] Sethna [who succeeded Bhabha as AEC Chairman] opposed this continuously. As a result, one of the last office orders [first AEC Chairman Homi] Bhabha wrote to A.S. Rao (who was in charge of the Health and Safety Division in BARC) directed him to reassign a certain engineer from the plutonium plant as the latter was being too tough about strict compliance with health and safety practices. Sethna won. (Parthasarathi 2007: 17–18)

A different example comes from the Narora reactor, and was revealed by a member of the nuclear establishment to Surendra Gadekar, the editor of *Anumukti* (Sahgal 1998). Once, a worker with a Geiger counter, an instrument used to measure radiation, went to the canteen for tea. His counter suddenly started ticking fast, indicating a high level of radioactivity. On investigating he found that the radioactivity was coming from the fire used for preparing the tea. On further investigation it was discovered that the wood being burnt in the fire had originally been used for scaffolding inside the plant, and had got contaminated. Rather than being stored as low-level waste (LLW), it had been sold to a contractor, who in turn had sold it to the canteen.

In all, the accidents described here and the other pieces of evidence reveal poor safety and accident-risk-management practices on the part of the DAE. First, organizational leaders did not place a high priority on safety in design. This is suggested by both the placement of power supply lines together without fire protection at Narora and, at KARP, the absence of functional redundancy in methods to prevent high-level waste (HLW) coming into tanks that were designed to hold only LLW. Second, as shown by repeated occurrences of similar precursor events as well as other costly accidents, there was inadequate learning from failures. Third, the KARP accident demonstrates that the relationship between management and workers was not healthy. As suggested below, one likely reason for these failings is the confidence that nuclear officials had in the safety of their reactor, despite reasons to think otherwise.

RISK ASSESSMENT

Studies of risk perception around the world have revealed that most people have a multi-dimensional conception of risk that is based on characteristics such as the familiarity of the hazard, whether exposure to the hazard is undertaken voluntarily, features of the technology such as its susceptibility to disastrous accidents, inequities in risks and benefits, and the long-term implications of exposure to the hazard (Slovic et al. 1982). In India, this would likely include concerns about how nuclear power would be managed in a country which has had a number of corruption scandals taint the political class and its institutions. Concerns may also surround a legal system that still fails to adequately address environmental and health disasters like the one that occurred in Bhopal in 1984, and environmental regulations that are frequently disregarded and manipulated. The noticeable lack of accountability and transparency in the nuclear establishment's operations is also likely to influence the perception of risk (see Chapter 12 by Claire Mays).

In contrast, the nuclear establishment's general world-view appears to be characterized by a great deal of what might be called 'techno-optimism'. For example, Indian nuclear officials have kept stating that the reactors being constructed or proposed for construction in locations like Koodankulam and Jaitapur are newer and more advanced than the ones in Fukushima, therefore they would not undergo any accidents. In their risk assessments officials appear to narrowly focus only on the technology aspect of nuclear power rather than the wider context.[4] This technocratic outlook predisposes the nuclear establishment to ignore various risks associated with nuclear power.

Examining the DAE's attitude towards the production of radioactive wastes is indicative of this tendency to overlook the risks associated with nuclear power. It is widely acknowledged that dealing with radioactive waste is one of the major negative attributes of nuclear power, and this has been an important factor in the decision by some European countries to phase out nuclear power. More immediately, many countries have found dealing with the spent fuel accumulating at various reactor sites to be a major problem.

---

[4] This happens even in arenas where the wider context is obviously important. Discussions of liability in the context of nuclear accidents, for example, focus only on compensation payments and not issues like healthcare. When the Nuclear Liability Bill was being drafted, the health ministry was not involved and later said that the country did not possess the capacity to manage a radiological emergency.

The DAE, on the other hand, has a two-fold response. First, it maintains that spent fuel is not a waste but 'a resource to extract plutonium from' (Chidambaram 1996). Extraction of plutonium is done through the process of reprocessing, wherein the spent fuel is chopped up, dissolved in concentrated acid, and then various solvents are added to separate out different elements. Besides plutonium and uranium, reprocessing also produces three waste streams classified on the basis of their radioactive content as high-level, intermediate-level and low-level wastes (HLWs, ILWs, and LLWs). The largest component (by volume) is LLW that comprises over 80 per cent by volume of the waste stream; however, this only contains about 0.1 per cent of the total activity from the spent fuel. ILW accounts for over 10 per cent by volume and contains about 1 per cent of the radioactivity (Rodriguez 1996). HLW constitutes about 2 per cent by volume but contains nearly 99 per cent of the total radioactivity.

As its second response to the question of dealing with radioactive wastes, the DAE focuses primarily on the HLW and goes on to claim that because it reprocesses spent fuel, waste volumes are reduced so much that there is no problem with storing it for several decades until a geological repository is established to bury these wastes. This is somewhat disingenuous because it ignores the other two categories of waste. Of particular concern is the LLW produced during reprocessing, because it is released into the oceans or the atmosphere and is therefore a potential source of radioactivity which can reach human beings. Traces of these are routinely found in the soil, vegetation, fish, and so on. For example, the levels of iodine-129 in soil samples at a distance of 1.5 km away from the small-sized Trombay reprocessing plant are over 50 times higher than the background levels (Doshi et al. 1991).

RISK COMMUNICATION

The DAE's ideas on risk communication fall short of the general norms of public engagement and transparent deliberations needed for the creation of trust (see Chapter 12 by Claire Mays). There have been a growing number of public protests at several sites earmarked for new nuclear reactors and uranium mining projects, where local people have refused to accept the DAE's assertions that these facilities would be safe and their health would not be impacted. These protests suggest that the

DAE suffers from a lack of credibility, and weaknesses in the regulatory system, described later, only serve to exacerbate this.

One particular weakness in the DAE's attitude towards risk communication is the refusal to even acknowledge that nuclear facilities might pose some risk, albeit at a low level, to the health of the population in the vicinity. A good illustration is in the case of the Jaduguda uranium mines and mills, and their impacts on public and occupational health. In the last decade or so, a few independent epidemiological studies have found discernibly higher levels of poor outcomes in various health indicators, such as numbers of congenital deformities, among the inhabitants of the villages near Jaduguda, as compared to control villages a little further away (Gadekar et al. (unpublished); Vishnu 2010). When confronted with such data, the nuclear establishment has a standard set of responses. These range from outright denial: '[T]here is no health hazard in and around Jaduguda caused by our uranium mines' (Biswas 1999); to dismissing the significance of the observation: '[C]ongenital malformations occur the world over' (Malhotra 2001); or finding some alternate explanation, '[I]llnesses are largely due to malnutrition and an unhealthy lifestyle' (Vishnu 2010); or to invoking scientific studies of radiation effects: '[H]ealth effects of radiation have been the subject of detailed study for the past several decades. The United Nations Scientific Committee of the Effects of Atomic Radiation publishes periodic reports on it. None of these ever recorded that radiation can cause such symptoms' (Parthasarathy 2007). Occasionally, there is also talk about how such claims are made by those who are opposed to India achieving technological progress: '[T]hese reports are uninformed and, in some cases, part of a campaign to stop India from pursuing its nuclear research and power generation' (P.K. Iyengar in *Hindustan Times* as cited in Gadekar (1993)).

These responses suggest that DAE personnel cannot even contemplate the possibility that nuclear facilities could be linked to ill health. Further, anyone pointing to negative impacts related to nuclear power, let alone explicit criticism, is accused of being anti-nationalistic.

Another aspect of risk communication, or lack thereof, by the nuclear establishment has been its refusal to even discuss its activities with populations that could be potentially impacted. Since decision-making has not involved these populations, this has frequently resulted in protests and sometimes the abandonment of these projects. This pattern has been dubbed DADA (Decide, Announce, Defend, and Abandon) by scholars (Mackerron and Berkhout 2009).

One such example of DADA in India has been the DAE's attempt to deal with the disposal of HLW and spent fuel. Since the 1950s, countries around the world with nuclear facilities have explored different options for nuclear waste disposal and most have settled on burying these wastes in geological repositories. Despite decades of effort, however, no repositories have actually been constructed and operated. Those countries that have actually made progress in identifying a site for geological waste have realized the importance of public acceptance and initiated site selection processes that include significant public stakeholder involvement (NEA 2008). Important among them are Finland and Sweden, and to a lesser extent, Canada and the United Kingdom (Feiveson et al. 2011).

The nuclear establishment in India has not just eschewed public stakeholder involvement but has been remarkably opaque about its plans. In March 1997, the inhabitants of Sanawada village near Pokhran found that a number of people had come to the area near their village and were drilling the ground. When asked, they were told that the Minerals Exploration Corporation Limited (MECL) was drilling for precious stones (Sinha 2000). Later, environmentalists discovered that MECL was doing the drilling for BARC and that Sanawada was being considered as a potential nuclear waste storage location (DTE 2000). Apparently even the Chief Minister of Rajasthan did not know of these plans. When this news became public and protests ensued, the central government declared that it had not taken a decision on the disposal of nuclear wastes (PTI 2000).

More recently, in February 2012, the AEC Chairman announced that the DAE was going to set up an underground lab to study the suitability of the surrounding rock to host a deep underground repository (PTI 2012). The AEC Chairman listed a number of criteria (one of them being, 'a rock formation that is geologically stable, totally impervious and without any fissures') but not one of these had anything to do with obtaining the consent of the local population.

In sum, the DAE violates many of the canons of risk communication (Kasperson 1986; Flynn et al. 1993; Slovic et al. 1991). One consequence has been a lack of trust among populations living close to nuclear facilities. This is especially true near proposed nuclear facilities, for example, at the Meghalaya uranium deposits (Karlsson 2009). In many cases, this has led to strong opposition to the establishment of the facility, most spectacularly through the intense and sustained protests surrounding the commissioning of the Koodankulam nuclear plant.

EXPLORING THE REASONS

Writing from the outside, it is hard to conclude anything definitively about why the record of safety in India's nuclear facilities has been poor, and the nuclear establishment does not deal with risk adequately. Nevertheless, some tentative suggestions are offered here.

No-risk Ideology

To understand this gamut of problems with nuclear power in India, one has to begin with how the nuclear establishment views the risk of accidents. Nuclear power, as Charles Perrow famously argued nearly three decades ago, is an 'interactively complex' and 'tightly coupled' system that is prone to 'normal accidents' (Perrow 1984). Rather than acknowledge that there is an ever-present risk that accompanies such a hazardous technology, the dominant view within the Indian nuclear establishment is that there is no risk of accidents. This is illustrated by the current AEC Chairman's assertion that nuclear reactors in India are 100 per cent safe, or, as he said elsewhere, the probability of an accident is one in infinity, that is, zero (PTI 2011a).

In line with this misguided belief that accidents are impossible, leaders of the nuclear establishment went even further and denied the very nature of what happened at Fukushima. The Chairman and Managing Director of the NPC claimed, 'there is no nuclear accident or incident in Japan's Fukushima plants. It is a well-planned emergency preparedness programme which the nuclear operators of the Tokyo Electric Power Company are carrying out to contain the residual heat after the plants had an automatic shutdown following a major earthquake' (PTI 2011b). The AEC Chairman said, 'It was not a nuclear accident...immediately after the earthquake, the nuclear reactor shut down and nuclear chain reaction stopped' (PTI 2011a). Such utterances reveal the lengths to which the nuclear establishment goes to maintain its ideology in the face of evidence.

The belief in the absence of risk is not merely a case of maintaining a public persona. In fact, the former chairman of NPC has stated that it is 'important' that 'the people (operating the nuclear plant) should be confident about safety' (Subramanian 2000). This suggests that the confident view of safety should be deeply internalized. Since there is little openness in the activities of the nuclear establishment, and by and large workers in various nuclear facilities live in fairly close-knit communities, there is a significant likelihood that elite views on nuclear risk will permeate throughout the establishment.

It is worth recalling one of the many paradoxes about safety that those who study accidents point out: '[I]f an organization is convinced that it has achieved a safe culture, it almost certainly has not' (Reason 2000).

Lack of Accountability

A second reason for the poor track record of the nuclear establishment is that it has not been held liable for its many failures. Even though there have been several revelations about radiation leaks, safety errors, and workers being subject to high levels of radiation, so far none of these resulted in any major policy changes. By and large, the regulatory authorities, that is, the AERB and the Pollution Control Boards (PCB), have been more concerned about keeping nuclear facilities operational rather than public health. So far, no reactors have been shut down for exceeding radiation limits in effluents. None of these issues have been subject to any meaningful debates in the Parliament or Legislative Assemblies.

As the current Minister for Environment and Forests, Jayanthi Natarajan, was to despair publicly:

> I have been a Member of the Parliamentary Consultative Committee for Defence and Atomic Energy, and have tried time and again to raise issues relating to public safety, both at Parliamentary Committee hearings, and in the Rajya Sabha, and have achieved precious little for my pains. Since I was an MP at the time, and a pretty aggressive one, I had to be dealt with. But they simply drowned me with totally obscure and incomprehensible scientific terms and explanations, which sounded impressive, and meant nothing. The rest was simply not forthcoming because they claimed it was 'classified'. I have repeatedly

raised the issue of the hazards of radiation leaks, safety procedures, and environmental contamination, that might flow from the atomic power station at Kalpakkam, but have always received the bland and meaningless reply that the radiation was 'within acceptable limits'. (Natarajan 2003)

Weaknesses in Regulation

An additional problem so far has been its regulatory structure. Until 1972, the DAE did not have a separately identifiable organization or personnel for reviewing the safety of its nuclear installations (Gopalakrishnan 2002). The first reactor, Apsara, did not even undergo a formal safety analysis (Sundararajan et al. 2008: 2). Eventually, AERB was set up in 1983, but under the administrative and financial purview of the Atomic Energy Commission. This places structural limits on the AERB's effectiveness. As common experience would indicate, it is hard to criticize one's boss or force action in ways that he or she does not want.

Further, the AERB has always been constrained by its lack of technical staff and testing facilities. As Gopalakrishnan, former chairman of the AERB, has observed:

95 per cent of the members of the AERB's evaluation committees are scientists and engineers on the payrolls of the DAE. This dependency is deliberately exploited by the DAE management to influence, directly and indirectly, the AERB's safety evaluations and decisions. The interference has manifested itself in the AERB toning down the seriousness of safety concerns, agreeing to the postponement of essential repairs to suit the DAE's time schedules, and allowing continued operation of installations when public safety considerations would warrant their immediate shutdown and repair. (Gopalakrishnan 1999a)

A good example of the inadequacy of the regulatory structure comes from the Kaiga nuclear power plant. On 13 May 1994, the inner containment dome of one of the units collapsed during reactor construction, due to inadequate quality control and faulty design (Pannerselvan 1999). According to DAE officials it seems that 'while inputs such as cement and steel had been tested for quality, that was not the case with the concrete blocks as a whole' (Mohan 1994). Construction workers have accused the contractors of various malpractices in construction (Hayanur 1994).[5]

But the underlying failure was that of regulation. According to Gopalakrishnan, the head of the AERB at the time of the dome collapse:

> Senior NPC civil engineers and the private firms which provide civil engineering designs and construction drawings to the DAE have had a close relationship. In this atmosphere of comradeship, the NPC engineers did not carry out the necessary quality checks on the designs they received before passing them on to the Kaiga project team. The AERB also did not check this, because it had almost no civil engineering staff with it. Serious design errors went undetected and these eventually led to the failure of the dome. (Gopalakrishnan 1999b)

The Kaiga dome collapse was also an example of direct interference in the activities of the AERB. According to Gopalakrishnan: 'When, as chairman, I appointed an independent expert committee to investigate the containment collapse at Kaiga, the AEC chairman wanted its withdrawal and matters left to the committee formed by the NPC [Managing Director]. The DAE also complained to the [Prime Minister's Office] who tried to force me to back off' (Pannerselvan 1999).

Following the Fukushima accidents, in September 2011, the Indian government introduced the draft Nuclear Safety Regulatory Authority (NSRA) Bill in the Parliament to create a new organization that would regulate nuclear activities in the country. The NSRA would replace the AERB. As of February 2012, the draft Bill is being discussed by the parliamentary committee on science, technology, environment, and forests.

Looking at the content of the Bill and the context under which the NSRA has been created, it seems unlikely that it will lead to an effective separation between the regulatory authority and the nuclear establishment. Many of the key processes involved in ensuring effective regulation will continue to be controlled by the AEC. The power for crucial steps like the appointment of members is vested with the central government. But for most purposes, the authority empowered to act on behalf of the central government is the AEC. The AEC Chairman

[5] Though unproven, corruption among contractors involved in nuclear construction activities has been alleged. Besides at Kaiga, these allegations have been made in the case of Koodankulam (Jayaraman and Sundar Rajan 2011).

will also be one of the key members of the Council of Nuclear Safety that will set the policies with respect to radiation and nuclear safety that will fall under the purview of the NSRA. Further, as evidenced by Gopalakrishnan's observation, there is little expertise outside the nuclear establishment on technical issues relating to nuclear facilities.[6]

★ ★ ★

Nuclear power in India has been a risky enterprise, marked by numerous small accidents and near misses. Yet, reading the literature put out by the DAE or statements made by senior officials, one would be hard-pressed to even suspect that there is the slightest risk to either workers or the general public from any of the many nuclear facilities in India.[7] As the examples in this chapter illustrate, there is much reason for concern about the risk of accidents at nuclear facilities, as well as radioactive contamination and the resulting impact to public health in areas near these facilities. This state of affairs is not helped by the absurd confidence that is displayed by establishment officials.

Can anything be done about this? The problems we have enumerated permeate throughout the DAE and its many attendant institutions. This means that there would have to be a thorough overhaul of all these institutions. The political power of the nuclear establishment is such that this is not likely to happen unless the very nature of decision-making in the country changes substantially. And for the same reason, perhaps one way that such change might come about is as a result of powerful social movements. However, such movements, as in

---

[6] Even within the nuclear establishment, the amount of expertise available is limited, a consideration that is especially of concern because of the diversity of nuclear reactor designs being imported. This has been commented on even by Jairam Ramesh, the former Minister of Environment and Forests (Goswami 2011).

[7] For example, in its submission to the International Atomic Energy Agency (IAEA) as part of its responsibilities under the 1994 Convention on Nuclear Safety, the DAE stated that: 'Safety is accorded overriding priority in all activities. All nuclear facilities are sited, designed, constructed, commissioned and operated in accordance with strict quality and safety standards.... As a result, India's safety record has been excellent in over 260 reactor years of operation of power reactors and various other applications' (Government of India 2007).

the case of the recent (at the time of this writing) protests against the Koodankulam reactor might well call for a complete abandonment of nuclear power, rather than reforming the nuclear establishment, and its approach to risk.

BIBLIOGRAPHY

Anand, S. (2003). 'India's Worst Radiation Accident', *Outlook*, 28 July, pp. 18–20.

——— (2005). 'DAE: Slow Reactors To Impending Doom?', *Outlook*, 17 January, available at http://www.outlookindia.com/article.aspx?226227, last accessed on 19 November 2013.

Anonymous (2003). 'BARC says Kalpakkam Reprocessing Plant Will Soon be Starting', *Press Trust of India*, 11 July.

Atomic Energy Regulatory Board (AERB) (2001). *Annual Report 2000–2001*. Mumbai: Atomic Energy Regulatory Board.

——— (2004). *Annual Report 2003–2004*. Mumbai: Atomic Energy Regulatory Board.

Babar, A.K., R.K. Saraf, A. Kakodkar, and V.V. Sanyasi Rao (1989). *Probabilistic Safety Assessment of Narora Power Project*. Mumbai: Bhabha Atomic Research Centre.

Bagla, Pallava (2011). 'Why Nuclear Reactors are "100 Per Cent Safe"', 20 March, available at http://www.ndtv.com/article/india/why-nuclear-reactors-are-100-per-cent-safe-92815, last accessed on 19 November 2013.

Banerji, Rishi (2011). 'Kakrapar Workers Victims of Radiation Were Not Given Safety Kits.' *Daily News and Analysis*, August 7, available at http://www.dnaindia.com/india/report_kakrapar-workers-victims-of-radiation-were-not-given-safety-kits_1573526, last accessed on 19 November 2013.

Bigley, Gregory A., and Karlene H. Roberts (2001). 'The Incident Command System: High Reliability Organizing for Complex and Volatile Task Environments', *Academy of Management Journal*, 44(6): 1281–300.

Biswas, Soutik (1999). 'Nuclear Fallout', *Asia Week*, 20 June.

Chidambaram, R. (1993). 'The Inevitable Option for Future' Interview with R. Chidambaram, AEC Chairman. *Frontline*, 29 November, pp. 99–104.

——— (1996). '"India is not isolated", interview with AEC Chief R. Chidambaram', *Frontline*, 29 November, pp. 86–9.

Doshi, G.R., S.N. Joshi, and K.C. Pillai (1991). 'I in Soil and Grass Samples Around a Nuclear Reprocessing Plant', *Journal of Radio analytical and Nuclear Chemistry Letters*, 155(2): 115–27.

Down to Earth (DTE) (2000). 'Down with the Dump', Special Report, *Down to Earth*, 30 June.

Feiveson, Harold, Zia Mian, M.V. Ramana, and Frank Von Hippel (eds) (2011). *Managing Spent Fuel from Nuclear Power Reactors: Experience and Lessons from Around the World*. Princeton: International Panel on Fissile Materials, available at http://www.fissilematerials.org/blog/2011/09/managing_spent_fuel_from_html, last accessed on 19 November 2013.

Flynn, James, Paul Slovic, and C.K. Mertz (1993). 'The Nevada Initiative: A Risk Communication Fiasco', *Risk Analysis*, 13(5): 497–502.

Gadekar, Surendra (1993). 'Discussion', *Anumukti*, 6(5): 23–9.

Gadekar, Surendra, Shreekumar, and Sanghamitra Gadekar (unpublished). 'Health Impacts of Uranium Mining in Jaduguda, India'.

Ghosh, G. (1996). 'Operational Experiences: Nuclear Power Stations'. *Electrical India*, pp. 29–33.

Glasstone, Samuel, and Alexander Sesonske (1981). *Nuclear Reactor Engineering*, Vol. 3. New York: Van Nostrand Reinhold.

Government of India (2007). *National Report to the Convention on Nuclear Safety*. New Delhi: Government of India.

Gopalakrishnan, A. (1999a). 'Issues of Nuclear Safety', *Frontline*, March: 13–26.

——— (1999b). 'Of the Shortcomings, The Risks', *Frontline*, May: 8–21.

——— (2002). 'Evolution of the Indian Nuclear Power Program', *Annual Review of Energy and the Environment*, 27: 369–95.

Goswami, Urmi (2011). 'Review Jaitapur and Large Nuclear Parks: Jairam Ramesh', *Economic Times*, 7 April, available at http://articles.economic times.indiatimes.com/2011-04-07/news/29392568_1_nuclear-power-anil-kakodkar-nuclear-park, last accessed on 19 November 2013.

Havanur, Sanjay (1994). 'The Dome of Death', *Anumukti*, 7(6): 4–5.

Jayaraman, Nityanand, and G. Sundar Rajan (2011). 'Answers to Some FAQs About Koodankulam and Nuclear Power', *Dianuke*, 22 November, available at http://www.dianuke.org/faqs-about-koodankulam-and-nuclear-power, last accessed on 19 November 2013.

Judd, A.M. (1981). *Fast Breeder Reactors: An Engineering Introduction*, Vol. 1. Oxford and New York: Pergamon Press.

Karlsson, B.G. (2009). 'Nuclear Lives: Uranium Mining, Indigenous Peoples, and Development in India', *Economic & Political Weekly*, 44(34): 43.

Kasperson, Roger E. (1986). 'Six Propositions on Public Participation and their Relevance for Risk Communication', *Risk Analysis*, 6(3): 275–81.

Knief, Ronald Allen (1992). *Nuclear Engineering: Theory and Technology of Commercial Nuclear Power*. New York: Hemisphere Publishing Corporation.

Koley, Jaharlal, S. Harikumar, S.A.H. Ashraf, S.K. Chande, and S.K. Sharma (2006). 'Regulatory Practices for Nuclear Power Plants in India', *Nuclear Engineering and Design*, 236: 894–913.

Krishnan, Lina (2007). 'Jaduguda Fallout', *Himal*, April.

Kumar, Ashwin, and M.V. Ramana (unpublished). 'Nuclear Safety in India: Theoretical Perspectives and Empirical Evidence'.

La Porte, Todd R. (1996). 'High Reliability Organizations: Unlikely, Demanding and at Risk', *Journal of Contingencies and Crisis Management*, 4(2): 60–71.

La Porte, Todd R., and Gene Rochlin (1994). 'A Rejoinder to Perrow', *Journal of Contingencies and Crisis Management*, 2(4): 221–7.

Mackerron, Gordon, and Frans Berkhout (2009). 'Learning to Listen: Institutional Change and Legitimation in UK Radioactive Waste Policy', *Journal of Risk Research*, 12: 989–1008.

Malhotra, S.K. (2001). 'No Radiation Hazards at UCIL', *Nuclear India*, July/August.

Mohan, M. Madan (1994). 'Kaiga Questions: A Gaping Hole in Safety Standards', *Frontline*, 17 June: 84–5.

Natarajan, Jayanthi (2003). 'Classified Dangerous', *New Sunday Express*, 29 July.

Nuclear Energy Agency (NEA) (2008). *Moving Forward with Geological Disposal of Radioactive Waste*. Paris: Nuclear Energy Agency, OECD.

Nowlen, S.P., M. Kazarians, and F. Wyant (2001). *Risk Methods Insights Gained From Fire Incidents*. Division of Risk Analysis and Applications, Office of Nuclear Regulatory Research. Washington, DC: US Nuclear Regulatory Commission.

Pannerselvan, A.S. (1999). 'Close to a Critical Mess', *Outlook*, 8 November.

Parthasarathi, Ashok (2007). *Technology at the Core: Science and Technology with Indira Gandhi*. New Delhi: Pearson-Longman.

Parthasarathy, K.S. (2007). 'An Open Letter to the People of Meghalaya', *The Shillong Times*, 12 June.

Perrow, Charles (1984). *Normal Accidents: Living with High Risk Technologies*. New York: Basic Books.

Press Trust of India (PTI) (1999). 'Govt. Admits Mishap at RAPS Unit Last Year', *Press Trust of India*, 8 December.

——— (2000). 'No Decision on Nuke Waste Disposal Site', *Press Trust of India*, 27 July.

——— (2011a). 'AEC Chief Puts Odds of N-Plant Accidents at '1-in-Infinity', *The Hindu*, 10 November.

——— (2011b). 'Japan Nuclear Crisis: No Nuclear Accident in Fukushima, Say Indian N-Experts', *Economic Times*, 15 March, available at http://articles.economictimes.indiatimes.com/2011-03-15/news/28691538_1_japan-nuclear-crisis-nuclear-accident-nuclear-operators, last accessed on 19 November 2013.

——— (2012). 'Scouting for Sites to Store N-waste: AEC Chief', *The Hindu*, 15 February.

Rahman, Azizur, and Jayanta Basu (1999). 'Living in Death Shadow', *Sunday*, 4 April.

Raj, K., K.K. Prasad, and N.K. Bansal (2006). 'Radioactive Waste Management Practices in India', *Nuclear Engineering and Design*, 236: 914–30.

Ramana, M.V. (2007). 'Heavy Subsidies in Heavy Water', *Economic and Political Weekly*, 42(34): 3483–90.

Ramana, M.V., and Ashwin Kumar (2010). 'Safety First? Kaiga and Other Nuclear Stories', *Economic and Political Weekly*, 45(7): 47–54.

Ramsey, Charles B., and Mohammad Modarres (1998). *Commercial Nuclear Power: Assuring Safety for the Future*. New York: Wiley.

Reason, James (2000). 'Safety Paradoxes and Safety Culture', *Injury Control and Safety Promotion*, 7(1): 3–14.

Rodriguez, Placid (1996). 'Chemical Engineering and Fast Breeder Reactor Technology', in Y.B.G. Varma, C.D.P. Rao, A.R. Balakrishnan, and M.S. Ananth (eds), *Advances in Chemical Engineering*. Delhi: Allied Publishers.

Sagan, Scott (1993). *The Limits of Safety: Organizations, Accidents and Nuclear Weapons*. Princeton: Princeton University Press.

Sahgal, Bittu (1998). 'Nuclear Fantasy: Not Everyone in India is Enthralled by the "Hindu Bomb"', *New Internationalist*, August.

Shankar, Ravi (2008). 'Those Years...These Months...', *Nuclear India*, January–February: 18–19.

Sinha, Rajesh (2000). 'Some Dumpyard, This', *Indian Express*, 8 May.

Slovic, Paul, Baruch Fischhoff, and Sarah Lichtenstein (1982). 'Why Study Risk Perception?', *Risk Analysis*, 2(2): 83–93.

Slovic, Paul, James Flynn, and Mark Layman (1991). 'Perceived Risk, Trust, and the Politics of Nuclear Waste', *Science*, 254(5038): 1603–7.

Smith, Adam (2001). *An Inquiry Into the Nature and Causes of the Wealth of Nations*. London: Electric Book Company.

Sonowal, C.J., and Sunil Kumar Jojo (2003). 'Radiation and Tribal Health in Jadugoda: The Contention Between Science and Sufferings', *Studies of Tribes and Tribals*, 1(2): 111–26.

Srinivas, Madhusudan (1993). 'The Narora Fire and the Communication Gap', *Frontline*, 7 May.

Subramanian, T.S. (2000). 'Confident about Safety: Interview with V.K. Chaturvedi', *Frontline*, 18 August: 89–91.

——— (2003). 'The Kalpakkam "Incident"', *Frontline*, 16 August.

Sundararajan, A.R., K.S. Parthasarathy, and S. Sinha (eds) (2008). *Atomic Energy Regulatory Board: 25 Years of Safety Regulation*. Mumbai: Atomic Energy Regulatory Board.

Telegraph correspondent (2008). 'Blame Game Over UCIL Toxic Gas Leak', *The Telegraph*, August 18.

Tiwari, Amit (2008). 'UCIL Pipe Bursts, Sprays Nuclear Waste', *Hindustan Times*, 18 August.

Tiwari, Manish (1999). 'A Deformed Existence', *Down to Earth*, 15 June.

The Times of India (ToI). (1999). 'Kaiga-II Will Go Commercial in a Month', *The Times of India*, 25 October.

Venkatesh, M.R. (2003). 'BARC Admits Radiation Error', *Telegraph*, 7 August.

Vinod, Gopika, R.K. Saraf, A.K. Ghosh, H.S. Kushwaha, and P.K. Sharma (2008). 'Insights From Fire PSA for Enhancing NPP Safety', *Nuclear Engineering and Design*, 238 (9 September): 2359–68.

Vishnu, G. (2010). 'High-grade Energy, Low-grade Safety', *Tehelka*, 25 September.

11

MARC POUMADÈRE

Before and After Fukushima

The Many Fronts of Managing the Nuclear Power Option

In 1986, when the Chernobyl accident occurred, Hans Blix, the Director of the International Atomic Energy Agency (IAEA), stated that a nuclear accident somewhere is a nuclear accident everywhere. Some 25 years later, after the Fukushima nuclear plant accident in Japan, this statement still appears to be true. Immediate reactions appeared from all parts of the world expressing widespread concerns about nuclear risk, almost as if the accident had occurred in each country's backyard. These reactions even superseded the deaths and economic losses caused by the devastating earthquake and tsunami that hit Japan. Images of the devastated plants in Japan exposed people around the world to the vulnerability and danger of nuclear power technology, raising or increasing public concern. Most governments rapidly echoed those criticisms and public concern, with positions ranging from promises to reinforce plant safety to reconsidering new programmes and even, as in the notable case of Germany, phasing out nuclear power as a source of energy production. In India, the Kudankulam nuclear plant has been under construction for years and only recently have protests really begun, in response to the fear and uncertainty planted in the minds of the local population after Fukushima.

Previous analysis (Poumadère 1991) had shown that the social acceptance of the eventuality of nuclear accidents is very low—much lower than for any other possible type of accident. This fact is perhaps what prompts nuclear technocrats and politicians to provide themselves and others with a reassurance that nuclear accidents are not supposed to happen. More precisely, there are strong pressures from all sides to produce probabilistic risk evaluations that fit the level of social acceptability of nuclear accidents. It is common to analyse the relationship between the public, on the one hand, and nuclear technocrats and government, on the other, in terms of opposing interests. At some level, however, the relationship is de facto of a collusive nature: low social acceptability produces low risk probabilities.

In the aftermath of Fukushima nothing would be the same for nuclear energy. Increased public concern and additional costs for improving safety have somewhat undermined the future of nuclear energy. Nonetheless, dangers from climate change are pressing for lower CO_2 emissions worldwide, and growing energy demands in countries like India maintain the viability of the nuclear energy option. Nuclear energy has a very low CO_2 impact, and for that reason it can play a worldwide and national role in the energy mix. However, this manner of framing the issue of nuclear energy does not always disguise all the problems that are associated with it.

Since contemporary society is inundated with information, which it processes in a practical and heuristic manner that sometimes oversimplifies information and introduces various biases (Rouquette 1998), the acceptance of nuclear energy is profoundly influenced by how these issues are framed to the public. In the risk domain, framing refers to the perceptual filters, worldviews or assumptions which guide the collective definition and interpretation of specific issues (Miller 2000). According to Jasanoff (2005), the framing of an issue should provide a conceptual language allowing the public and local populations to understand how policy decisions are made. The immediate rejection of nuclear power, as a stigmatized entity related to weapons, war, explosions, and contamination, can be instantly nuanced when nuclear energy is framed as a solution for mitigating climate change, or as a means of securing domestic energy supplies (Knight 2008). However, if the public is not overly concerned about the dangers of climate change, but more worried about nuclear reliability and vulnerability, unsolved waste issues, and the appropriate risk governance models to manage these risks (see Chapter 12 by Claire Mays), then they may resist this climate change framing. Nuclear energy can prompt strong visceral reactions, particularly in populations neighbouring nuclear power plants (NPPs), as seen at Kudankulam. Assessing the acceptability of nuclear power can help governments understand better how and on what level to engage with the public. For example, are there concerns about competence and corruption? Is the public primarily worried about the equitable distribution of risks and benefits, and the nature and direction of society's development? Are there fears over the governance of nuclear power and the lack of transparency and accountability in the system? Or is it the case that nuclear energy is not seen to be the only, or the most desirable option, to meet the growing energy gap?

In this chapter, we examine the technical, economic, political, organizational, and psychological fronts of nuclear power, with the aim of mapping issues for India to examine in nuclear energy governance. We first evaluate the overall legacy of nuclear energy, and its future, in light of Fukushima. We then highlight the value of in-depth risk perception studies which can uncover some of the reasons behind the public's appreciation of nuclear energy, with its notable variation across time, countries, and different sections of society. The role of national culture is analysed amongst the possible explanations for the patent differences which can be observed across nations in terms of public appreciation of nuclear energy. Meanwhile, the management of NPPs as complex organizations requires specific attention to build and maintain an appropriate safety culture. Understanding Indian cultural attributes and patterns of behaviour in relation to decision-making and authority is indispensable to the safe management of NPPs as complex organizations. Unlike the reactors at NPPs, a safety culture cannot be imported from other countries, but needs to be developed to suit the local and cultural conditions. Nuclear energy is not simply the remit of engineers but demands the interdisciplinary research skills of psychologists, sociologists, risk communication experts, among others, to forge a more socially acceptable and responsible nuclear energy regime. A further step would be to consider risk governance approaches to include stakeholders (Non-governmental Organizations or NGOs, local residents, and other interested groups). Public information is also an issue, from a dual perspective—from that of the general public at the national level, but also from that of local populations who live in the vicinity of the plant (or future plant). This distinction is seldom made and it might be of particular interest for India considering the extent and diversity of local communities.

While these might not be the only issues that need to be considered, we believe that they cover a large part of the complex spectrum of the situation upon which present and future decisions will be made regarding the nuclear power option. Can this background be useful for India, considering its strongly developing nuclear energy programme? At first glance, one could say that decisions vary a lot from one country to another and over time, and it is not possible to learn much from such diversity. However, the diversity of experience and decisions could provide useful insights and help India better define its own decision path in regard to nuclear energy.

NUCLEAR ENERGY: LEGACY AND FUTURE

The invention of nuclear energy brought the promise of a means for producing cheap and abundant electricity. During the second half of the 20th century, however, this new technology became associated with the risk of low probability, but high-impact accidents. The fear of such accidents led to early public opposition to nuclear programmes in democratic countries (Freudenburg and Rosa 1984), movements that varied by country due to cross-cultural factors (Slovic et al. 2000). The public's confidence in nuclear energy fell further after the accidents at the Three Mile Island (TMI) plant in the United States in 1979 and in Chernobyl in the former USSR in 1986. The credibility crisis (Poumadère 1991) that followed put the future of nuclear energy in question. Countries such as Sweden and Germany decided to gradually phase out their use of nuclear energy, while public support declined to permanently low levels. In 2005, the situation began to change. Higher oil prices, the announcement of greater global electricity demands, and increased warnings of the dire effects of climate change brought attention back to nuclear energy. Furthermore, the development of third-generation reactors ensured more reliable technology. It appeared that the decades-long nuclear energy winter might come to an end. In India, nuclear energy was considered an option that could play a major role in its evolving energy production mix.

Proponents of nuclear energy have emphasized its positive records on safety, the environment, and pricing. In the 25 years between the Chernobyl and Fukushima accidents, approximately 9,000 reactor-years of operation produced electricity in 31 countries without accident. The level of fatalities per output caused by nuclear operations is lower than that of other means of energy production or other industrial activities (OECD 2010). Furthermore, a nuclear reactor is said to emit 60 times less CO_2 than a coal power plant. Scientists now largely agree on the methods for handling spent fuel and reprocessed high-level nuclear waste. Finally, since the cost of uranium fuel represents only 5 per cent of the price of each KWh produced, nuclear energy prices are much less volatile than those of fossil fuels.

Despite these benefits, several difficulties remain. The issue of NPPs as terrorist targets is raised and can stand as a large public concern. Countries must decide how to apply nuclear governance methods equitably across the nation and across generations. Furthermore, there is debate about the true cost of nuclear energy, whether to take into account costs of dismantling plants or responding to accidents. Parties independent of the nuclear industry assess costs significantly higher than previously thought. This debate about costs is one that has arisen in India as well. In Jaitapur, activists claim that the environmental impact assessment (EIA) report is flawed because of the absence of a specific plan for decommissioning. They also say that the cost of electricity generated from the Jaitapur nuclear power plant (JNPP) would be in excess of Rs 9 per unit, compared to the current rate of Rs 4 per unit. This does not include the costs of managing radioactive waste and decommissioning. It has been noted in the Rajya Sabha that as far as the cost difference between hydro, thermal, and all the other available options vis-à-vis nuclear electricity is concerned, nuclear power is thrice as costly (Rediff News 2010). Uncertainty about the costs of nuclear energy continues to constrain its future, according to financial analysts (Spiegel and McArthur 2009). Financial risks become a concern in both the banking and political sectors when private power plant operators are involved, as in the US. This could become a concern in India as well. In addition to these concerns and uncertainty, there is the risk of nuclear proliferation as a result of the illegal trade of nuclear elements for armament purposes.

Before Fukushima, it was thought that the number of nuclear plants in operation could double in the years to come. Since then, however, the International Energy Agency has predicted that only half as many plants will be built. Even though third-generation reactors are technically ready for implementation, few are currently under construction. International research into a fourth-generation of nuclear reactors is underway, but their application is constrained by a limited timeframe. According to IPCC (2007), in order to avoid increased climate change, it is critical for us to change our methods of energy production in the next 10 years. Given this short time-span, nuclear energy developments will most likely focus on building new nuclear production units and adequately training personnel.

Some countries like India might face the problem of lacking well-enough trained personnel. Furthermore, post-Fukushima concerns have increased the cost of nuclear energy due to the call for additional measures aimed at improving accident prevention and protection. In France, the post-Fukushima report issued by the Autorité de Sûreté Nucléaire (ASN) (the French Nuclear Safety Authority) (ASN 2011) lists the steps to be undertaken to upgrade the safety of all the country's reactors, entailing multi-billion euro investments. While France's rapid response has been welcomed (Nature 2012), activist groups such as Greenpeace France (Greenpeace 2012) point out the limits of these technological risk assessments. Fairly laudatory comments have been made about France's rapid response, with hopes that other countries will follow a similar path (ibid.). While in France, these planned safety improvements are expected to restore public trust, in neighbouring Germany, the government did not put much hope into changing the very low social acceptability of nuclear risks in Germany and decided to phase it out.

VARIATIONS IN PUBLIC APPRECIATION OF NUCLEAR ENERGY

The fate of nuclear energy depends not only upon technical factors, but also social and political considerations—especially, public opinion. The attitudes towards nuclear energy range from ambivalence to complete commitment, and are rooted in different value systems and cultural worldviews and vary according to demographic variables.

They are not immutable, but change in response to external events (Fukushima), the discursive context within which they are debated/ framed, and even in response to how researchers phrase their questions (Pidgeon et al. 2008).

Fukushima appeared to cement and provide added justification to pre-existing negative attitudes towards nuclear energy in countries such as Germany, Italy, and Switzerland, which have decided to completely phase out nuclear power. A poll of 24 countries, immediately after Fukushima, conducted by the Ipsos Research Institute came to the conclusion that whilst the Fukushima crisis pushed already sceptical countries into more decisive action, it only sparked a temporary dip in public attitudes elsewhere, which eventually resettled at pre-Fukushima levels. Support for nuclear power in Britain fell in June 2011, yet since then it has bounced back and even strengthened by three points—a finding supported by Pidgeon (2011) whose results from tracking data indicate: 'Fukushima had little impact on overall UK public concern about nuclear power'. Similarly, the reaction in America has been more muted than expected. Research by Pew (2011) in America found that the proportion favouring increased use of nuclear power fell from 47 per cent to 39 per cent between October 2010 and March 2011, suggesting that there is still a strong core support for nuclear power. This can be explained by studies that have shown that information corroborating a previously established point of view will be preferred over facts that favour a contradiction of this stance. The establishment of support or rejection towards nuclear energy finally depends less on knowledge than on an individual's political background (Costa-Font et al. 2008). The patchwork of policies and decisions in the EU is evidence of this and the public's varied and inconsistent involvement around the nuclear issue.

Political rhetoric has increasingly stressed the role that nuclear power can play in mitigating climate change and securing energy supplies, particularly since the 1970 OPEC (Organization of Petroleum Exporting Countries) oil crisis and rising oil and gas prices. Nuclear power now spans the globe, with 439 nuclear reactors in operation in 31 countries, about 40 new units under construction, and 230 projects under consideration. According to the Eurobarometer (EU 2008), Europeans have become more accepting of nuclear energy since 2005. The percentage of the population either 'totally' or 'fairly' in favour of nuclear energy production has risen seven points to 44 per cent, while the percentage of those opposed has fallen by 10 points and now stands at 45 per cent. This trend is especially apparent in UK, where 35 per cent of the public now favours nuclear energy against just 26 per cent who do not (Knight 2008). One explanation for these relatively high acceptance rates may be that people living in countries that already have nuclear programmes tend to be more tolerant toward nuclear production; they are often more exposed to debates about nuclear power and waste disposal and generally better informed. Those who live near nuclear plants illustrate the so-called 'proximity effect', by which their proximity to nuclear units makes them more likely to consider nuclear energy acceptable; they come to see it through the lens of 'ordinariness' (Pidgeon et al. 2008). The same study revealed that a dichotomous categorization of being 'pro' or 'con' toward nuclear energy does not capture the full range of residents' attitudes; instead, they can best be expressed through four main perspectives: 'Beneficial and Safe', 'Threat and Distrust', 'Reluctant Acceptance' and 'There's No Point Worrying'. However, it appears that the proximity effect may apply to NPPs more than to other types of industry. A recent study conducted near Dunkerque in northern France compared the views of populations living near a large NPPs and to industrial plants, which are considered dangerous by the EU Seveso Directive. The study found that the proximity effect had indeed produced a favourable attitude toward the nearby NPPs, but not toward the industrial plants (Gonthier et al. 2008).

According to an Massachusetts Institute of Technology (MIT) study on the 'Future of Nuclear Power', American public opinion of energy sources is largely shaped by concerns over environmental damage and electricity costs (Ansolabehere 2007). The study shows a decline in support for oil and coal, despite the latter's moderate price, and a slight increase of those in favour of nuclear power, when compared with the first MIT Energy survey from 2002. Another study on value orientations and risk perceptions of nuclear power (Whitfield et al. 2009) finds a significant shift in American attitudes; while still far from fully supportive of nuclear energy, the views are now much less negative than in the past. This change can perhaps be attributed to the nuclear industry's new public relations strategy, which attempts to engage the public in a conversation about the regional and national needs for proposed facilities and calls on community involvement in the installation process. Beyond the immediate benefits to the nuclear industry in facilitating nuclear installations (Chandler 2008; Kidd 2008), this new communications approach could lead to lasting shifts in views of nuclear energy (Kidd 2008; Pidgeon et al. 2008).

However, there are still enduring memories from nuclear accidents of the past, such as TMI and Chernobyl, and doubts remain relating to the unsolved questions of nuclear waste management. While there have been continuous improvements in nuclear safety regulations (the active role of IAEA in that domain is widely recognized to be efficient, and at the national level most countries have established an independent nuclear agency that controls all aspects of nuclear safety), as of today an efficient method of waste disposal has yet to be achieved—a fact that contributes to the negative image of nuclear energy (OECD 2010). For example, among respondents holding a negative opinion of nuclear energy (EU 2008), 39 per cent affirmed that they would change their stance given a permanent and reliable solution for radioactive waste, however, 48 per cent reported that they would not change their opinion, regardless. This statistic shows us that nuclear power can still prompt a particularly negative reaction in parts of the population. Logically, the Fukushima accident will push this negative image further, at least for a certain period of time. One important issue for India will be to strengthen its working relationship with the IAEA. Unfortunately, it has to be noted that India, along with other large countries like the US and China, has rejected the IAEA proposal to implement more stringent controls upon operating NPPs worldwide.

Public attitudes towards nuclear energy have also shifted with the rise in popularity of alternative clean energy options—raising doubts over the desirability of nuclear power as a tool for mitigating climate change. In Europe (EU 2008), populations were broadly in favour of other renewable energy sources (80 per cent in support of solar energy, 71 per cent of wind energy and 65 per cent of hydroelectric energy), and showing mostly negative attitudes towards nuclear energy (45 per cent in opposition, 20 per cent acceptance but not support). In Britain, for example, support for replacement nuclear new builds has dropped to 36 per cent. A focus group study conducted in the UK by Bickerstaff et al. (2008) revealed that questions concerning the risk of radioactive waste provoked particularly emotive responses that were couched in a language of fear and dread. On the other hand, threats from climate change were perceived to be removed in both time and space. A second set of questions relating to trust in the government pointed to some serious misgivings about the government's motivations for promoting nuclear energy, believing science and policy to be too bound up with big business, and veiled in secrecy. However, when nuclear energy was presented as a solution for mitigating climate change, the majority of focus group participants reconsidered their resolutely negative stances and *reluctantly accepted* nuclear power as the 'lesser of two evils'. A fifth of participants were uncomfortable with this risk–risk trade-off arguing that other policy framings existed, such as a temporary reliance on nuclear power until better alternatives became viable.

How do the different framings of nuclear power resonate amongst various sections of India's society? Does the risk of climate change or the everyday reality of extended power cuts outweigh the perceived risks of nuclear power? Or is trust in the government's competency, fairness, and integrity so broken that these risks do not seem worth taking? S.P. Udayakumar, co-ordinator of the People's Movement Against Nuclear Energy, characterizes the current Kudankulam protests as 'a classic David–Goliath fight between the "ordinary citizens" of India and the Indian government supported by the multinational companies, imperial powers, and the global nuclear mafia. They promise nuclear power, development, atom bombs, security, and superpower status. We demand risk-free electricity, disease-free life, unpolluted natural resources, sustainable development and a harmless future' (The Guardian 2012). The Indian government and nuclear establishment, on the other hand, have framed nuclear energy as 'the gateway to a prosperous future' (Abdul Kalam) and the 'only option' (Former AEC Chairman M.R. Srinivasan) to meet India's growing energy demands as it surges forward to take its place as one of the leading economies of the world.

What particular framings and risk–risk trade-offs would it be most relevant to investigate further in India? Western studies distinguish between the attitudes of men and women, along education levels, age, and social status, social values, and specific issues such as trust (towards scientists, the policy makers, or the engineers)—what other categories would be added in the Indian context to establish a larger picture of the risk scene? Monitoring public risk perception over time is particularly important to allow us to capture the population's reaction to major events (like the Fukushima incident) and how opinions are revised as new priorities and risks emerge. For instance, while there is relatively low support for climate policies in India currently (Brechin 2010), it would be important to monitor how this attitude evolves, considering India's climate vulnerability. Understanding the public's response to policy framings around nuclear power can enable the Indian government to mediate a more socially acceptable solution to India's energy crisis, and avoid the escalating costs and darkening public mood that has accompanied the nuclear power protests at Kudankulam and Jaitapur.

UNDERSTANDING THE ROLE OF NATIONAL CULTURES

Among the factors that might help explain the variations in public appreciation of nuclear energy, national cultures deserve particular attention.

Differences between European countries, which are very close in terms of economic development, serve as evidence that decisions about nuclear energy depend on more than technical and industrial factors. Additional cultural and political elements exist within each national context. Without any international governance of nuclear energy choices, these additional elements deeply influence decision-making. It is thus important for each nation to have a clear knowledge of each of these factors when engaging in the decision-making process on nuclear energy. Whilst India has a rather long-standing technical knowledge of nuclear power, has it supplemented this with its understanding of political and social processes? In Chapter 13 of this volume, Bouder points out several characteristics of the Indian political context: a discredited industry, a strong litigation culture, the permanence of community-based channels of trust, and a strong activist culture. On that basis, it is quite a challenge to imagine what kind of risk communication process could be the most effective in India.

While the Fukushima accident impacts public risk perception, it might be useful to look for stable elements which structure each national context. For instance, in France some specific cultural elements are worth noticing. A recent report (Marx 2011) shows that more than a quarter (26 per cent) of French CEOs were previously high-level public servants. This percentage is only 1 or 2 in Germany, the US, or the UK. Another French peculiarity is the existence of the Grandes Ecoles (literally translated as 'great schools'), which are higher education facilities that operate outside the more democratic university system. The majority of high ranking civil servants, industry executives, and politicians emerge from these schools, creating a *State nobility*, that is, a shared social group involved in decision-making both within the state and industry (Bourdieu 1998; Bourdieu and Passeron 2000). In terms of decision models, these elements show a link with the science-based decision model presented by Millstone (in Chapter 9 of this volume) that is typical of the French technocratic style—in place since the late 18th and early 19th centuries. As a result of these singularities, there is a continuity between the French state and industry with its shared engineering culture, a typical result being the state-controlled nuclear power system with a single operator and national nuclear industry. When compared, (Slovic et al. 2000), risk perceptions of nuclear energy appear very similar in France and in the US, but a striking difference appears in terms of general attitudes: in contrast to the low level of trust witnessed in the US, the French place much greater confidence in engineers and nuclear operators.

This can also explain the fact that, in spite of the results of recent risk perception surveys, the French nuclear programme seems stable. Results of a thorough risk perception survey conducted six months after Fukushima (IRSN 2012) show a sharp increase in the French population regarding nuclear risks as high (as compared to previous periods and with a data base starting in 1988). Now, 55 per cent of the population considers the nuclear risk as high and only 24 per cent trusts the public officials to protect them. And more than 80 per cent wishes that a safety assessment of French NPPs be performed on a pluralist basis (that is, open to NGO and civil society) and by international experts. However, the same survey reveals that trust in science remains unchanged and high (76 per cent), and 67 per cent of the French population (an unprecedented high level) agrees that energetic independence and the presently low cost of electricity are arguments in favour of nuclear power. During the campaign for the presidential election in April and May 2012, nuclear power was a mild issue for the two preeminent candidates. In contrast, nuclear power is strongly opposed by the Ecologist candidate (who is currently credited to have less than 3 per cent of the votes). Only two issues appear under discussion. The first of which revolves around either replacing older NPPs with new ones or extending their life span. The second is about closing the Fessenheim plant, the oldest French NPP in operation, which is subject to seismic and flooding risks, and has been under scrutiny for the adequacy of its design. The local population has protested *against* the closing of this NPP.

These types of elements, specific to a given national culture, are important to recognize, as they influence not only decision-making in regards to the implementation of nuclear programmes and public appreciation, but also everyday management of the safety culture in NPPs and engagement with communities who live in the vicinity of the plant. As India is a very large country, it is likely that powerful cultures exist locally and it is not certain how these different cultures blend, if at all, at the national level. Yet, it is at this 'supra-local' level that decisions are made regarding nuclear power. This ought to be further studied in India, along with risk perceptions and the attitude of people towards scientists/experts.

MANAGING NUCLEAR PRODUCTION: SAFETY CULTURE AND RISK COMMUNICATION

Safety Culture

Operational and management constraints of nuclear energy production are highly similar from one country to another as they are defined by technological characteristics. The successful launching of a long range intercontinental ballistic missile in April 2012 shows India's capacity to master complex technological systems. Yet it is important to integrate cultural specificities—whether these reflect the specific conditions found in each plant, or the local and national cultures. In-depth field work with NPP workers reveals various forms of commitment towards the plant and the reactor. It would be interesting to better know what could be the imaginary dimensions associated with nuclear technology in different areas of India. On the eve of installation of new 3rd-generation NPPs, the social and psychological dimensions of safety behaviour, and the complex adjustments of local communities, are among the areas of knowledge that should not be left aside.

The same year that the Chernobyl accident occurred, the IAEA (1986) coined the Safety Culture concept and then put forward very central guidelines: safety should be given the attention it requires at all organizational levels; NPP workers are encouraged to actively question decisions in their work environment, rather than applying them passively (IAEA 1991). The latter instruction can be difficult to apply, as the organization of a NPP is highly hierarchical and relies upon formalized processes. In other words, the rule is to apply the rules, while, at the same time keeping, alive the capacity to assess situations at each organizational level. The IAEA recommendations are universal and should be applied to all NPPs all around the world. Yet, we can imagine that the concrete application of these guidelines would vary from one country to another—and even from one plant to another. The challenge here will be to rely upon local leadership styles and organizational values to implement the IAEA recommendations. In that perspective, action-research programmes were developed early on in French NPPs, through monitoring of safety practices along with teambuilding, which aimed to decentralize risk analysis in everyday working life (Mays and Poumadère 1989). Similar analyses were developed in the UK as well (Turner and Pidgeon 1997), and the critical review recently made by Guldenmund (2010) shows the richness of the safety culture concept. How can such a safety culture be developed in India? As it is the case in other countries with a strongly hierarchical organization, it might be difficult to challenge your superiors, as was pointed out in M.V. Ramana's chapter (Chapter 10 of this volume). Thus India will need to enhance organizational learning. This means it will need trained personnel not only in engineering but also in managerial fields.

Risk Communication

On the front of risk communication and public information, two levels ought to be distinguished: firstly, the general public, and secondly, the local populations who live near existing or future NPPs. As is observed in this statement, the central issue of public information relating to nuclear accidents was tackled early on: 'Although the case in favour of concealing nothing from the public appears to be unanswerable, there is, nevertheless, a duty to study the psychological principles of the presentation of anxiety-raising information in relation to the capacity of the public to endure it' (WHO 1958: 44).

This statement by experts from the World Health Organization (WHO) encapsulates the dilemmas associated with public information about nuclear risks fairly well—information is a must, yet the goal is not to raise anxiety, so the capacity of the public to cope with bad news enters into play and ought to be assessed.

This coping capacity is generally appreciated on the cautious side by governments, and it might vary according to national/cultural factors and according to how the public accommodates nuclear risk. For instance, in France, up until the Chernobyl accident, there was a widespread belief that nuclear disasters were not supposed to happen (Poumadère 1991) and communication with the public disregarded any eventuality of an accident. This communication doctrine changed in 1990 with the official announcement of the results of a probabilistic risk assessment (PRA) of an accident at level 5 (similar to TMI). The announcement stated that the probability of an accident was about 1 per cent; this applies to all 56 French reactors, and covers a period of 20 years. With this information, a taboo was broken—the possibility that an accident could occur was acknowledged. In addition, nuclear operators now systematically inform the media about any incident which occurs inside NPPs.

The advantages of such risk communication are numerous. The first one is in line with developing *risk literacy* in society—zero risk does not exist, accidents happen, tools such as PRA are available. In addition, the shock of the accident, should it occur, might be less traumatic than if it had been totally inconceivable and outside of the population's mental representation. Finally, acknowledging the possibility of a major accident facilitates prevention and protection measures based upon *realistic worst case scenarios*. On that same ground, populations' preparedness for coping with accidental situations can be better developed and their resilience improved. On the operational goals' level, risk information should engage populations to behave responsibly and to take care of themselves in case of an accident, which will lower the workload of emergency forces and health units, while limiting panic and organizational chaos (Paton and Johnston 2001).

On that basis, it appears that Ramana (Chapter 10 of this volume) is accurate on several grounds for criticizing the DAE Secretary who stated that Indian reactors are 100 per cent safe. However, maybe the DAE Secretary was uncertain and cautious about the capacity of the

Indian population to endure potentially anxiety-raising information, especially in the aftermath of a major nuclear accident such as Fukushima. A more realistic information policy could be developed, associated with the history of India as a nuclear country. Ramana (ibid.) additionally mentions various accidents which have occurred in Indian nuclear facilities. It would be useful to know how these events were reported in the media and if, for instance, the International Nuclear Event Scale (INES) was used. The INES scale is a practical risk communication tool and rather simple to implement. It is widely used to rank each incident or accident and plays the role of a common language among all involved: policy persons, the public, nuclear management, the media, and NGOs. If the INES scale is not well known, information should focus on it, using examples of lower level incidents to contrast with major cases such as TMI, Chernobyl, and Fukushima. India should consider using the INES scale as part of an appropriate communication policy, which allows full information while avoiding generation of public anxiety.

The situation is different when considering local populations confronted with the issue of living near an existing or future NPP. In most cases, if not all, a *new* NPP is first regarded by residents as a territorial intrusion or an inappropriate land use. However, the construction and the later operation of a new plant often means improvement of local infrastructure and creation of jobs in the local community. If this does not happen, it is understandable that local communities complain bitterly. Either of these negative and positive effects can prevail in perceptions at different moments of the siting process. In the long run and in addition to risk issues, one concern involves the impact of the facility upon land and housing prices. A commonly heard complaint in Jaitapur was that neighbouring land prices rose, so the compensation package was not sufficient for people to buy other land. However, based upon a meta-analysis of the after-effects of various facilities, Kiel and Williams (2007) show that a new facility does not translate systematically into a decrease or an increase of neighbouring land prices. Context-specific variables enter into play. For government officials and developers, attention to these variables is among the goals of risk mitigation as was the case during the siting process of the International Thermonuclear Experimental Reactor (ITER) in the French context. While, from a technological point of view, risk mitigation is a primary step (through more effective risk reduction technologies), risk mitigation should include governance as well, with items such as residents' open access to information, residents' participation in risk management, and penalties in case of faulty management (Poumadère 2001).

From the point of view of local communities, important issues ought to be identified *before* engaging in the communication process. For instance, if India is predominantly a rural country, is there some divide between the rural culture and that of experts or policymakers coming from big cities? Does this divide lead to deep misunderstandings caused by differences in perception of the issues at hand?

An illustration of these possible discrepancies appears in the account of protests against the Kudankulam nuclear power project (Outlook 2011). Villagers complained that they had not been properly informed about a trial run with 'dummy fuel' and were worried when they heard loud noises, described as 'drowning out the roar of the night sea', from the plant. Clearly, prior information would have helped the villagers feel better prepared for the trial—and the noise would have been less worrisome. But it is likely that this was not a priority for experts for whom the trial run was only a technical step among others. One cannot expect engineers to be risk communication experts and it would be counterproductive to let them play that role alone, as further evidence shows. In Kudankulam, activists claim that the central expert panel members had not talked to any section of the Tamil public nor have they tried to allay the fears and concerns of the people. They also alleged that the 38-page report of the Expert Group has 'ignored our question on liability, and has given no specific or scientific information on nuclear waste, and vague information on the fresh water needs of the KKNPP' (Hindustan Times 2012). The Central Expert Group at Kudankulam counters that the locals have a lot of 'misconceptions' about the project and radiation and they were calling off talks with the activists as they have already completed their job. They said: '[C]reating fear in the minds of public with partial information and selected video clippings on Fukushima is mischievous and not in the interest of the local public and the nation,' (DNA 2011). This sequence shows how impossible the communication can become unless roles have been prepared well in advance. Technical experts need training or need to have colleagues who are trained in risk communication.

These examples show that specific and sensitive attention ought to be given to the *needs and identity* of local populations. Recognizing the expression of cultural codes, identities, practices and resources through knowledge systems is central to effective communication (Freire 1973). One of the advantages of nuclear energy is to produce amounts of electricity which will reach large populations sometimes living far away from the plant. There too a division can appear between those who are more closely exposed to the risks and those who are less exposed while benefiting from the nuclear production of electricity. In the decision-making process, policymakers ought to include, whenever feasible, representatives from those two populations, who would acknowledge their differences and attempt to balance the risk/benefit equation with them. It is among the general goals of policy to compensate any unequal distribution of risks when it cannot be avoided. In many countries, democratic processes are being developed to accommodate the complex requirements of nuclear operations in a better way. It is likely that this will happen in India as well, the question being how fast it will happen and through which changes within the political establishment.

Finally, and following the right-to-know principle, local populations must be actively informed about the nature of the risk to which they are exposed, and about the actions they should take to protect themselves in case of an accident. In addition to this first step, it would be useful to consider what populations 'need to know', and pay attention to the more ambivalent 'wish to know' of specific communities (Poumadère and Bertoldo 2010). Empowerment of the local population is also an aim, to develop the capacity of dialogue on a more realistic basis. For instance, attention could be given to improving the quality of life of the local community. From a practical point of view, it might be possible to use in India some guidelines developed in France (Poumadère and Mays 2003):

- Each player on the risk scene is attentive to avoid depriving others of their understanding of the situation;
- Science and the irrational are not seen to be mutually exclusive—they can exist side by side in the construction of a risk situation;
- Scientists put their skills to the service of community risk construction, rather than opposing that construction—science is 'on tap, not on top';

- No player spends time and energy asserting that his worldview is right and that he can prove the others wrong—not even those who will ultimately be proved right by events;
- Pre-existing or emergent concerns, doubts, or worries about various objects in the environment are not dismissed, but taken on board as the starting point for expertise and evaluation;
- Such openness may be shared by commissioned experts, who are invited to avoid imposing *a priori* conclusions based upon their previous expertise or experience. Rather, they engage with local expertise as if they were researchers embarking upon some new experiment.

★ ★ ★

Debates over nuclear power bring out issues of safety, energy independence, climate change, waste management, and the social acceptability of risk. With each of these issues come options that must be carefully considered. The situation is further complicated by the difficult balance needed between mitigating risks and meeting the growing demand for energy, both within national contexts and around the world. The way in which various actors and stakeholders present nuclear energy to the public will play a large role in determining the future of nuclear technology deployment. We can already observe the implementation of different styles of institutional processes and risk governance that vary according to national context.

We recall in this chapter, that nuclear power had a well-established identity before the Fukushima accident and, although this is more arguable, that it has a future as well. In the short term, the negative impact upon the image of nuclear energy prevailed in public perception and this was directly echoed by several governmental decisions. Furthermore, the increased attention to safety and vulnerability will augment costs and make nuclear power less attractive in the energy mix sought after in many countries worldwide. The long-term future is more uncertain. At this point, several stances can be observed: the phasing out of nuclear energy, the limiting or delaying of new programmes, and the continued goal of developing nuclear energy with improved safety. The important point here is that there will be no common position across all countries, as some might phase out while others will continue nuclear power use. In contrast to Germany, which decided to phase-out its nuclear production, it is unlikely that Finland and France, where third-generation reactors are under construction, will renounce their nuclear programmes. Other European countries such as Sweden and the UK plan to carry on nuclear production of electricity as well. Decision-making is challenging as well for emerging economies where the need for energy is growing rapidly and nuclear production remains an option. For instance, India is considering developing what would become the largest single-location nuclear power project in the world near Jaitapur.

Several questions also came up during the course of our discussion that India might need to address, such as: How does the Indian public respond to the government's framing of the nuclear energy issue? What are the predominant fears and concerns of different sub-sections of society, at the national level and near NPPs? Has there been adequate training in the risk communication field? What are the actions engaged to improve the risk literacy in society? Are rather simple communications tools such as the INES scale widely known and used by the media and other actors? Are realistic worst-case scenarios being developed to better prepare preventive and protective measures? As India is predominantly a rural country, is there some deep divide between the rural culture and that of experts or policymakers coming from big cities to talk to the villagers?

Not to be forgotten is the everyday management of existing and future NPPs. While industrial reliability and inspections keep the probability of an accident relatively low, safety culture ought to be developed in each context to further decrease these odds. Extensive experience of operating NPPs exists in both the US and the EU. NPP technology will be imported by India from several countries. While it is possible to learn from other countries' safety culture, it cannot be imported and India has to develop its own. Research is needed into the social and psychological dimensions of safety behaviour in India, and what may be the cultural elements underlying this. As for public information, special attention should be given to local populations who live in the neighbourhoods of NPPs. Empowerment and improvement of the everyday quality of life, as defined by each community, are the goals which should be met. If India can learn from these lessons and implement appropriate changes in its practices, nuclear energy can become a safer, viable, and a more socially acceptable part of its evolving energy portfolio.

BIBLIOGRAPHY

Ansolabehere, S. (2007). 'Public Attitudes Toward America's Energy Options: Report of the 2007 MIT Energy Survey'. Cambridge, MA: Center for Energy and Environmental Policy Research.

ASN (2011). 'Evaluations complémentaires de sûreté [Additional Safety Assessments]. Rapport de l'Autorité de Sûreté Nucléaire', p. 520. Paris, France: Autorité de Sûreté Nucléaire (ASN). available at http://www.asn.fr/index.php/Les-actions-de-l-ASN/Le-controle/Evaluations-complementaires-de-surete/Rapport-de-l-ASN, last accessed on 19 November 2013.

Bickerstaff, K., I. Lorenzoni, N.F. Pidgeon, W. Poortinga, and P. Simmons (2008). 'Reframing Nuclear Power in the UK Energy Debate: Nuclear Power, Climate Change Mitigation and Radioactive Waste', *Public Understanding of Science*, 17: 145–69.

Bourdieu, P. (1998). *The State Nobility: Elite Schools in the Field of Power*. Stanford, California: Stanford University Press.

Bourdieu, P., and J.C. Passeron (2000). *Reproduction in Education, Society and Culture*, 2nd edition. London: Sage.

Brechin, S.R. (2010). 'Public Opinion: A Cross-national View', in C. Lever-Tracy (ed.), *The Routledge Handbook of Climate Change and Society*. London: Routledge.

Chandler, S. (2008). 'Management Response to an Unexpectedly Controversial Consultation on Military Nuclear Waste Disposal', in C. Mays, R. Bertoldo, B. de Marchi, and L. Pellizzoni (eds), Proceedings of the 3rd Workshop of the Risk Bridge EC FP6 Coordination Action. Gorizia, Italy.

Costa-Font, J., C. Rudisill, and E. Mossialos (2008). 'Attitudes as an Expression of Knowledge and "Political Anchoring": The Case of Nuclear Power in the United Kingdom', *Risk Analysis*, 28: 1273–87.

Cour des comptes (2012). Les coûts de la filière électronucléaire [Costs of the electronuclear branch in France]. Cour des Comptes, rapport public thé matique, Janvier 2012, p. 430, available at http://www.ccomptes.fr/fr/CC/documents/RPT/Rapport_thematique_filiere_electronucleaire.pdf, last accessed on 19 November 2013.

DNA (2011). 'Expert Panel, Anti-Kudankulam Activists Rule Out Further Talks', *Daily News and Analysis*, available at http://www.dnaindia.com/india/report_panel-clears-kudankulam-nuclear-plant_1644330, last accessed on 19 November 2013.

EPA (2011). 'Fact Sheet. Proposed Mercury and Air Toxic Standards', Environmental Protection Agency, USA, available at http://www.epa.gov/mats/pdfs/proposalfactsheet.pdf, last accessed on 19 November 2013.

EU (2008). 'Eurobarometer. Attitudes Towards Radioactive Waste'. *Special Eurobarometer 297/Wave 69.1–TNS Opinion & Social*. Brussels: European Commission.

Freire, P. (1973). 'Extension or Communication', in P. Freire (ed.), *Education for Critical Consciousness*. New York: The Seabury, pp. 91–164.

Freudenburg and Rosa (1984). *Public Reactions to Nuclear Power: Are There Critical Masses?* Boulder, Colorado: American Association for the Advancement of Science, Westview.

Gonthier, F., P. Hellequin, and H. Flanquart (2008). *Perception du risque industriel par les populations du Dunkerquois [Industrial risk perception by populations in the Dunkirk area]*. Dunkerque: Institut des Mers du Nord, Université du Littoral.

Greenpeace (2012). 'Sûreté nucléaire en France post-Fukushima: Analyse critique des Évaluations complémentaires de sûreté (ECS) menées sur les installations nucléaires françaises après Fukushima. [Nuclear safety in France after Fukushima: Critical analysis of additional safety assessments (ASE) performed upon French nuclear units after Fukushima]', 178 pages, Greenpeace: France, available at http://energie-climat.greenpeace.fr/les-58-reacteurs-nucleaires-francais-aussi-fragiles-que-ceux-de-fukushima, last accessed on 19 November 2013.

Guldenmund, F.W. (2010). '(Mis)understanding Safety Culture and Its Relationship to Safety Management', *Risk Analysis*, 30: 1466–80. doi: 10.1111/j.1539-6924.2010.01452.x, last accessed on 19 November 2013.

Hindustan Times (2012). 'Koodankulam Plant: Activists Seek Jaya's Help to Scrap Project', *Hindustan Times*, available at http://www.hindustantimes.com/india-news/koodankulam-plant-activists-seeks-jaya-s-help-to-scrap-project/article1-774782.aspx, last accessed on 19 November 2013.

IAEA (1986). 'International Nuclear Safety Advisory Group: Summary Report on the Post-Accident Review Meeting on the Chernobyl Accident'. Report No. 75-INSAG-1, Safety Series, International Atomic Energy Agency.

———— (1991). International Safety Advisory Group (INSAG-4). Safety Culture. Report No. 75-INSAG-4, Safety Series, International Atomic Energy Agency.

IPCC (2007). 'Climate Change 2007: The Physical Science Basis'. Working Group I. Fourth Assessment Report (AR4), Intergovernmental Panel on Climate Change (IPCC). London: Cambridge University Press.

IPSOS Social Research Institute (2012). 'After Fukushima: Global Opinion on Energy Policy', available at http://www.ipsos.com/public-affairs/sites/www.ipsos.com.public-affairs/files/Energy%20Article.pdf, last accessed on 19 November 2013.

IRSN (2012). 'Plus de 30 ans d'opinion des Français sur les risques nucléaires, Édition spéciale du Baromètre IRSN 2012' (French for 'Over 30 years of the French Public's Perceptions of the Risks from Nuclear Power: Special Edition of the Barometer IRSN 2012'), available at http://www.irsn.fr/FR/IRSN/Publications/barometre/Documents/IRSN_Barometre-2012_Edition-speciale-30-ans.pdf, last accessed on 10 April 2014.

Jasanoff, S. (2005). *Designs on Nature: Science and Democracy in Europe and the United States*. Princeton, New Jersey: Princeton University Press.

Kiel, K.A., and M. Williams (2007). 'The Impact of Superfund Sites on Local Property Values: Are all Sites the Same?', *Journal of Urban Economics*, 61(1): 170–92.

Kidd, S. (2008). 'Nuclear Acceptance', *IAEA Bull*, 50: 32–3.

Knight, R. (2008). 'Did You Say Yes?', *IAEA Bull*, 50: 36–8.

Marx, E. (2011). 'Route to the Top. A Transatlantic Comparison of Top Business Leaders'. Report, Heidrick & Struggles, 6 December, available at http://www.palgraveconnect.com/pc/doifinder/10.1057/9781137008121, last accessed on 19 November 2013.

Mays, C. and M. Poumadère (1989). 'Decentralizing Risk Analysis in Large Engineered Systems: An Approach to Articulating Technical and Socio-organizational Dimensions of System Performance', *Risk Analysis*, 9(4).

Miller, J.D. (2000). 'The Public Understanding of Science and Technology in the United States: A Report to the National Science Foundation', Science and Technology Indicators, 2000. Washington, DC: National Science Foundation.

Nature (2012). 'Getting Tough on Nuclear Safety', *Nature*, 481: 113–202. doi: 10.1038/481113a, last accessed on 19 November 2013.

OECD (2010). *The Security of Energy Supply and the Contribution of Nuclear Energy*. Paris: OECD.

Outlook (2011). 'Kudankulam Nuclear Power Project', *Outlook India*, available at www.outlookindia.com/article.aspx?278934, last accessed on 19 November 2013.

Paton, D., and D. Johnston (2001). 'Disasters and Communities: Vulnerability, Resilience and Preparedness', *Disaster Prevention and Management*, 10(4): 93–111.

Pew Research Centre for the People and the Press (2011). 'Opposition to nuclear power rises amid Japanese crisis', available at http://www.people-press.org/2011/03/21/opposition-to-nuclear-power-rises-amid-japanese-crisis/, last accessed on 10 April 2014.

Pidgeon, N. (2011). 'Learning the Lessons of Fukushima', *People and Science*, December 2011, p. 20.

Pidgeon, N., I. Lorenzoni, and W. Poortinga (2008). 'Climate Change or Nuclear Power: No Thanks! A Quantitative Study of Public Perceptions and Risk Framing in Britain', *Glob Environ Change*, 18: 69–85.

Poumadère, M. (1991). 'The Credibility Crisis', in Segerstahl, B. (ed.), *Chernobyl: A Policy Response Study*. Berlin: Springer.

——— (2001). 'Public Acceptance and Beyond: The Meaning of Risk in Context', Invited presentation, International Thermonuclear Experimental Reactor (ITER) Project, French Atomic Energy Commissariat (CEA), Cadarache, France, pp. 28–9.

Poumadère, M., and, R. Bertoldo (2010). 'Risk Information and Minority Identity in the Neighbourhood of Industrial Facilities', *Catalan Journal of Communication and Cultural Studies*, 2(2): 213–29, doi: 10.1386/cjcs.2.2.213_1, last accessed on 19 November 2013.

Poumadère, M., and C. Mays (2003). 'The Dynamics of Risk Amplification and Attenuation in Context: A French Case Study', in N. Pidgeon, R. Kasperson, and P. Slovic (eds), *Risk Communication and Social Amplification of Risk*. Cambridge: Cambridge University Press, pp. 209–42.

Rediff (2010). 'Why the Jaitapur Nuclear Plant Must Be Opposed', *Rediff News*, available at http://www.rediff.com/news/column/why-the-jaitapur-nuclear-plant-must-be-opposed/20101229.htm, last accessed on 19 November 2013.

Rouquette, M.L. (1998). *La psychologie politique. [Political Psychology]*. Paris: PUF.

Slovic, P., J. Flynn, C.K. Mertz, M. Poumadère, and C. Mays (2000). 'Nuclear Power and the Public: A Comparative Study of Risk Perception in France and the United States', in O. Renn and B. Rohrmann (eds), *Cross-Cultural Risk Perception: A Survey of Empirical Studies*. Amsterdam: Kluwer Academic Press.

Spiegel E., and N. McArthur (2009). *Energy Shift. Game-changing Options for Fueling the Future*. New York: McGraw Hill.

The Guardian (2012). 'Dramatic Fall in New Nuclear Power Stations After Fukushima', *The Guardian*, available at http://www.guardian.co.uk/environment/2012/mar/08/fall-nuclear-power-stations-fukushima, last accessed on 19 November 2013.

Turner, B., and N. Pidgeon (1997). *Man-Made Disasters*, 2nd edition. Oxford: Wykeham.

Whitfield, S.C., E.A. Rosa, A. Dan, and T. Dietz (2009). 'The Future of Nuclear Power: Value Orientations and Risk Perception', *Risk Analysis*, 29: 425–37.

WHO (1958). 'Mental Health Aspects of the Peaceful Uses of Atomic Energy'. Technical report series: No. 151, p. 53. Geneva: World Health Organization.

12

CLAIRE MAYS

Sustainable Management of Radioactive Waste

What Can India Learn from Stakeholder Engagement in the West?

ANGRY PROTESTS OR STAKEHOLDER ENGAGEMENT?

Ten thousand citizens in the streets; two thousand fishermen on fast; roads blocked to prevent seven hundred engineers from reaching their work at the nuclear plant; villagers on stretchers in hospital, assaulted, because they took their deep concerns out into the sunlight. These are images from Kudankulam in 2011 and early 2012, where local people, afraid for the physical safety and the livelihood of future generations, opposed the commissioning of the 1,000 megawatt nuclear power plant, which has been under construction there for 20 years. Fukushima, the nuclear disaster in Japan sparked by natural catastrophe in March 2011, is casting its long shadow over this region. Highlighting the experience that resonates in protestors' minds, a December 2011 newspaper cartoon[1] shows the Grim Reaper carrying his bloody scythe down the road from Bhopal to Kudankulam.

[1] Available at http://www.dianuke.org/wp-content/uploads/2011/12/Devil-Eng.jpg, last accessed on 17 March 2014.

The political struggles in the background at Kudankulam are complex, far too complex for this Western observer to come to grips with. Yet, the stark images say something very clear and very familiar: people are deeply affected in their community, their minds, and their very body by the prospect of living in the neighbourhood of a risky facility. They come forward again and again, stronger and stronger, demanding to be part of the decision-making. As their concern and insistence put more and more pressure on the plans, ideas, and governance structures that are in place, something breaks. Sometimes it is the health and safety of the protestors, and the peace of their community. Sometimes it is the project to which they are opposed that breaks. At other times, it is the entire philosophy and approach followed up until then by the authorities.

In the 1980s, 1990s, and 2000s, such breakdowns happened to programmes and projects for the management of nuclear waste in Western countries. Top-down initiatives by government and industry to site and operate radioactive waste storage facilities encountered strong societal resistance, and societal demand prevailed. Confrontations on the streets or in the courts led to the overturning of centralized plans. In France, the UK, Canada, Belgium, Sweden, the US, and elsewhere, national programmes had to be reset to zero. Extensive and intensive dialogue with stakeholders had to be undertaken so that parliaments, ministries, and radioactive waste management (RWM) organizations could construct a more acceptable decision-making and siting approach.

Presently, after years of government and industry adjustment, consultation, and search for a new way, the philosophy and approach emerging in the West focus on *partnership* between civil society and radioactive waste managers (OECD-NEA 2010a). Gradually officials have come to understand that stakeholder engagement is preferable to technocracy and confrontation. This is in line with international treaties like the Aarhus Convention,[2] making public participation in environmental decision-making a fundamental right. A RWM facility requires not only a technical license but also a *social* license to be earned and maintained (Nash 2010). Today when villagers and committees around the nuclear construction sites Kudankulam and Jaitapur urgently voice

[2] Available at: http://www.unece.org/fileadmin/DAM/env/pp/documents/cep43e.pdf, last accessed on 17 March 2014.

their concerns about ecology, displacement of population, future waste management, and indeed the exercise of democracy, this Western experience is one that India could well learn from.

In Europe and North America, while massive protests were not always seen, still a high degree of emotion was common within communities when the suggestion of hosting a RWM facility was placed on the table (for example, see Mays and Poumadère [1996]; OECD-NEA [2000]). It should not be said that this emotion is entirely a thing of the past, and that societal concerns about RWM have been solved across the board. However, there is a sure trend in the West to honour and to harness community commitment, with national authorities asking regional and local communities what they require in order to play a role in managing the wastes of energy consumption. Rendering service to the national population by hosting waste is increasingly made into an opportunity for communities to grow and to improve their sustainability and indeed their well-being (OECD-NEA 2010a; CIP 2009). More and more, closed-ended and short-term plans are replaced by an open learning and decision-making process designed to be built up iteratively over a period of years, so that when a RWM storage or disposal facility is finally sited and constructed, it will be in full understanding, agreement, and confidence. Community members are giving of their time and energy to see that the right questions—moral, technical, and economic—are asked and the right things are done to ensure safety. Governments and industry increasingly recognize that this kind of deep cooperation is the best way forward and that their new local partners, far from being irrational or hindering progress, are making RWM solutions better.

After a review of facts and images relating to RWM in India, this chapter will highlight the central lessons learnt in the West. We identify the essential features leading to societal confidence in the management of radioactive waste. The chapter is not about nuclear plant siting or safety, nor about communication between public authorities and civil society around nuclear power (interested readers can see Chapters 10 and 11). We do not delve into likenesses or differences between the physical risks of radioactive waste and those of nuclear power plant operation. But we do respond to the example of the intense emotion—and moreover, the extreme commitment—inspired when a risky facility is introduced into the community at Kudankulam or Jaitapur.

RADIOACTIVE WASTE IN INDIA: STATUS AND OUTLOOK

In choosing to meet national energy supply needs through the nuclear generation of electricity, a nation has also chosen to generate radioactive waste. Like waste arising from medical treatments, food processing, desalination of sea water, military activities, and R&D using radioactive materials (all present in India), the waste from nuclear power generation must be managed in dedicated facilities meeting the highest standards of safety. These facilities must be capable of containing and isolating the toxic waste from human beings and the living environment over time periods that range from some ten human generations (for waste with low or intermediate levels of radiation) to several hundreds of thousands of years (for the most highly irradiated or 'high-level' spent fuel waste—the latter also requiring the most substantial barriers to separate it from the biosphere).

Some may view that because of its emphasis on recycling, the Indian model for nuclear electricity generation spawns relatively limited amounts of highly radioactive waste, and that this most dangerous waste will not be present in sizable quantity for many years. India struck out for energy independence in the 1950s, developing a unique 'three-stage programme' of nuclear power generation. First drawing conservatively upon the small native reserve of relatively low-grade uranium ore, then progressing through the fast breeder stage where nuclear fuel is reprocessed, the programme aims to culminate by 2050 in the use of 'vast and abundant thorium resources in advanced nuclear power reactors' (DAE 2011). Under this model, much radioactive material is recaptured to fuel energy production in the subsequent stage.

However, India's so-called closed nuclear fuel cycle is not waste-free. The reprocessing of spent fuel at each stage produces waste that requires handling, interim storage and final disposal. Moreover, dramatic evolutions in the Indian nuclear energy landscape today suggest that substantial volumes of spent fuel or high-level radioactive waste may be produced earlier than anticipated. A 2008 Nuclear Suppliers Group waiver allows once-excluded India to buy foreign uranium for civil applications. Most significantly, India targets much greater reliance on atomic power. At the Nuclear Security Summit convened by US President Obama in April 2010, Prime Minister Dr Manmohan Singh stated the ambition to increase India's installed capacity more than sevenfold from today's 4,120 MWe (megawatt electric) to 35,000 MWe by the year 2022 and 60,000 MWe by 2032 (Ravi 2010). In this goal, India today has nearly completed the construction at Jaitapur and Kudankulam of two 1,000 MWe light water reactors in cooperation with the Russian Federation, and signed agreements with Areva to buy French technology, fuel and services for a total of six 1,650 MWe European Pressurized Reactor (EPR) units of which the first two are planned to operate by 2018 (Business Line 2010).

While the EPR in particular is designed to produce less waste by burning uranium more efficiently, waste from the new reactors will accumulate faster than with existing indigenous reactors.

> [I]f India is to ramp up its [total] nuclear power generation to, say, 20 GW [20,000 MWe], there will be a sharp rise in waste generated, and the requirement for management of high-level waste would go up [from today's approximately 2.8 tonnes] to 14 tonnes a year, or storage of 96 tonnes of vitrified waste a year. This will keep accumulating over the life of the power plant. (Balakrishnan 2009)

In spite of these formidable statistics, the Indian authorities are not presently preoccupied with the issue of managing radioactive waste. Environment Minister Jairam Ramesh said early in 2011: 'Today, we don't have a waste management problem. We will have it by the year 2020–2030... The second stage of the three stage cycle (of using nuclear fuel) enables us to deal with much of the waste as is being generated today' (Times of India 2011). High-level, long-lived waste that cannot be recaptured is lying today in temporary on-site storage at nuclear facilities. The draft national RWM policy foresees that 'solidified waste products will be emplaced in a suitably engineered deep geological repository' (Raj et al. 2006), which corresponds to the international reference solution (OECD-NEA 2008a; NAS-NRC 2001). Like other countries, India is involved in a multi-decade programme to develop the technical concept and to identify and investigate sites for deep underground disposal. 'The process of identifying potential sites for a repository is currently underway with crystalline rock being looked at as the favoured geologic formation. The Kalpakkam (Tamil Nadu) site, underlain by granite, is under consideration along with several abandoned mines' (Mohan and Aggarwal 2009: 962).

International experience proves that government, waste producers and the organizations tasked with RWM should look ahead and pay attention not only to the scientific and technical context, but also to the societal challenges of managing radioactive waste (NAS-NRC 2001; OECD-NEA 2000). As Kudankulam and Jaitapur protests show, obtaining a social license (and not just a technical authorization) for nuclear activities of any type will be even more crucial in the aftermath of the Fukushima disaster. Indian federal and state authorities should seize the opportunity now, while interest in nuclear issues is high, to establish the groundwork for public confidence in RWM.

FACTORS THAT MAY INFLUENCE CONFIDENCE IN INDIAN RWM

On the face of it, does Indian RWM appear worthy of societal confidence? On the basis of events and debates in the national news, what image could citizens reasonably form of the processes and structures in place to manage nuclear affairs and assure safety? This is the context of any effort to inform Indian citizens or to associate the national or local publics in governance of RWM. A quick review uncovers items that may weigh negatively or positively on societal confidence.

POTENTIALLY NEGATIVE INFLUENCES UPON CONFIDENCE IN RWM

Safety issues in RWM are an integral challenge to public confidence the world over. Incidents and accidents will always raise legitimate questions of whether a nuclear establishment is set to ensure safety. The death of a 35-year-old man in New Delhi (and the hospitalization of six others) in 2010 after handling radioactive metal—labelled by the International Atomic Energy Agency (IAEA) as the world's most serious case of radiological exposure since 2006—brought to light the gaps in the handling of waste materials. The 'Mayapuri orphaned source' had been auctioned for scrap along with other contaminated spring cleaning items from the University of Delhi. This accident highlighted government failure to establish and enforce adequate controls against the circulation of domestic and foreign radioactive material as scrap (Ravi 2010; Yardley 2010).

Western nations have reinforced the independence of RWM safety authorities (OECD-NEA 2012a). India's Atomic Energy Regulatory Board (AERB) is subordinated to the Department of Atomic Energy (DAE), raising great doubts as to its effective independence; worse, there are serious misgivings about the new Nuclear Safety Regulatory Authority (NSRA) proposed by legislative bill which 'will have fewer powers and less independence than the present authority' (Gopalakrishnan 2011a, 2011b). Additional concerns are raised by the lack of separation between the nuclear industry and the Atomic Energy Commission (AEC), the principal nuclear regulatory body, as well as by the nuclear industry's military connections.

In every country, knowledge and research capabilities, by both operators and regulators, should be demonstrably up to the task of RWM. This is a concern as fewer graduates go into the nuclear field. In India, the concentration of relevant scientific expertise within the DAE, with little independent expertise in universities and elsewhere, may throw into question the quality, reliability, and autonomy of the knowledge driving RWM projects. If the nation proceeds with plans to build 44 nuclear plants over the next decade, Pricewater-houseCoopers estimates that 10,000 to 19,000 skilled people must be added, while India's top universities and special DAE-approved graduate programmes are graduating only about 150 nuclear specialists a year (Timmons 2011). With technological diversity coming into the nuclear power programme, Minister Ramesh raised the issue of India's 'domain knowledge', stating that 'Regulatory expertise takes times to build and in any case is not available easily' (Goswami 2011).

Studies on the 'social amplification of risk' (Pidgeon et al. 2003) suggest that the mere fact of controversy, protest, and opposition, like that surrounding Kudankulam and Jaitapur, seeds worry that could diminish confidence in operators' ability to handle radioactive waste. Another controversy today concerns legislation to cap civil liability in case of a nuclear accident. Pointing to widespread economic damage by Fukushima, critics charge that compensation payable by Indian industry under the August 2010 Bill would be sadly below the mark (Devraj 2011). Yet, foreign suppliers claim that they in turn are exposed to unlimited liability. Government rules offered in response were judged 'unlikely to satisfy US objections even as they trigger criticism at home for...dilution of Parliament's legislative intent in enacting a tough liability law' (The Hindu 2011). While nuclear reactor risks are greater than those typically associated with RWM facilities, the liability controversy signals instability, which could hamper confidence.

Lack of institutional transparency and accountability is always counted as a significant challenge to public confidence. India's DAE does not publish the operational statistics of reprocessing plants, nor is it subject to audit by the Comptroller and Auditory General (CAG) of India. It is unclear whether India's nuclear energy production is linked to weapons production, and with no Indian signature on the Non-proliferation Treaty and other IAEA conventions, her three reprocessing plants escape from international safeguards. The AERB 'has been historically structured to avoid public scrutiny and public participation such as we see in the functioning of new infrastructure regulators in India' (Mohan and Aggarwal 2009: 963). India's Right to Information Act, 2005, does not cover the nuclear sector, and the NSRA Bill, tabled in 2011, recommends the exclusion of yet-to-be-established nuclear safety agencies from transparency obligations (Freedominfo.org 2012).

Public participation in RWM has emerged in the West as a primary factor in developing societal confidence. Mohan and Aggarwal (2009) claimed that India needs a 'more comprehensive policy of public participation in both [nuclear power plant] construction and disposal of waste', and noted:

> With the expected massive capacity addition from nuclear energy in the next couple of decades, this may be the opportune time that the [Indian] public be informed and taken into confidence [about waste management]. There is an urgent need for a comprehensive nuclear energy policy and a communication plan covering all aspects of development, related use, and a plan for final disposal of nuclear waste. (ibid.: 963–4)

Yet, the draft national policy for RWM has not been widely circulated for public discussion (Balakrishnan 2009; Mohan and Aggarwal 2009). The DAE has placed online a detailed map of atomic energy establishments in India but no institutional website, however, gives indications that there may be any programme in India today to carry out public consultation, local stakeholder participation or other civic involvement in RWM.

Even if officials judge there is no immediate waste problem, it is an issue that people are concerned about and thus needs to be debated openly. People's representatives at Kudankulam and Jaitapur have decried the lack of clarity on RWM plans in the review or environmental assessment documents provided for those plants (Ramya [undated]; Deshpande 2011). Their criticisms transmit a clear societal demand for information, foresight, and shared governance. These elements have been ratified in the West as essential features of RWM.

POTENTIALLY POSITIVE INFLUENCES UPON CONFIDENCE IN RWM

The Indian context does offer some factors which may lay groundwork for public confidence in RWM projects. The country is making progress in positioning its nuclear energy programme in a global context, developing international collaborations and aligning itself with best practice. Following the Fukushima disaster, India moved appropriately to assess the vulnerability of atomic energy installations. Public figures are talking about openness, independence, learning, and deliberation— all prime factors for developing societal confidence in RWM. In a letter to the Prime Minister, the then Environment Minister Jairam Ramesh urged that public perceptions of nuclear safety be taken into account, and suggested a need to 'give serious thought to making AERB a fully independent organization drawing its powers directly from Parliament' (Goswami 2011). He also reflected: 'Learning a lesson from Japan incident and keeping in view the [Jaitapur] villagers apprehensions, at the moment special emphasis should be on evolving a fool proof safety system and nuclear options should be more deliberated and debated' (Sharma 2011). Similarly, legislator and vice chairman of the National Disaster Management Authority, S. Reddy, stated: 'We have to own up to the deficiencies and gaps that exist and find solutions. We have to win the confidence of the people. They have the right to make demands and it is for the government to address this... There is need for transparency in our dealings' (Deccan Herald 2012).

All these facets could contribute to a positive view of authorities as increasingly responsive to public concerns, and give hope that secrecy, non-accountability, and exclusively top-down decision-making in the nuclear domain could become things of the past. The Bt brinjal consultations held in 2010 show that India's environment ministry has indeed made strides to include civil society in environmental governance. On such a basis, greater confidence in the RWM system could be built up.

India's nuclear energy programme is closely linked with national autonomy and prestige, as the 3-stage technology drawing on abundant indigenous thorium stocks was conceived for energy independence. Former president Abdul Kalam paints nuclear power, combined with 'youth power', as India's 'gateway to a prosperous future' as the 'leading economy of the world', by seizing the 'opportunity to emerge as the energy capital [and] the first...to realise the dream of a fossil fuel-free nation' (Kalam and Singh 2011). At the same time, India's traditional independence may seem weakened by the 2010 agreements for EPRs to be operated by the Nuclear Power Corporation of India Limited (NPCIL), with fuel supplied by France. The development of a strong, modern national RWM programme, which is visible, open, and responsive, could reassure citizens that India has not relinquished its autonomy or progressive position in the nuclear domain.

INTERNATIONAL ADAPTATIONS TO THE SPECIAL NATURE OF RADIOACTIVE WASTE

There is a particular dimension to radioactive waste that may influence people's views: RWM events, facts, and objects have weighty symbolic meaning.

> In all cultures the word 'waste' is associated with negative symbolism. Waste is by definition something that is no longer wanted. It evokes images of dirtiness and impurity that spoil the landscape, have no economic value and may even be a threat. While radioactive waste probably shares those associations, it also has its own specific symbolic dimension... Waste connected to nuclear tends to draw the image of death and decay, an aura of threatening mystery or destructiveness. By association, the practice of managing radioactive waste has also taken on a negative symbolic value. It seems connected with powerful industries, secretive and unconcerned by the interests of communities hosting installations. The past lack of transparency by nuclear institutions has entailed fears and a sense of power imbalance among stakeholders. Thinking about communities and nuclear waste could seem like thinking about David versus Goliath, or good versus evil. (OECD-NEA 2011)

Structural aspects of India's nuclear programme reviewed above are likely to influence public confidence, positively or negatively. Perception of these aspects may carry over to new RWM arrangements. Officials can aim to reinforce successes and correct past shortcomings by specifically including public involvement, transparency, independent regulation, and a focus on building host community's well-being. In Western contexts, those important features have helped to overcome the negative symbolism of waste and radiation. The new Council Directive[3] that is to be transposed into the law of each European nation, stimulates member states to create a flexible and adaptable reference RWM policy framework, and to establish and update a precise waste inventory. Further, it strives to reinforce regulatory independence, and provide transparency by ensuring effective public information and opportunities for local authorities and also the public to participate in the decision-making processes.

It may be useful to give special attention to connotations of waste and radioactivity in the Indian context—research should say whether these are similar or different to perceptions in other places, and whether particular adjustments are needed in public communication and action on RWM in order to dispel negative connotations. Particularly as India has so many different languages and cultures, government and academia should investigate how people perceive radioactive waste as well as governance processes—and adjust strategies accordingly.

In Western countries, both official vocabulary and actual management approaches have been refined to reflect the peoples' preferred values. For instance, in Canada, the National Waste Management Organization no longer uses the word 'expert' which suggests an irreducible gap between the public and some highly trained individuals possessing all the answers; the word 'specialist' reflects better the fact that each stakeholder might bring a particular contribution to the RWM process while still needing to learn from other stakeholders. In France, where 'final disposal' was found to suggest an unwanted image of walking away from waste, terminology and management concepts have been revised to centre on the ability to *monitor* the future facility, to *reverse*

---

[3] Council Directive 2011/70/Euratom of 19 July 2011, establishing a community framework for the responsible and safe management of spent fuel and radioactive waste.

decisions, and also to *retrieve* waste should that become necessary. The term 'compensation' places the accent on harm to be offset or loss to be repaid; in the UK an 'involvement package' instead supports communities deliberating on whether they might host a RWM facility—and part of that deliberation is structuring a 'benefits package' to foster community sustainability. In Sweden, the accent is placed on 'added value' that a high-tech RWM facility should bring to a community and its region over the long-term. Two municipalities were competing candidates to host a geological repository. When a site located in one municipality was deemed preferable, the other municipality by prior negotiated agreement received 75 per cent of the added value programming support. This arrangement acknowledged the decade of hard work invested in deliberations by that municipality. By supporting economic planning and development, the added value programme improves the outlook for long-term community sustainability (OECD-NEA 2012b).

Moreover, a revolution is coming about in how RWM facilities themselves should be built and viewed. Safety used to be assured by fencing-off sites, producing an ugly, threatening presence that actually spoilt people's sense of security. The philosophy is beginning to evolve to say: '[D]o not set RWM facilities apart, but make them a part of the community'. Amongst the ways in which this can be achieved are: designing a modern surface building that can be marked out as a symbol of the country's technological progress and a proud feature of the community's landscape; planning to include visitors' centres, museums or even (such as in Belgium) a 'radioactivity theme park' so people can understand and 'see' what is managed (people fear the unknown and what they cannot see); and designing a multifunctional facility so that the community, now or later, can benefit from other uses of the infrastructure. Moreover, technical operators are cooperating with local stakeholders who want to be part of the design and monitoring of facilities. All in all, there is a movement to foster a durable relationship between the host community and the RWM facility, because the installation will be there for many generations (OECD-NEA 2007, 2008b).

CONFIDENCE FACTORS AS FOUND IN THE WEST

The Forum on Stakeholder Confidence (FSC) of the OECD Nuclear Energy Agency has reviewed RWM successes and failures in Europe and North America. The outcome is a large set of publications[4] about decision-making processes that can garner broad societal approval and support, and remain sustainable across the many generations touched by RWM. They show how the 'decide-announce-defend' approach has been replaced by 'engagement, interaction, and cooperation', allowing national RWM problems to find local solutions. Among the lessons learned by the FSC is that technical soundness and procedural fairness are of comparable importance in developing RWM solutions.

Stakeholder confidence is never established 'once and for all', and it must be earned on a continual basis. Three characteristics prove essential for development of confidence in an RWM concept and facilities:

1. *Decision-making should be performed through visible, iterative processes, providing the flexibility to adapt to contextual changes,* for example, by implementing a stepwise approach that provides sufficient time for developing a competent and fair discourse.

Countries like Finland and France have developed legislation that clearly outlines steps in developing RWM, involving civil society stakeholders at each step. The laws provide clarity about the stages of the programme (measured in decades not months), the roles of those involved, and their opportunities to influence outcomes. Milestones mark the points where preceding steps can be reviewed and adjusted if necessary, and where new phases can be refined. Canadian legislation places the accent on formally assessing the acceptability of RWM plans and projects at each step, first on a broad national level, and, progressively, in cooperation with identified communities. In the UK, the legislation was built up through a participative process, resulting in a clear stepwise RWM plan that is highly adaptable to changes in understanding and in preferences as technical research and community deliberations unfold.

In the stepwise processes implemented in the Western countries, there are now more checkpoints, allowing potential host communities and national institutions to confirm their confidence in what has been done up to date. As well, there are more off ramps, allowing the search to be redirected if technical factors show that a site is

---

[4] Available at http://www.oecd-nea.org/rwm/fsc; see in particular many 2-page flyers condensing useful information in plain English and other languages.

unsuitable—but also, allowing candidate communities to withdraw from consideration if full support from local residents cannot be achieved. In such a case, government is committed to respect the community choice and open the call for volunteers in a new siting process. While these are rich nations, they have learnt through experience that investing in participation and partnership, and working hand in hand with concerned citizens comes in much cheaper than trying to run them over or ignoring them.

2. *Collective learning should be facilitated*, for example, by promoting interactions between various stakeholders and specialists.

In Sweden, local communities approached by the waste management implementer to host a spent fuel repository insisted on their need to test proposed RWM plans and assumptions for themselves. The municipal councils called for financial support to build their competence with the help of third-party experts, and obtained it from the national Nuclear Waste Fund (a financing system wisely set up in the 1980s by Parliament and based on fees from nuclear operators; Kärnavfallsfonden 2011). With strong cooperation from the implementer, the safety regulator, and national organisms, the people's representatives conducted hearings over the course of the years. Questions were asked that 'stretched' the implementer. Looking for, and developing answers, on the sometimes quite complex queries brought forward by the municipalities as well as Non-governmental Organizations (NGOs), gradually improved confidence that the operator's RWM solution was solid. A cooperative process between government, technical stakeholders and citizens to look into both technical issues and socioeconomic concerns is becoming best practice in the West.

3. *Public involvement in decision-making processes should be facilitated*, by promoting constructive and high-quality communication between individuals with different knowledge, beliefs, interests, values, and worldviews.

In Belgium, local partnerships were formed between the implementer and candidate communities. Elected officials and local volunteers worked side by side with industry agents to develop a low-level waste disposal facility concept that integrated technical and societal requirements. Dedicated working groups looked into safe design, site emplacement, safeguarding local health, and economic and cultural impacts (OECD-NEA 2007, 2010a; COWAM 2 2006). The partnerships submitted their reports to their municipal council who, on that basis, confirmed local willingness to host the facility under specified conditions.

PARTNERSHIP ARRANGEMENTS

The main features of RWM partnership arrangements were identified by surveying 13 Western countries (OECD-NEA 2010a, 2010b). While the composition of local partnerships and the tasks they have to carry out vary widely, all share a high level of empowerment. Typically, partnership arrangements enable the local communities:

- To access, evaluate, and disseminate information;
- To consult experts of their choice and to build up their own expertise in order to assess the project;
- To make suggestions on facility design features, infrastructure, etc., and influence the implementer's work;
- To design benefit packages to ensure social and economic improvement to the community in the short and long term;
- To deliberate and provide recommendations to higher-level authorities;
- To stay abreast of research performed by the implementer, its consultants, the regulators, etc.;
- To monitor the performance of the various players.

Other favourable characteristics seen in national programmes with a partnership approach include voluntarism (candidate communities are incentivized to come forward), local veto power (up until a defined stage in project development), and benefits to support local engagement and sustainability. Highly practical information on how to set up, fund, and operate a RWM local committee is available in a 'Roadmap' written in collaboration with people from nine European countries (COWAM 2 2006).

MOVING TOWARDS CONSTRUCTIVE DEMOCRACY: THE EXAMPLE OF COWAM IN PRACTICE (CIP)

Can lay people representing local communities really bring valued inputs to highly trained professionals of waste management and policy? Can their dialogues produce materials that are useful to RWM decision-making? An innovative project supported by the European Commission showed they can, in early days of RWM planning just as in advanced stages before actual construction of a repository. Moreover, evaluation of these dialogues brought to light not just participative arrangements, but a new concept of 'constructive democracy'.

The Community Waste Management in Practice, or COWAM in practice (CIP)[5] platform brought together national radioactive waste managers (policy actors, industry agents, and regulators) with local counterparts in five European countries (France, Romania, Slovenia, Spain, and UK). The CIP process (2007–9) enabled each national multi-stakeholder group to identify issues important for the good governance of RWM in their own context, and then to conduct cooperative research into these issues.

The groups worked out that it was important to look into how communities are affected by RWM and how, instead of submitting to the dictate of plans made elsewhere, they can be empowered to integrate a proposed facility into their own territorial development plan. CIP participants highlighted the need to reinforce democracy on the local level such that citizens can have a real say, and they wanted also to address how safety can be assured over the centuries that a RWM installation will be present in a community.

The CIP groups found that in order to obtain a morally correct and effective social license for RWM, local and regional stakeholders must be directly involved in the governance process. They must be strengthened to play their continuing role over the course of decades. This implies that governments must move away from top-down approaches to concentrate instead on policies and structures that facilitate cooperation among the full diversity of stakeholders (CIP 2009). These suggestions are more ambitious in their scope than the local partnership arrangements outlined above. They propose a fundamental transformation of our framework of inclusive governance to one which thoroughly embraces core democratic principles.

Constructive democracy (Lavelle et al. 2010) is an alternative political model that moves away from the traditional models of representative democracy ('one man, one vote') or even participatory democracy (where authority sets aside limited times and places at which citizens can be part of decision-making). Constructive democracy transforms the relationship between stakeholders, putting public and private,

[5] The relevant material can be accessed at www.cowam.com/CIP.html, last accessed on 17 March 2014.

central authority, and civil society actors on an equal footing, with collective responsibility to take care of issues of mutual concern. It promotes self-organization and knowledge-gathering by civil society to rise to its role. CIP showed that constructive democracy can function in the area of RWM.

CIP participants acknowledged that championing a shift in mindsets and altering the balance of power and responsibility in patterns of relationship requires dogged perseverance and commitment on all sides. Should the Indian radioactive waste managers aspire straightaway to transform relationships between authority and the population, to aim for such a radical form of constructive democracy? Whatever be the answer, it would be justifiable for Indian managers to begin to gradually develop relationships with the local communities that are sure to be affected by RWM—both current nuclear host communities and those close to sites that may be investigated for a repository or other management facilities. These communities should be encouraged to identify their local interests and aspirations, so that they can move seamlessly into exploratory partnerships when RWM decision-making moves into a more active phase. On the national level, government, legislators, and policy actors should engage stakeholders in sketching out a stepwise RWM plan and fair process that will empower communities at term to play a competent role in governance.

CONCLUSION: GAINING SOCIAL LICENSE TO MAKE RWM SUSTAINABLE

Across the world, when the technological project for managing radioactive waste goes 'out of doors', seeking a candidate site to host an installation, local publics react with vigour. Typically conflict has been seen between 'technocrats' and civil society, and repositories have been regarded as most unwelcome potential neighbours (Slovic et al. 1994; Slovic 2000; Mays 2004). In Europe and North America, hard lessons have been learned over the past three decades. Top-down efforts to site storage or disposal facilities in local communities met with failure, sometimes setting the entire national RWM programme on its ear. France, Canada, and the UK, among others, have had to start over from square one in the face of public rejection—viewed as the refusal of a social license for official plans (OECD-NEA 2003, 2010a).

Social licensing is part of a sustainability approach. For any industrial or political practice to be sustainable, we need to make sure that the 'triple bottom line' of ecological, economic, and societal/ethical systems can carry it. Sustainable management of radioactive waste depends not only on safe technical design and dedicated funding, but also on the ability to align RWM with societal values—and moreover, to make hosting a facility an integral part of a community's quality of life over the long-term.

Worldwide, governments and the nuclear power establishment have gradually understood that the public must be engaged early on and in a meaningful way.[6] Increasingly, it is being recognized that civil society is not an enemy, but a vital partner in ensuring the safety and sustainability of waste management solutions. Local communities should be not just 'affected' by RWM, but should also take their rightful place to become influential in decision-making, and enjoy sustainable well-being across the generations during which radioactive waste requires attention (CIP 2009).

The social licensing process may be different in each country, but in essence it implies engaging civil society in shaping and assessing plans related to energy production and waste, and in taking enlightened decisions about how to manage the related risks. Principles have been identified for building inclusive governance processes, characterized by continuous learning and adaptation to meet societal requirements (OECD-NEA 2004). Western nations have recognized the need for citizen empowerment through engagement and partnership, in leaving behind a form of token participation focused on public information and limited consultation (OECD-NEA 2010b). Strides have been made to foster a durable relationship between RWM facilities and their host communities, by maximizing the potential of the facility to fit in, adapt to and also contribute directly to the host community's preferred way of life (OECD-NEA 2007, 2008b).

[6] This understanding is coherent with the 1998 Aarhus Convention (United Nations/Economic Commission for Europe Convention on Access to Information, Public Participation in Decision-making and Access to Justice in Environmental Matters) which increasingly is used as a standard against which the effective participation of civil society in RWM is compared; available at http://www.anccli.fr/Europe-International/ACN-Convention-d-Aarhus-et-nucleaire-Aarhus-Convention-Nuclear, last accessed on 17 March 2014.

Despite the Environment Minister Ramesh's view—as shared with the nuclear establishment—that RWM is not an immediate problem, recent protests in Jaitapur and Kudankulam illustrate that people are concerned that they have been kept in the dark. There is a strong demand from civil society to move into responsible dialogue, as part of 'faith in democracy' (Economic Times 2012). The protests make a very real case for ensuring that both nuclear power plants and RWM facilities in India hold a social license to operate.

What shape will public confidence in RWM take in India? Is it sufficient to have proper technical regulation and control in place to reassure passive citizens, as an AERB Newsletter (Thomas and Rao 2009) suggested—or must active stakeholder engagement be planned and carried out? Will the authorities continue to assume that technical experts hold all the keys to RWM, or will information, reflection, and planning be shared with the citizenry? Will the authorities form partnerships with civil society organizations and affected local publics to build a constructive democratic approach, fostering sustainable communities while solving the waste problem? In short, should Western best practices be attempted in India?

India has the opportunity now to anticipate the social licensing process for RWM by studying, preparing, and testing stakeholder engagement in this area. It is not a vain goal in the Indian context. Feasible in India, as many of the chapters in this volume have shown, is community control and development of assets, in partnership with other stakeholders, so that they will be appropriate to local conditions and contribute to the cultural, economic, psychological, social, and spiritual well-being of the community and the sustainability of the environment.

Many questions remain open, among them: What is the current level of confidence among Indians in the institutions and decision-making processes for the management of radioactive waste? How great—or small—is civic demand to be involved in that management? Even without answers to those questions, the author was encouraged to notice, in the two days of exchange at the 2011 'Risk Management in India' conference, that stakeholder engagement and constructive democracy certainly have their place on the subcontinent. The conference papers collected in this volume (the chapters) show that there is an apt cultural basis in India to achieve a world-class RWM governance process. India has a high level of political awareness, an active civil society and demonstrated the ability to cooperate across classes and challenge established authority. There is a record of stakeholder consultation and a strong tradition of self-government on the village level. Combined with citizens' natural attachment to their local landscape and desire for well-being across the generations, these mental and democratic qualities will stand India in good stead when it rises to the need for stakeholder engagement in RWM.

BIBLIOGRAPHY

Banerjee, S. (2010). Statement by D.S. Banerjee, Chairman of the Atomic Energy Commission and Leader of the Indian Delegation, International Atomic Energy Agency 54th General Conference, Vienna, 22 September, available at www.dae.gov.in/gc/gc54.doc, last accessed on 1 March 2012.

Balakrishnan, B. (2009). 'The Challenge of Radioactive Waste Management', *Business Line*, 14 November, available at www.thehindubusinessline.com/todays-paper/tp-opinion/article1069280.ece?ref=archive, last accessed on 1 March 2012.

Business Line (2010). 'India, France Ink pact for Areva Reactors, Fuel', *Business Line*, 7 December, available at www.dae.gov.in/press/npcil071210.pdf, last accessed on 1 March 2012.

CIP (COWAM in Practice) (2009). 'European-Level Guidelines for the Inclusive Governance of Radioactive Waste Management'. Paris: Mutadis; Institut Symlog, available at www.cowam.com/IMG/pdf_CIP-EUG_version_finale_telechargeable.pdf, last accessed on 1 March 2012.

COWAM 2 (2006). 'Roadmap for Local Committee Construction: Better Paths Towards the Governance of Radioactive Waste'. Paris: Mutadis; Institut Symlog, available at www.cowam.com/IMG/pdf_Cowam_2_WP1_ROADMAP_for_Local_Committee_Construction.pdf, last accessed on 1 March 2012.

DAE (2011). *Nuclear India*, Jan–June, 44(7–12), available at http://dae.nic.in/writereaddata/ni/ni0611.pdf, last accessed on 19 November 2013.

Deccan Herald (2012). 'Weak Links in Security of India's N-Plants', *Deccan Herald*, 20 January, available at www.deccanherald.com/content/220803/weak-links-security-indias-coastal.html, last accessed on 1 March 2012.

Deshpande, V. (2011). 'No Safety Study Undertaken on Jaitapur Project: Justice Shah', *The Hindu*, 23 May, available at www.thehindu.com/news/national/article2040287.ece, last accessed on 1 March 2012.

Devraj, R. (2011). 'India: Fukushima Revives Debate over Nuclear Liability', *International Press Service*, 30 March, available at http://www.ipsnews.net/2011/03/india-fukushima-revives-debate-over-nuclear-liability/, last accessed on 1 March 2012.

Economic Times (2012). 'Kudankulam Nuclear Power Plant: Udayakumar Says Protesters are "Ready for Talks"', *The Economic Times*, 26 March, available at http://articles.economictimes.indiatimes.com/2012-03-26/news/31240221_1_protesters-indo-russian-nuclear-project-anti-nuclear-activists, last accessed on 1 March 2012.

Freedominfo.org (2012). 'India Proposes RTI Act Exemption on Nuclear Safety', 3 February, http://www.freedominfo.org/2012/02/india-proposes-rti-act-exemption-on-nuclear-safety, last accessed on 1 March 2012.

Gopalakrishnan, A. (2011a). 'Why should Jaitapur be Made a Guinea Pig For Untested Reactor?', *Daily News and Analysis*, 17 March, available at www.dnaindia.com/print710.php?cid=1520843, last accessed on 1 March 2012.

———(2011b). 'A Nuclear Regulator Without Teeth', *The Hindu*, 16 September, available at www.thehindu.com/todays-paper/tp-opinion/article2457556.ece, last accessed on 1 March 2012.

Goswami, U.A. (2011). 'Review Jaitapur and Large Nuclear Parks: Jairam Ramesh', *The Economic Times*, 7 April, available at https://articles.economictimes.indiatimes.com/2011-04-07/news/29392568_1_nuclear-power-anil-kakodkar-nuclear-park, last accessed on 1 March 2012.

IAEA (International Atomic Energy Agency) (2011). 'Temperature of Spent Fuel Pools at Fukushima Daiichi Nuclear Power Plant—Updated', *Fukushima Nuclear Accident Update*, 18 March, 06:10 UTC, available at https://iaea.org/newscenter/news/2011/fukushima180311.html, last accessed on 1 March 2012.

Kalam, A.P.J., and S.P. Singh (2011). 'Nuclear Power is our Gateway to a Prosperous Future', *The Hindu*, 6 November, available at www.thehindu.com/opinion/op-ed/article2601471.ece, last accessed on 1 March 2012.

Kärnavfallsfonden (2011). *The Nuclear Waste Fund's Activity Report for 2010*. Stockholm, available at http://www.karnavfallsfonden.se/download/18.40946aa91373db03843e9/1336994994179/, last accessed on 19 November 2013.

Lavelle, S., G. Hériard Dubreuil, S. Gadbois, C. Mays, and T. Schneider (2010). 'Constructive Democracy and Governance of Technology' (in French), *revue gouvernance*, 7(2), Feb. 2011, available at http://www.revuegouvernance.ca/article-fr.html?article_id=79&page_id=45&&&lang_id=2, last accessed on 1 March 2012.

Mays, C., and M. Poumadère (1996). 'Uncertain Communication: Institutional Discourse in Nuclear Waste Repository Siting', in V. Sublet, V. Covello, and T. Tinker (eds), *Scientific Uncertainty and Its Influence on the Public Communications Process*. Dordrecht: Kluwer, NATO ASI Series D Behavioural and Social Sciences, Vol. 86.

Mays, C. (2004). 'Where Does it Go: Siting Methods and Social Representations of Radioactive Waste Management in France', in Boholm, A. and R. Löfstedt (eds), *Facility Siting: Risk, Power and Identity in Land-use Planning*. London: Earthscan, pp. 21–43.

Mohan, M.P.R., and V. Aggarwal (2009). 'Spent Fuel Management in India', *Journal of Risk Research*, 12(7–8): 955–67.

NAS-NRC (National Academy of Sciences-National Research Council) (2001). *Disposition of High-level Waste and Spent Nuclear Fuel: The Continuing Societal and Technical Challenges*, Committee on disposition of high-level radioactive waste through geological isolation, National Academy of Sciences and C. Mays (co-author). Washington, D.C.: National Academy Press, available at www.nap.edu/catalog.php?record_id=10119, last accessed on 1 March 2012.

Nash, K.E. (2010). 'Plan for the Long-term Management of Canada's Used Nuclear Fuel', Submission to the Blue Ribbon Commission on America's Nuclear Future, available at www.brc.gov/sites/default/files/meetings/attachments/k_e_nash_summay_of_presentation.pdf, last accessed on 1 March 2012.

OECD-NEA (Organisation for Economic Cooperation and Development-Nuclear Energy Agency) (2000). *Stakeholder Confidence and Radioactive Waste Disposal*, FSC Inauguration Workshop, Paris, France, 28–31 August. Paris: OECD.

——— (2003). *Public Confidence in the Management of Radioactive Waste: The Canadian Context*, Workshop proceedings, FSC Workshop, Ottawa, Clarington, and Port Hope, Canada, 14–18 October 2002. Paris: OECD.

——— (2004). *Learning and Adapting to Societal Requirements for Radioactive Waste Management: Key findings and experience of the Forum on Stakeholder Confidence*. Paris: OECD.

——— (2007). *Fostering a Durable Relationship Between a Waste Management Facility and its Host Community: Adding Value Through Design and Process*. Paris: OECD.

——— (2008a). *Moving Forward with Geological Disposal of Radioactive Waste: A Collective Statement of the NEA Radioactive Waste Management Committee*. Paris: OECD.

——— (2008b). 'Towards Waste Management Facilities that Become a Durable and Attractive Part of the Fabric of Local Community–Relevant Design Features', 2-page flyer, available at www.oecd-nea.org/rwm/fsc/docs/Towards-waste_management_EN_A4.pdf, last accessed on 1 March 2012.

OECD-NEA (Organisation for Economic Cooperation and Development-Nuclear Energy Agency) (2010a). *Partnering for Long-term Management of Radioactive Waste: Evolution and Current Practice in Thirteen Countries*. Paris: OECD.

———— (2010b). 'From Information and Consultation to Citizen Influence and Power: 10-year Evolution in Public Involvement in Radioactive Waste Management', 2-page flyer, available at http://www.oecd-nea.org/fsc/docs/EVOLUTION-EN-v4.pdf, last accessed on 1 March 2012.

———— (2011). 'More Than Just Concrete Realities: The Symbolic Dimension of Radioactive Waste and its Management', 2-page flyer, available at www.oecd-nea.org/fsc/docs/symbolic-dimension-of-waste.pdf, last accessed on 1 March 2012.

———— (2012a). *The Role and Image of the Safety Authorities in Radioactive Waste Management: Evolution over the Last Decades*. Paris: OECD.

———— (2012b). 'Actual Implementation of a Spent Nuclear Fuel Repository in Sweden: Seizing Opportunities', Synthesis of the workshop; Gimo, Forsmark and Östhammar, Sweden, 4–6 May 2011. Paris: OECD.

Pidgeon, N., R. Kasperson, and P. Slovic (eds) (2003). *The Social Amplification of Risk*. Cambridge: Cambridge University Press.

Raj, K., K.K. Prasad, and N.K. Bansal (2006). 'Radioactive Waste Management Practices in India', *Nuclear Engineering and Design*, 236(7–8): 914–30.

Ravi, Chaitanya (2010). 'The Nuclear Safety Culture in India: Past, Present, and Future', *IPCS Special Report*, No. 90, May 2010, available at www.ipcs.org/pdf_file/issue/SR90-Chaitanya.pdf, last accessed on 1 March 2012.

Ramya (undated). 'Kudankulam Nuclear Power Plant: The Issues', *Jeywin Blog*, available at http://www.jeywin.com/main/Kudankulam-nuclear-power-plant-%E2%80%93-the-issues, last accessed on 1 March 2012.

Sharma, A. (2011). 'Press Pause on Jaitapur, Says Jairam Ramesh', *Hindustan Times*, 23 April, available at www.hindustantimes.com/India-news/Punjab/Press-pause-on-Jaitapur-says-Jairam-Ramesh/Article1-688875.aspx, last accessed on 10 March 2012.

Slovic, P. (2000). *The Perception of Risk*. London: Earthscan.

Slovic, P., J. Flynn, and R. Gregory (1994). 'Stigma Happens: Social Problems in the Siting of Nuclear Waste Facilities', *Risk Analysis*, 14(5): 773–8.

Sri Raman, J. (2010). 'Sarkozy's India Visit: The Nuclear Fallout', *Truthout*, 22 December, available at http://archive.truthout.org/sarkozys-india-visit-the-nuclear-fallout66129, last accessed on 1 March 2012.

The Hindu (2011). 'New Rules Give Some Relief to Nuclear Suppliers', *The Hindu*, 16 November, available at www.thehindu.com/news/national/article2633545.ece, last accessed on 1 March 2012.

Times of India (2011). 'Nuclear Waste Not an Immediate Problem for India: Ramesh', *The Times of India*, 3 January, available at http://articles.timesofindia.indiatimes.com/2011-01-03/pollution/28363012_1_nuclear-waste-waste-management-nuclear-energy, last accessed on 1 March 2012.

Thomas, George, and S.N. Rao (2009). 'Regulatory Aspects of Radioactive Waste Management in Nuclear Facilities', *AERB Newsletter*, (January–June) 22(1). Atomic Energy Regulatory Board.

Timmons, H. (2011). 'A Country Searching for Engineers to Serve Its Nuclear Needs', *New York Times*, 14 April, available at www.nytimes.com/2011/04/15/business/global/15engineers.html?_r=1, last accessed on 1 March 2012.

Yardley, J. (2010). 'Scrap Metal Radiation Raises Concerns in India', *New York Times*, 23 April, available at www.nytimes.com/2010/04/24/world/asia/24india.html?_r=1, last accessed on 1 March 2012.

13

FREDERIC BOUDER

Can Health and Safety Regulators Respond to Changing Societal Expectations?

On 3 December 1984, the town of Bhopal, Madhya Pradesh, was affected by a leak of poisonous methyl isocyanate (MIC) at a Union Carbide plant. The accident, which cost the lives of thousands, would soon go down in history as the Bhopal gas tragedy. It probably holds the sad record of being the worst industrial disaster ever. In post-Bhopal India, the number of fatalities may be on the decline in some sectors thanks to educational programmes, technological improvements, and worker awareness (Preetha 2011). Yet, insufficient health and safety protection claims numerous lives each year. Examples abound. In 2008, India was hit with a major fire in a petrochemical complex in Maharashtra, which caused several deaths. In 2009, at least 41 workers were buried alive in Orissa when a chimney under construction at the coal-fired power plant for Vedanta's Korba aluminium complex collapsed. In 2011, one of the worst rail accidents occurred when a speeding Delhi-bound Kalka Mail derailed, killing at least 35 people and injuring over 200. Of course major incidents of this kind are only the tip of the iceberg as routine activities typically cause the largest number of fatalities. In practice, India needs to cope with myriad health and safety hazards, caused by industrialization, a thriving mining sector and haphazard urbanization.

In the West, the rapid economic development of the 1960s and the 1970s also produced many incidents—from Windscale and Three Mile Island, to the pollution produced by the burning of coal in power plants (acid rain); offshore oils spills (Santa Barbara and Torrey Canyon); the disposal of toxic wastes (Love Canal, Nuneaton); health hazards to workers (asbestos and vinyl chloride); and the safety of ethical drugs (Thalidomide, Oraflex) (Vogel 1986: 222). Some of the major accidents of the 1970s concerned particularly dreaded activities, such as the nuclear meltdown at Three Mile Island in the US, or, in the Netherlands, the release of propane at a chemical production unit in South Limburg that killed 14 people (Ale 2005). Occasionally, accidents cause major and long-lasting environmental damage, such as the Exxon Valdez disaster in 1989 and the BP oil spill in the Gulf of Mexico in 2010.

Accidents typically catch the public's attention; jeopardizing public trust and heightening public concerns about possible negligence on the part of businesses and regulators (Löfstedt 2005). The result, in the West, has been specific calls for action leading to the development of various regulatory regimes. These frameworks may bring benefits to workers, the public and even businesses. Yet they often come at a price, which requires the performance of cost–benefit, risk–benefit and risk–risk trade-offs. For example, 'banning a particular solvent may increase the use of a more hazardous one' or 'reducing airborne concentration of substances in the workplace by exhaust ventilation may increase risk in the community' (Le Guen 2007: 110). What are the options in front of India? Can rapid economic development continue whilst ensuring that this process is combined with risk reduction? Will laudable efforts to reduce fatalities put economic and technological development at risk and burden industry with cumbersome and inefficient red tape? Is risk management manageable or is it a 'luxury' that India cannot yet afford?

This chapter presents an analysis of the key challenges to health and safety regulation in the 21st century. It starts with introducing the crucial distinction between hazard-based and risk-based regulations and looks into their advantages and disadvantages. Then, the chapter delves into the different 'styles' and 'models' that have emerged in the West to deal with risk and uncertainty. The critical question of how these models may respond to global democratization calls is then addressed.

Finally, the chapter presents some conclusions and recommendations with particular attention to the Indian context.

RISK-BASED OR HAZARD-BASED APPROACH?

Four years after the Bhopal tragedy, Jasanoff observed that 'Investigating journalists revealed that workers at the Bhopal plant were inadequately trained and quite unaware that improper handling of MIC could set a disastrous runaway reaction in motion' (Jasanoff 1988). Sloppiness and negligence is often at the heart of many health and safety disasters. What, therefore, is the best course of action to prevent such tragedies from happening again? Gupta calls for a move towards 'inherently safer design' (Gupta 2002), which basically implies that hazardous activities should be avoided altogether. Mannan et al. (2005) prefer to stress the need for risk management. They highlight the insufficient efforts made in India to reduce the frequency and severity of incidents. Karthikeyan took a similar view when he called for better capacity-building (Karthikeyan 2004). Discussions about whether risks should be avoided or managed mirror the central debate about whether safety regulation should be based on risks or hazards, which, the author understands, has become a pivotal and hotly contested debate in India (for an illuminating discussion on risk versus hazard, see Löfstedt (2011)).

What are the key differences between hazard-based and risk-based approaches? Although the terms 'hazard' and 'risk' may be used interchangeably in everyday language, the conceptual difference between the two terms is of paramount importance. A hazard is the potential for a substance, activity, or process to cause harm, independent of the frequency or magnitude of the harm caused. The term hazard refers, therefore, to the built-in capacity to cause harm (Royal Society 1992). Risk, on the other hand, is defined as the probability of occurrence of harm. The notion of risk therefore implies a combination of likelihood and severity. Hazard-based management is concerned with containing or preventing the occurrence of harm, independent of the likelihood and severity of the hazard. Risk-based approaches, on the other hand, rely on the best scientific estimates of the probabilities and potential effects of a plausible hazard (Stirling 1998, 2003; Klinke and Renn 2002). The Royal Society (1983) report defined risk management as 'procedures by which the Government and regulatory bodies "determine what controls are needed, whether these controls are reasonable, and are in fact carried out, and whether they and their costs are acceptable to the public"' (ibid.: 149).

Löfstedt (2011) has shown that regulators may follow one or the other approach, or sometimes may combine both. Recent bans in France and Denmark of baby bottles made of Bisphenol A (BPA), on the grounds that the substance *may* cause cancer, is typical of a hazard-based approach which did not consider how likely or how big the risk may be. Hazard-based approaches are based on the avoidance of something deemed inherently unsafe, which is equivalent to taking a strong precautionary stance. Risk-based methods, on the other hand, imply that we tolerate the risks that we wish to mitigate. The central notion of risk 'tolerability' in this context refers to a willingness to live with a risk so as to secure certain benefits and in the confidence that it is being properly controlled. This was put very eloquently by the UK Health and Safety Executive (HSE):

> To tolerate a risk means that we do not regard it as negligible or something we might ignore, but rather as something we need to keep under review and reduce still further if and as we can. For a risk to be 'acceptable' on the other hand means that for purposes of life or work, we are prepared to take it pretty well as it is. (HSE 1988: 2)

For example, the modus operandi in British regulation and case law requires balancing the 'risk' (there is no general definition of the process for calculating the value of preventing a fatality) and sacrifices (money, time, and trouble) involved when taking measures to avert risk. This approach is grounded in the view that activities are not usually either 'safe' or 'not safe', but they can be made to be 'safe enough' (McQuaid 2007). If the sacrifice appears to be disproportionate when compared to the benefits from reducing the risk, then the requirement has been met and implementing additional measures is not required (Walker 2001). This view is similar to Granger Morgan's classical definition: '[T]he optimal level of risk is that at which the marginal cost of risk reduction equals the marginal reduction achieved in societal cost' (Morgan 1990: 17).

What are the pros and cons of each approach? A risk-based approach stimulates evidence-based decision-making. It helps to design a process that on the basis of the best up-do-date knowledge seeks to maximize benefits while minimizing harm. For instance, a cost–benefit analysis can help determine the reasonable amount to spend on eliminating the risk of an explosion. Marks has observed, 'assessing risk involves developing predictive mathematical models, using interpretation of data that are based on scientific assumptions and knowledge of how data were created' and using these predictions 'for developing strategies that affect many people in society' (Marks 2007: 7). Risk assessment stimulates the disciplines that support decisions, such as statistics, toxicology, or distinct methods, for example, economic valuation methods such as Quantitative Risk Assessment (QRA). The same logic extends to the regulatory arena with techniques such as regulatory impact assessments and risk–benefit analysis.

Risk-based approaches, however, are not problem-free. Their focus on probability and magnitude of harm tends to neglect equity issues in relation to time (future generations), space (the Not In My Back Yard or NIMBY issue), or the specific vulnerabilities of social groups (Kasperson et al. 1988). This last point may prove to be particularly challenging in a socially heterogeneous county like India, where large segments of the population live in poverty. Looking into the issue of asbestos regulation, Linda Waldman (2011) observes:

> [S]cience and medical opinions regarding asbestos are the preserve of the elite and expert opinion works systematically to exclude local understandings of disease and risk while shaping government policy (p. 16). Political awareness of asbestos is shaped by economic interests…. For many Indians, asbestos is a product of modernization and a means of enhancing economic growth. Asbestos roofs are what poor people desire as symbols of their financial success and modernization (p. 73)…. Despite the widespread recognition that asbestos is carcinogenic, regulatory structures use different scientific and medical framings to assess risk, determine appropriate legislation, gauge people's suffering and set commensurate compensation. Official framings of asbestos risk tend to exaggerate the formulaic, scientific calculation of likelihoods and outcomes, while downplaying situations where knowledge about outcomes and likelihood are not as clearly defined (Stirling 2009) (p. 13).

Another issue is the technical nature of the knowledge generated to support evidence-based decisions. This tends to empower experts at the expense of decision-makers (politicians) and citizens, with the risk that social uncertainties may be misrepresented as technical ones (Johnston 1980; Wynne 1987). The fact that empowered experts, like the rest of us, have their own biases makes it all the more problematic. For instance, risk assessors tend to omit issues that they have decided are too disinteresting, difficult to quantify, speculative, or likely to be misinterpreted (Hattis and Kennedy 1986).

Similar to risk-based methods, many hazard-oriented methods found in the UK, for example the BATNEEC (Best Available Technology Not Entailing Excessive Cost) and Best Practical Environmental Option (BPEO) methods found in the environmental field have been technical and highly quantitative (Fairman 2007: 120). Yet, the main advantage of judging on the basis of the inherent safety of a technology or substance is that in most cases the decision-making process is kept fairly simple. The character of most hazard-based decisions, like banning chemicals, does not require complex assessment and testing. The simple criterion is that a substance *may* cause harm. In the UK, for example, flammables do not undergo probabilistic assessments as health and safety experts claim that these are not sufficiently reliable. The consequence is that a distinctively hazard-based management model has been developed by the HSE with, as would be expected, little consideration of acceptability. Arguably, hazard-based decisions also make it easier for governments to test for public opinion. It is much easier to find out whether the majority is 'pro' or 'against' a specific technology, for example nuclear energy.

One key problem with hazard-based approaches is that they tend to discard benefits. Removing baby bottles made of BPA from the market may not be a major issue because many alternatives are available; however, removing a new vaccine that can save lives is much more problematic, both ethically and practically. Hazard-based approaches also tend to overlook risk–risk trade-offs. For example, people have come to fear that disinfectants such as chlorine in the drinking water may induce cancer. The concern may be justified, although the risk is obviously very small. Should regulators therefore stop using chemicals to disinfect the water? The answer will inevitably be very different in countries where there is plenty of fresh water and a small population, such as Iceland, compared to a densely populated country with major sanitation issues, like India.

Essentially, the priority given to risk or hazard assessment methods— for example, discussions about the need for probabilistic assessment—is far more than a technical debate. These methods reflect broader societal and political choices about the risks that a given society is ready to take (Finkel and Golding 1995). For example, Swedish regulators are likely to maintain their precautionary ban on BPA on the basis that: '[I]t is unacceptable that young children are exposed to the risk.'[1] On the other hand, they will continue to battle for temporary EU exemptions (renewed every five years) on Baltic herring and salmon containing high levels of Polychlorinated Biphenyls (PCBs) and dioxin, because they are considered to be national delicacies (Löfstedt 2011). Factors such as previous crises (like the BSE (Bovine Spongiform Encephalopathy) crisis in the UK), national economic interest and heritage may condition the regulator's response to uncertainty. For instance, the management of the Hepatitis B scare in France was heavily influenced by the legacy of public health failures, most notably the contamination of haemophiliacs with Human Immunodeficiency Virus (HIV)-tainted blood in the 1980s and early 1990s. When the risk of a link between the Hepatitis B vaccine and multiple sclerosis was discussed the regulator immediately stopped the vaccination campaign as a precautionary measure (Bouder 2006).

In the Indian context, both hazard-based and risk-based regulations have their pros and cons. The 'technicalization of politics' that comes with probabilistic risk assessment may help to counter the inefficiencies of the politicized decision process (like in the case of Bt cotton, or even Bhopal). When the independence of science is guarded from vested interests and government control, through science academies for example, injecting more science into the decision-making system can reduce the scope for arbitrary decisions and corruption. In the current politicized environment, risks are predominantly borne by the poorer and marginalized sections of society. The definition of a societal risk criterion that properly factors these vulnerabilities into calculable estimates could improve the fair distribution of risks and benefits. On the other hand, what the HSE calls a protection approach (inherently hazard-based), may help to obtain quick but decisive safety gains. One can understand that in a country where regulation has not proved very effective (look at Bt cotton and Bhopal), where the risk assessment

---

[1] Quote from Andreas Carlgren in a press release of the Swedish Ministry for the Environment, 'Government Preparing Ban on Bisphenol A in Baby Bottles', 29 July 2010.

process has predominantly reflected economic/commercial interests (Bt brinjal—a case in point) and risks are distributed unequally that the public may be more inclined to adopt a hazard-based approach. In a developing country, however, banning certain technologies or projects could be political (and economic) suicide.

RISKS AND BENEFITS: COMPARING COUNTRIES APPROACHES

Bhopal activists shared concerns about how to deal with technological uncertainties (Jasanoff 2007). Risk is also at the centre of current controversies about the building of two nuclear plants at Kudankulam (Tamil Nadu) and Jaitapur (Ratnagiri district). In both situations, the clash between local residents and activists on the one hand and experts and public authorities on the other, have led to an apparent dead-end. A number of common features suggest poor risk-management practices. Risk assessment techniques and decision-making practices remained largely opaque. The views and preferences of the local population were generally neglected or misrepresented. Authorities and experts have wrongly assumed that their evaluation of the risks and benefits of the new plants was sufficient, and that opponents were only driven by demands for financial compensation. Health, environmental, and economic concerns were largely neglected, which points to a very narrow appreciation of risks and benefits on the part of experts.

Has India learnt from Bhopal? Although technical risk estimates and calculations have been developed, the institutional capacity to identify hazards and prevent or deal with emergency incidents has not evolved at the rapid pace of technological and economic development (Waldman 2009). Failure is partly due to the inadequate implementation of new policies. There are severe shortages of resources, toxicological information, and skilled personnel, and the poor quality of the industrial infrastructure makes it all but impossible to bring about real changes (Bowonder et al. 1994). Ravi Rajan talks about 'missing expertise' which 'refers to the phenomenon wherein the production of the potential for risk is not matched by a concomitant creation of expertise and institutions with the wherewithal to help mitigate a crisis, should one ensue' (Rajan 2002: 237). In that respect, India may be compared to other rapidly industrializing countries (Porto and Freitas 1996).

What should be done to prevent such clashes in the future? Ultimately, India will have to improve its approach to risk from its own experiences. Yet, comparative analysis can be a valuable ally to achieve this goal (Jasanoff 2005). In our view, one of the most important advantages of comparative studies is that they encourage a reflexive appraisal of one's model, with the effect of spreading good practice and innovation. Comparative risk studies tell us that specific regulatory cultures and styles in different countries and sectors have shaped distinct routes towards socially-acceptable decisions (Kelman 1981; Jasanoff 1986; Vogel 1986; Rothstein et al. 2011). Many agencies in the US, the Netherlands, and the UK consider that a risk involving less than a 10^{-6} chance of death is acceptable. This number is the so-called *de minimis* number (Hattis and Kennedy 1986). Above this threshold, approaches differ. For example, the US takes a broad view of risk–benefit assessment (including socioeconomic considerations). Similarly, in the UK and the Netherlands, the interpretation of legal requirements to maintain risks 'as low as reasonably practicable' (ALARP) has led to risk-based assessments becoming the norm in health and safety regulation, with noticeable exceptions (for example, flammables in the UK). In other countries, like Germany, probabilistic assessment is accepted but it is not linked to a weighing of risks against benefits. Unlike the UK practice of encouraging the 'duty holder' (for example, the operator of an industrial facility) to balance risks, costs, and benefits to determine the best course towards risk reduction, German regulators encourage compliance with pre-established acceptability levels. These levels are defined on the basis of the 'best available' and 'state-of-the-art' technology. The 'state-of-the-art' safety assessment for the regulation of dangerous substances is attained by three levels of acceptability (Okstad and Hoskstad 2001):

- Basic level of acceptability, defined as commonly recognized standards.
- State-of-the-art safety technology, as above and also taking into account recent advances in sciences.
- State-of-the-art science, as above and also taking into account recent scientific, technical, and management research, including testing.

These features make the German approach more 'safety-oriented' than 'risk-oriented'. Finally, France has resisted the trend towards probabilistic risk management. The comparison between the Netherlands and France is highly illustrative. In the Netherlands, the 1953 flooding (Delta Commission 1960) and number of accidents that took place in the 1970s (Ale 2005; Beroggi et al. 1997) have framed its modern risk approach. The Dutch model focuses primarily on the probability of the loss of human life, in which incidences of death form the main indicator. Interestingly, the risk of injury is also taken into account. In addition to material costs, other factors, such as recreational values, agriculture, and operational losses are also integrated (Beroggi et al. 1997). In France, the nuclear sector commonly uses probabilistic assessment methods, especially so to prepare danger studies. Yet, outside of the nuclear sector, predictive mathematical models have been considered controversial in the public arena because they challenge the primacy of elected institutions (Borraz 2008, Borraz and Gilbert 2008; Rothstein et al. 2011). In the French system, which may be called 'fiduciary' (Renn 2007), elected patrons and those to whom they delegate responsibilities are the only legitimate authorities that make risk decisions. As a consequence, the probabilistic model 'consciously adopted by the Dutch Parliament or the British HSE to guide risk decisions' has been 'consciously avoided by French regulators outside the nuclear sector' (Poumadère and Mays 1997: 34). Figure 13.1, presents a typology and a summary of the various systems analysed in this chapter. Despite the unavoidable level of generalization, the classification may stimulate a debate about possible

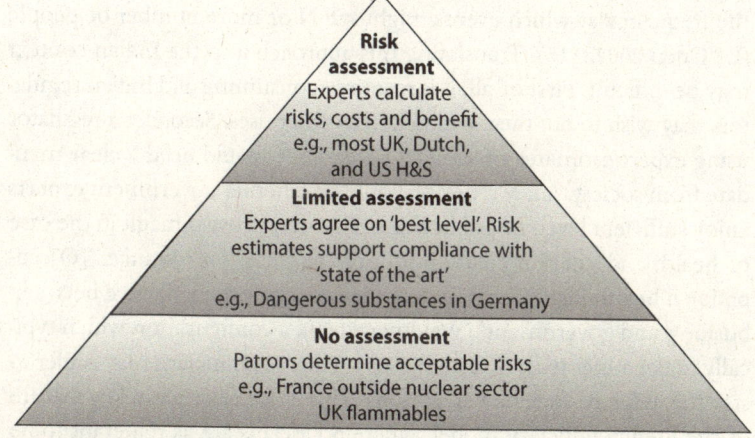

FIGURE 13.1   Typology of Risk Decision Criteria

routes in the Indian context. Where would India fit? A preliminary hypothesis, which would need to be tested, is that India tends towards the fiduciary model where politicians and administrators retain the upper hand in the decision-making process.

DEMOCRATIZING RISK MANAGEMENT: THE POINT OF NO RETURN?

In practice, countries and sectors have come up with very different ways to include 'society' into decisions about risk. For example, the notion of 'societal cost' may be interpreted in different ways. If societal cost is defined as the sum of individual costs, then conventional cost/benefit methods such as the 'quality-adjusted life years' (QUALYs) saved may guide decision-making. If societal cost also covers qualitative 'concerns' in a given population—such as dying from a dreaded cause like cancer, or the death of a child as opposed to the death of an adult—then specific methods may be defined to capture those concerns. There are various ways to systematically include societal concerns into the risk decision process. In the US, deliberative mechanisms have often been preferred. In Europe, health and safety regulators have sometimes taken a more technical route. Especially in the UK (Bouder et al. 2007), the Netherlands (Ale 2005), and Norway (Aven and Vinnem 2005), statistical estimates of public acceptance have been commonplace. The HSE has used, for example, the so-called FN curves, obtained by plotting the frequency at which events might kill N or more number of people (Le Guen 2007: 116). Translating this approach into the Indian context may be difficult. First of all, it is resource-consuming and Indian regulators may wish to put their statisticians to other uses. Secondly, a regulator using expert estimates of societal acceptance would need a clear mandate from society. A key criterion could be whether government experts enjoy sufficient levels of public trust. This may prove difficult in the case of health and safety regulation in India because, for instance: '[O]ccupational health institutions have tended to support an alliance between business and government' (Waldman 2009), a configuration which typically undermines trust (Löfstedt 2005). Thirdly, politicians may prefer to stay the judge of societal perceptions. This is, for example, a key feature of the French fiduciary model, where politicians are as reluctant to be bound to societal views as they are to be bound to the risk estimates of experts. Table 13.1, which is based on an in-depth review of regulatory practices in five countries, attempts to combine the typologies of countries' approaches to risk and deliberation. It shows a clear correlation (so causation remains to be established) between the regulator's appetite for risk-based practices and for the inclusion of public views.

Deciding which risks should be tolerated has proved the most controversial aspect of risk management (Renn 2007). As Fischhoff and Fischhoff eloquently put it:

> At times stigmatized risks are created deliberately. Their creators, whether in government or industry, hope that few people will know or strongly (and effectively) object to their actions... Often, and perhaps increasingly, though, institutions are discovering unexpectedly that they have created socially unacceptable risks. DDT, nuclear power, and even opiates are once-promising enterprises that have raised fundamental objections among significant publics. (Fischhoff and Fischhoff 2001)

Can expertocratic models still produce socially acceptable outcome? At a practical level, UK regulators have dealt with the 'dread' factor (Slovic 1987) associated with the risk of cancer by doubling the value of preventing a fatality from cancer. This approach would have been

TABLE 13.1   Approaches to Deliberation: A Typology

Fiduciary Avoidance Model	Consensual Containment Model
Elected officials and bodies determine the acceptable risks. No official individual risk estimates; weak mechanisms to include public views: **France**	Consensual agreement among experts on the 'best level'. Individual risk estimates support compliance with best technological solution: **Germany**
Consensual Control and Assessment Model	**Risk Assessment Model**
Engineering safety approach focussing on reduction. Thresholds supported by individual risk estimates + societal risk criterion: **Netherlands**	**Pluralistic**: Individual risk estimates looking at risk, costs and benefits, including through open mechanisms to include public views: **USA**
	Consensual: Individual risk estimates looking at risk, costs and benefits (in theory). Weak deliberation mechanisms: **UK**

Source: Bouder (2008).

unthinkable in a country like France. At a theoretical level, the discredit of expertocratic solutions has led to the emancipation of the non-expert (Latour and Woolgar 1979; Pinch and Bijker 1984; Bijker et al. 1987; Wynne 1989, 1991, 1996; Bijker 1997). Many scholars interested in the relationship between science and society suggest that the new risk-management models should be 'democratic' and participatory (Irwin 1995; Irwin and Wynne 1996; Jasanoff 1997; Wynne 1989, 1996).

The need to engage with the public is particularly important when trust in the regulator and science is low (Löfstedt 2005). The Indian context conveys powerful arguments in favour of a deliberative model of governance. Critical factors include: a discredited industry (Dinham and Sarangi 2002), a strong litigation culture (Galanter 1985), the permanence of community-based channels of trust (Das and Das 2003), and a strong activist culture (Galanter 1985; Jasanoff 1988, 2007).

One practical challenge for democratizing decision-making—in India or elsewhere—is the need to define acceptable risk–benefit trade-offs for each member of society (Fischhoff 1994). This becomes particularly arduous when decision-makers neglect and do not keep pace with changing societal expectations. Notwithstanding the above-mentioned nuclear controversies which perfectly illustrate the point, India has been recently subject to a Genetically Modified Organism (GMO) controversy of a much larger magnitude, the Bt brinjal case. For Bijker, this particular case illustrates a very big drift in society and the decline of the 'unquestioned high status' enjoyed by Indian scientists and engineers (Sekhsaria 2010).

The risk assessment methodology put forward by the US National Research Council (NRC) offers one of the most systematic views on how to put this democratic imperative at the heart of risk-management (see Figure 13.2). The NRC approach combines scientific 'appraisal' with 'broader value-based assessment' (NRC 1983, 1996). In other words the qualitative and quantitative aspects of the risk analysis are conducted simultaneously with an input from stakeholders.

Yet, exporting the NRC model outside the US may require some adaptation. The NRC approach has not emerged out of a vacuum—it was born and tested in the US. The fact that America is marked by a political culture characterized by pluralism rather than consensus (Eckstein 1960; Salisbury 1979) proved to be a favourable background (Vogel 1986). US environmental legislation (EPA 2000, 2004) and

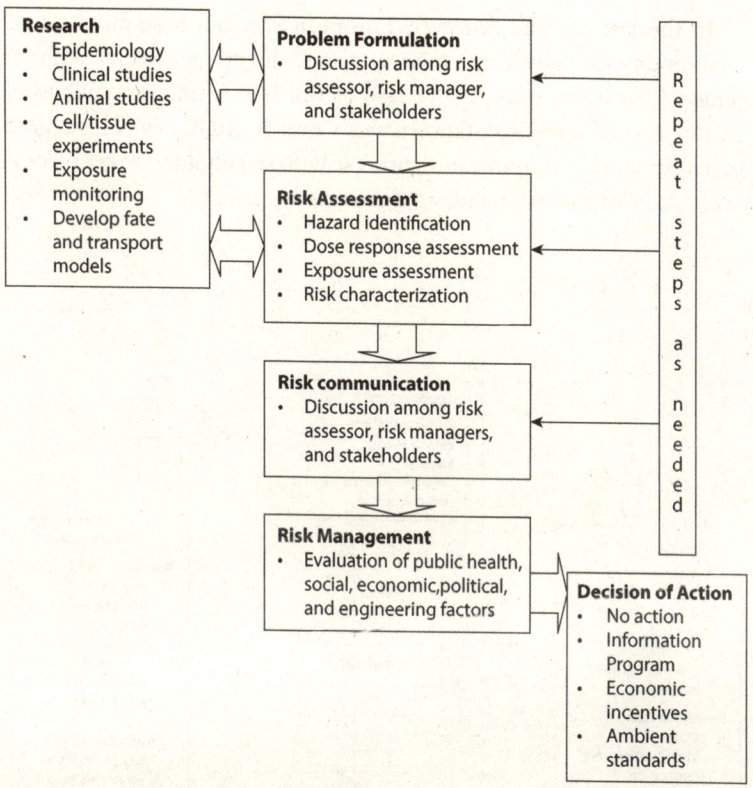

FIGURE 13.2   The NRC Risk Management Model
Source: Bouder (2008); adapted for HSE 2010.

Health and Safety regulations have introduced deliberative practices, which satisfy demands for public scrutiny and address worries about interest capture. An Occupational Safety and Health Administration (OSHA) official, interviewed for a recent study, confirmed that this view is still valid:

> We don't get into cosy relationships. Public hearings are much more formal than EPA hearings for example. Compared to the EPA, OSHA is very confrontational, especially if you consider how little we do. Witnesses often get crossed-examined and industry and unions get involved. And then, final rules are subject to judicial review and in one case ('Ergonomics') the US Congress even voted that OSHA could not put a rule into place'. (HSE 2010)

In the last decade, however, European scholars have also formalized models that give a much larger role to direct interactions with the public. This is for example the case of the 2005 framework published by the International Risk Governance Council (IRGC), which suggests that a two-way communication process with stakeholders takes place at every stage of the risk-handling chain (see Figure 13.3)

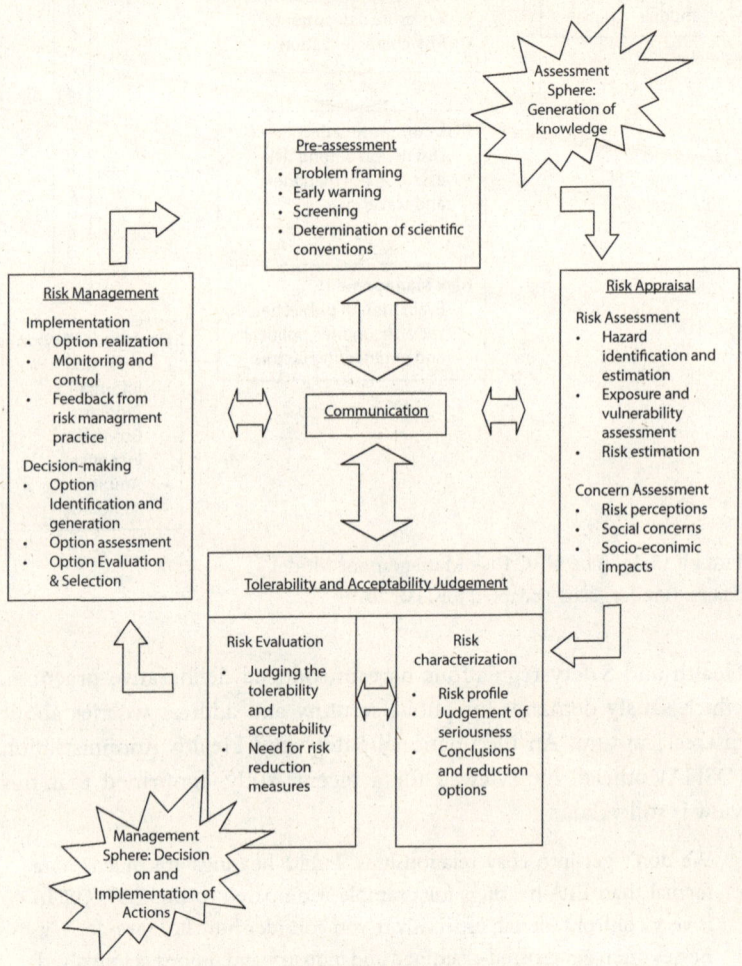

FIGURE 13.3   The Risk Governance Framework
Source: Adapted from the IRGC White Paper No. 1 'Risk Governance: Towards an Integrative Approach'.

European regulators have also favoured public involvement and participation in order to regain trust after the scandals and mishaps of the 1990s, in particular the BSE crises in the UK, the Diozine-contaminated chicken mishap in Belgium and the HIV-tainted blood scandal in France (Löfstedt 2005; Löfstedt et al. 2011). These changes, however, have happened mostly in the food and environmental areas. By and large, regulatory practices in the Health and Safety field have remained non-deliberative. Examples include the persistence of decisions made behind closed doors, or expectations that the complex statistical estimates of public acceptance (see the previous section) will suffice.

There are clear signs, however, that European regulators will need to take the bigger picture on board and involve citizens more directly, especially when confronted with a crisis situation. The management of the Buncefield incident recovery in the UK offers a good example of ways to involve the public after a major incident. In the early hours of Sunday, 11 December 2005, a number of explosions occurred at the fifth-largest oil-products' storage depot in the UK, the Buncefield Oil Storage depot. HSE's response would forever change the Organization's approach to risk communication. In view of the magnitude of the material damage (fortunately no one died in the explosion) deemed 'the largest incident of its kind in peacetime Europe' (Sky News 2005), HSE used its legal powers to launch, in addition to the criminal inquiry, an independent investigation into the circumstances of the incident. The Major Incident Investigation Board (MIIB) in the Buncefield incident was chaired by Lord Newton of Braintree. Lord Newton is a well-respected and consensual Westminster figure. The Board immediately appointed a local liaison officer who maintained a constant link between the enquiry and local residents. Eight timely reports were issued with concrete recommendations, and the first only a few weeks after the incident. MIIB members maintained an open door policy throughout the enquiry and met the local population. Among the critical factors of success one may highlight (HSE 2010):

- Frequent dialogues with regulators, industry, and media as well as key politicians
- MIIB's moderating role to avoid confrontation between the key parties

- The separation between the investigation and the criminal case
- A pacified debate concentrating on the root causes of the incident
- A strong scientific dimension throughout the investigation process
- Partnerships with independent members of the public trusted in their community
- Respect for the opinion of local policymakers, even when they were critical of the investigation in principle

This example suggests that relatively simple steps can sometime make a big difference. It also suggests that the devil is often in the details. For example a 15-member experts group was established in October 2011 to interact with the local people in and around the Kudankulam nuclear power plant project. How respected and well-known were its members in the local community? Did they listen to local concerns or did they patronize ordinary members of the public? In other words depending on its capacity to build trust the panel may turn out to be a risk-attenuator or, on the contrary, a risk-amplifier.

TAKING RISK SCIENCE ON BOARD: CONCLUDING NOTES

Accidents occurring in other countries are testimony that the Bhopal gas tragedy could have happened in the US, Europe or any other part of the world (Gupta 2002). When the prevalent view is that regulations simply impair scientific progress governments may easily overlook the simple measures that minimize technological risks. On the other hand, the systematic search for absolute safety, supported by hazard-based frameworks often leads decision-makers to forget that they need to balance risks and benefits and that reducing one risk may increase other risks (Graham and Wiener 1995). For example, how do old pesticides compare to new ones, and how do the risks of pesticides compare with the risks of GM crops? If these comparisons remain ill-informed, and unfocused, India may lose the economic and social benefit of technological development whilst creating unnecessary risks. In practice, risk analysis has been successfully applied in the West to a myriad of hazards including pesticides in food, pollutants in the air, chemicals in ground and water, nuclear waste, and the like. In many situations, these methods, combined with regulatory safeguards and guidance, have allowed countries to reap the benefits of technological progress while improving safety standards (Sunstein 2002, 2003).

Risk, however, is more than statistics and assessment, and experts can no longer ignore societal factors. Europe and India are places where the objective of combining risk-based methods with effective citizen involvement may be more difficult to achieve than in other places, especially the US. The reason is that, unlike in Europe or in India, structured consultation and deliberation mechanisms are deeply rooted in the American political and administrative culture. In Europe, new participatory experiments have led to many hiccups. Examples include the French debate on industrial risks (Essig 2002), and the GM Nation debate in the UK (Hails and Kinderlerer 2003; Horlick-Jones et al. 2007). In both these cases, the consultation exercise attracted mostly NGOs members radically opposed to the technology, while the general public remained indifferent. The process became highly conflictive, while the negative outcome—a stigmatization of GM Crops (GMOs)—did not reflect the general opinion. India might experience similar disappointment if insufficient efforts are made to organize public involvement in a way that builds rather than destroys trust in the process. However, just like Europe, India has no other choice. Public engagement is particularly important in the Indian context as regulators, industry, politicians, and even the media have been rocked by scandals and corruption scams. It is made even more challenging by the strong litigation culture that tends to destroy, rather than build trust among key actors (Löfstedt 2005; Löfstedt et al. 2011).

The question therefore is: what can be done to avoid failure and combine high standards of protection with a more open system? Rather than 'reinventing the wheel', I suggest beginning by taking on board 50 years of risk research, especially from the cognitive sciences. Robust studies have looked at factors that impact on the perception of risks (Fischhoff et al. 1978; Slovic et al. 1980; Slovic 1987), feelings (Loewenstein et al. 2001), trust (Slovic 1993; Renn and Levine 1991) and the amplifications and attenuation of risks by the media (Kasperson et al. 1988; Pidgeon et al. 2003). The result of these developments is that making risk judgments and decisions involves looking at people's 'expressed preferences' in relation to risk-related situations (Fischhoff et al. 1978, 1981; Slovic et al. 1981; Slovic 1987, 1992).

Fischhoff argues that taking risk perception on board should lead to a two-way model of non-persuasive communication rather than 'spin'. This observation is very important to support a coherent system of exchanges among stakeholders. To implement this objective, a number of recommendations follow:

- The first step for an organization is to understand perception. For example, Indian companies and regulators may, at a relatively low cost, conduct risk perception studies to map-out and understand critical players' attitudes as well as lay people's perceptions and expectations. They are likely to come across negative as well as positive views about risks and benefits.
- The second step is to test for trust. Trust is typically determined by perceived fairness, competence, and efficiency (Renn and Levine 1991). Relatively simple studies can be conducted to see who is trusted or not, what drives trust down and what actions need to be taken to re-build trust. During a crisis, involving highly trusted individuals as early as possible—be they scientists, NGOs or others—can help in solving risk disputes amicably, as seen in the Buncefield case.
- The third and final step is to translate this knowledge into bridging the gap between expert and non-expert views of expected risks and benefits. Simple risk communications based on concrete examples and narratives—for example what may happen if one does not wear a hardhat on a construction site—are often helpful to fostering meaningful interactions.

These positive outcomes can only be obtained when experts, government officials, and other powerful executives lead by example, in terms of both their personal and professional ethics, and learn to take heed of lay people's concerns. This may be more challenging in countries where disparities in levels of education and income are immense. Yet, building social trust is an absolute necessity to prevent—or at least mitigate controversies and failures. It is arrogance, not risk management, which is a luxury experts in India and elsewhere can no longer afford.

BIBLIOGRAPHY

Ale, B.J.M. (2005). 'Tolerable or Acceptable: A Comparison of Risk Regulation in the United Kingdom and in the Netherlands', *Risk Analysis*, 25(2): 231–41.

Aven, T., and J.E. Vinnem (2005). 'On the Use of Risk Acceptance Criteria in the Offshore Oil and Gas Industry, Reliability Engineering and System Safety', 90: 15–24.

BBC News (2007). 'HSE Failing to Probe Accidents', *BBC*, 27 July, available at http://news.bbc.co.uk/1/hi/uk/6918532.stm, last accessed on 19 November 2013.

Beroggi, G.E.G., T.C. Abbas, J.A. Stoop, and M. Aebi (1997). 'Risk Assessment in the Netherlands'. Unpublished report, in Pfister, G. and O. Renn (eds), *Reports on Risk Regulation Procedures in Several Countries*, introduction to discussion paper No. 91, Stuttgart: Akademie für Technik folgenabschätzung in Baden-Württemberg.

Bijker, W.E. (1997). 'Democratization of Technology—Who are the Experts?', in M. Kerner (ed.), *Rise of the Laity: Democracy and Expert Knowledge in the Technological World* (in German), pp. 133–55. Aachen: Thouet Verlag.

Bijker, W.E., T.P. Hughes, and T.J. Pinch (1987). *The Social Construction of Technological Systems: New Directions in the Sociology and History of Technology.* Cambridge, Massachusetts: MIT Press.

Borraz, O. (2008). *The Politics of Risk* (in French). Paris: Presses de Sciences Po.

Borraz, O., and C. Gilbert (2008). 'When the State takes Risks' in O. Borraz and V. Guiraudon (eds), *Public Politics, France in the Framework of European Governance* (in French), pp. 337–57. Paris: Presses de Sciences Po.

Bowonder, B., J.X. Kasperson, and R.E. Kasperson (1994). 'Industrial Risk Management in India Since Bhopal', in Sheila Jasanoff (ed.) *Learning from Disaster: Risk Management after Bhopal*, pp. 66–90. Philadelphia: University of Pennsylvania Press.

Bouder, F. (2006). 'A Contribution to Transnational Risk Analysis: Comparative Analysis of Risk Perception Related to Human Health Issues', in I.K. Richter, Sabine Berking, and R. Müller-Schmid (eds), *Risk Society and the Culture of Precaution.* Basingstoke: Palgrave Macmillan.

——— (2008). 'Defining a Tolerability of Risk Framework for Pharmaceutical Products in a Context of Scientific Uncertainty', PhD dissertation, King's College London.

Bouder, F., D. Slavin, and R.E. Löfstedt (eds) (2007). *The Tolerability of Risk: a New Framework for Risk Management.* London and Sterling (VA): Earthscan.

Broughton, E. (2005). 'The Bhopal Disaster and its Aftermath: A Review', *Environmental Health: A Global Access Science Source*, 4(6): 1–6.

Das, J., and S. Das (2003). 'Trust, Learning, and Vaccination: A Case Study of a North Indian Village', *Social Science & Medicine*, 57(2003): 97–112.

Delta Commission Report (1960). Contribution II 1-5. Mathematics Centre. Observations about Storm Floods and Tide Movements (in Dutch) Section 3, The Hague: State publications.

de Souza Porto, M.F. and C.M. de Freitas (1996). 'Major Chemical Accidents in Industrializing Countries: The Socio-Political Amplification of Risk'. *Risk analysis*, 16(1): 19–29.

Dinham, B., and B. Sarangi (2002). 'The Bhopal Gas Tragedy 1984 to?: The Evasion of Corporate Responsibility', *Environment and Urbanisation*, 14(1): 89–98.

Eckstein, H. (1960). *Pressure Group Politics*. Standford, California: Standford University Press.

Environmental Protection Agency (EPA). (2000). *Risk Characterisation Handbook*. Washington, D.C.: EPA.

——— (2004). *Risk Assessment Principles and Practice*. Washington, DC: EPA.

European Commission—Scientific Committee for Food. (2002). *Opinion of the Scientific Committee on Food: Update on the safety of Aspartame*. Brussels: DG SANCO-Scientific Committee on Food.

Essig, P. (2002). 'National debate on Industrial Risks (in French): October–December 2001: Report to the Prime Minister'. *Série Les Rapports*. Paris: La Documentation Française.

Fairman, R. (2007). 'What makes Tolerability of Risk work', in F. Bouder, D. Slavin. and R. Löfstedt (eds), *The Tolerability of Risk: A New Framework for Risk Management*. London and Sterling, VA: Earthscan.

Finkel, A., and D. Golding (eds) (1995). *Worst Things First? The Debate over Risk-Based National Environmental Priorities*. Washington, DC: Resources for the Future.

Fischhoff, B. (1994). 'Acceptable Risk: A Conceptual Proposal', *Risk: Health, Safety and Environment*, 1: 1–28.

Fischhoff, B., P. Slovic, and S. Lichtenstein (1978). 'How Safe is Safe Enough? A Psychometric Study of Attitudes Towards Technological Risks and Benefits', *Policy Sciences*, 9: 127–52.

Fischhoff, B., S. Lichtenstein, P. Slovic, S.L. Derby, and R.L. Keeney (1981). *Acceptable Risk*, p. 185. Cambridge: Cambridge University Press.

Fischhoff, B., and Fischhoff, I. (2001). 'Will they hate us?: Anticipating unacceptable risks', *Risk Management*, 3(4), 7–18.

Galanter, M. (1985). 'Legal Torpor: Why So Little Has Happened in India after the Bhopal Tragedy', *Texas International Law Journal*, 20: 273–94.

Graham, J.D., and J.B. Wiener (eds) (1995). *Risk Versus Risk: Tradeoffs in Protecting Health and the Environment*. Cambridge, MA: Harvard University Press.

Gupta, J.P. (2002). 'The Bhopal Gas Tragedy: Could it Have Happened in a Developed Country?', *Journal of Loss Prevention in the Process Industries*, 15(1): 1–4.

Hails, R., and J. Kinderlerer (2003). 'The GM Public Debate: Context and Communication Strategies: Science and Society', *Nature Reviews Genetics*, 4: 819–25.

Hattis, D., and D. Kennedy (1986). 'Assessing Risks from Health Hazard: An Imperfect Science', *Technology Review*, 89(4): 60–71.

Health Council of the Netherlands (1995). 'Not all Risks are Equal', Publication No. 1995 06E, Committee on Risk Measures and Risk Assessment. Hague: Health Council of the Netherlands.

——— (1996). 'Risk is More than Just a Number', No. 1996 03E, Committee on Risk Measures and Risk Assessment. Hague: Health Council of the Netherlands.

Health and Safety Executive (HSE) (1988). *The Tolerability of Risks from Nuclear Power Stations*. Sudbury: HSE Books.

——— (2002) [2001]. *Reducing Risks, Protecting People*. Sudbury: HSE Books.

——— (2010). 'Improving Health and Safety, An Analysis of HSE's Risk Communication in the 21st Century', prepared by King's College London, Research report No. RR785. Sudbury: HSE Books.

Health and Safety Laboratory (HSL) (2005). 'Review of Public Perception of Risk, and Stakeholder Engagement', HSL/2005/16, Report prepared by J. Williamson and A. Weyman, available at http://www.hse.gov.uk/research/hsl_pdf/2005/hsl0516.pdf, last accessed on 5 January 2011.

——— (2006). 'Public Perception of Risk Gauging Tool', SOFS/06/1, Report prepared by A. Weyman and P. Bibby. Unpublished.

Horlick-Jones, T., J. Walls, G. Rowe, N. Pidgeon, W. Poortinga, G. Murdock, and T. O'Riordan (2007). *The GM Debate: Risk, Politics and Public Engagement*. London: Routledge.

House of Lords (2000). Report of Select Committee on Science and Technology, *Science and Society*. London: The Stationery Office.

Irwin, A. (1995). *Citizen Science: A Study of People, Expertise and Sustainable Development*. London: Routledge.

Irwin, A. and B. Wynne (1996). *Misunderstanding Science? The public reconstruction of Science and Technology*. Cambridge University Press.

Jasanoff, S. (1986). *Risk Management and Political Culture*. New York: Russell Sage Foundation.

——— (1988). 'The Bhopal Disaster and the Right to Know', *Soc.Sci.Med.*, 27(10): 1113–23.

——— (1997). *Science at the Bar: A Twentieth Century Fund Book*, volume 9 of Twentieth Century Fund Books/Reports/Studies. Massachusetts: Harvard University Press.

——— (2005). *Designs on Nature, Science and Democracy in Europe and the United States*. Princeton University Press: Princeton and Oxford.

——— (2007). 'Bhopal's Trials of Knowledge and Ignorance', *ISIS*, 98(2): 344–50.

Jenkins, S. (2006). 'Those Who Walk Under Trees are at Risk from These Terrorizing Inspectors', *The Guardian*, Friday, 17 November 2006.

Johnston R. (1980). 'The Characteristics of Risk Assessment Research', in J. Conrad (ed.), *Society, Technology and Risk Assessment*. London: Academic Press.

Karthikeyan, B. (2004). 'Process Safety Management in India', Paper presented in International Conference on 'Bhopal and its Effects on Process Safety' at IIT, Kanpur.

Kasperson, Roger E., Ortwin Renn, Paul Slovic, Halina S. Brown, Jacque Emel, Robert Goble, Jeanne X. Kasperson, and Samuel Ratick (1988). 'The Social Amplification of Risk: A Conceptual Framework', *Risk Analysis*, 8: 177–87.

Kelman, S. (1981). *Regulating America, Regulating Sweden: A Comparative Study of Occupational Safety and Health Policy*. Cambridge, MA: MIT Press.

Klinke, A., and O. Renn (2002). 'A New Approach to Risk Evaluation and Management: Risk-Based, Precaution-Based and Discourse-Based Strategies', *Risk Analysis*, 22(6): 1071–94.

Latour, B., and S. Woolgar (1986) [1979]. *Laboratory Life: The Social Construction of Scientific Facts*. Princeton: Princeton University Press.

Le Guen, J.-M. (2007). 'Applying the HSE's Risk Decision Model: Reducing Risks, Protecting People', in Bouder, F., D. Slavin, and R.E. Löfstedt (eds), *The Tolerability of Risk: A New Framework for Risk Management*. London and Sterling (VA): Earthscan.

Loewenstein, G., E. Weber, C. Hsee, and E. Welch (2001). 'Risk as Feelings', *Psychological Bulletin*, 127: 267–86.

Löfstedt, R.E. (1997). 'Risk Evaluation in the United Kingdom: Legal Requirements, Conceptual Foundations and Practical Experiences with Special Emphasis on Energy Systems', in G. Pfister, and O. Renn (eds). 'Reports on Risk Regulation Procedures in Several Countries', introduction to discussion paper No. 91, Stuttgart: Akademie für Technik folgenabschätzung in Baden-Württemberg. Unpublished report.

——— (2005). *Risk Management in Post-Trust Societies*. Basingstoke: Palgrave.

——— (2011). 'Risk Versus Hazard Assessment—How to Regulate in the 21st Century: Two Case Studies', *European Journal of Risk Regulation*, 2(2): 149–68.

Löfstedt, R., F. Bouder, J. Wardman, and S. Chakraborty (2011). 'The Changing Nature of Communication and Regulation of Risk in Europe', *Journal of Risk Research*, 14(4): 409–29.

Mannan, M.S., H.H. West, K. Krishna, A.A. Aldeeb, N. Keren, S.R. Saraf, Y.S. Liu, and M. Gentile (2005). 'The Legacy of Bhopal: The Impact Over the Last 20 Years and Future Direction', *Journal of Loss Prevention in the Process Industries*, 18: 218–24.

Marks, H.M. (2007). 'Contemplating Risk Assessment: A Critique of NRC (1983, 1996)', *Human and Ecological Risk Assessment*, 13: 7–19.

McQuaid, J. (2007). 'A Historical Perspective on Tolerability of Risk', in F. Bouder, D. Slavin, and R. Löfstedt (eds), *The Tolerability of Risk: A New Framework for Risk Management*. London and Sterling, VA: Earthscan.

Major Incident Investigation Board (MIIB) (2008a). 'The Buncefield Incident', 11 December 2005, the final report of the Major Incident Investigation Board, available at http://www.buncefieldinvestigation.gov.uk/reports/index.htm#final, last accessed on 19 November 2013.

Major Incident Investigation Board (MIIB) (2008b). 'Recommendations on Land Use Planning and the Control of Societal Risk Around Major Hazard Sites', available at http://www.buncefieldinvestigation.gov.uk/reports/comahreport3.pdf, last accessed on 19 November 2013.

Morgan, G. (1990). 'Choosing and Managing Technology-Induced risk', in T.S. Glickman and M. Gough (eds), *Readings in Risk*. Washington, DC: Resources for the Future, pp. 17–28.

National Research Council (NRC) (1983). *Risk Assessment in the Federal Government: Managing the Process*. Washington, DC: National Academy Press.

———— (1994). *Science and Judgement in Risk Assessment*. Washington, DC: National Academy Press.

———— (1996). *Understanding Risk*. Washington DC: National Academy Press.

Okstad, E., and P. Hokstad (2001). 'Risk Assessment and Use of Risk Acceptance Criteria for the Regulation of Dangerous Substances', Proceedings of the European Conference on Safety and Reliability – ESREL 2001, Politecnico di Torino, Italy, 16–20 September, I: 117–24.

Pidgeon, N., R.E. Kasperson, and P. Slovic (eds) (2003). *The Social Amplification of Risk*. Cambridge, UK: Cambridge University Press.

Pinch, T.J., and W.E. Bijker (1984). 'The Social Construction of Facts and Artefacts: Or How the Sociology of Science and the Sociology of Technology Might Benefit Each Other', *Social Studies of Science*, 14: 399–441.

Poumadère, M., and C. Mays (1997). 'Energy Risk Evaluation in France', in G. Pfister and O. Renn (eds), 'Reports on Risk Regulation Procedures in Several Countries', introduction to discussion paper No. 91, Stuttgart: Akademie für Technik folgenabschätzung in Baden-Württemberg-Unpublished report.

Powell, D., and W. Leiss (1997). *Mad Cows and Mother's Milk*. Montreal: McGill-Queen's University Press.

Rajan, R. (2002). 'Missing Expertise, Categorical Politics and Chronic Disasters—the Case of Bhopal' in S. Hoffman and A. Oliver-Smith (eds), *Catastrophe and Culture: The Anthropology of Disaster*. Oxford: James Currey, and Santa Fe: School of American Research (SAR) Press.

Ratzan, S. (ed.) (1999). *The Mad Cow Crisis: Health and the Public Good*. London: University College London Press.

Renn, O. (2007). 'Concepts: Towards an Integrative Risk Approach', in F. Bouder, D. Slavin, and R. Löfstedt (eds), *The Tolerability of Risk: A New Framework for Risk Management*. London and Sterling, VA: Earthscan.

Renn, O., and D. Levine (1991). 'Credibility and Trust in Risk Communication', in R.E. Kasperson, and P.J. Stallen (eds). *Communicating Risk to the Public: International Perspectives*. Amsterdam: Kluwer.

Rhodes, R.A.W. (1981). *Control and Power in Central-local Government Relationships*. Farnborough, Hants: Gower.

Rimington, J. (1993). 'Coping with Technological Risk: A 21st Century Problem', Royal Academy of Engineering, CSE Lecture.

Rothstein, H., O. Borraz, and M. Huber (2011). 'From the "Neurotic" to the "Rationalising" State: Risk and the Limits of Governance' in C. Meyer and C. de Franco (eds), *Forecasting, Warning, and Transnational Risks: Is Prevention Possible?* Basingstoke: Palgrave Macmillan.

Royal Society (1983). 'Risk Assessment: A Study Group Report'. London: The Royal Society.

——— (1992). 'Risk: Analysis Perception and Management'. London: The Royal Society.

Salisbury, R. (1979). 'Why No Corporatism in America', in P.C. Schmitter, and G. Lehmbruch (eds), *Trends Towards Corporatist Intermediation*. Beverly Hills, California: Sage Publications.

Sekhsaria, P. (2010). 'Questioning the "Scientist" Theory', Interview of Wiebe Bijker, *The New Indian Express*, 21 November.

Sky News (2005). 'Fire Rages after Blasts at Oil Depot 11 December 2005', *Sky News*, available at http://news.sky.com/skynews/Home/Sky-News-Archive/Article/20080641205711, last accessed on 19 November 2013.

Slovic, P. (1987). 'Perception of Risk', *Science*, 236: 280–5.

——— (1993). 'Perceived Risk, Trust and Democracy', *Risk Analysis*, 13: 675–82.

Soundariya Preetha, M. (2011). 'Industrial Accidents on the Decline', *The Hindu*, 26 July.

Stirling, A. (1998). 'Risk at a Turning Point?', *Journal of Risk Research*, 1(2): 97–109.

——— (2003). 'Risk, Uncertainty and Precaution: Some Instrumental Implications from the Social Sciences', in F. Berkhout, M. Leach, and Scoones (eds), *Negotiating Change*, pp. 33–76. London: Edward Elgar.

Sunstein, C. (2002). *Risk and Reason: Safety, Law, and the Environment*. New York: Cambridge University Press.

——— (2003). 'Beyond the Precautionary Principle, Public Law and Legal Theory', Working paper No. 38. Chicago: Law School, University of

Chicago, available at http://law.uchicago.edu/Lawecon/index.html, last accessed on 3 August 2007.

Vogel, D. (1986). *National Styles of Regulation: Environmental Policy in Great Britain and the United States*. Ithaca and London: Cornell University Press.

Vrijling, J.K., P.H.A.J.M van Gelder, L.H.J. Goossens, and H.G. Voortman (2004). 'A Framework for Risk Criteria for Critical Infrastructures: Fundamentals and Case Studies in the Netherlands', *Journal of Risk Research*, 7(6): 569–79.

Waldman, L. (2009). '"Show me the Evidence": Mobilisation, Citizenship and Risk in Indian Asbestos Issues', IDS Working paper, 2009 (329), Sussex: Institute of Development Studies.

——— (2011). *The Politics of Asbestos: Understandings of Risk, Disease and Protest*. London: Earthscan.

Walker, T. (2001). 'Tolerability of Risk: Its Use in the Nuclear Regulation in the UK', available at www.ilk-online.org/download/en/walker_en.pdf, last accessed on 2 September 2003.

Wynne, B. (1987). 'Uncertainty—Technical and Social', in H. Brooks, and C.L. Cooper (eds), *Science and Public Policy*. Oxford: Pergamon.

——— (1989). 'Sheep Farming After Chernobyl: A Case Study in Communicating Scientific Information', *Environment*, 31, 10–15.

——— (1991). 'Knowledges in Context', *Science, Technology, & Human Values*, 16(1).

——— (1996). 'May the Sheep Safely Graze?' in S. Lash, B. Szerzynski and B. Wynne (eds), *Risk, Environment and Modernity: Toward a New Ecology*. London: Sage Publications.

About the Editors and Contributors

EDITORS

RAPHAELLE MOOR is a consultant based in London working in the area of disaster risk management and climate change adaptation. Over the last 4 years her research has concentrated on issues of capacity, expertise, and institutions in the fields of risk and resilience. She has an MSc in development studies from the London School of Economics and a BA in Philosophy, Politics, and Economics from the University of Warwick. She managed the UKIERI's (UK India Education and Research Initiative) 'India at Risk' project at the Indian Institute of Management Bangalore for over two-and-a-half years.

M.V. RAJEEV GOWDA is Professor, Economics and Social Sciences at the Indian Institute of Management Bangalore. He has a PhD in Public Policy and Management from the Wharton School, University of Pennsylvania. His research focuses substantially on how people and societies manage risk-related conflicts. He is also active in Indian politics and also writes on India's electoral system. He serves as a Director on the Central Board of the Reserve Bank of India and is a Carnegie Council Global Ethics Fellow. An avid quizzer, Dr Gowda was national runner-up on BBC TV's *Mastermind India* in 2001.

CONTRIBUTORS

AJAY BAILEY is Assistant Professor at the Population Research Centre at the Faculty of Spatial Sciences, University of Groningen. He is an anthropologist and a cultural demographer by training. His main research interests include high-skilled migration, global households, culture, access to healthcare, and mixed methods. He currently supervises master's and PhD researchers on these topics. His doctoral research was on 'Culture, risk and HIV among migrant and mobile men in Goa'. He currently teaches qualitative research methods at the Population Research Centre and in workshops in Europe and India.

FREDERIC BOUDER is Assistant Professor, Department of Technology and Society Studies, Maastricht University. He has developed policy-oriented research on risk communication and risk regulation, with a strong transatlantic and comparative dimension. His research interests concentrate primarily on developing new models of regulation and communication that reflect the changing nature of regulatory environments. Dr Bouder has developed expertise in several areas, including occupational safety, pharmaceutical, chemical, nuclear risks and sustainable development. His research has been supported by ESRC, BIS, GO Science, the European Medicines Agency and DEFRA.

MATHEW IDICULLA is a graduate fellow at the Law, Governance and Development Initiative at Azim Premji University, Bangalore, and a research associate in the Major Collaborative Research Initiative 'Global Suburbanisms: Governance, Land, and Infrastructure in the 21st Century', funded by Social Science and Humanities Research Council, Canada, housed at the CITY Institute, York University, Toronto. He graduated with a BA, LLB from Christ College, Bangalore University and has worked with the Centre for Public Policy at Indian Institute of Management Bangalore and the Centre for Budget and Policy Studies as an intern. His work is focused on areas where public law, politics and public policy converge and has widely researched on the changing urban governance regimes of post-liberalized India.

ROHIT JIGYASU is a conservation architect and risk management consultant from India, currently working as UNESCO Chair professor at the Institute for Disaster Mitigation of Urban Cultural Heritage at Ritsumeikan University, Kyoto, Japan and Senior Advisor at the Indian

Institute for Human Settlements (IIHS). He is elected member of the Executive Committee of International Council on Monuments and Sites (ICOMOS) and president of ICOMOS International Scientific Committee on Risk Preparedness (ICORP). He has a post-graduate in Architectural Conservation from School of Planning and Architecture, Delhi and PhD from Norwegian University of Science and Technology, Trondheim, Norway.

BANEEN KARACHIWALA has been associated with various organisations at the national and international level for the last seven years, providing support in research, documentation and programmatic interventions in the fields of health and development. Her special interests lie in the areas of human rights, maternal and child health. She has a Master's degree in Medical and Psychiatric Social Work from the Tata Institute of Social Sciences, Mumbai, India.

ASHA KILARU is a public health researcher based in Bangalore, India. She works with different networks and people's movements on social justice in health, primarily in the area of maternal and child health at the state as well as at the national level. She is a state working group member of the Karnataka circle of the People's Health Movement and has served on advisory boards for the Government of Karnataka. Asha was working at Belaku Trust when she led the study on the 'Quality of obstetric care in rural South India: Understanding women's perceptions, decision-making and providers' perspectives'.

SHANTI MAHENDRA is a public health research and communications specialist. She has substantial experience in field-based research and programmatic work and has specialist skills designing, implementing, managing, monitoring and evaluating programmes on maternal, newborn, child and adolescent health. Shanti has also worked extensively in the area of knowledge translation to support evidence-based policymaking. She has worked with local and international implementing agencies, academic and research institutions and the World Health Organisation. Shanti has worked on projects in India, Nepal, Bangladesh and Sierra Leone, and has co-authored several publications on maternal health.

ZOE MATTHEWS, originally a statistician and demographer, currently works on international health, specializing in health systems with a particular focus on reproductive, maternal, newborn and child health.

She is a professor of Global Health and Social Statistics at the University of Southampton, UK. Since 2011, she has been working on a five year DFID-funded programme called 'Evidence for Action for maternal and newborn health' based in six African countries. Before that she served as Head of Social Statistics and Demography at Southampton University. She also worked at both the World Health Organisation and the UK Department for International Development.

CLAIRE MAYS is a social psychologist and research consultant at Institut Symlog de France. Since 1992, she has focused on multi-stakeholder communications and empowerment in the management of radioactive waste, through field studies and action research. Claire co-authored the US National Academy of Sciences National Research Council BRWM major study 'Disposition of High-level Waste and Spent Nuclear Fuel: The Continuing Societal and Technical Challenges' (2001). She has acted as social science consultant to the OECD NEA Forum on Stakeholder Confidence and served as a leader of the COWAM programs supported by the European Commission.

ERIK MILLSTONE is Professor, Science Policy at the University of Sussex, England. His first degree was in Physics, followed by three in Philosophy. Since 1974, he has been researching into the causes, consequences and regulation of technological change in the food and chemical industries. His focus has extended over food additives, pesticides and veterinary medicines, as well as BSE, GM foods and obesity. Since 1988 he has been researching the role of scientific experts, evidence and advice in public policy-making. Much of his current research focuses on the drivers of technological change in agriculture for developing countries.

MARC POUMADÈRE, programme director of the Institut Symlog, France, has been engaged as a social scientist in risk research for almost 30 years. He has theoretical and applied experience of technological, environmental and health risks. He designed action research for operating nuclear units in France. He has served as an advisor of the World Health Organisation; conducted health risk assessment of radiofrequencies for the French Agency for Food, Environmental and Occupational Health & Safety; and defined priorities for EURATOM fission research and training (Horizon 2020). He is an associate professor at the Ecole Normale Supérieure and also teaches risk management at Mines ParisTech.

M.V. RAMANA, a physicist by training, is with the Nuclear Futures Laboratory and the Program on Science and Global Security at the Woodrow Wilson School of Public and International Affairs, Princeton University. He works on the future of nuclear energy in the context of climate change and nuclear disarmament. Ramana is the author of *The Power of Promise: Examining Nuclear Energy in India* (Penguin Books, 2012) and co-editor of *Prisoners of the Nuclear Dream* (Orient Longman, 2003). He is a member of the International Panel on Fissile Materials and the Science and Security Board of the *Bulletin of the Atomic Scientists*.

RANJANI RAMASWAMY obtained her Masters in Cultural Reporting and Criticism (CRC) from New York University (NYU). She has over four years mainstream journalism experience, in publications like the *Indian Express* Mumbai (health and human rights). She has also worked as a consultant and researcher with the Strategic Foresight Group (Middle East, health, global foreign policy) and with Amnesty International USA and New York University Law School Magazine (human rights, health, global policy). Her research interests focus on studying the impact of media on various social outcomes. She has also taught media studies and journalism at various colleges in Mumbai.

BHARGAVI S. RAO is Coordinator (Education)/Trustee of Environment Support Group (ESG), a not-for-profit research, training, campaign and advocacy initiative in Bangalore, India. Her qualifications include an MPhil in biology; she has undertaken research work in cell biology at the Indian Institute of Science and also taught in leading colleges and schools. At ESG she has advanced a variety of innovative experiential education programmes and guided a range of research initiatives in support of public interest campaigns. She actively works to bridge critical knowledge gaps of communities at risk as part of their empowerment process.

LEO F. SALDANHA is Coordinator/Trustee of Environment Support Group, a not-for-profit research, training, campaign and advocacy initiative in Bangalore, India. He has a background in environmental sciences and has advanced a variety of public interest litigations, primarily in the area of environmental law and policy, decentralisation and democratisation of decision making and in reclaiming the commons. He has taught in a variety of experiential education programmes and been part of a range of environmental and social science research initiatives.

He co-authored the book *Green Tapism* along with team members at ESG. His articles have appeared in many leading newspapers, journals and magazines.

SEMA K. SGAIER is a Senior Program Officer with the Bill and Melinda Gates Foundation. Sema leads the Male Circumcision Initiative and manages HIV prevention programs across Africa. Previously, she managed the Avahan program in India (the foundation's HIV prevention initiative) in the states of Karnataka, Manipur and Nagaland. She has also been working on the immunization and the monitoring and evaluation portfolios. Sema has a BSc in Molecular Biology and Genetics from Bogazici University (Turkey), a MA in Neuroscience from Brown University and a PhD in Cellular and Molecular Biology from New York University. She conducted her Postdoctoral training at Harvard Medical School.

Index

Heide Simonis

Unter Männern

Heide Simonis

Unter Männern

Mein Leben in der Politik

Verlag C. H. Beck

© Verlag C. H. Beck oHG, München 2003
Satz: Fotosatz Janß, Pfungstadt
Druck und Bindung: Ebner & Spiegel, Ulm
Gedruckt auf säurefreiem, alterungsbeständigem Papier
(hergestellt aus chlorfrei gebleichtem Zellstoff)
Printed in Germany
ISBN 3 406 50959 2

www.beck.de

Inhalt

Vorwort

Einen Flohmarktführer werde ich irgendwann auch noch schreiben! Aber das muss warten, bis ich mehr Zeit für ausgiebige Feldstudien und internationale Vergleiche habe. Jede Idee hat ihre Zeit. Jetzt hat mich die Bitte gereizt, einmal auf mein bisheriges Leben, politisch und privat, zurückzublicken und etwas gründlicher über einige Aspekte der Politik nachzudenken, die im Alltagsgeschäft leider zu oft im Hintergrund bleiben.

Die Arbeit an den letzten Seiten dieses Buches war überschattet vom Irak-Krieg, der am 20. März begann. Seinen Ausbruch habe ich, obwohl wir über Wochen darauf vorbereitet wurden, fast wie eine persönliche Niederlage erlebt. Als die Nachricht von den ersten Bombenabwürfen auf Bagdad kam, fühlte ich mich wie betäubt von einem Gefühl der Ohnmacht und war zugleich erschreckt über die unglaubliche Mischung aus Naivität und Machtdenken, die die amerikanische Führung an den Tag legte. So wie mir ist es vielen anderen Menschen hier bei uns und anderswo auf der Welt auch gegangen. Dieser Krieg, dessen militärischer Sieg sich beim Schreiben dieser letzten Zeilen abzeichnet, ist und bleibt dennoch eine moralische Niederlage für die Nationen, die Saddam Hussein gegenüber demokratische westliche Werte zu verteidigen meinen.

Zu den gravierenden Langzeitschäden, die dieser Krieg jetzt schon verursacht hat, gehört die Beschädigung der UNO. Indem sie ohne Legitimation des Sicherheitsrates handelten, haben die Amerikaner und Briten mit ihrer so genannten «Koalition der Willigen» die Autorität der Institution untergraben, die in mühsamen diplomatischen Anstrengungen nach dem Zweiten Weltkrieg von den Völkern aufgebaut worden war, gerade um zu verhindern, dass sich in internationalen Auseinandersetzungen das «Recht des Stärkeren» durchsetzt. Besonders beunruhigend ist es, dass wir nicht wissen, wie sich dieser Krieg auf die anderen Völker des Vorderen Orients auswirken wird. Es ist zu befürchten, dass er den Nahen Osten gefährlich destabilisiert und überall fundamentalistischen Strömungen weiteren Auftrieb geben wird.

Ich nehme an, dass die Amerikaner und vor allem die Engländer sich langfristig wieder um die UNO und Europa bemühen werden. Viel gravierender als der Riss in den transatlantischen Beziehungen erscheint mir die Frage, wie es im Irak weitergehen wird, wenn Husseins Regime entmachtet ist. Vermutlich wird eine jahrelange Präsenz der Vereinten Nationen nötig sein. Schauen wir nach Afghanistan und nach Bosnien – überall hat es sich erwiesen, dass die bewaffnete Aktion, auch wenn sie nach militärischen Kriterien erfolgreich war, als solche weder zu Frieden noch zu geordneten politischen Verhältnissen geführt hat. Dazu sind jahrelange Anstrengungen nicht zuletzt derjenigen erforderlich, die aufgrund ihrer Intervention Verantwortung für die jeweilige Region tragen. Ich denke, Amerikaner und Briten werden irgendwann mit einem furchtbaren Kater aus ihrer Siegesgewissheit aufwachen. Der Golfkrieg im Jahre 1991 hat die Weltpolitik nicht so dramatisch verändert, wie die Friedensbewegung damals glaubte. Aber dieser Krieg im Jahr 2003 könnte einen Wendepunkt in der Geschichte markieren: hin zu einem neuen Gleichgewicht der politischen Verhältnisse im Nahen Osten, wenn wir Glück haben. Leider ist das Gegenteil genauso gut möglich: der Beginn großer Unruhen, die den gesamten Nahen Osten erfassen könnten. Am Ende dieses Szenarios stände der viel beschworene «clash of civilizations». Eine schreckliche Vision, die wir nie Wirklichkeit werden lassen dürfen.

Ich bin froh über den konsequenten Anti-Kriegs-Kurs, den die Bundesregierung im Irak-Konflikt von Anfang an eingenommen hat. Dagegen scheint mir die Haltung der Opposition wenig überzeugend, und vor allem Angela Merkels unkritische Unterstützung der amerikanischen Führung ist peinlich. Sie tut damit weder sich selbst noch ihrer Partei und nicht einmal den Amerikanern einen großen Gefallen.

Entscheidend ist, dass so schnell wie möglich mit humanitärer Hilfe und dem Wiederaufbau des zerstörten Irak begonnen wird. Es geht dabei um Trinkwasser, um Nahrungsmittel und Medikamente, um Impfstoffe, die den Ausbruch von Seuchen verhindern, und Ähnliches mehr. Je schneller der Krieg beendet ist, desto eher wird man wirkungsvoll helfen können; je länger er andauert, desto dramatischer sind seine Folgen. Ich hoffe, dass die UNO beim Wiederaufbau des Irak wieder den ihr gebührenden Platz einnehmen wird, ohne diesen Krieg dadurch nachträglich zu legitimieren. Und ich wünsche mir, dass die Menschen in Deutschland, gerade weil sie mehrheitlich den Krieg ablehnen, zu großzügiger Hilfe für die irakische Bevölkerung bereit sein werden.

Im Vorfeld des Krieges erschien es mir besonders zynisch, wie von manchen fast ausschließlich über seine wirtschaftlichen Folgen räsoniert wurde. Man diskutierte darüber, wie sich ein kurzer und wie sich ein längerer Irak-Krieg auf die Ölpreise und die Börse auswirken werde. Man fragte nicht nur nach den Kosten für die amerikanische Wirtschaft, sondern auch danach, wer anschließend das große Geschäft mit dem Wiederaufbau machen werde. Tendenziell sind für die Weltwirtschaft wohl eher negative Auswirkungen zu befürchten – jedenfalls wird dieser Krieg den lang erhofften Aufschwung in Deutschland nicht beflügeln. Ich glaube aber, dass die Menschen bei uns durchaus sehen, dass die negativen Einflüsse in diesem Fall von außen kommen und nicht der Wirtschaftspolitik dieser Regierung anzulasten sind.

Der negative Einfluss der Weltkonjunktur darf allerdings

nicht die Tatsache verdecken, dass wir in Deutschland eigene wirtschaftliche Strukturprobleme haben, die wir sobald wie möglich lösen müssen. Bundeskanzler Gerhard Schröder hat mit seiner lang erwarteten Rede vom 14. März den Reformkurs klar umrissen und die Zügel fest in die Hand genommen. Inhaltlich stehe ich hinter seinen Plänen. Manches war allerdings noch nicht konkret beschrieben, da müssen Details noch ausgearbeitet werden, aber generell befürworte ich seine Richtung. Am wichtigsten und zugleich am schwierigsten durchzusetzen sind sicher die notwendigen Veränderungen im Gesundheitswesen. Möglicherweise lassen sich die Beiträge für die Krankenkassen relativ schnell senken; damit sie aber nicht sofort wieder steigen, brauchen wir strukturelle Reformen, die auf vielen Ebenen stattfinden müssen, und das wird Zeit brauchen.

Ich halte auch die Zusammenlegung von Arbeitslosen- und Sozialhilfe für einen richtigen Schritt. Die SPD ist schließlich angetreten, um die Gesellschaft so zu gestalten, dass jeder und jede Arbeit findet und für sich selbst sorgen kann. Arbeitslosen- und Sozialhilfe haben dabei eine dienende Funktion. Allerdings müssen wir uns vorwerfen lassen, dass wir im Augenblick nicht allen, die es wollen, auch Arbeitsplätze verschaffen können. Das muss unser vorrangiges Ziel sein, und um dorthin zu gelangen, müssen wir erst einmal ein paar dicke Brocken wegschaffen, die noch im Wege liegen, vor allem die zu hohen Lohnnebenkosten und viele bürokratische Reglementierungen. Auf einige nötige Reformschritte gehe ich in diesem Buch ausführlicher ein.

Natürlich ist es schmerzhaft, dass auch die Empfängerinnen und Empfänger kleinerer Einkommen von den Reformen betroffen sein werden. Umso mehr verschlägt es mir manchmal die Sprache, wie einige Unternehmer in dieser Situation eine geradezu unanständige Gier entwickeln und am liebsten überhaupt keine Steuern mehr bezahlen wollen. Derweilen schaut der normale Arbeitnehmer auf seine Lohnabrechnung und kann die Höhe der Abzüge nicht fassen. Er kann, anders als

Unternehmer, den hohen Abgaben nicht ausweichen. Man kann es nicht oft genug wiederholen: Bei uns sind keineswegs die Steuern zu hoch, sondern die Lohnnebenkosten. Doch viele Unternehmer scheinen nicht registriert zu haben, dass ihnen inzwischen schon viele Zugeständnisse gemacht worden sind, Zugeständnisse steuerlicher Art, beim Kündigungsschutz, in Bezug auf flexiblere Arbeitszeiten. Trotzdem bauen sie weiter Arbeitsplätze ab und beharren auf noch weniger Steuern. Sie wollen, wie alle anderen auch, dass der Staat mehr für Bildung und Ausbildung tut und die Infrastruktur erhält; er soll mehr Lehrer und Polizisten einstellen und die Bundeswehr besser ausstatten – und all das mit weniger Steuereinnahmen?

Es war an der Zeit, dass der Kanzler klare Worte gefunden hat. Es war gut, dass er keine Ausflüchte gesucht und die wirtschaftlichen Probleme klar beim Namen genannt hat. Wenn er das angekündigte Tempo bei der Umsetzung durchhält, dann könnte sich durchaus bald die Wende zum Besseren einstellen. Es gibt zwar noch Widersprüche, aber insgesamt ist die Disziplin in der SPD größer als zuvor, weil jetzt alle wissen, dass es hohe Zeit und die letzte Chance dieser Regierung ist.

Problematisch ist natürlich, dass nun alles gleichzeitig geschehen muss. Die Menschen werden die schmerzhaften Einschnitte jetzt unmittelbar erleben. Und es wird eine gewisse Zeit dauern, bis die ersten Erfolge sichtbar werden. Es kann daher passieren, dass wir, nachdem wir uns endlich zu den nötigen Reformschritten aufgerappelt haben, erst einmal nur die Unzufriedenheit auf allen Seiten ernten werden. Aber dieses Risiko müssen wir eingehen, denn wir dürfen nicht noch mehr wertvolle Zeit verstreichen lassen.

Die negativen Ergebnisse der schleswig-holsteinischen Kommunalwahlen vom 2. März habe ich als herbe Niederlage erlebt. Dieses schlechteste Ergebnis für die schleswig-holsteinische SPD seit 1946 hatte ich in meinen finstersten Befürchtungen nicht erwartet. Zwar hat die CDU insgesamt nur 9000 Stimmen dazugewonnen – das ist bei 2,25 Millionen Wahlberechtigten gar nicht so viel. Die Wahlbeteiligung von 52 Prozent, die niedrigste, die es in Schleswig-Holstein bei einer Kommunalwahl je gegeben hat, deutet darauf hin, dass unsere Wählerinnen und Wähler einfach zu Hause geblieben sind. In manchen Wahlbezirken, in denen wir gewöhnlich besonders viele SPD-Stimmen haben, hat es eine Wahlbeteilung von unter 30 Prozent gegeben! Ganz offensichtlich wollten uns die eigenen Wähler einen Denkzettel verpassen. Es hilft nichts, für diese Niederlage nur die Politik der Bundesregierung verantwortlich zu machen, obwohl das in der allgemeinen Situation nahe liegend wäre, oder auf kommunale Gegebenheiten hinzuweisen, die hier und da für das schlechte Ergebnis mit verantwortlich sein mögen. Wir dürfen jetzt auf keinen Fall zu lange unsere Wunden lecken; wir müssen als Landes-SPD und als Landesregierung die Mitverantwortung für das schlechte Ergebnis übernehmen und uns verstärkt um das kümmern, was wir in der Landespolitik besser machen können.

Ich hatte mein Kabinett schon vor der Wahl, zu Beginn des Jahres, umgebildet, um unsere Arbeit effizienter zu machen. Deswegen konnten wir uns auch gleich auf die zentrale Frage konzentrieren: Wo setzen wir nach der Wahl notwendige Schwerpunkte unserer Politik? Für mich steht, wie ich an anderer Stelle in diesem Buch noch ausführe, eindeutig die Bildungspolitik im Vordergrund. Vor allem möchte ich, dass wir den Unterrichtsausfall an unseren Schulen gegen null reduzieren. Wir haben uns in diesem Zusammenhang ein flexibles Instrument ausgedacht: Statt ein paar neue Stellen für Lehrerinnen und Lehrer zu finanzieren, die nur wenigen Schulen zugute kommen und den Unterrichtsausfall landesweit kaum vermindern würden, stellen wir den Geldwert von rund 200 Lehrerstellen für die ausgefallenen Stunden zur Verfügung und überlassen es den Schulen selbst, aus einem «Pool» von Nichtlehrern und pädagogischen Fachkräften Abhilfe zu schaffen. Mit Hilfe solcher «Pools», für deren Finanzierung wir zusätzliche 19 Millionen Euro bereitstellen, werden wir es hoffentlich schaffen, dass Kinder die Möglichkeit haben, von morgens um sieben Uhr bis nachmittags um zwei Uhr in ihrer Schule zu bleiben. In dieser Zeit können sie zum Beispiel ein Mittagessen bekommen, unter Aufsicht Schularbeiten machen und spielen. Für dieses Angebot der Betreuten Grundschule müssen die Eltern allerdings einen eigenen Beitrag zahlen. Die Betreuung übernehmen zum Teil ehrenamtliche Kräfte, zum Teil auch aus dem «Pool» stundenweise bezahlte Fachkräfte. Daneben können sich Halbtagsschulen auch zur Ganztagsschule entwickeln; dazu sind überwiegend Lehrkräfte erforderlich. Damit ziehen wir zum einen Konsequenzen aus den schlechten Ergebnissen der PISA-Studie und verbessern das Bildungsangebot. Gleichzeitig geben wir so berufstätigen Eltern die Gewissheit, dass ihre Kinder auch nach Schulschluss und bei Unterrichtsausfall etwas Sinnvolles tun.

Ein anderer Schwerpunkt der Bildungspolitik ist die verstärkte Förderung der Hochschulen. Wir stellen ihnen die finanziellen Mittel zur Verfügung, damit sie die jüngsten Tarifsteigerungen im öffentlichen Dienst auffangen können. Im Gegenzug müssen sie sich an die Empfehlungen einer von den Hochschulen und der Landesregierung eingesetzten Kommission halten, die verschiedene Strukturreformen zur Effizienzsteigerung in der schleswig-holsteinischen Hochschullandschaft vorgeschlagen hat.

Zu meiner Kandidatur für das Amt der Ministerpräsidentin im Februar 2005 stehe ich auch weiterhin. Ich wünsche mir, dass wir das Ruder bis dahin wieder herumreißen. Irgendwann müssen die Verhältnisse in Schleswig-Holstein und in Deutschland einfach wieder besser werden. Ich hoffe, dass dies bald geschieht, und werde dafür alles tun, was in meinen Kräften steht. Am meisten wünsche ich mir, dass sich etwas von dem Aufbauwillen einstellen möge, den unsere Eltern und Großeltern nach 1945 bewiesen haben, als es ihnen doch erheblich schlechter ging. Wenn die mit so einer verzagten und lustlosen Haltung an den Wiederaufbau herangegangen wären wie wir heute an die nötigen Strukturreformen, dann säßen wir wohl jetzt noch zwischen Trümmern. Wir müssen raus aus dem Jammertal – und zwar aus eigener Kraft und nicht, weil irgendwo das Wunder geschieht, auf das die meisten mehr oder minder resigniert zu warten scheinen – das Wunder, dass die Weltwirtschaft wieder anzieht, dass in Amerika die Konjunktur anspringt, weil der Irak-Krieg doch nicht so lange gedauert hat wie befürchtet. Wir sollten stattdessen auf unsere eigenen Kräfte vertrauen, denn es geht darum, unsere Gegenwart und Zukunft zu bauen und unseren Kindern eine Gesellschaft zu sichern, in der sie gern leben.

Im Vorwort zu einem Buch, das mein Leben in der Politik zum Gegenstand hat, habe ich all denen zu danken, die mir an entscheidenden Stellen meines Weges begegnet sind und weitergeholfen haben. Dazu gehören vor allem mein Mann und meine beiden Schwestern, natürlich auch mein Vater und viele Freundinnen und Freunde, die ich im Einzelnen nicht namentlich aufzählen kann. Mein besonderer Dank gilt Gerhard Hildenbrand und Linda Pieper, die mich bei der Arbeit an diesem Buch unterstützt haben.

Bordesholm, Ende April 2003

1

Eine persönliche und politische
Zwischenbilanz

Jubiläen sind ambivalente Ereignisse. Einerseits ist es natürlich schön, gefeiert zu werden – und sich selber in diesem Zusammenhang vielleicht verstohlen auf den Rücken zu klopfen und zu diesem oder jenem Erfolg in der zurückliegenden Zeitspanne zu beglückwünschen. Andererseits ist ein Jubiläum aber auch eine Herausforderung, Vergangenheit, Gegenwart und Zukunft einmal grundsätzlicher zu betrachten, als das politische Alltagsgeschäft es normalerweise zulässt. Das Jahr 2003 beschert mir gleich zwei solcher Ereignisse: im Mai den zehnjährigen Amtsantritt als Ministerpräsidentin, im Juli meinen 60. Geburtstag. Der eine Jahrestag regt zu einem Rückblick auf das eigene Leben an, der andere zu einer politischen Zwischenbilanz.

Die letzte Dekade des 20. Jahrhunderts war eine Zeit tiefgreifender Veränderungen, auf der internationalen Bühne ebenso wie bei uns in Deutschland. Mit dem Zusammenbruch der Sowjetunion verschwand das politische Ost-West-Koordinatensystem, an das wir uns in den Jahrzehnten zuvor gewöhnt hatten, und es herrschte erst einmal allgemeine Desorientierung. Seit dem Zweiten Weltkrieg hatte sich die Welt ganz gut im atomaren «Gleichgewicht des Schreckens» eingerichtet, das zwar labil war, aber dennoch eine Art Sicherheit bot, die in der Gewissheit lag: «Wer zuerst schlägt, stirbt als zweiter». Nun schien mit dem

Ende des «Kalten Krieges» zunächst eine Ära weltweiten Friedens möglich. Im vergangenen Jahrzehnt haben dann die USA als einzig verbliebene Supermacht ihre Hegemonialstellung zügig ausgebaut – und spätestens seit den Anschlägen vom 11. September 2001 auf das World Trade Center ist nichts mehr, wie es vorher war. Während ich dieses Buch schreibe, schwindet die Hoffnung auf eine diplomatische Lösung der Irak-Krise jeden Tag mehr – und es ist derzeit ganz unmöglich abzusehen, wie sich selbst eine nur kurze und militärisch erfolgreiche Offensive der Amerikaner auf den politisch aufgewühlten Nahen Osten und die Weltpolitik insgesamt auswirken wird. Unter anderem könnte es zu schweren Rückschlägen für die Weltwirtschaft und zu noch mehr Terrorakten überall auf der Welt kommen.

Tatsache ist, dass die vorrangige Beschäftigung mit der Frage: Krieg gegen den Irak – ja oder nein? politische Energien bindet, die eigentlich dringend nötig wären, sich mit den anderen drängenden Problemen des 21. Jahrhunderts zu beschäftigen, insbesondere solchen, die sich nur auf internationaler Ebene lösen lassen: Wie kann der fortschreitende Globalisierungsprozess so gestaltet werden, dass er für möglichst viele Menschen positive Auswirkungen hat, statt die Schere zwischen Reich und Arm, Nord und Süd, weiter zu vergrößern? Wie können wir den drohenden Umweltproblemen, vor allem der Klimaveränderung, der Wasserknappheit und der Zunahme von Extremereignissen wie Stürmen und Überschwemmungen, wirksam begegnen? Wie gehen wir mit dem rasanten Wachstum der Weltbevölkerung um? Können wir uns auf weltweit verbindliche Regeln und von allen anerkannte Institutionen zur Verhinderung von Kriegen und zur Sanktionierung von Verbrechen und Völkermord einigen? Gelingt es uns, Hunger und Elend in der Dritten Welt zu verringern und die dadurch ausgelösten Flüchtlingsbewegungen zu stoppen? So viele Fragen – und damit sind nur einige der drängenden Weltprobleme aufgelistet!

Bei uns in Deutschland hat sich in den letzten Jahren eine

Art Weltuntergangsstimmung breit gemacht, die weniger mit diesen Weltproblemen als mit der schwachen Wirtschaftskonjunktur, den gestiegenen Arbeitslosenzahlen, der Ebbe in den öffentlichen Kassen und dem drohenden Kollaps unserer Sozialversicherungssysteme zu tun hat. Die schwächelnde Weltwirtschaft wirkt sich angesichts unserer internationalen Verflechtung massiv auf unsere Wirtschaft aus. Darüber hinaus hat niemand die problematischen Auswirkungen der Wiedervereinigung Deutschlands auf die Wirtschaft richtig eingeschätzt. Hinzu kommt, dass wir in der vergangenen Dekade die notwendige Anpassung an die demographische Entwicklung und die veränderten wirtschaftlichen Bedingungen verschlafen haben. Wir hätten uns viel Ärger und Enttäuschungen ersparen können, wenn wir die Zeichen der Zeit eher erkannt und überlegt darauf reagiert hätten. Jetzt zwingt uns die schiere Notwendigkeit, Dampf zu machen. Nichts wäre fataler, als weiter so zu wursteln wie bisher und nur hier und da ein paar Reparaturen vorzunehmen. Wir müssen jetzt grundlegende Reformen anpacken. In seiner Regierungserklärung vom 14. März 2003 hat Bundeskanzler Schröder die großen Reformbereiche genannt: Arbeitsmarkt, das ganze Gesundheitssystem, Rente und die Finanzausstattung unserer Kommunen. Politiker und Politikerinnen müssen in diesem Zusammenhang den Mut haben, sich unbeliebt zu machen.

Jeder Mann, jede Frau, die sich in den letzten Jahren ein bisschen um Politik gekümmert hat, weiß, dass unser Sozialversicherungssystem, die Gesundheitskassen, das Rentensystem, die Arbeitslosen- und Pflegeversicherung, in ihren Grundfesten ächzen. Der Grund liegt auf der Hand: Sie alle sind auf Wirtschaftswachstum angelegt und müssen zusammenbrechen, wenn es einerseits immer weniger Arbeitnehmer gibt, die in die Systeme einzahlen, andererseits aber immer mehr Alte, Kranke und Arbeitslose, die finanzielle Unterstützung benötigen. Dabei werden die Auswirkungen der Umkehrung der Alterspyramide erst ab dem Jahre 2010 voll wirksam ...

Die Möglichkeiten einer Reform des Sozialversicherungs-systems sind im Grunde begrenzt. Wenn weniger hineinkommt als herausgeht, dann kann man erstens versuchen, die Einnahmeseite zu verbessern, das hieße in diesem Fall: die Beiträge erhöhen oder die Zahl der Beitragszahler vermehren. Weitere Beitragserhöhungen der Kranken- und der Rentenversicherung aber verbieten sich, weil sie die schon hohen Lohnnebenkosten noch weiter in die Höhe treiben würden. Stattdessen sollten wir unsere Reformen darauf konzentrieren, dass wieder mehr Menschen in die Sozialversicherungssysteme einzahlen. Stichworte sind hier: Arbeitslose wieder in Jobs bringen, ein modernes und zukunftsfähiges Zuwanderungsgesetz verabschieden oder die Bemessungsgrundlage verbreitern, indem Beamte und Selbstständige einbezogen werden. Man kann zweitens versuchen, die Ausgaben zu senken, wobei sich wieder zwei Möglichkeiten des Sparens anbieten: zum einen eine Effizienzkontrolle bei den bisherigen Leistungen, indem man Doppel- und Fehlversorgung abstellt – zum anderen eine Kürzung der Leistungen. Ich denke, dass beide Möglichkeiten ergriffen werden müssen. Und schließlich gibt es noch eine dritte, grundsätzlich andere Lösung, die darin besteht, unser Sozialversicherungssystem auf eine neue Basis zu stellen, das heißt, es von den Arbeitgeber- und Arbeitnehmerbeiträgen abzukoppeln und ganz anders zu finanzieren – etwa über eine erhöhte Mehrwertsteuer. Wie so etwas funktioniert, zeigt uns zum Beispiel unser Nachbar Dänemark.

Bei den anstehenden Reformen muss eine soziale Grundsicherung für alle weiterhin gewährleistet sein. Aber wir müssen auch fragen, wie weit einzelne Personen das Recht haben, diese Sozialversicherungssysteme auf Kosten der Gemeinschaft auszunutzen, und wir müssen uns mit dem Gedanken an mehr Eigenbeteiligung vertraut machen – sowohl was die Alterssicherung als auch was die Gesundheitsversorgung angeht. So wird die gesetzliche Rentenversicherung in den nächsten Jahrzehnten nur noch eine Grundversorgung gewährleisten können, auf deren

Basis jeder, jede Einzelne zusätzlich Eigenvorsorge betreiben muss. Bisher wird vom Angebot der «Riester-Rente» zwar mit steigender Tendenz, aber immer noch zu wenig Gebrauch gemacht, was wohl damit zusammenhängt, dass die Sache kompliziert ist und unübersichtlich wirkt. Andererseits haben längst noch nicht alle verstanden, dass sie sich zusätzlich privat versichern müssen – und das könnte irgendwann ein böses Erwachen geben.

Wir haben in Deutschland ein qualitativ hochwertiges Gesundheitssystem, und diese Qualität wollen wir auch erhalten, aber wir müssen sehen, dass eine Gesundheitsversorgung auf höchstem Anspruchsniveau nicht zum Nulltarif zu haben ist. Über- und Mehrfachversorgung könnten mit Hilfe einer Chipkarte, eines elektronischen Patientenausweises, vermieden werden, auf der die Daten des jeweiligen Patienten gespeichert sind. Das würde auch die Effizienz der Behandlung steigern. Es muss dann nicht mehr jeder Facharzt mit Anamnese und Diagnose von vorn beginnen. Wir führen in Schleswig-Holstein zur Zeit einen Modellversuch mit solchen Patientenkarten durch, von denen ich mir große Einsparungen verspreche.

Außerdem vertrete ich schon seit langem die Ansicht, dass auch Beamte in die Sozialkassen einzahlen sollten. Ihre besonderen Privilegien gegenüber Angestellten und Arbeitern sind nicht länger zu rechtfertigen. Für eine entsprechende Reform müssten wir allerdings das Grundgesetz ändern, und dafür sehe ich im Augenblick noch keine Mehrheiten. Doch irgendwann in der näheren Zukunft wird dieser Schritt getan werden müssen, ebenso wie eine generelle Reform des Beamtenrechts. Das derzeitige System ist ein historisches Relikt, das den öffentlichen Dienst belastet und nicht mehr zeitgemäß ist.

Bei den Krankenkassen wird zur Zeit über neue Tarifmodelle nachgedacht. So soll es etwa Beitragsrückerstattungen für Mitglieder geben, die innerhalb eines bestimmten Zeitraums keinen Arzt aufgesucht haben. Oder etwa Tarifvergünstigungen für diejenigen, die sich regelmäßig bestimmten Vorsorgeuntersuchungen unterziehen. Ich meine, dass es hier keine Denkverbote geben sollte, auch wenn jeder einzelne Vorschlag noch einmal sorgfältig geprüft werden muss, nicht nur unter dem Gesichtspunkt der praktischen Durchführbarkeit, sondern unter der Frage, ob nicht etwa das Solidaritätsprinzip ausgehöhlt wird. Ich finde Zuschläge für Menschen gerechtfertigt, die von sich aus erhöhte Gesundheitsrisiken eingehen. Wer zum Beispiel risikoreiche, unfallträchtige Sportarten betreibt, sollte dafür eine Zusatzversicherung abschließen müssen. Inzwischen werden auch Vorschläge diskutiert, nach denen Sondertarife eingeführt werden sollen für Menschen, die rauchen, zu viel trinken oder extremes Übergewicht haben. Doch einmal abgesehen davon, dass die Grenzen etwa zwischen «normalem» und «kritischem» Alkoholkonsum oder «selbstverschuldetem» und «krankhaftem» Übergewicht nur schwer zu ziehen sind, würde die praktische Durchführung zu einer unerträglichen Schnüffelei im Privatleben und auch sonst auf schier unüberwindbare Schwierigkeiten stoßen. Wer etwa sollte die Eingruppierung in die verschiedenen Tarifgruppen vornehmen, wer den Lebenswandel der Menschen überprüfen? Für mich scheidet diese Möglichkeit deshalb aus.

Der Einwand, dass wir mit unterschiedlichen Tarifen eine Zweiklassen-Medizin schaffen, führt allerdings nicht weiter: Zum einen gibt es schon längst Ansätze zu einer Zweiklassen-Medizin, etwa bei der Zahnarztbehandlung und beim Zahnersatz, wo sich ein Beamter mit Beihilfe und privater Zusatzversicherung etwas ganz anderes leisten kann als ein normaler AOK-Patient. Zum anderen können wir uns bei der gegenwärtigen Höhe der Beitragszahlungen und der gegenwärtigen Zahl der Beitragszahlenden das derzeitige Versorgungsniveau nicht länger leisten. Entweder muss das medizinische Versorgungsniveau für alle sinken, oder die Krankenkassen garantieren nur noch eine Grundversorgung. Für Sonderwünsche, die darüber hinausgehen, sollte man durch eine private Zusatzfinanzierung aufkommen. Schwierig bleibt es dann aber immer noch festzulegen, welche medizinischen Leistungen wir in den Katalog der medizinischen Grundversorgung aufnehmen wollen und welche als Extras definiert werden müssen.

Das Bundesgesundheitsministerium hat den Auftrag bekommen, bis Mitte 2003 Reformpläne für die Krankenversicherung vorzulegen. Die so genannte Rürup-Kommission wird weiter gehende Reformpläne für die sozialen Systeme insgesamt präsentieren. Sie werden hoffentlich die Grundlage für eine strukturelle Neuordnung unserer Sozialversicherung bieten, die wir dann umgehend beschließen und umsetzen können.

Diejenigen, die einen Arbeitsplatz haben, sind gut dran, verglichen mit den Arbeitslosen, vor allem den Langzeitarbeitslosen, die häufig leider nur eine geringe Chance haben, wieder eine Stelle zu bekommen. Bei Tarifverhandlungen müssen stärker als bisher auch die Interessen der Arbeitslosen berücksichtigt werden. Produktivitätszuwächse müssen auch ihnen zugute kommen. Auf dem Arbeitsmarkt darf es nicht zugehen wie beim Busfahren: Wer drin ist, schreit «Tür zu!». Unser vordringliches Bemühen muss es sein, möglichst vielen wieder einen Arbeitsplatz zu verschaffen. Dabei sollten wir aber so ehrlich sein, uns – auch öffentlich – einzugestehen, dass in absehbarer Zeit nicht mit einem nennenswerten wirtschaftlichen Wachstum zu rechnen ist. Auch dann nicht, wenn wir zügig die notwendigen Arbeitsmarktreformen in Gang bringen. Erst ein Wachstum oberhalb von 2 Prozent pro Jahr wirkt sich arbeitsplatzschaffend aus und ist zur Zeit nicht drin. Wenn aber keine nennenswerten Zuwächse zu verteilen sind, dann geht es eigentlich nur noch um das Umverteilen des Vorhandenen.

Im Übrigen geht es auch vielen anderen Ländern zur Zeit nicht besonders gut. Zwar sehen in den meisten EU-Staaten einige Zahlen und Statistiken etwas besser aus als bei uns, aber auch die wirtschaftliche Situation der Amerikaner ist schlecht, und den Japanern geht es deutlich schlechter als uns. Wir erleben unsere Situation auch nur vor dem Hintergrund eines halben Jahrhunderts raschen wirtschaftlichen Wachstums als so beklagenswert. Dabei stellt sich sehr wohl die Frage, ob nicht ebendiese letzten Jahrzehnte eher die Ausnahme waren und jetzt eine gewisse Normalisierung eingetreten ist. Zumindest müsste jedem klar sein, dass es in dem Stil und Tempo vergangener Jahre und Jahrzehnte nicht unbegrenzt weitergehen kann.

Die allgemeine wirtschaftliche Situation in Deutschland ist zur Zeit nicht besonders gut, aber sie ist auch keinesfalls so schlecht, wie die allgemeine Stimmung es zu belegen scheint. Diese Stimmung ist deswegen so gefährlich, weil wirtschaftliche Konjunktur und Psychologie aufs Engste miteinander verbunden sind. Wir bräuchten daher eine neue Aufbruchstimmung, das Bewusstsein, dass wir in einer zwar unsicheren, aber auch aufregenden Zeit leben, in der es darum geht, Weichen neu zu stellen und die Grundlagen für die Zukunft zu gestalten. Wir haben in den vergangenen Jahrzehnten unser Anspruchsniveau gewaltig erhöht und sind so zum Teil bequem geworden. Nun aber werden manche aus ihrer Trägheit aufgerüttelt. Sie reiben sich die Augen und begreifen erst allmählich, dass es nicht so weitergehen wird wie bisher, dass einschneidende Veränderungen erforderlich sind, die tendenziell auch ihren Besitzstand bedrohen – und da macht sich bei vielen Panik breit. Zwar wird die Notwendigkeit von Reformen von den meisten Menschen generell anerkannt – aber kaum wird eine Maßnahme angekündigt, da schreit die entsprechende Lobbygruppe auf: «Warum gerade wir! Nicht mit uns!» So wird dann der «Schwarze Peter» ständig hin und her geschoben.

Wir dürfen uns in dieser Situation aber nicht darauf beschränken festzustellen: «Es ist alles ganz schrecklich, und es wird immer noch schrecklicher werden!» Missstände und Fehlentwicklungen müssen aufgezeigt werden, und das ist schon lange genug geschehen. Nun ist es an der Zeit, die Probleme auch wirklich anzugehen.

In diesem Zusammenhang hat Bundeskanzler Schröder

nicht das erreicht, was er sich vorgenommen hatte. Lange Zeit war er zu sehr auf Konsens bedacht. Er hat versucht, alle wichtigen Akteure bei anstehenden Entscheidungen einzubinden. Seine Erwartung war, dass sich im Austausch zwischen ihm als Moderator und den beteiligten Gruppen eine Lösung herausbildet, die alle mittragen können. Das ist eine demokratische Verfahrensweise und hat manches für sich. Nur erfordern solche Prozesse in der Regel viel Zeit – und die haben wir nicht mehr. Wir stehen in vielen Fragen vor ebenso dringenden wie zwingenden Entscheidungen und können es uns einfach nicht leisten, geduldig abzuwarten, bis der große Konsens hergestellt ist. Gerade erst hat das Scheitern des Bündnisses für Arbeit, Ausbildung und Wettbewerbsfähigkeit auf Bundesebene uns die Grenzen des Konsensmodells ganz klar vor Augen geführt. Ich persönlich wünsche mir mehr, deutlichere und klarere Vorgaben, wie Gerhard Schröder sie in seiner Regierungserklärung vom 14. März 2003 gemacht hat.

Bereits im Jahr 2000 hat man mich in einem Interview gefragt: «Müsste man den Menschen nicht ehrlich sagen, dass die besten Jahre für Deutschland vorüber sind?» Ich habe darauf geantwortet – und das ist immer noch meine Überzeugung: «Die besten Jahre müssen keineswegs vorüber sein – aber ganz bestimmt sind für uns Deutsche die bequemsten Jahre zu Ende.» Es ist die Pflicht der Politiker, dies laut und deutlich auszusprechen, statt die Menschen immer wieder damit zu vertrösten, dass es übermorgen oder im nächsten Halbjahr vielleicht von selbst schon wieder besser aussieht. Ich bin überzeugt davon, dass man mit Ehrlichkeit in der Politik langfristig weiter kommt als mit falschen Versprechungen und populistischen Parolen; die Wahrheit kann den Menschen sehr wohl zugemutet werden. Wenn sie die Lage wirklich begriffen haben, sind sie auch bereit, ihre Illusionen aufzugeben, mit dem Jammern aufzuhören und wieder anzupacken. Mehr Ehrlichkeit in der Politik ist auch eine Chance, der verbreiteten Politikverdrossenheit entgegenzuwirken, die auf Dauer für eine Demokratie gefährlich werden kann.

Was die Reform der Sozialversicherungssysteme angeht, haben wir auf Länderebene keine großen Gestaltungsmöglichkeiten. Unsere Anstrengungen in Schleswig-Holstein müssen sich im Augenblick vor allem auf zwei Bereiche konzentrieren: auf die Bekämpfung der Arbeitslosigkeit und auf Reformen im Bildungssektor. Eine Landesregierung hat keinen Einfluss auf die Höhe der Lohnnebenkosten, aber sie kann sehr wohl Impulse für den Arbeitsmarkt geben, neue, effizientere Wege bei der Arbeitsvermittlung zu gehen und Bürokratie im Verhältnis Staat–Wirtschaft–Gesellschaft abzubauen. Nach den ernüchternden Ergebnissen der so genannten Pisa-Studie bemühen wir uns in Schleswig-Holstein um ein verbessertes Angebot an Ganztagsschulen, und wir fördern die Idee einer größeren Selbstständigkeit und Profilierung der Schulen, unter anderem durch selbstständige Budgetierung.

Auch Schleswig-Holstein hat mit der schwierigen wirtschaftlichen Gesamtsituation zu kämpfen; die Arbeitslosigkeit ist mit einer Quote von 10,3 Prozent (Stand: Januar 2003) viel zu hoch. Dennoch hat es in den letzten Jahren einen richtigen Entwicklungsschub gegeben. Schleswig-Holstein ist nicht mehr das bäuerliche Bundesland im äußersten Norden, mit dem Image, langsam, gründlich, aber etwas zurückgeblieben zu sein. «Die hängen immer hinten am Tampen dran» – so sahen uns die anderen früher. Die Menschen in Schleswig-Holstein sind im letzten Jahrzehnt merklich selbstbewusster geworden. Bei manchen zukunftsweisenden Techniken – wie etwa der Informationstechnik, der Medizintechnik, den erneuerbaren Energien – sind wir ganz stark. Die Menschen hier sehen ihr Land nicht mehr als das «Ende der Welt» – im Gegenteil: Sie öffnen sich für die baltischen Staaten, für Nord- und Osteuropa. Dabei hat das Verschwinden des Eisernen Vorhangs eine wichtige Rolle gespielt, und die EU-Osterweiterung wird diese Entwicklung weiter verstärken. Die Exportwirtschaft, die wir in Schleswig-Holstein im vergangenen Jahrzehnt in Richtung EU-Länder, nach Nordamerika, nach Asien und in den Nahen Osten aufgebaut haben, kann sich sehen lassen.

Eine Online-Umfrage vom März 2002 hat ergeben, dass Schleswig-Holstein, neben Bayern, das Bundesland ist, in dem die Menschen am liebsten leben. Die Identifikation mit dem eigenen Land hat sicher viel mit der Schönheit seiner Landschaft, mit der Lebensart und dem Temperament seiner Menschen zu tun. Doch es drücken sich darin auch allgemeines Einverständnis mit der gegenwärtigen Situation und positive Zukunftserwartungen aus, und darüber freue ich mich besonders.

Ich will die Probleme, die wir zur Zeit in Deutschland und natürlich auch in Schleswig-Holstein haben, nicht schönreden. Doch ich gestehe, ich bin stolz darauf, dass ich in den zurückliegenden zehn Jahren meiner Amtszeit das neue Erscheinungsbild dieses Landes in einigen entscheidenden Punkten mit prägen konnte. Die große Gesundheitsinitiative, mit der wir unser Standbein «Gesundheitswirtschaft» stärken wollen, die Modernisierung der Verwaltung, den Ausbau der Windenergie, die Exportförderung, die Öffnung des Landes in den Ostseeraum als vielfältigen und viel versprechenden Wirtschafts- und Kulturraum rechne ich zu den Erfolgen meiner Politik. Sicher gibt es andere Bereiche, in denen notwendige Veränderungen noch besser und vor allem auch schneller laufen könnten. An wirklich einschneidende Niederlagen kann ich mich aber nicht erinnern. Ich hätte mir größere Fortschritte beim Umbau des öffentlichen Dienstes gewünscht, insbesondere eine Öffnung der Grundsätze des Beamtentums; doch solche Reformen sind wohl erst in Zukunft und dann nur durch gemeinsame Anstrengung aller Länder und des Bundes möglich.

Runde Geburtstage erinnern natürlich auch und besonders an das eigene Alter. Zwar bildet man sich selber immer gern ein, man werde nicht älter – altern tun nur die anderen –, oder man bemerkt es erst dann, wenn man Freunde und Bekannte nach langer Zeit wiedersieht. So ging es mir im vergangenen Herbst bei einem Klassentreffen in Nürnberg, vierzig Jahre nach dem Abitur. Wir hatten uns zehn Jahre lang nicht gesehen. Da gab es dann zu Anfang den verblüfften Blick rundum: «Mein Gott, sind die alt geworden!» Man ändert sich ja selbst in seiner eigenen Wahrnehmung nur allmählich und eher fließend, solange nicht heftige Lebenskrisen scharfe Einschnitte schaffen.

Natürlich habe ich mich in den zehn Jahren, in denen ich das Amt der Ministerpräsidentin ausübe, verändert. Ich bin ein Stück unduldsamer und zugleich auch ein Stück gelassener geworden – so widersprüchlich das auch klingen mag. Ich kann auch heute noch wie von einer Tarantel gestochen unter die Decke gehen, wenn zum Beispiel eine Akte, die ich brauche, nicht gleich gefunden wird. Vor allem im eigenen Haus, in der Staatskanzlei, geht mir vieles nicht schnell genug. Aber nach außen hin habe ich manchmal, verglichen mit früher, eine Engelsgeduld, vor allem, wenn ich merke, dass die Menschen es nicht böse meinen, vielleicht eine Sache nur nicht gleich verstehen. Durch langjährige Erfahrung rücken manche Dinge eher an ihren eigentlichen Platz und erscheinen dann in einem anderen Licht. Angesichts wirklicher Katastrophen, wie etwa der großen Überschwemmungen in Ostdeutschland im vergangenen Sommer, denke ich häufiger als früher: Warum regst du dich eigentlich über Kleinkram auf, der zwar ärgerlich, aber so intensive Gefühle doch nicht wert ist!

Die wichtigste Veränderung meines Selbstbildes im Laufe der letzten zehn Jahre besteht sicher darin, dass ich die Rolle der «Landesmutter» akzeptiert habe, gegen die ich mich anfangs heftig sträubte. Landesmutter – das klang für mich so bieder und gediegen, machte irgendwie alt. Früher, als Abgeordnete, gefiel ich mir manchmal in der Rolle eines Enfant terrible der Politik, das gerne ins Fettnäpfchen trat und auch der eigenen Partei gegenüber kritische Positionen einnahm. Bevor ich Ministerpräsidentin wurde, befand ich mich immer in Rollen, in denen ich Partei ergreifen musste in Kontroversen und Konflikten: als Mitglied des Haushaltsausschusses, als Finanzministerin, als diejenige, die seitens der Länder die Tarifverhandlungen für den öffentlichen Dienst führte und die 1992/93 den ersten Solidarpakt mit den neuen Ländern mit ausgehandelt hat. Das waren Rollen, in denen entschieden werden musste nach dem Motto: «Du bekommst etwas, und du bekommst nichts – und du bekommst lange nicht so viel, wie du glaubst!». In der Rolle der «Landesmutter» steht dagegen das moderierende Element im Vordergrund: Alle Individuen und alle Gruppen im Land haben das gleiche Recht darauf, mit ihren Interessen berücksichtigt oder zumindest angemessen wahrgenommen zu werden; der Ausgleich selbst ist die Wahrung des Gemeinwohls.

Die Lust am politischen Geschäft ist bei mir nach wie vor da, und zwar ungemindert. Auch wenn es reichlich zähe Prozesse und immer wieder auch unerfreuliche Situationen und schwierige Probleme gibt – meistens macht mir meine Arbeit Freude. «Ich bin Politikerin geworden, weil ich Zoff liebe», «Mich fasziniert Macht» – mit solchen Aussagen wurde ich früher oft zitiert. Eigentlich aber lautet meine zentrale Devise: «Ich will meine Arbeit möglichst gut machen.» Trotzdem ist mir von der alten Streitlust genug geblieben; ich scheue die Auseinandersetzung nicht. Sonst würde ich auch nicht ab und an mal gegen den Kanzler der eigenen Partei aufmucken, wenn es mir notwendig erscheint, und dann dafür öffentlich Dresche beziehen. Aber die Freude am Zoff ist nicht meine Leitmelodie; sie wird überlagert durch eine andere Grundhaltung: Es kommt mir mehr darauf an, Menschen zu überzeugen, sie zum Mitmachen und zum Engagement zu ermutigen. Ich will ihnen vermitteln, dass sie eigentlich gern mittun sollten und froh sein werden, wenn sie sich dazu entschieden haben – und dass dann nur noch wenig Grund zum Meckern bleibt.

Rein äußerlich hat sich mein persönliches Leben im vergangenen Jahrzehnt weniger verändert als in den unruhigen Zeiten davor. Doch zehn Jahre in diesem Amt formen und prägen, und sie bleiben nicht ohne Auswirkung auf die privaten Lebensverhältnisse. Ich hoffe, dass ich etwas weiser geworden bin. Ich bin wohl auch etwas eleganter geworden. Hüte trage ich immer noch gern – obwohl da das Problem mit der Frisur ist. Sosehr ich Hüte mag: Es ist nicht besonders schön, wenn man irgendwohin kommt und einem die Haare am Kopf kleben.

Bei meinem 50. Geburtstag, als ich gerade mal fünf Wochen im Amt war, fragten sich viele, laut oder leise: Wird sie es schaffen? Heute traut man mir wahrscheinlich alles zu. Im rückwärts gerichteten Blick scheint das eigene Leben sehr gradlinig auf den Punkt hinauszulaufen, an dem man sich jeweils gerade befindet. Aber so war es in meinem Fall keineswegs. In meiner Kindheit und Jugend war ich weit davon entfernt, mir das Leben einer Politikerin für mich vorzustellen. Zufälle und Umwege spielten eine große Rolle, bis ich an die Politik geriet und richtig in ihr aufging. Und selbst als ich schon mit Leib und Seele Politikerin war, in meiner Bonner Abgeordnetenzeit, hätte ich mir kaum die Rolle einer «Landesmutter» für mich vorstellen können.

2

Eine nicht ganz einfache Kindheit
und Jugend

Meine Kindheit kann man bestimmt nicht in die heile Welt der Bilderbuchfamilien einordnen, und meine Biografie lässt sich kaum nach dem beliebten Muster erzählen: «Schon früh zeigte sich, was in ihr steckte, schon früh ahnte man, dass sie einmal eine erfolgreiche Politikerin sein würde.» Aber sie ist möglicherweise ein Beispiel dafür, dass auch Umstände, die eigentlich beschädigend sind, zu positiven Triebkräften in der eigenen Entwicklung werden können. Geliebt und unterstützt von einem eher sanften Vater, aber gegängelt und gedeckelt von einer mit ihrem Leben unzufriedenen Mutter, der man nichts wirklich recht machen konnte, gab es bei mir schon früh ein trotziges Aufbegehren, ein: «Jetzt erst recht! Das wollen wir doch mal sehen!» – Ich denke, so wurde der Grundstein gelegt für eine Art von Widerstandskraft und Durchhaltevermögen, die mir in meinem späteren Leben als Politikerin durchaus nützlich waren.

Ich wurde 1943 in Bonn geboren, als Älteste von drei Schwestern. Doris, «Dodo», kam ein Jahr nach mir, und Barbara, die Jüngste, zwei weitere Jahre später. Mein Vater hatte nach dem Abitur mit einem Jurastudium begonnen, sich aber nach wenigen Semestern freiwillig zur Luftwaffe gemeldet. Er wurde Sturzkampfflieger und ist noch kurz vor Kriegsende degradiert worden, weil er von einer Krankenstation im Osten ohne Befehl einige Krankenschwestern mitgenommen hatte, um sie in Sicherheit zu bringen. Anschließend geriet er in englische Gefangenschaft, aber nur kurz, und kam dann als gebrochener Mann nach Hause, ohne Studienabschluss, ohne Beruf, den Anforderungen des Alltags nicht sonderlich gut gewachsen.

Meine Mutter nahm daraufhin unser aller Leben fest in die Hand. Sie war gegen Kriegsende erst von Bonn nach Königsberg gezogen, wo sie sich in der Nähe ihrer Schwiegerfamilie sicherer glaubte. Als aber die russische Front näher rückte, zog sie den ganzen Weg wieder zurück, mit dem großen Treck aus Königsberg, über Österreich, bis nach Bonn hinauf. Ich finde das eine großartige Leistung, mit einem kleinen Kind an der Hand, gleichzeitig hochschwanger, durch viele Strapazen hindurch. Meine jüngere Schwester wurde während der Flucht in Schlesien geboren.

Wir sind in Bonn dann erst einmal bei meinen Großeltern untergekommen, alle zusammen in einem einzigen Zimmer. Mein Vater kehrte aus der Kriegsgefangenschaft zurück, und bald war das dritte Kind unterwegs. Von allen Berufen, die es gab, hat er sich dann ausgerechnet den eines Handelsvertreters ausgesucht, der eigentlich überhaupt nicht zu ihm passte. Er kam zwar einigermaßen damit zurecht, aber für meine Mutter war das unterhalb ihrer Würde. Sie wünschte, dass er sein Jurastudium wieder aufnähme, was ihm zunächst, als ehemaligem aktiven Offizier, aber gar nicht möglich war. Nach einiger Zeit wurden dann spezielle Kurzstudienprogramme für Wiedereinsteiger angeboten, für Familienväter, die Offiziere gewesen waren. Meine Mutter meldete ihn an der Universität an; sie war es auch, die beantragte, dass seine bisherigen sechs Semester anerkannt wurden. Sie musste ihn allerdings lange bearbeiten, bis er bereit war, seine Existenz als Handelsvertreter aufzugeben. Er brachte dann das Kurzstudium zwar zügig hinter sich, fand aber anschließend erst einmal keine Stelle. Meine Mutter hat ihn dann noch zur Promotion getrieben. Er war dreißig

Jahre, als ich geboren wurde; mit zweiundvierzig Jahren hat er dann endlich sein Studium beendet. Auch das spiegelt einiges wider vom Schicksal dieser Generation.

Meine Eltern entstammten ganz verschiedenen sozialen Schichten, ein Unterschied, der vor dem Krieg noch sehr bedeutsam war. Mein Vater kam aus einer Kaufmannsfamilie; sein Vater besaß ein bekanntes Herrenausstattergeschäft. Meine Mutter dagegen kam aus einer Handwerkerfamilie; sie war das dreizehnte Kind und damit das erste Mädchen nach vielen Geburten und mehreren Totgeburten. Sie wuchs sehr verwöhnt heran, doch erlaubten ihr die Eltern nahezu gar nichts. Der Nationalsozialismus gefiel ihr daher zunächst nicht schlecht, denn er brachte ihr viele neue Freiheiten. Auf einmal durfte sie zum Sport, zum Rudern; sie durfte mit auf Zeltfahrten gehen und fand das herrlich, und endlich konnte sie auch an Bällen der Studentenverbindungen teilnehmen. Vorher war so etwas völlig unmöglich gewesen, denn da waren nur die Töchter der «Alten Herren», der ehemaligen Verbindungsstudenten, zugelassen. Für sie war das etwas sehr Erstrebenswertes, sie sehnte sich nach einem sozialen Aufstieg. Meine Eltern haben sich in Brest, in Westfrankreich, kennen gelernt, wo mein Vater stationiert und meine Mutter kriegsverpflichtet war.

Mein Vater war stark durch die nationalkonservative Gesinnung seines Elternhauses geprägt. In der Nachkriegszeit litt er unter seiner beruflichen Situation ebenso wie unter der fordernden Lebenstüchtigkeit meiner Mutter. Da er sein Studium nicht abgeschlossen hatte, legte man ihm nahe, er müsse aus seiner studentischen Verbindung austreten – das traf ihn tief, denn diese Gruppierung war für ihn ein wichtiger Teil seines Lebens. Er war preußisch in seiner Pflichtauffassung, aber zugleich auch ein sehr sensibler Mensch; er konnte sich besser in seine Töchter einfühlen als unsere Mutter. In seinem Herkunftsmilieu war es klar, dass ein Mann die Familie zu ernähren hatte. Deswegen verbot er auch meiner Mutter zu arbeiten, als er endlich einen angemessenen Beruf gefunden hatte, im

Arbeitsamt in Bonn. Sehr zu meiner Verwunderung hat sie sich das gefallen lassen. Wenn sie etwa Lehrerin oder Ärztin gewesen wäre, hätte man vielleicht noch über eine Fortsetzung ihrer Berufstätigkeit reden können, hieß es zu Hause – aber Sekretärin? Dabei war meine Mutter immerhin über längere Zeit die zweite Sekretärin von Konrad Adenauer.

Sie war sehr tüchtig; sie mochte ihren Job, und sie hätte es bestimmt geschafft, Berufstätigkeit und Familie zu vereinbaren, aber das war für meinen Vater unvorstellbar, obwohl er alle seine Töchter das Abitur machen und sie studieren ließ. Die spätere Entscheidung meiner Mutter, zu Hause zu bleiben, war für niemanden gut. Sie hasste die Hausarbeit, sie kochte nicht gern; sie überließ die meiste Arbeit uns Kindern. Nachdem sie nicht mehr berufstätig sein konnte, hat sie viel Energie dazu benutzt, Migräne zu bekommen – ein vielleicht unbewusstes Manöver, die Aufmerksamkeit unseres Vaters auf sich zu ziehen. Der sagte immer zu uns: «Entweder man ist krank, dann legt man sich ins Bett und hält den Mund. Oder man ist gesund, dann tut man seine Arbeit und jammert ebenfalls nicht.» Er war aber zu schwach, unserer Mutter gegenüber zu dieser Haltung zu stehen. Die bekam einen Migräneanfall, wenn ihr etwas nicht passte; sie litt dann unüberhörbar und unübersehbar, und wir standen alle um sie herum, mein Vater an der Spitze: «Muttelchen, was können wir für dich tun?» Ihr Lieblingssatz in späteren Jahren war: «Ihr habt ja alle studiert – und ich bin hier nur die Minna!»

Meine frühesten Erinnerungen stammen aus meiner Zeit in Kinderheimen. Ich hatte als Kind schweres Asthma und musste deswegen von meinem dritten Geburtstag an oft ins Kinderheim. Doch da ist noch ein anderes Erinnerungsbild, das älter sein könnte: Ich sitze in einer Zinkbadewanne in der Küche unserer ersten Bonner Wohnung, und meine Eltern streiten, über meinen Kopf hinweg, wie so oft. Dann ist da die Erinnerung an eine schreckliche Nacht im Kinderheim, wo ich einen schlimmen Asthmaanfall hatte und niemand kam, um mir zu helfen.

Sonst war immer jemand angestürzt gekommen. Ich dachte damals, ich müsste ersticken ...

Es waren viele Kinderheimaufenthalte, mal für ein paar Wochen oder Monate, mal für ein halbes oder ein drei viertel Jahr, in Bad Soden, in Freudenstadt, Garmisch-Partenkirchen und zuletzt im Westerwald. Im Westerwald waren meine beiden Schwestern mit mir im Heim; unsere Mutter war zu dieser Zeit berufstätig, und das Heim mit angeschlossener Volksschule, die wir beiden Älteren besuchten, lag so nah bei Bonn, dass sie uns von dort aus an den Sonntagen besuchen konnte.

Ich bin oft gefragt worden, ob ich mich in den Kinderheimen nicht einsam und verlassen gefühlt hätte. Kann sein, dass ich manches verdrängt habe, doch ich kann mich an solche Gefühle nicht erinnern. Ich war in den meisten Heimen ganz gern und habe mich der neuen Umgebung schnell angepasst. Meine Mutter erzählte später, ich hätte sie, als ich zu Ostern oder Weihnachten aus Freudenstadt zurückkam, gefragt: «Ei, was schwätzesch du denn so komisch?» So fremd war mir mein rheinisches Zuhause geworden. Ich erinnere mich aber sehr wohl daran, dass ich meistens froh war, wenn ich nach den Zwischenaufenthalten von dort wieder fortkonnte. Denn es gab häufig Krach mit meiner Mutter. Wenn ich mich heute frage, wo denn eigentlich die tieferen Gründe gelegen haben, dann komme ich zu dem Ergebnis, dass meine Mutter eine sehr unglückliche Frau gewesen sein muss.

Meine ein Jahr jüngere Schwester Dodo war Mutters Augapfel. Sie hatte andere Durchsetzungsstrategien als ich. Sie setzte sich hin, klein und mickrig, und aß einfach nichts. Meine Mutter bat: «Noch ein Löffelchen!» Doch Dodo saß da und presste die Lippen zusammen. Dann bekam sie das Essen mit Gewalt hineingestopft, man konnte sehen, wie ihre Backe anschwoll, dick und dicker wurde. Eine ganze Stunde konnte das so gehen, bis sie auf einmal – popp! – alles wieder ausspuckte. Trotzdem war Dodo Mutters Liebling. Vielleicht, weil sie in der schlimmsten Zeit geboren und schon krank auf die Welt gekommen war; sie hatte Diphtherie, sie hatte eigentlich immer irgendetwas, aber sie war und blieb Mutters Kind. «Affenliebe ist nichts dagegen!», sagte mein Vater. Dodo war lange für viele Dinge zu schwach, und sie besaß großes Geschick darin, sich vor anstehenden Arbeiten zu drücken. Wir anderen beiden mussten immer viel tun, in der Küche helfen, putzen, Knöpfe annähen; Dodo aber war zu zart für diese Welt. Ich kann mich trotzdem nicht erinnern, sie deswegen gehasst zu haben; sie hatte nämlich die nette Eigenschaft, immer alles auf sich zu nehmen, wenn wir anderen etwas angestellt hatten. Wenn es gegen die Eltern ging, haben wir drei immer fest zusammengehalten.

Mit meiner jüngsten Schwester, Barbara, hatte ich viel mehr Streit. Sie war ein Wonneproppen, rund, blauäugig, strahlend, mit einem umwerfenden Charme und einer großen Klappe. Sie konnte aber auch ein richtiges Biest sein. Man hatte uns beigebracht, wir sollten immer alles teilen. Wenn Barbara etwas geschenkt bekam, Schokolade zum Beispiel, vergaß sie nie zu fordern: «Für Heide und Dodo auch!» – aber sie ließ einen dann nur widerstrebend abbeißen und hielt Daumen und Zeigefinger immer so weit oben, dass man kaum eine Chance hatte. Dodo verzichtete unter diesen Umständen, doch ich habe sie bei solchen Gelegenheiten schon mal gebissen.

Wenn Dodo das Mutterkind war, so war ich das Vaterkind, ich nehme an, der ausgleichenden Gerechtigkeit wegen. Vater hat seine drei Töchter gleichermaßen gern gehabt, keine wurde zurückgesetzt, aber um mich hat er sich von Anfang an besonders gekümmert, vielleicht weil er glaubte, dass ich es besonders nötig hätte.

Als ich zehn Jahre alt war, holte unsere Mutter uns nach Hause; ich sollte im vierten Schuljahr einer Bonner Schule auf die Aufnahmeprüfung für das Gymnasium vorbereitet werden. Danach bin ich nur noch ein paarmal kurz nach schweren Asthmaanfällen in Heimen gewesen. Die nächtlichen Asthmaanfälle hörten nach der Pubertät weitgehend auf; ich bekam nur noch dann Anfälle, wenn ich mich aufregte, und später, in den ersten Jahren meiner Ehe, ist auch dies schließlich ganz verschwunden.

Ich hatte in dieser Zeit meiner Jugend kein gutes Selbstbild. Mit zehn, elf Jahren tat ich in kürzester Zeit einen gewaltigen Wachstumsschub; seitdem fand ich mich hässlich, mager, viel zu groß – in dieser Zeit überragte ich nicht nur meine Schwestern um einiges, sondern ich war überhaupt die Längste in der Familie. Ich bekam oft keine Luft und fühlte mich danach sehr schlapp, mir wurde auch immer leicht schwindlig. Wenn ich morgens zu schnell aufstand, lag ich manchmal gleich wieder am Boden. Dodo passierte das auch; die konnte sogar auf Bestellung in Ohnmacht fallen, wenn sie etwas tun sollte, das ihr nicht passte. Ich fühlte mich in dieser Zeit als krankes Kind; ich musste immer furchtbar viel liegen, in den Heimen ebenso wie zu Hause. Früher war man der Ansicht, Asthmakinder müssten sich schonen, heute rät man eher zu leichter Bewegung, was mir viel angemessener erscheint. Das schlechte Verhältnis zu meinem eigenen Körper änderte sich erst spät, während des Studiums, in der Ehe.

Wegen der Heimaufenthalte habe ich viele verschiedene Schulen besucht. Wir sind auch mehrmals umgezogen, erst nach Hamburg, und schließlich lebten wir in Nürnberg, wo ich endlich einmal sechs Jahre hintereinander, bis zum Abitur, auf ein und dieselbe Schule ging – eine Mädchenschule natürlich, wie es damals üblich war. Ich war keine besonders gute Schülerin. Drei Viertel des Schuljahres habe ich die Dinge ziemlich schleifen lassen; dann war Elternabend, es gab zu Hause ein Donnerwetter; anschließend riss ich mich zusammen und hatte wieder bessere Noten, bis zur nächsten Versetzung. So kam ich immer durch. Am meisten Spaß machte mir Mathematik, ich mochte auch die Mathelehrerin; sie nahm mich, wie ich war. In die Klassengemeinschaft fand ich anfangs nur schwer hinein, denn die anderen waren ja schon ein paar Jahre zusammen, und alle sprachen fränkisch. Immerhin wurde ich dann irgendwann zur Klassensprecherin und später auch zur stellvertretenden Schulsprecherin gewählt – wohl, weil ich gut reden konnte. Vielleicht hatte ich damals schon die ersten Alphatierchen-Anwandlungen.

In meiner Freizeit habe ich viel und ziemlich wahllos gelesen, schon als Kind, weil ich so viel liegen musste, alles Mögliche bunt durcheinander, von Enid Blyton über Karl May bis zu Hedwig Courths-Mahler. Die Vorstellung unserer Mutter war, dass der Nachmittag für die Schulaufgaben und anschließend für Arbeiten im Haushalt da war. Ich liebte Musik, aber es wäre zu teuer gewesen, ein Instrument spielen zu lernen. In die Tanzstunde durfte ich nicht. Wir waren eigentlich alle immer zu Hause, das war die damals verbreitete und auch von meinen Eltern geteilte Vorstellung von Familienleben: immer alles zusammen zu machen. So etwas kennt man heute nur noch aus komischen Filmen. Wir gingen zusammen spazieren, wir aßen zusammen, wir spielten sonntags miteinander Canasta. Das war durchaus auch schön. Doch es war unvorstellbar, dass eine von uns Dreien mal gesagt hätte: «Ich möchte jetzt gern etwas anderes machen, ganz für mich allein, ohne die Eltern.»

Eigentlich muss dieser Versuch, die Fiktion vom wunderbaren Familienleben aufrechtzuerhalten, für die Erwachsenen wohl ebenso anstrengend und qualvoll gewesen sein wie für die Kinder. Mein Vater bekam ohnehin nur selten einen Satz dazwischen, wenn seine vier Frauen redeten. Er saß dabei und hörte sich das an, und alle halbe Jahr platzte ihm mal der Kragen. Später sind die Eltern dann manchmal ohne uns Kinder, weil es zu teuer gewesen wäre, uns mitzunehmen, zum Skilaufen gefahren, mit schlechtem Gewissen. Dabei waren wir richtig froh darüber, endlich einmal allein ohne sie zu Hause zu sein.

1962 machte ich Abitur. Eigentlich wollte ich Physik studieren, in München – aber für meine Mutter kam es überhaupt nicht in Frage, dass ich allein in eine andere Stadt ging. «Studiere doch Volkswirtschaft», meinte sie, «dein Vater ist auch Volkswirt – das ist doch ein schönes Studium!» Also habe ich in Nürnberg mit der Volkswirtschaftslehre angefangen. Allerdings lag der Schwerpunkt dort eher auf der Betriebswirtschaft, und die interessierte mich nicht sonderlich. Glücklicherweise bekam mein Vater wenig später ein berufliches Angebot in Kiel, und die Universität Kiel hatte einen hervorragenden Ruf in Volkswirtschaft. So sind wir dann alle zusammen nach Kiel gezogen. Wir lebten zu dieser Zeit noch bei den Eltern, meine jüngeren Schwestern und ich. Meine Mutter war der Ansicht, dass eine junge Frau ihr Elternhaus erst mit der Heirat verlässt. So war es dann auch bei mir.

Ich hatte zu dieser Zeit noch keine klaren Berufsvorstellungen, doch ich wollte auf jeden Fall erwerbstätig sein, mein eigenes Geld verdienen, nicht so leben müssen wie meine Mutter. Ich hätte dieses Angebundensein nicht ertragen können. Später hatte ich dann auch den meisten Streit mit meinem Mann in den Zeiten, in denen ich kein eigenes Geld verdiente. Ich wollte auch unbedingt heiraten, denn Heiraten bedeutete für mich Selbstständigkeit, während Kinder nicht unbedingt zu meinem Zukunftsbild gehörten, jedenfalls nicht an oberster Stelle. Ich hatte da ja das nicht ganz gelungene Beispiel meiner Mutter vor Augen. Auf jeden Fall wollte ich erst einmal eine Weile arbeiten, egal was – nur nicht als Lehrerin. Meine damaligen Vorbehalte gegenüber dem Lehrerberuf rührten wahrscheinlich gerade daher, dass meine Mutter ihn so anpries: «Wenn du dann erst mal Kinder hast, lässt sich das gut vereinbaren, du bist ja dann nur halbtags von zu Hause weg...» Eine meiner Schwestern ist übrigens Lehrerin geworden; die andere hat Soziologie, Psychologie und Französisch studiert.

Das Studium hat mir viel Spaß gemacht, vor allem in Kiel. Damals war es, anders als heute, auch noch möglich, das breiter anzulegen und ein richtiges Studium generale zu machen. Als Studentin entwickelte ich ein besseres Selbstgefühl; ich zog mit einer Clique herum, in der ich anerkannt war, sicher nicht wegen meiner hervorragenden wissenschaftlichen Leistungen oder meiner herausragenden Schönheit. Doch ich fühlte mich akzeptiert und fand es wunderbar, mir meine Tage endlich selbst einzuteilen. Zum ersten Mal in meinem Leben konnte ich frei durchatmen. Unsere Clique bestand fast nur aus Studenten; die wenigen Studentinnen, die es damals in diesem Fach gab, hatten meist den Schwerpunkt Betriebswirtschaft. Das waren in der Regel Unternehmertöchter, die den väterlichen Betrieb übernehmen sollten. Die Abbrecherquote gerade unter den Frauen war sehr hoch.

Ich genoss mehr Freiheiten als zuvor – aber so etwas wie abends ausgehen, während der Woche, war noch immer nicht möglich; meine Mutter übte da eine strenge Kontrolle aus. Es war der Beginn der 60er Jahre, also die Zeit noch vor der sexuellen Liberalisierung. Ich kann mich gut daran erinnern, wie ich meinen Hausarzt darum bat, mir die Pille zu verschreiben. Ich war damals noch nicht verheiratet, aber schon mit meinem späteren Mann zusammen. Der Arzt hat mich nur von oben bis unten angeguckt und rundheraus «Nein!» gesagt – «Nein, so etwas verschreibe ich Ihnen nicht!» Vor meinem Mann hatte es einige kleine Flirts gegeben, aber er war der Erste und Einzige, den ich heiraten wollte. Udo ähnelte, in seiner liebevollen und geduldigen Art, meinem Vater. Als wir uns kennen lernten, war er Assistent an der Universität und ich noch Studentin; ich fand ihn durchaus nett, wenn auch zunächst ein bisschen dröge. Einmal brachte er mich von einem Fest, auf dem ich etwas zu viel getrunken hatte, nach Hause; das fand ich sehr ritterlich, und von da an erwärmte ich mich für ihn. Anfangs haben wir uns viel gestritten. Als Wissenschaftler fand er mich als Studentin zu leichtfertig. Einmal kam ich zu ihm, um mir für eine Seminararbeit ein Thema zu holen, und er fragte erwartungsvoll: «Wofür interessieren Sie sich denn?» Ich erwiderte: «Ist mir ganz egal, geben Sie mir irgendein Thema, das Sie gerade übrig haben.» Er war entsetzt über diese Flapsigkeit; wahrscheinlich hatte er eine Antwort wie: «Ich finde die ‹planification› in Frankreich so wahnsinnig interessant!» erwartet. Aus dieser Seminararbeit hat sich dann übrigens auch das Thema meiner Diplomarbeit entwickelt, die sich mit planwirtschaftlichen Elementen in freien Marktwirtschaften befasste. Aber die Diplomarbeit hat dann nicht mehr mein Mann betreut, sondern ein Kollege von ihm, denn zu dieser Zeit hatten wir schon eine Beziehung miteinander.

Udo warnte auch meinen Vater: «Halte sie bloß davon ab, jetzt schon das Examen zu machen, sie wird durchfallen!» Das ärgerte mich, und ich erklärte: «Wollen wir doch mal sehen, wer hier durchfällt!» Udo holte mich nachmittags von den Examensklausuren ab und wollte wissen, was ich im Einzelnen geschrieben hatte; fast alles, was ich ihm erzählte, war seiner Meinung nach unzureichend oder falsch. «Das solltest du doch besser wissen!», rief er jedes Mal, bis ich ihm verboten habe, mich abzuholen. Ich habe dann aber doch das Examen bestanden – und wir haben bald danach geheiratet.

Udo war immer der Brillantere, was die Wissenschaft angeht, der Seriösere von uns beiden. Dennoch wollte er, dass ich promoviere, und in unseren ersten gemeinsamen Jahren haben wir auch ein paar wissenschaftliche Arbeiten zusammen verfasst; aber es stellte sich bald heraus, dass das nicht gut funktionierte. Wir hatten zu unterschiedliche Vorstellungen und Arbeitsstile; die gemeinsame Arbeit fortzusetzen, wäre das Ende unserer Ehe gewesen. Ich habe um jede meiner Formulierungen gekämpft – er wollte immer meine Sätze optimieren. Er sagte: «Wie willst du das denn beweisen?», und ich sagte: «Warum muss man denn immerfort alles beweisen wollen?» Wir haben dann irgendwann einen Schlussstrich gezogen, ich suchte mir mein eigenes Betätigungsfeld – die Politik. Das war eher intuitiv, aber offenbar eine kluge und richtige Entscheidung, für uns beide allemal die beste Form, produktiv mit Konkurrenz umzugehen. Er ist auf seinem Gebiet gut, ich bin es auf einem anderen; jeder von uns braucht die eigene Domäne. So können wir auch die besonderen Fähigkeiten des anderen jeweils neidlos anerkennen.

Was ich an meinem Mann so schätzte und noch immer schätze, sind seine Zuverlässigkeit und seine ruhige Art. Wir haben höchst gegensätzliche Temperamente, aber wir haben ähnliche weltanschaulich-politische Wertvorstellungen. Natürlich bin ich nach all den Jahren in der Politik pragmatischer als er, und deswegen frage ich immer gleich: «Kann man diese Idee auch umsetzen?», während er sich um die Umsetzung seiner Ideen nicht unbedingt zu kümmern braucht und deswegen häufig auch grundsätzlicher argumentiert. Aber unser gedanklicher Austausch ist immer sehr fruchtbar geblieben.

Meine Eltern mochten Udo. Natürlich wusste meine Mutter zu bemängeln, dass er kleiner ist als ich. Sie hatte mir gegenüber immer aufgetrumpft: «Du kriegst sowieso keinen Mann – und wenn, dann ist der nichts Besonderes.» Ich trug damals noch hohe Absätze, so dass ich Udo um ein ganzes Stück überragte. Das war aber unerhört; ich erinnere mich, dass sich Leute auf der Straße nach uns umdrehten. Mich hat es nie gestört, und auch Udo machte es nichts aus; er hat ein gutes Selbstbewusstsein. Meine Mutter hat später, wenn sie anderen meinen Mann beschreiben sollte, immer gesagt: «Er ist kleiner als Heide und fährt bei Rot über die Ampel.» Aber sie war natürlich durchaus beeindruckt, dass da ein seriöser Mann auftauchte, der mich heiraten wollte. Er war ihr allerdings wiederum schon ein bisschen zu seriös; er führte gern ernsthafte Gespräche, die sie nicht sonderlich interessierten. Mein Vater und Udo dagegen mochten einander sehr, und mein Mann bedauert es noch heute, dass es ihm nie so richtig gelungen ist, einmal mit meinem Vater allein bei einem Glas Bier ausgiebig und intensiv zu diskutieren, ungestört von den Frauen.

Ich war es, die Udo den Heiratsantrag machte – einer musste die Sache ja in die Hand nehmen. Es war an Silvester, wir feierten wie immer bei meinen Eltern, und ich dachte: «Irgendwann muss mal Schluss damit sein, dass alles bei meinen Eltern stattfindet!» Ich habe ihn dann gefragt, ob er mich heiraten wolle, allerdings nur unter der Bedingung, dass ich das Examen bestehe. Er hat kurz trocken geschluckt und dann «Ja» gesagt. Dieser Hochzeitstag! Ich glaube bestimmt, dass mein Mann sich heimlich wünschte, er hätte sich vorher den Fuß gebrochen. Ich sehe uns heute noch vor mir: Er sitzt da, blass, klein, im dunklen

Anzug, und ich daneben mit einem Pillbox wie Jackie Kennedy und einem rosa-lila Ding von Kleid. Ich glaube kaum, dass wir der Klischeevorstellung eines soeben verheirateten glücklichen Paares entsprachen. Aber es war der Aufbruch in einen neuen Lebensabschnitt, eine neue Phase der Freiheit. Neun Semester hatte ich studiert, im Sommer 1967 legte ich an der Universität Kiel das Examen ab. Nun war ich Diplom-Volkswirtin, gerade vierundzwanzig; wir heirateten im Juli, und wenige Wochen später waren wir schon in Afrika.

3

Neue Erfahrungen in fremden Welten

Zu Beginn unserer Ehe hatte ich noch keine klaren Vorstellungen von meiner eigenen beruflichen Zukunft. Nur endlich fort aus dem Elternhaus, unabhängig und selbstständig werden! Das stand für mich an oberster Stelle. Mein Mann hatte schon vor der Hochzeit ein Angebot aus Sambia bekommen, in einem Beraterteam von Präsident Kenneth Kaunda zu arbeiten. Davon versprachen wir uns beide interessante Erfahrungen, denn natürlich war klar, dass ich ihn dorthin begleiten würde. So war ich zunächst einmal anderer Planungen enthoben.

Vorher hatten wir noch eine zweiwöchige Hochzeitsreise nach Italien unternommen. Schon auf der Fahrt in den Süden gab es den ersten Streit. Ich wollte über Nürnberg fahren, um ihm die Stadt meiner Schuljahre zu zeigen – er wollte über Freiburg fahren, das er seit seiner Studienzeit besonders liebte. Da er am Steuer saß, setzte er sich einfach durch, und ich legte ihm eine handfeste Szene hin. Doch danach haben wir diese Reise beide noch sehr genossen. Ich fand es wunderbar, endlich einmal allein zu verreisen. «Allein» hieß für mich: nur wir beiden, zu zweit, denn bis dahin hatte ich ja niemals ohne meine Eltern Ferien gemacht. Anschließend, im Herbst 1967, brachen wir dann nach Sambia auf.

Sambia hatte erst 1964 die politische Unabhängigkeit erlangt. Es war und ist arm, abhängig von Kupfer, einem Rohstoff, dessen Weltmarktpreis in den vergangenen Jahrzehnten dramatisch eingebrochen ist. Dann gab es ein bisschen Kleinindustrie – und das war schon alles. Udos Beratertätigkeit dort war eigentlich auf drei Jahre anberaumt: Er als Volkswirt sollte zusammen mit einem Städteplaner und einem Landwirt gemeinsam Projekte zur Entwicklung des Landes entwerfen. Schon bald stellte sich heraus, dass sie nur für den Papierkorb arbeiteten, dass ihre Arbeit keine politische Auswirkung haben würde. Zwischen ihnen, als Deutschen, und dem Präsidenten standen die englischen Abteilungsleiter der Ministerien und die südafrikanischen Manager der Kupferindustrie. Das Land war noch immer eine versteckte «Kolonie». So ging der Aufenthalt nach eineinhalb Jahren schon zu Ende.

Dabei lebten wir beide in Lusaka durchaus angenehm; mein Mann verdiente gut. Wir wohnten in einem Compound House, mit Garten und einheimischem Personal. Udo wurde mit dem Dienstwagen abgeholt, und ich konnte mir ein kleines Auto kaufen. Weil ich keine Arbeit mit dem Haushalt hatte, habe ich mir bald einen Job gesucht, Deutschunterricht an der Universität gegeben und anschließend eine Stelle bei der Sambian Airways angenommen.

Wenn wir uns so eingerichtet hätten wie die meisten Deutschen in Lusaka, dann hätten wir in den eineinhalb Jahren unseres Aufenthalts dort von der sozialen Wirklichkeit des Landes nicht viel mitbekommen. Die Deutschen bildeten eine geschlossene Gesellschaft für sich, und wenn man keine besonderen Anstrengungen unternahm, lernte man eigentlich nur Deutsche kennen. Sie luden sich gegenseitig ein, gingen am Sonntag zu einem deutschen Brunch und anschließend in den deutschen Club; sie trieben miteinander Sport und kauften alle in derselben Hand voll Geschäfte ein. Wer zum Essen ausging, besuchte immer eines der beiden Lokale, die an Lusakas einziger langer staubiger Hauptstraße lagen, und stieß dort fast nur auf Europäer. Wenn man etwas weiter hinausfuhr, gab es noch ein drittes Restaurant. Man traf ständig und überall auf dieselben alten Bekannten.

Im einzigen Metzgerladen gab es zwei Theken. An der einen erhielt man die üblichen Fleisch- und Wurstwaren, an der anderen wurde «dog's food», verkauft, Hundefutter, und hier standen die Einheimischen an. Zwar sah man keine Schilder «nur für Weiße» – «nur für Schwarze» mehr, aber «dog's food» bewirkte genau das Gleiche. Das Sambia, das wir kennen lernten, war noch immer eine koloniale Gesellschaft. Auch bei der Sambian Airways arbeiteten überwiegend Europäer und nur wenige schwarze Afrikaner. Ich war dort als Assistentin einer Stabsstelle zugeordnet.

In meiner Freizeit bin ich nicht in die Clubs der Europäer gegangen, weil die Gespräche dort mich bald langweilten. Stattdessen arbeitete ich in Frauenprojekten mit, an denen sich auch Einheimische beteiligten. Die meisten dieser Projekte waren kirchlich initiiert. Sambia ist fast vollständig christlich, und die Kirche hat dort eine große Bedeutung. Ich habe im Kirchenchor gesungen und in Selbsthilfegruppen mitgearbeitet. Darüber erfuhr ich einiges von den strukturellen Problemen des Landes, und ich fing an, mich intensiver für Entwicklungshilfe zu interessieren. Die Statistiken zur Situation der Frauen und insbesondere die über die Säuglingssterblichkeit waren erschreckend. Wir weißen Frauen versuchten, die schwarzen Frauen davon zu überzeugen, dass sie ihre Babys nicht mit pulverisierter Fertigmilch ernähren, sondern wieder lange stillen sollten. Sobald die Frauen dort ein bisschen Geld hatten, kauften sie nämlich Trockenmilch, weil es so schön bequem war, die nur einfach anzurühren. Doch vielen war nicht klar, dass man das dazu benötigte Wasser vorher unbedingt abkochen und die Fläschchen sterilisieren muss. Die Babys auf den Werbefotos für Pulvermilch sahen trügerisch rund und glücklich aus, aber viele, die damit ernährt wurden, erkrankten und starben. Wir haben versucht, etwas dagegen zu unternehmen, durchaus mit einem bescheidenen Erfolg. Für mich war die Arbeit in diesen Gruppen ein erstes intensives, emotional motiviertes politisches Engagement. Überhaupt schärfte diese erste größere und längere Distanz zu Europa meinen Blick für die Probleme des Nord-Süd-Gefälles und die Unzulänglichkeiten der Entwicklungspolitik.

Nach eineinhalb Jahren in Lusaka beschlossen mein Mann und ich dann aber doch, unsere Zelte in Sambia abzubrechen. Es war auf Dauer einfach nicht befriedigend für ihn, nur Geld zu verdienen und bequem zu leben, dabei aber politisch überhaupt nichts zu bewirken. Alle Pläne, die er entwickelt hatte, blieben in irgendwelchen Kanälen stecken. Eigentlich hatten wir noch vorgehabt, eine «große» Afrikatour zu machen, doch wurde es am Ende eine interessante, aber «kleine» Tour. Denn das Reisen war damals sehr mühsam, und das ist es wohl bis heute geblieben. 1969 kehrten wir nach einer Schiffsumrundung Afrikas nach Kiel zurück.

Udo bekam eine von der Deutschen Forschungsgemeinschaft finanzierte, auf ein Jahr befristete Stelle, und ich suchte mir erst einmal einen Job als Sekretärin. Briefe tippen, Ablage und Termine machen, Kaffee kochen – was eine Sekretärin eben so macht. Hauptsache, ich verdiente mein eigenes Geld. Wir hatten eine geräumige, großzügige Altbauwohnung bezogen. Ich hätte nicht wie andere junge Paare in hutzeligen kleinen Wohnungen leben können, denn kleine Zimmer lösen in mir sofort Beklemmung aus, Erinnerungen an meine früheren Asthmaanfälle. Ich brauche hohe Räume und offene Türen. Die Altbauwohnung in Kiel war in Ordnung, doch vieles war jetzt für uns ganz anders als in Lusaka. Nun erst fiel mir auf, dass mein Mann von seiner Mutter ziemlich verwöhnt worden war; er tat zu meiner Überraschung im Haushalt keinen Handschlag. In Afrika hatte das keine Rolle gespielt, denn dort hatte ja der «Boy» sämtliche Hausarbeiten erledigt. Doch jetzt entwickelte sich dieser Teil unseres Alltags zu einer Quelle potenzieller Konflikte. Wir konnten dann aber glücklicherweise nach einigen heftigen Auseinandersetzungen ein paar grundsätzliche Verabredungen treffen. Außerdem beschäftigten wir eine Hilfe, die zweimal wöchentlich kam, und ich bestand von Anfang an darauf, sämtliche Haushaltsgeräte anzuschaffen, die zur Arbeitserleichterung beitragen. Alle riefen: «Zu zweit braucht ihr ja wohl keine Spülmaschine!» Doch für mich war das eine Strategie, überflüssige Spannungen zwischen uns beiden zu vermeiden.

Heute ist mein Mann wirklich sehr bereitwillig in allen diesen Dingen. Er kauft ein, wenn ich ihn darum bitte, er leert die Mülleimer, füllt die Waschmaschine, macht die Betten. Aber es gibt immer noch diese Situation, dass er am Schreibtisch sitzt, in seine Arbeit vertieft; ich bitte ihn um etwas, er ruft: «Ich komme gleich!» – und dann vergehen Stunden. «Gleich» bedeutet bei ihm eben etwas ganz anderes als bei mir.

In diesen ersten Jahren unserer Ehe war ja nicht nur Afrika exotisches Neuland, sondern auch das Zusammenleben als Paar. Die Beziehung zwischen meinem Mann und mir hat viele Phasen durchlaufen und viele Veränderungen erfahren, aber spannungsvoll ist sie immer gewesen. Das hängt vermutlich in erster Linie mit mir, und das heißt mit meinem schwierigen Verhältnis zu meiner Mutter, zusammen. In meinem Elternhaus hatte ich immer das Gefühl, gegen tatsächliche oder vermeintliche Wände zu laufen, ich musste mich ständig gegen Einengung wehren und um Freiraum kämpfen. Noch heute kann ich ausrasten, wenn ich das Gefühl habe, mein Mann will mir Vorschriften machen. Ich habe sehr lange gebraucht, bis ich mich selber ein bisschen durchschaut und gemerkt habe: Da laufen doch immer die gleichen Prozesse bei dir ab. Insgesamt hatte uns Sambia vor diesem Hintergrund beim Einstieg in unsere Ehe gut getan. Wir waren von familiären Einflüssen weit entfernt, niemand konnte uns in unser Leben hineinreden, und so hatten wir die Chance, uns recht gut zusammenzuraufen.

Meine Eltern lebten nach wie vor in Kiel, ebenso Dodo, die inzwischen ihre eigene Wohnung bezogen hatte. Barbara hatte geheiratet und war mit ihrem Mann nach Göttingen gezogen. Udo und ich führten nun wieder ein einigermaßen normales Leben, mit den akademischen Zirkeln im Umkreis der Uni als

Bezugsgruppe. Das war für meinen Geschmack ein viel zu homogenes soziales Umfeld, nur um weniges anregender als die geschlossene Gesellschaft der Deutschen in Lusaka. Doch als es anfing, mir zu eng zu werden, ergab sich schon wieder eine neue aufregende Veränderung: Wir gingen nach Japan.

Japan galt damals als das erfolgreichste Land auf seinem besonderen Weg in die hochindustrialisierte Gesellschaft. Udo hatte seine Doktorarbeit über die ökonomische und politische Situation Chinas geschrieben und mit Sambia ein Entwicklungsland näher kennen gelernt. 1970 wurden vom japanischen Staat zwölf Stipendien für Wissenschaftler auf der ganzen Welt ausgeschrieben – und eines davon bekam mein Mann.

In diesem Fall war es offiziell nicht vorgesehen, dass ich ihn 1971 nach Tokio begleitete; ein Japaner nahm damals für einen ein- bis zweijährigen Auslandsaufenthalt seine Familie nicht mit. Von dem winzigen Stipendium konnten wir dort auch zu zweit nicht leben, obwohl man uns ein kleines Appartement im Gästehaus der Universität zugewiesen hatte. Also suchte ich mir sofort wieder Arbeit. Durch Vermittlung eines Mannes, der mit Udo zusammen studiert hatte und im japanischen Außenministerium tätig war, erhielt ich zunächst die Möglichkeit, am Goethe-Institut Deutsch zu unterrichten, und dazu hatte ich auch einige Privatschüler. Was unseren Lebensstandard betraf, war unser Aufenthalt in Japan das vollkommene Kontrastprogramm zu dem in Sambia. Wir lebten sehr einfach und bescheiden, mitten im pulsierenden Alltagsleben von Tokio.

Schon bald bekam ich ein Arbeitsangebot, das mich mehr reizte als der Sprachunterricht. Die Firma Triumph International hatte das erste deutsch-japanische Joint Venture gestartet. Zu dieser Zeit trugen die Japanerinnen noch keine BHs, denn nach ihren Schönheitsvorstellungen sollte alles flach sein unter dem Kimono; sie trugen auch keine Strumpfhosen, das wäre viel zu umständlich gewesen, wenn sie zur Toilette mussten. Denn da sind die vielen Bänder und Gürtel, Oberkimono, Unterkimono, kein einziger Knopf. Damals trug die traditionelle

Japanerin unter dem Kimono nahezu nichts. Angesichts solcher Gepflogenheiten war es nicht ganz einfach, in diesem Land BHs und Strumpfhosen zu verkaufen, und erste Versuche in dieser Richtung hatten sich als Flop erwiesen. Man hatte es sich auch reichlich einfach gemacht mit der Planung. Weil die Japanerinnen kleiner sind als die Europäerinnen, hatte man einfach versucht, alle Modelle nur etwas zu verkleinern. Doch damit war es keineswegs getan, denn die Japanerinnen sind auch anders gebaut. Sie haben flachere Becken, weniger Busen, kürzere Beine – «Rettichbeine», sagten die japanischen Männer, was nicht besonders schmeichelhaft klingt.

Nun saß ich also in der Marketingabteilung von Triumph International und sollte Verkaufsstrategien entwickeln. Ich war gar nicht schlecht darin! Ich habe mir erst einmal wissenschaftliche Literatur besorgt. Außer den Unterschieden in Größe, Körperbau und Gewicht mussten noch andere kulturelle Unterschiede berücksichtigt werden. Die Japanerinnen mögen ganz andere Farben als wir, am liebsten so eine Art Muschelfarbe, wie mit Milch übergossen. Damals zumindest hätten die wenigsten einen kirschroten Kimono angezogen oder schwarze Negligés getragen. Also haben wir nicht nur ganz anders geschnittene Strumpfhosen entwickelt, sondern auch ein vollkommen neues Farbspektrum eingeführt. Ich habe die dazugehörige Strategie entworfen und die Verkaufskampagne mitgeleitet, die dann auch recht erfolgreich war.

Persönlichen Kontakt mit Japanerinnen hatte ich dagegen nur wenig. Deren Aktivitäten waren zu dieser Zeit noch weitgehend auf das Haus beschränkt. In unserer Firma arbeiteten nur einige und dann in untergeordneten Positionen; sie pflegten vollkommen andere Umgangsformen. Einmal hatten wir ein Treffen mit japanischen Kollegen in einem Teehaus. Während wir dort auf Matten am Boden saßen, öffnete sich die Tür, und die Gattin einer der Männer kam herein, warf sich auf die Knie und verbeugte sich. Das war wohl Teil einer ganz normalen Begrüßungszeremonie, doch für Europäerinnen ist so etwas

eher beklemmend und kaum eine Basis für eine tiefere Freund-
schaft. Ich selbst hatte überwiegend mit Männern zu tun, auch
während ich noch Deutschunterricht gab. Die japanischen
Männer hatten mit mir wohl ihre Probleme. Für eine Frau war
ich zum einen viel zu groß, ich überragte die meisten Japaner
um Kopfeslänge. Deren Köpfe lagen in der U-Bahn dann
immer an meiner Brust, wenn man dort in der Rushhour dicht
zusammengepfercht stand. Ich war außerdem zu schlaksig,
hatte eine vorstehende Nase, zu große Füße, machte keine netten Trippelschrittchen, und ich sprach und lachte einfach viel
zu laut. Die Japanerinnen nehmen beim Lachen immer ver-
schämt die Hand vor den Mund, lauthals herauszulachen, gilt
als sehr gewöhnlich. Für die japanischen Männer war ich einfach keine richtige Frau. Da ich aber auch kein Mann war, bil-
dete ich eine Sonderkategorie: sozusagen alle Scheußlichkeiten
zusammen.

Ich bin später, als ich schon Ministerpräsidentin war, noch
einige Male in Japan gewesen, und jedes Mal ist mir dieses Land
aufs Neue gleichermaßen bekannt und fremd erschienen, viel
fremder als China. Viele japanische Rituale erscheinen uns komisch, zum Beispiel diese Verbeugungen. Wenn ein Japaner
den Status eines neuen Gesprächspartners noch nicht kennt,
verbeugt er sich und verbeugt sich und sucht dabei aus den
Augenwinkeln nach einem kleinen Hinweis auf die soziale Stellung des anderen. Das Verbeugen nimmt kein Ende, bis endlich
eine Visitenkarte auftaucht, die ihm Aufschluss und damit Er-
leichterung verschafft. Vorher kann er noch nicht mit dem anderen reden, nur ein bisschen murmeln, da auch Wortwahl und
Satzkonstruktion vom Status des Gesprächspartners abhängig
sind.

Ich fand den Aufenthalt in Japan dennoch sehr interessant
und habe mich dort durchaus gut gefühlt; allerdings hätte ich
nicht viel länger bleiben können. Vor allem die sprachliche
Barriere hat mich sehr beeinträchtigt. Es hätte aber angesichts
des zeitlichen begrenzten Aufenthalts nur wenig Zweck gehabt,

Japanisch zu lernen. Die Worte lernt man schnell, doch Ausländer haben große Schwierigkeiten mit den Feinheiten der Satzkonstruktion und mit den in verschiedenen sozialen Situationen angemessenen Ausdrucksweisen. Es gibt nicht nur eine Männer- und eine Frauensprache, es gibt auch viele subtile Sprachcodes, die für uns unendlich schwer zu begreifen sind. Einmal wurde ich von einem japanischen Bekannten zum Essen eingeladen. Er fragte, wo und was ich denn essen wolle, unterbreitete verschiedene Vorschläge, und ich machte den riesigen Fehler zu erwidern, dass mir alles gleichermaßen angenehm sei. Diese Antwort brachte den Mann in allergrößte Schwierigkeiten, denn nun wusste er erst recht nicht, was mir eigentlich am liebsten war, und er versuchte lange, irgendeinen Hinweis zu erhalten, indem er seine Vorschläge wiederholte und andere hinzufügte. Wenn ich nicht ganz unjapanisch entschieden hätte: «Gehen wir doch einfach dahin!», dann ständen wir vielleicht noch heute da. Es ist sehr anstrengend für uns Europäer, in einem Kulturkreis zu leben, der in seinen sprachlichen und körperlichen Ausdrucksformen derart indirekt und so viel kontrollierter ist als der unsere. Der Kontakt mit Afrikanern war in dieser Hinsicht wesentlich einfacher; sie sind offen und direkt im Ausdruck ihrer Gefühle und Gedanken.

Damals war Japan noch ein Wirtschaftswunderland und das große wirtschaftliche Vorbild für uns und andere. Noch deutete nichts darauf hin, dass die japanische Wirtschaft einmal in die kritische Situation kommen würde, in der sie sich heute befindet. Allerdings waren wir über manches doch sehr erstaunt. Zum Beispiel gab es zu dieser Zeit in der Weltstadt Tokio noch keine integrierte Kanalisation, die Abwässer flossen vielfach noch durch offene Straßenkanäle – wie bei uns im Mittelalter. Dennoch waren die Japaner die Ersten, die in ihren ökonomischen Planungen das Konzept der «Lebensqualität» berücksichtigten, bevor dann auch bei uns davon gesprochen wurde.

Die verschiedenen Dimensionen der Lebensqualität und entsprechender Indikatorensysteme interessierten meinen Mann besonders. Als wir 1972 nach Kiel zurückkehrten, bekam er gleich ein Habilitationsstipendium und begann, darüber zu arbeiten. 1973 erhielt er den Ruf auf eine Professur für Ökonomie an der Technischen Universität Berlin. Ich fand, nun sei es auch bei mir endlich an der Zeit für einen richtigen Beruf, und ich suchte mir eine Stelle beim Arbeitsamt. Solange mein Vater dort noch tätig gewesen war – einige Jahre als Direktor des Kieler Arbeitsamtes –, mochte ich mich nicht bewerben. Doch als er an die Bundesanstalt für Arbeit in Nürnberg versetzt wurde, bewarb ich mich als Berufsberaterin in Kiel. Das war durchaus interessant, obwohl es schon damals, Mitte der siebziger Jahre, eine schwierige wirtschaftliche Phase gab, in der Leute mit Ausbildungswünschen zu uns kamen, für die einfach keine Stellen existierten.

Interesse für Politik hatte ich schon während des Studiums entwickelt. Damals war ich zu Wahlversammlungen und anderen politischen Veranstaltungen gegangen. Außerdem hatte ich nebenher immer wieder Vorlesungen zu Politik und Zeitgeschichte gehört, die nicht direkt mit meinem Fach zu tun hatten. Die Studentenclique, mit der ich in dieser Zeit zusammen war, besuchte gemeinsam die Veranstaltungen von Reimut Jochimsen, dem jungen, neu nach Kiel berufenen Professor für Volkswirtschaftslehre, der offen auch politische Fragen diskutierte. Einige dieser Jochimsen-Schüler haben später verantwortungsvolle Positionen in Wirtschaft und Politik übernommen.

1969, nachdem wir aus Sambia zurückgekehrt waren, war ich in die SPD eingetreten. Ich hatte schon in Afrika den Vorsatz gefasst, mich zu Hause politisch zu engagieren und unter anderem für eine bessere Entwicklungspolitik einzusetzen. Der aktuelle Anlass für meinen Beitritt war allerdings die Mitarbeit bei einer Wahlkampagne, die, im Rückblick betrachtet, gar nichts Spektakuläres an sich hatte. «Karlchen» Schiller, der damalige Wirtschaftsminister, hatte den Vorschlag gemacht, die D-Mark aufzuwerten. Kein normaler Durchschnittsbürger verstand so richtig, wozu das gut sein sollte, doch es war das große Wahlkampfthema. Also gründeten wir eine Wählerinitiative, die es sich zur Aufgabe machte, jedem, der anrief, am Telefon zu erklären, was eine Aufwertung bedeutet. Jedes Mitglied unserer Gruppe hatte sich dafür zweimal am Tag zwei Stunden zur Verfügung gestellt. Damals habe ich zum ersten Mal gemerkt, dass mir politische Diskussionen Spaß machen, dass es mir gefällt, Menschen zu überzeugen und ihnen wirtschaftliche Zusammenhänge so zu erklären, dass sie sie wirklich verstehen. Wenn man mit abgehobenen Äußerungen daherkommt wie «Die Elastizität der Exporte nimmt ab», dann wollen die meisten gar nicht mehr zuhören. Noch heute gehe ich ab und zu in Schulklassen, um Kindern am Beispiel ihres Taschengeldes zu erklären, was ein ausgeglichener Haushalt ist oder warum auch der Staat auf Dauer nicht mehr ausgeben kann, als er einnimmt. Mir hat die Aktion um die D-Mark-Aufwertung so gefallen, dass ich mich zusammen mit einigen anderen aus der Wählerinitiative entschied, in die SPD einzutreten, zumal sie aus meiner Sicht die einzige Partei war, die das Thema Entwicklungspolitik ernst nahm.

Mir wurde bald klar, dass die Politik genau das richtige Betätigungsfeld für mich war. Die Treffen des Ortsvereins allerdings waren anfangs etwas ernüchternd. In der einen Ecke saßen die gestandenen Parteimitglieder, die Honoratioren, in der anderen Ecke hockte das junge Gemüse, das immer nur motzte – zu denen gehörte ich. Es stand von vornherein fest, dass die Alten politisch eher rechts waren und die Jüngeren links. Zunächst einmal bekam man ungeliebte Aufgaben wie die der Ortsvereinskassiererin zugewiesen. Natürlich gab es auch informelle, gut eingespielte Strukturen, die dazu dienten, die Neuen außen vor zu lassen. Offiziell wurde beispielsweise bis gegen elf Uhr getagt. Dann äußerte jemand: «Anständige Menschen brauchen ihren Schlaf», und man ging auseinander. Erstaunlicherweise wurden dann aber anschließend völlig andere Dinge gemacht, als wir vor elf Uhr gemeinsam besprochen hatten! Wenn wir uns beschwerten, liefen wir gegen Wände. Das Geheimnis bestand darin, dass sich die Eingeweihten nach der offiziellen Sitzung immer noch in einem Hinterraum der Kneipe zusammensetzten, in dem dann die eigentlichen Entscheidungen getroffen wurden. Als ich dieses Prinzip begriffen hatte, bin ich auch in den Hinterraum gezogen und habe stets bis zum bitteren Ende ausgeharrt. Das hat dann zu mancher Auseinandersetzung mit meinem Mann geführt, wenn ich erst um zwei, halb drei Uhr nach Hause kam. Udo sagte: «Musst du denn eigentlich immer die Letzte sein?» Und ich versuchte, ihm zu erklären, dass ich einfach das Letzte mitkriegen musste, das da verhandelt wurde. Er ist übrigens erst sehr spät SPD-Mitglied geworden; von Anfang an war zwischen uns klar, dass die Politik meine Domäne sein würde, so wie seine die Wissenschaft war.

Inzwischen ist es wohl etwas besser geworden mit diesen Endlos-Sitzungen in den Ortsvereinen, jedenfalls hier bei uns in Schleswig-Holstein. Es gibt ja nun auch viel mehr Frauen in der Politik, Mütter mit kleinen Kindern, die sich solche Unsitten nicht mehr gefallen lassen und darauf bestehen, dass verbindlich abgestimmt wird und die Treffen nicht mehr die halbe Nacht dauern. Trotzdem spielen informelle und halboffizielle Strukturen immer noch eine große Rolle.

Meine politische Karriere wäre beinahe schon damals, ganz am Anfang, gescheitert. Ich riss immer sofort die Gosche auf und wurde gleich zur Kreistagsdelegierten gewählt, nach dem Motto: «Dann kann sie ja mal zeigen, ob sie das besser kann.» Dort riss ich den Mund wieder auf. Es traf sich, dass gerade die Devise ausgegeben worden war: «Wir wollen mehr Frauen aus allen gesellschaftlichen Schichten haben.» Jemand kam zu mir und fragte: «Willst du in der Kommunalpolitik etwas werden?», und ich sagte natürlich: «Na klar!» Ein anderer hielt dagegen: «Sie versteht doch überhaupt nichts von Kommunalpolitik!» Daraufhin erklärte ich vergnügt: «Stimmt – aber das kann man ja wohl lernen!» So landete ich schließlich auf einem der letzten Listenplätze für die bevorstehende Kommunalwahl. Dieser Platz war eigentlich hoffnungslos. Ich konnte nicht erwarten, von diesem Platz aus ins Rathaus einzuziehen. Aber ich empfand das schon als Erfolg vor dem Hintergrund, dass ich ja relativ neu war und wirklich keine Ahnung hatte.

Gleich nach der Wahl gingen wir nach Japan. Durch ein paar Zufälle rutschten dann Leute vor mir aus der Liste; einige, weil sie bei der Landtagswahl als Direktkandidaten gewählt worden waren, andere verschwanden aus anderen Gründen. Plötzlich hieß es: «Heide Simonis ist die nächste Nachrückerin.» Heide Simonis aber weilte mit ihrem Mann in Japan. Ich habe dann einen Brief geschrieben: «Liebe Genossen, ich bitte euch, das Mandat für mich zu reservieren!» Eigentlich geht so etwas gar nicht; wundersamerweise haben sie es trotzdem getan. Vielleicht war es damals lockerer, weil es sich nur um eine Kommunalwahl handelte und so wenig Frauen aktiv waren. Jedenfalls hätte meine politische Karriere schon hier, ganz am Anfang, enden können. So aber wartete das Mandat tatsächlich auf mich, als wir aus Japan zurückkehrten; und ich habe meinen Platz im Rathaus mit großer Begeisterung eingenommen.

Im Kieler Rat gab es damals 30 SPD-Abgeordnete, darunter nur drei oder vier Frauen. Meine Bezugsgruppe war die kleine Schar der Linken. Wir haben manche Schlacht geschlagen, allerdings die meisten verloren, weil wir in der Minderheit waren. Wenn ich heute daran denke, welche Themen und Auseinandersetzungen uns damals so weltbewegend erschienen, dass wir uns tage- und nächtelang, manchmal über viele Wochen, darüber erhitzten! Aber auch das muss man mal mitgemacht haben.

1975 wurde ich überraschend als Landtagskandidatin aufgestellt. Unsere Leute hatten sich so zerstritten, dass der rechte Flügel dem linken nicht mehr traute und umgekehrt; die Spannungen wurden so groß, dass es schwer war, miteinander einen Wahlkampf zu führen. Der Kandidat des einen Flügels warf die Brocken hin, und die Genossen sahen sich verzweifelt nach jemandem um, der für beide Seiten tragbar war; sie haben dann

mich ausgeguckt, weil ich von außen kam. Aus dem Landtags-
mandat wurde dann zwar nichts, aber es war knapp; ich hätte es
beinahe geschafft – mein CDU-Rivale hatte nur rund 300 Stimmen Vorsprung.

1976 kam dann das Mandat für den Bundestagswahlkampf.
Bis dahin hatte ich meine Energien noch ziemlich gleichmäßig
zwischen meinem Job als Berufsberaterin und der Politik verteilt. Wenn es damals mit Bonn nicht geklappt hätte, hätte ich
mir vermutlich noch einmal einen anderen Beruf gesucht,
denn auf Dauer wäre mir die Beratung wohl zu einseitig geworden. Eine Freundin von mir arbeitete im psychologischen
Dienst, und eine Zeit lang hatte ich das als weitere Entwick-
lungsmöglichkeit erwogen. Aber eigentlich war die Politik für
mich genau das Richtige. Sie ist vielseitig in den Anforderungen, und sie bietet viele verschiedene Tätigkeitsfelder; ich wusste gleich, sie würde mir nie langweilig werden.

Man hatte mir im Kreis Rendsburg-Eckernförde, meinem
ländlich strukturierten Wahlkreis, nur wenig Chancen bei der
Bundestagswahl eingeräumt. Mein Gegner war ein erfolgrei-
cher Lobbyist, ein Bauernführer mit fester, großer Anhänger-
schaft. Gegen so jemanden kann man nur einen Kandidaten
mit ähnlicher Hausmacht aufstellen – oder eben jemanden, der
ganz anders ist. Etwas Ähnliches wie ihn aber hatte die SPD
nicht, und so entschied man sich zum Kontrastprogramm: Ich
war eine Generation jünger, und ich war eine Frau. Wir hatten
mit Achtungserfolgen gerechnet, doch alle waren der Meinung: «Gewinnen kann sie nicht.» Dabei hatte ich nur eine
Chance als Direktkandidatin; über die Liste hätte ich es nicht in
den Bundestag geschafft, denn da lag ich ziemlich weit hinten.
Es ist schwer zu sagen, warum es dann tatsächlich geklappt hat –
die Schleswig-Holsteiner wählen manchmal anders, als man
denkt. Vielleicht war es wirklich der Bonus der jungen Frau, das
Image des Kessen, noch Unverbrauchten. Mein CDU-Gegner
soll später behauptet haben, ich hätte ihn nur geschlagen, weil
ich mit einer ziemlich durchsichtigen Bluse Wahlkampf ge-

macht hätte. Aber ich bin sicher, dass ich es auch im Roll-kragenpullover geschafft hätte.

Am Abend des Wahltags, als die Ergebnisse durchgegeben wurden, war ich zusammen mit meinem Mann im Landeshaus. Es waren nicht mehr viele der Kandidaten dort; die meisten waren schon in ihren Wahlkreisen, um ihre Anhänger zu trös-ten oder mit ihnen zu feiern, je nachdem. Es dauerte lange mit den genauen Daten an diesem Tag. Damals wurde noch richtig per Hand gezählt, und weil sie sich beim letzten Mal peinlicher-weise verzählt hatten, wollten sie diesmal ganz sichergehen. Udo und ich standen etwas einsam in der Gegend herum. Dann liefen auf einmal die Ergebnisse meines Wahlkreises über den Ticker: «Gewonnen hat die SPD.» «Das bin ja ich!», rief ich und stieß meinen Mann in die Seite. Ich konnte es noch gar nicht so richtig fassen. An diesem Abend trug ich ein langes Kleid, und neben mir hörte ich eine Frau naserümpfend sagen: «In diesem Fähnchen hat die gewonnen!» Es war eine Riesenüberra-schung, für uns beide wie für alle anderen.

4

Endlich richtig mitmischen!
Abenteuer Bundestag

Ich war gerade mal 33 Jahre alt, als ich im September 1976 zum Mitglied des Bundestags gewählt wurde, und schon wenig später, im Oktober, betrat ich zum ersten Mal das Bundeshaus in Bonn, das nah am Rhein gelegene Hochhaus. Während der nächsten elf Jahre sollte ich nun zwischen Bonn und Kiel hin- und herpendeln. Das bedeutete, wenn nicht ausnahmsweise Parlamentsferien waren, ein zweigeteiltes Leben; drei bis fünf intensive, arbeitsreiche Tage in Bonn, und der Rest der Woche bestand aus oft nicht minder anstrengenden Tagen in Kiel. Das Wochenende musste ich nun zwischen meiner Arbeit im Wahl- kreis und meinem Mann teilen.

Wir hatten uns, weil meine Wahl so unwahrscheinlich schien, vorher gar nicht richtig überlegt, welch gewaltige Veränderun- gen der Sprung nach Bonn mit sich bringen würde. Immerhin waren wir inzwischen schon daran gewöhnt, eine Wochenend- ehe zu führen, denn Udo hatte drei Jahre zuvor einen Lehrstuhl an der Technischen Universität Berlin angenommen. Er hatte dort eine kleine Wohnung gemietet, und manchmal genoss ich einen kurzen Abstecher nach Berlin. Aber in der Regel verbrach- ten wir die Wochenenden in Schleswig-Holstein. Ich hatte bei meiner Aufstellung für die Wahl versprochen, in meinen Wahl- kreis zu ziehen, und deswegen wohnen wir seit 1977 in Bordes- holm, einen schönen historischen Ort südlich von Kiel.

Das politische Bonn, in dem sich nun der größte Teil meines Lebens abspielte, war ein ganz anderes als das Bonn meiner Kindheit. Ich betrat eine völlig neue Bühne, eine andere Welt. Es begann damit, dass man jeden Morgen von einem Wagen der Fahrbereitschaft abgeholt und ins Bundeshaus gebracht wurde – ein völlig neues Lebensgefühl. Erst nach einer Weile lernte ich, dass es sich empfahl, ein angemessenes Trinkgeld zu zahlen – die Fahrer ließen Abgeordnete, die dies nicht taten, immer gern länger warten. Ich hatte ein Büro in der berühmten 17. Etage des «Langen Eugen» – dort, wo alle Parteilinken saßen – und außerdem zwei Mitarbeiterinnen, von denen die eine für die Bonner Angelegenheiten, die andere für den Wahlkreis in Schleswig-Holstein zuständig war. Und dann ging es los mit den Sitzungen, den Arbeitskreisen und Gruppentreffen, den Sprechstunden und all den anderen Terminen...

Das Gefühl, dabei zu sein, mitmischen zu können, hat mir von Anfang an Freude gemacht, obwohl es natürlich einige Zeit dauerte, bis ich halbwegs begriff, nach welchen Regeln gespielt wurde. Da waren zunächst die ganz banalen technischen Probleme: Wo bestellt man hier im Haus die Flugtickets für eine Reise? Wie stellt man es an, eine Dienstreise ins Ausland zu bekommen? Manche schienen immer Dienstreisen zu machen, andere durften offenbar nie. Eine große Hilfe bei all diesen Dingen war mir der Kollege Norbert Gansel, der mich in der ersten Zeit unter seine Fittiche nahm. Für ihn war es bereits die zweite Legislaturperiode, und er erklärte mir gleich: «Du wirst ein ganzes Jahr damit verlieren, nur das simple Wer, Was, Wann, Wo und Warum zu kapieren.»

Norbert Gansel, Horst Jungmann und ich taten uns im «Nordpool» zusammen, einer kleinen Aktions- und Bürogemeinschaft. Wir sahen uns am linken Rand der Fraktion, fanden uns radikal und innovativ, pflegten einen intensiven Gedankenaustausch, stärkten und stützten uns gegenseitig. Das war eine gute Sache für mich, nicht nur, weil es die anfängliche Phase der Desorientierung verkürzte, sondern auch, weil es dabei half, die eigene politische Identität in dieser Umgebung zu finden. Es dauerte schon eine Weile, sich im Spannungsfeld der verschiedenen formellen und informellen Bonner Gruppierungen zurechtzufinden. Da gab es die Gruppierungen mit größerem politischen Einfluss, in die man nicht ohne weiteres hineinkam, und es gab jene, in denen man unbedingt dabei sein musste.

Jeder Abgeordnete hat in einem Ausschuss mitzuarbeiten. Von Anfang an schien mir der Haushaltsausschuss am interessantesten, doch die Zuteilung zu den Ausschüssen wurde vom Fraktionsvorsitzenden Herbert Wehner persönlich vorgenommen, und der fand es wohl ziemlich anmaßend von mir, dass ich mich als Neuling gleich um so etwas Wichtiges bewarb. Die Neuen wurden nämlich immer dahin gesteckt, wo sonst niemand hinwollte. Ich kam aus Schleswig-Holstein, einem Agrarland, also schob er mich erst einmal in den Landwirtschaftsausschuss. Der galt deswegen als schwierig, da schon damals viele Dinge von Brüssel aus gesteuert wurden und man meist nur abnicken konnte. Typischerweise saßen eine ganze Reihe von Frauen in diesem Ausschuss. Ich habe aber nicht locker gelassen und Herbert Wehner wiederholt bedrängt: «Merk mich doch wenigstens als Stellvertreter vor, wenn im Haushaltsausschuss jemand ausfällt!» Erstaunlicherweise klappte es dann ziemlich schnell, schon nach wenigen Wochen. Das zeigt, wie wichtig es in der Politik ist, vielleicht gerade für Frauen, nicht zu lieb und zu brav zu sein, sondern durchaus ein bisschen penetrant und vor allem immer am Ball zu bleiben.

Ich stürzte mich also Hals über Kopf in die Arbeit im Haushaltsausschuss, in das Bonner politische Leben überhaupt, und fand alles sehr interessant und aufregend. Ich kam gar nicht dazu, mich einsam zu fühlen. Zunächst einmal war ich bei Bekannten untergekommen, anschließend hatte ich kurze Zeit eine gemeinsame Wohnung mit einer Bundestagsmitarbeiterin, dann aber suchte ich mir eine eigene kleine Wohnung im Bonner Stadtteil Pützchen. Ich besaß keinen Fernseher, denn es gab gar keine Zeit, in der ich hätte fernsehen können. Ich bin in meinen Bonner Jahren höchstens dreimal im Kino gewesen. Noch ein paar Seiten eines Buchs, vor dem Einschlafen – mehr war nicht drin. Man muss dieses Leben einfach mögen, um es in seiner Intensität auszuhalten, aber ich wusste gleich: «Das ist es!» Ich empfand die politische Arbeit als ein lustvolles Spiel und genoss es, mittendrin zu sein, auch wenn es anfangs eher die Illusion der Macht war als tatsächliche Macht.

Ich kann mich noch genau an meine erste Rede im Bundestag erinnern. Ich war Berichterstatterin für das Haushaltskapitel «Jugend und Familie». Klar, dass man mir ausgerechnet dieses Kapitel zugeschoben hatte: wenn schon als Frau im Haushaltsausschuss, dann eben für «Jugend und Familie». Ich musste meine Jungfernrede abends nach acht Uhr halten, ich war sehr aufgeregt, und an einer bestimmten Stelle hatte ich ein richtiges Blackout. Zwar lag das Redemanuskript vor mir, aber ich fand in der Aufregung die richtige Zeile nicht wieder. Dabei hatte ich mich so auf meine erste Rede gespitzt, ich wollte Weltbewegendes sagen, und nun war es, als würde sich der Boden vor mir auftun. Dazu muss man sich die Atmosphäre im Bundestag vorstellen, es war unruhig, laut, alle waren müde, es gab dumme Zwischenrufe. Später gewöhnt man sich an so was, aber damals fühlte ich mich grässlich. Ich habe ganz schnell aus diesem Vorfall gelernt und von da an nur noch Redemanuskripte verwendet, die in großer, gut leserlicher Type geschrieben sind, oft nur Stichworte, so dass man den Faden leicht wiederfindet, wenn man zwischendurch aufsieht und das Publikum anschaut.

Ich erinnere mich noch an ein anderes Drama aus den ersten Monaten im Haushaltsausschuss. Es war mir inzwischen gelungen, innerhalb des Haushaltsausschusses von «Jugend und Familie» zum «Wirtschaftshaushalt» zu wechseln, der mich weit mehr interessierte, und ich war Berichterstatterin unserer Gruppe. Zunächst wurde innerhalb der Gruppe diskutiert: Welche Ausgaben sollen erhöht, welche reduziert, welche Posten neu aufgenommen, welche ganz gestrichen werden? In dieser Diskussion hatte die Gruppe mir meine vorher lange und sorgfältig überlegten Argumente in der Luft zerrissen, und ich war am nächsten Tag dazu verdonnert, im Haushaltsausschuss den Mehrheitsbeschluss vorzutragen und zu vertreten, der gar nicht meiner ursprünglichen Meinung entsprach. Ich habe das auch ganz brav gemacht. Damals war Otto Graf Lambsdorff der zuständige Minister – und der argumentierte nun ständig gegen mich, und zwar mit genau den Argumenten, mit denen ich am Abend zuvor in der Gruppe untergegangen war. Und plötzlich haben die anderen dann all diese Argumente, als sie von Lambsdorff kamen, akzeptiert und zu allem Überfluss noch so getan, als sei genau das unser Konsens gewesen! Sie sind mir in den Rücken gefallen, und ich musste zum zweiten Mal die Seite wechseln. Als sich dieses Theater beim fünften und sechsten Posten wiederholte, bin ich aufgestanden, habe den ganzen Kram genommen und ihn vor meinen Obmann hingeworfen: «Macht euren Mist allein, mich seht ihr hier nicht wieder!», und bin aus dem Saal gerannt. Sie waren einigermaßen sprachlos, haben mich dann zurückgeholt, und von da an durfte ich die Sache so vortragen, wie ich sie selber von Anfang an ausgearbeitet hatte. Hinterher haben sie mir zwar gesagt, ich hätte da ja etwas hysterisch reagiert. Aber im Prinzip fanden sie es letztlich wohl doch gut, dass ich mich gewehrt hatte.

Natürlich war ich am Anfang für die meisten Herren im Haushaltsausschuss «die Kleine». Es gab eine feste Sitzordnung, die die Hackordnung widerspiegelte. Wer neu war, musste erst einmal ganz am unteren Ende des großen Karrees, dicht bei der Tür, Platz nehmen. Mit der Zeit rückte man dann langsam nach oben hin auf, wo die Altvorderen thronten. Der arme Mensch, der bei der Tür hockte, hatte die lästige Aufgabe, vor den Abstimmungen sämtliche Mitglieder zusammenzutrommeln. Die Leute liefen während der endlos langen Sitzungen immer wieder nach draußen, um eine Zigarette zu rauchen, zu telefonieren, dies und das miteinander zu besprechen. Für die

Abstimmungen war es aber wichtig, dass sich alle im Raum befanden. Also schaute mich der Obmann auffordernd an und verkündete: «Abstimmung!» So rannte ich denn los, über den Gang und rief: «Abstimmung!» Lief zu den Telefonen: «Abstimmung!» Aber was, wenn Kollegen auf der Toilette sind? Denen musst du natürlich auch Bescheid sagen! Also riss ich die Tür der Herrentoilette auf und brüllte: «Abstimmung!» hinein. – Ob das heute noch so läuft, weiß ich nicht, heute werden sie vermutlich andere Rituale haben. Aber damals war ganz klar: «Wenn das Mädel hier mitmischen will, dann muss es auch diese Dinge machen!»

Wir «Haushälter» waren eine ganz eigene Gemeinschaft. Wir waren damals 33 Abgeordnete im Haushaltsausschuss, aus allen Parteien. Ich war die erste und anfangs die einzige Frau, später kamen dann noch einige dazu. Obwohl ich vielleicht nicht so aussehe, war und bin ich doch eine richtige Papierfresserin: Es machte mir Spaß, mich durch Papier- und Aktenberge zu wühlen, und es fiel mir nicht schwer, mir Zahlen und Fakten zu merken, Fakten in Zahlen umzusetzen. Ich interessierte mich auch für den Kleinkram, den andere einfach lästig finden. Nach einer gewissen Anlaufzeit fand ich mich richtig gut zurecht, und ich war auch imstande, mich durchzusetzen. Allerdings war der Haushalt als politisches Steckenpferd damals noch nicht sonderlich in Mode. Das Thema «Sparen» interessierte weder die Öffentlichkeit noch die anderen Abgeordneten sonderlich. Man kann leidenschaftlich darüber diskutieren, ob und wie viel neue Panzer angeschafft werden sollen, vielleicht auch über die Rentenreform. Aber es ist schwierig, über den Haushalt als solchen flammende Reden zu halten. Die meisten finden diese Dinge eher trocken und langweilig. Das merkte ich jedes Mal, wenn ich nach Hause in meinen Wahlkreis fuhr; ich musste dann stets noch ein paar Informationen aus anderen Ausschüssen bereithalten, um meinen Leuten etwas Handfesteres erzählen zu können. Heute hat sich das ein bisschen geändert. Seit die Menschen

begriffen haben, dass man auf Dauer nicht auf einen über-
schuldeten Staat bauen kann, ist das Thema Finanzen salon-
fähig geworden.

Die «Haushälter» blieben meist für sich, sie hatten etwas
«Asoziales». Ich erinnere mich an manche Sitzung, die bis um
ein, zwei Uhr nachts dauerte. Danach haben wir dann meist
noch zusammen ein Bier in der «Papierkneipe» getrunken, so
nannten wir das Archiv neben dem Sitzungssaal, im 25. Stock
des Bundeshauses, und nicht selten wurde dabei weiterdisku-
tiert. Die anderen Abgeordneten waren um diese Zeit längst zu
Hause oder bei Treffen außerhalb, vielleicht auch von irgendwelchen Interessenverbänden zum Essen eingeladen. Wir aber
hockten in der «Papierkneipe». In der arbeitsintensivsten Zeit,
wenn die Haushaltsberatungen anstanden, zwischen der Som-
merpause und Weihnachten, habe ich meine Kollegen im
Haushaltsausschuss öfter gesehen als meinen Mann. Ich reiste
am Montagabend an, am Dienstag tagten wir vormittags noch
in der Fraktion. Spätestens mittags ging es los mit den Haus-
haltsdiskussionen, den ganzen Mittwoch und Donnerstag, immer von morgens neun bis tief in die Nacht. Wenn dann im
Januar der Haushalt durchgebracht war, wurde es etwas ruhiger.
Dann beschäftigten wir uns mit den Berichten des Bundesrech-
nungshofs, und es blieb auch schon mal Zeit, abends mit
jemandem essen zu gehen oder eine Kneipe in der Stadt zu besuchen.

Natürlich neigt man immer dazu, das, was man gerade tut,
für das Wichtigste auf der Welt zu halten. Das ist auch gut so –
denn wenn nicht die Jungen und die Neuen ihre Arbeit wichtig
nehmen, wer soll es sonst tun? Später lernt man dann ganz von
selbst zu relativieren, man wird politisch reifer, nachdem man
reichlich Niederlagen hat verdauen und Kompromisse hat eingehen müssen.

Der Haushaltsausschuss war meine wichtigste Bonner Bezugsgruppe und innerhalb dieses Ausschusses natürlich die
Kollegen aus der eigenen Partei bzw. aus der Koalition. Es gab

ein paar freundschaftliche Beziehungen: So war ich mit einem Kollegen befreundet, der später Oberbürgermeister von Saarbrücken wurde, und mit einer Frau, die nach mir zum Haushaltsausschuss stieß und dann leider früh an Krebs verstarb. Aus dieser Zeit stammt auch meine freundschaftliche Verbundenheit mit Klaus Gärtner, der mit mir nach Kiel ging, als ich das Finanzministerium übernahm, und dort später Chef der Staatskanzlei wurde. Überwiegend hatte man ein kumpelhaftes Verhältnis zueinander, im Übrigen durchaus auch zu den Abgeordneten der Opposition. Das jahrelange gemeinsame Brüten über den Finanzen schaffte eine gewisse Verbundenheit. Wenn ich heute Michael Glos (CSU) treffe, dann begrüße ich ihn: «Michael, altes Haus, sieht man dich auch mal wieder!» und er erwidert: «Na, wie geht's, Heide, du alter Gangster?» Ich duze auch Theo Waigel; immerhin haben wir jahrelang Tage und halbe Nächte miteinander verbracht, und bei der Zusammenarbeit spielt nicht nur das Parteibuch eine Rolle, sondern auch, wie man sich jeweils zusammenrauft. Wenn allerdings die Leute von der Opposition der Meinung waren, wir gäben zu viel Geld für Asylanten aus, und wir fanden, dass das so richtig sei, dann half es bei solchen politischideologischen Meinungsverschiedenheiten natürlich nicht zu sagen: «Du bist doch sonst ein ganz netter Kerl, nun stimm mal in unserem Sinne ab!»

Meine andere wichtige Bezugsgruppe war der «Leverkusener Kreis» – so nannte sich die informelle Gruppierung der Linken in der Fraktion, zu der außer mir Norbert Gansel, Karsten Voigt, Volker Hauff, Peter Conradi und andere gehörten. Innerhalb der Partei hießen die Linken «Frankfurter Kreis». Aber die größte und einflussreichste Gruppe innerhalb der SPD-Fraktion waren die so genannten «Kanalarbeiter», die, von uns aus gesehen, eher rechts standen. Zu ihnen gehörten unter anderen Annemarie Renger, Anke Fuchs, Helmut Wieczorek und Jürgen Linde. Sie gruppierten sich um Egon Franke, den späteren Minister für innerdeutsche Angelegenheiten, der zeitweise Vorsitzender der IG Bau war – daher der Name «Kanalarbeiter». Für unsere Arbeit im Haushaltsausschuss war es allerdings oft egal, ob jemand ein «Kanaler» war oder ein «Leverkusener»; das hörte auf zu zählen, wenn man miteinander 40 000 Haushaltsposten durchgehen musste. Außerdem gab es noch eine andere, eher regionale Gruppierung, zu der ich gehörte: Das war die so genannte «Wesergang» (später «Küstengang»), die der Abgeordnete Ernst Walthemathe gegründet hatte. Zu ihr zählten sich alle Abgeordneten, die aus dem Norden kamen und mit Werften und Schiffen zu tun hatten. Sie hatten verständlicherweise in manchen politischen Auseinandersetzungen ähnliche Interessen.

Am Anfang hatte ich große Antipathien gegen die Kanalarbeiter und ihren etwas rüden politischen Stil. Sie waren die mächtigste Gruppe in der Fraktion und entschieden oft einfach nach Gutdünken – Daumen rauf oder Daumen runter –, ob jemand die Chance bekam, etwas zu werden oder nicht. Sie fackelten nicht lange, wer nicht für sie war, war gegen sie und ging bei der Verteilung der Posten leer aus. Berühmt-berüchtigt war das traditionelle Spargelessen, das die «Kanaler» einmal im Jahr veranstalteten, eine Dampferfahrt auf dem Rhein mit großem Spargelgelage. Daran nahm natürlich auch der Kanzler teil. Doch ich – wie viele andere aus den niederen Rängen – wurde dazu in all meinen Bonner Jahren nicht ein einziges Mal eingeladen. So versuchten wir, mit unserem kleinen «Leverkusener Kreis» eine Gegenmacht zu den mächtigen Kanalarbeitern zu organisieren.

Diejenigen, über deren Arroganz ich mich damals geärgert habe, sind inzwischen längst verstorben oder im Ruhestand; die «Kanalarbeiter» gibt es als Gruppierung nicht mehr, und der «Seeheimer Kreis», zu dem die Konservativen der Partei sich später zusammenfanden, pflegt erfreulicherweise einen anderen Stil. Inzwischen hat man auch auf dieser politischen Ebene ein bisschen mehr über Kommunikation gelernt, und das Verhältnis zwischen den verschiedenen Gruppierungen ist entspannter geworden. Man hat mir erzählt, dass sie heutzutage sogar Emissäre austauschen.

Die «Kanaler» hatten wohl ein Vorurteil gegen mich, weil ich Beamtentochter war, also aus der Mittelschicht stammte und zudem studiert hatte. Die meisten von ihnen kamen aus der Gewerkschaftsbewegung, sie sahen sich als richtige Malocher, die sich über den Betriebsrat hochgekämpft hatten. In ihren Augen hatte ich keine Ahnung von der wirklichen Welt und deren Nöten. Sie sagten öfter herablassend: «Kindchen, komm du mal in meinen Wahlkreis, da werden sie dir was erzählen!» Sie fanden, alle müssten die Welt mit ihren Augen sehen. Aber natürlich traf ich auf genügend Leute, die die Welt so sahen wie ich.

Jede politische Bühne hat ihre eigenen Gruppierungen und Kräfteverhältnisse, ihre ganz eigene Gruppendynamik jenseits der demokratisch gewählten Vertretungen, die entscheidend ist für das Funktionieren der Macht. Es gibt Abgeordnete, die sehr fest in solche Gruppierungen eingebettet sind, und es gibt andere, die sich eher am Rande aufhalten und zwischen den verschiedenen Gruppierungen bewegen, weil sie in dieser Sache eher zur Meinung der einen und in einer anderen Sache eher zur Meinung der anderen Gruppierung neigen. Und immer wenn man eine neue politische Bühne betritt, ist es ganz wichtig, erst einmal herauszufinden: Wer bestimmt hier das Spiel? Zu wem will ich mich gesellen? Wo finde ich Verbündete für meine Ideen? Wer mitmischen will, muss ein Gespür dafür entwickeln, wo und wie die unterirdischen Wasseradern der politischen Entscheidungsbildung verlaufen. Es reicht nicht, gute Ideen zu haben, man muss auch wissen, wie man sie durchsetzt. Das bedeutet immer wieder, Verbündete zu suchen – und um die zu finden, muss man gelegentlich auch Kompromisse machen. Sonst sitzt man während seiner Abgeordnetenjahre nur auf seiner Bank, ohne viel zu bewegen. Allerdings gibt es zentrale Überzeugungen, bei denen man weiß: Hier will und werde ich keine Kompromisse eingehen, weil ich sonst als Person, weil wir sonst als Gruppe an

Glaubwürdigkeit verlieren. Doch auch diese zentralen Punkte stehen nicht für alle Ewigkeit; sie müssen immer wieder neu überdacht und ausgehandelt werden.

Ich hegte großen Respekt für Herbert Wehner, wegen seiner unglaublichen Leistung, einen so heterogenen Haufen wie die SPD-Fraktion zusammenzuhalten. Ich bewunderte seine Disziplin, seine Präsenz und auch seine Fähigkeit, aus dem Stand zu reagieren, wenn jemand in einer wichtigen Angelegenheit wackelte oder wenn es im Bundestag mal wieder hoch herging. Richtig geschwärmt habe ich, wie natürlich alle Parteilinken, für Willy Brandt, der ja unsere Galionsfigur war. Deswegen hat es mich auch besonders geschmerzt, dass mir meine etwas vorlaute Kritik an ihm, kurz vor seinem Rücktritt, den Ruf der Vatermörderin eingetragen hat. Dieser Vorfall führte zur schlimmsten Krise in meiner Abgeordnetenzeit.

Willy Brandt wollte im März 1987 Margarita Mathiopoulos zur Pressesprecherin der Partei machen, und das fanden wir fast alle unmöglich. Nicht die Tatsache, dass sie Griechin, jung und eine Frau war, sondern dass sie keine Ahnung hatte, gar keine Ahnung von innerparteilichen Fragen haben konnte, weil sie parteilos war. Jemand, der von außen kommt, kann einfach nicht wissen, wie eine Partei funktioniert. Eine Partei ist ein Tendenzbetrieb, und eine Parteisprecherin muss zum Beispiel die Stimmung in den Ortsvereinen genau kennen. Beim Regierungssprecher sieht das anders aus, diese Aufgabe kann auch sehr gut von jemandem wahrgenommen werden, der parteilos ist. Wir waren alle unzufrieden mit Willy Brandts Entscheidung, wir saßen abends in größerem Kreis in der Kneipe zusammen und schimpften drauflos. Aber ich war dann die Einzige, die diese Kritik lauthals vor einer Kamera, in ein Mikrofon hinein wiederholte: «Wie konnte er nur! Das ist ja wohl das Letzte!» Ich hatte mir nicht viel dabei gedacht.

Doch auf einmal wurde dieses Statement überall wiederholt und immer wieder groß herausgestellt – und da wurde es plötzlich eisig still um mich. Diejenigen, die vorher noch meiner

Meinung gewesen waren, zogen sich empört von mir zurück. Auf einmal hieß es nur: «Wie konnte sie unserem Parteivorsitzenden öffentlich so in den Rücken fallen!» Natürlich war diese Kritik auch berechtigt, denn man muss als Politikerin unterscheiden können zwischen kritischen Bemerkungen, die nach innen und im eigenen Kreis geäußert werden, und solchen, die nach außen an die Öffentlichkeit gehen. Korrekt wäre es gewesen, Willy Brandt meine Meinung direkt und persönlich zu sagen. Ich ärgere mich selbst ja heute auch darüber, wenn ich Kritik an mir aus dem eigenen Lager den Tageszeitungen entnehmen muss.

Ich versuchte dann, in weiteren Interviews meine Aussage zu modifizieren, aber mit jeder weiteren Korrektur wurde es nur noch schlimmer. Es war ein gefundenes Fressen für die Presse, und das Theater nahm kein Ende. Aus diesem Vorfall habe ich auch etwas gelernt: Wenn man sich in dieser Weise vergaloppiert hat, wäre es besser, jemand käme daher und würde einen erst mal kurz k. o. schlagen, damit man für die nächsten Tage aus dem Verkehr gezogen ist und in kein Mikrofon sprechen kann. Aber damals tat das keiner, und ich wurde von den eigenen Leuten wie ein Outcast behandelt.

Natürlich war die Kritik an mir berechtigt, aber die Reaktion der Partei war überzogen. Eine junge Gans hatte etwas Dummes gesagt – die angemessene Reaktion der Genossen wäre gewesen: «Heide, jetzt halt mal eine Weile die Goschen, und das nächste Mal überlegst du dir, was du sagst!», und anschließend hätte man zur Tagesordnung übergehen sollen. Stattdessen wurde ich zur Meuchelmörderin hochstilisiert. Natürlich spielten in diesem Zusammenhang auch andere politische Hintergrundfaktoren eine Rolle. Willy Brandt trat bald darauf zurück, natürlich nicht meinetwegen. Wahrscheinlich war ihm schon länger bewusst, dass es auch Kritik in den eigenen Reihen gab, und er war schon vorher an dem Punkt, die Sache beenden zu wollen. Der Wirbel um seine Wunschkandidatin Mathiopoulos war da nur das letzte I-Tüpfelchen.

Ich aber war noch lange danach geächtet, niemand mochte mit mir gesehen werden; ich war das Kind, mit dem keiner mehr spielen wollte. Dabei hatte ich doch nur laut ausgesprochen, was viele andere damals auch dachten. Endlich hat dann Günther Jansen, der damalige Landesvorsitzende der SPD in Schleswig-Holstein, auf dem Parteitag ein paar erlösende Worte gesagt: «Also, Heides Verhalten war nicht in Ordnung, aber irgendwann muss mal Schluss damit sein, ihr das immer wieder vorzuhalten.» Ich hatte nur noch mit eingezogenem Kopf dagesessen, danach konnte ich endlich wieder aufatmen.

Es gibt im politischen Leben immer wieder mal hässliche Situationen, die man einfach durchstehen muss. Wenn man sich entschieden hat, dass man deswegen nicht zurücktreten will und wird, dann muss man einfach eine Weile die kalten Winde aushalten, die einem ins Gesicht wehen. Ich hatte eine Dummheit begangen, aber nichts Ehrenrühriges getan, und deswegen sah ich auch keinerlei Anlass, mein Mandat aufzugeben. Also musste ich da einfach durch. Es ist schließlich auch nicht besonders angenehm, vor vielen tausend Werftarbeitern zu stehen, die um ihren Arbeitsplatz fürchten, und ihnen mitzuteilen, dass die Landesanteile an der Werft verkauft werden müssen, was ihre Zukunft ungewisser macht. Es ist auch nicht lustig, die Proteste und Prügel einer Gewerkschaft auszuhalten, wenn man entscheidende Haushaltskürzungen vorgenommen hat. Auch da hilft nichts, als sich zu sagen: «Da mööt wie dörch!»

Andere wären vielleicht zusammengebrochen, wenn sie so wie ich damals allein im eisigen Regen gestanden hätten. Aber vielleicht erweist es sich in solchen Situationen dann doch als nützlich, dass ich eine schwierige Kindheit hatte – ich musste oft eine gewisse innere Einsamkeit aushalten, und das stählt. Zum Glück konnte ich mich auf meinen Mann verlassen, der mir auch heute noch bei Krisen ähnlicher Art das «Händchen hält». Auch meine Schwestern stützen mich in solchen Situationen; sie rufen etwas öfter an und erzählen von ganz anderen

Dingen, um mich abzulenken. Und dann gibt es da immer noch eine innere Stimme, die mir sagt: «Durchhalten! Alles in allem machst du deine Sache nicht schlecht. Du bist zäh, du schaffst das!» – und irgendwann kommen wieder freundlichere Tage.

Auf dem Hintergrund dieses Vorfalls, der mir noch lange anhing, war es ziemlich mutig von Björn Engholm, mich 1987 als Finanzministerin für sein Schattenkabinett zu nominieren.

5

Frauenpower –
der weibliche Griff nach der Macht

Es gab vor mir in der Bundesrepublik Deutschland nur eine einzige andere Finanzministerin, Birgit Breuel in Niedersachsen. Deren Einstieg in dieses Amt wurde durch ihren persönlichen Hintergrund erleichtert; man traute ihr, als Tochter des Bankiers Alwin Münchmeyer, irgendwie zu, mit Geld umgehen zu können. Aber 1987 war es für die Sozialdemokraten im Allgemeinen und für eine SPD-Frau im Besonderen noch ganz schön schwierig, an diesen Posten zu gelangen. «Kann die das denn überhaupt?», wurde gefragt, offen oder verdeckt. Heute würde wahrscheinlich niemand mehr grundsätzlich die Qualifikation von Frauen für dieses Amt bezweifeln, nur weil sie Frauen sind. Björn Engholms Entscheidung für mich war also in mehr als einer Hinsicht mutig.

In meiner politischen Laufbahn bin ich immer wieder mit der Tatsache konfrontiert worden, eine Frau zu sein. Immer wieder hieß es: Sie ist die jüngste Frau, die erste Frau, die einzige Frau – die jüngste Abgeordnete im Bundestag, das erste und eine Zeit lang einzige weibliche Mitglied des Haushaltsausschusses, die erste und bisher einzige Ministerpräsidentin. Diese Apostrophierung schafft natürlich einen anderen Erwartungs- und Beurteilungsrahmen als für die männlichen Kollegen. Man musste immer damit rechnen, besonders scharf unter die Lupe genommen zu werden – fast als sei Weiblichkeit ein

Defekt, der durch besondere Leistungsfähigkeit überkompensiert werden müsse.

Derzeit gehören dem Deutschen Bundestag 198 Frauen an, mehr als je zuvor, und ihr Anteil ist während der letzten Legislaturperioden kontinuierlich auf 33 Prozent gestiegen. 1976, als ich nach Bonn ging, waren wir insgesamt nur 36 Frauen (7 Prozent) im Bundestag. Das war ein bloßes Händchen voll linker und noch viel weniger konservativer weiblicher Abgeordneter, und die politischen Lager trennten uns damals noch viel nachdrücklicher. In der Politikergeneration vor mir gab es nur ein paar Frauen, an denen man sich orientieren konnte. Hildegard Hamm-Brücher beeindruckte mich sehr durch ihr Selbstbewusstsein und die selbstverständliche Eleganz, mit der sie auftrat. Sie war die große Alte Dame des Parlamentes – erst nur die große und später die große Alte Dame. Ich bewunderte ihre souveräne Entscheidung beim Misstrauensvotum gegen Helmut Schmidt im September 1982, wo sie den Mut hatte, sich gegen ihre eigene Partei zu stellen. Damals sind wir uns etwas näher gekommen, und seitdem reden wir uns mit dem Vornamen und Sie an, was bei ihr schon sehr viel bedeutet.

Dann war da auch noch Rita Süßmuth, für die die meisten Frauenpolitikerinnen schwärmten. Ihr bin ich allerdings nur selten begegnet, weil ich mich nicht mit den ausgesprochenen Frauenthemen befasst habe. Zu den herausragenden Frauen meiner eigenen Generation gehörte damals schon Renate Schmidt, doch auch mit ihr hatte ich nicht allzu viele Berührungspunkte, weil sie zu ganz anderen Zirkeln gehörte als ich. Ihr Schwerpunkt war die Sozialpolitik, und den Sozialpolitikern begegneten wir Haushälter immer mit der allergrößten Reserve. Die neigten dazu, immer nur teure Forderungen zu stellen, ohne zu fragen, woher das Geld kommen sollte – glaubten wir.

In den Anfangszeiten meiner parlamentarischen Karriere, in den späten 70ern und den frühen 80er Jahren, war in Bonn wie in Kiel die Frauenbewegung sehr aktiv. Mein Verhältnis zu den Feministinnen war damals ambivalent, um nicht zu sagen schwierig. Es gab immer wieder heftige Zusammenstöße und Konflikte. Sie warfen mir vor, eine «männliche Frau» zu sein. Tatsache ist, dass ich, von den Jahren im Elternhaus und in der Mädchenschule einmal abgesehen, weitgehend in Männergruppen agiert habe, und mein Politikstil ist sicher davon beeinflusst. In den politischen Gruppen, in denen ich gearbeitet habe, hätte ein typisch «weibliches Verhalten», etwa ein schöner Augenaufschlag, ganz bestimmt nichts genützt; es verlangte schon andere Anstrengungen, um sich durchzusetzen. Man musste, gerade als Frau – und das gilt auch heute noch –, sehr kompetent sein, nicht nur gut informiert, sondern auch sachlich überzeugend argumentieren können. Vor allem aber muss frau zäh sein und einiges einstecken können. Wer zu zart besaitet ist, hält es in der Politik nicht lange aus. Denn Misserfolge gibt es jede Menge und immer wieder. Das mag gerade für die Frauen meiner Generation ein besonderes Problem gewesen sein – die jungen Frauen, die heute in die Politik gehen, tun sich damit ganz sicher leichter.

Ich erinnere mich an Auseinandersetzungen mit Feministinnen in Kiel, die sich für Frauenhäuser einsetzten, und an heftige Zusammenstöße auf Frauenkongressen, zu denen ich in dieser Zeit manchmal eingeladen wurde. Die Vorwürfe liefen immer darauf hinaus, dass ich mich als Parteifrau den Spielregeln der Männer anpassen würde. Auch kam es mir nicht in den Sinn, mich über die bösen, ausbeuterischen Männer zu beklagen, mit denen ich zusammenarbeitete, denn ich hatte nun mal keinen Anlass zu behaupten, dass ich während meiner politischen Karriere in meiner Eigenschaft als Frau besonders schlecht von ihnen behandelt worden wäre. Obwohl ich natürlich einräumen würde, dass es manchen Politikerinnen so ergangen ist. Außerdem glaubte ich nicht daran, dass Frauen die besseren Menschen sind, ich hatte keine Männergewalt erlebt, ich war keine Mutter – und ich trug nicht die richtigen Klamotten. All das führte dazu, dass mir die tonangebenden Feministinnen oft mit tiefem Misstrauen begegneten. Vor allem mit meiner Garderobe bin ich bei ihnen immer wieder angeeckt, denn ich mochte weder die lila Latzhosen noch die Wallekleider, die damals in der Frauenbewegung beliebt waren; ich habe mich immer gern ein bisschen eleganter angezogen. Den Sozialdemokraten dagegen war meine Kleidung manchmal zu modisch; sie entsprach auch dort nicht ganz dem Komment. Jede Gruppe hat eben ihren eigenen Kleiderkodex.

Für einige radikale Feministinnen verkörperte ich also eine Zeit lang das Feindbild der «männlichen» Frau, die sich bei den Männern anbiedert, statt sich mit den Schwestern zu solidarisieren. Es war eine Zeit, in der in der Frauenbewegung sehr lautstark die Solidarität der Unterdrückten proklamiert wurde. Viele Frauen wollten sich am liebsten immer nur als Opfer sehen, im Kreis hocken, Selbsterfahrung betreiben, gemeinsam jammern und ihre Wunden lecken, und sie taten sich schwer mit Frauen wie mir, die sich offen dazu bekannten, Macht und Erfolg haben zu wollen. Das war insofern eine verrückte Situation, als es doch eigentlich zu den erklärten Zielen der Frauenbewegung gehörte, dass mehr Frauen in die Politik gehen sollten, um die gesellschaftlichen Verhältnisse zu verändern. Tatsächlich aber begegnete den Politikerinnen aus den Reihen der Feministinnen am Anfang oft mehr Feindseligkeit als Unterstützung. In späteren Jahren schwächten sich die Gegensätze zwischen den angeblich männlich orientierten Parteifrauen und den Feministinnen dann allmählich ab. Beide Seiten haben sich einander angenähert.

Der Frauenbewegung kommen ohne Zweifel große Verdienste zu. Der Feminismus hat die Öffentlichkeit wach gerüttelt, und auch die Selbsterfahrungsgruppen haben eine wichtige Bedeutung für den allgemeinen Bewusstseinswandel gehabt. Die wachsende Sensibilität für die Benachteiligung der Frauen kam später auch den Frauen zugute, die in den politischen Parteien und Institutionen arbeiteten. Ohne die Frauenbewegung hätte es zum Beispiel die Quote nicht gegeben – eine politische Forderung, die ich anfangs für überflüssig hielt, deren Notwendigkeit mir aber mit zunehmender Erfahrung immer einsichtiger wurde. Ich wollte keine Quotenfrau sein, sondern mich als Individuum durchsetzen, wollte durch meine eigene Leistung politische Positionen erreichen. Doch wenn man heute die Situation der Frauen bei den Grünen und der SPD betrachtet und sie mit der bei CDU und FDP vergleicht, bei denen es keine Quote gibt, dann sprechen die Zahlen für sich. Im Bundestag sind zur Zeit mehr als die Hälfte der grünen Abgeordneten Frauen (58 Prozent), bei der SPD immerhin mehr als ein Drittel (38 Prozent); die CDU dagegen hat nur 22 Prozent und die FDP nur 21 Prozent weibliche Abgeordnete. Inzwischen bin also auch ich davon überzeugt, dass es ohne ein Reißverschluss-System nicht geht.

Die Situation der Frauen in der Politik hat sich in den letzten beiden Jahrzehnten deutlich verbessert; es hat einen wirklichen Veränderungsschub gegeben. Die jüngeren Frauen sind lockerer und nicht mehr so feministisch-fundamentalistisch in ihren Ideen; ein viel breiteres Verhaltensspektrum für weibliche Abgeordnete ist möglich geworden. Außerdem haben die jüngeren Frauen heute allgemein ein unverkrampfteres Verhältnis zur Macht; sie sehen es nicht mehr als «männlich» an, Lust an der Macht zu haben. Sie betrachten es als individuelle Entscheidung jeder einzelnen Frau, ob sie beruflich Karriere machen oder sich in die Politik stürzen will. Bei den Frauen der jüngeren Generation mag es allerdings zum Problem werden, dass sie im Gegensatz zu den Feministinnen der frühen Jahre strukturelle Karrierehindernisse manchmal gar nicht mehr oder erst zu spät als solche erkennen. Denn noch immer ist es eine augenfällige Tatsache, dass bei uns erfolgreiche Frauen seltener Kinder haben. Das gilt nicht nur für den Bereich der Politik.

Nicht nur der Frauenanteil im Parlament nimmt sich heute viel erfreulicher aus als vor zwanzig, dreißig Jahren, auch der Umgangsstil untereinander hat sich verändert. Es hat immer mal wieder Initiativen gegeben, bei denen die weiblichen Bundestagsabgeordneten über die Parteigrenzen hinweg kooperierten. Die Fristenlösung beim Paragraphen 218 ist ja nur auf diese Weise zustande gekommen. Zu manchen Themen kann man jetzt im Bundestag richtig Frauengruppenarbeit machen. Die weiblichen Abgeordneten sind wohl auch mit- und untereinander solidarischer als früher. Natürlich bleiben die alten Kämpfe zwischen denen, die etwas werden wollen – doch solche Kämpfe gibt es eben zwischen Männern und Männern, zwischen Männern und Frauen und zwischen Frauen und Frauen; sie gehören einfach zur Politik dazu. Daneben existiert aber doch ein gegenseitiges unausgesprochenes Übereinkommen, dass wir Frauen uns nicht auch noch gegenseitig fertig machen müssen.

Trotz dieser positiven Entwicklungen sind allerdings noch immer erschreckend wenig Frauen in den zentralen politischen Machtpositionen. Auf Bundesebene hat es bei uns bis jetzt keine Finanzministerin gegeben, noch keine Wirtschaftsministerin, keine Verteidigungsministerin, keine Innen- und keine Außenministerin. Das sind innerhalb des Kabinetts in der Regel die mächtigsten Ressorts und somit wohl die letzten Bollwerke der männlichen Macht. 1995 habe ich einmal bei einem Interview gesagt (es ging um die so genannte «K-Frage»): «In zehn Jahren wird Deutschland von einer Frau regiert.» So wie es jetzt ausschaut, muss ich da wohl noch einmal zehn Jahre drauflegen! Allerdings dürfte es wohl so sein, dass die Spitzenpositionen in der Wirtschaft für die Frauen noch schwerer zu erobern sein werden als die in der Politik. Und was die Machtpositionen in den Medien angeht, sieht es kein bisschen besser aus. Wo ist die Chefredakteurin einer bedeutenden Zeitung oder Zeitschrift? Eben erst wurde die erste Intendantin einer Rundfunkanstalt gewählt (RBB). Innerhalb der Wirtschaft wird es für Frauen bei den Banken am schwierigsten werden. Ich vermute, dass es bei uns eher eine Bundeskanzlerin geben wird als eine Bankensprecherin. Denn Geld ist Macht – nicht nur das Geld, das man besitzt, sondern vor allem die Möglichkeit, über die Geldströme in einer Gesellschaft zu bestimmen.

Vermutlich wird es auch noch lange dauern, bis Frauen bei uns Spitzenmanagerinnen in einem Großunternehmen werden, das in der Rüstungsindustrie angesiedelt ist. Und in der Politik wird vermutlich der Posten des Verteidigungsministers als Letzter von einer Frau besetzt, denn auch die Entscheidungsmacht über das Militär scheint eine eiserne männliche Bastion zu sein. Frankreich ist da mit Michèle-Marie Alliot allerdings schon weiter.

Eher noch hat eine Frau bei uns die Chance, Bundeskanzlerin zu werden. Denn in diesem Amt geht es, zumindest in Friedenszeiten, vor allem um die Fragen: Ist die Person fähig, Deutschland im Ausland zu repräsentieren? Wie kommt sie mit den Wirtschaftsbossen und den Gewerkschaftsführern zurecht? Kennt sie sich mit den Abläufen in der Verwaltung aus, und beherrscht sie den politischen Apparat? Ist sie fähig, zwischen den großen gesellschaftlichen Interessengruppen zu moderieren? – Ich denke, dass man bei uns, in der Öffentlichkeit wie in den Parteien, nach der gesellschaftlichen Entwicklung der letzten zwanzig Jahre eher bereit ist, diese Fähigkeiten auch einer Frau zuzutrauen als etwa die Fachkompetenz für militärische Logistik oder die psychologische Führungskompetenz für eine noch überwiegend männliche Wirtschafts- und Bankenwelt.

Wenn man sich die wenigen gewählten weiblichen Staatschefs des 20. Jahrhunderts anschaut, stößt man häufig noch auf das alte Muster, dass Witwen oder Töchter männliche Staatsoberhäupter beerbt haben. Das gilt für Sirimavo Bandaranaike und Indira Gandhi ebenso wie für Benazir Bhutto. Bandaranaike in Sri Lanka war die erste gewählte Premierministerin der Welt, von 1960 bis 1965 – aber sie hätte diesen Posten wohl nie bekommen, wenn sie nicht die Witwe des 1959 ermordeten Premiers gewesen wäre. Auch Indira Gandhi wäre ohne ihren Vater Nehru in einem Land wie Indien kaum Staatschefin geworden. Sie erwarb sich in ihrer Rolle als Tochter viele politische Erfahrungen, indem sie ihrem verwitweten Vater zuarbeitete und ihn auf seinen diplomatischen Reisen begleitete. Nach

Nehrus Tod war sie dann von 1966 bis 1977 und noch einmal von 1980 bis zu ihrer Ermordung 1984 Premierministerin. Benazir Bhutto, die erste Premierministerin eines islamischen Landes (von 1973 bis 1979), hatte ebenfalls einen Vater, der vor ihr Premier war; er war ein Jahr vor ihrem Amtsantritt ermordet worden. Dieses Muster hat immer noch Ähnlichkeit mit der Erbfolge in Monarchien, wo – wie etwa bei Maria Theresia von Österreich – mangels geeigneter männlicher Thronfolger gelegentlich auch Frauen zum Zuge kamen, weil es einer Dynastie oder einem Clan darum ging, an der Macht zu bleiben.

Ein wirklich neues Muster zeigt sich in politischen Karrieren wie denen von Golda Meir, Margaret Thatcher und Gro Harlem Brundtland – das waren Frauen, die demokratisch legitimiert und durch eigene Leistung an die Spitze ihrer Länder kamen, auch im 20. Jahrhundert noch eine Seltenheit. Golda Meir, Tochter ukrainischer Juden, von den USA aus 1921 in Tel Aviv eingewandert, gehörte 1948 zu den Gründungsmitgliedern des Staates Israel; sie war zunächst Ministerin für Arbeit und Soziales, dann Außenministerin und von 1967 bis 1974 Ministerpräsidentin Israels. Margaret Thatcher, Tochter eines Kolonialwarenhändlers aus der Kleinstadt Grantham, war erst Erziehungs- und Wissenschaftsministerin und dann von 1979 bis 1990 britische Premierministerin. Gro Harlem Brundtland, ursprünglich Ärztin, war zunächst Umweltministerin und zweimal, von 1986 bis 1989 und noch einmal von 1990 bis 1996, Norwegens Ministerpräsidentin.

Dabei erscheint Brundtlands Karriere in Norwegen weniger erstaunlich als Thatchers Aufstieg in Großbritannien. Denn Brundtland war die Kandidatin der Linken in einem Land, das sehr fortschrittlich über die Frauenrolle denkt, und sie verkörperte in dieser Hinsicht einen breiten Konsens. Zeitweilig gab es in ihrem Kabinett mehr Ministerinnen als Minister. Die skandinavischen Länder sind uns in Sachen Gleichstellung der Frau ohnehin um einiges voraus, aber in puncto Chancengleichheit existiert auch innerhalb von Deutschland ein merkliches Nord-

Süd-Gefälle. In Schleswig-Holstein gab es nicht nur die erste Ministerpräsidentin, sondern auch die erste Bischöfin, und auch in meinem Kabinett war der Frauenanteil schon einmal fast halbe-halbe. Zur Zeit haben wir eine Chefin der Staatskanzlei, eine Stellvertretende Regierungssprecherin, eine Bildungsministerin, eine Justizministerin, eine Sozialministerin, eine Staatssekretärin für Justiz – mit mir zusammen also sieben Frauen unter zwanzig Personen am Kabinettstisch.

Bei Margaret Thatcher ist es auf den ersten Blick schwerer zu verstehen, wie sie es im traditionsbewussten England schaffen konnte, erst an die Spitze der konservativen Partei und von dort in die Downing Street Nummer 10 zu gelangen. Sie hat sich in ihrem äußeren Erscheinungsbild und ihrem Auftreten immer sehr an die traditionelle Frauenrolle gehalten; in ihrem politischen Stil und ihren Durchsetzungsstrategien war sie dagegen knallhart und durchaus «männlich», wenn man die alten Stereotypen bemühen will. Sie verfügte über eine große Sachkompetenz, über Ehrgeiz, einen zähen Willen und eiserne Disziplin. Das Phänomen ihres Aufstiegs ist aber wohl in erster Linie damit zu erklären, dass sie sich dem Verhaltenskodex der bürgerlichen Mittelschichten perfekt angepasst hatte. Vermutlich haben die Engländer sie weniger als Frau wahrgenommen denn als eine vollkommene Verkörperung britischer Mittelschichtswerte. In der Figur ihrer Königin, der Verkörperung der britischen Monarchie, hatten sie ja in gewisser Weise auch schon ein Vorbild – und immerhin war England im 19. und frühen 20. Jahrhundert Vorreiter der Frauenrechtsbewegung.

Wir sind in Deutschland und in Europa noch weit entfernt von einer Gesellschaft, in der die politischen Spitzenpositionen zwischen Männern und Frauen einigermaßen gleichgewichtig verteilt sind. In den mittleren Ebenen der Hierarchien sieht es zwar deutlich besser aus als noch vor einer Generation, und das gilt nicht nur für die Politik, sondern für alle Bereiche des öffentlichen Lebens, auch in der Verwaltung, der Wirtschaft, dem Kulturbetrieb, den Universitäten. Aber im Augenblick sieht es so aus, als ob bei uns die Schieflage in den Spitzenposten eher wieder zunimmt. Es ist jedenfalls nicht so, dass sich überall die Türen für Frauen weit geöffnet hätten.

Dass immer noch zu wenig Frauen in die Politik gehen, liegt natürlich auch an der Form, wie Politik gemacht wird. Man trifft sich abends um acht, man trifft sich zu Wochenendseminaren und -tagungen, Parteitage finden grundsätzlich an den Wochenenden statt. Politisches Engagement bedeutet also Verzicht auf ein Stück Privatleben, bedeutet weniger Familienleben mit Ehemann und Kindern, weniger Geselligkeit mit Freundinnen und Freunden. Dazu sind nur wenige Frauen bereit. Sie denken: «Diese endlos zerredeten Abende will ich mir nicht antun, auch nicht diese grauenvollen Marathonsitzungen an den Wochenenden!» Noch schwieriger wird es, wenn sie Kinder haben und ohnehin schon Probleme genug, ihre Berufstätigkeit und ihren Alltag mit Familie zu organisieren. Beruf plus Kinder plus parteipolitische Karriere – das ist dann oft wirklich zu viel Stress. Jede parteipolitische Karriere erfordert nämlich Zeit; und noch mehr Zeit braucht es, um in Spitzenpositionen zu gelangen.

Ich beobachte immer wieder, dass Frauen, die ehrgeizig und erfolgreich sind, die viel geschafft haben, sofort ihre Ambitionen zurücknehmen, wenn sie Kinder bekommen. Die Mutterrolle reduziert nicht unbedingt ihren Arbeitseinsatz. Doch sie müssen jetzt ihre Zeit anders einteilen, und sehr häufig verändern sich in dieser Phase die Prioritäten und damit auch ihre Motivation von Grund auf. Gut, da ist immer wieder das schwierige Problem der Kinderbetreuung. Aber das erklärt nicht alles. Denn wenn es auf einem Parteitag Kinderbetreuung gibt und man erwarten könnte, dass die Mütter mit ihren Kindern in Scharen herbeieilen, dann stellt sich heraus, dass diese Möglichkeit nur von ganz wenigen genutzt wird. Deswegen haben wir die Kinderbetreuung während der Parteitage schon wieder aufgegeben.

Manchmal sind es auch die Ehemänner oder Partner, die sich

beschweren. Sie erwarten, dass ihre Freundinnen oder Frauen zu Hause sind, wenn sie heimkommen. Umgekehrt ist das weit weniger selbstverständlich. Viele Männer nehmen für sich selbst in Anspruch, berufliche Fortbildungen oder Zusatzschichten zu machen, wann immer sie es für nötig halten oder die eigene Karriere es verlangt. Bei ihren Frauen akzeptieren sie das umgekehrt nicht unbedingt. Und wenn es nicht einmal der Beruf ist, der zusätzliche Zeit in Anspruch nimmt, sondern etwas Freiwilliges wie ein politisches Engagement, dann haben dafür die meisten Ehemänner noch weniger Verständnis: «Muss das denn sein, dass du da immer hinläufst?», heißt es dann.

Doch sobald Frauen genügend Interesse an der Politik haben, um diese Hürden zu überwinden, haben sie in der Regel ausgesprochen gute Chancen. Dann gelangen sie oft sehr rasch in Ämter, und wenn sie am Ball bleiben, können sie durchaus auch Ministerin, Parlamentspräsidentin und vielleicht auch Ministerpräsidentin werden.

Je höher es auf der Karriereleiter geht, desto hartnäckiger halten sich allerdings die alten Machtmechanismen zwischen den Geschlechtern. Ganz oben gilt noch immer, dass eine Frau am ehesten dann eine Chance bekommt, wenn der Mann vor ihr gescheitert aus der Kurve getragen wurde und sich im Augenblick kein anderer findet, der die Sache übernehmen will. In einer solchen Konstellation bin auch ich Ministerpräsidentin geworden. Ähnlich war es, als Angela Merkel CDU-Parteivorsitzende wurde. Insgeheim wird dann von den Konkurrenten billigend in Kauf genommen, dass frau mit der Sache doch nicht fertig werden wird. Mann hält sich dann, während frau versucht, den Karren aus dem Dreck zu ziehen, im Hintergrund zum Sprung bereit, für den Augenblick, in dem sie vielleicht doch scheitert. So hat Angela Merkel nach der Spendenaffäre von Helmut Kohl der CDU wieder Selbstbewusstsein gegeben, und doch musste sie anschließend gegen den Kanzlerkandidaten Edmund Stoiber das Feld räumen – so weit ein vertrautes Muster. Jetzt sieht es allerdings so aus, als habe sie ihren vorläufigen Verzicht strategisch klug genutzt, indem sie sich gleich nach der letzten Bundestagswahl ihr Wohlverhalten von Stoiber honorieren ließ, sich mit seiner Rückendeckung auch den Posten der Fraktionschefin sicherte, gegen den Konkurrenten Friedrich Merz. So kann sie sich in dieser Runde eine größere Hausmacht aufbauen und hat damit bei der nächsten Wahl durchaus realistische Chancen, Kanzlerkandidatin zu werden.

Frauen tun sich schwer mit dem Aufbau von Gruppen und Seilschaften, die ja beim Karrieremachen in der Politik wie anderswo eine wichtige Rolle spielen. Vielleicht sind Seilschaften im ursprünglichen Sinn ohnehin etwas eher Männliches. Seilschaft bedeutet ja, dass derjenige, der oben bzw. vorn ist, andere nachzieht, die ihn im Gegenzug stützen. Einer ist die Nummer eins, die anderen ordnen sich ihm unter; er fördert sie und baut sich so zugleich eine Hausmacht auf. Vielleicht haben die Männer das schon bei den Neandertalern so gemacht: Der Älteste und Stärkste geht als Boss voran und sichert das Terrain, die anderen folgen ihm nach Rang und Status, vom stellvertretenden Boss bis zu den Wasserträgern. Dieses hierarchische Prinzip schlägt sich auch im Militär und in vielen anderen Männerbünden nieder. Bei den Frauen will aber oft keine den Boss machen; vielleicht sind sie sich auch der Gefolgschaft der anderen nicht so sicher, wenn sie es in dieser Weise versuchten. Frauen neigen eher zum Knüpfen von Netzwerken, die mehr horizontal als vertikal angelegt sind, jedenfalls den Statusunterschied zwischen den Beteiligten nicht akzentuieren. Netzwerke verlangen mehr Kommunikation als Seilschaften, und das kriegen Frauen auch ganz gut hin, weil sie viel mehr reden als Männer – angeblich mindestens doppelt so viel am Tag. Die schweigsamen Herren sind dagegen in ihren Seilschaften gut aufgehoben, in denen von vornherein klar ist, wer weiter oben und wer weiter unten ist und was man in dieser Position zu tun hat – da muss dann nicht mehr viel geredet werden.

Vielleicht kann man in der Politik ohne Seilschaften auskommen, Netzwerke aber braucht es auf jeden Fall. Frauen tun sich manchmal noch schwer damit, die nötigen Zweckbündnisse einzugehen, um Mehrheiten zu bekommen. Manchmal muss man Kompromisse mit Personen oder Gruppen finden, die man nicht besonders mag. Frauen sagen dann eher: «Iieehh – mit denen will ich nicht, über die hab ich mich so geärgert!» Dahinter steht oft noch die Vorstellung, man müsste andere hundertprozentig lieben, um sich mit ihnen zu verbünden. Männer dagegen können ganz kühl sagen: «Den brauch ich – also trink ich jetzt mit ihm ein Bier und rede mit ihm.» Zwei, die sich gestern nur mit dem Hintern angeguckt haben, laufen dann plötzlich Arm in Arm herum.

Viele Frauen haben noch ein weiteres Handicap beim Aufstieg in der Politik. Sie tun sich schwer damit, im entscheidenden Augenblick vorzutreten und zu sagen: «Hier bin ich! Wählt mich, ernennt mich, nehmt mich für diese Funktion!» Sie warten oft darauf, dass andere sie vorschieben: «Wir finden dich so gut, du solltest das unbedingt machen!» Frauen sagen seltener: «Ich will das! Ich kann das!», sondern lieber: «Mein Ortsverein hat mich vorgeschlagen.» Entsprechungen gibt es auch in anderen Bereichen. Viele Frauen haben zum Beispiel Schwierigkeiten, zum Chef zu gehen, um eine Beförderung oder eine Gehaltserhöhung zu verlangen. Sie hoffen darauf, dass der Chef zu ihnen kommt und sagt: «Seit Jahren beobachte ich mit Wohlgefallen, wie wunderbar Sie arbeiten – deswegen möchte ich Ihnen heute eine Verdoppelung Ihres Gehalts anbieten!» Darauf können sie lange hoffen. Dass das Selbstbewusstsein der Frauen in diesem Punkt immer noch zu wünschen übrig lässt, kann man auch den Frauenzeitschriften entnehmen, die ihren Leserinnen unermüdlich Ratschläge für ein offensiveres Verhalten erteilen.

Untersuchungen auf verschiedenen Ebenen in Politik, Wirtschaft, Verwaltung haben gezeigt, dass Frauen einen eher teamorientierten Führungsstil entwickeln. Männer sagen: «Da will ich hin; alles hört auf mein Kommando!» Frauen sagen: «Da wollen wir doch alle hin, stimmt's?», und sie versuchen, die

Gruppe auf diese Weise zu motivieren. Dieser Unterschied gilt tendenziell immer noch, obwohl sich Frauen inzwischen etwas vom härteren Führungsstil der Männer abgeguckt haben und Männer jetzt häufiger auch teamorientierte Verhaltensweisen erlernen. Beide Führungsstile haben übrigens ihre Berechtigung. Wer immer nur darauf achtet, dass die Gruppe beieinander bleibt, dass es allen gut geht und die Schwachen nicht abgehängt werden, der kommt nicht besonders gut voran. Es gibt Zeiten, in denen man knallhart sagen muss: «Das Ziel müssen wir erreichen, in kürzester Zeit, und zwar alle!» Man kann nicht ständig warten, bis sich der letzte Lahme aufgerafft hat, und alle Energien dabei verbrauchen, ihm gut zuzusprechen. Es gibt aber auch Situationen, in denen es in erster Linie darauf ankommt, einigend und integrierend zu wirken. – In der Politik ist wahrscheinlich der Mensch besonders erfolgreich, dem es gelingt, den traditionell männlichen mit dem traditionell weiblichen Führungsstil zu vereinbaren bzw. angemessen zwischen beiden zu variieren.

Ich bin der Meinung, dass Durchsetzungs- und Konfliktlösungsstrategien schon früh in der Schule erlernt werden sollten, und zwar von Jungen wie von Mädchen. Jungen haben oft die Angewohnheit, gegen Hindernisse anzugehen wie ein Stier, mit gesenktem Kopf und geballter Kraft. Mädchen dagegen ziehen sich gern zurück, weil ihnen Konflikte unangenehm sind; das übertriebene Harmoniebedürfnis hängt ihnen dann lebenslang als Klotz am Bein.

Natürlich gibt es inzwischen viele selbstbewusste Frauen, die sehr gut wissen, was sie wollen und können. Aber es gibt immer noch zu viele Frauen, die sich zu viel gefallen lassen. Allerdings werden die Durchsetzungsstrategien von der sozialen Umgebung beim einen oder anderen Geschlecht durchaus anders wahrgenommen. Ein so genannter «männlicher», das heißt ein offener, direkter und vielleicht aggressiver Stil wird an Frauen häufig noch negativ bewertet. Das Fordernde wird bei ihnen als unangenehm, laut und schrill angesehen, und sie fahren zum

Teil immer noch besser damit, wenn sie ihre Argumente charmant verpacken. Was Männer untereinander für «okay» halten, vielleicht sogar als «stark» bewundern, erscheint ihnen bei Frauen als «zickig». Da heißt es dann: «Die nervt, die stresst» – und das mögen die Jungens gar nicht.

Für die Frauen meiner Generation war es in der Politik nicht gerade karriereförderlich, sich auf die so genannten «Frauenthemen» zu kaprizieren. Herkömmlich hat man ihnen stets die «weichen» Ressorts zugeschoben, Frauen, Familie, Jugend, Gesundheit, Soziales – eine Ausdehnung der typisch weiblichen Zuständigkeiten vom privaten in den öffentlichen Bereich. Ich bin keiner bewussten Strategie gefolgt, als ich mich um die Mitarbeit im Haushaltsausschuss bewarb und auf die Finanzpolitik spezialisierte. Ich fand das einfach am interessantesten, es schien mir die größte Herausforderung. Aber es erwies sich durchaus als nützlich. Politikerinnen sind, wenn sie Karriere machen wollen, immer noch gut beraten, sich in eher männerdominierten Bereichen Kompetenz zu erwerben. Über die Frauenpolitik kann frau jedenfalls kaum Wirtschaftsministerin werden. Umgekehrt müssen inzwischen auch Männer, wenn sie politisch erfolgreich sein wollen, die Interessen der Frauen im Blickfeld haben. Gerhard Schröder hat bei seinen Auftritten im Wahlkampf nicht nur mit der Stellungnahme zum Irak-Konflikt Punkte gemacht, sondern immer auch dann gewaltigen Applaus bekommen, wenn er die moderne Frauenrolle angesprochen und mehr Unterstützung bei der Vereinbarkeit von Familie und Beruf versprochen hat. Für Edmund Stoiber waren die Frauen kein Thema, und das hat ihn Stimmen gekostet. Es gibt mehr Wählerinnen als Wähler, und mehr Frauen als Männer haben Schröder gewählt.

Es gibt noch eine andere wichtige Verhaltensregel für Frauen, die in der Politik etwas werden wollen: Sie sollten sich nie zu auffällig oder betont weiblich anziehen. Das scheint eine unwesentliche Äußerlichkeit, ist aber von großer Bedeutung. Ich habe die unausgesprochenen Kleidervorschriften zu Beginn meiner politischen Karriere nicht sonderlich ernst genommen und mich häufig darüber hinweggesetzt. Das hat reichlich Probleme mit sich gebracht. Ich kann Politikerinnen nur empfehlen, alles zu vermeiden, was ihren Kollegen, ihren politischen Gegnern oder der allgemeinen Öffentlichkeit einen Vorwand gibt, an ihrem Äußeren herumzumäkeln und ihr Aussehen zu kommentieren, statt sich politisch mit ihnen auseinander zu setzen.

Also: Nicht zu aufdringlich geschminkt sein! Nicht in zu engen Kleidern oder zu kurzem Rock erscheinen! Am besten sind das klassische unauffällige Kostüm, noch besser der Hosenanzug, gedeckte Farben, keine geblümten Kleidchen, nur ja keine Spitze und keine Rüsche. Das bedeutet leider tatsächlich eine Annäherung an den langweiligen Kleidungsstil der Männer. Bisher fehlt immer noch die Modevariante für Frauen, in der sie seriös und dennoch nicht als verkleidete Männer erscheinen. Ich trage inzwischen überwiegend dunkle Hosenanzüge oder Kostüme, damit kann man nichts verkehrt machen. Besonders problematisch ist es, wenn eine Frau sich sexy gibt, denn dann wird sie sofort als weniger kompetent wahrgenommen. Sollte sie sexy auftreten und zugleich unleugbar kompetent sein, dann wird sie von Männern (und anderen Frauen!) mit Sicherheit als extrem gefährlich erlebt und deswegen schnell ausgegrenzt. Sich deshalb nun gleich hässlich zu machen wie eine kleine graue Maus, ist aber auch keineswegs förderlich – und ja auch nicht nötig.

Natürlich sind nicht alle Frauen an politischer Macht oder Karriere interessiert. Zum Glück haben sich die Zeiten aber insofern geändert, als sie es zumindest heute eher zugeben dürfen, wenn sie so etwas anstreben. Die Zurückhaltung mancher Frauen erklärt sich daraus, dass das Streben nach Macht auch unbequeme Seiten hat. Sobald man um sie kämpft, kriegt man auch ganz schön Zunder. Das ist anstrengend und gelegentlich beunruhigend, hat aber auch seine lustvollen Seiten. Sonderbarerweise wird die Frage «Wollen Sie das wirklich? Ist Ihnen wirklich wohl dabei?» nie einem Mann gestellt.

Frauen haben manchmal davor Angst, dass Macht sie in den Augen der anderen unweiblich werden lässt. «Macht macht Falten», scheinen sie insgeheim zu denken. Wer mächtig ist, wird eben nicht nur bewundert, sondern auch beneidet und attackiert. Für Männer wächst mit der Macht noch ihre Chance, geliebt zu werden, vielleicht nicht von anderen Männern, die respektieren oder fürchten sie eher, aber dafür von Frauen, die dazu neigen, Macht an Männern erotisch zu finden, egal wie der Betreffende im Einzelnen aussieht oder sich aufführt. Mächtige Frauen aber werden keineswegs mehr geliebt – weder von den Männern noch von anderen Frauen. Sie müssen sich im Gegenteil gewaltig anstrengen, damit sie trotz ihrer Macht noch attraktiv wirken. Es gibt genügend Beispiele dafür, dass Ehen auseinander brechen, weil die Ehemänner es nicht ertragen, wenn ihre Frauen einen höheren Sozialstatus oder ein größeres Einkommen haben als sie selbst.

Traditionell haben sich die Frauen deswegen häufig damit begnügt, an der Macht ihrer Männer teilzuhaben. Viele Ehefrauen von Spitzenpolitikern organisieren ihr ganzes Leben um den Job ihres Mannes herum; sie kümmern sich um seine Termine, nehmen Anrufe entgegen, erledigen einen Teil der Büroarbeit, betreiben Wahlkampf für ihn, verteilen Zettel, kleben Plakate. Sie konzentrieren sich ganz darauf, den Mann zu stützen und ihm den Rücken freizuhalten. Umgekehrt findet man das extrem selten, und eine Politikerin kann sich schon mit einem Ehemann glücklich schätzen, der ihr politisches Engagement akzeptiert. Schlimmstenfalls heißt es: «Musst du schon wieder weg? Wer ist dir nun wichtiger – ich oder deine Politik?» Natürlich gibt es hier und da ein paar Schätzchen unter den Männern, aber in der Regel fällt es ihnen noch schwer, Frauen in ihren Karrieren zu ermutigen oder zu stützen.

Doch vielleicht vollzieht sich auch hierin allmählich ein Wandel. Jedenfalls stelle ich fest, dass ich viel Beifall von Frauen bekomme, wenn ich diese Dinge stellvertretend für sie ausspreche. Und natürlich freut es mich, dass es viele Menschen gibt, die mich mögen, nicht nur im eigenen politischen Lager. Natürlich gibt es auch genug, die mich nicht mögen – das ist völlig klar. Aber mir begegnen immer wieder Frauen und Männer, die sagen: «Ich wähle zwar Ihre Partei nicht, weil ich andere politische Ansichten habe – aber ich finde es gut, wie Sie sind und wie Sie das machen. Machen Sie weiter so!»

6

Herrin der leeren Kassen –
Finanzministerin im Kabinett Engholm

Uwe Barschel hatte im Herbst 1987 wegen seiner Diffamie-rungskampagne gegen Björn Engholm vom Amt des Minister-präsidenten zurücktreten müssen. Nachdem die SPD die vor-gezogenen Landtagswahlen gewonnen hatte, konnte Björn Engholms Kabinett Ende Mai 1988 die Arbeit aufnehmen – und damit wurde ich zur Herrin über Schleswig-Holsteins leere Kassen.

Engholm hatte, bevor mir die unglückliche Geschichte mit Willy Brandt und Margarita Mathiopoulos passiert war, schon einmal in dieser Richtung Interesse an mir signalisiert; wir hat-ten ein paar Gespräche geführt, doch damals stand seine Regie-rungsübernahme noch in den Sternen. Nach meinem folgen-schweren Ausrutscher distanzierte sich Björn Engholm spürbar von mir, und ich glaubte, mit meinen Ambitionen sei es nun ein für alle Mal vorbei. Willy Brandt, der aus Lübeck kam, war in Schleswig-Holstein sehr beliebt, und ich schien deswegen für Björn Engholm untragbar geworden. Aber dann waren viele kleine Zufälle am Werk, die in der Politik nicht selten eine Rolle spielen: Die Wahl in Hamburg war anders ausgegangen, als man zuvor gedacht hatte; die SPD gewann dort noch einmal ganz knapp, und das bedeutete, dass der Mann, den sich Björn inzwischen als Finanzminister ausgeguckt hatte, auf seinem Pos-ten in Hamburg bleiben würde. Völlig unerwartet erhielt ich nachts um halb zwölf einen Anruf. «Willst du in meinem Kabinett mitarbeiten?», fragte Björn Engholm. Ich sagte sofort: «Ja. Aber nur als Finanzministerin. Denn das ist das, was ich wirklich gut kann.» So wurde ich also Ministerin in Engholms Schattenkabinett.

Die Chancen, dass wir die Landtagswahl gewinnen würden, waren nicht überwältigend; sie standen etwa halbe-halbe. In der ersten Runde, 1987, gab es dann auch ein Patt, und richtig klappte es erst bei der Wahlwiederholung 1988. Meine letzten beiden Jahre in Bonn, als eine Veränderung der politischen Machtverhältnisse in Schleswig-Holstein schon in der Luft lag, waren nicht gerade einfach. Ich war nicht Fisch noch Fleisch, nicht mehr ganz hier und noch nicht richtig dort. Die Pattsituation in Schleswig-Holstein verlängerte diesen unangenehmen Zustand. Die anderen um mich herum fragten sich: «Geht sie nun, oder bleibt sie? Sollten wir nicht schon mal anfangen, ihre Posten hier anders zu verteilen? Schließlich steht zu befürchten, dass sie nur noch halbherzig mitarbeitet und mittendrin aufhört.»

Tatsächlich habe ich mich in dieser Übergangszeit schon viel mit den besonderen finanziellen Problemen Schleswig-Holsteins befasst, und je mehr ich absehen konnte, was da auf mich zukommen würde, desto mulmiger wurde mir. Einerseits war es natürlich großartig, Finanzministerin zu werden, ein schönes Erfolgserlebnis zumindest. Aber das Gefühl, aufs Äußerste herausgefordert zu sein, wog zunächst stärker als die Bestätigung. Tatsächlich hatte ich reichlich Manschetten, als ich mein neues Amt antrat. Schleswig-Holstein war in einer so schwierigen Lage, hoch verschuldet, wirtschaftlich teilweise rückständig, und die SPD war bei der Wahl mit Versprechungen angetreten, die eingelöst werden mussten. Ich hätte mir natürlich auch einen netten, einfacheren Posten im Kabinett wünschen können. Das Wirtschaftsministerium hätte mich auch interessiert, aber jeder weiß, dass Wirtschaft ohnehin zur Hälfte aus Finanzen besteht und zur anderen Hälfte aus Psychologie. Ich dachte mir: «Jemand, der so zuschlägt wie du, ist der geborene Finanzminister.» Ich würde es einfach schaffen müssen.

Ich übernahm ein Ministerium, in dem viele CDU-Mitglieder arbeiteten. Das war zunächst nicht ganz einfach. Die leitenden Mitarbeiter im Ministerium sind ja Beamte und nicht etwa politisches Personal, das von den jeweiligen Regierungen einfach ausgetauscht werden kann. Man kann auch nicht dem ganzen Haus, das ja hinter einem stehen sollte, den Kampf ansagen. Also musste ich zunächst einmal herausfinden: Mit wem kann man hier zusammenarbeiten? Wer ist tüchtig und kompetent, wer ruht sich in seinem Beamtensessel aus? Wer gehört zu den loyalen Mitarbeitern, auf deren Vorlagen ich mich verlassen kann? Wer hat neue, pfiffige Ideen, wer ist fähig, sich auch Alternativen zu alten eingefahrenen Mustern auszudenken?

Manches habe ich erst mühsam lernen müssen. Da gab es zum Beispiel Mitarbeiter, die versuchten, einem Reden unterzuschieben, die schon ein paar Jahre alt waren, die schon der Vorvorgänger irgendwo gehalten hatte. Dann las ich die, stutzte, wunderte mich: «Moment mal – das ist doch nicht SPD-Position? Jedenfalls ist es ganz bestimmt nicht meine Position!», und anschließend war ein grundsätzliches Gespräch mit dem jeweiligen Mitarbeiter fällig. Andere Fachreferenten ritten auf ihren Steckenpferden herum und lieferten langweilige ellenlange Abhandlungen, ohne auch nur einen interessanten neuen Gedanken, ohne ein Fünkchen einer zündenden Idee. Die erste Rede, die ich als Finanzministerin vor Steuerberatern halten musste, war eine von dieser Art: knochentrocken und nicht enden wollend. Vor mir gähnten die Steuerberater, und ich selber schlief bei meinem Vortrag auch fast ein. Ich habe dann mittendrin aufgehört und erklärt: «Ich denke, Sie wissen alles, was hier in meinem Manuskript steht, viel besser als ich – also machen wir an dieser Stelle einfach mal Schluss und diskutieren. Ich will Ihre Meinung hören.» Da ging ein Ruck durch die schlummernde Runde; sie haben mich angestarrt und konnten es nicht fassen. Wenn ich meine Rede bis zum bitteren Ende gehalten hätte, hätte ich es mir wohl gründlich mit ihnen verdorben. Auf diese Weise wurde es noch eine lebhafte Veranstaltung.

Bei der ersten Orientierung hat mir Klaus Gärtner sehr geholfen, den ich als Staatssekretär ins Finanzministerium geholt hatte. Ich hatte ihn bei unserer gemeinsamen Arbeit im Haushaltsausschuss des Bundestages als kompetent und guten Kämpfer erlebt, auf den ich mich unbedingt würde verlassen können. Doch es war für mich nicht ganz einfach, ihn durchzusetzen, da er FDP-Mitglied war. Zum Glück kannten einige unserer Leute ihn von früher, aus anderen Zusammenhängen, und stellten ihm ein gutes Zeugnis aus. Auch Hans-Jochen Vogel setzte sich für ihn ein, indem er an die Fraktion schrieb: «Der Mann ist in Ordnung, er ist ein Sozialliberaler mit einem eigenen Kopf.»

Damals fand sich schon weitgehend das Team zusammen, das mich fünf Jahre später, als ich Ministerpräsidentin wurde, auch in die Staatskanzlei begleitete. Neben Klaus Gärtner waren das Jutta Ziehm, meine persönliche Sekretärin, die mich schon seit 1977 bei der Betreuung meines Wahlkreises unterstützt hatte, Knud Büchmann, mein Büroleiter, und Gerhard Hildenbrand, der 1988 Pressesprecher des Finanzministeriums und später dann Regierungssprecher wurde. Ich nenne dieses Team gern «mein Küchenkabinett»: Menschen, mit denen ich gut zusammenarbeiten, auf deren Loyalität ich mich unbedingt verlassen kann und die mir auch manche meiner Schwächen nachsehen.

Damals, als erstmals eine SPD-Regierung in Schleswig-Holstein antrat, wehte ein Wind des Aufbruchs, und ich finde immer noch, dass unsere ersten Haushalte sich wirklich sehen lassen konnten. Zumindest ist es uns gelungen, ein weiteres Anwachsen der Schulden zu bremsen. Für eine gewisse Zeit wechselte Schleswig-Holstein im Finanzausgleich der Länder sogar von der Nehmer- zur Geberseite. Die finanzielle Situation verschlechterte sich dann aber erneut, als mit der Wiedervereinigung Deutschlands die fünf neuen Bundesländer dazukamen.

Von Anfang an war Sparen angesagt: die beste Voraussetzung, sich gleich überall im Land unbeliebt zu machen. Noch bevor ich angetreten war, hatte es eine Riesenschlagzeile in der «Bild»-Zeitung gegeben: «Heide Simonis will das Musikfestival kippen.» Davon konnte natürlich keine Rede sein, aber ich hatte den Fehler gemacht, in einem Interview laut über ein paar Modifikationen nachzudenken, ohne das später noch einmal gegenzulesen. Meines Wissens hatte ich in diesem Interview gar nichts über das Musikfestival gesagt, sondern mich nur gegen eine Ballettschule ausgesprochen, die im landeseigenen Herrenhaus Salzau untergebracht war und uns eine Menge Geld kostete. Ich fand, sie würde für Schleswig-Holstein wenig bringen. So etwas kann man in Hamburg machen, aber bei uns wäre das Geld viel sinnvoller für den Ausbau der bereits bestehenden und qualitativ sehr guten Kunstinstitutionen eingesetzt: für die Muthesius-Hochschule für Kunst und Gestaltung, die als staatliche Kunsthochschule anerkannt werden soll, und für die Musikhochschule in Lübeck.

Doch da war nun diese gewaltige Schlagzeile, und ich hatte es ziemlich schwer, weil ich tatsächlich bei den Ausgaben für das Musikfestival bremsen musste. Das Schleswig-Holstein Musik Festival ist eines der großen kulturellen Events im Lande, und sein Leiter Justus Frantz war sehr beliebt. Er stammt aus Schleswig-Holstein, ist charmant und kann sich gut verkaufen. Er hat seine eigenen Marktstrategien entwickelt, und wenn man ihm sagt: «Wir haben genau fünf Millionen für das Festival», dann probiert er wie beim orientalischen Basar erst einmal, ob er nicht doch zehn Millionen herausschlagen kann. Dabei gerieten wir in eine Situation hinein, bei der die Sache zu explodieren drohte. Es wurde immer mehr Geld ausgegeben, das wir einfach nicht hatten. Meine Haltung war natürlich äußerst unpopulär. Die gesamte Presse schrie auf: «Heide Simonis will unseren armen Justus niedermachen und überhaupt das ganze Musikfestival abschaffen!» Aber es half alles nicht, da musste ich durch.

Überall einfach nur rigoros zu streichen, das wäre nicht besonders konstruktiv gewesen. Zu diesem Zeitpunkt war ein strikter Sparkurs auch in der eigenen Partei noch keineswegs so akzeptiert wie heute – zumal die SPD vor den Wahlen neue Programme und Projekte versprochen hatte und es vor allem der Westküste wirtschaftlich ziemlich schlecht ging. Andererseits wäre es unverantwortlich gewesen, so weiterzumachen wie bisher. Also entwickelten wir die Strategie: «Alternativ statt additiv» – jedes Ministerium, das ein Projekt finanziert haben wollte, musste dafür etwas anderes streichen. In der damaligen Situation hätte man sonst, wenn die anderen mit Ideen und Plänen kamen, die sie finanziert sehen wollten, immer nur sagen müssen: «Geht nicht, kein Geld!», und das hätte nur Ärger gegeben. So versuchten wir, die guten Ideen gemeinsam mit den jeweiligen Fachreferaten weiterzuentwickeln und sie dahin zu bringen, das betreffende Projekt mit Geldern aus einem anderen ihrer Töpfe zu bestreiten, indem sie die Gelder im eigenen Haus umschichteten. Oder wir versuchten, sie zu animieren, sich Kooperationspartner in der privaten Wirtschaft zu suchen. Wir haben die verschiedenen Ministerien immer wieder angeregt: «Tut euch bei diesem oder jenem Projekt mit Privaten zusammen, macht ein Angebot, geht auf den Markt – dann lässt sich das durchführen!» So haben wir mit Erfolg manche Unternehmung in «public-private partnership» angestoßen.

Übrigens habe ich nie von meinem Vetorecht als Finanzministerin Gebrauch gemacht, mit dem man alles verhindern kann, was andere sich überlegt haben. So ein politisches Instrument benutzt man nur einmal, um dann alle anderen für immer gegen sich zu haben. Es bietet keine wirklich konstruktiven Lösungen. Solche lassen sich immer nur durch gemeinsames Nachdenken und in vertrauensvoller Kooperation finden.

Mir war es wichtig, als Finanzministerin ernst genommen zu werden. Sparen war eisernes Gebot, durfte aber nicht zum Selbstzweck werden. Ich wollte im Kabinett Engholm nicht als die Pfennigfuchserin dastehen, sondern das Denken in Entwicklungskategorien unterstützen. Nicht nur: «Das geht nicht, das können wir uns nicht leisten!», sondern: «Wo wollen wir hin? Was wollen wir erreichen? Wie können wir die dazu notwendigen Prozesse in Gang bringen?» Ich bin damals schon viel im Land gereist und habe mir nicht nur einen Einblick in Werften und landwirtschaftliche Betriebe verschafft, sondern mir auch selber ein Bild von vielen einzelnen Projekten und sozialen Einrichtungen verschaffen können.

Schleswig-Holstein war zu dieser Zeit noch stark von der Landwirtschaft und vom Schiffbau geprägt, und vor allem um die Werften stand es nicht gut. Die haben nicht nur keinen Gewinn gemacht, sondern ständig größere Verluste, die sich zu irrwitzigen Summen addierten. Uns war klar: Wir dürfen nicht nur am Schiffbau kleben, auch andere Wirtschaftsbereiche müssen aufgebaut, gestärkt und gefördert werden. Übrigens kann man dies inzwischen, infolge der Globalisierung, schon wieder in neuem Lichte sehen: Der Schiffbau ist heute auch Hochtechnologie und hat als solcher trotz riesiger Probleme durchaus Zukunft, aber eben nicht mehr regional und national, sondern nur noch in internationaler Zusammenarbeit.

Das Finanzministerium hat damals viele Initiativen gemeinsam mit dem Wirtschaftsministerium auf den Weg gebracht. Der Wirtschaftsminister, Franz Froschmaier, kam von der Europapolitik, aus Brüssel, und in Zusammenarbeit mit ihm ist der Anschluss Schleswig-Holsteins an Europa gelungen. Froschmaier hat uns auf manche Geldtöpfe aufmerksam gemacht, die es schon lange gab, die aber bisher vom Land nicht genutzt worden waren.

Wir haben in dieser Zeit auch den Mittelstand «entdeckt», der vorher auf der politischen Agenda fast gar nicht existent war. So haben wir zum Beispiel Beratungsdienste für mittelständische Unternehmer aufgebaut. Dabei spielte die Neukonstruktion unserer Landesbank zusammen mit der WestLB eine wichtige Rolle. Die neue Bank sollte helfen, verstärkt auch Exporte zu finanzieren. Damals hieß es: «So eine Bank brauchen wir hier nicht, denn wir exportieren doch fast gar nicht.» Das hat sich inzwischen gründlich geändert, inzwischen exportiert Schleswig-Holstein sehr wohl, vor allem in die Ostseeregion, und zunehmend auch in andere Teile der Welt. Björn Engholm hat damals die Ostsee-Anrainerstaaten, die vor unserer Haustür liegen, als unsere zukünftigen politischen und ökonomischen Partner entdeckt. Anfangs, als der Eiserne Vorhang noch existierte, haben sich viele darüber schlapp gelacht, sie waren der Ansicht, dort gebe es nichts zu tun für die Exportwirtschaft. Wir nannten diesen Handelsraum, den wir neu beleben wollten, anfangs das «Mare Hanseaticum»; doch weil das vielleicht einen kleinen imperialistischen Beigeschmack haben könnte, änderten wir die Bezeichnung in «Mare Balticum».

Nachdem der Eiserne Vorhang gefallen war, haben wir unsere Kontakte zu Estland, Lettland, Litauen und Polen rasch ausgebaut, heute gibt es intensive, lebendige Handels- und Kulturbeziehungen mit diesen Ländern. Witzigerweise korrigiert man uns jetzt, wenn wir nach Danzig kommen: «Was wollt ihr ausbauen? Die Magistrale Balticum? Wir nennen das hier bei uns Magistrale Hanseaticum.» Wir haben diesen Ländern zunächst kleine Hilfen angeboten, wie etwa eine Agrarberatung oder eine Finanzberatung. Es kamen auch Anfragen von weiter entfernten Ostblockstaaten. So haben wir z. B. zusammen mit der Gesellschaft für Technische Zusammenarbeit Georgien geholfen, auf nationaler Ebene ein Budgetwesen aufzubauen. Später haben wir uns dann mehr auf unsere unmittelbaren Nachbarländer konzentriert. Das «Mare Balticum» ist ja auch eine politische Vision, Teil der Osterweiterung Europas, in der die skandinavischen und osteuropäischen Länder einen wichtigen Platz haben.

Die Regierung Engholm hat für viele wirtschaftliche Entwicklungen die Weichen gestellt. Wir hatten den Ehrgeiz, dieses Land weiterzuentwickeln, uns selbst und allen anderen zu beweisen, dass hinter Hamburg nicht etwa der südliche Teil des nördlichen Urals beginnt, sondern dass da ein lebendiges, waches Land ist, mit einer eigenen Geschichte und Kultur, aber auch mit zukunftsfähigen Ressourcen und Kompetenzen.

In meine Zeit als Finanzministerin des Landes Schleswig-Holstein fallen noch zwei große, beinahe geschichtsträchtige Aktionen: Zwischen 1991 und 1993 war ich bei den Tarifverhandlungen für den öffentlichen Dienst die Vorsitzende der Tarifgemeinschaft der Länder, und von 1992 bis 1993 gehörte ich mit zu den Finanzministern, die nach der Wiedervereinigung den ersten Finanzausgleich mit den neuen Bundesländern aushandelten.

In der Geschichte der Bundesrepublik hat es im öffentlichen Dienst zwei große Streiks gegeben: Der eine fand unter Willy Brandt und Heinz Kluncker statt und dauerte vier Tage, und der andere fand 1992 unter Heide Simonis und Monika Wulff-Matthies statt und hat rund zwei Wochen gedauert. Der Vorsitz für die Länder bei den Tarifverhandlungen steht immer derjenigen Partei zu, die im Bundesrat die Mehrheit hat, und das war damals gerade die SPD. Niemand übernimmt diese Rolle gern, eben weil man sich dabei selten beliebt macht. Alle anstehenden Posten wurden zwischen den Ländern rasch und gütlich verteilt. Als Letztes hieß es: «Und da wäre dann noch die TdL – die Tarifgemeinschaft der Länder –, wer möchte das denn machen?» Alle schwiegen vornehm und betreten. Für mich galt: «Da mööt wie dörch!», und ich meldete mich.

Bei diesen Tarifauseinandersetzungen hat es richtig gerappelt, und ich habe mich beim öffentlichen Dienst wohl ziemlich unbeliebt gemacht. Man nahm mir übel, dass ich, obwohl SPD- und selber auch ÖTV-Mitglied, so wenig konziliant sei. «Wie kannst du nur, du Verräterin!», hieß es da. Doch für mich war klar, dass Frau Wulff-Matthies und ich in dieser Auseinandersetzung nun mal unsere festen Rollen als Kontrahentinnen hatten. Sie konnte mir nichts schenken, nur weil sie die liebe Heide nicht kränken wollte, und ich konnte ihr nichts schenken, weil ich die liebe Monika nicht verletzen mochte.

Die ÖTV hatte – wie immer – sehr viel gefordert, und die

Länder hatten – wie immer – sehr wenig angeboten, und schon bald flog die ganze Sache auseinander. Es kam zur Schlichtung, wobei auch der Schlichtungsvorschlag aus unserer, der Sicht der öffentlichen Arbeitgeber, noch viel zu hoch lag. Für die Länder ist schon jedes halbe Prozent, um das die Gehälter anwachsen, eine kleine Katastrophe, denn bei uns machen die Personalkosten ca. 40 Prozent des Haushalts aus – beim Bund sind es nur 11 Prozent und bei den Kommunen etwa 27 Prozent. Dabei können die Kommunen immerhin noch über Gebühren neue Einnahmen erzielen, eine Möglichkeit, die die Länder nicht haben. Deswegen mussten wir auch um jedes Prozent feilschen; wir konnten den Schlichterspruch auf keinen Fall annehmen. Die Tarifverhandlungen haben sich ein gutes halbes Jahr hingezogen; zum Streik kam es zwischen der Schlichtung und dem Friedensangebot, und erst dann haben wir uns auf halber Strecke zwischen den beiden Angeboten einigen können.

Ich bin froh, dass sich die zeitraubenden Rituale der Tarifverhandlungen inzwischen ein bisschen geändert haben, denn sie sind äußerst schwerfällig und energieverschleißend und dienen nicht zuletzt dazu, ein großes Spektakel zu inszenieren. Obwohl alle Gesten des Schlagabtausches schon vorher allen klar sind, müssen sie nach dem immer gleichen unverrückbaren Muster ablaufen. In der ersten Runde erklärte die ÖTV, dass und warum sie den alten Tarifvertrag kündigte, und sie nannte ihre Forderungen. Dazu mussten dann alle Delegationsmitglieder anreisen, ein Nachmittag, eine Übernachtung, ein Vormittag ging dahin, obwohl doch vorher schon klar war, was sie sagen würden. Anstatt dass nun die Gegenseite, die öffentlichen Arbeitgeber, auf derselben Sitzung ihr Angebot und ihre Argumente vorgetragen hätten, wurden alle wieder nach Hause geschickt, es mussten erst einmal drei Wochen vergehen – und dann rückten alle wieder zur zweiten Runde an, mit demselben Zeit- und Kostenaufwand. Das Ganze scheint nur dem Zweck zu dienen, den eigenen Leuten hinterher erzählen zu können:

«Immer wieder haben wir bis nachts um drei zusammengesessen, ich habe gekämpft wie ein Löwe, bin fast tot umgefallen vor Müdigkeit – aber ich habe um keinen Punkt hinter dem Komma nachgegeben!» Was schon vorher feststand. Das ließe sich alles viel effizienter regeln, indem man etwa mehrere Verhandlungsschritte bei einem Treffen zusammenfasste.

Der erste Finanzausgleich der Länder nach der Wiedervereinigung ist 1993 unterschrieben worden, und das war wirklich eine Verhandlung von historischer Bedeutung, an der ich teil hatte. Der damalige Bundesfinanzminister Theo Waigel und seine «Viererbande» handelten die Einzelheiten aus. Dazu gehörten Gerhard Mayer-Vorfelder, der Finanzminister von Baden-Württemberg, Heinz Schleußer, der Finanzminister von Nordrhein-Westfalen, Georg Milbradt, der Finanzminister von Sachsen, und Heide Simonis, die Finanzministerin von Schleswig-Holstein, nach dem Verteilungsschlüssel: ein reiches CDU-regiertes Flächenland und ein reiches SPD-regiertes Flächenland, ein armes CDU- und ein armes SPD-Land. Wir haben damals wirklich gute Arbeit geleistet, auch wenn das Ergebnis war, dass wir hinterher ziemlich viel für die wirtschaftliche Einheit zahlen mussten und die finanzielle Situation Schleswig-Holsteins damit noch problematischer wurde. Zu diesem Zeitpunkt gingen wir, allen voran Theo Waigel und der Präsident der Treuhandgesellschaft, Detlev Carsten Rohwedder, noch davon aus, dass in die Treuhand ein Vermögensplus von 600 Milliarden DM eingebracht werden würde. Die Länderfinanzminister haben damals Theo Waigel angebettelt, den Ländern einen Teil des prospektiven Treuhandvermögens zu überlassen, aber der wollte alles für den Bund. Zum Glück, kann man jetzt nur sagen, sonst ginge es den Ländern heute noch schlechter, obwohl das kaum vorstellbar scheint. Tatsächlich belief sich das Treuhandvermögen dann ja auf Schulden in Höhe von 250 Milliarden DM.

Als Björn Engholm mich zur Finanzministerin in sein Schattenkabinett berief, hatte ein Kumpel im Bundestag gefrotzelt:

«Da wirst du dann aber richtig arbeiten müssen!» Ich war darüber ziemlich empört gewesen. Was hatte ich denn, bitte schön, all die Tage und halben Nächte im Haushaltsausschuss getan? Und doch behielt er insoweit Recht, als in diesen Jahren nicht nur die Verantwortung, sondern auch die Arbeit gewaltig zunahm, und die Anforderungen wuchsen, je länger ich im Amt war. Trotzdem hatte ich als Finanzministerin noch ein bisschen Freizeit und so etwas wie ein Privatleben. Es gab noch Wochenenden ohne Termine. Samstags konnte ich manchmal über einen Flohmarkt bummeln und weitere wunderbare überflüssige alte Kaffeekannen und Brotschneidemaschinen für meine Sammlung erwerben. Gelegentlich ging ich noch abends mit meinem Mann ins Kino und weinte an den herzzerreißenden Stellen. Ab und an trafen wir Freunde zum Essen in einem Lokal. Ich lud sogar noch jeden zweiten Monat Gäste ein, weil ich so gerne koche. Und einmal im Jahr veranstalteten wir eine große Party. Mit diesen Vergnügungen war Schluss, als ich einigermaßen plötzlich Ministerpräsidentin wurde.

7

«Das ganze schöne Land in der Hand einer einzigen Frau»

Plötzlich war ich Ministerpräsidentin. Am 4. Mai 1993 trat Björn Engholm von seinem Amt als Ministerpräsident des Landes Schleswig-Holstein zurück, und am 19. Mai übernahm ich das Amt, also beinahe von heute auf morgen. Am Anfang war es ein Gefühl, als wäre ich bei Nacht und Nebel von einem Dampfer ins kalte Wasser geschubst worden. Trotzdem hatte ich die Zuversicht: «Du kannst schwimmen, du wirst es schaffen, oben zu bleiben.»

Björn Engholm hatte nach Uwe Barschel in Schleswig-Holstein als Garant für Integrität und Offenheit gegolten, in seinen Rollen als Parteivorsitzender, als Kanzlerkandidat und als Ministerpräsident. Zuvor hatte die Affäre um Barschel uns alle sehr aufgewühlt. Im Bundestag hatten die anderen Abgeordneten bis dahin gern liebevoll spöttelnd von «Schläfrig-Holstein» geredet; nun hieß es auf einmal: «Ihr da oben habt es aber ganz schön faustdick hinter den Ohren!» – und das war gar nicht schmeichelhaft gemeint. Ich erinnere mich noch genau an die Pressekonferenz, bei der Barschel sein Ehrenwort gab. Damals war ich überzeugt davon, dass er nicht gelogen haben könne. Denn er hatte einen ähnlichen sozialen Hintergrund wie mein Vater, und der hatte mir vermittelt, dass man dem Ehrenwort eines Ehrenmannes absolut vertrauen kann. Das alles fand noch in der Zeit vor der öffentlichen Diskreditierung des

Ehrenwortes statt. So schien es mir empörend und ungeheuerlich, dass Uwe Barschels Ehrenwort eine Lüge kaschierte. Doch später, nachdem man ihn tot in der Badewanne eines Schweizer Hotels aufgefunden hatte, empfand ich auch Mitleid mit seiner unglücklich verstrickten Person, zumal die merkwürdigen Umstände dieses Todes ja nie ganz aufgeklärt worden sind. Ich habe die Affäre damals, von Bonn aus, eher aus der Distanz erlebt, doch sie war natürlich zentrales Gesprächsthema der Landes-SPD, wenn ich zu Hause in Kiel war.

Björn Engholm erschien anfangs im Kontrast zu Uwe Barschel wie eine Lichtgestalt. Er stand für Wahrhaftigkeit und einen Neuanfang, er war fast schon designierter Kanzlerkandidat, hochbeliebt im Land, ein begehrter Gesprächspartner für Repräsentanten aus Kultur und Wirtschaft. Er war kultiviert und weltoffen, und in seinem Kabinett herrschte so etwas wie Teamgeist. Umso größer war dann für uns alle der Schock, als sich herausstellte, dass auch er nicht ganz die Wahrheit über die Machenschaften gesagt hatte, die zum Sturz Barschels führten – oder zumindest die Wahrheit ein paar Tage zu lang zurückgehalten hatte. Aus der «Barschel-Affäre» war inzwischen die «Schubladen-Affäre» geworden: Barschel hatte im Herbst 1987 zurücktreten müssen, weil sein Medienreferent Reiner Pfeiffer dem «Spiegel» anvertraut hatte, er habe im Auftrag Barschels Diffamierendes über Engholms Privatleben aufspüren sollen. Später stellte sich heraus, dass der damalige SPD-Landesvorsitzende Günther Jansen über einen Mittelsmann Pfeiffer eine größere Geldsumme hatte zukommen lassen. Jansen sagte aus, er habe Pfeiffer aus Mitleid unterstützen wollen, und zwar mit Geldern, die er privat in der Schublade gesammelt habe. Viele konnten es einfach nicht glauben, dass Björn Engholm über diese Transaktion informiert gewesen sein sollte, und ich weiß bis heute nicht genau, was im Einzelnen abgelaufen ist. Jedenfalls geriet Engholm so unter Druck, dass er zurücktreten musste.

Was macht eine Partei, wenn sie in solchen Momenten ganz schnell jemanden nach vorn holen muss? Ich war als Finanzministerin im Land relativ bekannt und trotz des Zwanges, sparen zu müssen, einigermaßen beliebt – und ich war auf jeden Fall frei von dem Verdacht, etwas von den Affären gewusst zu haben, da ich in der fraglichen Zeit noch in Bonn gewesen war. Ich war eine Frau, das hatte es auf diesem Posten noch nie gegeben, und in der verzweifelten Situation erhoffte man sich gerade von dieser Novität die Rettung. Es musste alles sehr schnell gehen; die Partei konnte sich nicht viel Zeit lassen mit einer Entscheidung – und so entschied man sich ganz schnell für mich.

Es waren noch zwei, drei andere Namen im Gespräch, Kollegen, die sich durchaus berechtigte Hoffnungen machen konnten. Unter normalen politischen Bedingungen wären sie entweder mit Björn Engholm nach Bonn gegangen, oder sie hätten gute Chancen gehabt, in Kiel seine Nachfolge anzutreten. Sie hätten ihre Sache sicher auch gut gemacht. Aber man einigte sich auf mich, um auf jeden Fall ein Kontrastprogramm zu haben – es war eine von den Situationen, in denen es zur Abwechslung einmal nützlich ist, eine Frau zu sein.

Ich hatte anfangs einige Bedenken, nachdem ich zu diesem Posten gekommen war wie die Jungfrau zum Kinde. Die Menschen im Lande mochten Björn Engholm; er ist auch heute noch bekannt und beliebt; ich werde immer mal wieder nach ihm gefragt. Viele Menschen waren richtig verdattert über den plötzlichen Wechsel an der Spitze. Nie werde ich die Veranstaltung des Bauernverbandes vergessen, bei der ein älterer Mann auf mich zukam und kopfschüttelnd sagte: «Eene eenzige Frau regeert dat wunnerschöne Land ganz alleen. Oh ne, dat dörf doch nicht sin!» – Is awer so worn! Es war ein kleiner Bauer, dem man ein Leben harter Arbeit ansah, mit großen Händen und zutiefst kummervollem Gesichtsausdruck, und aus seiner Äußerung sprach tiefe Verwirrung und Resignation. Es war spürbar, dass er nichts gegen mich persönlich hatte, sondern nur so etwas wie den Untergang des Abendlandes fürchtete. Vielleicht waren damals nicht alle so skeptisch wie er, aber es schlug mir keineswegs nur Begeisterung entgegen.

Deswegen war der erste Wahlkampf meiner Amtszeit, für die Kommunalwahlen im April 1994, nicht ganz einfach. Es begegnete mir auch eine Menge an Irritation und Ärger aus den eigenen Reihen, an der Basis. «Wir strengen uns hier vor Ort an, und die Dinge laufen prima», hieß es, «dann kommt ihr mit eurem Mist in Kiel und macht uns alles kaputt.» Das waren natürlich verständliche Frustrationen, und es war wichtig, sie ernst zu nehmen, sich diesem Ärger zu stellen, damit die engagierten Leute nicht in die innere Emigration gingen.

Ministerpräsidentin zu sein, bedeutet, über alle politischen Belange des eigenen Landes informiert zu sein, sich um sie alle zu kümmern; es bedeutet, Landesinteressen über Parteipolitik zu stellen und sie gegenüber dem Bund zu vertreten, dessen Interessen keineswegs immer kompatibel sind. Man muss Politik im und für den Alltag machen, aber auch Weichen stellen für die zukünftige Entwicklung. Man plant und gestaltet vieles, anderes ist auch nur Organisation, Verwaltung, Repräsentation, und manchmal steht – wie beim Untergang des Holzfrachters «Pallas» vor Amrum oder bei der BSE-Krise – die Bewältigung von unvorhergesehenen kleineren oder größeren Katastrophen im Vordergrund der Arbeit.

Sachlich fühlte ich mich durch den neuen Posten nicht überfordert. Ich hatte schon als Finanzministerin Einblick in viele Bereiche, welche die anderen Fachministerien beschäftigten. Außerdem fällt es mir nicht schwer, mir neue Fakten und Zusammenhänge rasch anzueignen. Ich habe so eine Art Teppichmusterwissen: Die Struktur von Sachverhalten prägt sich mir fest ein, neue Daten lassen sich jeweils rasch in das gespeicherte Muster einbauen. Ich vergesse zwar manche Einzelheiten schnell wieder, aber solange ich die Informationen benötige, sind die Fakten in der Regel präsent.

Eine der ersten und unangenehmsten Aufgaben bestand darin, das Kabinett umzubesetzen. Der Wirtschaftsminister kam neu hinzu; der Sozialminister wurde Finanzminister; es gab eine neue Sozialministerin. Meine erste Kabinettsliste ist in einem Lokal auf der Speisekarte entstanden, direkt nach meiner Nominierung auf dem Parteitag. Wir aßen dort im Kreise von drei Ehepaaren, anschließend hatte mein Mann mit den Ehefrauen der anderen einen «bunten Abend», und wir Übrigen setzten uns beiseite und begannen, erste Überlegungen anzustellen.

Die anstehenden Entlassungsgespräche allerdings habe ich allein geführt. Es fällt mir auch heute nicht leicht, einem Menschen sagen zu müssen: «Wir können nicht mehr miteinander arbeiten.» Damals ahnten es einige schon, andere hat es doch unerwartet getroffen. Ein solches Gespräch ist immer eine harte Situation, manchmal auch eine Kränkung, da müssen nicht noch Zuschauer zugegen sein. Weder die Minister in meinem Kabinett noch meine engeren Mitarbeiter müssen in jedem Punkt denken wie ich, sie müssen auch nicht den gleichen Arbeitsstil haben. Darauf lege ich keinen Wert. Aber ich brauche das Gefühl, dass die Chemie stimmt. Wenn das nicht der Fall ist, dann hat es einfach keinen Zweck, weil ich mich auf diese Menschen nicht verlassen könnte.

Mit mir wechselte mein «Küchenkabinett», die kleine Gruppe meiner engsten Mitarbeiter, vom Finanzministerium in die Staatskanzlei über: meine langjährige Sekretärin Jutta Ziehm und mein Fahrer Klaus Göttsche. Klaus Gärtner wurde Chef der Staatskanzlei, Gerhard Hildenbrand Regierungssprecher und Knud Büchmann Büroleiter. Sie alle haben mir geholfen, in der neuen Umgebung mit den neuen Aufgaben schnell zurechtzukommen. Es ist in einer solchen Position ganz wichtig, im nächsten Umkreis Menschen zu haben, auf die man sich absolut verlassen kann. Sonst muss man sich ja dauernd überlegen: «Was und wie viel darf ich sagen? Wie soll ich es sagen? Könnte dies oder das vielleicht falsch aufgefasst werden?» Wenn man sich auch in seinem nahen, täglichen Umfeld ständig kontrollieren müsste, dann besteht die Gefahr, dass man auf Dauer ein bisschen komisch wird – und komisch ist noch das Mindeste.

In meiner ersten Zeit als Ministerpräsidentin wurde ich zum Liebling der Presse. Interviews, Porträts und Kommentare rückten dabei gern die mehr oder minder dekorativen Äußerlichkeiten in den Mittelpunkt. Immer wieder ging es um meine persönlichen Eigenarten und Vorlieben – «Kodderschnüss und Temperament», «Häuptling Flinke Zunge», «Ein Mundwerk wie ein Schwert, das Sitzfleisch eines tibetanischen Gebetsmönchs, ein Gedächtnis zum Fürchten» –, um meine Vorliebe für Hüte und Schmuck – «selbst die englische Queen, die Königin der Filzdeckel, würde bei diesem Kopfputz vor Neid erblassen», «vierzehn Ringe an zehn Fingern und kunstvolle Ohrgehänge», «Sie trägt gern Brillen im Straßenkreuzer-Format» –, um meine Hobbys und Ähnliches – «Vorliebe für Flohmärkte und Sammelleidenschaft für Haushaltskrimskrams», «sie besitzt 280 Servietten, 360 Handtücher, 40 Tischdecken, 120 Kaffeekannen, alles auf dem Flohmarkt erstanden» –, die Zahlen in diesem Zusammenhang variierten beliebig.

Der Tenor war im Großen und Ganzen wohlwollend, aber wir hatten wirklich viel damit zu tun, dazwischen auch die politische Botschaft zu platzieren: «Sie präsentiert nicht nur ihre Hüte, sie kann auch was; sie sitzt nicht nur herum mit ihren Ringen an den Fingern, sie tut auch was. Sie hat Ideen für dieses Land und Lösungen für seine politischen Probleme anzubieten.»

Mir ist immer wieder nachgesagt worden, ich hätte meine etwas unkonventionellen Eigenarten bewusst genutzt, um ein Image aufzubauen: «Wenn keine protokollarischen Termine anstehen, regiert sie schon mal barfuß und in Jeans», konnte man lesen, und: «Die Landesmutter aus dem hohen Norden inszeniert sich gerne unkonventionell. Ist sie wirklich so, oder setzt sich da nur jemand gekonnt in Szene?» Natürlich inszeniert man sich auch; man kann gar nicht anders, wenn das ständig von außen an einen herangetragen wird. Aber ich habe mich nicht in einer bestimmten Weise verhalten, um einem künstlich fabrizierten Image zu entsprechen. Ich war schon vorher so, und es wäre mir extrem schwer gefallen, mich grundsätzlich zu ändern und mich so steif und förmlich zu verhalten, wie es manche wohl mit der Rolle eines Ministerpräsidenten verbinden. Ich sehe keinen Sinn darin, mich vierundzwanzig Stunden am Tag staatstragend zu geben. Und wenn die Leute gern wissen wollen, mit was für einem Menschen sie es zu tun haben – warum soll man dann nicht zu dem stehen, was einen sowieso ausmacht? Inzwischen haben die Menschen hier im Land eine gewisse Abweichung vom Protokoll als eigenen Stil akzeptiert, den sie nicht negativ bewerten, sondern zumeist als eine lebendige Auflockerung betrachten. Heute achte ich allerdings auch darauf, dass ich bei Außenterminen förmlicher angezogen bin als bei Terminen im Haus.

Bis zum März 1996 verdankte ich mein Amt noch dem Rücktritt Engholms. Dann aber standen die nächsten Landtagswahlen an. Nun würde sich zeigen, ob es mir gelungen war, die Bevölkerung Schleswig-Holsteins von mir und meiner Arbeit zu überzeugen. Die SPD war immer noch ziemlich zerstritten; wir kämpften natürlich für eine absolute Mehrheit. Aber mir war klar, dass wir eins auf die Finger bekommen würden, zumal gerade erst der Untersuchungsausschuss zur «Schubladen-Affäre» seine Arbeit beendet hatte, bei der die Partei nicht gut wegkam. Die Wahl war im März, und im Februar lag der Abschlussbericht vor. So etwas wird von der Opposition ja immer gern bis unmittelbar vor die nächste Wahl hingezogen.

Auf diesem Hintergrund konnte ich mit dem Ergebnis der Landtagswahl – knapp 40 Prozent für die SPD – durchaus zufrieden sein. Allerdings mussten wir eine Koalition mit den Grünen eingehen, und das erwies sich erst einmal als recht schwierig, da die Grünen direkt von der Position der außerparlamentarischen Opposition an den Kabinettstisch wechselten. Sie hatten noch all die typischen Kinderkrankheiten einer Partei, die bisher nie in der Regierungsverantwortung gestanden hat. Allzu häufig wurden bei ihnen, kaum war etwas im Kabinett entschieden worden, anschließend Sondersitzungen einberufen, und auf denen wurden die grünen Minister von ihren eigenen Landesausschüssen mehr als einmal zur Schnecke gemacht.

Zu Beginn der Legislaturperiode waren einige Mitglieder der SPD-Fraktion geradezu begeistert von der rot-grünen Idee, sie sahen darin das Gesellschaftsmodell der Zukunft. Solche Erwartungen sind inzwischen einer eher nüchternen und pragmatischen Herangehensweise gewichen, obwohl sich die zweite Legislaturperiode mit den Grünen (ab 2000) eindeutig angenehmer und professioneller gestaltet als die erste. Die beiden grünen Minister und ihre Staatssekretäre, die jetzt mit am Kabinettstisch sitzen, sind ausgesprochen kooperative Partner – nicht in dem Sinne, dass sie mich höflich fragen: «Wie hätten Sie es denn gern?», und sich dann entsprechend verhielten. Aber wenn wir gemeinsam eine Sache erarbeitet haben, dann stehen sie auch dazu, und es geht nicht immer wieder von vorne los wie in der vorangegangenen Legislaturperiode.

Ein großer Fehler dieser ersten Regierung mit den Grünen bestand darin, dass wir einen viel zu detaillierten Koalitionsvertrag ausgehandelt hatten (er umfasste genau 84 Seiten; im Jahr 2000, zu Beginn der zweiten gemeinsamen Legislaturperiode, schafften wir es dann mit nur 39 Seiten). Nicht nur, dass uns dieser Vertrag selbst unendlich viel Zeit gekostet hat, er machte auch die politischen Alltagsgeschäfte äußerst schwierig und umständlich, da man im Einzelnen immer wieder nachschauen musste, wie in welchem Fall genau vorzugehen sei, was wir – laut Vertrag – durften und wo uns die Hände gebunden waren.

Bald gab es mit den Grünen einen langen und nervenzehrenden Kampf um den Bau der A 20, der geplanten Ost-West-Autobahn, die Mecklenburg-Vorpommern mit Schleswig-Holstein und Niedersachsen verbinden soll. Die Grünen lehnen die A 20 grundsätzlich ab. Nun lässt sich über den Sinn und Unsinn von Straßenbau immer streiten, aber diese neue Autobahn ist meiner Ansicht nach wirklich notwendig. Sie soll von der polnischen Grenze über die Elbe, durch Niedersachsen bis ins Rheinland führen. Sie hätte eine Entlastungsfunktion für die A 7, die sich an Sommerwochenenden gelegentlich in die längste Parkstrecke der Welt verwandelt. Doch diese Straße ist und bleibt ein Dorn im Auge der Grünen; sie haben darüber schon einmal fast die Koalition platzen lassen. Sie erklärten ganz schnell alles zum Naturschutzgebiet, was in der Nachbarschaft der geplanten Strecke liegt. Der Straßenbau ist in diesen Bereichen damit zwar nicht ganz verboten, aber wir müssen nach EU-Recht erst beweisen, dass wir diese Straße brauchen und warum sie genau an dieser Stelle verlaufen muss. Das dauert lange, und auch die vielen Einspruchsmöglichkeiten, die es in Deutschland bei solchen Bauvorhaben gibt, verzögern und verteuern die Sache ganz ungemein. Es ist übrigens bemerkenswert, dass die Grünen genau in den Gebieten, die an der geplanten A 20 liegen, bei den Kommunalwahlen 1998 ziemlich verloren haben.

Wenn ich die beiden Legislaturperioden rückwirkend aus der Distanz betrachte, so würde ich sagen: Mein Einstieg im Jahr 1993 war nicht einfach, doch dann lief es recht gut bis 1996; in der zweiten Legislaturperiode ab 1996 gab es Anfangsprobleme mit den Grünen und die aufreibenden Querelen um die A 20. Davon abgesehen, war ich selbst auch einigermaßen zufrieden, bis zum Untergang der «Pallas», der uns wegen des schlechten Krisenmanagements hart traf. Vielleicht hat jede Legislaturperiode ihre «Pallas», ihre ganz besonderen kleineren oder größeren Katastrophen.

Die «Pallas», ein Holzfrachter, war bei einem gewaltigen Sturm vor Dänemark leckgeschlagen. Sie fuhr unter der Flagge der Bahamas, der Kapitän war ein Pole, und die Mannschaft kam aus aller Herren Länder. Die Dänen ließen das Schiff nicht in einen ihrer Häfen einlaufen. Es trieb steuerlos auf unsere Küste zu, setzte sich vor Amrum auf einer Sandbank fest und brannte dann tagelang. Wir waren nicht vorgewarnt worden und haben zu spät und zunächst nicht sehr effizient reagiert. Wir haben aus diesem Vorfall gelernt und werden künftig in vergleichbaren Situationen schnell und angemessen reagieren.

Nach meiner Wiederwahl 1996 hatte die Presse plötzlich ein neues Lieblingsthema: die K-Frage. In Bonn trugen zu dieser Zeit teils vor, teils hinter den Kulissen Scharping, Lafontaine und Schröder ihre Kämpfe um die Kanzlerkandidatur aus, und die Journalisten kamen auf die abstruse Idee, mich zu fragen, ob ich mich denn nicht auch in die Arena begeben und bei den Sandkastenspielen der Jungs mitmachen wollte. Es gab Schlagzeilen wie: «Wird diese Frau der erste Kanzler?», «Warum machen Sie nicht den Kanzler, Frau Simonis?»

Dabei lag auf der Hand, dass ich vom Wahnsinn hätte besessen sein müssen, wenn ich mich da reingehängt hätte. Es war ganz klar, dass zu diesem Zeitpunkt die Karten längst vergeben waren, auch wenn es zwischen den dreien noch länger ein Kampf mit offenem Ausgang war. Lafontaine hatte eine starke Stellung in der Partei; er war ein charismatischer Redner, der ganze Parteitage herumreißen konnte. Schröder und ich hatten gemeinsam, dass wir beide an Scharping herumgemeckert hatten, wofür wir auch beide Prügel bezogen. Lange Zeit hätte ich am ehesten auf Lafontaine getippt. Aber es gab auch deutliche Hinweise aus den großen Landesverbänden, dass sie auf Schröder setzten, weil sie in ihm den Mann der Wirtschaft sahen. Den meisten war klar: Wir Sozialdemokraten müssen unsere Wirtschaftskonzepte neu überdenken. Alte Klassenkampfparolen wie: «Wir Linken stehen auf Seiten der Arbeiterschaft gegen das Kapital, und deswegen kooperieren wir nicht mit den Unternehmern» sind für die Zukunft untauglich. In dieser Hinsicht hatte Schröder einen gewissen Vorsprung vor Lafontaine.

Fest stand nur eines: Jeder, der da noch hätte mitmischen wollen, hätte sich nur eine blutige Nase geholt. Und man hätte mich zu Recht des Größenwahnsinns bezichtigt, wenn ich gesagt hätte: «Warum eigentlich nicht?» Ich hatte ja gerade erst als Ministerpräsidentin Fuß gefasst.

Das war also wieder so ein Beispiel für einen Journalismus, der plötzlich aus heiterem Himmel Ideen mit Sensationswert in die Welt setzt. Wenn eine es schon geschafft hat, als Erste

Ministerpräsidentin zu werden, dann kann man der auch zutrauen, dass sie jetzt gegen die drei Männer losgeht! Die Tatsache, dass ich ohne eigenes Zutun plötzlich Gegenstand solcher Spekulationen war, hängt sicher damit zusammen, die einzige Frau in meinem Amt zu sein. Wenn man das einzige Exemplar einer Gattung ist, fehlen die Bezugskoordinaten für einen Vergleich, was dazu führen kann, dass man einerseits schnell hochgejubelt, andererseits aber auch gnadenlos abqualifiziert wird.

Bei der nächsten Landtagswahl im Jahr 2000 hatte ich Volker Rühe als Gegenkandidaten und zunächst einmal keinen leichten Stand. Die SPD stand, nach dem zunächst wenig überzeugenden Start der rot-grünen Bundesregierung, insgesamt ziemlich wackelig da, und das schlägt meist voll auf das Land durch. Volker Rühe war in Schleswig-Holstein ähnlich bekannt wie ich, vielleicht nicht ganz so beliebt. Aber er war ein neuer Mann mit einem bundespolitischen Namen, der selbstbewusst auftrat. Doch dann sind ihm im Laufe des Wahlkampfes Fehler unterlaufen, die mich gewundert haben. Sie machten deutlich, dass er sich im Land doch nicht besonders gut auskannte. Nach und nach bekamen die Menschen das Gefühl: «Der ist ja hier nur auf der Durchreise; in Wirklichkeit will er nach Bonn. Er will sich hier nur zum Ministerpräsidenten wählen lassen, um Kanzlerkandidat der CDU zu werden.» Diese Diskussion hätte er gar nicht aufkommen lassen dürfen. Außerdem hat er wohl, nach allem, was man hörte, im Landesverband der CDU manchen Streit vom Zaun gebrochen, so dass die Begeisterung seiner Partei, für ihn Wahlkampf zu machen, sich bei vielen bald auf ein Pflichtgefühl reduzierte. Natürlich habe ich dann auch durch die CDU-Spenden-Affäre Aufwind bekommen, das muss man nüchtern anmerken, wie auch dadurch, dass die Bonner SPD wieder Tritt gefasst hatte. So kam ein positiver Doppeleffekt für mich zustande.

Ich hatte bei den Befragungsprofilen nicht nur in den «weichen Faktoren» einen hohen Vorsprung vor Volker Rühe – so

etwas wie: auf die Menschen zugehen, ihre Probleme wahrnehmen, mit ihnen reden –, sondern ich schnitt auch bei den «har-
ten Faktoren» wie Kompetenz, vor allem Wirtschaftskompetenz,
ganz gut ab. Diese Kombination hat es dann wohl gebracht.

So konnte ich im Jahr 2000 mit 43 Prozent SPD-Stimmen ein
ordentliches Wahlergebnis hinlegen, eine erfreuliche Steige-
rung gegenüber 1996 (da waren es 39,8 Prozent gewesen).
Diesmal hatten wir auch die Koalitionsvereinbarungen zügig
unter Dach und Fach, und alles lief recht gut. Doch dann tauch-
te da plötzlich, wie aus heiterem Himmel, in der Presse die Ver-
mutung auf, ich sei amtsmüde.

Ich weiß nicht, wer das in die Welt gesetzt hat. Ich war 57 Jahre alt, und mit einmal war das ein Thema. Kurt Biedenkopf
feierte als Ministerpräsident Sachsens gerade seinen 70. Geburtstag, und Bernhard Vogel aus Thüringen wurde 68 Jahre
alt. Bei ihnen aber wurde das Alter nur erwähnt, um ihre besondere Vitalität und Tatkraft herauszustreichen. Ich habe mich
damals gefragt, wie solche Geschichten in der Presse zustande
kommen. Werden sie bewusst von jemandem lanciert? Oder rä-
sonieren Journalisten laut an ihren Stammtischen, und dann
schreibt einer vom anderen ab? Es war noch gar nicht so lange
her, dass mir die gleiche Presse die Kraft und den Ehrgeiz zuge-
traut hatte, Bundeskanzlerin werden zu wollen – und nun kipp-
te diese Einschätzung fast übergangslos ins Gegenteil. Plötzlich
wollten alle Anzeichen von Müdigkeit festgestellt haben, wofür
es keinerlei objektiven Grund gab. Eine Zeit lang hat mich das
ziemlich geärgert. Ich dachte: «Eigentlich bist du doch be-
kloppt, all diese vielen Termine zu absolvieren; du könntest es
dir ebenso gut zu Hause bequem machen und die Beine hoch-
legen, wenn es ohnehin nur heißt, du seist müde – egal, wie du
dich ins Zeug wirfst.» Zum Glück bin ich dieser Versuchung
nicht erlegen, nicht zuletzt deswegen, weil ich einfach viel zu
gern unterwegs bin und mit den Menschen rede.

Vielleicht lag der Fehler darin, dass ich in den ersten Jahren
als Ministerpräsidentin den Eindruck erweckt habe, ich könnte

wirklich jede Veranstaltung im Lande besuchen. Als Fachministerin ist man nur für das zuständig, was mit dem eigenen Haus zu tun hat, aber für eine Ministerpräsidentin ist eigentlich alles wichtig: jede Eröffnung einer größeren Veranstaltung, jede Initiative, jedes Projekt, alles, was die Menschen Interessantes auf die Beine stellen. Und eigentlich interessiert mich auch das meiste. Aber die Woche hat nun mal nur sieben Tage und der Tag nur vierundzwanzig Stunden. Und selbst wenn ich, wie es manchmal der Fall ist, von morgens früh um acht bis nachts um zwölf und von Sonntag bis Sonntag unterwegs bin – selbst dann bleiben immer reichlich Termine, die abgesagt werden müssen. Vielleicht sind die Betroffenen besonders enttäuscht, weil ich anfangs den Eindruck erweckt habe, dass ich mich um alles persönlich kümmere und überall hinkomme.

Eine andere Ursache für das Gerücht von der Amtsmüdigkeit könnte darin gelegen haben, dass nach der Wahl fünf Minister zurückgetreten waren, zwei von den Grünen und drei der unseren. «Der gehen schon die eigenen Leute laufen», hieß es. Dabei war das nur ein zufälliges Zusammentreffen sehr verschiedener persönlicher Gründe, von denen ich jeden im Einzelnen gut verstehen konnte. Einer war über sechzig und fand, er habe nun genug von der Politik. Der nächste wollte sich stärker um sein Kind, um die Familie kümmern. Der Wirtschaftsminister hatte ein attraktives Angebot aus der Wirtschaft, in die er immer hatte zurückkehren wollen. Und die Grünen hatten über den Wechsel ihrer Minister selbst entschieden. All diese gesammelten Rücktritte boten natürlich ein unerfreuliches Bild und beschäftigten die Öffentlichkeit eine Weile.

Wie auch immer: Der Vorwurf, ich sei amtsmüde, hat mich gewurmt, zumal es auch eine geraume Zeit dauerte, bis er wieder aus der Presse verschwand – im Übrigen auf ähnlich unerklärliche Weise, wie er entstanden war. Es könnte allerdings sein, dass dabei die BSE-Krise eine gewisse Rolle gespielt hat, denn in diesem Zusammenhang wurde mir von allen Seiten in der Presse ein gutes Krisenmanagement bescheinigt.

8

Politik und Presse –
eine Hassliebe

Medienschelte ist zu einem beliebten Sport bei Politikern geworden. Alle Politikerinnen und Politiker beklagen sich, wenn sie zu wenig Aufmerksamkeit bekommen, und natürlich auch, wenn nicht genau das über sie publiziert wird, was sie sich wünschen. In diesem Zusammenhang hört man dann oft das Klagelied über den Verfall des politischen Journalismus. In diesen Chor will ich nicht einstimmen – zumal Presse, Hörfunk und Fernsehen mit mir über große Strecken nicht unfreundlich und meistens fair umgegangen sind. Politik und Medien brauchen einander, so viel steht fest. Allerdings haben sich die Medien seit den Jahren, als ich in die Politik ging, tatsächlich verändert, und diese Veränderungen sind nicht unproblematisch.

Am auffälligsten ist, wie sehr das Tempo der Berichterstattung zugenommen hat. Nichts ist so alt wie die Nachricht von gestern, und jede Zeitung, jeder Sender will die Nase vorn haben. Früher rechnete man dabei noch in Tagen, heute in Stunden und manchmal sogar in Minuten. Der Wettbewerbsdruck ist groß, denn es gibt viele Medien, die miteinander um die Aufmerksamkeit des Publikums buhlen. Dabei ist die allgemeine Hektik noch durch die modernen Kommunikationstechniken wie Internet und E-Mail verstärkt worden.

Es liegt auf der Hand, dass der beschleunigte Umschlag von Nachrichten auch auf Kosten der Qualität der Berichterstattung gehen muss. Solide Recherchen erfordern nun einmal Zeit, und diese Zeit findet sich im journalistischen Alltagsgeschäft offensichtlich immer seltener. Journalisten werden eher für ihr Tempo als für ihre Gründlichkeit belohnt, und deswegen werden immer häufiger komplexe Sachverhalte nur verkürzt dargestellt. Der solide Hintergrundbericht ist die Ausnahme geworden.

Neben dem gestiegenen Tempo ist noch eine andere große Veränderung zu beobachten, die Tendenz zu einer personalisierten und gefühlsbetonten Berichterstattung. Natürlich hat es auch vor zwanzig, dreißig Jahren Boulevardblätter gegeben, die stark vereinfachten und emotionalisierten. Neu ist, dass diese Entwicklung auch vor den seriöseren Medien nicht Halt zu machen scheint. Die Effekthascherei hat zugenommen. Oft zählt die Verpackung mehr als der Inhalt. Das ist sicher ein allgemeines Zeitgeistphänomen, das durch die Konkurrenz der Medien untereinander verschärft wird. Das reizüberflutete Publikum kann sich auf lange und differenzierte Zeitungsartikel kaum mehr einlassen, und in der Informationsschwemme haben griffige Formeln, marktschreierische Schlagzeilen und Sensationsberichte die größte Chance, wahrgenommen zu werden. Ideen und politische Positionen interessieren vor allem, wenn sie an Personen festgemacht werden können.

Natürlich sind Politik und Medien in unserer Gesellschaft aufeinander eingespielt. Sie beeinflussen sich gegenseitig, und auf diese Weise werden Trends verstärkt. Die Art, wie Politik sich darstellt, beeinflusst die Berichterstattung; umgekehrt nehmen die Medien durch das, was sie auswählen, und durch die Art, wie sie es berichten, Einfluss auf die Selbstdarstellung der Akteure. Politiker und Politikerinnen wollen das Beste an Werbung für sich herausholen und kommen dem Medientrend entgegen, indem sie auch ihrerseits stärker vereinfachen und sich selber mehr inszenieren als früher; auch sie stellen häufig die Verpackung über den Inhalt. Der Populismus nimmt zu, Zwischentöne sind kaum noch gefragt.

In Berlin beklagen sich zur Zeit viele darüber, dass alte Spielregeln verloren gegangen sind, die früher im Umgang von Politik und Presse galten. Da gibt es die so genannten «Hintergrundgespräche». Früher konnte man den Journalisten auch vertrauliche Informationen geben, die dazu beitragen sollten, Informationen besser einzuordnen. Man konnte sich absolut darauf verlassen, dieses oder jenes bitte noch nicht zu zitieren, etwa weil Dinge noch im Fluss sind, weil empfindliche Prozesse dadurch gestört werden könnten – und im Allgemeinen hielten sich die Journalisten daran. Sagt man heute: «Ich vertraue Ihnen das jetzt an, möchte Sie aber bitten, es nicht zu drucken» – dann könnte man diese vertraulichen Informationen manchmal ebenso gut gleich an die Rathaustür nageln.

Ein neues Phänomen ist auch die Verbreitung des voyeuristischen «Schlüsselloch-Journalismus». Das private Leben öffentlicher Personen wird immer mehr in den Medien ausgebreitet, während es früher weitgehend ausgespart blieb. In England, im Presseimperium von Rupert Murdoch, ist diese Tendenz noch ausgeprägter als bei uns; und so, wie der Medienmarkt sich im Augenblick entwickelt, wird das wohl auch hier noch extremere Formen annehmen. Der Kampf um Quoten und Marktanteile ruft nach Sensationen und Skandalen, vorzugsweise nach solchen, die im privaten Bereich angesiedelt sind. Die sind für einfache Menschen allemal interessanter, weil leichter nachzuvollziehen als politische Sachverhalte. Deswegen haben sie einen größeren Marktwert. Die personalisierte politische Berichterstattung führt auch dazu, dass Politiker und Politikerinnen heute auf der Sympathieskala viel abrupter mal rauf- und mal runtergeschrieben werden. Wer gestern noch bejubelter Presseliebling war, kann morgen schon ganz tief im Keller sein.

Aufgabe des politischen Journalismus in einer Demokratie ist in erster Linie die solide Berichterstattung. Über Zeitungen, Zeitschriften, Hörfunk und Fernsehen soll die Öffentlichkeit so über Politik informiert werden, dass sich die mündige Bürgerin, der mündige Bürger ein eigenes Urteil bilden können, das dann zur Grundlage ihres eigenen politischen Handelns wird. Dabei kommt den Medien auch eine wichtige Kontrollfunktion zu. Sie sollen Politik transparent machen, in dunkle Ecken hineinleuchten, Probleme aufspüren, Fehler aufdecken.

In dieser Rolle hat der politische Journalismus einen großen Einfluss und, damit verbunden, natürlich auch eine große Verantwortung, die bei der Jagd nach Auflagen und Quoten nicht leichtfertig vergessen werden darf. Stößt die Presse tatsächlich auf einen politischen Skandal, dann muss natürlich aufgedeckt und aufgeklärt werden. Sollte sich aber herausstellen, dass es sich nur um eine Seifenblase handelt, dann sollte man sie nicht Tag für Tag immer wieder aufblasen, mit der Wiederholung alter Geschichten, die scheinbar neue «Enthüllungen» enthalten, nur um die Suppe noch eine Weile länger am Köcheln zu halten – vorzugsweise bis zum nächsten Wahltermin.

Schon die Formulierung von Schlagzeilen kann eine unzulässige Beeinflussung der öffentlichen Meinung bewirken. So etwas hat stattgefunden, als plötzlich überall von meiner angeblichen «Amtsmüdigkeit» zu lesen war. Nur ein paar Schlagzeilen, in denen die angebliche Müdigkeit und Lustlosigkeit der Ministerpräsidentin erwähnt wird, und schon verselbstständigt sich diese Behauptung.

Im Zusammenhang mit tatsächlichen oder scheinbaren politischen Skandalen spielen die Medien eine zentrale Rolle. Manchmal entwickelt sich aus einer relativ geringfügigen Angelegenheit, aus einer unbedachten Äußerung eines Politikers, einem Versäumnis, einem Fehler in kürzester Zeit ein Riesending. Dann gibt es viel öffentliches Geschrei, in das alle einstimmen, viel Gemache und Gedöns – und wenn man hinterher fragt: «Was ist da eigentlich tatsächlich passiert?», dann weiß es niemand so genau. In einer politisch aufgeladenen Situation kann mit ein bisschen Nachhilfe einiger Medien eine Mücke zum Elefanten werden.

Umgekehrt ist es manchmal erschreckend, wie politisch hochbedeutsame Affären und Skandale in kürzester Zeit wieder in

Vergessenheit geraten, auch ohne dass sie angemessen aufgeklärt wurden. Wie viele von den Menschen, die das Zeitgeschehen einigermaßen aufmerksam verfolgen, können sich noch genau erinnern, was es eigentlich mit der «Schubladen-Affäre» in Schleswig-Holstein auf sich hatte? Sogar die «Parteispenden-Affäre» um Helmut Kohl ist fast vollständig vergessen. Ähnlich ist es mit den «Jüdischen Vermächtnissen» in der CDU von Roland Koch. Die Verfallszeiten von politischen Affären sind ein Thema für sich. Häufig scheint es, man braucht nur ein hinreichend dickes Fell, um die Anfangsphase zu überstehen, dann schafft man es auch, die Sache ganz auszusitzen, egal, wie schwerwiegend die politischen Fehler waren, die da gemacht wurden.

Problematisch finde ich es auch, wenn sich Teile der Presse für bestimmte Zwecke einspannen lassen, egal ob es dabei gegen meine oder gegen eine andere Partei geht. Natürlich können Blätter bestimmten politischen Parteien oder Gruppierungen näher stehen als anderen, aber für eine Person oder politische Position einzutreten, sollte nicht dazu führen, die Gegenspieler auf unfaire Weise fertig zu machen.

Die «Bonusmeilen-Affäre» im Sommer 2002 war in meinen Augen ein solches Beispiel für den Missbrauch von Pressemacht. Unstrittig handelte es sich bei der privaten Nutzung von Bonusmeilen um persönliches Fehlverhalten von Abgeordneten, die sich ja zu einer anderen Regelung verpflichtet hatten – das soll hier nicht schöngeredet werden. Doch die scheibchenweise «Enthüllung» durch die «Bild»-Zeitung, die einen Abgeordneten nach dem anderen aufspießte (und durch einen sonderbaren Zufall vorzugsweise immer Grüne oder SPD-Abgeordnete), war eine Kampagne, die in den letzten Wochen des Wahlkampfes nur darauf angelegt sein konnte, ein politisches Lager zu beschädigen. Diese Taktik war durchschaubar, zumal die ganze Sache ins politische Sommerloch platziert wurde. Doch obwohl das Spiel in der Öffentlichkeit von vielen durchschaut wurde, hat es partiell Wirkung gezeigt, etwa im Rücktritt des grünen Bundestagsabgeordneten Cem Özdemir. Und es wäre vermutlich noch mehr hängen geblieben, wenn nicht die Flutkatastrophe in Ostdeutschland die «Bonusmeilen-Affäre» von einem Moment auf den anderen buchstäblich aus den Nachrichten geschwemmt hätte.

Als Grüner hatte Cem Özdemir natürlich noch ein besonderes Problem. Nach wie vor verbinden viele Menschen mit den Grünen den Anspruch, eine ganz andere Politik zu machen, mit einem hohen moralischen Anspruch. Wenn dann ein Grüner selbst bei unmoralischem Tun ertappt wird, ist es besonders peinlich und zählt in den Augen der Öffentlichkeit doppelt. Während Özdemir wirklich über die Bonusmeilen gestolpert ist, lag der Fall Gregor Gysi ganz anders: Gysi ist von seinem Amt als Berliner Wirtschaftssenator zurückgetreten, weil er offensichtlich ohnehin kein Interesse mehr daran hatte. Für ihn waren die Bonusmeilen nur ein Anlass zum Rücktritt.

Bei Rudolf Scharping würde niemand auf die Idee kommen zu sagen, er sei das Opfer einer Pressekampagne geworden. In seinem Fall gab es über einen längeren Zeitraum eine Häufung von Ungeschicklichkeiten und Peinlichkeiten, die ihn alle zusammengenommen das Amt gekostet haben. Bei ihm war die «Affäre Hunziger» um Kleidungsrechnungen und verschwiegene Honorare nur der berühmte Tropfen, der das Fass zum Überlaufen brachte. In diesem Zusammenhang konnte man aber wieder einmal beobachten, dass in den Augen der Öffentlichkeit die Fehltritte am schwersten wiegen, die sich auf Vorgänge beziehen, die der Mann oder die Frau auf der Straße sich selber gut vorstellen kann. Die Leute sagen sich: «Ich kann mir im Jahr höchstens einen Anzug leisten, aus dem Kaufhaus – und der kleidet sich für über 50 000 Mark einfach so neu ein – nein, das ist ja unglaublich!» Oder sie sagen: «Ich muss mir meinen Urlaub auf Mallorca mühsam zusammensparen – und diese Abgeordneten nehmen Mama, Papa, Oma und Opa auf Bonusmeilen kostenlos mit auf den Flug nach Bangkok – unerhört!» So etwas empört die Bürger vermutlich tiefer als politisches Fehlverhalten in Bereichen, in die sie weniger Einblick haben, weil sie komplex oder weit entfernt von ihren alltäglichen Erfahrungen sind. Um einen gravierenden politischen Skandal wirklich beurteilen zu können, muss man in der Regel erhebliches Hintergrundwissen und politische Kenntnisse haben. Wenn es dagegen um den Lebensstil geht, dann spielen der Vergleich und manchmal auch der Neid die entscheidende Rolle. Auch im Falle Scharpings wird es in kürzester Zeit vergessen sein, worum es politisch ging. An die Urlaubsbilder von ihm und seiner Lebensgefährtin im Swimmingpool auf Mallorca werden sich die Leute dagegen noch lange erinnern.

Ich will noch einmal festhalten, dass bei uns keineswegs der gesamte Medienbetrieb zu personalisierten Sensationsberichten und zum Aufblähen von Skandalen neigt. Ganz überwiegend wird fair und seriös berichtet. Doch nicht nur in der Boulevardpresse kommt es immer wieder zu ärgerlichen Vorgehensweisen, gegen die man sich nur schwer wehren kann. Da gibt es Blätter, die mit schöner Regelmäßigkeit ausgerechnet am Freitagnachmittag mit einer riesigen Fragenliste zur Pressestelle kommen und erwarten, dass man diese innerhalb weniger Stunden beantwortet – zu einem Zeitpunkt also, wenn kaum noch jemand im Hause und der Rest der Belegschaft schon auf dem Sprung ins Wochenende ist. Da sollen Mitarbeiter noch aufwändig Akten zusammensuchen, Fakten recherchieren, damit solide geantwortet werden kann. Wenn sich so ein Vorgehen wiederholt, im Zusammenhang mit prekären Sachverhalten (wie bei uns zuletzt im Zusammenhang mit der so genannten «Affäre Pröhl»), dann liegt es nahe, System und Absicht dahinter zu vermuten. Will man nicht, dass einem aus flüchtigen oder gar fehlerhaften Antworten ein Strick gedreht wird, dann muss man die Mitarbeiter wieder und wieder bitten, am Wochenende Überstunden zu machen. Das ist unerfreulich und zermürbend – und ganz bestimmt kein Ausdruck von fairem Journalismus.

Natürlich muss nicht nur berichtet werden, die Argumente der Politiker müssen auch unter die Lupe genommen, kommentiert und bewertet werden. Wenn etwas aufzuklären ist, hat die Presse ein Recht auf Information und die Aufgabe, die Dinge aufzuklären. Selbstverständlich muss sie in diesem Zusammenhang auch unbequeme Fragen an Politikerinnen und Politiker stellen; so weit ist das alles in Ordnung. Aber ärgerlich wird es, wenn immer die gleiche falsche Geschichte gedruckt wird, selbst wenn man sich den Mund dabei fusselig geredet hat, die Einzelheiten richtig zu stellen.

Ein gezieltes Aufblasen von Nichtigkeiten zu Skandalen ist auch deswegen ärgerlich für Politiker, weil es dem Alltagsgeschäft so viele Energien entzieht. Man muss oft einen riesigen Aufwand betreiben, um Kleinigkeiten zu recherchieren: Wann genau fand dieses oder jenes Gespräch statt? Wer war im Einzelnen dabei? Wer hat was zu wem gesagt? Natürlich ist es klar, dass so etwas manchmal sein muss, wenn ein berechtigter Verdacht auf politisches Fehlverhalten besteht, auf Mauscheleien, Begünstigung und Vetternwirtschaft. Umso ärgerlicher aber, wenn nur der heißen Luft wegen auf Kosten der Steuerzahler viele Mitarbeiter auf Trapp gehalten werden, die sich eigentlich mit anderen Dingen beschäftigen müssen. Noch problematischer an der Sensationsberichterstattung scheint mir, dass sich auf Dauer in der Öffentlichkeit der Eindruck einstellen könnte, sämtliche Politiker und Politikerinnen seien ausnahmslos eine Gaunerbande. Das kann langfristig das Vertrauen in die Demokratie erschüttern.

Die Medien haben durchaus auch die Macht, in der Bevölkerung bestimmte Stimmungen zu schüren. Das konnte man sehr gut bei der Unterschriftenkampagne gegen die doppelte Staatsbürgerschaft vor den Landtagswahlen 1999 in Hessen beobachten. Da entstand, nicht nur durch die Menschen, die in den Fußgängerzonen herumstanden und Unterschriften sammelten, sondern auch durch die Art, wie über diese Kampagne berichtet wurde, eine regelrechte «Ausländer-raus!»-Stimmung. Große Teile der Presse machten sich zum Sprachrohr einer bestimmten Meinung und haben sie auf diese Weise noch einmal kräftig unterstützt.

Doch alles in allem haben wir ein relativ gut funktionierendes Pressesystem. Zwar können gelegentlich unfaire Kampagnen einzelnen Politikern schon schwer zu schaffen machen und sie kürzer- oder längerfristig beschädigen. Ich bin allerdings überzeugt davon, dass die Presse bei uns keinen Rücktritt eines Politikers erzwingen kann, wenn nicht wirklich etwas gegen ihn vorliegt, gewissermaßen aus dem blauen Himmel heraus, nur aufgrund einer lancierten Kampagne, weil man jemanden nicht leiden kann und ihn oder sie weghaben will. Es mag vorstellbar sein, dass manche Blätter so etwas versuchen – aber es gibt dann ja bei uns immer noch genügend andere Zeitungen und Zeitschriften, die als Gegengewicht fungieren. Und das ist doch ein beruhigender Gedanke.

Im Zusammenhang mit den beiden Fernsehduellen von Schröder und Stoiber ist im vergangenen Herbst viel und grundsätzlich über die Rolle der Medien im Wahlkampf diskutiert worden. Zahlreiche Stimmen haben die «Amerikanisierung» des deutschen Wahlkampfes beklagt, die Stilisierung der politischen Auseinandersetzung zum Medienevent. Ich finde, dass diese neue Form aber auch eine Chance ist, die Öffentlichkeit zu informieren und zur Wahl zu motivieren, nicht nur die Duelle selbst, sondern auch die Berichterstattung darüber. Gewiss hat man dabei nicht viel Neues von den beiden Politikern erfahren, aber für diejenigen, die sich sonst nicht intensiv mit Politik befassen, bot sich so immerhin eine Gelegenheit dazu. Zahlreiche Menschen haben sich mit Freunden getroffen, um die Duelle im Fernsehen anzuschauen, und dies zum Anlass genommen, über politische Fragen zu diskutieren, ausgiebiger, als das sonst üblich ist. Für die Presse bot die Zusammenfassung der Argumente beider Seiten noch einmal die Möglichkeit, diese im Einzelnen zu vergleichen und zu bewerten. Dabei war keineswegs nur von den Krawatten, der Redegewandtheit und dem Stil der Selbstdarstellung der Kandidaten die Rede, wie vielfach polemisch behauptet wurde. Gerade was diese Fernsehduelle anging, hatte ich den

Eindruck, dass darüber in der Presse recht seriös und differenziert berichtet wurde.

Wahrscheinlich wird diese Form sich auch bei uns auf Dauer durchsetzen. Sicher ist die Personalisierung nicht ganz unproblematisch vor dem Hintergrund, dass wir in unseren Wahlen nicht den Kanzler, sondern die Parteien wählen. Es scheint aber immer mehr, als ob die Menschen Personen brauchen, an denen sie Positionen festmachen können. Man wird kaum die 15 Millionen Menschen, die im vergangenen Herbst die Fernsehduelle angeschaut haben, dazu bringen, die Parteiprogramme zu lesen. Wir leben nun einmal in einer Mediengesellschaft, und deswegen wird man wohl kaum von dieser Form des Wahlkampfevents wieder wegkommen.

In Schleswig-Holstein gibt es im Wahlkampf eine ähnliche Befragung der beiden Spitzenkandidaten, auf NDR 3. Ich halte das für eine gute und nützliche Veranstaltung. Bei dieser Sendung wird fair verfahren und anschließend sachlich darüber berichtet – das gilt im Wesentlichen auch für die konservativen Journalisten, wenn sie über die SPD schreiben. Im Übrigen ist es ja keineswegs so, dass die Journalisten der eigenen Seite immer besonders seriös berichteten und nur die aus dem anderen politischen Lager in dieser Hinsicht zu wünschen übrig ließen.

Ich würde mir für die Zukunft wünschen, dass das Privatleben von Politikern und Politikerinnen wieder mehr respektiert wird. Auch sie haben das Recht auf eine geschützte Privatsphäre. Für mich gehört zu diesem geschützten Bereich auch, wie viel Geld jemand für seine Garderobe ausgibt, wo er oder sie einkauft, was er oder sie in ihrer Freizeit macht, mit wem er oder sie befreundet ist, wo man essen geht oder was wer gern isst. Grundsätzlich ist es, wenn ich mein Einkommen rechtmäßig und anständig erworben habe, meine Privatangelegenheit, ob ich meine Klamotten secondhand kaufe oder in einer Edelboutique, ob ich die Dinge neu oder heruntergesetzt erwerbe, ob ich sie mir selbst kaufe oder mir von meinem Mann schenken lasse. Natürlich haben manche Politiker selber mit

Schuld daran, wenn Presseleute dauernd vor ihrer Haustür hocken. Wer sich vorab die Journalisten für die Homestories ins Haus geholt hat, darf sich nicht wundern, wenn er die Geister, die er rief, nicht mehr los wird.

Nicht nur die Politiker betreiben in regelmäßigen Abständen Medienschelte, auch die Presse ergeht sich immer wieder gern in Politikerschelte. Das gehört offenbar zum Spiel. Zwischen Politik und Presse besteht eine Art Hassliebe. Die Presse braucht uns, um berichten zu können, und wir brauchen die Presse, damit über uns berichtet wird.

Das Bild, das die Öffentlichkeit von Politikern hat, wird überhaupt erst durch die Medien vermittelt. Das öffentliche Bild formt sich über einen längeren Zeitraum hinweg. Man inszeniert sich bei öffentlichen Auftritten natürlich auch ein bisschen, immer auf dem Hintergrund der Person, die man tatsächlich ist. Beim Transport durch die Medien wird dann einiges akzentuiert, anderes bleibt eher stecken. Schon während sich so ein öffentliches Bild formt, wirkt es von außen wieder auf einen zurück. Ich bemerke zunehmend, wie dieses Bild die Erwartungen der Menschen prägt, mit denen ich zu tun habe, und damit auch wieder auf mein eigenes Verhalten einwirkt. Es entsteht eine Art Rückkoppelungsprozess: Man handelt von nun an auch auf der Vorlage dieses Bildes – das heißt, zum Teil erfüllt man die Erwartungen, die sich daran knüpfen, zum Teil versucht man auch, es da zu korrigieren, wo es nicht stimmig oder auf ärgerliche Weise falsch ist. Solche Korrekturen werden allerdings im Laufe der Zeit immer schwieriger, wenn das öffentliche Bild sich einmal verfestigt hat. Von den anderen werden dann nämlich nur noch die Lebensäußerungen registriert, die in das schon vorhandene Bild passen.

So werde ich selbst immer «die mit dem Hut» bleiben, ob ich nun im Einzelfall tatsächlich mit einem Hut daherkomme oder nicht. Ich werde auch immer die sein, die auf Flohmärkten unendliche Mengen von Krimskrams erwirbt, selbst dann, wenn ich damit aufhörte oder meine Wohnung von allem Trödel ganz leer räumte. Ähnliches gilt auch für weniger äußerliche Zuschreibungen. Das öffentliche Bild tendiert dazu, sich zu verselbstständigen, und hat dann ein gewisses Beharrungsvermögen. Man hat später nur wenig Möglichkeiten, etwas daran zu ändern. Insgesamt ist es einfacher, neue Facetten hinzuzufügen – die aber einigermaßen stimmig sein müssen –, als welche fortzunehmen oder in ihr Gegenteil zu verkehren.

Als Finanzministerin war ich die Sparerin mit der eisernen Disziplin und der schnellen Zunge. Im Laufe des letzten Jahrzehnts hat sich das Bild der «Landesmutter» über das der großen Sparerin geschoben; das Etikett mit der flinken Zunge blieb dagegen erhalten. Man registriert das und anerkennt auch, dass ich mich für soziale Initiativen im In- und Ausland einsetze, für UNICEF beispielsweise, für die Unterstützung der Bevölkerung Afghanistans. Die Menschen haben ein Bild von mir als einer Politikerin, die ihre Belange ernst nimmt, die sich um sie kümmert – und gerade in diesem Punkt ist es für mich erfreulich, dass hier Selbstbild und Fremdbild weitgehend übereinstimmen.

Natürlich finde ich mich nicht in allem wieder, was über mich gesagt oder geschrieben wird. Aber es wäre nicht gut, wenn zu große Divergenzen zwischen dem Bild, das man von sich entworfen hat, und dem tatsächlichen Verhalten beständen. Solche Widersprüche bemerken die Menschen sehr wohl und kreiden sie einem negativ an. Öffentliche Erklärungen über Werte und Moral zum Beispiel müssen zum privaten Verhalten passen. Wenn man als Politiker die große Bedeutung von Ehe und Familie preist, tut man gut daran, auch selber ein vorzeigbares Familienleben zu pflegen. Wer Transparenz in der Einkommenssituation von Politikern fordert, sollte seine eigene so gestalten, dass sie kritischen Blicken von außen standhält. Wer für eine neue Bescheidenheit plädiert, sollte sich nicht bei luxuriösen Eskapaden erwischen lassen. Am besten ist es, wenn möglichst wenig Unstimmigkeit besteht zwischen dem Bild, das gute Bekannte und Freunde von einem haben, und dem Bild, das sich die Öffentlichkeit von einem macht. Das heißt allerdings nicht, dass ich den Journalistinnen und Journalisten jedes Detail meines Privatlebens erzählen müsste. Ich verrate den Leuten durchaus, dass ich bei bestimmten Filmen gern weine und auch so manches Taschentuch dabei draufgeht – sie brauchen deswegen aber nicht alle meine Gemütsregungen genau zu kennen.

In dem Bild, das ich nach außen von mir entwerfe, erschöpft sich eben nicht die ganze Person. Man zitiert gewissermaßen ein paar Chiffren, die die Leute wieder erkennen, aber darüber hinaus gibt man nicht unbedingt alles von sich preis. Es schmeichelt ja durchaus auch, erkannt zu werden, wenn man irgendwohin kommt. Ich finde es immer heuchlerisch, wenn Politikerinnen und Politiker sagen: «Ich kann nirgendwo mehr hingehen! Alle erkennen mich draußen wieder!» Wir würden uns doch das Leben nehmen, wenn uns niemand mehr wieder erkennen würde!

Vielleicht ergibt sich gerade dadurch, dass man bestimmte schon verfestigte äußerliche Erwartungen erfüllt, auf die sich die allgemeine Aufmerksamkeit konzentriert, ein bisschen Platz für anderes, bei dem ich dann sagen kann: «Leute, das geht euch nun wirklich nichts an!» So kann ich mir einen Freiraum wahren. Manchmal erscheint der mir allerdings sehr klein. Aber grundsätzlich halte ich eine Übereinstimmung von Selbstbild und Fremdbild für erstrebenswert.

Eine Zeit lang behauptete der Oppositionsführer bei beinahe jeder seiner Reden: «Frau Simonis, von Ihnen geht die Arroganz der Macht aus ...» Das ist typischerweise nie in der Presse wiederholt und gedruckt worden. Denn ich bin nicht arrogant, und ich wirke auch in der Öffentlichkeit nicht so. In diesem Fall steuert das öffentliche Bild, das mit meiner Selbstwahrnehmung übereinstimmt, auch die Wahrnehmung der Presseleute, die über diesen Anwurf hinweghören. Würde der Oppositionsführer mir vorwerfen: «Sie sind immer viel zu schnell, Sie reden so schnell, und deswegen haben Sie wohl über dies und das noch nicht genug nachgedacht ...», dann könnte schon eher was hängen bleiben – allerdings ohne hohen Neuigkeitswert. Denn das rasche Reagieren, manchmal eine Stärke, aber manchmal auch eine Schwäche, ist wirklich eine allseits bekannte Eigenart von mir.

Das öffentliche Bild hat auch dazu geführt, dass im Zusammenhang mit der so genannten «Pröhl-Affäre» im Jahr 2001 niemand im Land wirklich glaubte, dass ich mich bereichert haben könnte. Die Menschen wissen, dass das nicht zu mir passt, dass ich meine Pflichten ernst nehme und diszipliniert meine Arbeit tue. Genauso wenig wäre vorstellbar, dass jemand plötzlich öffentlich behaupten könnte, ich sei faul und nähme die Dinge zu locker, ich kümmerte mich nicht genügend um die Probleme des Landes. Eine solche Kritik würde einfach nicht überspringen, niemand würde sie glauben.

9

Zehn Jahre Politik für Schleswig-Holstein

I n den vergangenen zehn Jahren ist Schleswig-Holstein mehr und mehr aus seinem Dornröschen-Schlaf erwacht – das sehe ich als wichtigste Leistung in meiner Zeit als Ministerpräsidentin an. Die Menschen hier haben lange mit großer Geduld das Image ertragen, in einem netten, freundlichen Land zu leben, das aber immer ein bisschen hintendran war, nur unzureichend vertraut mit den neuesten wissenschaftlichen, technologischen und wirtschaftlichen Entwicklungen. Schleswig-Holstein war das verträumte Urlaubsland, geprägt von Schiffbau und Landwirtschaft – und das war's. Im letzten Jahrzehnt haben wir einen großen Sprung in die Moderne gemacht, wir haben die Weichen für einen Strukturwandel und damit auch für eine neue Identität dieses Landes gestellt. Schleswig-Holstein ist nach wie vor ein beliebtes Reiseland. Das soll es auch in Zukunft bleiben, mit seinen vielen Naturschönheiten, den beliebten Nordseestränden und den Steilküsten der Ostsee, dem Nationalpark Wattenmeer, mit seinen herrlichen Inseln und vielen Halligen, Deichen und Prielen, den schönen, weiten, windzerzausten Landschaften. Aber darüber hinaus ist das nördlichste Bundesland auch zur Drehscheibe von Wirtschaft und Kultur nach Norden und Osten geworden, ein Land, in dem an Zukunftstechnologien und -produkten gearbeitet wird. Wir sind nicht mehr nur bescheiden nach innen, auf uns selbst ausgerichtet, wir gehen auch nach außen und bauen unsere

Kontakte aus. Wir sind inzwischen ein wichtiger Teil der neuen lebendigen Ostseeregion, wirtschaftlich wie kulturell besehen.

Als ich Anfang der 60er Jahre nach Kiel kam, bestimmten ausschließlich Marine und Werften das Bild dieser Stadt. Beide haben zwar immer noch einen großen Stellenwert. Aber neben ihnen haben andere Institutionen an Bedeutung gewonnen, die Universität zum Beispiel, die früher in der Öffentlichkeit und von der Wirtschaft kaum wahrgenommen wurde. Da hat sich gründlich was geändert. Inzwischen schaut auch die Industrie auf das, was sich in den Hochschulen tut; viele Unternehmen kooperieren mit Forschungsinstituten, beteiligen sich sogar an der Einrichtung neuer Fakultäten. Die Universitäten in Kiel und Lübeck genießen mit ihren hervorragenden Forschungsleistungen Weltruf.

Die Medizintechnik hat sich besonders rasant entwickelt. Einige Krankenhäuser haben sich auf die minimalinvasive Chirurgie und andere Hightech-Operationsverfahren spezialisiert. Die modernen Informations- und Kommunikationstechnologien haben Einzug in den Krankenhausbetrieb gehalten. In der Region Flensburg arbeiten Krankenhäuser und ein Netz niedergelassener Ärzte an einem Modellprojekt zur Entwicklung elektronischer Patientenkarten. Auf ihnen sollen alle wichtigen medizinischen Daten des Patienten verschlüsselt gespeichert werden: Daten und Ergebnisse bisheriger Untersuchungen und Eingriffe, Therapien, Allergien und so weiter. Ziel dieses Modellprojektes ist es, Doppeluntersuchungen und Fehlmedikationen zu vermeiden, Kosten zu sparen und zugleich den Patientinnen und Patienten eine hohe Qualität der medizinischen Versorgung zu garantieren. Ein wichtiger Beitrag zur aktuellen Diskussion um Kostensenkungen in unserem Gesundheitswesen.

Inzwischen arbeiten in der schleswig-holsteinischen Medizintechnik mit etwa 10 000 Beschäftigten in rund 200 Unternehmen mehr Menschen als auf den Werften – und in dieser Zahl sind die Hochschulen noch nicht berücksichtigt.

Gesundheit und Wellness sind Zukunftsmärkte, die wir für uns entdeckt haben. Mit der «Gesundheitsinitiative Schleswig-Holstein» hat die Landesregierung alle Akteure im Gesundheitssektor an einen Tisch gebracht, um Ideen und Projekte miteinander zu vernetzen. Nach zwei Jahren wirklich harter Arbeit ist diese Initiative so gut in Gang, dass es immer weniger Anstöße seitens der Regierung bedarf. Wenn so etwas ein Erfolg werden soll, dann müssen daran wirklich alle Akteure beteiligt werden: die Kliniken, die Reha-Einrichtungen, die Vertreter der Ärzteschaft, die Krankenkassen, die Universitäten sowie die Gewerkschaften, weil es ja auch um die Arbeitsplätze des Pflegepersonals geht. Damit wir nicht nur im eigenen Saft schmoren, haben wir auch unsere Kontakte nach außen intensiviert, vor allem die Zusammenarbeit mit Dänen und Norwegern. Es gibt jetzt eine norwegische «Patientenbrücke», das heißt: Patienten aus Norwegen, die dort nicht schnell genug behandelt werden können, kommen nach Schleswig-Holstein. Dänische Patientinnen und Patienten kommen zur onkologischen Behandlung nach Flensburg. Die Medizinische Universität Lübeck und die Universität Bergen in Norwegen sowie die Universität Tartu in Estland realisieren gemeinsame Forschungsprojekte, verbunden mit einem Austausch von Studierenden und Lehrenden.

Außerdem haben wir eine Wissenschaftsbrücke nach China geschlagen, zu unserer Partnerstadt Hangzhou, in der Nähe von Schanghai. Die erste Lebertransplantation, die in China Ende der 90er Jahre durchgeführt worden ist, wurde von einem chinesischen Professor vorgenommen, der in Kiel bei einem unserer Professoren studiert hat.

Ich würde für unsere Medizintechnik auch gern einen Markt im Nahen Osten erschließen. Die arabischen Länder entwickeln eine große Nachfrage nach medizinischen Produkten und Dienstleistungen. Wenn die Kontakte einmal geknüpft sind, könnten wir dorthin nicht nur Krankenhäuser, Maschinen, Geräte, Apparate verkaufen, sondern auch Informationstechnologie, Computerprogramme über optimale Abläufe im Operationssaal und Disease Management. Vieles von unserem Wissen muss an die dortigen Verhältnisse angepasst werden, weil es die zum Teil sehr strengen religiösen Vorschriften so erfordern. In Saudi-Arabien etwa dürfen Frauen keinen Nachtdienst machen; Frauen dürfen normalerweise keine Männer pflegen und Männer umgekehrt keine Frauen berühren. Das macht es nicht ganz einfach, eine 24-Stunden-Betreuung im Krankenhaus zu organisieren. Vieles, was bei uns extrem wichtig ist – Hygienevorschriften beispielsweise –, kann in armen Ländern nur schwer umgesetzt werden. Dafür darf wiederum in keinem arabischen Krankenhaus der Gebetsraum fehlen. Aus all dem folgt, dass man diesen Ländern nicht einfach unsere Vorstellungen von einem gut funktionierenden Krankenhaus überstülpen kann, sondern dass die Dinge neu durchdacht, entworfen, adaptiert werden müssen. Das ist ein Wachstumsmarkt, auf dem schleswig-holsteinische Unternehmen in Zukunft große Umsätze erzielen können.

Schleswig-Holstein hat sich in den vergangenen zehn Jahren auch ganz besonders um den Ausbau erneuerbarer Energien bemüht. Aus nahe liegenden Gründen steht dabei die Windenergie bei uns an oberster Stelle: Rund 2500 Windkraftanlagen decken bereits ein Viertel des Energiebedarfs in unserem Land – und wir wollen den Anteil auf 50 Prozent ausdehnen. Daneben bemühen wir uns um eine verstärkte Nutzung der Biomasse (Holz, Gülle, Stroh). In der vergangenen Dekade sind wir das Bundesland mit dem höchsten Anteil an Windenergie geworden, und wir stehen mit der Windenergie auch auf dem internationalen Markt sehr gut da. Wir exportieren inzwischen sogar nach Ostasien.

Medizintechnik und Windenergie – das waren auch die beiden Schwerpunkte, mit denen wir Schleswig-Holstein auf der «Expo 2000» vorgestellt haben. Die sechzehn Bundesländer durften jeweils für eine Woche den deutschen Pavillon gestalten. Für uns war das ein großer wirtschaftlicher Erfolg, denn wir konnten viele wichtige internationale Kontakte knüpfen. Auch auf der «CeBit» sind wir seit Jahren recht erfolgreich. Wir machen dort seit 1996 einen norddeutschen Gemeinschaftsstand, im Jahr 2000 zum Thema «Kommunikation im Gesundheitswesen», im Jahr 2001 zur «Modernisierung der Verwaltung», im Jahr 2003 unter dem Motto «e-government-Strategien für die effiziente Zusammenarbeit von Verwaltungen».

Im Zeitraum von 1991 bis 2000 ist die Exportquote der schleswig-holsteinischen Wirtschaft von 20,6 Prozent des Gesamtumsatzes im verarbeitenden Gewerbe auf 31,7 Prozent gestiegen. Damit liegen wir nur noch vier Prozentpunkte hinter der Quote des Bundes. Dieser Aufholprozess beweist, dass es schleswig-holsteinischen Unternehmen immer besser gelingt, sich auf den internationalen Märkten zu behaupten. Gerade die kleinen Unternehmen, die die Wirtschaft in unserem Land prägen, haben an diesem Erfolg großen Anteil. Ihre Exportquote stieg von 2 Prozent im Jahr 1990 auf 14,6 Prozent im Jahr 1999. Hier liegen noch erhebliche Potenziale, die wir nutzen wollen.

In den vergangenen zehn Jahren haben wir uns mit Erfolg darum bemüht, Hightech-Unternehmen aus Zukunftsbranchen in Schleswig-Holstein anzusiedeln. Seit 1996 haben sich zum Beispiel 25 Firmen aus der Biotech-Branche neu gegründet oder niedergelassen. Auch im Bereich der Informations- und Kommunikationstechnologie sowie in der Mikroelektronik und Mikrosystemtechnik hat sich viel getan. In Kiel wurde in «public-private partnership» ein Multimedia-Campus aufgebaut, der unter anderem als Ausbildungszentrale für Fachkräfte in den digitalen Medien und im Internet fungiert. In der Hansestadt Lübeck ist mit den «Media Docks» ein Unternehmenspark für neue Medien entstanden, in dem Forschung, Wirtschaft und Ausbildung miteinander vernetzt werden.

Wirtschaftsförderung und Strukturpolitik sollen und müssen trotz der Verschuldung des Landes ein Schwerpunkt unserer Anstrengungen bleiben, besonders der Arbeitsplätze wegen. Darüber dürfen aber die alten sozialdemokratischen Themen nicht vergessen werden: Im Zentrum bleibt für mich immer das Ziel, mehr soziale Gerechtigkeit zu verwirklichen. Dazu gehört zum Beispiel, allen Jugendlichen eine gute Schulbildung zu garantieren und sie beim Einstieg ins Erwerbsleben zu unterstützen. Ich denke, wir sind diesem Ziel durch unser «Bündnis für Ausbildung» ein gutes Stück näher gekommen. In diesem Bündnis arbeiten Wirtschaft, Kammern, Gewerkschaften, Arbeitsverwaltung und Landesregierung mit vereinten Kräften daran, jedem Jugendlichen, der ausbildungsfähig ist, auch einen Ausbildungsvertrag anzubieten. Es gibt inzwischen auch ausreichend Kindergartenplätze. 1988, als ich Finanzministerin wurde, war Schleswig-Holstein mit 51 000 Plätzen und einer Versorgungsquote von 59 Prozent noch Schlusslicht in Deutschland. Wir standen in dieser Hinsicht ähnlich schlecht da wie die anderen Länder, in denen lange die CDU regiert hatte. In der CDU vertrat man ja die Ansicht, es sei Privatangelegenheit der Mütter, sich um ihre Kinder zu kümmern. Heute haben wir in Schleswig-Holstein für Kinder zwischen drei Jahren und dem Schuleintritt eine Versorgungsquote von 93,8 Prozent erreicht (das sind 86 400 Kindergartenplätze).

Die Landwirtschaft spielt für Schleswig-Holstein nach wie vor eine große Rolle – und so hat sich bei uns in den Jahren 2000 und 2001 die BSE-Krise stark ausgewirkt. Wir haben viele große Betriebe mit extensiver Viehhaltung, die das besonders hart traf. Aber wir haben daraus gelernt und Konsequenzen für die Zukunft gezogen. Angeblich waren wir das erste Bundesland, in dem die Rinderseuche BSE auftrat. Später stellte sich dann heraus, dass die Bayern schon früher einen Fall von BSE hatten, den sie einfach lange verschwiegen haben, während wir damit direkt an die Öffentlichkeit gegangen sind, weil wir der Meinung waren, es sei unverantwortlich, die Verbraucher zu täuschen. Gleich nach BSE kam dann die Maul- und Klauenseuche ins Land, ein weiterer Schlag für die Landwirtschaft. Diesmal erwischten uns wirklich innerhalb kürzester Zeit fast alle Plagen.

Diese kleineren und größeren Katastrophen haben aber Gott sei Dank zu grundsätzlichen Diskussionen geführt. Natürlich musste erst einmal Aufklärungsarbeit geleistet werden. Wir mussten den Verbrauchern und Verbraucherinnen deutlich sagen, dass Qualität ihren Preis hat. Selbstverständlich sind die Leute zunächst nicht begeistert, wenn man ihnen sagt: Ihr kriegt nun mal für zwei Mark vierzig keinen handverlesenen Eiswein; und ein frei laufendes Huhn, das sich selber sein Futter sucht, kostet nun mal mehr als ein fließbandernährtes Käfighuhn – dafür schmeckt es auch um einiges besser. Und außerdem tut man auf diese Weise auch etwas für eine naturnahe, artgerechte Tierhaltung.

Gemeinsam mit der Wirtschaft haben wir ein integriertes System zur Qualitätssicherung landwirtschaftlicher Produkte entwickelt: die «Qualitätstore». Alle Beteiligten ziehen dabei an einem Strang: Dünger- und Futtermittelindustrie, Landwirte, Schlachtereien, verarbeitende Betriebe und Einzelhandel, und jeder von ihnen garantiert auf seiner Ebene die festgeschriebenen Sicherheits- und Qualitätsstandards. Der Landwirt garantiert beim Verkauf, dass seine Tiere ordentlich ernährt und gehalten wurden und dass er keine überflüssigen Medikamente zugefüttert hat. Der Schlachtbetrieb kauft ihm die Tiere nur mit dieser Selbstzertifizierung ab. Er selbst garantiert dem verarbeitenden Betrieb, dass er sein Fleisch nicht aus dubiosen Beständen gekauft hat und alle Hygienevorschriften einhält. Wer Fleisch zu Wurst oder Fertiggerichten weiterverarbeitet, muss dem Einzelhandel garantieren, dass seine Zutaten und Herstellungsverfahren den gesetzlichen Bestimmungen genügen. Und der Einzelhandel bestätigt schließlich per Zertifikat, dass er die Produkte richtig gelagert und ausgezeichnet hat.

So haben die Verbraucherinnen und Verbraucher die Gewissheit, dass das, was sie essen, zuvor durch mehrere «Qualitätstore» gegangen ist. Sie sollen sich darauf verlassen können, dass auf allen Stufen der Produktion, vom Feld bis zur Ladentheke, Qualitätskriterien eingehalten worden sind, und zwar unabhängig davon, ob sie im Supermarkt oder im Bioladen einkaufen. Alle beteiligten Betriebe unterwerfen sich freiwillig behördlichen Stichproben, die jederzeit erfolgen können. Landwirte wie Ernährungsindustrie tragen bei uns dieses Konzept gleichermaßen mit, denn schließlich haben sie hautnah gespürt, was es bedeutet, wenn die Menschen sich mit Grausen von ihren Produkten abwenden.

Auf Bundesebene wurde als Konsequenz aus der BSE-Krise das «Verbrauchergarantiesiegel» geschaffen, das Mindeststandards für Sicherheit und Qualität vorschreibt. Das schleswig-holsteinische Konzept der «Qualitätstore» geht jedoch noch über die Rahmenrichtlinien des Bundes hinaus. Wir haben unser Konzept der «Qualitätstore» 2002 auf der Grünen Woche in Berlin der Öffentlichkeit vorgestellt und dafür viel Zustimmung bekommen. Am 10. April 2003 haben wir dann das komplette Konzept der Öffentlichkeit vorgestellt. Mit diesem Datum startete landesweit die Produktion innerhalb des Systems der Qualitätstore. Jetzt kommt es darauf an, dass die Verbraucherinnen und Verbraucher dieses Qualitätssystem auch annehmen und die nötige Nachfrage schaffen.

Ganz besonders wichtig war für mich während meiner gesamten bisherigen Amtszeit unser breit angelegtes Projekt zur Modernisierung der Verwaltung. Wir haben eine große Initiative gestartet mit dem Ziel, die Verwaltung, nicht nur in den Ministerien, sondern in allen öffentlichen Ämtern weniger bürokratisch, dafür effizienter, kostengünstiger und kundenfreundlicher zu machen. Der erste Schritt bestand darin, dass wir in Vorrunden über das Image des öffentlichen Dienstes diskutiert haben: «Warum kommt das, was wir tun, so schlecht an – obwohl wir doch gute Arbeit leisten?» Dann haben wir uns mit einer Beratungsfirma zusammengetan. Zunächst einmal ging es um das Selbstbild und das Fremdbild des öffentlichen Dienstes: «Wie nehmen andere uns wahr? Wie sehen wir uns selber?» Immer wieder stellten wir fest, dass vieles, was Außenstehende an der Verwaltung kritisieren, zum Beispiel langwierige und umständliche Verfahren, einfach mit gesetzlichen Vorschriften zusammenhängt, an die wir gebunden sind. Nach dieser ersten Gesprächsphase haben wir dann Ideen für Veränderungen entwickelt, die sich auch innerhalb des Korsetts der gesetzlichen Vorschriften bewerkstelligen ließen. Es ging uns darum, nach außen hin zu vermitteln, dass die Verwaltungen moderne Serviceeinrichtungen sind, die dazu da sind, den Bürgerinnen und Bürgern mit ihren Anliegen weiterzuhelfen.

Bei der Ideenfindung haben wir gleich mit der Regierung selbst, sozusagen vor der eigenen Haustür, angefangen, indem wir die Mitarbeiterinnen und Mitarbeiter aller Ministerien baten, einmal alle die Aufgaben aufzuschreiben, die sie ständig erledigen müssen. Es ging also nicht darum, den anderen Ministerien von außen Vorschriften zu machen, sondern Ideen für Verbesserungen im eigenen Arbeitsbereich auf den Tisch zu legen. Da sind allein aus dem Innenministerium fast 1200 Verbesserungsvorschläge gekommen! Natürlich ließ sich nicht alles umsetzen, aber es waren doch viele wichtige Anregungen dabei, den alltäglichen Geschäftsablauf zu vereinfachen und zu beschleunigen. Bei der Bewertung der Vorschläge gab es keine Vorgaben von oben nach unten, sondern über jeden einzelnen von ihnen entschieden zunächst die Mitarbeiterinnen und Mitarbeiter selbst, bevor er zur endgültigen Entscheidung an die Lenkungsgruppe aus Ministern und Staatssekretären ging. Vorschläge, die in der ersten Runde abgelehnt worden waren, durfte auch die Lenkungsgruppe nicht wieder aufgreifen. Auf diese Weise haben wir eine hohe Identifikation mit dem Projekt erreicht. 1998 haben wir für dieses Projekt «Aufgabenanalyse/ Aufgabenkritik» den renommierten Modernisierungspreis der Verwaltungshochschule Speyer gewonnen. Die Jury hat den schleswig-holsteinischen Beitrag als besonders innovativ gewürdigt, weil unsere Methode in der Bundesrepublik bis dahin völlig neu war. Anschließend haben wir mit der Beraterfirma einen Lizenzvertrag geschlossen. Wenn sie in Zukunft einen der Vorschläge, die sie mit uns gemeinsam erarbeitet hat, an andere

verkauft, muss sie dem Land Schleswig-Holstein dafür Lizenz-
gebühren zahlen.

Viele Mitarbeiter haben dieses Projekt, das darauf zielt, be-
triebswirtschaftliche Kriterien bis zu einem gewissen Grad auch
im öffentlichen Dienst einzuführen, sehr positiv bewertet. In diesem Zusammenhang haben wir auch die Budgetierung einzelner
Institutionen eingeführt. Die Staatskanzlei zum Beispiel hat inzwischen eine Vollbudgetierung, das heißt, es steht ihr ein bestimmtes Budget zur Verfügung; innerhalb dieses Rahmens kann
eigenständig und stets von Neuem entschieden werden, wie viel
Geld für welche Dinge ausgegeben werden soll. So haben wir die
Freiheit zu beschließen, dass wir den Kauf neuer Büromöbel
noch eine Weile aufschieben, dafür aber im laufenden Jahr mehr
Geld für die Fortbildung unserer Mitarbeiterinnen und Mitarbeiter ausgeben wollen. Oder wir entscheiden, dass wir, statt Stellen
wiederzubesetzen, uns einmal in dieser oder jener Angelegenheit ein Gutachten von außen einholen wollen. Mit diesem System kann man viel flexibler auf die aktuellen Aufgaben und die
Bedürfnisse der Mitarbeiter und die Anforderungen des Parla-
ments als Haushaltsgesetzgeber reagieren.

Eine solche Budgetierung würde ich mir für viele Bereiche
der öffentlichen Verwaltung wünschen. Sie fördert die Eigen-
verantwortlichkeit und schafft eine bessere Wahrnehmung für
die Kosten öffentlicher Leistungen als das herkömmliche Vorgehen. Üblicherweise ist sehr rigide vorgegeben, welche Töpfe
für welche Zwecke bestimmt sind, und darüber hinaus stellt
man immer neue Anträge auf zusätzliche Gelder, die von den
vorgesetzten Behörden nach Kriterien, die man oft nicht nach-
vollziehen kann, bewilligt oder abgelehnt werden.

Ein gutes Beispiel dafür, was man mit dem Instrument der Budgetierung alles gestalten kann, sind die Schulen in Schleswig-Holstein. Es gibt bei uns schon viele Schulträger, die ihren Schulen
ein Sachbudget geben, über das sie in eigener Verantwortung verfügen können. So können sie selber für sie wichtige Schwerpunkte setzen. In der einen Schule müssen vielleicht die Lehrbücher

erneuert werden, bei der anderen steht der Kauf neuer Sportgeräte an, und die dritte wünscht sich einen Konzertflügel.

Schleswig-Holstein war das erste Bundesland, das 1995 die Diskussion um eine stärkere Eigenverantwortung begonnen und diese Idee an die Schulen herangetragen hat. Alle Schulen, die mit dieser neuen Arbeitsweise Erfahrungen gemacht haben, sind begeistert davon. Die Budgetierung von Schulen wird sich sicher in Zukunft durchsetzen, weil sie auch zur Profilbildung beitragen kann. Denn in Zukunft wird es weniger Schülerinnen und Schüler geben, und die Schulen werden mit unterschiedlichen Profilen um sie werben müssen. So mag zum Beispiel eine Schule für sich ins Feld führen, dass sie mit Computern und Laboren besonders gut für die naturwissenschaftlichen Fächer ausgestattet ist. Eine andere streicht vielleicht heraus, dass sie über einen Schulgarten verfügt, den die Schülerinnen und Schüler selbst bestellen, oder dass sie die besten Lehrer für die künstlerischen Fächer hat, dass dort Theaterstücke und Konzerte von den Schülern selbst gestaltet werden und so weiter.

Langfristig gehen unsere Überlegungen dahin, den Schulen auch in Bezug auf ihr Personal mehr Spielraum zu eröffnen. Wir haben mit einigen Schulen das Programm «Geld statt Stellen» begonnen. Sie können nun selbst entscheiden, ob sie Lehrkräfte oder anderes Personal für besondere Projekte einsetzen wollen. Unser Ziel ist es, die Schulen so weit wie möglich eigenverantwortlich über Personal und Sachmittel entscheiden zu lassen. Die Voraussetzungen dafür sind gut, da wir 1998 im Schulgesetz den Rahmen für mehr Eigenverantwortung geschaffen haben. In vielen Bereichen müssen die Schulen heute mit ihren Innovationen nicht mehr auf Modellversuche warten oder große Anträge stellen, denn das Schulgesetz gibt ihnen bereits einen breiten Gestaltungsspielraum. Doch ausfüllen müssen sie ihn schon selbst.

An diesem Punkt hat man am Anfang immer mit Widerständen zu tun. Das war auch bei der Modernisierung der Verwaltung nicht anders. Das Projekt der Landesregierung zur Modernisierung der Verwaltung hielten fast alle, die im öffentlichen

Dienst arbeiten, für eine gute Sache. Aber mit einem anderen Teil unserer Reformideen sind wir auf heftigen Widerstand gestoßen. Wir wollten weniger Beamte und mehr Angestellte im öffentlichen Dienst. Ich halte es für ganz wichtig, die Rolle der Beamten und den Sinn von Beamtenprivilegien neu zu überdenken. Kein Land in der Europäischen Union leistet sich überhaupt noch Beamte, außer Österreich und Deutschland (D: 2745 Beamte pro 100 000 Einwohner; A: 3160 Beamte pro 100 000 Einwohner). Das hat historische Gründe, die aber keine Geltung mehr haben, denn die meisten Aufgaben, die heute Beamte erledigen, könnten ebenso gut von Angestellten wahrgenommen werden. Langfristig wäre das mit Blick auf die im Landeshaushalt veranschlagten Summen für Pensionen erheblich kostengünstiger.

Ein Beispiel soll dies verdeutlichen: Ein Beamter im mittleren Dienst (Besoldungsgruppe A9), 40 Jahre alt, verheiratet, zwei Kinder, bekommt am Ende des Monats 2098,55 Euro ausgezahlt. Sein gleichaltriger Kollege, ein Angestellter in der vergleichbaren Vergütungsgruppe BAT Vb, ebenfalls verheiratet, mit zwei Kindern, bekommt dagegen nur 1848,09 Euro. Das ist zunächst einmal nur schön für den Beamten und ärgerlich für den Angestellten. Aber auf lange Sicht liegt hier auch ein immenses Problem für den Landeshaushalt. Denn wenn der Beamte nach 40 Dienstjahren in den Ruhestand geht, zahlt das Land seine Pension in Höhe von 71,75 Prozent des Gehalts, das er zuletzt verdient hat. Die Rente des Angestellten dagegen wird aus der solidarisch finanzierten Rentenversicherung gezahlt, ergänzt durch Bausteine der privaten Vorsorge und der Zusatzversicherung des öffentlichen Dienstes.

Im laufenden Landeshaushalt 2003 betragen die Pensionszahlungen rund 720 Millionen Euro. In den kommenden Jahren wird diese Summe weiter ansteigen, bis 2006 auf etwa 850 Millionen Euro – und dieser Trend wird sich in den folgenden Jahren weiter fortsetzen. Damit schrumpft der finanzielle Spielraum des Landes zur Gestaltung von Politik immer weiter. Deshalb bin ich der Ansicht, dass Beamte nur dort eingesetzt werden sollten, wo es wirklich um hoheitliche Aufgaben geht, um das Rechtswesen etwa oder die Polizei (nach Art. 33, Abs. 4 GG). Das Grundgesetz spricht nicht davon, dass Lehrer Beamte sein müssen, und ich sehe auch keinen stichhaltigen Grund dafür.

Diese Ideen sind natürlich auf heftigen Widerstand der Beamtenlobby gestoßen. Ich finde, es ist nicht einzusehen, warum Angestellte sehr viel mehr für ihre Sozialversorgung zahlen müssen, nämlich die Hälfte der Kranken- und Rentenversicherungsanteile, während Beamte so gut wie keinen Eigenanteil leisten. Beamte finanzieren auch die Arbeitslosenunterstützung nicht mit – sie können ja nicht arbeitslos werden. Die Vorrechte der Beamten sind nicht mehr zeitgemäß, sie sind in einer historischen Situation mit einer völlig anderen Staatsauffassung entstanden. Damals verdiente die Gruppe der Staatsdiener besonders wenig und war gleichzeitig zu rigider Loyalität verpflichtet, im Gegenzug übernahm der Fürst besondere Fürsorgepflichten für sie. Das sind heute alte Zöpfe.

Trotzdem mussten wir unsere Reformpläne an dieser Stelle aufgeben. Wenn ich zum Beispiel daran festgehalten hätte, Lehrer nicht mehr als Beamte, sondern als Angestellte einzustellen, dann würden die natürlich erst einmal in andere Bundesländer abwandern. Schließlich hat, wie ich eben beschrieben habe, ein Beamter am Monatsende deutlich mehr in der Tasche als ein Angestellter. Deshalb hat sich die Landesregierung im Sommer 2000 entschlossen, dieses Projekt zunächst zurückzustellen. Doch auch wenn unser Versuch einer «Entbeamtungspolitik» vorläufig gescheitert ist, können wir doch stolz darauf sein, dass Schleswig-Holstein seine Verwaltungsreform durchgeführt hat. Die Früchte dieser Reform beginnen wir jetzt zu ernten. Sie hat die öffentliche Verwaltung kundenfreundlicher gemacht und außerdem zu merklichen Einsparungen geführt. Andere Bundesländer sind uns inzwischen auf diesem Weg gefolgt.

Ich habe mich auf Bundesebene leider auch in einer anderen Sache nicht durchsetzen können, die den Interessen des Landes genutzt hätte. Ich hatte mich bei der Steuerreform für die Wiedereinführung der Vermögenssteuer oder zumindest für eine angemessene Erhöhung der Erbschaftssteuer eingesetzt, wie sie ja eigentlich auch im SPD-Programm vorgesehen sind. Tatsächlich ist dann aber vor allem in die Steuereinnahmen der Länder eingegriffen worden. Da war die SPD-Bundesregierung auf Kosten der Länder sehr großzügig – vielleicht weil damals noch nicht abzusehen war, was für Riesenlöcher es aufgrund der allgemein schwachen wirtschaftlichen Entwicklung in den Länderkassen geben würde.

Länder, Bund und Gemeinden teilen sich die großen Steuern: die Lohnsteuer, die Einkommenssteuer, die Umsatzsteuer, nach einem bestimmten Schlüssel, der von Mal zu Mal neu ausgehandelt wird. Bundessteuern sind im Wesentlichen die Tabak-, die Schaumwein-, die Versicherungs- und die Mineralölsteuer. Ländersteuern sind im Wesentlichen die Körperschafts-, die Vermögens- und die Erbschaftssteuer, die Abgaben von Spielbanken und außerdem die Kfz-Steuer. Die Kommunen sind ebenfalls beteiligt an der Einkommenssteuer, außerdem haben sie die Gewerbe-, die Hunde-, die Vergnügungs- und die Schanksteuer. Die gegenwärtige Bedrängnis der Kommunen hängt vor allem mit den gesunkenen Einnahmen aus der Gewerbesteuer und den gleichzeitig gestiegenen Kosten für die Sozialhilfe zusammen.

Die im Sommer 2000 beschlossene Steuerreform sah erst einmal gut aus, weil insgesamt 30 Milliarden Euro Steuererleichterung dabei herausgesprungen sind, die die Menschen jährlich mehr im Portemonnaie haben. Das ist eine stolze Summe. Doch leider ist diese Steuerersparnis von den meisten kaum zur Kenntnis genommen worden und inzwischen wieder vollständig aus dem Gedächtnis verschwunden, weil sie von anderen Entwicklungen überlagert wurde. Als wir die Steuerreform beschlossen, konnte noch niemand etwas von den Terroranschlägen in den USA am 11. September 2001 und ihren Folgen für die Weltwirtschaft ahnen. Auch war noch nicht abzusehen, welche neuen gewaltigen Anstrengungen die Länder für Bildung, Schulen und Hochschulen würden unternehmen müssen, nachdem die PISA-Studie uns auf sehr drastische Weise einen Spiegel vorgehalten hat. Aus leeren Kassen können wir aber keine Bildungs- oder Schulreform finanzieren. Die Körperschaftssteuer, die die großen Unternehmen an die Länder zahlen, ist völlig versiegt, von 22 Milliarden Mark auf einen Minusbetrag geschrumpft. Deswegen wäre es gut, wenn wir eine Vermögens- oder wenigstens eine neu geregelte Erbschaftssteuer hätten. Diese Steuer bedeutet wirklich keine riesigen Einschnitte für diejenigen, die erben, wegen der großen Freibeträge, die in diese Regelung eingebaut sind. Es muss schon ein ziemlich großes Haus sein, wenn man als Erbe von der Steuer überhaupt etwas merkt, und dann beginnt sie auch erst einmal mit niedrigen Sätzen.

Die Bundesländer brauchen einfach mehr Geld. Nach dem 11. September 2001 sind fast alle Investitionen zurückgegangen, einige Auslandsmärkte sind mehr oder weniger zusammengebrochen. Es lief schon vor diesem Datum nicht besonders gut, doch der Geldzufluss auf dem amerikanischen Markt war so groß, dass man es in den USA nicht recht zur Kenntnis nahm; und danach kam es erst richtig dicke, mit dem Crash auf dem Neuen Markt. Dabei hatten sich dessen Schwächen schon vorher abgezeichnet; weitsichtige Wirtschaftsexperten hatten schon frühzeitig darauf hingewiesen, dass es sich beim New Market zum Teil um ein Cappuccino-Gebilde handelte – viel Luft und wenig Substanz. Doch dann kam alles auf einmal, der 11. September und der Zusammenbruch des Neuen Marktes, und daran haben wir immer noch zu knabbern. Noch immer hat die Stimmung in der Wirtschaft sich nicht gebessert, der Einzelhandel klagt, dass die Leute nicht mehr konsumieren. Klamotten? Brauchen wir nicht! Anderer Krimskrams? Muss nicht sein! Sogar mit dem Ausgehen in Kinos und Restaurants und beim Reisen sind die Leute zurückhaltender geworden.

Die Steuerreform ist jetzt erst einmal gelaufen, und wir müssen sehen, wie wir mit unseren Finanzen auf der gegebenen Basis zurechtkommen. Jetzt stehen erst einmal andere dringend notwendige Reformen an, so zum Beispiel die Umgestaltung und Sicherung unserer sozialen Systeme, vor allem der Kranken- und Rentenversicherung, auch die Pflegeversicherung steht nicht gut da. Außerdem müssen wir uns um die Reform des Arbeitsmarktes kümmern. Die Palette reicht vom Kündigungsschutz über das Arbeitslosengeld bis hin zur Sozialhilfe. Für uns Sozialdemokraten wird das doppelt schwer: In einer wirtschaftlichen Flaute, in der die Menschen ohnehin schon verunsichert sind, müssen wir ihnen weitere Einschnitte zumuten. Und die in früheren Jahrzehnten gern gewählte Ausflucht in die Verschuldung ist zu Recht durch die Maastricht-Kriterien versperrt.

Das Verhältnis zwischen Bund und Ländern ist nicht immer einfach, auch wenn die eigene Partei regiert. Als wir in Bonn noch in der Opposition standen, konnten wir herausstreichen: «Seht, was für ein frischer Wind bei uns in Schleswig-Holstein herrscht! Unter der CDU-Regierung stagnierte alles, aber jetzt kommen wir in Fahrt!» Und man konnte frei darüber sinnieren, wie wunderbar man es machen würde, wenn die SPD auch im Bund an der Regierung wäre. Nun gestaltet sich das alles nicht ganz einfach, weil die Zeiten insgesamt schwieriger geworden sind.

10

So viel Markt wie möglich,
so viel Staat wie nötig!

Der stürmische Wandel von Wirtschaft und Gesellschaft, der das vergangene Jahrzehnt bestimmte, hat auch uns Sozialdemokraten dazu gebracht, das Verhältnis von Staat und Wirtschaft neu zu überdenken. Die alten staatswirtschaftlichen Konzepte sind schon länger aufgegeben worden. Ohnehin sind die beiden extremen Modelle der reinen Staatswirtschaft und der reinen Marktwirtschaft nur noch Gedankenfiguren, die niemand mehr ernsthaft vertreten kann. Sicher haben die Sozialdemokraten vor 30 Jahren noch andere Ansichten über die ideale Wirtschaftsform gehabt – das gebe ich gern zu, und ich nehme mich selbst davon nicht aus. Inzwischen hat es in der SPD aber nicht nur einen Generationenwechsel, sondern auch einen politischen Paradigmenwechsel gegeben, der die Veränderungen in der Gesellschaft widerspiegelt. Doch die Tatsache, dass wir uns von der Idee des dirigistischen Wirtschaftens verabschiedet haben, heißt keineswegs, dass der Staat sich nun überall zurückziehen sollte.

Wenn man sich die neoliberalen Ideen anschaut, die in der FDP und in Teilen der CDU/CSU propagiert werden, dann bestände die Aufgabe des Staates lediglich darin, wenige rudimentäre Aufgaben der «Daseinsfürsorge» – wie etwa die Bereitstellung von Polizei, Gerichtsbarkeit, Schulen und Straßenbau – zu übernehmen und sich ansonsten möglichst wenig in die Wirtschaft einzumischen, damit die Märkte ihre Eigengesetzlichkeit entfalten können. Freie Bahn der Wirtschaft!

Dieser Ansatz mag vielen auf den ersten Blick plausibel erscheinen, zumal die planwirtschaftlichen Systeme der Vergangenheit so gründlich gescheitert sind. Gleichwohl wissen beide großen Volksparteien – bis vielleicht auf die Abteilung Wirtschaft in der CDU – gleichermaßen, dass der Staat sich gar nicht gänzlich aus der Wirtschaft verabschieden darf. Er könnte es nicht einmal, zumindest nicht von heute auf morgen. Auch die international bestehenden Verflechtungen und vertraglichen Verpflichtungen verbieten das.

Die Anhänger des Neoliberalismus behaupten, man müsse nur aufhören mit staatlichen Interventionen, mit Subventionen und Regulierungen, dann würde die Konjunktur wieder anspringen und die Wirtschaft von selbst laufen. Aber ich fürchte, sie liefe in diesem Fall ganz bestimmt in die falsche Richtung. Wir Sozialdemokraten sind der Meinung, dass es nicht nur der minimalen Daseinsfürsorge durch den Staat bedarf, sondern ebenso seiner lenkenden Hand – und das bedeutet auch: seiner Umverteilungshand. Die Prinzipien soziale Gerechtigkeit, Freiheit und Gleichheit, der Schutz der Schwächeren durch den Staat, werden von Sozialdemokraten und ihren Wählerinnen und Wählern höher eingeschätzt als von der FDP und ihrer Klientel. Aber auch die CDU – und für die CSU gilt das noch stärker – kommt nicht darum herum, die Alltagsprobleme der kleinen Leute ernst zu nehmen. Auch sie müssen die kleinen und mittelständischen Firmen schützen und können es sich nicht leisten, den ganz Großen vollkommen freie Hand bei der Durchsetzung ihrer Interessen zu lassen.

Andererseits ist manche Kritik am staatlichen Interventionismus berechtigt. Ein erster korrigierender Eingriff zieht oft die zweite und dann wieder die nächste Korrektur nach sich. Gleichwohl kann niemand wirklich wollen, dass der Staat sich vollständig aus der Wirtschaftspolitik zurückzieht. Die Frage ist, wie viel Staat brauchen wir, um die Freiheit des Einzelnen zu sichern, und auf der anderen Seite steht die Frage, wie viel Staatsinterventionismus gefährdet gerade diese Freiheit. Eigentlich hat die SPD sich erst in der Ära Schröder vom staatswirtschaftlichen Denken gelöst. Der Konflikt zwischen Schröder und Lafontaine spiegelte noch etwas vom Gegensatz zwischen alten sozialdemokratischen Wirtschaftskonzepten und dem neuen Weg der Sozialdemokratie wider. Die SPD-Ministerpräsidenten stehen in dieser Hinsicht hinter Gerhard Schröder, was mit der Einsicht in schiere Notwendigkeiten zusammenhängt. Die Erfahrung ist oft eine gewichtigere politische Lehrmeisterin als die ideologische Grundorientierung. Man wird relativ schnell pragmatisch, wenn man feststellt, dass die Menschen nicht gegängelt werden wollen und dass es extrem teuer wäre, wollte man sie trotzdem gängeln. Außerdem liefe man Gefahr, so sehr mit Interventionen und Korrekturen beschäftigt zu sein, dass keine Kapazitäten mehr frei wären für Innovationen und richtungweisende Projekte.

Dennoch vollzieht sich der Rückzug des Staates aus der Wirtschaft nur in kleinen Schritten. Oft geht es wie bei der Echternacher Springprozession, drei Schritte nach vorn und zwei zurück, einer schon mal seitwärts, dann vielleicht wieder mal fünf nach vorn und nur zwei zurück, zum Teil auch gegen massiven Widerstand. Denn es ist keineswegs so, dass der Rückzugsprozess des Staates aus der Wirtschaft in allen Teilen der SPD die gleiche Unterstützung erfährt. Aber im Großen und Ganzen ist die SPD inzwischen auch in ihrem Programm eine Partei, die größere wirtschaftliche Freiräume schaffen will, Freiräume allerdings, in denen bestimmte Spielregeln eingehalten werden müssen.

Die Schwierigkeiten beim Rückzug des Staates aus der Wirtschaft lassen sich gut am Beispiel der Werften aufzeigen. Seit es eine starke Konkurrenz aus Indien, Brasilien und Korea gibt, sind manche unserer Werften nicht mehr voll wettbewerbsfähig. Und schon ist es aus mit der Devise, der Staat solle sich nicht in die Wirtschaft einmischen. Immer wieder fordern Arbeitnehmer wie Arbeitgeber, einmal die einen, einmal die anderen lauter, dass den Werften aufgeholfen werden müsse. Zum Glück sind die Werften in Schleswig-Holstein inzwischen alle privatisiert.

Sicherlich gibt es eine Reihe von Beispielen für missglückte staatliche Interventionen in den letzten Jahren. So kann man sich darüber streiten, ob es klug war, der Firma Holtzmann noch einmal einen staatlichen Kredit zu geben, der das Unternehmen dann doch nicht retten konnte. Viele behaupten, sie hätten das schon von Anfang an gewusst. Aber immerhin saßen damals im Vorstand der Firma Holtzmann Manager, die ein «Schweinegeld» verdienten; und als die erklärten, dass sie das Schiff mit ein paar Millionen wieder flott bekämen, da durfte man doch eigentlich annehmen, dass sie etwas von ihrem Job verständen. Sie haben mit Hilfe des Betriebsrats ihre Arbeitnehmer auf die Straße getrieben, und als die Menschen dort «Gerhard, hilf uns!» riefen, musste der Bundeskanzler handeln. Kann man ihm das vor diesem Hintergrund verübeln? Ist er der Schuldige, weil er die Banken noch einmal zu Krediten überredete, die Rettung des Unternehmens aber trotzdem nicht klappte? Es gehört zu den zentralen Ungerechtigkeiten in unserer Gesellschaft, dass bei Firmenpleiten die Manager relativ ungeschoren davonkommen. Sie beziehen weiter ihre Spitzengehälter, und sie bekommen womöglich noch riesige Extrasummen gezahlt, wenn es ihnen gelingt, einen Betrieb durch den Abbau von zigtausend Stellen vorübergehend zu sanieren, während sich die einfachen Arbeitnehmer auf der Straße wiederfinden.

Selbst da, wo sich im Prinzip alle einig sind, dass das Engagement des Staates reduziert werden sollte, ist die Durchführung oft problematisch. So haben wir alle im Grunde dem Gedanken zugestimmt, dass die Bundeswehr kleiner und effizienter werden muss und dass zu diesem Zweck Standorte geschlossen werden müssen. Aber wenn es dann konkret um einzelne Kasernen geht, rufen alle: «Nicht bei uns!» Man war sich einig, dass die verbleibenden Standorte möglichst gleichmäßig auf alle Bundesländer verteilt werden sollten, und schon erklärten die Vertreter der alten Bundesländer: «Natürlich sollen die neuen Bundesländer auch ihre Standorte bekommen – aber bitte nicht unsere!» Bei solchen Prozessen merkt man dann, dass die verschiedenen an einer Entscheidung beteiligten politischen Akteure oft gar nicht so weit auseinander liegen in ihrem Ansatz – der Teufel steckt dann immer noch im Detail der Umsetzung.

Ich bin der Auffassung, dass der Staat sich nicht zu sehr in das Wirtschaftsgeschehen einmischen sollte. Die Aufgabe der Wirtschaftspolitik liegt für mich darin, für alle Beteiligten günstige Rahmenbedingungen zu schaffen, positive Anstöße zu geben und darüber hinaus «Türöffner» für internationale Kontakte und neue Exportmärkte zu sein.

Viele politische Rahmenbedingungen enthalten bereits mehr oder minder klare Handlungsvorgaben für die wirtschaftlichen Akteure. Das gilt zum Beispiel für die Richtlinien der Europäischen Union, die landwirtschaftliche Hilfen an bestimmte Bedingungen knüpfen. Früher wurde den Bauern das Getreide in jeder Menge zu einem garantierten Preis abgenommen, und dies führte dazu, dass immer mehr produziert wurde, in einem solchen Ausmaß, dass Überschüsse vernichtet werden mussten. Es gab die berühmt-berüchtigten Butterberge, Fleischberge und Milchseen. Wenn es von Seiten der EU nur noch Subventionen für Landwirte gibt, die auch umweltpolitische Auflagen erfüllen, dann bedeutet auch dies Einfluss auf das Unternehmerverhalten. Baut man die Subventionen für ein Produkt ab, dann hat auch dieses eine steuernde Wirkung. Nun mag mancher Landwirt sich fragen: «Warum soll ich noch Getreide anbauen, wenn ich dafür gar nichts mehr bekomme?»

Ein häufiger Vorwurf an den Staat lautet, er habe die revolutionären Entwicklungen der Globalisierung der Wirtschaft überhaupt noch nicht richtig zur Kenntnis genommen, er hinke mit seiner Subventionspolitik einer völlig veränderten ökonomischen Wirklichkeit hinterher. Dass die Politik viel langsamer ist als die Wirtschaft, sei eine Hauptursache unserer derzeitigen wirtschaftlichen Misere. Diese Behauptung mag zwar nicht ganz falsch sein, sie ist aber auch nicht ganz richtig. Denn die Politik muss notwendig in manchen Anpassungsprozessen langsamer sein. Auch wenn ich die Auffassung teile, dass der Staat sich weitgehend aus der Wirtschaft zurückziehen sollte, kann dies nicht von heute auf morgen geschehen. Das lässt sich gut am Beispiel des Kohlebergbaus zeigen. Die Stützung der Kohle sei wettbewerbsverzerrend und zugleich klimaschädigend, so heißt es zu Recht. Die Subventionen müssten vollständig abgebaut werden, schlussfolgern die Anhänger der reinen Marktwirtschaft wie die Umweltschützer. Einmal abgesehen davon, dass ein solcher Schritt aufgrund bestehender Staatsgarantien gar nicht sofort möglich ist, könnte er bedeuten, dass Tausende auf einen Schlag arbeitslos würden und eine ganze Region auf einmal wirtschaftlich zerstört wäre. Also befürworten die aktiven Sozialdemokraten den schrittweisen Abbau der Subventionen, begleitet von Bemühungen, Beschäftigungsalternativen aufzubauen. Bei einem solch allmählichen Vorgehen, einem sanften Strukturwandel, hinkt man der Einsicht in die notwendigen Veränderungen natürlich immer hinterher, doch man macht zugleich Fortschritte. Als ich im Haushaltsausschuss des Bundestages saß, in den 70er und 80er Jahren, belief sich die Kohleförderung noch auf riesige Milliardenbeträge, und diese Subventionen galten als heilige Kuh, die nicht angetastet werden durften. Das ist inzwischen nicht mehr der Fall, wenn auch noch immer erhebliche Summen in diesen Bereich fließen.

Die Anhänger der Theorie der reinen Marktwirtschaft würden mit den Achseln zucken und sagen: «Was soll's? Weg mit den Subventionen, der Markt wird's richten. Lass die Leute ruhig arbeitslos werden und die Region schrumpfen. Langfristig entstehen von selbst wieder neue wettbewerbsfähige Branchen. Qua ‹unsichtbarer Hand› wird sich das alles von selbst wieder einspielen.» Aber in solchen Fällen des raschen Umbruchs ist es immer der Staat, der anschließend die Scherbenhaufen zusammenkehren und die Fürsorge für die Menschen übernehmen muss, deren Existenz zuvor durch den Zusammenbruch ganzer Wirtschaftszweige zerstört wurde. Das kümmert die Privatwirtschaft dann nur wenig. Denn die Arbeitslosen- und Sozialhilfe für die Menschen, die keine neuen Jobs finden, geht zu Lasten des Staatssäckels, ganz abgesehen davon, dass die Kommunen obendrein noch viele andere soziale Probleme mit ihnen haben.

Der Glaube, dass die wirtschaftlichen Prozesse sich optimal einspielen, wenn man die Märkte nur sich selbst überlässt, ist zudem naiv und höchst gefährlich. In jüngster Vergangenheit hat uns die wirtschaftliche Entwicklung der neuen Bundesländer und der Zusammenbruch des Neuen Marktes genügend Beispiele dafür geboten, welche Desaster das freie Spiel der Kräfte schaffen kann. Am Anfang hieß es: Die neuen Bundesländer brauchen sich nur dem freien Markt zu öffnen, dann entstehen dort blühende Landschaften. Stattdessen haben wir vielfach erlebt, was es bedeutet, wenn man abrupt und ohne Abfederung rein marktwirtschaftlichen Prozessen ihren Lauf lässt.

Man ging damals – wie gesagt – davon aus, dass die gesamte Wirtschaft der ehemaligen DDR rund 600 Milliarden Mark wert sei. Immerhin rangierte sie vor ihrem Zusammenbruch auf Platz 17 der Liste aller Industrieländer. Es stellte sich dann allerdings heraus, dass es in Wirklichkeit minus 250 Milliarden waren. Wenn man gleich gewusst hätte, dass da nicht viel wettbewerbsfähige Substanz ist, dann wäre manches anders gelaufen. Man hätte völlig andere Strategien entwickeln müssen. Zum Beispiel hätte man viel mehr in die Innenstädte investieren müssen. Damit wären grandiose Fehlinvestitionen an anderer Stelle vermieden worden. Jetzt finden wir zwar Einkaufsmärkte auf der grünen Wiese am Stadtrand, mit Großparkplätzen, Friseur für Mutti, mit Kinderparadies und McDonald's, auf der anderen Seite aber sind die Innenstädte verödet. Die

Supermärkte draußen werden wohl schon bald nicht mehr so nett aussehen und nicht mehr so attraktiv sein. Nötig gewesen wäre ein ganzheitliches Städtebausanierungsprogramm, dass die Innenstädte belebt und attraktiv macht. Ein Euro Innenstadtsanierung zieht bis zu acht Euro Investitionen in anderen Bereichen· nach sich. Diese einfache Weisheit ist vielfach nicht bedacht worden. Natürlich ist man hinterher immer schlauer.

Die Sozialdemokraten hatten bei der «Wende» ein anderes Konzept. Wir wollten die großen Kombinate nicht ganz zerschlagen, sondern sie so zerlegen, dass daraus wirtschaftlich tragfähige kleinere Einheiten hätten werden können. Wir waren überzeugt, dass es einfacher ist, auf Bestehendem aufzubauen, als alles platt zu machen. Das, was an staatlichen Hilfen angeboten wurde, nachdem sich die Treuhand richtig ausgetobt hatte, ist zwar auch nicht besonders überzeugend gewesen. Aber diese Maßnahmen kamen ja auch eher als eine Art Notfeuerwehr, als es genau genommen für optimale Lösungen schon zu spät war.

Wenn jemand wie Lothar Späth mit seinem Engagement in Jena als ökonomischer Wunderknabe gefeiert wird, weil er gewisse Erfolge vorweisen kann, muss man auch hier genauer hinschauen. Ich halte es nicht unbedingt für eine Superleistung, mit 3,6 Milliarden Mark Finanzspritze von der Treuhand aus einem maroden Betrieb mit 27 000 Mitarbeitern einen gesunden Betrieb mit 1 500 Mitarbeitern zu machen. Außerdem kann man Späths Vorgehen wohl kaum als ein rein marktwirtschaftliches Verfahren bezeichnen. Auch hier musste der Staat einspringen, nicht nur mit finanzieller Unterstützung, sondern auch bei der Versorgung der vielen Entlassenen, der neuen Arbeitslosen.

Ganz offensichtlich war es ein Fehler, die Anpassung der Ostwirtschaft an die Westwirtschaft dem freien Markt ohne geeignete Spielregeln zu überlassen. In den neuen Bundesländern ist eine ausgesprochen schwierige Situation entstanden, weil zahlreiche jungen Leute wegen der hohen Arbeitslosigkeit abwandern und damit den wirtschaftlichen Abwärtstrend verstärken. Wir werden ehrlich zugeben müssen, dass wir den meisten Menschen im Osten Deutschlands in absehbarer Zeit nichts anderes als den zweiten Arbeitsmarkt anbieten können. Es ist ja eine grundsätzliche Frage, was man in den Regionen anfängt, in denen aufgrund der Abwanderung nicht mehr viele Menschen leben. Ein bisschen Tourismus, ein bisschen Dienstleistung, ein bisschen Infrastrukturausbau, das sind oft nur Tropfen auf den heißen Stein. Notwendig wäre die Neugründung von kleinen und mittelständischen Unternehmen, vor allem in der Informations- und Kommunikationstechnologie. Denen müsste auch finanziell stärker unter die Arme gegriffen werden. Nun sollen ja die Kreditanstalt für Wiederaufbau und die Deutsche Ausgleichsbank zusammengelegt werden, eine Maßnahme, die ich begrüße. So muss man nicht mehr zu zwei verschiedenen Banken laufen, sondern bekommt den Service aus einer Quelle. In diesem Zusammenhang ist auch geplant, Existenzgründern, die von den ängstlich gewordenen Banken derzeit nur zögerlich behandelt werden, mit einer Art Risikokapitalbeteiligung den Start zu erleichtern. Viele Banken haben in den zurückliegenden Jahren der Goldgräberstimmung zum Teil ihr Kapital leichtfertig in fragwürdige aufgeblähte Projekte gesteckt und viel verloren, jetzt sind sie übervorsichtig geworden und behandeln den kleinen Handwerksmeister so, als wäre der an der Misere schuld.

Der Staat kann es sich nicht leisten, das Desaster, dass die freien Kräfte des Marktes gelegentlich hinterlassen, einfach zu ignorieren. Genau deswegen kann der notwendige Strukturwandel auch nicht abrupt, sondern nur in kleinen Schritten erfolgen. Er muss ihn immer gestalten und extreme negative Auswirkungen abfedern. Damit will ich natürlich nicht sagen, dass die Anpassungsschritte im Einzelnen nicht auch schneller sein könnten.

Der Glaube an die «unsichtbare Hand» des freien Marktes,

die von selber alles richten wird, ist in jüngster Zeit auch durch die Entwicklung am Neuen Markt in Frage gestellt worden. Der Neue Markt konnte sich vollkommen frei entfalten, doch was dabei herausgekommen ist, haben wir jetzt erlebt: eine Kapitalvernichtung von gigantischem Ausmaß. Mancher neue Aktionär ist regelrecht arm geworden, obwohl sich die meisten Aktienkäufer marktgerecht verhalten haben. Viele Leute sind von den Analysten in risikoträchtiges Verhalten hineingetrieben worden, keineswegs von staatlichen, sondern von privat agierenden Analysten. Die zuckten dann hinterher nur die Achseln: «Da habt ihr eben Pech gehabt!» Natürlich war es auch psychologisch verständliches Wunschdenken, das die Aktionäre glauben ließ, die Kurse würden immer weiter steigen. Nur wenige haben sich die Frage gestellt, ob denn die Zuwächse in der Realwirtschaft diesen Kursanstieg überhaupt rechtfertigen, und dann kam für viele das böse Erwachen. Es kann kaum erstrebenswert sein, dass sich solche wilden Marktverhältnisse auf andere Wirtschaftsbereiche ausdehnen.

Es spricht auch Bände, zu welchen Fantasiepreisen die UMTS-Lizenzen von den großen Telekommunikationsfirmen ersteigert wurden. Alle Beteiligten scheinen damals geglaubt zu haben, dass es sich hier um Produkte handelt, die sich in Kürze jedermann und jedefrau würde zulegen wollen. Alle würden sich beispielsweise die Fußballweltmeisterschaften im Handyformat anschauen wollen. Auch die Banken haben offenbar geglaubt, dass UMTS in kürzester Zeit enorme Gewinne einspielt. Sie haben den Bietern Kredite in unglaublicher Höhe bereitgestellt, ohne genau zu wissen, wie der Markt aussieht, wie die Produktion im Einzelnen vor sich gehen sollte, ohne realistische zeitliche Perspektive. Dies hat sich alles nach den Gesetzen des Marktes abgespielt. Und doch wird jetzt Finanzminister Eichel dafür kritisiert, dass er den Bietern zu viel Geld für die Lizenzen abgenommen habe. Die Regulierungsbehörde hatte als Minimum einen dreistelligen Millionenbetrag für die sechs Lizenzen haben wollen, und sie hat hundert Milliarden bekommen.

Kann man dafür dem Finanzminister die Schuld in die Schuhe schieben? Liegt die Verantwortung nicht ganz und gar bei den beteiligten Firmen und bei den Banken, die den Bietern Kredite in unverantwortlicher Höhe fast nachgeworfen haben? Alle hatten sie einen Vorstand und einen Aufsichtsrat, die hätten Einhalt gebieten müssen.

Bei dem Run auf die UMTS-Lizenzen war keine Staatsregulierung im Spiel, es tobte nur der freie Wettbewerb auf dem freien Markt. Die Tatsache, dass dabei vollkommen überhöhte Summen für eine neue Technologie geboten wurden, hat in Schleswig-Holstein die Firma Mobilcom ins Straucheln gebracht und könnte für über 1000 Menschen den Verlust des Arbeitsplatzes bedeuten, wenn man die Beschäftigten der Zulieferfirmen in die Schätzung einbezieht. Der Neue Markt hat auch Firmen in den Strudel seines Zusammenbruchs gerissen, die vorher ganz ordentlich dastanden. Und viele Aktionäre, die sich in den letzten Jahren an der Börse verspekuliert haben, werden als gebrannte Kinder vermutlich nie wieder Aktien kaufen.

Ich würde gern einmal die Rolle der Banken bei der ungünstigen Entwicklung der Wirtschaft in den letzten Jahren genauer unter die Lupe nehmen lassen, nicht nur bei uns und in den USA, sondern auch in Thailand, Indonesien, Argentinien und anderswo. In vielen Fällen haben die Banken bei den großen Wirtschaftskrisen durch unseriöse Kreditvergabe eine entscheidende Rolle gespielt. Auch die vielen falschen Testate und gefälschten Unternehmensbilanzen, die zu den großen Firmenpleiten in den USA geführt haben, sind der so gelobten freien Marktwirtschaft zuzurechnen. Auch für die Konkurse des Immobilienhändlers Schneider und des Mediengiganten Kirch ist das Kreditgebaren der beteiligten Banken mit verantwortlich. Im Falle Schneider sind sie betrügerisch reingelegt worden. Doch auch so etwas dürfte eigentlich nicht passieren, wenn man eine ordentliche Marktanalyse macht. Jedenfalls fällt es auf, dass die Banken bei Kleindarlehen die Bonität ihrer Kunden sehr viel penibler prüfen.

Historisch gesehen, hat durch den Untergang der staatswirtschaftlichen Systeme der Kapitalismus erst einmal freie Bahn bekommen; vom «Ende der Geschichte» fabulierte ein amerikanischer Autor. Doch vielleicht wird es jetzt mehr solcher Exzesse des freien Marktes geben, die uns dann erst die Notwendigkeit einer neuen Form der sozialen Marktwirtschaft – und das weltweit – sichtbar machen. Der amerikanische Ökonom Paul Krugmann führt die jüngsten Wirtschaftskrisen in Asien, Lateinamerika und Japan nicht etwa auf fehlendes marktwirtschaftliches Verhalten der entsprechenden Länder zurück, sondern darauf, dass sie sich zu schnell und übergangslos auf den freien Markt eingelassen haben.

Es ist ein Fehler zu glauben, man müsse die Dinge nur dem freien Spiel der Kräfte auf dem Markt überlassen, dann werde sich alles schon von selbst wieder richten. Sicher kann man darüber streiten, wo der Staat eingreifen muss, ihn aber zum wirtschaftspolitischen Eunuchen zu machen, ergibt keine Perspektive, schon gar nicht in einem Land mit historisch gewachsenen Institutionen – schon gar nicht in einem sozialdemokratisch regierten Bundesland.

Was aber können wir tun, um unsere schwächelnde Wirtschaft zu beleben und zukunftsfähig zu machen? Das Rezept, das man von der Opposition am häufigsten hört, lautet: «Die Steuern senken!» Das klingt in den meisten Ohren wie Musik und macht seine Verfechter beliebt, vor allem in Wahlzeiten. Kaum jemand zahlt gern Steuern. Zwar wollen alle gute staatliche Leistungen, doch Steuern zu zahlen, ist eine andere Geschichte. Der Staat soll die materielle und institutionelle Infrastruktur bereitstellen, die Bildung fördern, Kleinkindbetreuung und Ganztagsschulen flächendeckend anbieten, Wissenschaft auf hohem Niveau fördern; er soll dafür sorgen, dass das Straßennetz ausgebaut und in Stand gehalten wird, dass die Müllabfuhr funktioniert und dass Polizei und Gerichtsbarkeit gewährleistet sind. Alles das wird wie selbstverständlich erwartet – aber gleichzeitig sollen die Steuern gesenkt werden. Das wäre, wenn überhaupt, nur durch eine ständige Erhöhung der Staatsschulden zu finanzieren. Diesen Weg sind wir in der Vergangenheit allzu lange gegangen. Noch höhere Staatsschulden können und sollten wir den kommenden Generationen aber nicht zumuten; und auch die in der EU vereinbarten Stabilitätskriterien schieben dem einen Riegel vor.

Radikale Marktwirtschaftler empfehlen, noch mehr Staatsaufgaben zu privatisieren, Arbeitslosen- und Sozialhilfe zu kürzen und die staatliche Verwaltung weiter zu verschlanken. Denn wenn der Staat weniger Aufgaben zu erfüllen habe, brauche er auch weniger Steuereinnahmen. Folglich könne man die Steuern senken. Dann werde die Wirtschaft auch in erwünschtem Maße wachsen, was wiederum die Arbeitslosigkeit senken und die Menschen in den Stand setzen würde, mehr private Vorsorge für Alter und Krankheit zu betreiben. Diese Kur scheint manchen auf den ersten Blick plausibel, aber so einfach funktionieren Wirtschaft und Gesellschaft nun einmal nicht.

Was die Privatisierung vormals staatlicher Großunternehmen betrifft, besteht schon seit längerem weitgehend Übereinstimmung zwischen SPD und CDU/CSU, mit geringen Akzentunterschieden. Der Prozess der Privatisierung ist ja auch längst schon in vollem Gange. Die Energieversorgung wird inzwischen fast nur noch von privaten Unternehmen betrieben. Bahn und Post sind dereguliert, mit gewissen Übergangsbedingungen. Die Subventionierung des Kohlebergbaus wird immer weiter zurückgeführt. Noch ist die Staatsquote in Deutschland etwas höher als in anderen Ländern, höher als in England, doch schon niedriger als in Schweden. Die Engländer haben in der Thatcher-Ära viele frühere staatliche Betriebe radikal privatisiert, bis hin zu den Gefängnissen, mit allerdings zum Teil bedenklichen Folgen. So zeigt sich jetzt zum Beispiel bei der englischen Bahn, dass die Privatisierung zu einer Vernachlässigung des Schienennetzes geführt hat; es befindet sich in teils katastrophalem Zustand, weil sich niemand mehr dafür verantwortlich fühlt.

Wegen solcher und anderer Beispiele aus anderen europäischen Ländern warnen wir Sozialdemokraten in Sachen Privatisierung davor, das Kind mit dem Bade auszuschütten. Auch besteht immer die Gefahr, dass private Unternehmer sich die Filetstücke aus den bisher staatlichen Betrieben heraussuchen, ebendie, mit denen es viel zu verdienen gibt, während andere, für das Gemeinwohl wichtige Teilbereiche als Stiefkinder auf der Strecke bleiben.

In den «guten alten Zeiten», als die Post noch das Monopol für die Telekommunikation hatte, war klar, was eine Telefoneinheit kostete. Es gab nur eine Form und eine Farbe des Telefonapparates, später dann drei Farben zur Auswahl. Irgendwelche Extras waren nicht möglich, und wer an seiner Telefonanlage selber irgendetwas veränderte, dem kam die hoheitlich organisierte Post aufs Haupt. Von diesem Zustand haben wir uns inzwischen, angestoßen durch die EU, weit entfernt. Vieles ist liberalisiert und dereguliert worden, mit der Folge, dass es jetzt eine riesige Auswahl von Geräten und Anlagen gibt und dass die Telefongespräche nur noch wenige Cent kosten. Auch der Service ist, zumindest was den Fernsprechbereich angeht, besser geworden. Allerdings ist gleichzeitig – und das ist die Kehrseite der Privatisierung – die Gelbe Post, vor allem der Paketservice, schlechter und auch teurer geworden. Das zeigt wieder, dass man sehr genau darüber nachdenken muss, was im Einzelnen passiert, wenn staatliche Monopole privatisiert werden. Es gehört zu unserem Kulturverständnis, dass der Staat jedem Bürger, jeder Bürgerin, egal, wo sie leben, den gleichen Post-Mindestservice garantiert. Da muss dann die Allgemeinheit den kostenintensiven, unrentablen Teil übernehmen, um zu gewährleisten, dass der Frau auf der Hallig und dem Mann auf der Alm der Brief persönlich vom Postboten zugestellt wird.

Den «schlanken Staat» können wir inzwischen kaum mehr durch weitere Privatisierung erreichen, denn es gibt gar nicht mehr viel zu privatisieren. Das geht nur noch auf dem Weg über eine effizientere öffentliche Verwaltung. Es gibt im Verhältnis

zwischen Staat und Bürger noch immer einen Wust an Formalitäten, der für viele einen großen Zeitaufwand und reichlich
Ärger bedeutet – und zugleich für die staatliche Verwaltung
einen enormen Kostenfaktor darstellt. Bei einem Wohnort-
wechsel beispielsweise muss man sich im Einwohnermeldeamt
ab- und anmelden, man muss das Auto ab- und wieder anmelden und vieles andere mehr. Das ließe sich sehr vereinfachen,
indem eine einzige Stelle gegen eine Gebühr alle diese Dinge
für den Betreffenden per Computer erledigte. Auch der Umgang mit der Krankenversicherung, das Beantragen der Rentenversicherung könnte wesentlich vereinfacht werden; das
Informationszeitalter bietet grundsätzlich viele Möglichkeiten
zum Abbau unnötiger Formalitäten.

Im Verhältnis zwischen Staat und Wirtschaft kann und muss
sich vieles ändern, Antragsverfahren, Anmeldungen, rechtliche
Genehmigungen könnten wesentlich vereinfacht und die notwendigen Verfahren verkürzt und beschleunigt werden. So will
es mir nicht in den Kopf, dass es bei uns im konkreten Fall dreißig Jahre dauern kann, bis der Bau einer Straße genehmigt
wird. Zu viel Bürokratie ist ein ernsthaftes Hindernis für die
Wirtschaft, vor allem für kleine und mittelständische Betriebe.
Wir haben uns in Schleswig-Holstein daher darangemacht,
Genehmigungswege drastisch zu verkürzen. Wir bieten auch
Hilfen für Investitionswillige an, Führer durch den Behörden-
dschungel, in denen aufgelistet ist, was sie beachten müssen,
welche Papiere sie benötigen, wo und wie sie an diese kommen.

Auch durch den Abbau sozialstaatlicher Leistungen könne
und müsse der Staat sparen, so wird von neoliberalen Politikern
gefordert. Ich bin der Ansicht, dass der Staat verpflichtet ist, ein
Mindestmaß an Daseinsfürsorge gegenüber seinen Bürgerinnen und Bürgern zu gewährleisten. Verweigert man die, dann
fallen immer mehr Menschen in die Armut, wie das in den USA
der Fall ist. Dort erhalten sie keine ärztliche Versorgung, wenn
sie sie brauchen, bekommen zwar Lebensmittelkarten (anstelle
der Sozialhilfe), damit sie nicht verhungern, aber sie werden an

den Rand der Gesellschaft gedrängt, übrigens auch viele Mütter mit Kindern, denen dann für ihre Zukunft wenig Chancen bleiben. Wenn das die «Welt von morgen» sein soll, dann kann ich nur sagen: nicht mit uns; in einer solchen Gesellschaft möchte ich nicht leben. Um das zu vermeiden, müssen wir den Sozialstaat leistungsfähig erhalten. Dazu brauchen wir dringend eine Reform der Sozialversicherungssysteme, damit sie wieder auf einer festen Grundlage stehen.

Es ist durchaus möglich, die Arbeitslosen- und Sozialhilfe effizienter zu gestalten und dadurch Ausgaben zu sparen. Die vom Bundeswirtschaftsminister geplante Zusammenlegung dieser beiden finanziellen Hilfen ist da schon ein wichtiger Schritt. Es muss aber auch möglich sein, in Extremfällen dem einzelnen Arbeitslosen oder der Sozialhilfeempfängerin zu sagen: «An dieser Stelle ist Schluss!» Denn schließlich muss das Geld, das umverteilt wird, auch von anderen erarbeitet werden. Das ist ebenfalls ein Gebot der sozialen Gerechtigkeit.

Auch wenn wir unsere Bemühungen verstärkt darauf richten, bestimmte Staatsausgaben zu senken, bleiben immer noch genügend Aufgaben, für die wir stetige Steuereinnahmen brauchen. Die generelle Klage über eine zu hohe Besteuerung in Deutschland ist nicht gerechtfertigt. Wenn man sich die steuerliche Belastung insgesamt anschaut, dann ist sie bei uns nicht höher als anderswo, obwohl das immer wieder behauptet wird. Nach Berechnungen der OECD hatte Deutschland im Jahr 2001 mit 21,7 Prozent die niedrigste Steuerquote in Europa (wenn man die Sozialversicherungen herausrechnet). Weltweit hatte nur Japan mit 17,2 Prozent eine niedrigere Rate, und Japan ist schon seit Jahren kein besonders geglücktes Beispiel für eine wirtschaftliche Erfolgsstory.

In Deutschland gibt es außerdem unendlich viele steuerliche Ausnahmeregelungen, die die reale Steuerlast reduzieren. Die Frage ist berechtigt: «Warum nicht gleich die Steuersätze senken, wenn dafür die Ausnahmeregelungen gestrichen werden?» Damit könnte unser Steuersystem ungleich durchschaubarer und verständlicher werden. Ein undurchsichtiges Steuersystem ist immer auch ein Stück weit ungerecht, weil bestimmte Personengruppen das Gestrüpp der Bestimmungen und Ausnahmen besser durchschauen als andere und davon profitieren. Steuern sollten einfach und nachvollziehbar sein, so sagt es jedes Lehrbuch. Doch das sind sie bei uns in Deutschland leider nicht. Ähnlich sehe ich die Subventionen. Es macht meist wenig Sinn, mit der einen Hand zu nehmen und mit der anderen zu geben. Wir könnten Steuern senken, wenn wir Subventionen abbauen.

Allerdings halte ich den Glauben von FDP und CDU, die Konjunktur werde ganz von selbst wieder anspringen, wenn die Steuern gesenkt würden, für naiv. Jedenfalls hat sich diese Annahme in den letzten Jahren, in denen Steuern gesenkt worden sind, als falsch erwiesen. «Weil die Steuersenkungen noch viel zu gering waren!», behauptet die Opposition. Auf Bundesebene wurden in der ersten rot-grünen Legislaturperiode, mit der ersten Stufe der Steuerreform, Steuersenkungen in Höhe von 30 Milliarden Euro jährlich für Privathaushalte beschlossen. Trotzdem lässt die Konjunktur zu wünschen übrig. Wir beobachten schon länger, dass es zwischen Steuerhöhe und Wirtschaftswachstum keinen eindeutigen Zusammenhang gibt. Demnächst sollen bei uns noch zwei weitere Stufen der Steuerreform zusätzliche Steuersenkungen bringen (bis zum Jahr 2005 bis zu 60 Milliarden Euro jährlich für Privathaushalte, Mittelstand und Großunternehmen zusammen), die nur zeitlich verzögert erfolgen, weil so die staatliche Hilfe für die Opfer der Flutkatastrophe vom Sommer 2002 finanziert wird. Wie weit sich diese zusätzlichen Steuersenkungen als wachstumsfördernd auswirken werden, bleibt abzuwarten. Es wird nicht unerheblich auch von der weiteren Entwicklung der Weltwirtschaft abhängen.

Wir bewegen uns nämlich nach Ansicht vieler Wirtschaftsexperten weniger am Rande einer Inflation als einer Deflation – wenn wir Pech haben. Das könnte bedeuten, dass die Konjunktur trotz Steuersenkungen, trotz Reduzierung der Lohnnebenkosten und trotz weiterer Deregulierung nicht anspringt. In Japan waren die Kreditzinsen in den 90er Jahren auf nahe null reduziert, und es wurde trotzdem nicht investiert. Auch bei uns gibt es in einigen Bereichen schon Kreditzinsen von null. Wenn man ein neues Auto kaufen beziehungsweise leasen will, zahlt man bei einigen Marken für den Kredit nichts mehr. Ob das den Absatz fördert? Ganz offenbar greifen in der jetzigen volkswirtschaftlichen Situation viele der alten Instrumente nicht mehr, die früher geholfen haben.

Die rot-grüne Bundesregierung muss sich allerdings vorwerfen lassen, bei der Steuerreform bestimmte Entwicklungen falsch eingeschätzt zu haben. Bei der Senkung der Körperschaftssteuer war man davon ausgegangen, dass die Unternehmen die Altsteuerrückzahlungen, die ihnen zustehen, über mehrere Jahre verteilt geltend machen würden. Stattdessen haben die meisten diese Abschreibungen auf zwei Jahre konzentriert. Statt Einnahmen aus der Körperschaftssteuer zu erzielen, muss der Finanzminister Altsteuern an die Unternehmen zurückzahlen. Diese Einbrüche waren unvorstellbar hoch und wurden nicht richtig eingeschätzt. Die Körperschaftssteuer war einmal eine Haupteinnahmequelle des Staates mit etwa 22 Milliarden Mark und ist zur Zeit (2002) zu einem Minusposten von 1,5 Milliarden Euro geworden. Deshalb wird jetzt wieder über eine Mindestkörperschaftssteuer für Unternehmen diskutiert. Durch eine solche Mindeststeuer könnten die staatlichen Einnahmen aus der Körperschaftssteuer wieder auf 7–11 Milliarden Euro ansteigen. Was wir dringend brauchen, ist eine Verstetigung der Steuereinnahmen, was eine solide Planung des Staatshaushaltes erst möglich macht.

Außer dem etwas simplen Steuerrezept empfehlen die Marktwirtschaftler zur Ankurbelung der Wirtschaft gern, den Faktor Arbeit billiger und den Arbeitsmarkt flexibler zu machen. «Die Löhne in Deutschland sind einfach zu hoch!», heißt es immer wieder. Oder es werden die zu hohen Lohnnebenkosten beklagt. Der Arbeitsmarkt sei insgesamt zu wenig flexibel: Übertriebene Arbeitnehmerrechte, forciert durch die Gewerkschaften (so etwa die Lohnfortzahlung im Krankheitsfall, ein zu rigider Kündigungsschutz usw.), würden die Unternehmerinitiative lähmen. Viele der notwendigen Reformen würden durch die Macht der Gewerkschaften verhindert, die noch dem Klassenkampfdenken des 19. Jahrhunderts verhaftet seien.

Der Bundeswirtschaftsminister hat eine Diskussion um die Lockerung des Kündigungsschutzes für Unternehmen mit weniger als fünf Mitarbeitern begonnen. Über diesen Vorschlag kann man durchaus nachdenken, denn eine größere Flexibilität in dieser Hinsicht könnte das Leben kleiner Betriebe erleichtern. Generell halte ich den Kündigungsschutz und die Mitspracherechte der Mitarbeiter aber für wichtige soziale Errungenschaften, an denen wir festhalten sollten.

Die Lohnnebenkosten sind in Deutschland im OECD-Vergleich tatsächlich sehr hoch. Wollten wir sie drastisch senken, stellt sich allerdings sofort die Frage: Wie finanzieren wir dann die Sozialversicherungssysteme? Unser Plan war und ist es, über die so genannte Ökosteuer den Rentenkassen aufzuhelfen. Wenn statt der Löhne aber bestimmte Ressourcenverbräuche besteuert werden, könnte man die Beiträge zur Sozialversicherung stabilisieren, vielleicht sogar senken.

In vielen anderen Ländern werden die Sozialversicherungssysteme über die Mehrwertsteuer gespeist, zum Beispiel in Schweden. Dort liegt der Mehrwertsteuersatz bei 25 Prozent, bei uns bei 16 Prozent. Mit diesen Einnahmen werden die Leistungen finanziert, für die bei uns Arbeitgeber und Arbeitnehmer mit ihren Sozialversicherungsanteilen aufkommen. Der Vorteil der mehrwertsteuerfinanzierten Sozialversicherung liegt darin, dass alle daran beteiligt sind, die Reichen wie die Armen – wobei jemand, der sich einen schicken Pelzmantel leistet oder ein schnelles Auto, über die Mehrwertsteuer mehr in die Sozialversicherung einzahlt als jemand, der im Billigladen einkauft oder weiter Fahrrad fährt.

Zur Senkung der Lohnnebenkosten ist auch eine grundlegende Reform des Gesundheitswesens und der Krankenversicherung erforderlich. Auch hier ließe sich schon eine Menge durch Effizienzsteigerungen erreichen. So bin ich zum Beispiel eine Verfechterin der Idee der elektronischen Patientenausweise, zu der wir in Schleswig-Holstein einen Modellversuch durchführen. Solche Patientenkarten würden helfen, Mehrfachuntersuchungen und Mehrfachverschreibungen zu verhindern, und dadurch enorme Kosten sparen.

Zur Zeit arbeitet das Bundesgesundheitsministerium auf Hochtouren an solchen Ideen, und auch die Rürup-Kommission denkt über grundlegende Reformen der Sozialversicherungssysteme nach. Ich bin zuversichtlich, dass wir noch in dieser Legislaturperiode bei der Senkung der Lohnnebenkosten sichtbare Fortschritte erzielen werden.

Marktwirtschaftler wiederholen immer wieder, es sei vor allem die Macht der Gewerkschaften, die mit ihren Forderungen die Entwicklung unserer Wirtschaft blockierten. Damit es wieder ein nennenswertes wirtschaftliches Wachstum gebe, solle es mehrere Nullrunden bei den Tarifverhandlungen geben, die Lohnzuwächse sollten sich nicht am Preisniveau oder den Unternehmensgewinnen orientieren, sondern an der Arbeitsproduktivität und so weiter.

Hierzu ist zunächst festzuhalten, dass es genügend Beispiele dafür gibt, dass Gewerkschaften über zwei, drei und mehr Jahre auf höhere Lohnforderungen verzichtet haben. Wenn daraus keine neuen Arbeitsplätze entstanden, wenn bestehende Arbeitsplätze sogar abgebaut wurden, dann kann man den Gewerkschaften nicht verübeln, dass sie bei der nächsten Tarifverhandlung erklären: «Noch mal legt ihr uns damit nicht rein!» Die Gewerkschaften haben, dies sollte man nicht vergessen, über längere Zeit, in der die Unternehmen riesige Gewinne eingefahren haben, zum Teil Lohnverzicht geübt und sich auf Lohnrunden nahe null eingelassen.

Ich bin durchaus bereit, darüber nachzudenken, ob die

Flächentarifverträge, die für die großen Unternehmen der Industrie, zum Beispiel für die Autoindustrie, genauso gelten wie für das Kleinunternehmen um die Ecke, wirklich der Weisheit letzter Schluss sind. Da wäre es möglicherweise sinnvoller, stattdessen Mindestbedingungen, einen Rahmen, auszuhandeln und den einzelnen Betrieben darüber hinaus Gestaltungsfreiheit zu lassen. Es gibt auch Betriebe – ein Beispiel in Schleswig-Holstein ist die Firma Motorola in Flensburg –, die ihren Mitarbeitern im sozialen Bereich zusätzliche Angebote machen. Da wird dann zwar nicht der Lohn erhöht, aber dafür zum Beispiel das Preis-Leistungs-Verhältnis in der Kantine verbessert. Das sind Anreize für die Mitarbeiter, sich in ihrem Betrieb wohl zu fühlen, die sich indirekt auch auf das Portemonnaie der Arbeitnehmer auswirken.

Bislang interessieren sich, so scheint mir, die Gewerkschaften noch zu wenig für solche qualitativen Extras. Die Firma Motorola bietet beispielsweise auch Betriebskindergärten an. Die Mütter können ihre Kinder zur Arbeit mitbringen, und es vermittelt ihnen ein gutes Gefühl zu wissen, dass der Sprössling in Reichweite, im Nebengebäude, gut beaufsichtigt spielt. Für das Wohlbefinden im Alltag sind solche Dinge oft wichtiger als eine monatliche Einkommenssteigerung um 20 Euro, die in null Komma nichts wieder ausgegeben ist.

Es ist und bleibt ein Problem der Gewerkschaften, dass sie in der öffentlichen Meinung die Interessen derer vertreten, die (noch) Arbeit haben, und kaum die der Arbeitslosen, die Stellen suchen. Damit sei nicht gesagt, dass die Arbeitslosen den Gewerkschaftlern völlig egal wären, aber in erster Linie nehmen sie eben die Interessen ihrer zahlenden Mitglieder wahr – und die sind definitiv andere als die der Arbeitslosen.

Manchmal sind Arbeitnehmer durchaus dazu bereit, auf Lohnzuwachs zu verzichten, wenn dafür neue Stellen eingerichtet werden. Nach einem ähnlichen Prinzip funktionierte das «5000 × 5000»-Modell bei VW, das ein Erfolg wurde. Die VW-Arbeiter waren allerdings nur deswegen zum Lohnverzicht zu motivieren, weil sie unmittelbar erleben konnten, welche positiven Auswirkungen ihr persönlicher Verzicht hatte. Es ist eine alte Beobachtung, dass Menschen vor allem dann zu gemeinschaftsorientierten Handlungen bereit sind, wenn sie sehen können, dass ihr eigenes Verhalten unmittelbare positive Folgen für andere hat. Wenn der Zusammenhang dagegen abstrakt, indirekt und mehrfach vermittelt ist, tun sie sich verständlicherweise schwer.

Insgesamt hat die Macht der Gewerkschaften im Zeitablauf eher nachgelassen. Zwar war ver.dis Streikdrohung bei den Tarifverhandlungen im Januar 2003 noch einmal eine große Machtdemonstration. Immerhin gelang es dabei, den öffentlichen Arbeitgebern Lohnerhöhungen abzuringen, die für Länder und Kommunen höchst problematisch sind. Dennoch sind Mitgliederzahl und Einfluss der Gewerkschaften tendenziell rückläufig. Außerdem wandelt sich auch bei den Gewerkschaften allmählich die Einstellung, und neue Einsichten in die veränderten wirtschaftlichen Bedingungen setzen sich durch, vor allem bei den kleineren Gewerkschaften. Da gibt es also durchaus welche, die neuen Ideen gegenüber aufgeschlossen sind. Bei den größeren, bürokratisch organisierten Gewerkschaften dauert das offenbar etwas länger.

Vehement möchte ich der Auffassung widersprechen, dass wir in Deutschland zu viel Mitbestimmung hätten und diese Mitbestimmung die Unternehmerinitiative lähme. Natürlich mag es hier und da Auswüchse geben. Die muss man abstellen. Doch eines ist sicher: Die Mehrzahl der Unternehmen, die einen Personalrat haben, sollten diesem eigentlich auf den Knien danken. Denn der Personalrat erledigt nicht selten eine Menge unerfreulicher Aufgaben für die Betriebsleitung, gerade dann, wenn der Betrieb in Schwierigkeiten steckt. Wenn das Management seinen Betriebsrat ordentlich behandelt und ihm die relevanten Daten offen legt, die z. B. einen Personalabbau unabdingbar machen, dann nehmen die Betriebsräte auch an den unangenehmen Verhandlungen mit den Mitarbeitern, die gehen müssen, teil. Die Betriebsräte machen sich Gedanken über die soziale Abfederung und helfen in Einzelfällen, was wiederum das Geschäft der Unternehmer erleichtert und dem Frieden im Betrieb und damit auch der weiteren Produktivität zugute kommt. Wie kooperativ Betriebsräte sein können, haben wir in Schleswig-Holstein am Beispiel der Werften erlebt. Wenn da etwa am Freitag ein Schiff reinkommt, das am Sonntag wieder rausmuss, dann ist es der Betriebsrat, der die Leute zusammentrommelt und ihnen sagt: «Leute, wir malochen jetzt hier, bis die Sache gelaufen ist!» Und dann arbeiten sie, wenn es sein muss, auch mehr als zwölf Stunden am Tag, am Samstag oder Sonntag.

Als der Handy-Hersteller Motorola vor einiger Zeit in wirtschaftliche Turbulenzen geriet, zeigte sich, dass eine flexible Arbeitszeit eingeführt werden musste, um auf dem Weltmarkt konkurrenzfähig zu bleiben. Die Betriebsleitung kam zu dem Schluss, dass der Standort in Flensburg nur gehalten werden könne, wenn in dieser Fabrik an 365 Arbeitstagen pro Jahr, sieben Tagen pro Woche und 24 Stunden pro Tag gearbeitet würde. Man tüftelte aus, wie das mit vier Schichten hinzukriegen war, und der Betriebsrat wurde an diesen Planungen beteiligt und hat ihnen zugestimmt. Denn den Betriebsräten war klar, dass der Betrieb andernfalls nach Schottland abwandern würde, wenn die Belegschaft nicht mitzöge.

Auf dem Hintergrund solcher und ähnlicher Beispiele finde ich es unsäglich, wenn in der öffentlichen Diskussion von Guido Westerwelle, Friedrich Merz und anderen der Popanz aufgebaut wird, Betriebsräte und Gewerkschaften seien grundsätzlich nicht in der Lage, an vernünftigen Lösungen mitzuwirken. Es ist einfach ein altes Vorurteil, ihnen ständig Blockadehaltung vorzuwerfen. Ich behaupte sogar, dass kooperierende Betriebsräte, die in Krisen mit der Unternehmensleitung zusammenarbeiten, ein Standortvorteil für Deutschland sind, der Investitionsentscheidungen positiv beeinflusst. Die Identifika-

tion der Arbeitnehmer mit ihrem Betrieb, eine hohe Betriebs-
bindung sind neben einer guten Ausbildung eindeutige Vorzü-
ge des «Standorts Deutschland», die wir uns von politischen
Scharfmachern nicht schlecht reden lassen sollten.

11

Das tägliche Geschäft des Regierens

Manchmal wollen Menschen, die mir auf Veranstaltungen begegnen, von mir wissen, was es denn eigentlich bedeute, ein Bundesland zu regieren. Schulkinder fragen mich: «Was tut so eine Ministerpräsidentin den ganzen Tag?» An einem normalen Tag, wenn keine politischen Krisen anstehen und ich auch nicht auf einer längeren Reise bin, habe ich ungefähr acht bis neun Termine, Innentermine und Außentermine. Wir mischen das gern, um die Sache aufzulockern. Ich gehe möglichst einmal am Tag nach draußen; manchmal werden auch zwei oder mehrere Außentermine gebündelt. Zweimal im Jahr unternehme ich ausgedehntere Reisen durch Schleswig-Holstein, gewöhnlich in den Sommerferien, um einzelne Firmen, Institutionen und Organisationen gründlicher kennen zu lernen. Vor kurzem fand eine solche Reise unter dem Gesichtspunkt «Gesundheit» statt. Ich informierte mich darüber, welche Projekte und Initiativen es in diesem Bereich gibt, was verschiedene Firmen an Produkten und Dienstleistungen im Gesundheitssektor anbieten und was ihre Probleme sind. Zu solchen Reisen laden wir auch die Presse ein.

Viel Zeit wird von den regelmäßig wiederkehrenden Innenterminen beansprucht. Einmal wöchentlich finden Kabinetts- und Fraktionssitzungen statt, außerdem eine Abteilungsleitersitzung, die die Chefin der Staatskanzlei allein leitet, wenn ich es zeitlich nicht mehr schaffe. Relativ regelmäßig gibt es Presse-konferenzen, bei denen wir Journalisten über Regierungsent-scheidungen unterrichten. Manchmal werden solche Presseblö-cke auch an Außentermine angehängt, dann haben vor allem Journalisten unserer regionalen Medien Gelegenheit, Fragen zu all dem zu stellen, was sie interessiert. Hinzu kommen viele einzelne Interview-Wünsche von überregionalen Medien, die ich möglichst zu erfüllen versuche.

Kabinettssitzung ist das ganze Jahr hindurch jede Woche dienstags ab halb elf; in den Parlamentsferien fällt sie schon mal aus. An diesen Sitzungen nehmen die sieben Ministerinnen und Minister, drei Frauen und vier Männer, sowie ihre Staatsse-kretäre beziehungsweise Staatssekretärinnen teil. Alle haben sich zuvor schon mit der Tagesordnung beschäftigt und sie vor allem daraufhin geprüft, ob und bei welchen Punkten es Wider-spruch oder Ärger geben könnte. Ich lasse in den Kabinettssit-zungen bewusst viel Diskussion zu, damit sich niemand hinter-her beschweren kann, er oder sie sei bei einer Entscheidung überfahren worden. Wir stimmen auch nicht einfach ab nach dem Motto: «Wer ist dafür und wer dagegen?» Wenn wir feststel-len, dass es in einer Sache keinen Konsens gibt, dann war das eine erste Lesung; die Angelegenheit wird dann noch einmal zur weiteren Überarbeitung geschickt. Wir haben allerdings einen Arbeitsplan, in dem festgelegt ist, was wir in Schleswig-Holstein im ersten, zweiten und jedem weiteren Quartal errei-chen wollen, das heißt, in einem bestimmten zeitlichen Rah-men muss eine Entscheidung fallen.

Natürlich gibt es auch aktuelle Tagesordnungspunkte, die sich durch bundespolitische Themen ergeben. Zum Beispiel: Wieweit sind wir bereit und in der Lage, zum Wiederaufbau Afghanistans beizutragen? In welchem Umfang soll oder muss Schleswig-Holstein sich an der Zwangsarbeiterentschädigung beteiligen? Wir diskutieren unsere Haltung zum Lauschangriff oder zur Rasterfahndung. Es handelt sich dabei um Themen, die gerade den Bundestag beschäftigen oder die von den zuständigen Ministerien oder der Staatskanzlei deswegen auf die Tagesordnung gebracht werden, weil sich demnächst der Bundesrat damit befassen wird. Also müssen wir diskutieren, wie Schleswig-Holstein dazu steht. Es gibt die «Tagesordnung ohne Aussprache», das sind Themen, die vorher einvernehmlich abgestimmt worden sind. Daneben gibt es Tagesordnungspunkte, über die weiter diskutiert werden muss, außerdem die Rubrik «Verschiedenes». Manchmal stellt sich heraus, dass bei einem der Punkte unter «Verschiedenes» doch noch Gesprächsbedarf besteht. Dann packen wir ihn für die nächste Woche auf die Tagesordnung.

Kabinettsvorlagen werden in der Regel federführend von einem Ministerium erarbeitet und müssen mit den anderen betroffenen Ressorts zuvor abgestimmt werden. Alle Vorlagen – ob strittig oder einvernehmlich – laufen vor den Kabinettssitzungen über den Schreibtisch der jeweiligen «Spiegelreferenten» in der Staatskanzlei, die sich um die Verbindung und Koordination zwischen den Ministerien kümmern. Sie beurteilen die Vorlagen sowohl sachlich als auch politisch. Dabei müssen sie immer den gesamtpolitischen Zusammenhang im Blick haben: die Regierungserklärung, den Koalitionsvertrag und das Arbeitsprogramm der Landesregierung. Die «oberste» Koordinierung hat allerdings die Staatskanzlei, die den Überblick über alle anstehenden Vorhaben behalten muss.

Wenn sich bei einer Kabinettsvorlage die betroffenen Ressorts nicht einigen können, muss auf der Ebene der Staatssekretäre oder Minister ein Schlichtungsgespräch geführt werden. Erst wenn auch die sich nicht einigen konnten, darf die Kabinettsvorlage strittig ins Kabinett, jedoch nur, wenn die Staatskanzlei zustimmt. So etwas kann zum Beispiel bei politischen «Knackpunkten» zwischen Rot und Grün vorkommen. Dort müssen wir dann versuchen, zu einer politischen Lösung zu kommen. Wenn das nicht möglich ist, war dies die erste Lesung, und die Sache muss nach einem weiteren Schlichtungsversuch noch einmal auf den Tisch.

Natürlich könnte ich bei solchen Konflikten auch mit einem Machtwort entscheiden, aber darüber würde vielleicht die Koalition platzen. Außerdem ist es nie gut, wenn jemand am Kabinettstisch das «Gesicht verliert», und das könnte leicht geschehen, wenn ich bei einem politischen Dissens von vornherein einer Partei Recht gäbe. Die andere Partei würde frustriert sein, ihre Unzufriedenheit nach außen tragen, und daraus würden zusätzliche Probleme entstehen. Natürlich kann ich durchblicken lassen, dass mir ein Argument zunächst einmal mehr einleuchtet als ein anderes, aber wenn es Schwierigkeiten gibt, dann bin ich lieber vorsichtig. Als Ministerpräsidentin muss ich dafür sorgen, dass alle Kabinettsmitglieder die Entscheidung am Ende mittragen. Deswegen machen wir auch nie Abstimmungen, in denen die Mehrheit ganz einfach über die Minderheit siegt. Ich halte nichts davon, einen «gordischen Knoten» mit Hauruck zu durchschlagen. Es ist vielmehr wichtig, die Balance zu wahren, die mit dem Koalitionspartner und die im Kabinett.

Wahrscheinlich unterscheiden sich unsere Kabinettssitzungen nicht sehr von Konferenzen, wie sie fast jeder Mensch aus seinem eigenen Lebensbereich kennt – ob es sich nun um Besprechungen in einem Wirtschaftsunternehmen, um eine Lehrerkonferenz oder die Redaktionssitzung einer Zeitung handelt. Nicht nur die geregelten Verfahrensabläufe bestimmen die Atmosphäre, sondern auch gruppendynamische Faktoren. Im Allgemeinen ist die Stimmung bei uns recht gut und trotz der festen Rednerliste und der förmlichen Garderobe relativ locker. Jeder hat seine Tee- oder Kaffeetasse vor sich, und es gibt auch eine Kleinigkeit zu essen. Jeder hat seine besseren und seine schlechteren Tage, und manchmal ist man müde und ertappt sich bei unpassenden Gedanken wie «Muss die eigentlich jetzt so rumzicken?» oder «Was hat der heute für eine unmögliche Krawatte an!».

Wir stehen meist unter einem gewissen Zeitdruck, da wir mittags gegen zwei Uhr fertig sein müssen, um anschließend in der

Fraktion berichten zu können, was beschlossen wurde. Doch manche Kabinettssitzungen dauern sehr lange. Den Haushalt des nächsten Jahres zum Beispiel kann man nicht in drei Stunden durchziehen. Gelegentlich machen wir in solchen Fällen Kabinettsklausuren, einen ganzen Tag lang, mit Übernachtung, bis zum nächsten Abend, und dann wird wirklich hart gearbeitet, manchmal auch die halbe Nacht hindurch. Zweimal, einmal im Jahr 1995 und noch einmal 1998, haben wir auf einem Schiff getagt, auf der Fähre nach Oslo. Da hieß es: «Keiner verlässt den Saal!» Niemand konnte von Bord gehen. Also mussten wir zusammenbleiben und arbeiten. Solche Marathonsitzungen finden aber nur dann statt, wenn es um den Haushalt geht oder um besonders schwierige und anspruchsvolle Themen.

So haben wir uns zum Beispiel zu einer Klausur zum Thema Gentechnologie zusammengesetzt. Das war zwar im Bundesrat nur ein Zustimmungs- und nicht etwa ein Einspruchsgesetz. Was der Bundestag erlaubt, können wir in Schleswig-Holstein nicht verbieten. Aber wir wollten uns doch darüber unsere eigenen Gedanken machen. So haben wir Fachleute für die kontroversen Positionen eingeladen, Experten pro und contra embryonale Stammzellenforschung, und wir haben mit Naturwissenschaftlern, Soziologen, Psychologen und einer Bischöfin zusammengesessen. Interessanterweise sind wir dabei zu einem Ergebnis gekommen, das dem von Berlin ziemlich ähnlich ist. Wir stellten den Konsens her: Verbrauchende Stammzellenforschung ja – aber es dürfen nicht extra für diese Forschung Stammzellen produziert werden. Wir haben uns allerdings schwer getan mit dem Teil der Berliner Entscheidung, der den Import von Stammzellen erlaubt, obwohl die Herstellung im Inland weiter verboten bleiben soll.

Solche Kabinettsrunden, bei denen wir uns die Zeit nehmen, gründlicher über wichtige Themen nachzudenken und zu diskutieren, obwohl das im Lande keine unmittelbaren politischen Folgen hat, können wir uns natürlich nicht so oft leisten, wie wir möchten. Ein-, zweimal im Jahr treffen wir uns zu solchen Runden; manchmal versuchen wir auch, eine Stunde vor unseren normalen Sitzungen einem bestimmten Thema zu widmen. Dann diskutieren wir zum Beispiel ausführlicher über Arbeitsmarktpolitik oder über besondere Vorfälle in Pflegeheimen.

Unabhängig von den Kabinettssitzungen gibt es dann und wann Gesprächsrunden zwischen Politik und Fachleuten zu aktuellen, für Schleswig-Holstein wichtigen und brisanten Fragen. Ich lade dann beispielsweise, zusammen mit den jeweiligen Fachministern, zu einem Gespräch über Sozialpolitik ein, speziell über Pflegeheime. Außer der zuständigen Gesundheitsministerin sind bei einem solchen Gespräch die Träger von Pflegeheimen vertreten, die uns über die Zustände dort berichten, sowie Ärzte, die über die Krankheiten informieren und die Eingruppierung der Pflegebedürftigen in die verschiedenen Pflegestufen vornehmen. Bei diesen Gesprächen geht es in erster Linie um Information und Austausch, um das, was wir Politikerinnen und Politiker vom Sachverstand der Expertinnen und Experten lernen können.

Wir haben in den letzten Jahren vier große Gesprächsrunden über die Ostseeregion organisiert, über unsere Zusammenarbeit mit den anderen Ostseeländern bei den Themen Verkehr, Kommunikation und Wirtschaft, an denen zahlreiche Experten und Expertinnen, auch aus der Wissenschaft, teilgenommen haben. Außerdem haben wir immer wieder Dialogrunden mit Gewerkschaften, mit Unternehmern sowie mit beiden Akteuren zusammen. Früher liefen diese Gespräche immer sehr formalisiert ab; sie wurden wochenlang vorbereitet. Davon sind wir inzwischen abgerückt zugunsten einer «Runde ohne Block und Bleistift», wie ich das nenne. Ich frage dann: «Was bewegt euch? Welche Probleme beschäftigen euch zur Zeit?» Solche Gespräche sind in der Regel spannend und kreativ; daraus ergeben sich oft wichtige Anregungen für die praktische Politik.

Die Themen zu solchen Gesprächsrunden werden aus dem Mitarbeiterkreis vorgeschlagen. Auf diese Weise ist zum Beispiel unsere große Gesundheitsinitiative entstanden. Wir hatten uns in Vorrunden mit der Frage beschäftigt, welche Themen in Zukunft für Schleswig-Holstein wirtschaftsbestimmend sein könnten, und kamen dabei zu dem Ergebnis, dass nach den Schwerpunkten «Verkehr», «Freizeit und Fun», «elektronische Datenverarbeitung» das Thema «Gesundheit und Wellness» in den Mittelpunkt rücken würde. Also haben wir dazu eingeladen, in mehreren Runden. Solche Initiativen übernimmt dann das Planungsreferat der Staatskanzlei. In diesem Fall waren mehrere Ministerien daran beteiligt, in erster Linie natürlich die Sozial- und Gesundheitsministerin, aber auch die Bildungsministerin, die für die Hochschulen zuständig ist, der Wirtschaftsminister, weil Firmen in unserem Land tangiert sind, die damalige Landwirtschaftsministerin als Zuständige für Tourismus und Nahrungsmittel. Auf diese Weise war bei der Gesundheitsinitiative das halbe Kabinett involviert.

Ich arbeite gern in kleineren Runden, die zügig und sensibel reagieren können. Wenn man merkt, dass in der Öffentlichkeit ein Thema hochkocht, dann kann man sich auf diese Weise schnell die ersten Informationen bei denjenigen holen, die etwas von der Sache verstehen. Der Rahmen, den Björn Engholm in seiner «Denkfabrik» den Experten geboten hat, war möglicherweise glänzender; er hatte vielleicht auch mehr Medienwirkung. Unser Rahmen ist bescheidener, aber auf diese Weise können wir öfter vor Ort sein und auch mehr Menschen deutlich machen, dass wir uns um ihre Probleme kümmern.

In solchen Runden erlebe ich Politik als besonders interessant, als motivierend und als gestaltende Kraft, nicht nur als zähes Alltagsgeschäft, als bloßes Reagieren auf äußere Geschehnisse und Anforderungen oder als reines Krisenmanagement, was oft genug der Fall ist.

Zu meinen regelmäßigen Terminen gehören auch die Sitzungen aller deutschen Ministerpräsidenten, die sich mindestens viermal im Jahr treffen; darüber hinaus kann es weitere Sondersitzungen geben. An diesen Runden nehmen auch die Chefs der jeweiligen Staats- und Senatskanzleien teil. Jedes Bundesland hat ein Jahr lang den Vorsitz, das heißt, es muss die Treffen organisieren. Mindestens zweimal jährlich ist dabei der Kanzler anwesend. Die Sitzungen der Ministerpräsidenten finden in der Regel in Berlin statt, doch die erste des Jahres ist immer im jeweiligen Vorsitzland. Dabei wird man auch eingeladen, das Land ein bisschen kennen zu lernen. Eineinhalb bis zwei Tage wird dann zügig gearbeitet, von morgens bis abends, meist in freundlicher Atmosphäre, und abends können ausnahmsweise die Ehepartner dazukommen.

Die Tagesordnung ergibt sich aus den Vorschlägen der Ministerpräsidenten. Zu bestimmten Themen werden gelegentlich auch die Fachminister eingeladen. Manchmal einigt man sich sehr schnell über die Diskussionspunkte, auf Zuruf, weil sie für alle sichtbar anliegen. Es gibt aber auch Sitzungen mit schwierigen Themen, die von den Chefs der Staats- und Senatskanzleien penibel vorbereitet werden. Bei diesen Sitzungen tagen in der Regel die (SPD-geführten) A-Länder und die (CDU/CSU-geführten) B-Länder gemeinsam. Die Vorbesprechungen am Morgen finden dagegen nach A- und B-Ländern getrennt statt, weil hier die Strategien für den Tag abgesprochen werden.

Manchmal finden sich die Ministerpräsidenten auch zu den so genannten «Treffen im Kaminzimmer» zusammen, bei denen es um heikle Angelegenheiten geht, die zunächst einmal nicht an die Öffentlichkeit dringen sollen. Die Finanzminister fürchten sich jedes Mal, wenn es heißt, dass es ein solches Treffen am Kamin geben soll. Denn sie wissen, dass die Ministerpräsidenten dann nicht nur über Dinge sprechen, die die Welt bewegen, sondern vor allem über Angelegenheiten, die viel Geld kosten. Einmal haben wir beispielsweise bei einem solchen Kamingespräch nach einer Härtefallklausel im Asylrecht gesucht.

Es gibt Härtefälle, die mich wirklich ins Mark treffen. Da lebt zum Beispiel eine Familie von Bürgerkriegsflüchtlingen seit sieben Jahren in einem Dorf in Schleswig-Holstein; die Kinder sind dort aufgewachsen, der Mann hat eine Stelle bei der Gemeinde bekommen, die Familie ist integriert – und nun sollen sie zurück in ihr Herkunftsland. Manchmal rückt dann der gesamte Gemeinderat mit dem CDU-Bürgermeister an, um uns klar zu machen, dass wir diese Leute doch jetzt unmöglich wieder zurückschicken können, zumal die Kinder plattdeutsch reden. «Die gehören doch jetzt nach Schleswig-Holstein!», heißt es, «denen könnte man doch irgendwann die deutsche Staatsbürgerschaft geben!» Doch das Gesetz ist eindeutig, und es besagt, dass Bürgerkriegsflüchtlinge wieder in ihre Heimat zurückmüssen, wenn die Gewalttätigkeiten dort beendet sind. Andere Beispiele für Härtefälle liegen vor, wenn jemand durch Gewalt so traumatisiert ist, dass es ihn oder sie zerstören würde, wenn sie zurückmüssten, oder wenn jemand schwer krank ist und bei uns die Chance zu einer Krankenhausbehandlung hätte, die im Heimatland nicht möglich ist.

Angesichts solcher Schicksale habe ich mich beim «Treffen im Kaminzimmer» für eine Härtefallklausel eingesetzt, die im Einzelfall das Gesetz aufheben kann. Eine solche Klausel war dann auch im Zuwanderungsgesetz enthalten, das Bundestag und Bundesrat Anfang 2002 verabschiedet haben. Nachdem das Bundesverfassungsgericht Anfang 2003 entschieden hat, dass das Gesetz nicht rechtmäßig zustande gekommen sei, ist jetzt auch die Frage der Härtefallregelung wieder offen. Ich hoffe sehr, dass wir diesen zentralen Punkt auch im zweiten Anlauf verankern können.

Grundsätzlich ist es sehr sinnvoll, zwischen Bürgerkriegsflüchtlingen und Asylbewerbern zu unterscheiden. Die meisten Kriegsflüchtlinge gehen ohnehin von selbst gern wieder in ihre Heimat zurück, wenn die Kriegshandlungen beendet sind, vor allem dann, wenn sie nicht zu lange andauerten. Die Situation der Asylbewerber ist eine grundsätzlich andere. Sie müssen triftige Gründe dafür angeben, dass sie in ihrer Heimat nicht mehr leben können, ohne Gefahr für Leib und Leben befürchten zu müssen.

Das Asylverfahren ist schon bürokratisch genug, und ich kann verstehen, dass sich viele Leute darüber ärgern, dass diese Prozedur in der Vergangenheit endlos lange dauerte, oft viele Jahre, mit verschiedenen Einspruchsmöglichkeiten, dem ewigen Hin und Her. Und natürlich gibt es auch die so genannten Wirtschaftsflüchtlinge, die Asylanträge stellen. Menschen, die zu uns kommen, weil sie hier auf ein besseres Leben hoffen, die ihre Papiere wegwerfen und dann auf einmal keine Sprache der Erde mehr verstehen, so dass man gar nicht weiß, wohin man sie zurückschicken könnte. Also werden sie zunächst einmal geduldet, bis man ihre Herkunft und Identität recherchiert hat. Das ist sicherlich nicht in Ordnung, schon deswegen nicht, weil dadurch andere, die unseren Schutz tatsächlich dringend benötigen, auf Ablehnung stoßen. Zwar können auch Menschen, die aus wirtschaftlichen Gründen ihre Heimat verlassen, verzweifelt sein. Doch das Asylrecht ist nur dazu da, Leib und Leben vor Gewalt zu schützen. Den wirtschaftlichen Problemen müssen wir mit den Mitteln der Entwicklungshilfe begegnen und dadurch, dass wir die Bedingungen der wirtschaftlichen Globalisierung diskutieren und besser zu gestalten versuchen.

Das ist nur ein Beispiel für die heißen Themen, die «im Kaminzimmer» erörtert werden, selbst wenn es da gar keinen Kamin mehr gibt. «Am Kamin» bedeutet: im kleinen Kreis, in dem man offener reden kann, ohne jedes Wort auf die Goldwaage legen zu müssen.

In meinem politischen Leben gibt es halbwegs «normale» Wochen und daneben die «hammerharten» Wochen, Wochen, in denen sich Abend für Abend und Sonntag bis Sonntag ein Termin an den anderen reiht. Auch die normalen Wochen haben oft ein ziemlich arbeitsreiches, bunt zusammengewürfeltes Programm. Innerhalb weniger Tage empfange ich eine Delegation chinesischer Journalisten und nehme an einem Sponsorenessen für das Musikfestival teil. Ich führe ein Gespräch mit den Hauptpersonalräten und unterstütze den

Wahlkampf in einem anderen Bundesland. Ich besuche eine Schule, um mit den Schülern über Konsequenzen der PISA-Studie zu diskutieren, oder eine Einrichtung für behinderte Kinder, um einen Förderbescheid zu überreichen. Ich eröffne einen Kongress oder weihe eine neue wichtige Institution ein. Ich besuche und besichtige Betriebe, Krankenhäuser, Zeitungsredaktionen. Regelmäßig treffe ich mich mit der Minderheitenbeauftragten, die für die Dänen, die Friesen, die Sinti und Roma sowie für die deutsche Minderheit in Dänemark zuständig ist.

Zeitaufwändige Termine sind die Treffen zur Vorbereitung größerer Reden, an denen außer mir der Redenschreiber oder die Redenschreiberin, die Chefin der Staatskanzlei, der Regierungssprecher und weitere Mitarbeiter teilnehmen. Es wird darüber diskutiert, an welchen Stellen für eine Rede noch einmal zugearbeitet werden muss, welche Daten, Fakten und weiteren Informationen noch benötigt werden. Wir sitzen zusammen und überlegen, was in diesem Zusammenhang gesagt werden sollte, was ich vielleicht schon vorher an anderer Stelle zu diesem oder einem ähnlichen Thema in der Öffentlichkeit gesagt habe, was jetzt auf keinen Fall gesagt werden darf, weil erst einmal die Kabinettsmitglieder oder das Parlament ein Recht darauf haben, es zu erfahren. Da wähle ich dann die Formulierung, dass sich die Regierung gerade mit dieser Angelegenheit befasst und die Ergebnisse beizeiten bekannt geben wird. Von mir aus spreche ich in den Reden am liebsten nur über das, was beschlossene Sache ist, aber ich werde natürlich häufig auch zu Dingen befragt, die noch im Fluss sind, und auch solche Fragen müssen beantwortet werden. Das ist nicht selten eine Gratwanderung, und deswegen ist es so wichtig, dass an der Vorbereitung größerer Reden mehrere Menschen mit Durchblick beteiligt sind. Die erste Sammelphase dauert gelegentlich bis zu zwei Stunden, dann verfasst der Redenschreiber einen Entwurf, den der Regierungssprecher, die Staatssekretärin, der Büroleiter durchlesen, und anschließend setzen wir uns noch einmal zusammen, und jeder gibt seinen Senf dazu: «Mir ist da ein Widerspruch aufgefallen!» Oder: «So kann das auf keinen Fall stehen bleiben!» Oder: «An dieser Stelle bloß nicht angreifen, sondern nett sein zu den Leuten!»

Für mich bestimmte Post, «An die Ministerpräsidentin!», kommt direkt in meinem Büro an und wird vom Büroleiter an mich oder direkt an die zuständigen Mitarbeiterinnen und Mitarbeiter weitergeleitet. Beschwerden wird im Einzelnen nachgegangen, zunächst einmal, indem bei dem Ministerium nachgefragt wird, in dessen Arbeitsbereich die Angelegenheit fällt. Darüber hinaus habe ich noch einen Mitarbeiter, der sich unter anderem speziell mit privaten Einzelschicksalen befasst. Da sind Menschen, die sich über konkrete Missstände beklagen, und solche, die existenzielle Hilfe benötigen. Sie wenden sich an mich, weil sie nicht mehr weiterwissen, das Gefühl haben, zwischen allen Stühlen zu sitzen oder von den Mühlen der Bürokratie zermahlen zu werden. Natürlich kann ich mich nicht um jeden dieser Menschen persönlich kümmern, aber solche Briefe wandern nicht in den Papierkorb, sondern die zuständigen Mitarbeiter gehen jedem Fall nach und bemühen sich um Rat und Lösung.

Selbst an den normalen Tagen, in den eigentlich ruhigen Stunden, wenn ich in meinem Büro hinter dem Schreibtisch sitze, klingelt das Telefon alle paar Minuten, eine Mitarbeiterin steckt den Kopf zur Tür herein: «Da ist jemand von der Presse, nur ein Satz zu diesem oder jenem!», «Das und das müsste noch ganz schnell entschieden werden!», «Dieses Papier muss dringend unterschrieben werden!» Jemand anderes kommt herein mit der Frage: «Was hältst du davon? Nur ganz kurz, ganz schnell.»

Überall um mich herum hängen große Fahnen, auf denen «Eilig! Eilig!» steht. Ich weiß gar nicht, warum alles immer so eilig sein muss. Zum Glück kann ich ganz gut relativ lange ruhige Nerven und den Überblick behalten. Man braucht allerdings eine gewisse Fähigkeit zur Simultaneität; man muss vieles gleichzeitig sehen und erledigen können und dabei zugleich die unwichtigeren Dinge zurückstellen und ausblenden können. Meistens geht es hektisch und manchmal eben ganz besonders hektisch zu. Die Unterschriftenmappe nehme ich meist mit ins Auto, auf dem Weg zum nächsten Außentermin, weil es sonst gar nicht zu schaffen wäre. Wenn etwas Unvorhergesehenes eintritt, wie zum Beispiel eine unerwartete Einladung ins Kanzleramt oder aber eine Beerdigung, an der ich teilnehmen muss, dann geht ein unglaubliches Rödeln durch meinen Terminkalender, dann muss A nach B geschoben werden und B nach C, das eine von oben nach unten, weit in den Abend, das andere in die Mittagspause oder die übernächste Woche. Meine Terminreferentin tut mir dann richtig leid. Sie ist echt damit ausgelastet, meine Termine zu organisieren: Zusagen oder Absagen zu geben, Termine zu verschieben oder neu anzuordnen. Ich bin eigentlich ganz gut darin, rasch von einem Thema auf das nächste, von einem Problem auf ein anderes umzuschalten. Manchmal erfordert das aber eine gewaltige Kraftanstrengung.

12

Der Preis des Amtes

Erst als ich Ministerpräsidentin wurde, begann die totale Vereinnahmung des eigenen Lebens. Vorher war zumindest noch manchmal Zeit für kleine private Gänge, fürs Einkaufen, für Flohmarkt oder Kino, für Besuche von Freunden. Mittlerweile kann ich mich kaum noch daran erinnern, wann ich zuletzt für Freunde gekocht habe. Auch ein Buch zu lesen, ist für mich zu einem seltenen Vergnügen geworden, von den Ferien natürlich abgesehen. Es gibt beinahe kein Wochenende ohne berufliche Termine, und wenn ausnahmsweise einmal wirklich nichts ansteht, dann sage ich zu meinem Mann: «Gott sei Dank! Endlich eine Atempause!», und will niemanden sehen. Ich beklage mich nicht darüber; es gehört dazu. Schließlich hat mich niemand gezwungen, Ministerpräsidentin zu werden. Natürlich könnte ich darauf bestehen, nur ausnahmsweise Wochenendtermine wahrzunehmen. Aber viele Veranstaltungen von Partei, Verbänden und Vereinen finden nun einmal am Wochenende statt, und ich will die vielen Menschen, die zu Recht erwarten, dass ich mich für ihre Aktivitäten interessiere und um ihre Sorgen kümmere, nicht enttäuschen.

So ist es vielleicht ganz gut, dass meine eigene Familie nur aus mir und meinem Mann besteht, der sich zudem sehr gut allein beschäftigen kann. Man hat mich oft gefragt, warum wir keine Kinder haben. Das war nicht bewusst geplant, es hat sich so ergeben, weil immer einer von uns beiden etwas Lebensentscheidendes vorhatte. Erst musste ich mein Examen machen, dann meinen Mann ins Ausland begleiten. Dann wollte sich mein Mann habilitieren, und ich wollte endlich mal einen richtigen Beruf ausüben. Dann trat mein Mann seine Professur in Berlin an. Und als ich Abgeordnete in Bonn wurde, war erst recht nicht an ein Kind zu denken. So kam dies und das, bis die Zeit zum Kinderkriegen vorüber war. Es war alles in allem eher ein fortwährendes Aufschieben denn eine klare Entscheidung gegen Kinder. Man sagt sich, es ist ja noch viel Zeit, und gerade jetzt stehen erst einmal andere Dinge im Vordergrund. Doch natürlich bedeutete dieses Aufschieben auch, dass der Kinderwunsch für mich nie eine hohe Dringlichkeit hatte, denn sonst hätte ich die Prioritäten sicherlich anders gesetzt. Ich mag Kinder. Deswegen engagiere ich mich zum Beispiel auch nach Kräften bei UNICEF; zudem haben wir mehrere echte wie unechte Patenkinder. Ich bin gern mit Kindern zusammen, aber manchmal auch ganz froh, wenn sie dann wieder gehen.

Vielleicht hing mein Zögern damit zusammen, dass ich im tiefsten Inneren glaubte, es sei besser, wenn ich keine Kinder hätte – ich fürchtete wohl, das schwierige Verhältnis zu meiner Mutter könne sich wiederholen. Nur eine meiner Schwestern hat eigene Kinder, die andere immerhin Stiefkinder. Zu Beginn meiner Ehe wäre ich dieser Aufgabe wohl nicht gewachsen gewesen. Bei der kleinsten Kleinigkeit konnte ich schon platzen. Ich kann mir nicht vorstellen, dass das Kindern gut bekommen wäre. Später, als ich ausgeglichener war und es vielleicht ganz gut gegangen wäre, war es schon zu spät.

Doch ich habe es eigentlich nie bedauert und zu keinem Zeitpunkt, wie manch andere Frauen, das schmerzliche Gefühl gehabt, etwas Wichtiges verpasst zu haben. Wahrscheinlich, weil mir mein Leben, so wie es ist, interessant genug erscheint. Ich mag Menschen ohnehin nicht, die ständig verpasste Chancen beklagen: «Hätte ich doch …», «Wenn ich bloß …» und «Wäre ich damals nicht …» Natürlich wäre es durchaus nett, wenn ich jetzt einen gut geratenen Sohn hätte, womöglich mit kleinen Enkeln, oder eine bildhübsche Tochter, die vielleicht gerade ihren Doktor, worin auch immer, macht. Aber, wie es im Volksmund heißt: Man kann nicht alles haben.

Seit dem Sommer 1977, kurz nachdem Rendsburg/Eckernförde mein Wahlkreis geworden war, leben mein Mann und ich in Bordesholm, einem schönen, größeren Dorf mit Geschichte, in einem Mietshaus, zusammen mit vier anderen Familien. Passanten, die vorübergehen, zeigen oft mit dem Finger darauf und sagen: «Hier wohnt Heide Simonis.» Demnächst müssen wir allerdings ausziehen, der Vermieter macht Eigenbedarf geltend. So werden wir vielleicht wieder eine Wohnung in Kiel nehmen. Eigentlich bin ich sowieso eher ein Stadtmensch, und wir hatten ohnehin geplant, in die Stadt zu ziehen, wenn wir älter werden, weil man dann immer schnell mit dem Taxi überall hinkommt.

Natürlich verändert sich das Leben in vielerlei Hinsicht, wenn man über eine längere Zeit ein solches Amt ausübt, auch man selbst verändert sich dabei. Manches – wie etwa das Schrumpfen der Freizeit, den Verlust an Privatheit – bemerkt man sehr rasch. Andere Veränderungen vollziehen sich eher allmählich und schleichend über die Jahre.

Am Anfang fiel es mir schwer, mich daran zu gewöhnen, dass ich von nun an auf Schritt und Tritt von Sicherheitsbeamten begleitet wurde. Ich bestehe allerdings darauf, dass sie, wenn ich mal Wäsche einkaufen will, vor dem Geschäft warten. Normalerweise folgen die Beamten einem immer in ein paar Schritten Abstand, aber das finde ich eher albern, und so bitte ich sie meistens, neben mir zu gehen. Inzwischen kennt sie in Kiel sowieso jeder.

Das größte Problem bei dieser Art von Lebensführung ist wohl der ständige Zeitdruck, der auf Dauer auch Auswirkungen auf die Persönlichkeit und die Haltung gegenüber dem Umfeld hat. Ein Termin reiht sich an den nächsten, und dabei muss ich mich ständig sehr rasch auf immer neue Anforderungen, veränderte Situationen, völlig unterschiedliche Themen und Gesprächspartner einstellen. Da bleibt oft nur noch wenig Zeit, über bestimmte Dinge einmal grundsätzlicher nachzudenken und die Gedanken neu zu sortieren. Wenn man lange im «Betrieb» ist, kommen die Floskeln ganz von selber. Man sagt erst einmal ein paar unverfängliche Sätze, und dann ist man «im Programm». Manchmal fühle ich mich wie ein Zirkuspferdchen: Kaum erklingt die Melodie, weiß ich, was angesagt ist. Wer noch neu im «Geschäft» ist, kann manchmal ins Stottern kommen; das werten die anderen leicht als Schwäche und freuen sich darüber, einen vermeintlich schwachen Punkt erwischt zu haben. Kein Wunder, dass viele Politiker und Politikerinnen, um dem zu entgehen, rasch ihre Spontaneität aufgeben und sich stattdessen in Floskeln flüchten.

Es bleibt nicht aus, dass der ständige Zeitdruck einen routinierter macht. Doch deswegen muss ich als Politikerin nicht unbedingt zur Maske werden, zu einer Schablone, die nur noch vorfabrizierte Äußerungen von sich gibt. Mein Eindruck ist, dass sich verschiedene Politikerinnen und Politiker in dieser Hinsicht doch erheblich unterscheiden, auch wenn sie ähnlich lange Berufserfahrung haben. Viele sind so kontrolliert bei ihren öffentlichen Auftritten, dass es schwer fällt, Schlüsse auf ihre Gedanken und Gefühle unter der glatten Oberfläche zu ziehen. Besonders extrem in dieser Hinsicht war Außenminister Hans-Dietrich Genscher, der Fragen selten wirklich beantwortete, sondern immer nur genau das sagte, was er schon vorher zu sagen beschlossen hatte.

Ich selbst war wohl nie besonders gut darin, meine unmittelbaren Reaktionen klug zu verbergen, dazu bin ich zu temperamentvoll. Sonst wäre mir auch der schwerwiegende Ausrutscher bei der Kritik an Willy Brandt nicht unterlaufen. Heute macht das Fernsehen es ohnehin schwieriger, andere über die eigenen Gedanken und Gefühle hinwegzutäuschen. Zwar kann man lernen, das gesprochene Wort zu kontrollieren, doch die Körpersprache lässt sich nicht so einfach manipulieren. Man hat mir zum Beispiel erzählt, ich hätte in einer Fernsehdiskussion mit dem hessischen Ministerpräsidenten Roland Koch überhaupt nicht verbergen können, was ich tatsächlich von ihm hielt. Und das lag nicht etwa an dem, was und wie ich es sagte, sondern offenbar an meiner Haltung und der Art, wie ich ihn angeschaut habe. Ich selber war dagegen der Ansicht, ich hätte mich in dieser Situation vollständig unter Kontrolle gehabt.

Es gibt Politikerinnen und Politiker, die nach außen hin sehr kontrolliert sind, souverän und ausgeglichen wirken, aber im vertrauten Kreis nicht selten explodieren. Gerhard Schröder zum Beispiel kann ja recht gut mit den Medien umgehen; es heißt, er wisse sehr genau, was die Leute hören wollen, und komme gut damit an, ihnen genau das zu sagen. Ich habe ihn aber auch schon in bärbeißiger Laune erlebt, und im engeren Kreis kann er durchaus sehr deutlich werden, wenn ihm etwas gegen den Strich geht. Ich denke, niemand kann ganz aus seiner Haut, und wer nun einmal ein mitteilsamer Mensch ist, wird auch in der Politik nicht zum großen Schweiger werden.

Wirklich kritisch wird es, wenn man beginnt, auch zu Hause und in privater Runde nur noch Worthülsen zu dreschen. Deswegen ist es gerade für Politiker in Spitzenpositionen ganz wichtig, verlässliche, gewachsene Beziehungen zu Menschen zu haben, die einem ehrlich Rückmeldung geben, auf die man sich verlassen kann, nicht nur in Krisenzeiten. Denn eine gewisse Einsamkeit entsteht allein schon dadurch, dass man keine Zeit mehr hat, Freundschaften zu pflegen, und dass das eigene Leben so verschieden ist von dem der meisten Menschen um einen herum. Bei mir sind es in erster Linie mein Mann und meine beiden Schwestern, mit denen ich reden kann, wenn es mal hart auf hart geht. Aber am liebsten mache ich die Dinge mit mir selber aus. Ich kann Freunden oder Bekannten nicht gut etwas vorjammern. Mit ihnen rede ich meist erst dann, wenn ich die Probleme für mich schon weitgehend geklärt habe.

Normalerweise telefoniere ich täglich mit meinem Mann und

oft mehrfach. Er nimmt Anteil an meinem Leben wie ich an seinem, auch wenn wir uns nicht alle Einzelheiten haarklein erzählen. Manchmal tut es einfach nur gut, ein bisschen Dampf abzulassen. Wenn ich stöhne: «Nichts als Ärger, lauter Idioten!», dann erwidert er: «Reg dich nicht auf, das wird schon wieder.» An den Wochenenden, wenn wir gemeinsam zu Hause sind, schlafe ich am liebsten die halbe Zeit, während er versucht, mich um den Bordesholmer See zu jagen. Spazieren gehen an der frischen Luft oder Fahrrad fahren, das ist seine Vorstellung von Erholung. Ihm ist das immer noch viel zu wenig Bewegung, und so holt er dann bei jeder Gelegenheit sein Rennrad aus dem Keller.

Natürlich entwickelt eine Ehe, die über Jahrzehnte als Wochenendehe gelebt wird, ihre eigenen Gesetzmäßigkeiten. Wir wissen zwar immer noch recht gut über das Leben des anderen Bescheid. Ich weiß zumeist, an was er gerade arbeitet, und er weiß, was mich besonders beschäftigt. Aber unsere Lebensbedingungen sind doch sehr verschieden. Er kann sich seinen Alltag so ganz anders, seinen Bedürfnissen entsprechend, einteilen. Wenn er abends von der Arbeit in seine kleine Berliner Wohnung kommt, dann liest er und macht es sich gemütlich. Vielleicht geht er auch noch zum Griechen essen und plaudert mit Freunden und Bekannten; ansonsten aber lebt er in seiner Wissenschaft. Manchmal bin ich auf all das ein klein bisschen neidisch.

Wir haben uns aber über die Jahre daran gewöhnt, dass wir beide, er und ich, viele Sachen allein machen. Beide entscheiden wir vieles allein, und alles in allem passt es uns so, wie es ist. Wir wissen und akzeptieren, dass wir beide Menschen sind, die um sich herum viel Raum brauchen. Udo braucht Ruhe für sich und seine Arbeit, seinen Schreibtisch, seine Bücher und Papiere, längere Phasen ungestörter Konzentration. Und ich brauche, schon auf Grund meiner Kindheits- und Jugenderfahrungen, auch viel Platz, eine große Wohnung, in der ich mich bewegen kann. Der größte Horror wäre für mich, wenn wir zu zweit in einem kleinen Appartement eng aufeinander leben müssten. An unserem Lebensstil hat sich durch Udos Emeritierung im Frühjahr 2003 zunächst nicht viel geändert. Er pendelt nach wie vor zwischen Bordesholm und Berlin, arbeitet weiterhin an seinem alten Institut, hält Vorträge und schreibt an Büchern und Aufsätzen. Bis jetzt habe ich jedenfalls nicht den Eindruck, dass er im Ruhestand ist. Seine Arbeit ist einfach so wichtig für ihn, dass der Übergang in eine andere Lebensphase sich vermutlich erst viel später und fließend vollziehen wird.

Mein Mann hat überhaupt kein Problem damit, dass ich bekannter bin als er. Aber manchmal ärgert es ihn, dass jeder Unsinn, den ich von mir gebe, in der Zeitung gedruckt wird, während Dinge, an denen er jahrelang und mit größter Sorgfalt gearbeitet hat, nur von wenigen Eingeweihten zur Kenntnis genommen werden. Diesen Ärger kann ich gut verstehen, und ich finde das auch sehr ungerecht.

Was ich an meinem Mann besonders schätze und immer geschätzt habe, ist seine Zuverlässigkeit und Loyalität. Er ist loyal gegenüber allen Menschen, die er mag – und mir gegenüber besonders. Das hat dazu geführt, dass er von Anfang an eigentlich alles akzeptiert hat, was zu mir gehört: meine Familie, die Schwestern, auch seine Schwiegermutter, die Anforderungen, die der Beruf an mich stellt. Er begleitet mich immer dann, wenn seine Anwesenheit unbedingt erwartet wird und wirklich wichtig ist, obwohl ihn mancher repräsentative Auftritt eher nervt. Nur hat er von Anfang an klar gemacht, dass seine Arbeit für ihn an erster Stelle kommt und dass er sich nicht auf die Rolle des hinterherdackelnden «Mannes an ihrer Seite» reduzieren lassen wird. Das kann niemand besser verstehen als ich, denn ich habe diese Rolle vor Jahren ja umgekehrt für mich auch abgelehnt.

Ich brauche auch in meinem beruflichen Alltag um mich herum Menschen, mit denen ich schon lange zusammenarbeite, von denen ich weiß, dass ich ihnen vertrauen kann. Denn zu den gefährlichen Deformationen, die das Leben als Spitzenpolitikerin mit sich bringen kann, gehört ein wachsendes Misstrauen gegenüber anderen. Es wird immer schwerer, allen unbefangen gegenüberzutreten, weil man schon viel Heuchelei und falsches Spiel erlebt hat. Im Laufe der Zeit fängt man an, hinter allem einen doppelten Sinn zu vermuten: «War das jetzt ein aufrichtiges Lob oder eine versteckte Kritik? Welche Absicht steckte hinter dieser speziellen Bemerkung?» Zum Glück geht es bei mir noch nicht so weit, dass ich, wenn mir jemand einen guten Tag wünscht, gleich den Dolchstoß von hinten vermute. Aber über die Jahre wird man doch, ob man es will oder nicht, verhaltener und wachsamer. Man entwickelt eine gewisse Vorsicht und Skepsis, man wittert auch Intrigen – und leider liegt man damit oft genug nicht falsch. Wenn das nicht zum Verfolgungswahn führen soll, dann braucht man in seiner unmittelbaren Umgebung Menschen, auf die man sich verlassen kann, bei denen man auch nicht jedes Wort auf die Goldwaage legen muss.

Ein anderes Problem des Politikerberufs besteht darin, dass man nach außen nicht zu viele Schwächen zeigen darf. Ich persönlich glaube zwar, dass einen die Menschen auch dann noch akzeptieren, wenn sie einen schon einmal schwach erlebt haben. Gleichwohl fürchten die meisten Kollegen nichts so sehr wie Anfälle von Schwäche in der Öffentlichkeit. Auch deswegen wird dieses Sich-selbst-Kontrollieren, dieses ständige Auf-der-Hut-Sein und Aufpassen, dass man nichts preisgibt, zur zweiten Natur. Vielleicht können Männer mit dieser Situation besser umgehen als Frauen, obwohl auch das nicht generell gelten dürfte. Denn ich kenne genügend sensible Männer, die an diesen Verhältnissen zerbrechen, und auch harte, starke Frauen, die recht gut damit fertig werden. Aber wahrscheinlich haben die Männer, weil sie schon länger im «Geschäft» sind, Rituale entwickelt, auf die sie in solchen Situationen zurückgreifen können, die ihnen helfen, sich von den eigenen Gefühlen zu distanzieren, Schwächen zu kaschieren und Stärke zu demonstrieren. Vermutlich hat das nichts mit der Natur der Ge-schlechter zu tun, sondern ist eher eine Frage der Erfahrung und der Gewöhnung. Ich will das zunächst einmal weder positiv noch negativ bewerten; ich stelle es einfach nur fest. Es hat gewiss manche Vorteile, alle Schwächen überspielen zu können. Doch auch dafür zahlt man einen Preis.

Politikern in Spitzenpositionen wird häufig vorgeworfen, dass sie nach und nach einen totalen Wirklichkeitsverlust erleiden. Es ist richtig, dass wir uns kaum mehr unter das normale Volk mischen, und wenn, dann nur noch in unserer besonderen Rolle, in der wir eben keine normalen Menschen unter anderen sind. Überall werden uns die Türen aufgehalten und die Hindernisse aus dem Weg geräumt. Wir müssen uns kaum mehr um die Organisation unseres Alltags kümmern. Ich erinnere mich daran, dass wir über diese Dinge schon diskutiert haben, als ich Bundestagsabgeordnete wurde. «Ihr wisst ja überhaupt nicht mehr, was ein Pfund Butter kostet!», sagten uns die Kritiker anklagend, «daran kann man doch sehen, wie abgehoben ihr lebt!»

Zugegeben, ich weiß nicht, was ein Pfund Butter im Moment kostet. Ich bestelle die Dinge telefonisch im Geschäft; sie werden geliefert oder für mich abgeholt; der Rechnungsbetrag wird überwiesen – also, ich weiß es wirklich nicht so genau. Ich fände es allerdings auch albern, wenn ich bei meinem Einkommen so tun würde, als ob ich wie eine Sozialhilfeempfängerin auf jeden Cent achten und hinter den Sonderangeboten her sein müsste. Ich registriere aber sehr wohl, dass es ein Privileg ist, ein gutes Einkommen zu haben und von Menschen umgeben zu sein, die meinen Alltag erleichtern. Ich halte das nicht für einen Realitätsverlust: Es ist ein Stück andere Realität als die anderer Menschen.

Tatsächlich erfahren wir wohl alle sehr unterschiedliche Arten von Alltagsrealität, je nach sozialer Schicht, Beruf, Geschlecht, Alter und Lebenssituation. Dass mein Alltag anders aussieht, macht mich aber keineswegs unfähig, im Interesse der anderen politisch zu handeln, solange ich mir stets bewusst bin, dass ihre Realität eine andere ist. Was ich tun muss, ist, ihnen zuzuhören, wenn sie von ihrem Leben erzählen. Es wäre eine Anbiederung, wenn ich behauptete, mir sei genau bekannt, wie ein Werftarbeiter in Kiel lebt. Das weiß ich natürlich nur aus Statistiken und Berichten, ich lebe nicht Tag für Tag in einer Werftarbeiterwohnung. Trotzdem weiß ich, wenn ich richtig zugehört habe, was die Werftarbeiter und ihre Familien bewegt, welche Sorgen sie haben. Und ich sage mir: Ich darf nicht aufhören, mich in die Lebenssituation der anderen hineinzuversetzen; ich muss versuchen, sie als Menschen wahrzunehmen, die ihre individuellen Sorgen und Probleme, ihre Träume und Hoffnungen haben.

Ich denke, man sollte als Ministerpräsidentin nicht so tun, als lebe man in einer Laubenpieperkolonie. Dann würde man nur unglaubwürdig. Bestenfalls kann man vergleichbare Situationen von früher kennen. Aber wenn man so tut, als wüsste man jetzt noch, wie es da im Einzelnen zugeht, dann ist das verlogen. Die Leute erwarten auch von einem Bundeskanzler oder einer Ministerpräsidentin einen bestimmten Lebensstil; der sollte nicht protzig, aber auch nicht schäbig sein, sondern eben angemessen. Gerhard Schröder hat man seinen Brioni-Anzug nicht übel genommen, weil er so teuer war, sondern vor allem, weil diese Form der Zurschaustellung nicht zu ihm und zum Amt passt.

Die Leute erwarten von uns Politikern nicht, dass wir uns anbiedern, sondern dass wir sie in ihrer Alltagswirklichkeit wahrnehmen. Sie wollen, dass man ihre Probleme zur Kenntnis nimmt. Indem ich auf all diese Veranstaltungen gehe, zeige ich ihnen, dass ich mich für sie interessiere, ihre Anliegen ernst nehme und sie weiterhin oder in Zukunft bei politischen Entscheidungen zu berücksichtigen versuche. Das führt dann dazu, dass die Termine wie verrückt den Kalender überwuchern, dass meine Terminreferentin immer noch etwas und noch etwas unterzubringen versucht und dass ich mich fast in Stücke reiße, um hierhin und dahin und am liebsten überallhin zu gehen. Wenn man an vielen Stellen präsent sein muss, kommt tendenziell das Aktenstudium zu kurz. Das kann ein echter Konflikt sein. Ich kann nicht mehr so viel lesen wie früher und muss mich oft auf Zusammenfassungen verlassen, die Mitarbeiter aus den Ministerien oder der Staatskanzlei für mich anfertigen. Doch auch die zur Kenntnis zu nehmen, verlangt Zeit, und es bleibt meist ein Balanceakt. Streiche ich einen Außentermin, muss jemand anders an meiner Stelle hingehen; gönne ich mir etwas Schreibtischzeit, verpasse ich möglicherweise eine wichtige Zusammenkunft. Bin ich eine gute Politikerin, wenn ich mich gründlich vorbereite, Hintergrundmaterial durcharbeite, alle Statistiken kenne? Oder wenn ich den Leuten durch meine Anwesenheit das Gefühl gebe, dass ich ihre Probleme und Sorgen ernst nehme und mich bemühe, ihnen weiterzuhelfen? Das sind offene Fragen.

Gerhard Schröder hatte vor einiger Zeit einmal hundert Frauen aus verschiedenen Vereinen und Verbänden eingeladen, die ihm die unterschiedlichsten Fragen stellten; anschließend wurde er von der Presse dafür kritisiert, dass er in dieser Runde häufiger sagte: «Darüber weiß ich nichts. Das kann ich jetzt nicht beantworten.» Man nannte ihn schlecht informiert, desinteressiert, auch arrogant. Aber wäre es in dieser Situation besser gewesen, auf alle Fragen irgendein unverbindliches Sprüchlein parat zu haben? Die Presse schien das von ihm zu erwarten. Da müssen die Journalisten dann aber wirklich aufpassen, dass sie nicht selber die Sorte von Politikern heranzüchten, über die sie dann anschließend hämisch herfallen: nämlich die leeren glatten Sprücheklopfer. Weder ein Kanzler noch eine Ministerin oder eine Oppositionsführerin, kein Politiker kann jederzeit über alles Bescheid wissen – und wenn sie oder er dies vorgibt, dann stimmt es nicht. Aber er oder sie kann zuhören, kann selber Fragen stellen, kann sagen: «Ich nehme das jetzt mit, was Sie da eben gesagt haben; ich werde mich darum kümmern.»

Durch die Spielregeln des politischen Lebens, an denen nicht nur die Politiker selber, sondern auch die Presse und die

Öffentlichkeit mit basteln, werden bestimmte Verhaltensformen bestärkt und andere erschwert – und hinterher beklagen alle gemeinsam die Deformation der Politiker und den Verlust an Menschlichkeit in diesem Metier. Es ist wohl kaum möglich, Verformungen und Defiziten ganz zu entgehen, die es übrigens in jedem Beruf gibt; aber ich denke, es korrigiert schon ein bisschen, sich wenigstens dieser Gefahren bewusst zu sein.

Ich gebe ohne weiteres zu, dass es bestimmt einmal im Jahr einen Anlass gibt, bei dem mir der Gedanke kommt: «Jetzt reicht's!» Dann gucke ich morgens nach dem Aufstehen in den Spiegel, finde, dass ich grauenhaft aussehe, und denke: «Das kann doch nicht wahr sein. Wofür tust du dir das an?» Das geschieht vor allem in Zeiten von anhaltendem Stress und fehlenden Erfolgserlebnissen, von endlos langen Sitzungen, bei denen es nicht vorangeht, wenn man dauernd zu spät ins Bett kommt, wenn sich unerfreuliche Kleinigkeiten häufen. Aber es sind meist nur kurze Augenblicksstimmungen, die auch rasch wieder verfliegen. So richtig an den Rand gekommen, dass ich tatsächlich erklären würde: «Macht doch euren Kram alleine!» – das bin ich eigentlich noch nie oder nur ganz selten mal, und auch da sah die Sache schon anders aus, nachdem ich mich einmal richtig ausgeschlafen hatte. Vielleicht spielt dabei die preußische Disziplin eine Rolle, die mein Vater uns anerzogen hat. Man schmeißt eben den Krempel nicht einfach hin, auch wenn es mal hart auf hart geht und sehr unerfreulich ist. Man beißt sich durch. Man gibt nicht auf. Man macht seine Arbeit bis zu Ende und geht nicht zwischendurch laufen.

Schwierig ist die Stille nach dem Sturm, wenn sich nach manchmal wochenlanger großer Anspannung und Hetze plötzlich winzige freie Zeitinseln auftun. Dann besteht die Gefahr, dass ich richtig in mich zusammenfalle, weil ich nervlich fertig bin. In solchen Situationen nehme ich mir meist meinen Quilt und arbeite daran; Quilten tut mir gut, es beruhigt und ist wie Meditation für mich. So habe ich im vergangenen Jahrzehnt schon viele Quadratmeter wunderschöner Decken gequiltet;

und fast jedes Jahr wurde ein solches kleines Kunstwerk fertig. Manchmal lese ich auch Krimis zur Entspannung. Solche Stimmungen entstehen zum Beispiel häufiger im Wahlkampf. Ich sage mir: «Bis zu dem und dem Tag musst du durchhalten!», und dieses Datum ist wie die Ziellinie bei einem Marathon. Wenn jemand auf die Idee käme, den Wahltermin um eine Woche zu verschieben, würde ich, glaube ich, zusammenbrechen. Man teilt sich dann wie beim Marathon seine Kräfte auf das Ziel hin ein, und dabei ist es schon wichtig, auf dem letzten Kilometer nicht völlig erschöpft zu sein. Schließlich muss man auch bei der letzten Wahlkampfveranstaltung noch fit, engagiert und interessiert sein. Doch wenn die Sache gelaufen ist, stellt sich ein extremer Zustand ein. Ich bin dann gelegentlich so überdreht, dass ich nicht mehr richtig schlafen kann, obwohl ich mich nach Schlaf sehne. Ich laufe auf Hochtouren, auch weil ich eine Überfunktion der Schilddrüse habe, ich kann dann kaum was essen und verliere kiloweise Gewicht. Es ist, als ob ich den Motor, der mich antreibt, nur schwer wieder auf eine niedrigere Umdrehungszahl bringen kann. Inzwischen erlebe ich das allerdings nicht mehr ganz so extrem wie früher, doch ich brauche noch immer Tage, bis ich mich nach solchen Extremsituationen wieder umgestellt habe und ruhiger geworden bin. Dann nehme ich mir meinen Quilt vor oder eine Krimi-Lektüre, und mein Mann überredet mich vielleicht zu einem Spaziergang oder zu einer Fahrradtour. Manchmal machen wir dann auch den heldenhaften Versuch, endlich mal wieder ins Kino zu gehen. Der Zustand dauert einige Tage, dann bin ich durch. Schließlich warten da schon die nächsten Dinge, um die ich mich kümmern muss.

Ähnlich sieht es in den Ferien aus. Das Programm der äußeren Aktivitäten, Sightseeing, Besuche, ist immer runtergeschraubt. Mein Bedürfnis, mir neue Dinge anzuschauen, ist in der ersten Urlaubsphase ziemlich gering. Vielleicht ist das auch der Grund, warum wir immer wieder in dieselbe Gegend, in die Toskana, fahren. In der ersten Woche liege ich meist platt wie eine Flunder und schlafe viel. In der zweiten Woche fühle ich mich schon besser, da nehmen dann das Lesen und das Kochen einen breiteren Raum ein, und in der dritten Woche erwacht das Interesse an der Umgebung. Da habe ich dann durchaus auch Lust, nach Siena, Florenz oder Lucca zu fahren, um mir schöne Dinge anzusehen. Zwar kennen wir die toskanischen Städte schon recht gut, doch selbst das Alte ist immer wieder neu und schön. Wir genießen es, durch die engen Gassen zu laufen, auf dem Marktplatz zu sitzen, einen Prosecco zu trinken und einfach dem Leben und Treiben zuzuschauen. Den größten Teil des Urlaubs verbringe ich allein mit meinem Mann. Dann und wann aber laden wir auch Freunde ein, damit wir sozial nicht ganz entwöhnt werden.

Natürlich habe ich mein Handy dabei, so dass man mich immer erreichen kann, wenn während des Urlaubs zu Hause etwas Besonderes geschieht. Doch von mir aus rufe ich bestenfalls jeden zweiten Tag in der Staatskanzlei an. Das muss reichen. Sonst ist es kein Urlaub.

13

Die Droge Macht –
Risiken und Nebenwirkungen

In jüngster Zeit ist der Beruf des Politikers zunehmend in Verruf geraten. Politiker und Politikerinnen seien zu bloßen Entertainern verkommen, heißt es. Sie seien eitel und nur an ihren Privilegien interessiert, die sie häufig genug missbrauchten. Sie klebten an ihren Posten und seien, einmal an der Macht, unfähig, einen anständigen Abgang zu finden. Sind wir wirklich so schlecht wie unser Ruf?

Wahrscheinlich starten die meisten Männer und Frauen, die in die Politik gehen, mit einer Idee – es muss nicht unbedingt gleich das große Wort «Vision» bemüht werden, das heute oft so inflationär verwendet wird. Aber ich unterstelle einmal, dass sie in der Mehrzahl irgendetwas erreichen, die Welt oder zumindest unsere Gesellschaft in irgendeiner Hinsicht verbessern wollen. Die Erfahrungen, die sie anfänglich motivieren, mögen sehr unterschiedlich sein, und deswegen sind auch die ersten Zielvorstellungen ganz verschieden. Bei mir war es der Aufenthalt in einem Entwicklungsland, die Entwicklungspolitik, die mich dazu brachten, in die SPD einzutreten. Bei anderen ist es vielleicht das Interesse an Jugendpolitik, an Familienpolitik, an Wirtschafts- oder Steuerpolitik.

Doch außer einem anfänglichen Interesse für ein bestimmtes gesellschaftliches Thema kommt bei allen, die in die Politik gehen, meist noch etwas anderes hinzu: ein starkes Geltungsbedürfnis. Wer das leugnet und behauptet, es seien nur die edlen Motive der Weltverbesserung und des Engagements für das Gemeinwohl im Spiel, ist sich selber gegenüber einfach nicht ehrlich. Man möchte Menschen überzeugen, man möchte sich selbst mitsamt seinem Programm darstellen. Man möchte beweisen, dass man Antworten auf diffizile Fragen hat und die besten Lösungen für die anstehenden gesellschaftlichen Probleme anbieten kann. Es ist also unbedingt auch ein Stück Eitelkeit dabei, wenn jemand Politiker wird.

Dieses Geltungsbedürfnis zeigt sich bei vielen schon früh. Viele Politikerinnen und Politiker, die ich kenne, sind bereits in ihrer Schulzeit als Klassensprecher oder Schulsprecherinnen aktiv gewesen. Sie haben bei der Schülerzeitung mitgearbeitet oder Jugendgruppen geleitet. Manche waren in der Gemeinde, andere in der Kirchenpolitik tätig. Ute Vogt zum Beispiel, die SPD-Landesvorsitzende in Baden-Württemberg, war Ministrantin, zu einer Zeit, als das für Mädchen noch die Ausnahme war, gegen den erbitterten Widerstand ihres gesellschaftlichen Umfeldes. Auf diese Weise regt sich wohl schon früh so etwas wie ein Alphatierchen-Verhalten: Es sind Menschen, die vorne stehen, den Ton angeben und sagen wollen, wo es langgehen soll. Die meisten Politiker sind übrigens eher Gruppenmenschen als Einzelgänger, obwohl es natürlich auch hier Ausnahmen gibt.

Der persönliche Ehrgeiz ist also eine wichtige Ausgangseigenschaft für die Entscheidung, in die Politik gehen zu wollen. Aber ich unterstelle einmal, dass bei den meisten, egal, ob sie von rechts oder links kommen, zumindest am Anfang Idealismus und ehrliche Überzeugungen vorherrschen. «Wenn wir erst drankommen, wird es mehr soziale Gerechtigkeit geben! Wir werden etwas für die Familien tun! Wir werden die kleinen Leute steuerlich entlasten! Wir werden die Arbeitsmarktpolitik so verändern, dass es deutlich weniger Arbeitslose gibt!» Erst im Laufe der Zeit erkennt man dann: So einfach ist das alles gar nicht. Spätestens an dieser Stelle muss man aufpassen, dass man nicht zum Zyniker wird. Zynisch finde ich die Haltung von Politikern, denen völlig klar ist, dass nichts von dem geschehen wird, was sie den Leuten erzählen, die aber trotzdem weiter das Blaue vom Himmel versprechen, statt ehrlich zu sagen: «Es wird länger dauern, als wir glaubten. Es sind Schwierigkeiten aufgetreten, mit denen wir nicht gerechnet haben. Wir können erst einmal nur Schritte in die gewünschte Richtung tun. Wir müssen womöglich ganz neue Wege suchen, die mehr Zeit brauchen.»

Die reinen Zyniker kommen meiner Erfahrung nach im Allgemeinen über eine kleinere Parteikarriere nicht hinaus. Die Menschen spüren es, wenn jemand selber nicht mehr an die Dinge glaubt, für die er sich angeblich einsetzen will, wenn er allein vom kühlen Machtkalkül getrieben wird. Und sie mögen es nicht.

Zum Ehrgeiz muss bei einer politischen Karriere die Bereitschaft hinzukommen, viel und lange zu arbeiten, womit vor allem auch zermürbende Kleinarbeit gemeint ist. Allerdings gibt es auch eher faule Politiker, die sich einen sonnigen Lenz machen und sich trotzdem gut verkaufen können – da nenne ich jetzt natürlich keine Namen. Es sind die Frohnaturen, die das spärliche Wissen, über das sie verfügen, in Hochglanzformat zur Geltung bringen und es als beeindruckende Fassade vor sich hertragen. Doch langfristig kommen die anderen denen schon auf die Schliche. Natürlich kann niemand in der Politik über alles Bescheid wissen. Ich gebe das für mich auch offen zu. Die Leute merken ja selbst, ob ich etwas nur ablese oder ob ich wirklich Bescheid weiß, weil ich mich intensiv damit beschäftigt habe oder vor Ort gewesen bin. Andererseits gibt es immer wieder Politiker, die mit einem Minimalaufwand an Faktenwissen durchs politische Leben kommen. Fast schon beneidenswert!

Politiker, vor allem Spitzenpolitiker, müssen im Allgemeinen schon deswegen viel arbeiten, weil sie sich ständig an den verschiedensten Stellen zeigen müssen. Dazu kommt die Arbeit in vielen Ausschüssen und Gremien. Das Aktenstudium nimmt dagegen eine vergleichsweise geringe Zeit ein. In diesem Beruf muss man einfach bereit sein, sich zu engagieren. Man findet es dann natürlich besonders ungerecht, wenn die Leute einen nicht lieben, obwohl man ihnen so viel Zeit geopfert und alles getan hat, was menschenmöglich ist. Eine 70-Stunden-Woche ist bei mir selbst keine Seltenheit, sondern die Regel. Und wenn hintereinander der dritte, vierte, fünfte Sonntag den Bach hinuntergeht, dann verfalle auch ich manchmal dem Selbstmitleid. Wieder einmal überhaupt keine Privatbeschäftigung, denke ich dann, in kein Buch hineingeschaut, nicht mal ein, zwei Stündchen im Garten gesessen! Zwar darf man die aufgewendete Zeit nicht eins zu eins mit Arbeitsleistung gleichsetzen. Aber es ist einfach eine große physische und psychische Anstrengung, bei vielen unterschiedlichen Anlässen präsent zu sein und sich für die Dinge zu öffnen, um die es dabei jeweils geht.

Vielleicht sind Politikerinnen und Politiker deswegen so stark vom Beifall abhängig, weil sie sich mit Haut und Haar in Aufgaben stürzen, die oft diffus bleiben, nicht klar umgrenzt sind und manchmal wie Endlosschleifen zu sein scheinen. So viel man auch macht, es ist nie genug; es könnte immer noch mehr und besser sein. Es gibt nicht immer klare Anzeichen dafür, ob man gut, weniger gut oder schlecht war. Als Sportler habe ich meine in Hundertstelsekunden messbaren Leistungswerte, an denen ich mich orientieren kann, und nicht nur die Begeisterung meiner Fans. Als Spitzenmanager der Wirtschaft kann ich mich an die Bilanzen, Umsätze und Gewinne halten. Als Politiker habe ich zum Teil nur vage, wenig konkrete Kriterien, kleine Schritte in die richtige Richtung, die ich mir zuschreiben kann, ab und an Beifall und ansonsten nur die Gunst der Bevölkerung, wie sie sich in den Wahlergebnissen ausdrückt.

Bei mir persönlich stellt sich das Gefühl ein, etwas geleistet zu haben, wenn ich die Leute «rumgekriegt» habe, wenn es mir gelungen ist, ihnen meine Position zumindest so klar zu machen, dass sie sagen: «Sie hat Recht. Da ist was dran!» Oder auch wenn sie meinen: «Das war eine schöne Rede!» Manchmal rechne ich es mir schon als besondere Leistung an, wenn es mir gelingt, in bestimmten Situationen die Ruhe zu bewahren und mich nicht wie Rumpelstilzchen vor Wut oder Ungeduld in der Luft zu zerreißen. Am Anfang der politischen Laufbahn will man sich am liebsten nur an den eigenen Zielen messen: «Wir haben dies und das erreicht, was wir uns vorgenommen hatten! Ich habe dies und das durchgesetzt, was ich versprochen hatte!» Aber größere und für alle sichtbare Erfolge sind in der Politik höchst selten, etwa spektakuläre Erfolge von der Art: «Es ist uns in der letzten Legislaturperiode gelungen, die Zahl der Arbeitslosen zu halbieren.» So etwas wie die Wiedervereinigung kann es zum Beispiel nur einmal geben.

Wenn ich meinen Wählern verkünden würde: «Seht mal her: Ich habe den Prozess der Modernisierung im öffentlichen Dienst eingeleitet!», dann fragen die: «Aha – und was habe ich davon?» Wenn ich ihnen daraufhin erkläre, dass die Ämter sich jetzt als Serviceunternehmen verstehen und Beamte und Angestellte im öffentlichen Dienst sich nun mehr um ihre Klientel bemühen, dann kriege ich garantiert von einem Wähler oder einer Wählerin zu hören: «Stimmt gar nicht! Ich war gestern auf dem Finanzamt, und die haben mich genauso angeblafft wie immer!» Worin die konkrete politische Leistung besteht, das lässt sich eben oft nur schwer vermitteln.

Es gibt aber auch die anderen Beispiele: Die Erfolge unserer Gesundheitsinitiative etwa sind deutlich sichtbar. Da haben viele erst gemäkelt, doch jetzt, nach der relativ kurzen Zeitspanne von zwei Jahren, läuft etwas, das sich auch in Zahlen fassen lässt, und es gibt verbreitet Zustimmung und Begeisterung. 16 Prozent aller Beschäftigten in Schleswig-Holstein arbeiten im Bereich «Gesundheit und Wellness». Wie sich das im Bruttosozialprodukt des Landes auswirkt, müssen wir erst noch sehen. Doch ich kann es schon jetzt durchaus als Erfolg verbuchen. Man stößt etwas an, manchmal läuft der Schlitten – doch manchmal bleibt er irgendwo stecken.

Dass die Dinge stecken bleiben, ist eine ziemlich häufige Erfahrung in der Politik. Auch darüber könnte man zum Zyniker werden. Alles geht so viel langsamer, als man möchte, immer wieder läuft man gegen Wände, übrigens auch in der eigenen Partei. Es ist ja ein frommer Kinderglaube zu denken, dass die Störenfriede nur immer bei den anderen sitzen. Anfangs habe ich das auch geglaubt: «*Wir* haben die richtigen Ideen, die wahren Lösungen, aber *die* stehen uns im Weg, wenn wir *die* nur erst abgelöst haben, dann können wir es *denen* beweisen.» Doch bald stellt man fest, wie viel Widerstände es auch in den eigenen Reihen gibt, wie viel Kraft es kostet, die eigenen Leute zu überzeugen und zusammenzuhalten. Auch in der eigenen Partei gibt es immer solche, die anderer Meinung sind, was im Grunde auch ihr gutes Recht ist. Eine offen ausgedrückte andere Meinung ist ja nichts Negatives. Aber da sind dann auch solche Partei-«Freunde», die hinterrücks gegen einen arbeiten und intrigieren. Plötzlich gibt es dann eine Schlagzeile: «Heide Simonis im eigenen Lager ohne Rückhalt!» So etwas ist natürlich überhaupt nicht lustig. Dann muss ich mich selber daran erinnern, dass das Spiel eben manchmal so läuft, muss mitspielen, obwohl das Kräfteverschleiß bedeutet. Um darüber nicht zur Zynikerin zu werden, brauche ich allerdings die Überzeugung, dass meine Position die bessere ist, und die Kraft, dies weiterhin nach allen Seiten deutlich zu machen.

Ich würde keinem jungen Politiker sagen: «Du wirst dich noch wundern!» Jeder und jede muss diese Erfahrungen für sich selbst machen. Ich sehe, wie sich unsere jungen Kandidatinnen und Kandidaten in Schleswig-Holstein mächtig ins Zeug legen. Noch kennt sie niemand so recht, und doch müssen und wollen sie ihre Botschaften an den Mann und die Frau bringen. Wenn ich denen sagen würde: «Ihr werdet euch wundern, was da noch alles auf euch zukommt!», dann würden die doch zusammenbrechen, falls sie mir überhaupt glaubten. Man braucht einfach dieses Stückchen Überzeugung, dass man die Welt zum Besseren verändern kann, sonst würde man nicht in die Politik gehen. Und diese Überzeugung darf auch nie ganz abhanden kommen, sonst hält man das alles nicht durch. In diesem Beruf darf man vielleicht nicht zu früh zu weise werden.

Politik besteht vor allem aus kleinen Schritten, die nur wenig ins Auge fallen und doch so wichtig sind. Nehmen wir zum Beispiel die nach der PISA-Studie erforderlichen Reformen im Schulwesen. Auch wenn wir sofort die notwendigen Veränderungen einleiten, wird es fünf bis zehn Jahre, eine ganze Schülergeneration lang, dauern, bis sie Früchte tragen. Die Eltern aber erwarten schon übermorgen sichtbare Verbesserungen. Man hat also hier gerade kein unmittelbares Erfolgserlebnis und darf trotzdem das Ziel nicht aus den Augen verlieren. Man muss ruhig bleiben, wenn einem die Eltern die Türen einrennen: «Tut etwas, sofort! Unsere Kinder sind nicht wettbewerbsfähig!» Die Aufgabe besteht dann darin, ihnen klar zu machen, dass so etwas Zeit braucht und dass sie, wenn sich ein Erfolg einstellen soll, selber mitmachen müssen. Wenn wir es schaffen, Schüler, Lehrer, Eltern, die ganze Gesellschaft an dem erforderlichen Veränderungsprozess zu beteiligen, dann ist das auch ein politischer Erfolg, an dem auch ich mich freuen kann.

Treten tatsächlich messbare Erfolge ein, dann ist es kaum möglich, sie ausschließlich für die eigene Leistungsbilanz zu verbuchen, weil viele daran mitgewirkt haben. Ich kann dann nicht erklären: «Ich habe diesen Missstand abgeschafft!», sondern eigentlich nur: «In der Zeit, in der wir die Regierungsverantwortung hatten, ist dieses und jenes besser geworden.» Natürlich gibt es auch Politiker, die sich keineswegs schwer damit tun, einen Erfolg, an dem viele gesellschaftliche Kräfte beteiligt waren, allein für sich zu reklamieren: «Ich habe das und das geleistet.» Aber das ist nicht rechtschaffen, das ist nicht mein Ding.

Meine Mitarbeiter machen mich gelegentlich darauf aufmerksam, dass ich in solchen Zusammenhängen seltener «ich» sage als andere Kollegen. Ich verwende viel häufiger das Wort «wir», und manchmal schreiben sie mir ein «ich» in die Reden, das ich dann doch durch ein «wir» ersetze. Vor allem die Formulierung «meine Landesregierung» bringe ich nur schwer über die Lippen, obwohl es natürlich de facto «meine» Landesregierung ist. Ich würde es in vielen Zusammenhängen als unbescheiden und aufgebläht empfinden, nicht darauf hinzuweisen, dass es ein Team ist, dass da gearbeitet hat und jetzt einen bestimmten Erfolg in der Sache für sich verbuchen kann. Außerdem sind zu jeder Zeit auch außerhalb dieses Teams noch eine ganze Reihe weiterer Menschen mit ihren Anstrengungen an jeder Veränderung zum Besseren beteiligt.

Weil in der Politik unmittelbare sachliche Erfolgserlebnisse rar sind, liegt die Gefahr sehr nahe, dass Politiker ihren Bekanntheits- und Beliebtheitsgrad in der Bevölkerung zur Hauptquelle der Bestätigung machen. Das kann sich so verselbstständigen, dass es ihnen am Ende nur noch um die Frage geht: «Wie komme ich an? Wie finden die mich? Wie beliebt bin ich?» – und nicht mehr um das politische Programm und seine Umsetzung.

Es trifft zu, dass sich der Typus des Politikers in den letzten zehn, zwanzig Jahren merklich verändert hat. Niemand könnte sich zum Beispiel heute als Fraktionschef noch so bärbeißig aufführen wie einst Herbert Wehner. Von Wehner wird erzählt, dass er einmal Karl Wienand, den parlamentarischen Geschäftsführer der Fraktion, zu sich bestellte und ihn dann einfach nur angeschwiegen hat. Wienand stand da, Wehner blieb in seine Akten vertieft und sagte einfach kein Wort. Er wollte testen, wie lange sich Wienand das gefallen ließe. Der hielt das aus und schwieg mit Wehner um die Wette, ein Machtspiel. Heute wäre eine solche Situation undenkbar. Der Jüngere würde sofort sagen: «Was soll das? Dafür bin ich ja wohl nicht hergekommen!» Hinter Herbert Wehners autoritärem Stil standen natürlich Lebensgeschichte und Lebensleistung, und wir 68er haben ihn brav ertragen. Aber die jüngeren Politikerinnen und Politiker sind selbstbewusster geworden, sie würden einen Fraktionschef nicht mehr akzeptieren, der ihnen ständig nur vorschreibt, wo es langgehen soll.

Ähnlich sieht es aus, wenn man Helmut Schmidts Auftreten in seiner Regierungszeit mit dem von Gerhard Schröder heute vergleicht. Helmut Schmidt war herrisch, er duldete keinen Widerspruch, wenn er seine Sachen durchzog. «Le Feldwebel» haben ihn die Franzosen nicht ohne Anerkennung genannt. Gerhard Schröder gibt sich viel werbender, offener, mediengerechter, in einem ständigen Balanceakt zwischen selbstbewusstem, machtbewusstem Auftreten einerseits und Konzilianz andererseits. Natürlich pflegte auch Herbert Wehner sein Image. Aber seine Adressaten waren ein kleiner Kreis: verschiedene Gremien, die Partei, das Parlament und nicht in erster Linie die Medien und die breite Öffentlichkeit. Heute würde ein Fraktionschef, der nur als ein Mythos für seine eigene Partei existiert, dessen Image nur aus dem Bild besteht, an dem seine Fraktionsmitglieder stricken, der ohne Außenwirkung in den Medien ist, sich nicht lange halten können. Er muss von sich aus nach außen gehen, den Medien ein Bild von sich anbieten.

Dabei wird das Auftreten von Politikern in verschiedenen Teilen der Bevölkerung durchaus unterschiedlich bewertet. Wir wissen zum Beispiel, dass bei der letzten Bundestagswahl Schröder bei Frauen, vor allem bei jüngeren Frauen, besser ankam als Stoiber, während Männer, die ihre Karriereplanung im Auge haben, positiver über Stoiber urteilten. In Schleswig-Holstein gab es 2000 ein ähnliches Phänomen: Die Frauen waren mehrheitlich für mich, und die jungen Männer waren eher für Volker Rühe. So etwas hängt mit Identifikation und Lebensentwürfen zusammen. Ein junger Mann findet sich selbst in einem siegesgewissen und machtbewussten männlichen Politiker eher wieder, während ich bei vielen Frauen für eine sozialere, familienfreundliche Gesellschaft stehe. Mit einem Programm wie «Vereinbarkeit von Familie und Beruf» kann man jungen Männern kaum imponieren. Die Schwierigkeit besteht darin, dass man beide Gruppen ansprechen muss, wenn man eine Wahl gewinnen will. Man kann nicht nur auf die einen abstellen und die anderen abschreiben.

Tatsache ist, dass sich die Politiker der alten Generation in den Medien nicht so inszenieren mussten, wie die von heute es tun. Dazu tragen natürlich Presse und Fernsehen ihren Teil bei. Früher stand das Privatleben der Politikerinnen und Politiker noch nicht so im Mittelpunkt. Nach meiner Erinnerung gab es über Willy Brandt nur eine einzige Homestory: Fotos von der Einschulung des jüngsten Sohnes, von Willy Brandt und seiner Frau Rut, wie sie ihn am ersten Schultag begleiten. Heute findet man in Illustrierten sogar Fotos von den Bildern, die an den Wänden der Privatwohnung hängen, und die Ehefrauen der Spitzenpolitiker, Frau Stoiber und Frau Schröder-Köpf, leisteten ihren eigenen Beitrag zum Wahlkampf. Da haben die amerikanischen Verhältnisse auf uns abgefärbt, was ich schon sehr bedenklich finde.

Natürlich ist es eine grundlegend andere Situation, ob ich mich nur im Kreis meiner Partei durchsetzen, mir dort Verbündete suchen und eine Hausmacht aufbauen muss oder ob ich direkt durch die Medien um die Gunst einer breiteren Öffentlichkeit werbe. Jeder Mensch will lieber gelobt als gerüffelt werden. Da die Medien beides so extrem tun und dadurch viel Einfluss ausüben, ist es nur zu verständlich, dass viele Politikerinnen und Politiker alles tun, um den Medien zu gefallen. Man fängt oft unbewusst an, sein Verhalten an ihnen auszurichten, um die begehrten Streicheleinheiten zu bekommen. Die Presse macht es einem auch schwer, sich einfach hinzustellen und zuzugeben: «Ich habe einen Fehler gemacht.» Wenn man einräumt, dass irgendetwas schief gelaufen ist, wird man von einigen Journalisten erbarmungslos fertig gemacht. Man beginnt deshalb sehr bald, sich bei allem, was man sagt und tut, zu überlegen: «Was könnte das morgen für Schlagzeilen bringen?» Natürlich muss man es schaffen, sich immer wieder ein Stück davon zu befreien oder die jeweiligen Schlagzeilen zu ertragen.

Doch ich gebe zu, dass auch ich mir inzwischen gut überlege, wofür ich eine negative Schlagzeile riskiere.

Vermutlich bringt die Art von Mediendemokratie, die sich inzwischen bei uns entwickelt hat, auch einen anderen Politikertypus hervor: Einerseits nehmen die glatten, gefälligen Typen mit Entertainerqualitäten zu, andererseits haben aber auch wieder diejenigen Erfolg, die sich widerborstig gerieren und den kalkulierten Tabubruch inszenieren. Das war Jürgen Möllemanns Strategie, der sich damit größeren Minderheiten populistisch anbiederte. Gerade weil das Glattpolierte so zugenommen hat, kann ein schriller Tabubruch dazu führen, dass man von der Öffentlichkeit wahrgenommen wird. Dadurch wird allerdings der Appetit der Medien und des Publikums auf noch Extremeres, Schrilleres nur noch größer. Es bedarf sozusagen immer stärkerer Reize, damit die Medienmaschinerie überhaupt anspringt.

Alles in allem bleibt der Politikertyp, der dabei herauskommt, rundpoliert. Es ist ja keineswegs bewiesen, dass Möllemann oder andere wirklich an alles glauben, was sie sagen. Die Art, wie sie sich öffentlich aufführen, ist oft schlichtes Kalkül. Sie wollen Schlagzeilen bekommen, und sie bekommen sie. Sie lassen die provokante Art, die sie an den Tag legen, auch sofort fallen, wenn sie politisch an der Macht sind. Sie verhalten sich oft nur nach dem Rat ihres Imageberaters: «Haben Sie heute schon ein Tabu gebrochen?» Sobald das spezielle Tabuthema ausgelutscht ist, suchen sie sich ein neues, von dem anzunehmen ist, dass sich damit mehr Aufmerksamkeit erzielen lässt. Wenn Möllemann das Verhalten der Israelis gegenüber den Palästinensern kritisierte, dann interessierte ihn in diesem Moment weder, was in diesem traumatisierten Volk vorgeht, in dem unschuldige Menschen durch Selbstmordattentäter umkommen, noch interessiert ihn die Situation der Palästinenser, die ebenfalls traumatisiert sind durch die Gewalt der Besatzer, die sie täglich erfahren. Möllemann benutzte den Tabubruch, um die eigene Person aufzuwerten.

Man kann nur hoffen, dass die Bevölkerung das durchschaut, obwohl solche Medieninszenierungen kurzfristig schon zu Stimmengewinnen führen können. Andererseits gibt es natürlich auch Beispiele dafür, dass die Menschen Politikern ihre Stimme geben, weil sie sie für aufrichtig und wahrhaftig halten. Es ist meine feste Überzeugung, dass man mit Ehrlichkeit am besten fährt, wenn man auf Theater verzichtet und sich so gibt, wie man tatsächlich ist. Auf Dauer, glaube ich, wird eine Masche von den meisten Menschen als solche durchschaut. Allerdings wenden sie sich dann vielleicht nicht nur von diesem einen Politiker ab, von dem sie sich betrogen fühlen, sondern gleich ganz von der Politik als solcher, und das ist problematisch. Die effekthascherische Art, um jeden Preis die Aufmerksamkeit der Medien zu erlangen, schadet also der Politik insgesamt. Sie trägt mit dazu bei, die gesamte Politikerkaste in Verruf zu bringen.

Macht bedeutet, Einfluss zu haben, Dinge bewegen zu können und deswegen bedeutsam zu sein. Da in der Demokratie die Macht davon abhängt, gewählt zu werden, muss, wer bedeutsam sein will, dafür sorgen, dass er öffentlich wahrgenommen wird. Die Könige früherer Zeiten erwarben ihre Position erblich und übten Macht von Gottes Gnaden aus. Sie mussten sich um Beliebtheit beim Volk nicht bemühen. Die Macht von Diktatoren und Warlords, von Häuptlingen und Clanchefs, von allen nicht demokratisch legitimierten Führern hängt davon ab, dass sie mächtige Bevölkerungsgruppen hinter sich haben und halten können. Sie erreichen das, indem sie den Angehörigen ihrer Führungseliten Privilegien versprechen und Posten zuschanzen. Solche Möglichkeiten gibt es für Politiker, die in einer Demokratie Machtpositionen anstreben, nicht oder nur sehr bedingt. Die eigene Position ist in erster Linie von der Wählergunst abhängig, und deswegen sind Politiker in einer Demokratie so besonders auf öffentliche Beliebtheit angewiesen. Seit es über das Fernsehen möglich ist, eine breite Öffentlichkeit direkt zu erreichen, ist der Wettbewerb um Bekanntheit und Beliebtheit schärfer geworden. Tatsächlich bekommen Politiker und Politikerinnen, wenn sie sich öffentlich selbst darstellen, immer mehr Ähnlichkeit mit Popstars und anderen Leitfiguren der Medienkultur.

Die Mediengesellschaft hat also neue Bedingungen geschaffen. Sogar die uralte Institution der englischen Monarchie muss heute ihre Existenz auf dem Wege der Medienpräsenz rechtfertigen. Auch in England haben die Leute zu fragen begonnen: «Was kriegen wir eigentlich für unser Geld, wenn die Königin nur hinter ihren Mauern sitzt und sich nicht rührt und regt? Sie sollte sich mehr für uns interessieren!» Selbst vor dieser Institution, die sich die Engländer vielleicht in erster Linie aus Denkmalschutzgründen leisten, macht die Demokratisierungswelle nicht Halt. Wenn die Menschen ihre Königin nicht mehr mögen, erlischt ihre Existenzberechtigung, und deswegen ist auch sie auf eine positive Darstellung in den Medien angewiesen.

Natürlich sind solche Entwicklungen nicht unproblematisch. Wenn Politiker vor allem deswegen gewählt werden, weil man sie mag und nett findet, dann besteht die große Gefahr, dass ihre medialen Auftritte für sie immer wichtiger, ihre Programme dagegen immer unwichtiger werden. Sie konzentrieren sich dann nur noch darauf zu erspüren, was die Leute wollen, um ihnen nach dem Mund zu reden. Sie haben zunehmend Angst davor, den Leuten unbequeme Wahrheiten zu sagen, und können es nicht mehr riskieren, irgendjemanden auf die Zehen zu treten. Je mehr aber das Gefallenwollen und die Selbstinszenierung in den Vordergrund rücken, desto enger wird der Gestaltungsspielraum für Politik. Das, was eigentlich Aufgabe der Politik ist, das Arrangement unterschiedlicher Gruppeninteressen, das Gestalten und Verbessern der Bedingungen des gesellschaftlichen Lebens, gerät so immer mehr in den Hintergrund.

Die vier Jahre einer Legislaturperiode sind keine lange Zeit. Erst einmal braucht es ein paar Monate, bis sich ein neues Kabinett mit einem neuen Parlament zurechtgefunden hat, und im letzten Jahr vor der nächsten Wahl geschieht in der Regel nichts mehr, was die Wählerinnen und Wähler vor den Kopf stoßen könnte. So bleibt dann nur eine kurze Spanne, in der die Regierung wirklich so handlungsfähig ist, dass sie auch größere Reformen und Veränderungen anpacken kann.

Würden sich Politiker, wenn ihre Amtszeit von vornherein begrenzt wäre, beispielsweise nur auf ein oder zwei Legislaturperioden, weniger um ihre Beliebtheit scheren und sich mehr auf die anstehenden Aufgaben konzentrieren? Ich bezweifle das. In den USA jedenfalls hat sich gezeigt, dass ein Präsident, der nicht mehr wiedergewählt werden kann, in seiner zweiten Amtszeit als «lame duck» durch die Gegend läuft. Er ist dann bemüht, sich so populär zu geben, dass er hinterher einen Platz im Wanderzirkus ehemaliger Prominenter findet, als Vortragsredner, als Ehrenvorsitzender oder als Aufsichtsratsmitglied. Bill Clinton bezieht jetzt für seine Auftritte enorme Honorare, und das nur, weil es ihm gelungen ist, sich rechtzeitig beliebt zu machen. Deswegen scheint mir eine Begrenzung der Amtszeit auch nicht das geeignete Rezept, Politiker souveräner zu machen. Sie müssten sich dann ja erst recht beizeiten darum kümmern, wo sie in der Zeit nach ihrer politischen Karriere noch unterkommen können.

Was macht eigentlich den Reiz der Droge Macht aus? Warum können Spitzenpolitiker, wenn sie einmal davon gekostet haben, so schwer davon lassen – trotz der vielen Arbeit, des Dauerstresses, der Intrigen, trotz der Medien, die einen immer mal wieder prügeln und manchmal sogar fertig machen wollen? Ein Teil der Faszination hängt sicher mit dem tatsächlichen Einfluss zusammen, den man hat, mit der Möglichkeit, Menschen und Themen zu bewegen. Es lässt sich fast immer etwas bewegen, wenn auch meist nicht so viel, wie man ursprünglich glaubte, und bestimmt nicht so schnell, wie man möchte. Dazu kommt dann der Kick, den man daraus bezieht, sich wichtig zu fühlen; abends nach Hause zu gehen mit dem Gefühl: «Da habe ich wieder gepunktet! Das habe ich wieder gut hingekriegt!» Das persönliche Motiv der Eitelkeit, die größer oder geringer sein mag, aber immer vorhanden ist, spielt, wie schon erwähnt, eine entscheidende Rolle. Die Belohnungen liegen nicht unbedingt in dem, was man neu anstoßen oder wirklich verändern konnte, denn das sind eher seltene Erfolgserlebnisse. Es ist auch nicht das Einkommen, denn das ist niedriger als bei vergleichbaren Positionen in der privaten Wirtschaft. Und gewiss haben die Spitzenmanager der Wirtschaft faktisch oft mehr Macht als Politikerinnen und Politiker. Unsere Belohnung besteht wahrscheinlich zu einem großen Teil darin, allseits wahrgenommen zu werden.

Deswegen ist wohl auch die Angst vor dem Ende der Macht so groß. Es ist die Angst, auf einmal ein «Niemand» zu sein. Als wäre man gar nicht da, wenn die anderen nicht mehr auf einen schauen und ständig auf einen reagieren. Die Angst vor der Leere und Stille, wenn plötzlich um einen herum keine Kameras und Mikrofone mehr sind, man von heute auf morgen keine Einladungen mehr bekommt. Wenn man bemerkt, dass die Leute, die früher immer hinter einem hergerannt sind, jetzt anderen nachlaufen. Winston Churchill hat nach Ende seiner politischen Laufbahn auf die Frage, was ihm fehle, geantwortet: «No transport, no information» – kein Dienstwagen mehr und abgeschnitten vom Informationsfluss.

Es gibt kein Netz, das einen in dieser Situation auffängt. Vielleicht würde es helfen, wenn man nach seinem Rücktritt vom politischen Amt einen Kreis von Menschen hätte, die einem vermitteln: «Du bist jetzt hier bei uns zwar nicht die Nummer eins, aber du bekommst doch Zuwendung und Wärme, und wir interessieren uns noch für dich als Person. Wir wollen auch deinen Rat noch hören und von deiner Erfahrung profitieren.» Nein, es geht ratzfatz, von jetzt auf gleich, und wer vorher auf Wochen nie einen Termin frei hatte, der steht plötzlich vor einem großen weißen Kalender mit leeren Tagen und fragt sich: «Was soll ich denn heute und morgen überhaupt machen?»

Ein Dilemma des Politikerlebens besteht auch darin, dass man durch die Umstände gezwungen wird, all die stabilisierenden Bezüge aufzugeben, aus denen normale Menschen ihre persönliche Sicherheit und Identität beziehen: Freundschaften, alltägliche Beschäftigungen, Hobbys. Nach und nach muss man den Wunsch nach intensiven freundschaftlichen Kontakten, nach Freizeit und Muße aufgeben, sonst könnte man seine politischen Aufgaben nicht bewältigen. Die meisten Alltagsbeschäftigungen, die dem Tag seinen Rhythmus geben, wie Einkaufen, Kochen, den Haushalt versorgen, werden Spitzenpolitikern abgenommen; man verlernt sie deshalb. Als Vollblutpolitikerin muss man den Wunsch nach einem selbstbestimmten Tagesablauf vergessen, man wird freiwillig zur Sklavin des Terminkalenders. So kommt einem allmählich die Fähigkeit abhanden, seinen Tag selbstbestimmt zu gestalten. Man gibt vieles auf, um sich mit Haut und Haaren ins «Geschäft» zu stürzen. Man wird zum Workaholic, und die einzige Belohnung, die einem hilft, Arbeitsbelastung und Stress durchzuhalten, ist das Gefühl, Dinge beeinflussen und bewegen zu können, das Gefühl der eigenen Wichtigkeit und Bedeutung. Genau dieses Gefühl wird einem dann abrupt mit dem Ende der politischen Karriere entzogen. Viele sind daran gescheitert, weil jetzt all die anderen Dinge fehlen, die helfen könnten, ein neues Leben zu beginnen, weil sie einem zuvor systematisch abgewöhnt worden sind.

Verständlicherweise haben die meisten Berufspolitiker und -politikerinnen vor dieser Situation Angst, und wenn es geschieht, macht es vielen furchtbar zu schaffen. Sicher mag es auch einige geben, denen es nicht so schwer fällt, die vor allem erleichtert sind und sagen: «Jetzt hab ich endlich wieder meine Ruhe!» Der Vorgänger von Ministerpräsident Ernst Albrecht in Niedersachsen, Alfred Kubel, soll so reagiert haben, als er zurücktrat: «Gott sei Dank! Nie wieder eine Schlaftablette, weil ich nicht abschalten kann! Endlich wieder ein selbstbestimmter Tagesablauf!» Inwiefern er das dann in den Wochen danach auch tatsächlich so erlebt hat, steht natürlich auf einem anderen Blatt. Aber es gibt genügend Politiker und auch Politikerinnen, die daran zerbrechen oder zumindest sehr lange brauchen, bis sie den Übergang geschafft haben. Die hämische Schadenfreude, die sie dabei oft begleitet, macht es bestimmt nicht einfacher. Anstelle von Verständnis und Unterstützung gibt es eher diese gehässigen Reaktionen: «Guck mal, der schafft es nicht! Schau mal, was für eine miese Figur sie bei ihrem Abgang macht!» Dann wird noch einmal genüsslich nachgetreten.

Ich muss dabei an einen alten Ritus bestimmter primitiver Gesellschaften denken, wie Sigmund Freud ihn beschreibt: Sie wählen sich einen Häuptling, und dem geben sie für eine gewisse Zeit alles, was er will, und noch viel mehr. Sie füttern ihn mit den erlesensten Leckerbissen, er wird dick und fett dabei, weil er keinen Schritt mehr zu machen braucht oder selber keinen Schritt mehr machen darf. Sämtliche Wünsche werden ihm von den Augen abgelesen, er lebt wie im Paradies. Doch nur für eine begrenzte Zeit, und wenn die um ist, wird er kurzerhand umgebracht. Denn während die anderen ihn verwöhnten, hat sich bei ihnen so viel Neid und Wut gesammelt, dass sie schließlich sagen: «Schluss! Fort mit ihm!» Manchmal kommt mir die Situation der langjährigen Spitzenpolitiker ganz ähnlich vor. Sie werden verwöhnt und gleichzeitig beneidet, und anschließend müssen sie einen ziemlich hohen Preis dafür zahlen. Sie werden zwar nicht physisch ermordet, aber wenn man sie vom Podest stößt, sind sie als öffentliche Personen schlagartig tot. Also verzichte ich lieber darauf, zu sehr verwöhnt zu werden. Vielleicht lebe ich dann weniger gefährlich.

Ich glaube, dass viele von uns davon träumen, einen selbstgestalteten Abschied hinzukriegen, natürlich unter viel Applaus, und dass sie sich den souveränen Übergang in einen anderen Bereich wünschen, in dem sie vielleicht nicht mehr ganz so im Mittelpunkt stehen, aber immer noch akzeptiert und geachtet sind. Die meisten klammern sich aus Angst vor dem großen

Loch danach an ihr Amt. So lange hat man daran gearbeitet, die Spielregeln zu beherrschen, all seine Schritte zu kontrollieren, um nur ja nichts Falsches zu machen, um dahin zu gelangen, wo man jetzt ist, an die Spitze, sich dort zu halten, nur ja nicht abzustürzen. Je mehr Energie man darauf verwandt hat, desto größer wird die Angst vor dem, was danach kommt. Doch so mag es dem Spitzenpersonal in anderen Berufssparten auch ergehen. Auch einen Chefredakteur wird es wurmen, wenn er plötzlich nicht mehr zu wichtigen Veranstaltungen eingeladen wird. Selbst Wirtschaftstycoone leiden darunter, wenn ihr Name plötzlich nicht mehr in der Presse genannt wird. Früher übten sie ihre Macht eher unsichtbar im Hintergrund aus, aber auch vor der Wirtschaft hat die Medienkultur nicht Halt gemacht. Manager wie Jürgen Schrempp oder Wendelin Wiedeking haben sich daran gewöhnt, ganz vorn im Rampenlicht zu stehen, und jeder, der auf einer Bühne steht, sei sie nun größer oder kleiner, hat diese Angst vor der Leere nach dem Abtritt. Bei einer normalen Pensionierung ist der Bruch im Leben nicht ganz so scharf; man kann dann ja noch weiter mit seinen alten Kollegen ein Bier trinken oder angeln gehen. Selbst im Showbusiness verlischt das Rampenlicht im Allgemeinen nicht von heute auf morgen, sondern eher allmählich: Die letzte Tournee war vielleicht kein ganz so großer Erfolg mehr, die letzte Platte hat sich nicht mehr ganz so gut verkauft, man bekommt nicht mehr so viele Engagements – so kann man sich nach und nach an eine andere Situation und Identität gewöhnen.

In manchen Kulturen gibt es so etwas wie den «Rat der Alten»: Der ausscheidende Politiker schließt sich einem Kreis von Elder Statesmen an, die der jüngeren Politikergeneration beratend zur Seite stehen. In der Wirtschaft wechselt das Vorstandsmitglied häufig in den Aufsichtsrat. Doch Vergleichbares ist bei uns in der Politik verpönt. Es gilt als schlechter Stil, dem Nachfolger reinzureden und gute Ratschläge zu erteilen, meiner Meinung nach auch zu Recht. Ich würde einem Nachfolger oder einer Nachfolgerin nie sagen, was und wie ich es an ihrer

Stelle gemacht hätte. Umgekehrt würde ein Nachfolger, der sich bei mir einen Rat holen würde, wohl eher unmöglich, denn das sähe nach mangelnder Souveränität aus. Wer also seinem Nachfolger gegenüber fair sein will, hält besser den Mund. Jede öffentliche Äußerung würde dem oder der Neuen schaden. Dadurch aber sind denen, die abtreten, die alten Bande radikal abgeschnitten; sie müssen sich wirklich ein ganz anderes Betätigungsfeld suchen.

Ein Rezept gegen den großen Absturz könnte darin bestehen, dass man sich schon früh Alternativen überlegt «für die Zeit danach», am besten auf dem Höhepunkt der eigenen Karriere. Doch wenn man das öffentlich tut, rufen alle: «Sieh mal da, Amtsmüdigkeit!» Und schon beginnen die Geier über dem Stuhl zu kreisen, noch während man darauf sitzt. Sobald es heißt: «Er oder sie bereitet ihren Abgang vor!», setzt man damit schon selber den Prozess in Gang, der zur Ablösung führt. Also lässt man das besser tunlichst bleiben, solange man noch mitmischen möchte.

Für mich ist es undenkbar, dass ich gar nichts mehr tue und nur noch meinen Ruhestand genieße, wie es so schön heißt, wenn ich einmal nicht mehr Ministerpräsidentin bin. Ich könnte mir vorstellen, dass ich mich wieder stärker in der Entwicklungshilfe engagiere, die für mich am Anfang meines politischen Lebens im Mittelpunkt stand. Institutionen wie der DAAD, der Senior Expert Service und andere bieten Jobs für begrenzte Zeiträume in Entwicklungsländern an. In diesen Jobs tut man etwas Nützliches; man ist konfrontiert mit neuen Herausforderungen, und man lernt interessante, engagierte Menschen kennen. Ich könnte mir auch eine beratende Tätigkeit vorstellen: Es würde mir ganz sicherlich Spaß machen, junge aufstrebende Manager und Politiker zu beraten, die erst lernen, sich im Gestrüpp des öffentlichen Lebens zurechtzufinden, oder auch speziell Karriereberatung für junge Frauen zu machen, ihnen Tipps zu geben, wie man auftritt, wie man sich durchsetzt.

Es kann wohl nicht schaden, sich auch dann, wenn man noch mitten im politischen Geschäft ist und noch keineswegs ans Aufhören denkt, die eine oder andere Alternative vorzustellen. So bewahrt man sich eine gewisse Souveränität und erinnert sich selber von Zeit zu Zeit daran, dass man nicht völlig identisch mit seinem Posten ist, sondern auch jenseits davon noch Lebensvorstellungen und Existenzmöglichkeiten hat.

14

Ein Blick nach vorn

Zur Zeit geschieht in der deutschen Politik viel, und noch mehr müsste geschehen. Das Schlimmste, was uns passieren könnte, wäre ein Andauern der Lähmung und der wechselseitigen Blockade verschiedener Initiativen und Interessengruppen. Wir müssen endlich aufhören zu lamentieren und die Dinge wirklich anpacken. Die Probleme und die Ziele sind einigermaßen klar, jetzt müssen wir uns auf Lösungswege verständigen, und dann können wir es auch schaffen, die Verhältnisse zu bessern. Mich ärgert, wie viel Energie Tag für Tag mit Kleinkram und Taktik, mit politischem Theater wie etwa dem Bundestagsuntersuchungsausschuss zum angeblichen Wahlbetrug und ähnlichen Dingen vergeudet wird.

Sicher brauchen größere Richtungswechsel im Denken, Paradigmenwechsel, wie sie jetzt nötig sind, eine gewisse Zeit, bis sie in den Köpfen der Allgemeinheit angekommen sind. Es dauert, bis wirklich alle begriffen haben, dass die Sozialversicherungssysteme kollabieren werden, wenn wir uns nicht bald etwas Neues einfallen lassen, oder dass es keine Alternative zum Sparen gibt. Sicher kann man den Menschen, weil solche Erkenntnisprozesse nur langsam vonstatten gehen, nicht von heute auf morgen riesengroße Sprünge zumuten, sondern nur Veränderungen in kleineren Schritten. Es ist auch verständlich, dass alle erst einmal die Einschnitte bemerken, die sie selbst betreffen, und dann in ein großes Geschrei ausbrechen. Niemand will zunächst einsehen, dass alle, auch die eigene Gruppe, ein bisschen abgeben müssen, dass jedem Einzelnen bestimmte Härten zugemutet werden müssen. Doch inzwischen sind wir hoffentlich an dem Punkt, wo das Jammern allmählich der Einsicht weicht, dass es ohne grundlegende Veränderungen nicht weitergehen kann.

Es scheint ein grundsätzliches Problem der Deutschen, dass sie zwar alles anders haben möchten – aber die Veränderung fürchten. Wasch mir den Pelz, aber mach mich nicht nass! Mir scheint, die Angst vor größeren Veränderungen sitzt bei uns tiefer als anderswo. Wahrscheinlich hängt sie damit zusammen, dass die Deutschen im 20. Jahrhundert zweimal von null anfangen mussten, durch eigene Schuld zwar, aber das ändert nichts an dem Gefühl der existenziellen Verunsicherung. Die Deutschen haben nach 1918 und nach 1945 ganz von vorn anfangen müssen, und die Menschen in der ehemaligen DDR sogar noch ein drittes Mal, nach der Wende 1989, und das keineswegs nur materiell, sondern auch weltanschaulich verstanden. Solche Erfahrungen, vor allem die Erinnerung an den Mangel und die Armut der unmittelbaren Nachkriegszeit, haben sich tief in das kollektive Gedächtnis gegraben und führen zu einem starken Wunsch nach Sicherheit und Erhalt des Status quo, zu einem grundsätzlichen Misstrauen gegenüber jeder größeren Veränderung.

Zum Glück haben die jungen Leute von heute diese Angst nicht mehr, sie sind unbefangener, risikofreudiger und weltoffener. Sie reisen überall auf der Welt herum, sind neugierig auf andere Gesellschaften und Lebensverhältnisse; sie haben so früh die Möglichkeit zu vergleichen. Sie finden im Allgemeinen auch die flexibleren Arbeitsformen der Zukunft nicht nur bedrohlich, sondern können ihnen Positives abgewinnen. Heute kommt es seltener vor als in den 70er Jahren, meiner Zeit als Berufsberaterin, dass junge Leute sich als Erstes erkundigen: «Wie sieht das später mal mit meiner Rente aus?», wenn sie Informationen über einen Beruf einholen. Heute fragen sie vor allem: «Interessiert mich die Sache, habe ich Spaß daran, was verdiene ich?» Und wenn sie merken, dass es nicht das Richtige für sie ist, erproben sie eben etwas anderes.

In diesem Zusammenhang erscheint das drohende Problem der Überalterung unserer Gesellschaft noch einmal in einem anderen Licht. Dieser demographische Trend zeichnet sich schon seit zwei Jahrzehnten ab, und doch haben wir es bisher versäumt, uns die gesellschaftlichen Konsequenzen in aller Deutlichkeit klar zu machen und uns auf sie einzustellen. Dass der Anteil der Alten gegenüber den Jungen in Zukunft gewaltig wachsen wird, hat nämlich nicht nur dramatische Folgen für unser Sozialversicherungssystem. Es wird nicht nur dazu führen, dass Kindergärten und Schulen um die wenigen Kinder und Jugendlichen konkurrieren und zum Teil schließen müssen, während Altersheime und Pflegedienste boomen werden. Der demographische Trend wird darüber hinaus auch atmosphärische Auswirkungen haben, die wir bisher noch gar nicht richtig einschätzen können: Wenn die Jungen in der Minderheit sind, werden uns auf Dauer auch mutige, kreative, innovative Ideen fehlen. Wir Älteren haben uns zumeist ganz gemütlich in den bestehenden Verhältnissen eingekuschelt. Wir haben unsere Lebenserfahrung und aus ihr bestimmte Schlüsse gezogen, wir wissen ziemlich genau, was wir nicht noch einmal erleben wollen, und das macht uns weniger wagemutig und reformfreudig. Damit eine Gesellschaft sich erneuert, bedarf es aber auch der Radikalität junger Menschen, die unbefangen sagen: «Das ist ja unterirdischer Schrott, was ihr da macht!», die die Dinge einmal aus einem völlig anderen Blickwinkel betrachten. Wenn die Jüngeren sich nicht entfalten können, weil überall die Älteren dominieren, ist eine soziale Erstarrung zu befürchten. Leider haben wir bisher nur wenig soziologische Kenntnisse darüber, wie sich überalterte Gesellschaften entwickeln. Unser einziges Beispiel ist Japan. Doch in Japan ist vieles so völlig anders als bei uns, dass wir die Erfahrungen von dort nicht eins zu eins auf uns übertragen können.

Neben der Überalterung werden uns in naher Zukunft noch stärker als bisher Probleme zu schaffen machen, die mit dem raschen technologischen Wandel verbunden sind. Während bahnbrechende technische Veränderungen früher Jahrzehnte brauchten, bis sie sich flächendeckend durchgesetzt hatten – denken wir an das Auto, das Telefon, den Fernsehapparat –, ist das bei den jüngsten Neuerungen – wie etwa beim Handy oder der Internetnutzung – in einem Zeitraffertempo von wenigen Jahren vor sich gegangen, begleitet von gewaltigen Umwälzungen nicht nur der Wirtschaft, sondern auch unseres Alltagslebens. Das Tempo des technologischen Wandels wird sich in den nächsten Jahren womöglich weiter beschleunigen. Vieles, was wir heute noch überwiegend real erledigen, werden wir demnächst nur noch virtuell und online ausführen. So sind Onlineshopping und Onlinebanking auf dem Vormarsch. Für mich selber kann ich mir manches zur Zeit noch nicht vorstellen: Ich käme nie auf die Idee, mir Klamotten über den Bildschirm zu bestellen, da möchte ich weiterhin beim Einkaufen das sinnliche Erleben des Anschauens, Anfassens, Anprobierens haben. Und was das Onlinebanking betrifft, so habe ich bisher noch gewisse Bedenken wegen der Sicherheit. Doch die Kenner der Szene prognostizieren, dass die Entwicklungen stürmisch weitergehen und unsere gesamte alltägliche Routine revolutionieren werden. Zwar mag es Sciencefiction bleiben, dass überall Roboter durch die Wohnungen laufen und sämtliche anfallenden Hausarbeiten selbstgesteuert erledigen. Doch in Zukunft werden wir vom Büro aus unseren Kochherd programmieren, damit das Essen fertig ist, wenn wir nach Hause kommen. Unser Kühlschrank wird uns, ohne dass wir hineinschauen, mitteilen, was wir einkaufen sollten. Und wir werden die Kinder beim Spielen per Monitor beaufsichtigen. Noch stärker werden sämtliche Arbeitsabläufe in Büro und Fabrik, in Wirtschaft und Verwaltung tangiert sein, die sich ja schon innerhalb der letzten Dekade stürmisch verändert haben. Sicher werden bestimmte Branchen und Firmen im Zuge dieser Entwicklung gute Umsätze und ein hohes Wachstum erzielen. Aber wir müssen uns auch darüber im Klaren sein, dass diesen Prozessen Hunderttausende Arbeitsplätze zum Opfer fallen können. Auch diesen Menschen müssen wir eine Perspektive geben.

Dem E-Commerce wird das E-Government folgen, die Onlinekommunikation zwischen Staat und Bürger, im Zusammenhang mit Meldeverfahren, Steuererklärung und vielem anderen mehr. Innerhalb der schleswig-holsteinischen Landesregierung ist im Umgang der Ministerien untereinander, beim Abgleichen von Vorlagen, die neue Kommunikationstechnologie schon jetzt nicht mehr wegzudenken. Aber das hat bisher kaum dazu geführt, dass die Dinge nun einfacher geworden wären, im Gegenteil. Stattdessen wächst der Wust von Papieren und Anfragen innerhalb der Verwaltung genauso wie der, der nach draußen geht. Das Ergebnis der informationstechnologischen Revolution ist eben keineswegs, wie man uns prophezeit hatte, das papierlose Büro, sondern eine Inflationierung der Papiermengen, weil nun auch noch die banalsten Dinge ausgedruckt und in Umlauf gebracht werden. Es ist ja so schön einfach und geht so wunderbar schnell!

Genauso wenig wie die Entstehung des papierlosen Büros hat sich eine andere Voraussage über die Auswirkungen der Telekommunikation erfüllt. Es hieß, dass die neuen Kommunikationsmittel räumliche Mobilität zum Teil überflüssig machen würden. Auch hier erleben wir eher das Gegenteil: Trotz des hochbeschleunigten virtuellen Informationsaustauschs steigt die Zahl der dringend notwendigen Konferenzen, der unbedingt erforderlichen Dienstreisen und beruflichen Treffen. Es ist zu hoffen, dass diese Phänomene, die wir jetzt beobachten, nur anfängliche Auswüchse sind, die sich nach einer Übergangszeit zurückbilden, wenn die Mehrzahl der Menschen gelernt hat, mit den neuen Technologien angemessen umzugehen.

Der technologische Wandel bringt nicht unbedingt und überall sogleich eine Produktivitätssteigerung mit sich, sondern vorübergehend vielleicht sogar erst einmal einen Produktivitätsverlust. Alle Mitarbeiterinnen und Mitarbeiter müssen immer wieder mit der jeweils neuesten Technik vertraut werden, und diese Zeit fehlt ihnen dann für die Erledigung ihrer eigentlichen Aufgaben. Bei einer sehr großen Geschwindigkeit des technologischen Wandels wäre sogar eine Situation denkbar, in der der größte Teil der eigentlichen Arbeitsenergie brachliegt, weil er auf immer neue Schulung und Fortbildung verwendet werden muss. Dann gäbe es zwar einen wachsenden Umsatz bei neuer Hard- und Software, aber ein Sinken der Arbeitsproduktivität insgesamt. Jüngere Leute schaffen die Umstellungen in der Regel schnell; je älter aber im Schnitt die Arbeitnehmer, desto mehr könnte dies als negativer Faktor ins Gewicht fallen.

In diesem Zusammenhang müssen wir uns auch mit der Gefahr auseinander setzen, dass sich in Zukunft die Gesellschaft noch stärker als derzeit schon in Technikverständige und Technikbedrohte spaltet. Auf der einen Seite stehen die kundigen «Technikfreaks», die über das neue Herrschaftswissen verfügen, auf der anderen die «Technikmuffel», die sich davon bedroht fühlen. Das gibt auch der Diskussion über soziale Gerechtigkeit eine neue Dimension. Als vergleichsweise harmloses Alltagsbeispiel kann die Onlinebestellung von Zug- oder Flugtickets dienen: Wer computerkundig ist und den entsprechenden Zugang besitzt, kann sich den zeitaufwändigen Gang zum Bahnhofsschalter oder ins Reisebüro sparen, hat die Sache rasch von zu Hause aus erledigt und kann das gewünschte Ticket zu einem vielleicht auch noch günstigeren Preis selbst ausdrucken. Gleichzeitig werden aber, seit es diese Möglichkeit gibt und die Bahn parallel dazu Personal abbaut, die Warteschlangen vor den wenigen geöffneten Schaltern immer länger. Die weniger Technikversierten, die ihre Fahrscheine auf dem «altmodischen Weg» kaufen, verbringen noch mehr leere Zeit in Warteschlangen, was sie den anderen gegenüber weiter benachteiligt. Wir müssen also jetzt und in Zukunft verstärkt dafür sorgen, dass alle die gleichen Qualifizierungschancen und vergleichbare Zugangsmöglichkeiten hinsichtlich der neuen Technologien haben oder erhalten. Der technologische Wandel kann, wie erwähnt, das Problem der Arbeitslosigkeit noch verschärfen, und deswegen müssen Reformen auf dem Arbeitsmarkt höchste Priorität haben. Die Zusammenlegung der Ressorts für «Wirtschaft» und «Arbeit» in einem Ministerium auf Bundesebene war ein richtiger Schritt, diese beiden Bereiche stärker zu koordinieren und zu integrieren. Auch in Schleswig-Holstein haben wir uns dazu im Frühjahr 2003 entschieden. Vorher gaben sich – vereinfacht gesagt – im Wirtschaftsministerium die Arbeitgeber die Klinke in die Hand und im Arbeitsministerium die Gewerkschaftsfunktionäre. Jetzt haben die Vertreter beider Lobbys ein und denselben Ansprechpartner. Das erhöht den politischen Handlungsspielraum.

Auch die Vorschläge der Hartz-Kommission zielen in die richtige Richtung. Allerdings betreffen die meisten dieser Vorschläge zunächst nur die Effizienz der Arbeitslosenvermittlung und schaffen nicht unbedingt neue Stellen. Wir wissen, dass es trotz der wirtschaftlich schwierigen Situation durchaus immer noch offene Stellen gibt. In Schleswig-Holstein werden zur Zeit 300 Arbeitskräfte im Bereich der Windenergie gesucht. Die Industrie sucht überwiegend qualifizierte Mitarbeiterinnen und Mitarbeiter, aber es gibt auch noch Nachfrage im Bereich der so genannten Niedriglohnjobs. So ist anzunehmen, dass durch eine effektivere Vermittlung die Zahl der Arbeitslosen reduziert werden kann.

Darüber hinaus müssen wir die Dienstleistungsbereiche weiter ausbauen und dort mehr Stellen schaffen, qualifizierte wie weniger qualifizierte. Wir müssen herausfinden, wie wir in den Bundesländern, innerhalb von Europa und auf dem Weltmarkt Produkte und Dienstleistungen anbieten können, die die anderen bisher nicht im Angebot haben. Schleswig-Holstein hat es zum Beispiel mit der Windenergie geschafft, ein eigenes spezifisches Profil zu entwickeln. Im Moment stehen die Staaten wirtschaftlich am besten da, die den höchsten Anteil von Serviceleistungen am Bruttosozialprodukt haben, so zum Beispiel Schweden und Finnland. Unsere Wirtschaft in Deutschland ist dagegen noch sehr stark vom produzierenden Sektor und von herkömmlichen Industrien bestimmt. Im Bereich der industriellen Produktion ist der Markt aber in großen Bereichen gesättigt, von dort kann nicht mehr viel Wachstum kommen; da sind oft nur noch Ersatzinvestitionen drin. Es gibt allerdings auch traditionelle Bereiche, für die man sich etwas Kluges, grundsätzlich Neues ausdenken könnte und sollte, wie etwa im Verkehrssektor. Unsere Straßen sind demnächst wirklich endgültig verstopft, und man müsste sich intelligente Alternativen einfallen lassen, beispielsweise ein effizienteres Zugsystem und integrierten Verkehr. Das wären Investitionen, die sowohl wirtschaftliches Wachstum als auch neue Arbeitsplätze schaffen würden.

Auch der Ausbau des Niedriglohnsektors darf kein Tabu mehr sein. Darin liegt eine zusätzliche Möglichkeit, die Arbeitslosigkeit zu senken. Wir haben uns zu lange vorgemacht, wir könnten alle Arbeitenden qualifizieren, aber man kann nun einmal nicht aus jedem Ungelernten einen Facharbeiter für Informatik machen. Das darf allerdings nicht zu amerikanischen Verhältnissen führen, wo die Leute zwei oder drei Niedriglohnjobs annehmen müssen, nur um sich über Wasser halten zu können. Schon jetzt bringen bei uns viele Verkäuferinnen so wenig Lohn nach Hause, dass von ihrem Einkommen allein die Familie nicht überleben kann. Wenn Niedriglöhne unterhalb der Sozialhilfe gezahlt werden, bieten sie keinerlei Anreiz mehr, eine Beschäftigung aufzunehmen. Ich meine, wir sollten weiterhin über «Kombi-Modelle» nachdenken, die einen gewissen Sozialhilfesatz mit der Möglichkeit verbinden, Jobs im Niedriglohnsektor anzunehmen. Das wäre ein Anreiz für die Arbeitgeber, Stellen zu schaffen, und für den Staat billiger als die fortgesetzte Finanzierung der Arbeitslosigkeit.

Deutschland ist immer noch Vizeweltmeister bei den Exporten, nach den USA und vor Japan. Ohne die Exporte ständen wir wirtschaftlich noch schlechter da. Der Erfolg unserer Exportwirtschaft zeigt, dass «Made in Germany» weiterhin einen guten Ruf genießt, er weist auf die hohe Qualität unserer Produkte hin. Deswegen ist es auch so wichtig, dass wir in Zukunft stärker in Qualifizierung und Bildung investieren. Die Ergebnisse der PISA-Studie waren da ein Alarmsignal zur rechten Zeit: An Bildung, Wissenschaft und Forschung dürfen wir nicht sparen, wir müssen Schulen und Hochschulen effizienter machen.

Vermutlich werden aber alle diese Maßnahmen nicht ausreichen, um vier bis fünf Millionen Arbeitslose unterzubringen. Wahrscheinlich müssen wir uns für die nächsten Jahre insgesamt auf ein geringeres Wirtschaftswachstum und damit auf eine gewisse Sockelarbeitslosigkeit einstellen. Es scheint, als ob ein Wachstum von über 2 Prozent erforderlich ist, wahrscheinlich sogar von mindestens 2,5 Prozent, um einen merklichen Effekt auf dem Arbeitsmarkt zu erzielen. Diese Zahl erreichen wir zur Zeit nicht, nicht zuletzt wegen der schwächelnden Weltwirtschaft.

Für mich ist deswegen die Idee der Förderung und der neuen Rolle der Zivilgesellschaft noch keinesfalls zu den Akten gelegt. Denn viele Menschen werden, statt arbeitslos zu sein, lieber Tätigkeiten in Bereichen übernehmen wollen, die der Allgemeinheit zugute kommen. So könnte beispielsweise ein arbeitsloser Ingenieur für ein geringes Entgelt Computerkurse an der Volkshochschule anbieten. Wenn diese Tätigkeit nicht angemessen, sondern nur quasi symbolisch bezahlt werden kann, wäre ein solches Modell allerdings nur im Verbund mit einer finanziellen Grundsicherung aller Bürgerinnen und Bürger zu realisieren, die wir langfristig nicht aus den Augen verlieren sollten.

An dieser Stelle wäre auch zu diskutieren, ob es nicht ohnehin sinnvoller wäre, das durch Beiträge finanzierte Sozialversicherungssystem aufzugeben zugunsten eines steuerfinanzierten Systems, das allen eine Grundrente bietet. Auf diese Grundrente könnte man dann die über eigene Erwerbsarbeit erworbene Rente und andere in Eigenverantwortung erworbene Zusatzsicherungen aufstocken. Ein solches Modell müsste zügig und gründlich überlegt werden, weil es weitreichende Folgen hat und nicht von heute auf morgen eingeführt werden kann. Eine Grundrente würde auch eine Entbürokratisierung mit sich bringen, weil an die Stelle verschiedener Bezüge (Arbeitslosenhilfe, Sozialhilfe, Rente), die wegen der Unterschiede in den Biografien kompliziert zu berechnen sind, nun ein Standardeinkommen träte.

Die Rürup-Kommission hat den Auftrag erhalten, Änderungsvorschläge für unser Sozialversicherungssystem vorzulegen, und ich hoffe, dass wir schon bald, auf jeden Fall noch in dieser Legislaturperiode, Reformen beschließen werden, die mehr sind als bloße Symptomkuriererei und in den Stürmen des sozialen Wandels dauerhaft bestehen.

Manche Zukunftsforscher entwerfen höchst düstere Szenarien. Sie malen uns das Bild einer zutiefst gespaltenen Gesellschaft, die im Wesentlichen in drei Gruppen zerfällt: Da sind erstens die gut Ausgebildeten, die in relativ gesicherten Vollzeitberufen Karriere machen, viel arbeiten und damit so gut verdienen, dass sie kaum Zeit haben, ihr Geld auch wieder auszugeben; diese Gruppe, in der jüngere Menschen, Singles und Kinderlose dominieren, soll in Zukunft nur noch etwa ein Drittel der Bevölkerung ausmachen. Daneben gibt es eine zweite, zahlenmäßig stärkere Gruppe, die ihren Lebensunterhalt in unsicheren Beschäftigungsverhältnissen verdient. Dazu gehören Menschen mit zeitlich befristeten Arbeitsverhältnissen, Honorarkräfte und Teilzeitarbeitende, die kleinen Selbstständigen und Scheinselbstständigen, die nur gelegentlich Jobbenden. Ihre Zahl wird nach allgemeiner Einschätzung in den nächsten Jahren noch erheblich zunehmen, sie könnten die Mehrheit der Bevölkerung ausmachen. Junge, flexible, dynamische Menschen werden mit diesen Arbeitsverhältnissen möglicherweise ganz gut zurechtkommen, sie werden auch Freiheitsräume für sich darin sehen und sie nutzen. Schwierig wird es allerdings für

weniger Leistungsfähige, die dem wachsenden Wettbewerbsdruck der neuen Form der Arbeitsgesellschaft nicht gewachsen
sind, weil sie irgendein Handicap haben, oder auch nur, weil sie
zusätzlich durch Familienpflichten in Anspruch genommen
sind, was ihre berufliche Flexibilität einschränkt. Für sie besteht
die Gefahr, dass sie in die dritte Gruppe abgleiten, in das Heer
der Langzeitarbeitslosen und Sozialhilfeempfänger. Die Gruppe könnte in Zukunft nach unterschiedlichen Prognosen ein
Fünftel, ein Viertel oder gar ein Drittel der Bevölkerung ausmachen. Hier finden sich die schlecht Ausgebildeten wieder,
die Jugendlichen ohne Schulabschluss, die Alten, Menschen
mit Behinderungen, die nicht integrierten Ausländer, allein
erziehende Eltern, vor allem Mütter.

Man könnte bei solchen Vorhersagen einigermaßen zynisch
zu dem Schluss kommen, dass der Staat in Zukunft nur dafür
sorgen müsse, dass diese Menschen mit einer minimalen
Grundversorgung einfach «ruhig gestellt» werden, damit sie
sich nicht zu einem Potenzial für sozialen Unfrieden und Gewalt entwickeln. Dazu mag ein Sozialhilfesatz ausreichen, der es
ihnen ermöglicht, ihre Tage mit Bier und Kartoffelchips vor
dem Fernseher zu verbringen und sich wahlweise zig Programme anzuschauen.

Eine solche Gesellschaft aber wäre eine Horrorvision für
mich. Deswegen haben wir schon vor Jahren mit der Diskussion
von Konzepten wie «Arbeit statt Sozialhilfe» und «Ausbildung
statt Sozialhilfe» begonnen. Dahinter steht die Idee von kom-
munalen Beschäftigungsgesellschaften, die Sozialhilfeempfängern einen Ausbildungs- oder Arbeitsvertrag im Bereich gemeinnütziger Arbeit bieten. Das sind nicht gerade Superjobs.
Aber sie verhindern, dass die Betroffenen ganz aus dem Erwerbsleben herausfallen. Denn sobald dies einmal geschehen
ist, verselbstständigt sich ein Mechanismus: Wer eine gewisse
Zeit arbeitslos war, verliert die Anpassungsfähigkeit an das normale Arbeitsleben. Er oder sie kann die Anforderungen an sich
und die eigene Leistungsfähigkeit nicht mehr angemessen ein-

schätzen. Dauerarbeitslose entwickeln ein anderes Zeitgefühl. Manche werden irgendwann unfähig, morgens um acht an einem Arbeitsplatz zu erscheinen und dort den ganzen Tag lang durchzuhalten. Ihre Kreativität, Energie und Anpassungsfähigkeit sind nur noch darauf ausgerichtet, sich unter den Bedingungen der Sozialhilfe durchs Leben zu schlagen. Das wird dann vielleicht sogar als Freiheit gesehen und die Arbeitswelt dagegen immer mehr als Zwang erlebt. Bald bestehen nur noch soziale Kontakte zu Leuten, die ähnlich leben, was den Teufelskreis schließt.

Die Langzeitarbeitslosigkeit ist deshalb so gefährlich, weil sie die Integration in neue Arbeitsverhältnisse immer schwieriger macht, je länger sie andauert. Auch werden die Arbeitslosen oft zum Stein des Anstoßes für andere, die regulär arbeiten. Ich erinnere mich an einen Fernsehbericht, in dem ein Sozialhilfeempfänger auftrumpfte: «Es gibt mir ein richtig gutes Gefühl, wenn ich morgens von meinen nächtlichen Kneipentouren nach Hause komme und dabei all den Dummen begegne, die jetzt zur Arbeit müssen! Ich dagegen hau mich dann gemütlich ins Bett, mein Geld reicht immer noch aus, mir einen guten Tag zu machen, mit dann und wann noch ein bisschen Schwarzarbeit.»

Da sprach sicher nicht der typische Arbeitslose. Doch diese Haltung drückt genau das aus, was den arbeitenden Durchschnittsbürger aggressiv macht, weil er glaubt, so seien sie alle. Und natürlich ist klar, dass es immer Menschen gibt, die sich vor unliebsamen Arbeiten zu drücken verstehen, wenn sie feststellen, dass sie sich auch anders ganz gut durchschlängeln können. Das darf ihnen aber auf jeden Fall nicht zu leicht gemacht werden. Doch vermutlich wird es schon aufgrund der Leere der öffentlichen Kassen in Zukunft immer schwieriger, sich in der viel zitierten sozialen Hängematte auszuruhen.

Ich meine, wir sollten an der alten sozialdemokratischen Tradition festhalten, der zufolge der Staat zwar die Rahmenbedingungen für Arbeit zu schaffen hat, der Einzelne aber die Verantwortung für sich selbst übernehmen muss. Der Sozialstaat ist verpflichtet, sich um die zu kümmern, die wirklich krank oder so eingeschränkt sind, dass sie nicht für ihren eigenen Unterhalt sorgen können. Alle anderen sollten für ihren Lebensunterhalt arbeiten können, und eine Gesellschaft sollte für sie alle bezahlte Arbeit haben, je nach ihren Fähigkeiten. In diesem Zusammenhang scheint es mir auch zumutbar, den Empfang von Sozialhilfe mit dem Ableisten von gemeinnütziger Arbeit zu verbinden, wie es in den skandinavischen Ländern zum Teil seit längerem schon gemacht wird.

Es war immer eine große Frage, welchen Anteil von ausgegrenzten und verzweifelten Menschen sich eine Gesellschaft leisten kann, ohne dass sie dabei ganz aus den Fugen gerät. Je größer solche Randgruppen werden, desto stärker werden der soziale Frieden und die allgemeine Lebensqualität bedroht, desto mehr nehmen Vandalismus, Kriminalität und Gewalt zu. Wo hohe Arbeitslosigkeit herrscht, da verfallen auch Wohnviertel und ganze Stadtteile. Man kann förmlich spüren, wie die Menschen gleichgültig und depressiv werden, wie sie das Interesse an sich selbst und ihrer unmittelbaren Umgebung nach und nach verlieren. Hausflure, Innenhöfe und Spielplätze verkommen zu Mülldeponien. Das Gras der Anlagen ist zertrampelt, die Bäume sind ramponiert, die Hochhäuser sehen trostlos aus. Die Menschen lassen sich gehen, und ihre Umgebung verwahrlost mit ihnen.

Umgekehrt nimmt der Vandalismus ab, wenn man in diesen Vierteln einen Park anlegt, die Spielplätze in Ordnung hält oder auch nur eine Bank hinstellt, wo sich ältere Leute bei ihren Spaziergängen hinsetzen können. Für solche und ähnliche Projekte kann die gemeinnützige Arbeit von Sozialhilfeempfängern sehr sinnvoll sein; sie erhöht die Identifikation der Menschen mit ihrem Viertel.

Wir haben in Kiel zwei große Wohnsiedlungen, die in ihren Anlagen eine Art «Sozialbüro» eingerichtet haben. Die Mitarbeiter der Sozialbüros beraten die Menschen, die dort leben, bei persönlichen Problemen, sie kümmern sich etwa um deren Sozialhilfe, sie organisieren auch Geburtstagsfeiern für die Kinder oder Grillfeste im Sommer, so dass die Leute nachbarschaftlichen Kontakt behalten und nicht allein in ihren Sozialwohnungen hocken. Das verbessert die Lebensqualität in solchen Wohneinheiten entscheidend; es wird nicht mehr so viel in den Fluren und an den Hauswänden herumgeschmiert, die Leute reden wieder miteinander. Die Umgebung ist nicht so zugemüllt, versifft und verdreckt, sondern schaut freundlich aus. Eine auf diese Weise gelebte soziale Gemeinschaft macht einen gewaltigen Unterschied.

Ich möchte jedenfalls nicht in einer Gesellschaft leben, in der es Slums an den Rändern der großen Städte gibt wie mancherorts in den USA. Wohnviertel, um die man sogar im Auto einen großen Bogen macht. Wenn man zufällig dort hineingeraten ist, verschließt man von innen per Knopfdruck die Autotüren, damit sie nicht von außen aufgerissen werden können, und drückt aufs Gas, um schneller wieder draußen zu sein. Da sind in manchen amerikanischen Städten diese herumlungernden Scharen arbeitsloser junger Männer, die aus Langeweile trinken und an Drogen geraten, Menschen ohne ordentliche Schul- und Berufsbildung, die keine Perspektive haben, viele Schwarze unter ihnen. Ein explosives Milieu, in das nur ein Funken geraten muss, um das Ganze hochgehen zu lassen. Wenn man früher nach New York fuhr, wurde man vor Harlem gewarnt. Heute kann man dort wieder spazieren gehen, doch es gibt inzwischen solche Slums im Westen der USA, aber auch in Straßburg, Marseille oder in den Ringstädten um Paris und London ist es zum Teil ähnlich unsicher und unerfreulich geworden. Bei uns gibt es zum Glück Vergleichbares noch nicht, und wir müssen unbedingt verhindern, dass es dazu kommt.

In diesem Zusammenhang könnten auch schlecht integrierte Zuwanderer zu einem Zukunftsproblem werden. Deswegen ist ein modernes Zuwanderungsgesetz so wichtig, das den unterschiedlichen Umgang mit Asylsuchenden und Wirtschaftsmigranten regelt. Es wäre längst in Kraft, wenn die CDU/CSU-Opposition es nicht vor den Bundestagswahlen im Herbst 2002 zum Gegenstand eines großen Polittheaters gemacht hätte. Immerhin haben wir es inzwischen geschafft, der Tatsache ins Auge zu sehen, dass Deutschland ein Einwanderungsland ist, was jahrzehntelang einfach verdrängt und geleugnet wurde. Außerdem haben wir inzwischen auch weitgehend akzeptiert, dass wir auf bestimmte Formen der Zuwanderung dringend angewiesen sind. Viele Bereiche unseres Wirtschaftslebens würden zusammenbrechen, wenn es die Zuwanderer als Arbeitskräfte nicht gäbe, und das Problem der Überalterung unserer Gesellschaft würde sich noch dramatischer darstellen. Hätten wir keine Saisonarbeiter aus Osteuropa, die Arbeiten übernehmen, die bei uns niemand mehr machen will, dann gäbe es auf unseren Märkten kaum noch Kirschen, Spargel oder Weißkohl zu kaufen.

Es ist selbstverständlich, dass wir politisch Verfolgten Asyl gewähren, das gehört zu den Werten unserer Verfassung. Bei den anderen Migranten, die in Deutschland ihr wirtschaftliches Glück suchen, haben wir das Recht, die Einwanderung unter dem Gesichtspunkt unseres eigenen wirtschaftlichen Interesses zu steuern. Grundsätzlich meine ich, dass jemand, der hier leben und arbeiten möchte, Deutsch können oder schnell lernen sollte; das ist eine wichtige Voraussetzung für eine erfolgreiche Integration. Dann wird sich eine gewisse kulturelle Konvergenz im Laufe der Zeit von selbst einstellen, auch wenn dieser Prozess immer mal wieder von gegenläufigen Tendenzen unterbrochen werden mag. Jetzt zum Beispiel kann man feststellen, dass einige Muslime, die schon seit Jahren bei uns leben und sich weitgehend angepasst hatten, sich wieder abgrenzen. Manch türkische junge Frau trägt betont wieder das Kopftuch, und hier und da erklärt ein türkischer junger Mann, dass er statt einer in Deutschland aufgewachsenen Frau lieber wieder eine aus Anatolien heiraten möchte, die nach traditionellen Vorstellungen erzogen worden ist. Ich meine, es ist ausschließlich eine persönliche Angelegenheit, wie ein Mensch sein religiöses und privates Leben gestaltet, solange es nicht gegen die Gesetze verstößt. Und wir sollten, so lange die Zuwanderer unsere Gesetze respektieren, umgekehrt auch ihre Bräuche und Eigenarten respektieren. Von einer kulturellen Vielfalt, die unsere eigene regionale Vielfalt ergänzt, können wir alle profitieren.

Auf internationaler Ebene können wir der Gefahr großer Wanderungsbewegungen am besten durch eine gute Politik in den Entwicklungsländern selbst begegnen, indem wir dazu beitragen, dass sich dort die Lebensverhältnisse bessern. Wenn es auf der Welt gerechter zuginge, wenn insbesondere das Gefälle zwischen unserem Wohlstand und der Armut dort nicht so groß wäre, dann wäre der Wunsch, die Heimat zu verlassen und anderswo nach Auskommen und Arbeit zu suchen, ohnehin weniger ausgeprägt. Also muss unsere Wirtschafts- und Außenpolitik darauf zielen, die Unterschiede zwischen Globalisierungsgewinnern und -verlierern zu minimieren. Denn natürlich würde auch ein modernes Einwanderungsgesetz nichts mehr nützen, wenn sich alle Armen der Welt auf einmal nach Europa aufmachten.

Viel vom gegenwärtigen Unfrieden in der Welt, auch der internationale Terrorismus, hängt mit den problematischen Folgen der Globalisierung zusammen, die eben keineswegs allen gleichmäßig mehr Lebensqualität und Wohlstand bringt. Das ist gewiss keine Entschuldigung für irgendeinen terroristischen Anschlag, und es ist zu Recht immer wieder darauf hingewiesen worden, dass die Terroristen in ihren eigenen Gesellschaften nicht zu den Ärmsten, sondern im Gegenteil zu den Privilegierten gehören. Doch ebenso ist es ein soziologisches Faktum, dass der Terrorismus in Gesellschaften mit gerecht verteiltem Wohlstand und sozialem Frieden auf Dauer keine Unterstützung findet. Terrorismus kann nur dort gedeihen, wo Terroristen ihn mit dem Verweis auf extreme soziale Ungerechtigkeit rechtfertigen können. Wenn große Teile der Welt am Rande des Existenzminimums leben, dabei aber durch die technischen Segnungen der Globalisierung immer den westlichen Lebensstil vor Augen haben, dann braucht bloß jemand den daraus resultierenden Frust und Zorn für seine Zwecke zu instrumentalisieren, und schon haben wir ein Problem riesigen Ausmaßes. In einer stärker zusammenrückenden Welt ist es gefährlich, wenn einige immer reicher und andere immer ärmer werden. Das gilt vor allem dann, wenn von den Reichen erhabene Werte wie Demokratie und Menschenrechte im Munde geführt werden, obwohl sie faktisch nur von Eigeninteresse geleitet werden. Gerade weil wir in unserer hochkomplexen Gesellschaft extrem verletzlich gegenüber terroristischen Anschlägen sind, muss es in unserem eigenen Interesse sein, den Prozess der Globalisierung weltweit in sozial verträgliche Bahnen zu lenken. Wir müssen Strategien entwickeln, die Spielregeln einer sozialökologischen Marktwirtschaft anstelle eines hemmungslosen Turbokapitalismus auch weltweit einzuführen. Wir dürfen uns nicht so verhalten, als sei die Globalisierung in dieser Form naturgesetzlich vorgegeben und politisch nicht gestaltbar. Zu den neuen Spielregeln globalen Wirtschaftens müsste es beispielsweise gehören, Finanzströme zu kontrollieren und keine Steuerparadiese mehr zuzulassen. In diesem Zusammenhang wird auch ein Schuldenerlass für die ärmsten der armen Länder diskutiert, was ich sehr begrüße. Es scheint mir auch sinnvoll, ein solches Entgegenkommen mit der Bedingung einer Demokratisierung in dem betreffenden Land zu verknüpfen. Es sollte auch sichergestellt werden, dass die frei werdenden Gelder wirklich zum Wohle der Bevölkerung und nicht für Waffenkäufe ausgegeben werden.

Dass fanatisierte Islamisten überall auf der Welt großen Zulauf haben, hängt nicht zuletzt mit der Tatsache zusammen, dass die Länder der Ersten Welt sich nicht genug um latente Konfliktherde in der Dritten Welt gekümmert haben. Da ist nicht nur der explosive Konflikt Israel–Palästina, sondern auch die religiös verwurzelten Konflikte in Kaschmir und Indien. Irland, nah genug vor unserer eigenen Haustür, ist ein gutes Beispiel dafür, wie religiös motivierte Konflikte jahrzehntelang schwelen und immer wieder neu aufflackern können. Ich fürchte, dergleichen wird in Zukunft auf der Welt nicht etwa ab-, sondern zunehmen, wenn sich ein Amerikanisches Empire etabliert, unter dem sich viele Völker ungerecht behandelt fühlen. Dann könnte der Terrorismus nicht nur weltweit stärker, sondern auch zunehmend mitten in die westlichen Gesellschaften getragen werden.

In einer wirtschaftlich globalisierten Welt zu leben, bedeutet eben nicht nur, dass wir Waren, Dienstleistungen und Kapital überall frei hinbewegen und daraus Nutzen für uns ziehen können. Es bedeutet auch, dass wir nicht hoffen können, bequem und friedlich auf unserer Wohlstandsinsel weiterzuleben, während es anderswo auf der Welt tiefe Krisen, Elend und Armut gibt. Mehr oder weniger schlägt das wieder auf uns zurück, und schon deshalb müssen wir ein vitales Interesse an einer sozial gerechteren Weltordnung haben.

Eines unserer Zukunftsprobleme könnte aber auch darin bestehen, dass wir im Kampf gegen den Terrorismus überreagieren in der Weise, dass Grundrechte eingeschränkt werden und die demokratische Grundordnung dadurch Schaden nimmt. Im Augenblick ist diese Befürchtung zum Glück noch nicht sehr real, sie könnte aber rasch konkreter werden, wenn auch bei uns terroristische Attentate zunähmen und die Bevölkerung nach höherer Sicherheit verlangte. Die bisherigen Maßnahmen zur inneren Sicherheit wie der Kleine Lauschangriff und die Rasterfahndung halte ich für vertretbar, obgleich ich der Ansicht bin, dass sie nicht im erwarteten Maß zum Aufspüren von Terroristen beitragen. Sie führen zunächst einmal zu einer gewaltigen Materialsammlung, die ohne einen großen Personalaufwand nur schwer nutzbar gemacht werden kann. Es ist allerdings auch nicht einfach, Maßnahmen zu finden, die bei der Vereitelung terroristischer Anschläge greifen, ohne dass sie das Klima eines Polizeistaates schaffen. Es wäre fatal, wenn die Polizei von nun an überall jeden fremd aussehenden Menschen auffordern würde, seine Papiere zu zeigen. Und es wäre grässlich, wenn in Zukunft nicht nur Militäranlagen und Atomkraftwerke, sondern auch U-Bahn-höfe, Kaufhäuser und Banken, Schulen und Kirchen bewacht werden müssten. So etwas könnte Terroranschläge nicht vollständig verhindern, weil es letztlich nie vollkommene Sicherheit geben kann. Es würde unserer zivilen Gesellschaft aber ein erschreckend anderes Gesicht geben.

Die geschärfte Aufmerksamkeit für die Probleme von morgen darf uns nicht den Blick auf die positiven Entwicklungen in unserer Gegenwart verstellen. Ich meine, wir haben durchaus auch Anlass zu Hoffnung und Optimismus. Ermutigend finde ich die Einstellung der jungen Menschen, die weitgehend ohne Zukunftsängste an ihr Leben herangehen. Eine gewisse allgemeine Politikverdrossenheit ist sicher zu konstatieren. Es ist zum Beispiel bedenklich, dass die Zahl der Menschen zunimmt, denen Wahlen eher gleichgültig werden. Doch im internationalen Vergleich stehen wir mit unserer Wahlbeteiligung insgesamt noch ganz gut da. Ich finde es positiv, wie das Engagement für die Gemeinschaft im lokalen Rahmen in den letzten Jahren wieder zugenommen hat. In Schleswig-Holstein gibt es kaum noch eine Stadt oder ein Dorf, wo nicht eine Agenda-21-Initiative existiert. Überall florieren Straßenfeste, von den Anwohnerinnen und Anwohnern selbst gestaltet; sie zeigen, dass den Menschen ihre nächste Umgebung keineswegs gleichgültig ist, dass sie sie liebens- und lebenswert gestalten wollen, vielleicht als Gegengewicht zu einer gewissen sozialen Kälte, die sie in größeren gesellschaftlichen Zusammenhängen wahrnehmen. Das sind kleine, nicht immer spektakuläre Prozesse, die ich gleichwohl für sehr bedeutsam halte.

An manchen Stellen hält sich in unserer Gesellschaft aber noch hartnäckig das alte Anspruchsdenken: Der Staat, der große Versorger, soll gefälligst alles richten! Auf der anderen Seite regt sich erfreulicherweise immer mehr bürgerschaftliches Engagement, und zwar in den verschiedensten lokalen Initiativen. In zahlreichen Ortschaften Schleswig-Holsteins gestalten ehrenamtliche Mitarbeiter und Mitarbeiterinnen so genannte «Tafeln», die überschüssige Lebensmittel in Geschäften und auf Märkten einsammeln und an Bedürftige verteilen. Dabei fällt auf, dass sich die Formen des sozialen Engagements und des Ehrenamtes auch verändern. Immer weniger Menschen sind bereit, sich jahrzehntelang beim gleichen Verein karitativ zu betätigen, immer mehr Engagierte finden sich zu einmaligen größeren Aktionen und kurzfristigen Initiativen zusammen. Tausende von Schülerinnen und Schülern beteiligen sich bei uns alle zwei Jahre an den sozialen Aktionstagen der Initiative «Schüler helfen leben». Besonders ermutigend fand ich auch die große Hilfsbereitschaft bei der Flutkatastrophe im Sommer 2002. Dabei denke ich nicht nur an die Spendenbereitschaft, sondern auch an die große Zahl der Menschen aus allen Teilen der Republik, die vor Ort helfen wollten. Es meldeten sich viel mehr, als tatsächlich eingesetzt werden konnten, ganze Schulklassen mussten abgewiesen werden.

Solche Phänomene zeigen, dass wir keineswegs nur eine Gesellschaft von spaßorientierten und selbstverwirklichungssüchtigen Egomanen geworden sind. Überhaupt scheint es, als begünstige der zunehmende Verteilungskampf auch einen gewissen Wertewandel in Richtung zu mehr Solidarität. Es findet eine Art «Wende nach innen» statt. Familie, Heiraten und Kinder großziehen wird für viele wieder ein zentrales Lebensziel. Die gute alte bürgerliche Familie ist allerdings zunehmend nur noch eine unter vielen Familienformen, und wir werden uns wohl in Zukunft immer mehr darauf verständigen, dass Familie da stattfindet, wo Kinder sind, egal, ob es sich um Mann und Frau, einen allein erziehenden Elternteil, zwei Frauen oder zwei Männer mit Kindern handelt. Generell erweist sich, dass Familie, in welcher Form auch immer, aufgewertet wird, wenn Menschen sich durch äußere Bedrohungen verunsichert fühlen. Man bleibt öfter mal wieder zu Hause und will es sich dort schön machen, man geht seltener aus oder verzichtet auf regelmäßige Auslandsreisen. Derzeit konsumieren die Deutschen deutlich weniger, sie üben sich zum Teil in einer neuen Bescheidenheit.

Auch wenn der Einzelhandel darüber klagt: Dieser Wertewandel hat auch seine positiven Seiten. Denn Glaube an ein Recht auf Wohlstand, die Idee der Besitzstandswahrung allein, reicht nicht aus, um eine Gesellschaft zusammenzuhalten. Wenn dies zur vorherrschenden Einstellung wird, dann lassen sich soziale Probleme nur lösen, solange es einen ständigen wirtschaftlichen Zuwachs gibt. So bequem konnten wir es uns in der Vergangenheit machen: Alle kriegen ein bisschen mehr, und dann ist Ruhe im Karton! Auch die, die ein bisschen weniger von dem Mehr abbekamen, waren einigermaßen zufrieden, weil es immer noch etwas mehr war als das, was sie vorher hatten. In der nahen Zukunft werden wir sozialen Frieden und Lebensqualität auf diese einfache Art nicht mehr herstellen können. Umso wichtiger wird es, uns auch auf andere Werte im Zusammenleben zu besinnen.

Den Politikern wird häufig vorgeworfen, wir hätten keine wirklichen Visionen mehr. Wir seien entweder populistisch und opportunistisch oder nur pragmatisch der kleinen Tagespolitik verhaftet. Natürlich ist es wichtig, umfassendere politische Ziele zu haben, und die haben wir Sozialdemokraten in unserem Parteiprogramm auch deutlich benannt. Für die tägliche politische Arbeit sind aber nicht die Visionen entscheidend, es kommt auf die vielen kleinen Schritte an.

Allerdings spielen Visionen eine wichtige Rolle in der öffentlichen Diskussion um den Strukturwandel unserer Gesellschaft. So etwa, wenn wir uns mit der Frage auseinander setzen: Wie machen wir unsere Gesellschaft zukunftsfähig? Wie gestalten wir unsere Sozialversicherungssysteme nach dem Prinzip «mehr Eigenverantwortung», ohne dass dabei die Idee der sozialen Gerechtigkeit ins Hintertreffen gerät? Wie passen wir uns dem Prozess der Globalisierung so an, dass unsere Wirtschaft wieder floriert, und befördern dabei gleichzeitig faire Spielregeln für die Weltwirtschaft? Wie kommen wir dem erhöhten Sicherheitsbedürfnis der Menschen entgegen, ohne dass dabei demokratische Grundrechte aufgegeben werden? Eine zentrale sozial-demokratische Vision ist und bleibt für mich eine gerechte Gesellschaft, eine Gesellschaft, in der insbesondere die Schere zwischen den großen und kleinen Einkommen nicht immer weiter auseinander klafft. Bei der generellen Notwendigkeit zum Sparen bedeutet das konkret: Da wir nun mal sparen müssen, sollten alle dazu beitragen – und die, die mehr haben, sollten auch mehr dazu beitragen.

Wir leben in einer Zeit, die nicht einfach, aber dafür auch ganz bestimmt nicht langweilig ist. Mein wichtigstes Ziel als Politikerin ist es, den angelaufenen gesellschaftlichen Modernisierungsprozess, der unser aller Leben verändern wird, weiter zu befördern und in gute Bahnen zu lenken – in Schleswig-Holstein, in Deutschland, in Europa und überall da in der Zeit, wo wir ihn mitgestalten können.